Louis Applebaum

Louis Applebaum

A Passion for Culture

Walter Pitman

THE DUNDURN GROUP
TORONTO · OXFORD

Editor: Dennis Mills
Copy-Editor: Brenda McLoughlin, First Folio Resource Group
Indexer: Ruth Pincoe
Design: Jennifer Scott
Printer: Transcontinental

National Library of Canada Cataloguing in Publication Data

Pitman, Walter
    Louis Applebaum : a passion for culture / Walter Pitman.

Includes bibliographical references.
ISBN 1-55002-398-5

1. Applebaum, Louis, 1918- 2. Composers — Canada — Biography. I. Title.

ML410.A648P68 2002   780'.92   C2002-902294-0

1   2   3   4   5   06   05   04   03   02

We acknowledge the support of the **Canada Council for the Arts** and the **Ontario Arts Council** for our publishing program. We also acknowledge the financial support of the **Government of Canada** through the **Book Publishing Industry Development Program** and **The Association for the Export of Canadian Books**, and the **Government of Ontario** through the **Ontario Book Publishers Tax Credit** program.

Care has been taken to trace the ownership of copyright material used in this book. The author and the publisher welcome any information enabling them to rectify any references or credit in subse-quent editions.

J. Kirk Howard, President

Printed and bound in Canada.⊕
Printed on recycled paper.
www.dundurn.com

Dundurn Press
8 Market Street
Suite 200
Toronto, Ontario, Canada
M5E 1M6

Dundurn Press
73 Lime Walk
Headington, Oxford,
England
OX3 7AD

Dundurn Press
2250 Military Road
Tonawanda NY
U.S.A. 14150

To Lou's beloved wife, Jan,
and to my cherished spouse, Ida.

Table of Contents

Preface

A biography of Louis Applebaum provides an opportunity to examine the ideas and behaviour of an extraordinary Canadian artist, composer, and administrator through a significant period of the nation's history, and particularly, its cultural development. Louis Applebaum was very much a man of the world he inhabited. He was a voracious reader of books, periodicals, and daily newspapers.[1] There was no ivory tower of academe to which he could retreat — nor would he have wished one. His constant crusade was to bring the arts and the affairs of humankind together. He had very early in his life seen the effect of poverty and despair, the impact of the tumult of war, and the injustice and havoc of rampant racism. Over a period of nearly six decades, he scripted music for hundreds of films and radio and television broadcasts — music that he believed would command people's attention, and increase their emotional reaction and intellectual concentration.[2] He was not interested in entertainment as mere titillation; however, he perceived that there was no boundary between learning and human enjoyment, and that in the midst of joy and laughter people could find better ways to live and love. Intellectual focus and moral direction typified his work. Although he wrote compositions for the recital hall, concert stage, and synagogue, his art never left behind matters of major import occurring in the daily events of his own time.

Unlike most artists, Louis became deeply involved in administrative responsibilities. He did so not because of the allure of enhanced income, but because of the same motivations that led him to write music, which had a social and communicative role. He believed that all the arts performed a societal role — that music, drama, dance and visual arts, whether on the live stage, in a gallery, or transmitted through technological media, could influence the lives of people for good purpose. People could be inspired to be collectively conscious; to create beauty for each other; and to be attracted to the values of justice and compassion. Through the arts, people could become more appreciative of the wonder of their lives and discover reasons for joy in their well-being. Because of his beliefs, Louis was drawn to projects and institutions that brought the arts to the conscious reflection of millions of people. He knew he was a good administrator and participated in the founding and continuing operation of a host of agencies and voluntary organizations dedicated to the arts and to the work of those who were his artist-colleagues. Through the examination of this man's career, one can glimpse the development of a unique culture above the 49th parallel on the North American continent.

Louis Applebaum was at the centre of the cultural explosion that took place in Canada in the middle and later years of the 20th century. He was involved in the founding years of the National Film Board — by far the most influential institution in the development of Canada's film industry — as well as the beginnings of the Stratford Shakespearean Festival — the largest and most significant theatrical presenter in this country. He was deeply engaged in the early years of the CBC, certainly the most pervasive and influential cultural institution in the land. He actively participated in the early development of the nation's two major arts funding organizations — the Canada Council and the Ontario Arts Council — taking responsibility for the leadership of the latter body for almost a decade. He was a significant contributor to the founding of the major performing arts venue in the nation's capital, the National Arts Centre, and to the commitment to music education at the University of Ottawa. He administered and influenced the future programming of one of Canada's earliest and most prestigious music festivals, in Guelph, Ontario, and chaired a Federal Cultural Policy Review Committee whose recommendations substantially affected the life of the country. As a composer, he was an active member of every organization associated with the making of music in Canada — the Canadian Music Council, the Canadian Music Centre and the Canadian League of Composers. He was also an important participant in the successful development of the major performing rights organization, SOCAN (Society of Composers, Authors and Music Publishers of Canada), and its predecessor, CAPAC (Composers, Authors and Publishers Association of Canada), both dedicated to making the role of being a composer in Canada financially feasible. Significantly, all these involvements (and many others undertaken throughout his career) were an expression of his altruistic service to those who could be termed members of the artistic community — a role that made him a most loved and respected figure in that community.

Yet Louis Applebaum nevertheless wanted to be remembered as a composer. When people heard his name, he wanted them to remember his fanfares before every performance at the Festival Theatre in Stratford, the music they recalled from the television presentation of Pierre Berton's *National Dream*, the lush lyricism accompanying Harry Rasky's film on Marc Chagall, *The Colours of Love*, the tension he created with the background music for Bill Mason's film, *Paddle to the Sea*, or the impact of his score on his first feature film success — *The Story of G.I. Joe*. He was sure that his final offering, the opera *Erehwon*, would eventually find a place in the memories of his fellow citizens.

He measured his contribution as a music maker in an integrated context with all his other work. Certainly he wanted his compositions to form a repertoire of offerings for orchestra, string quartet, choir, single voice or solo instrument, but he also wished his life-work to be judged on the broadest possible basis — the pursuit of personal excellence in communicating important ideas through artistic expression, and particularly through his work for radio, film, television, and live theatre, especially the Stratford Festival. His contribution to the development of the arts and artists in his nation was another aspect of his creativity. He wanted to change a society that failed to esteem its creative artists, including its composers, in the knowledge that such a change would herald the arrival of a cultural age. He believed passionately that a strong Canadian nation was a crucial element in the fashioning of a better world. For him, creativity was a fabric with many colours and textures, and his life as an arts administrator was as much an expression of that characteristic as his placing of notes on a page. His lyricism and his leadership were one. Indeed, his career is, in its totality, an extraordinary oeuvre devoted to the enhancement of his nation, its essential values of justice and equality, its creativity, its artistic expression, and the artists whom he believed were the greatest hope for a civil and humane future.

It was for all these reasons that, on his death in April 2000, he was mourned not only as a great Canadian musician but, equally as importantly, as a beloved colleague of countless artists from coast to coast. His compassion for the creative figures in every art form had been boundless. Their reciprocal respect and affection was infinite. His loss could not be measured, it could only be deeply felt.

Chapter One
The Crucial Years

In 1918 "the war to end all wars" came to its conclusion, and the full impact of this horrendous struggle — to be realized worldwide — had special importance to Canada. The nation had entered the war, indeed, had had the war thrust upon it as a colonial jurisdiction, automatically supporting the United Kingdom, its mother country. However, the enormous sacrifice of Canadian lives on the Western Front and the particularly courageous responses of Canadian soldiers to the horrific clashes over a few hundred yards of European soil had ironically forged a new nation. The politics of being Canadian would never be the same again.

In that same year, on April 3rd, Louis Applebaum was born of the union of Morris and Fanny Applebaum, East European Jewish immigrants who had found their way to Canada, Ontario, and Toronto before the Great War of 1914–18 had begun. The war had scarcely touched this young couple, just starting their lives in a new land; and they had brought forth a son. Louis Applebaum had become a member, not only of a family, but also of a significant minority group who had come to Canada in the early years of the 20th century. There had been few Jewish families in the Toronto of the 19th century. Then, in the last decades of that century, the policies of the Russian Empire had once again become severely racist. Efforts to "Russify" the Jews during the late 19th and early 20th century forced some 2 million Jewish people in the Russian Empire to leave family, friends and property and seek a new home in North America.[1]

Both of Louis's parents were Polish Jews, Poland being then very much a part of the Russian Empire. Morris had been born in 1895 in Nowa Slupia, one of a family of four brothers and a sister, and Fanny Freiberg had been born just four years later in Ostrievic. Stories about the ghastly month at sea abound in the Applebaum family, as with so many other families who came across the Atlantic in those years.[2] Morris, as a teenager, was brought by his father to Toronto in 1909. When his father, disillusioned and homesick, returned within a few months to Poland, Morris stayed in Canada. Fanny, too, had arrived with her father in 1911. Thus, Fanny and Morris were part of that flood of Jewish people who decided to seek economic well-being, as well as religious liberty, in Canada at the beginning of the new century.

By the 1890s, Montreal had a considerable community of Jewish people, while Toronto had only a handful and they were all but invisible. That was to change. Early immigration policy in Canada had attempted to direct all new arrivals to the new western provinces and territories, to make farmers of them and thereby strengthen the nation's agricultural base. But the farming experiences in Eastern Europe were often poor preparation for the North American west, and since most of the Jewish people came from urban settings, these efforts at rural settlement failed. And so it was to the city, to Toronto, that these travellers came, in sufficient numbers to create a welcoming community for those who were to follow.

> For Canadian Jews, no period was more dramatic than the thirty years between 1880 and 1910. In 1880 there were a handful of Jewish communities in a few parts of the country: by 1914, communities of Jews could be found in cities, small towns, and villages from coast to coast.[3]

By 1917, Morris and Fanny had met in one of many social centres which had sprung up in the Toronto Jewish community — had been attracted to one another, fallen in love, courted, and married. They became part of the new generation of Jews in Canada who were no longer peripheral but central to the cultural life of the rapidly growing capital city in a province on the verge of extraordinary economic development.

> By 1914, the acculturated Anglo-Jewish community of Canada had all but disappeared; gone was their serene, comfortable, stable world. In its place had emerged the new world of Canadian Jewry, the seething, crowded, chaotic, noisy Yiddish world of the Eastern European newcomer.[4]

As happened within many cities in North America during these years, families like the Applebaums joined a minority that came to have an enormous effect on the cultural life of their communities. Most were educated, indeed, had a sophisticated understanding of the mysteries of philosophy and theology. And many were musically literate. Even though Louis Applebaum was not born into a musical family, he became part of a musical community with a musical heritage. It was not surprising that a piano appeared in his home while he was a little child, or that he and his sister, Ruth, just four years younger, began taking music lessons at an early age. The sound of the Applebaum piano filtered out of screen doors to be joined by the sounds of other pianos in other parlours of other homes in the Jewish neighbourhood. Hockey and football had little resonance or attraction for Jewish youths looking for recreation, but music was another story. This extraordinary flood (the number of Toronto Jews grew by 600% from 1901 to 1911[5]) presented the city with a vast array of musicians who formed the base contingent for the Toronto Symphony Orchestra and virtually every musical ensemble in the city during the first decades of the 20th century. As well, the Jewish people became the attentive audiences and the generous financial supporters of Toronto's cultural institutions, far beyond their relative numbers to every other minority, in what became during the 20th century the most multicultural urban centre in the world.

Louis Applebaum was born in St. John's Ward, an area bordered by Yonge Street and University Avenue on the east and west and by College and Queen Streets on the north and south, that became known simply as "the Ward" as it became a predominantly Jewish "ghetto" in central Toronto. The term "ghetto" has taken on a pejorative connotation for good reason. The unspeakable events that overtook such concentrations of Jewish people in mid-20th-century Europe has made this word a reminder what can happen when intolerance is allowed to flourish. But for Jewish people coming from a strange land, many with limited resources, the near presence of a host of relatives and friends sharing a common past and a very present religious tradition provided a source of strength and confidence. Examples are legion of Jewish people who emerged from these ghettos to give leadership beyond their immediate family or even their synagogue congregation, to lend their strength to political and social efforts to build a decent society. Their emergence as contributors to the cultural life of the community, particularly in the discipline of musical composition and performance, is to be found across Canada.[6]

By Louis's elementary school years, the ghetto had shifted to the west and the Applebaums had moved to Beatrice Street, situated in a neighbourhood bounded by Spadina Avenue and Bathurst Street. The most explicit remaining feature of these early years is Toronto's Kensington Market, a treasure deeply valued by the city.

Louis's ghetto experience closely relates to everything he accomplished in his long life of creativity and service. He remembered his home as the venue for a constant flow of relatives and friends coming from the old world, staying for a few weeks or months and ultimately establishing them-

selves in the new community. "Uncle Lazer" or "Uncle Max" would myste-
riously arrive, and then leave after a while to be replaced by various cousins.
Louis remembered his childish efforts to teach them English, giving objects
with Yiddish names their English equivalents, and bringing a store of
English words to the attention of his bewildered relatives. "The table is a
table" was as profound a statement as his language-challenged relatives
could comprehend. These efforts were made doubly difficult as a grandmother on Fanny's side of the family had taken up residence and spoke only
Yiddish, thereby making this the main language at the dinner table. Indeed,
Louis himself did not learn to speak English until he went to public school.[7]

More than a family dwelling, his home became a community centre,
endowed with a particularly large kitchen. Besides the host of relatives
who were permanent or semi-permanent inhabitants (at one point, six
adults lived at Beatrice Street and there was only one bathroom), a constant stream of friends habitually dropped by in the evenings. The generosity of the Applebaum family became legendary. Louis's sister, Ruth,
who herself shared her room with her grandmother, remembers vividly
the day that tragedy struck a neighbouring family. Both parents died suddenly and the older brother, who was about to be married, felt he could
look after an orphaned younger sister, but not a younger brother. Louis
asked his mother, "Can Ben live with us?" The answer: "Yes, of course."
Louis shared his own room with the boy for years.[8]

Morris had found work virtually on arrival, in the needle-trades workshops of the T. Eaton Company, not only a major retail outlet but also the
dominant manufacturer of clothing in early 20th century Toronto.
Morris's father, Shiman, had been a hat-maker in Poland and the skills of
working with cloth had been passed from father to son.

Fanny's father made coats, and she too was expected to take up the needle as soon as she was mature. For many immigrants, coming to Canada presented an opportunity to escape the family connection with work on the
farm, in the fishing boat, or in the mine, but not for those who were Jewish.
Jews were expected to work in well defined areas of employment. Working in
the production of clothes and shoes, or as draymen who picked up the waste
goods of an entire city by horse and wagon, was considered appropriate
employment, and every imaginable informal stricture was devised to ensure
that people of Jewish origin would keep to their proper place in the economic
structure of Toronto. Then, in 1912, came the Eaton strike— in which
Jewish and non-Jewish workers stood together to secure better pay and decent
working conditions in what were essentially sweatshops. By this time, Morris
had developed a close friendship with Joseph Markovitz, a fellow employee
with whom he shared a common determination and ambition. Morris and

Joseph decided to "strike" out on their own, to forsake the Eaton empire, and to produce goods for sale in their own shop, which they called the Bell Cloak Company — selling mainly coats and suits for ladies. This family business also employed Fanny's brother and sister, who had followed her to Toronto, as well as Joseph's brother. In a rented store at 382 Parliament Street, they worked 12 hours a day — more if necessary. By the mid-20s, the business was doing well in the surge of prosperity that defined that decade. More important, it had the strength to survive the depression that followed.

Louis's sister, Ruth (given the childhood nickname "Ootoo" by her brother Louis and still answering to that name to countless acquaintances) remembers those years with both warmth and sadness. Louis would never claim to have risen from the debilitating misery of poverty, though he sought out ways to secure music lessons at the lowest possible cost — and on occasion piano studies had to be cancelled until the family cash flow was restored. The Applebaums were certainly not rich, nor could they claim to be well off. But both Morris Applebaum and Joe Markovitz were employers at a time when being a "boss" was as much a disadvantage as an advantage. The needle trade that had provided so much community cohesion after World War I was now rent by the tensions of Jews who found themselves, as employees, pitted against bosses who were their friends and co-religionists. Ruth remembers how a schoolmate shocked and hurt her with the retort, "You are rich!" during the days of the depression.[9] Ruth was speechless. She knew that her family was not starving in those hard times, but she was sure that they were not "rich" and unaffected by the poverty that she could see all around them. Morris's example of entrepreneurship, both in good and bad times, most certainly influenced Louis's life. Though Louis spent most of his career associated with public enterprise, he was unlike many artists in that he did not eschew the role of entrepreneur, seeing in the private sector opportunities that would have been quite inappropriate to pursue as a public servant.[10]

From the beginning of their partnership, the Applebaum and Markovitz families realized that they could achieve benefits of scale through purchasing duplicates of furniture or daily food. They bought connected homes on Beatrice Street that were virtually identical and filled their homes with the same furniture, the same accessories, and the same appliances. As Louis recalled, the houses were mirror images in every way.[11] Not forgotten either was the sharing that characterized the Applebaum-Markovitz relationship — even to the point of "mothballing" one car in winter so the families could share a single vehicle and cut costs.

At age five, Louis entered the neighbourhood elementary school, Clinton Public School. Louis had spent one year (1923-4) at King Edward

School before the move to Beatrice Street, but, although his time there certainly made an impact on his language skills, he was too young to have many memories of the school. The school population at Clinton was not as concentrated in its Jewishness as the schools in "the Ward," where both elementary schools were 87% Jewish.[12] Clinton turned out to be a more valuable place to learn for several reasons. First, much could be learned from the other minorities present at the school, yet because Jewish students could identify themselves as different, they established a network of special friends with whom they could share their sense of "differentness." Secondly, Clinton had been established as a school to which children with disabilities in hearing and speech could be sent. In the playground, Louis and Ruth learned something of what it was like to suffer from such a disability and both remembered it as an experience that had affected their response to human need. Finally, the school had a music program, although Louis remembered it as being embarrassingly inadequate. Despite Louis's protestation that Clinton could not claim any credit for his music career, the school turned to him in 1989 to write a song commemorating its centennial. More important, his experiences at Clinton led him to analyze the role of arts education in the elementary school with more tenacity and critical comment than any other composer, with the possible exception of R. Murray Schafer. Louis's own experience in the elementary classroom had no great impact on his life. In speeches to educators he suggested that children arrive in kindergarten filled with creative urges that are systematically beaten out of them by the time they reach Grade 7 — not a message that is universally appreciated.

Graduating from Clinton, Louis arrived, in 1931, at Harbord Collegiate, legendary for its nurture of those students whose passion was the creation or performance of music. By the 1920s Harbord had become a special home for Jewish youth who had been brought to Toronto in the influx of the early years of the century. It remained Toronto's Jewish secondary school even into the 1940s and '50s, until the next migration of Jewish people moved north to Forest Hill and North York.[13]

No school in Ontario could have presented Louis with a greater array of fellow students who were to become distinguished citizens. In his graduating class, one can find the names of Johnny Wayne and Frank Shuster, two of Canada's most famous entertainers,[14] and, in the following year, Sam Sniderman, who was to become "Sam the Record Man," Canada's most prolific purveyor of recorded music, and Eleanor Sniderman, who would establish a classical recording company in her own right. All of these people would play a role in Louis's career. But even more important, John Jacob Weinzweig, destined to become the dean of Canadian com-

18

posers, had attended Harbord just four years earlier and had made a lasting impression. Indeed, Harbord, and particularly Brian S. McCool, the head of the school's music department, could be said to have launched Weinzweig's career. Before attending Harbord, Weinzweig had not taken music seriously and it was McCool who "realized that I had genuine music talent and made me the orchestra's assistant conductor."[15] Harbord was the only school in Toronto at which this could have happened. McCool had established the "first high-school orchestra in the province of Ontario. Under his guidance, the orchestra developed a wide repertoire — most notably, performing Gilbert and Sullivan operas on an annual basis."

This repertoire was to have a great influence on Louis. At that time, however, he sang in the chorus, but remained otherwise invisible as a musical presence.[16] A few years later, Victor Feldbrill was to experience Harbord before his career as one of Canada's most distinguished orchestral conductors, and "at one time, no less than one quarter of the T.S.O. were Harbord graduates."[17] There were many others in the field of music and broadcasting who attended Harbord in later years and became a part of this extraordinary extended family: Morris Surdin, Steven Staryk, Ivan Fecan, Morley Safer, Alan Hamel, Toby Robbins and David Cronenberg. Louis imbibed the culture of excellence in the arts that pervaded this school and was a dedicated student, but he did not make his mark at Harbord in the way that John Weinzweig and Victor Feldbrill most certainly did.[18] McCool may have made a crucial intervention in the lives of these Canadian cultural "heroes," but Louis remembers the quality of advice in vocal technique of another teacher, Alistair Haig, who trained the chorus for Gilbert and Sullivan productions. Louis's involvement with these productions began in 1933 with a performance of the *Pirates of Penzance*, followed in 1935 with *The Gondoliers*, and in 1936 with *Iolanthe*. These were major initiatives, with full orchestra and chorus.

In addition to music, Harbord had much to offer its students. During the Harbord years, Louis's proficiency as a swimmer came to the fore. Like many secondary schools built in the early years of the century, Harbord had an indoor swimming pool, and Louis became a constant participant in aquatic activities. At one point, he was unable to play the piano for several weeks as a result of a finger broken in performing on the pool's diving board. By that time, he was over six feet tall, lanky and muscular, and his strength, speed, and endurance made swimming a natural sport for him. Throughout his life he maintained this athleticism seemingly with little effort, and although he had broad shoulders and considerable heft, he was never overweight. He could dominate a room physically and psychically. Ironically, many fellow students appreciated his athletic proficiencies in the Harbord pool and on the Beatrice Street tennis courts but were unaware of his real passion — music and its creation. That suited Louis just fine![19]

Even though Louis's career grew mainly out of his experiences outside the secondary school setting, he supported Harbord's Charitable Foundation throughout his life and, like Clinton, the school turned to Louis in 1992 for music to commemorate its centennial. The celebrations began with the opening of the museum-archives on October 24, 1991, at which it was announced that "we will be introduced to the centennial song which will be sung by the school choir with original music composed by Louis Applebaum, who selected the lyrics from about fifty entries in a prize-winning contest."[20]

Certainly, Harbord produced an environment in which Louis could be comfortable, one free from the anti-Semitism that ran rampant in Toronto in the 1930s. The school's aura of commitment to achievement gave confidence to a young man about to pursue a career in the arts which seemed to offer little hope of recognition in a land overwhelmed by the cultural outpouring of other nations, both from across the Atlantic and across the southern border.

The permanently influential moments of Louis's early years were spent in the company of a group of boys and girls with whom he shared, yes, his Jewishness, but also his enthusiasm for fun, for earning pocket-money, and for recreational activities such as playing cards and tennis, dancing, and partying. During their time at Harbord, these students also spent many hours helping one another with their studies. It was a context for living with confidence in an environment that, by the mid-1930s, was becoming increasingly hostile, not only in Nazi Germany but around the world. This group of some 15 or 20 young people maintained their intimate association through elementary and secondary school, leading to Louis's friendship with prosperous owners of Toronto businesses (Ben Silver), professional leaders (Dr. Harry Sheffer of the National Research Council), entertainers (Johnny Wayne and Frank Shuster), and most important by far — with a slim and comely woman who very early captured his heart and later became his wife, Jan Hershoff. As Louis's Beatrice Street home had been the immigration centre in the early years, it became the recreation centre in the 1930s as the Applebaum children matured into active high school students. Frank Shuster remembers the card games that tended to become so competitive that the shouting "could be heard blocks away."[21] Ruth states categorically "nothing was more important to Lou than his membership in that very 'exclusive' association. It came to include the people whom he regarded as his closest friends." To the end of Louis's life these friends continued to attend his workshops or concerts, as well as special occasions, birthday celebrations and wedding anniversaries.[22]

Louis had no sense of having been constantly at risk as a Jew in WASP-controlled Toronto. However, he remembered the environment of fear engendered by an altercation that took place in 1933 at Christie Pits — a park not far from his home where the most violent racial clash in this country's history took place at a baseball game between two teams, one of which was largely made up of Jewish players. Swastikas, thugs, and clubs were the order of the day and the clash went on for several hours. Louis recalled that groups of swastika-arm-banded toughs came into his neighbourhood with the express purpose of breaking windows and confronting any "Jew-boys" who might cross their path.[23]

Part of Louis's sense of confirmation and support came from attendance at a predominantly Jewish secondary school with a commitment to both music creation and performance as well as academic excellence, but by far the major contribution came from his acceptance in an extraordinary group of young people. One of their more enterprising activities was selling magazines outside Toronto, in Eastern Ontario in particular. The National Home Monthly (now defunct as a Canadian periodical), anxious to increase its subscriber base beyond Ontario's capital city, recruited Louis and his schoolmates to sell magazine subscriptions. Ben Silver was the "captain" of the team and the entrepreneurial force behind the scheme, and he received 10% of the profits. The rest went to the individual seller of each subscription. To find their way to towns in eastern Ontario, they needed a car. With the money these young entrepreneurs were prepared to invest, they bought an old crock of a car that had to be urged along the highways of the province with enormous injections of oil. This forced them to search out sources of cheap "used" lubricant. However, the car had ineffective brakes and hit a truck head-on, sending Harry Sheffer through the windshield and then to a local hospital for stitches. He carries the scar on his face to this day.[24] As a result of this somewhat disastrous, yet nevertheless adventurous, excursion into the marketplace, Louis was prepared later in life to become a private producer or executive, sometimes concurrently with his public-service roles.

Louis continued to live on Beatrice Street until he left home for New York in his early 20s. By that time, he had made the decision to devote his time and energy towards the composition of music. Perhaps in no other arts discipline is there such a perceived distance between the experiences of the creator and the form and nature of the work. We listen to music, but we rarely ask ourselves what personal experiences have led the composers to express themselves in that way. This leads to a considerable contrast in the influences that are assumed to motivate the composer of music, as compared to the novelist, the dramatist, or the visual artist.

During the years of Louis's attendance at elementary and secondary schools, Canada's understanding of itself was being fuelled by visual artists we have come to know as the Group of Seven and early and late associates such as Tom Thomson and Emily Carr. We are told that their landscapes had many sources of inspiration — some as a result of the roles the artists played as Canadian military illustrators of the carnage of World War I, but also as a result of their travels into the isolated lands of the Canadian North or the more remote regions of the west coast (sometimes supported by commissions directed towards bringing tourists north and west to keep Canadian railways and their hotels profitable), but all leading to the creation of distinctive images by which Canadians defined themselves in the early decades of the 20th century. It would not occur to us to attempt any assessment of the work of these artists without some clear analysis of their formative years. Nor would we attempt to appreciate Margaret Laurence, a writer with a rich western Canadian background, or Robertson Davies, whose education and early dramatic experiences in the U.K. made him unique, without that understanding of their roots. But music is seen as so "abstract,"[25] even so exotic, that it seems impervious to the influence of all but the most devastating early-life experiences of the composer-artist.

Louis Applebaum's role as a composer — to say nothing of his other roles as musician, arts administrator, conductor, and producer — can be traced to the streets of central Toronto, to the playground of Clinton Public School, and to the Assembly Hall of Harbord Collegiate, but, most of all, to his association with other Jewish young people who continued to be his friends and colleagues. In one case, this association brought him a life-partner who has shared both the triumphs and the defeats that are essential elements of a life in the arts. The moments of youth became transformed and were preserved in the very fibre of each composition, in the quality of each just decision, and behind the insight that produced every plan of action or recommendation to government. These are the building blocks of Louis's creativity that are identifiable and understandable in a career that dominated Canadian cultural response for the latter part of the 20th century.

Chapter Two

Moulding a Musician

The Applebaums acquired a piano when Louis was only nine years old. However, this was no parental vote of confidence in music as a possible career choice for the Applebaum children. Quite the contrary! Louis explained, "every Jewish kid took music lessons."[1] Indeed, every home of the developing urban middle class in Canada was expected to have a piano, with parents encouraging their children to learn the rudiments of performance. The early 20th century was the heyday of parlour piano music.

The Applebaums were caught up in this behaviour, as was the Markovitz family next door. However, no precursors in either Morris' or Fanny's families would support any notion of musical genes in the Applebaum children. Certainly not the slightest expectation existed that either Louis or Ruth would make their living as musicians — and certainly not as composers. Indeed, Louis's parents hoped that he would either be a physician or a lawyer — professions seen as the heights of ambition for Jewish children.[2] Unfortunately, in Canadian faculties of law and medicine, formal and informal processes of the time ensured that only a minority of the admissions were Jews. A few bright Jewish youths were accepted into both professions — enough to silence any radicals who might wish to initiate change — but the vast majority of admissions were the offspring of Christian citizens, preferably Protestant and English-speaking.[3]

Discrimination at its worst, at the very point of entrance to a career choice, faced every Toronto Jewish youth in the first decades of this century, and certainly Louis Applebaum was no exception. Ultimately, the piano, a piece of "middle-class" furniture for his parents, became a doorway to a lifetime career opportunity for him.

Only a fierce determination could have impelled any Canadian youth in the 1930s to follow a career in music. In the best of times, work in arts-related jobs was unrewarding employment, and the 1930s were the worst of times. Aspiring to be an instrumentalist was bad enough, but to plan a career as a composer was viewed as sheer madness. Canada was still frontier and colonial, and that mentality continued well into the mid-20th century. Authors and composers, if people thought about them at all, were seen as unusually gifted males who came from other countries on other continents and, in most cases, were dead.

This country's musical life, which existed mainly in eastern Canada and particularly in Ontario and Quebec, was very much an inherited tradition from France and Britain and, in smaller measure, from other lands inhabited by Jewish minorities. The most pervasive influence was, of course, that of the British church musicians who came from the U.K. from the late 1700s until the mid-1900s. Healey Willan, the most famous of these immigrants by far, arrived in Canada in 1913 at the age of 33. Willan was heavily endowed with compositional characteristics acquired through the study of the works of Stanford, Parry, Holst, and the Elgar — by then considered to be the creators of a new era in British music.

The most prolific performance tradition could be found in the Christian church, and that was the major source of inspiration for Canadian composers. Canada shared in the excitement of the revival of the massive oratorio, with large forces of singers and musicians, and this led directly to the formation of the Mendelssohn Choir in Toronto in the 1890s. The choir was the country's first arts organization of such size and significance, and it proudly remains in place to this day.

Military bands also gave some encouragement to musical composition, especially for celebratory events — the monarch's birthday or the anniversary of some memorable event. With a sparse number of professional musicians and performing organizations in Canada, few of whom could master the major works of the classical repertoire, the motivation for composition was meagre indeed. Composers, unlike visual artists and writers, are at the mercy of performers, and without a base of professional musicians to perform their work, their role is, to put it generously, tentative. Thus, as late as the 1930s, composers were mainly amateur musicians who wrote a few pieces on special occasions for local groups — usually parish choirs. This was not a thrilling context in which a young man could expect to find sufficient opportunity and resources to pursue a full-time commitment.

Music historian Clifford Ford recognized the difficulties imposed by Canada's enormous size, and the limits this placed on opportunities for communication, as well as the reality of cultural divergence, and especially the contrasting traditions of English and French Canada. In his book, *Canada's Music: An Historical Survey,* he attributed the sad state of the composer to the lack of composer organizations:

Without an organization, the composer group found little
or no spiritual, intellectual or economic security in the profession which effectively discouraged the individual from
taking up composition on a major basis, or caused those
few composers to leave the country, such as Calixa Lavalée
or Clarence Lukas.[4]

By the time Louis had graduated from high school, Healey Willan,
Arnold Walter, and Leo Smith had formed an organization — the Vogt
Society — to encourage the performance of Canadian works. It lasted
only a few years. It was not until 1951 that the Canadian League of
Composers was formed to give support to the nation's composers. (Louis
himself was to become one of the instigators of this organizational effort
and a member of its first executive.) In short, the writing of music attracted only the most dedicated and determined — some would say the most
foolhardy — only those committed to some higher ideal. For some, this
ideal was the glory of God. For others, it was a secular goal such as that
of giving Canada a body of music that expressed the meaning of being a
citizen in a strange and empty land. It was the latter vision that was to
attract Louis Applebaum.

An exciting and encouraging community, a loving family, an ongoing
association with peers who shared interests and passions, were all supportive and positive influences on the young Louis. However, the individual
who led him to see music as his life was his music teacher, Boris Berlin.
Louis began taking lessons on the piano at the age of nine, but after a few
months with a temporary teacher, Mary MacDonald, he moved on to
Boris Berlin and the die was cast.[5]

Boris Berlin had come to Canada in 1925. In Czarist Russia, he had
spent a childhood as a member of an aristocratic family. Berlin and his family had emerged penniless from the 1917 revolution, but he had been able
to survive by selling the jewels he had salvaged from his family's possessions
as he fled the newly created Soviet Union. He finally arrived in Geneva,
Switzerland, where a kindly aunt gave him lodgings and, although he had
already acquired an extensive musical education, he studied literature there,
and later in Germany. Post-war Europe was in such chaos and his own future
so tenuous that he decided to try his fortune in the new world. He arrived
in Toronto where, initially, he found little happening in the Jewish community to which he could attach himself. Ultimately he discovered an enclave
of fine musicians but, more important, he found an opportunity for
employment that had been denied him in Europe.[6] Teaching music to the
offspring of the burgeoning middle class was to be his future.

Soon after Berlin's arrival, he found his first job at the Hambourg Conservatory — one of Toronto's first music training institutions. It was the only source of music lessons, other than the Toronto Conservatory (which was sometime later to receive the unique honour of being designated "Royal"). From the outset, Berlin seemed to be everywhere — giving lessons in Jewish homes around Markham Street where he lived, or at St. Christopher House where Louis found he could secure a lesson for 25 cents rather than the $1 it cost at his own home or at Berlin's studio.[7] From the moment the Applebaums brought their son Louis to Boris Berlin, a bond developed that remained alive for some 70 years. To Berlin, Louis seemed "a very nice boy … a very good-looking boy … most congenial. I had a bad temper but never with Louis."[8] Fanny and Morris had made a most fortunate choice.

Louis and his sister, Ruth, along with the Markovitz daughters, were expected to take piano instruction — the results of which would give them joy throughout their lives. However, both Louis and Boris Berlin soon agreed that Louis would not be an outstanding performer. He was simply "not interested in the mechanics of learning to play the piano," though he eventually did become proficient at playing duets with Joe Markovitz's daughter. Louis was, Berlin states, "much more interested in creating music … always interested in making music … always improvising."[9] Louis states quite unequivocally "I never learned to play the piano properly … I was not interested in technique and I hated to practise."[10]

However, the selection of Boris Berlin proved extraordinarily fortunate for a youth who was to see his future as a creator rather than a performer. Berlin, unlike many teachers, found his satisfaction in teaching children rather than adults, and his main goal was "to make students love music … not just play the piano."[11] Also, his enthusiasm seemed directed towards contemporary composers. (At that time — and certainly to Toronto ears — Debussy was definitely avant-garde and Stravinsky's music was perceived as dissonant and unapproachable; piano recitals then kept very much to the mainstream of 18th- and early 19th-century composition, with Bach, Beethoven and Chopin being favourites.) So, with the guidance of his teacher and mentor, Louis's interest soon turned to composing, and he joined the ranks of Debussy, Ravel, and Stravinsky! Berlin had retained his connections with Europe's musical world, and he was able to secure copies of recent compositions by contemporary composers — a skill that enthralled the young Applebaum. Louis was able to study and hear Berlin play the compositions that were moving sound in new directions, and it was this that encouraged Louis to try his own hand at creating rather than performing.

These hours with Berlin, rather than what was going on at Harbord

Collegiate, became Louis's focus. Indeed, Berlin found "that Applebaum's brain was always filled with music ... he could sit down and write good music with seeming ease."[12] Berlin encouraged Louis to write songs, and his lessons increasingly concentrated on the mysteries of composition. At the appropriate moment, he suggested to Louis that he enter a competition sponsored by the Canadian Performing Rights Society, a precursor to CAPAC and SOCAN. Contestants had to submit a song for adjudication, and the winner would not only be awarded a prize of $150, but would receive it from the hands of Canada's governor general at Rideau Hall in Ottawa.

At 18, Louis was in his final year at Harbord. By this time a fellow member of the group with which he had been so closely associated for so many years had secured his romantic interest. Jan Hershoff was a petite, slim, lovely young woman whose beauty was matched by her intelligence and wit. Louis had known her back in his Clinton Public School days and she was very much a part of the teenage gathering of Jewish young people who had continued to attract one another's company at Harbord. The feelings of fondness were reciprocal and it was a gift from Jan, a volume of Heinrich Heine's poems including "Du Hast Diamenten und Perlen" ("You have diamonds and pearls") that provided Louis with inspiration for his contest entry. Berlin had encouraged Louis to enter the contest as a way of testing his talent and determination, but it did not cross his mind that an 18-year-old could actually win. Louis proceeded to do just that, and he was invited to go to Ottawa, much to the consternation of his mother, whose love bordered on obsessive protectiveness. But Louis went nonetheless, accompanied by his father who "took him by the hand to the nation's capital."[13] How appropriate that the governor general of the day was John Buchan, Lord Tweedsmuir, an author and advocate for the arts!

The effect of this success was immediate: Louis Applebaum decided to be a composer. It was a shock to the entire family. To pursue a career as a professional musician was unwise, particularly in the context of a savage depression. Yet performers did make money. Morris and Fanny had little expectation that a composer could survive in the 1930s and they were right about most aspirants. However, Louis was adamant. Now he knew how he would spend his creative energy. There were no restrictions on those who were Jewish in this line of work. Indeed, Jewish composers, Mahler being the most recognized figure, had dominated the world of serious music throughout Europe in the latter years of the 19th century and were at the centre of popular musical forms in the U.S. and Europe. Making music was something Louis could do, and could obviously do well. Fortunately, even in their perplexity and in the hard times that seemed to have no end, Louis's parents never failed to give support to his ambitions.

27

But what kind of composer was he to be? There was a broad range of musical forms from "serious" or classical, to light dance music, to musical comedy (just entering its golden age), to religious music. Louis saw himself as a serious composer, but found himself attracted to virtually every genre. Now, however, music-making was becoming inextricably linked to the new communications technologies that had recently been developed — radio and the phonograph in particular. In the 1920s, radio came to dominate the lives of Canadians, and did so until mid-century, and the ubiquitous phenomenon of the moving picture was about to transform behaviour and lifestyle. The connection between communications technology and music was not initially obvious, but it was not long before Louis Applebaum made that association, and it became the nucleus of his composing career. Composers of the 17th and 18th centuries depended on the royal courts and great houses of the aristocracy. By the late 1800s, the industrial revolution had spawned a new middle class — providing an audience for the works of Beethoven, Berlioz, Brahms, Wagner, and Tchaikovsky — and lush surroundings in great concert halls and opera houses abounded. Now, in the 20th century, a mass audience would be available through radio, movie houses, and, ultimately, the television screen. Louis Applebaum had decided to be a composer at the very time this shift was taking place.

In 1937 the context of Louis's lifework was already in place: information dispersal, dramatic presentation, and entertainment were all to be a part of the 20th-century communication revolution that sought to reach the minds and hearts of all men and women. Indeed, perhaps the greatest equality in the democratic tendencies of the 20th century has been that of universal access to the very best (and worst) of artistic creations. Louis's first step had to be that of broadening his understanding of music and developing his skill at creating it, and he enrolled in the University of Toronto's Faculty of Music. For Louis, the reasons for this choice of academic program were more practical than academic. The university was accessible to Beatrice Street by streetcar and, frankly, slightly cheaper than continuing his studies at the Royal Conservatory. When asked by the *Canadian Jewish News* why he had gone to the University of Toronto and to the Music Faculty in particular, he answered simply: "It was cheapest!"[14] Speaking many years later to the graduating class of the Royal Conservatory of Music, Louis expanded on that theme:

> I was a student in the Faculty of Music. One of the reasons I am in music was because the tuition fee for the Faculty of Music was the lowest in the University of Toronto. It was $40 and for that you got an examination and a few lectures

given by Sir Ernest MacMillan, Healey Willan and Herbert Fricker. The courses in Harmony, Counterpoint Fugue, Orchestration, and History, you did on your own, or studied privately with whomsoever you chose.[15]

There was also an inevitability about the move: the conservatories in North America, including the Conservatory in Toronto, trained young people to experience the delight of competent performance. On the continent, by contrast, conservatories that were more generously subsidized by the state prepared talented youth to become professional musicians and composers. Some able Canadian performing artists seeking a career in music found their way to these institutions, but that alternative was far from Louis's mind and budget.

Though the Conservatory was now of less use to Louis, the purposes of the University's Faculty of Music were perfectly in line with his interest and enthusiasm — teaching the art and craft of composition. "The older Canadian universities had inherited the British concept whereby degrees at both undergraduate and graduate levels were awarded only in academic compositional skills such as harmony and counterpoint"[16]

Composer John Beckwith was a student in this faculty some years after Louis had left, but there had been little change. He described its character and musical interests from its very beginning with considerable perception:

> … a fair picture of the original 1918 Faculty is one of a group of organist-composers of English outlook who were conservative but not entirely unaware of the wider musical world of their time. Suggesting a different context, J. Paul Green and Nancy Vogan, in their *Music Education in Canada*, 1991, characterize the early Faculty program as not just English but "Anglican" in contrast to the "Methodist" heritage of public school music in Ontario.[17]

Certainly Toronto's faculty included some of the great names of Canadian music, at least from the English-speaking community. First and very much foremost was Sir Ernest MacMillan, who also gave leadership to the Conservatory and was even more widely known as the conductor of the Toronto Symphony Orchestra and the Mendelssohn Choir. As Canada's most distinguished musician, his views on everything musical were sought and respected. Healey Willan, by then ensconced as organist and choirleader at St. Mary Magdalene's Church in central Toronto, was, and still is, regarded as the country's most prominent composer of church music. Herbert

Fricker, a splendid organist and choir leader, and Leo Smith, a musical schol-ar of considerable note, completed a stellar team that could have graced any faculty in any university. Unfortunately, virtually the entire faculty repre-sented only one section of the broad spectrum of music that was emerging by the mid 1930s. Their traditional and English outlook meant that none of the faculty reflected the latter years of 19th century Europe. Neither Webern, Schoenberg, nor Hindemith were countenanced; nor yet Igor Stravinsky and Aaron Copland. Louis had been brought along farther in the direction of contemporary music by Boris Berlin.

Furthermore, after the frantic life of a high-school student involved in extra-curricular activities, enmeshed in the social life of his friends and asso-ciates, searching out ways to contribute to the family income, Louis found the life of the undergraduate in the Music Faculty less than totally challeng-ing. In his splendid book on Sir Ernest Macmillan, Ezra Schabas describes the music education at the University of Toronto quite bluntly. After comment-ing on "the university's passive attitude toward music," Schabas continues:

> The Faculty of Music's two degrees, the Mus. Bac. and Mus. Doc., were based on the British system — final exam-inations and submissions alone determined success or fail-ure. Students could attend lectures and tutorials or not, as they wished. The Faculty of Music had few students and those it did have generally passed or failed their degree requirements with little fuss.[18]

It turned out to be less simple for Louis Applebaum. For the next three years, he attended the lectures and took instruction from individual faculty members. He found that his time was in no way monopolized by the faculty's expectations, and he filled his schedule by attending lectures given by other faculties, particularly in philosophy, psychology, history and English literature. From the very outset of his career as a composer for documentaries and drama, Louis would make intense use of this informal education. The experience created not only an adult learner *par excellence,* but also a thinker whose mind was always ready to embrace the "big pic-ture." Louis never allowed himself the luxury of dwelling on the narrow and the inconsequential — whether he was writing music for drama, film, TV, or radio productions, or administering an arts organization. He con-stantly sought to intellectually extend and find universal meaning in any enterprise in which he was engaged.

Louis's three years as an undergraduate added little to his reputation as a performer or a creator of "serious" music. He wrote all the exams (failing one in second year) and, in third year, obtained conditional standing in harmony and fugue. The last challenge in his final year was to write an original composition, and Louis chose to present a string quartet as his final exercise. The composition was written and submitted, but somehow lost. As a result he never received his degree and thereby joined a distinguished coterie of degree-deprived graduands — individuals who excelled but simply failed to comply with all the requirements for formal graduation with a piece of parchment.

In contrast to his undistinguished record at the Faculty, Louis's informal musical accomplishments received considerable attention in the university's press during his final year. Under the headline, "Varsity Symphony Orchestra Premieres Work by Student," an article informs the university community that "The University of Toronto Symphony Orchestra, in its annual concert next Wednesday, will present the world premiere of a "Piece for Orchestra" by Louis Applebaum, student in the Faculty of Music." Louis is quoted as stating modestly "that the "Piece for Orchestra" has no meaning. It is not program music. It was written expressly for the University orchestra with nothing else in mind. In my opinion, it is musically not very important and contains nothing new."[19] All this attention came to a student who, a few months later, failed to graduate. The reason can be found partly in the rather casual attitude taken by the Faculty of Music about evaluation and graduation. Following the Oxbridge tradition, lectures, degrees, and formal attendance were not really important. Indeed, one could sit the exams without having taken classes at all. Candidates were free "to study from curricular outlines and old exam papers and simply turn up for the exam …."[20] That Louis did not graduate simply did not matter. He did not follow up on the loss of the string quartet; his mind was soon filled with other things, in particular, his proposed studies in New York. Actually, Jan Applebaum, his wife of some 60 years, has a simpler explanation for this nonchalance about acquiring a degree: his love for her concentrated his attention on her constant presence rather than on the completion of his music studies. His preoccupation with his future life-partner, along with his plans for further education, made formal graduation seem less crucial, if not irrelevant. That, combined with an apparent lack of attention to such details on the part of the Faculty of Music, meant that Louis lived his life academically undistinguished until decades later, when he began to receive honorary doctorates.

Perhaps Louis's most important musical experience in these years took place outside the classroom. Louis had become a member of a Jewish fraternity, Beta Sigma Rho. His old colleagues, Frank Shuster and Johnny Wayne, had both entered the University of Toronto as well but were unable to afford the cost of joining the fraternity. A fellow student, Milton Shulman, recognized their potential as entertainers and was able to get them an entrée into the fraternity. In the mid-1930s, all the affiliated colleges (Victoria, University, Trinity, and St. Michael's), as well as the fraternities, put on some kind of special event, usually a dance, for the entire university community. There was a good deal of competition and Beta Sigma Rho decided not to mount a dance, but to go all out by presenting a major production of skits and musical numbers in a tradition established by the University College Follies — the *pièce de résistance* for undergraduate presentations on the University of Toronto campus at that time. Thus, the Beta Sigma Revue was born.

Wayne and Shuster wrote the script and the songs — a task that presented no challenge after several years in the "oola-boola" club at Harbord Collegiate. However, they decided to use the talents of their old friend and classmate Louis Applebaum and placed him in charge of musical production, as well as making him their accompanist. Wayne and Shuster's talents in the composition of songs was severely limited. In fact, they could compose only in the key of C. Louis found the original score so boring that he was given to developing more interesting arrangements of the melodies, even changing the key signatures, to extend the harmonic variety. This threw off the vocalizing of the two comics so completely that Shuster remembers shouting, "Lou, for God's sake, learn to play on the white keys!" At one point they fired Louis and brought in Shuster's sister, Geraldine, also a student of Boris Berlin, but a musician who had no propensity for shifting key signatures. The break was temporary, Louis was reinstated and the revue was a smashing success, outshining even the chief competitor for campus accolades, the U.C. Follies.[21]

As well as having an active campus life, Louis was faced with the task of relieving his parents' financial burden for his education. He worked as a teacher and social worker in Jewish social centres and summer camps. His work included being a recreational worker at the YMHA and a counsellor and musical activity director at the B'nai B'rith Camp on Lake Couchiching. During these undergraduate years, Louis also worked in various ways with Jewish music, both in his faith tradition and in more recreational contexts with young people he was serving. Yet he was determined to reach beyond the confines of one religious tradition, to embrace the sounds that inspired and brought joy to people of other faiths and no faith at all. At the same time, he never minimized the impact of the Jewish musical tradition on his music, openly reflecting on this question in an interview for *The Harbordite*.

> What is Jewish music? If I write a piano sonata, is this Jewish? Well, yes and no. Because it is a statement of my background it has to be inherently Jewish.[22]

Louis was to write music that spoke to many people of many faiths. Indeed, his arrangements of Christian Christmas carols have been heard around the world. He, like John Weinzweig, another Jewish music-maker, never became a "Jewish composer."

A later generation of composers was to produce a Srul Irving Glick, who brought forth very moving works that drew inspiration from the Jewish scriptures in his choral and instrumental works, and who overtly celebrated his Jewishness in all his musical compositions.[23] Yet Louis's own religious ties remained strong. He and Jan attended their synagogue and enjoyed their association with those who worshipped with them. His sister, Ruth, and her husband were founders of the Temple Sinai synagogue in Toronto. His grandson Jordan, with whom Louis was especially close, observed a few months before his death, "I see Lou as a man of great faith ... but not a religious man. He attends his synagogue because he is intellectually stimulated. He sees it as an exercise in historical study, in debate and discussion." Still, Jordan has no hesitation in stating that Louis drew his values and the guidelines for his personal behaviour from the deep well of Judaic religious tradition. In the same interview, describing Louis's career in motion picture, drama and television (where one often looks in vain for an indication of moral integrity), Jordan put this quite bluntly: "Louis will do only what he believes is right. If it seems wrong in his mind, he simply will not do it."[24] In later years, Louis and his sister, Ruth, attended the synagogue on the day of the death of both parents, and Louis insisted on a yearly visit to the graves of both Morris and Fanny. He and Jan kept the High Holidays of the Jewish faith and Louis always responded to any invitation to write a composition for his synagogue.[25] His obsessive interest in the political and social events going on around him, stemming from a Hebrew scripture tradition that simply would not let go, completely negated the image of the isolated artist.

In the summer of 1940 when Louis was working as a music director at Camp Arowhon, a summer camp in Algonquin Park, a dramatic event transpired. Louis's relationship with Jan Hershoff had matured through many years of association. Now the two were deeply in love. Jan had shared Louis's pride of accomplishment in winning a prize for the song he had composed, and it was a particularly sweet triumph as she knew she had been the inspiration and had participated by finding the perfect text. They had been waiting for years while Louis attended university and now they wanted to seal their commitment through marriage. It was a time of war and violence in the world, and Louis's future seemed somewhat chaotic as he sought further work that would enhance his opportunities to compose music, but Jan and Louis both felt that it was time for them to face these challenges together, as partners.

There were difficulties to overcome. Morris and Fanny Applebaum had great expectations for the sole male heir of their family and these did not include a hasty marriage to a young woman they found to be delightful and intelligent, but not sufficiently elevated in social class to be a spouse for their beloved Louis. As well, Louis's only income came from his modest employment as a part-time camp counsellor, social worker, and arts organizer in the Jewish community. To say it was modestly paid work would be a major understatement. At this point the only further education that made any sense would be available south of the border or across an ocean at an expense that would stretch the Applebaum budget beyond bearing. The path of true love and the road to a composing career were both strewn with rocks of many sizes.

That same summer, Jan was with her mother at Crystal Beach, west of Toronto. The only tolerable solution to the couple's difficulties seemed to be to resolve at least one issue immediately — their life together. They agreed to marry secretly and to reveal the fact only after Louis had completed his studies. However, the logistics of the wedding presented a distinct problem. The couple were now apart — at least for the summer. By the fall their separation might be even more long-lasting and the opportunity for closeness more tenuous. A speedy union would be workable only if they could both leave their summer abodes, meet in Toronto, find a rabbi to marry them and then make their way back to camp and family without suspicion being aroused. This they determined to do.

Louis had a day off coming to him as a camp administrator, and Jan convinced her mother that her presence in Toronto on a certain day was essential. Louis caught the train out of Algonquin Park and Jan took leave of her mother and made her way to Toronto where they met and took themselves to the home of Rabbi Sacks, who on July 19, 1940, dutifully performed the ceremony, with his son as witness.[26] After the brief ceremony, Louis and Jan went for a walk and Louis bought her a yellow rose. Expressions of eternal love, a restrained embrace in a crowded railway station, and Jan returned to her mother at Crystal Beach while Louis made his way back to Camp Arowhon. Louis told only one person — his close friend and fellow camp administrator, Frank Shuster. They were sitting together on the pier and Louis desperately wanted to tell someone of his happiness. With shock and disbelief, Shuster could only repeat again and again, "You can't have … it makes no sense!" [27] — not the reaction which Louis had anticipated but one that he would hear again from other sources.

Chapter Three

The Seductive Screen

The eventful summer of 1940 came to a close, but an even more dramatic autumn emerged. The two secretive newlyweds were now back in Toronto in their expected places — at home with their families and socializing with their friends. No one suspected. Very soon, surprising and exciting news captured the minds of the Applebaum family and distracted their attention from any unusual behaviours on the part of their son and his neighbourhood girlfriend. Louis had decided to seek a scholarship at the Juilliard School of Music in New York City, the very pinnacle on the North American continent for learning to be a musician — composer or performer. Though he had not distinguished himself at the University of Toronto or graduated with full honours, his submission of a musical composition had so impressed the Juilliard selection committee that, although a full scholarship was not forthcoming, he received an equally attractive offer from a senior staff faculty member who was to accept him for individual study. Louis eagerly enrolled at Juilliard with high hopes for a learning experience unavailable in his native land.

He left Toronto in the fall of 1940 to work with Bernard Wagenaar, a Dutch-born composer whose work was little played, but who had the capacity to arouse extraordinary awareness of the form and structure of "serious" music. Louis was immediately thrust into the full activity of a working composer and found himself writing music exercises endlessly, all connected to the process of adapting the methods of the masters to create his own personal sound. Not even his work with Boris Berlin, Sir Ernest MacMillan, or Healey Willan had prepared him for the pressure he was facing day by day. He discovered again the thrill of " working with someone who inspires you."[1] This experience was to be a pattern in his life, as at virtually each stage of his career he was to be inspired by some individual, such as Boris Berlin, John Grierson, Tyrone Guthrie, Hamilton Southam, Arthur Gelber, and Mavor Moore — all men whose vision drove them and their associates to accomplish more than they could have believed possible.

However, Louis's concentrated attention on Wagenaar's expectations was soon interrupted by the arrival on the Juilliard campus of one of America's most prominent composers, Roy Harris. He had been invited as a guest lecturer, and the Henry Street Settlement in New York was offering a scholarship to allow a promising young composer an opportunity to work with this musical giant. Applebaum received a friend's clipping from the *New York Times* informing him of this opportunity and immediately applied. His application was successful and meant that he now had made contact with a real "name" in the music creation enterprise. Harris, on his arrival in New York, organized a small class of graduate students, one, though technically still an undergraduate, being Louis Applebaum. Louis was attracted to the major characteristic of Harris's music — the "long line of lyrical exposition that draws the listener in" — a direct contrast to the more fragmented musical expressions of the Viennese School.[2] Unfortunately for Louis, this latter style had captured the commitment of his present mentor, Bernard Wagenaar. Harris, though only a temporary faculty member, also expected a constant flow of music composition from his rigorously selected students. Louis experienced yet again the closed mind of academe — teachers unable to welcome and celebrate difference. Neither Wagenaar nor Harris could countenance the work of the other. Indeed, Louis discovered that to bring a composition he had written influenced by Harris to the attention of Wagenaar, or vice versa, unleashed a torrent of recrimination that shocked the generous-minded, tolerant, but naïve Louis. Yet in the midst of all this tension and conflict, he gleaned a gem of philosophic advice from Roy Harris that he never forgot: "Find a musical path ... persist in it ... history may provide a fit ... . If so, you are on your way ... if not, then you have followed your own light ... to a fulfilling life."[3]

Finding that "fit" is the struggle in every creative artist's life and it was certainly a central focus of Applebaum's many-faceted career. Louis remained only six months in New York, returning in the early spring of 1941 to Toronto, but not before two dramatic explosions took place. One occurred in his personal life; the other provided a revelation of such impact that it decided the first phase of his working life and influenced his career as a composer forever.

Jan had remained in Toronto, still the "girlfriend" of the aspiring scholar whose life in New York was now concentrated on the task of completing his training as a composer. Both husband and wife were desperate to see each other. Jan saw an opportunity to visit her new husband; she had an aunt who lived not far away from Mrs. Wolkin's boarding house where

Louis had found inexpensive accommodation. They both began laying plans for a liaison. Once it became known that Jan was going off to New York, Louis's mother, Fanny, saw the inappropriateness of a young woman travelling alone to a large and dangerous city. Needless to say, she also wanted very much to see her only son, and invited herself to come along as a chaperone. The belated honeymoon tryst was now in jeopardy, and in the confusion, the secret of the marriage was revealed — much to the horror of both families.

The reaction of Louis's mother was predictable. The deed was done ... but it had to be seen to be done. The respectability of the family demanded that every member and every acquaintance, yes, the entire Jewish community of Toronto and beyond be informed by a process that has come down through the ages ... bridal showers, special receptions, and gatherings at which the bride and, on occasion, the groom would be present so that all would understand that Jan and Louis were indeed married, officially and forever. For Jan, this torture meant having to achieve acceptance into the Applebaum clan as well as assuaging the disappointments of her own family. These circumstances increased Louis's desire to return to Toronto and his new bride as soon as possible.

However difficult its beginning, the marriage brought joy and confidence to Louis at every stage of his life; but it would not be without tensions. The life of a freelance composer is often peripatetic; combined with the demands made on a conductor, a producer, a film-maker, and an arts administrator and advocate, it also required a great deal of night work. For Jan, a private person with her own compelling motivation as a visual artist, this life had much excitement and satisfaction that she could share with Louis; but it also included many weeks and months of inevitable separation and loneliness. More important, it required that she sublimate her own creative ambitions in order to serve the needs of a husband with a host of roles to perform, projects to complete, and places to be.[4] For generations of women this was expected; only in the last decades has the injustice been corrected — too late for Jan.

When Louis arrived in New York, all the talk in the city was about the World's Fair that had opened some months before. This was the planet's "last hurrah" while politicians and diplomats in Europe tried to restrain an aggressive Hitler and before the real violence of the war had reached the English-speaking world. This World's Fair provided a wonder for a young man just out of university in "small-town" Toronto. The exhibits predicted a future of glorious dimensions, with every technological expectation displayed in all its innocence. The Fair itself was a mammoth enterprise, setting the standard for post-war fairs until Montreal's "Expo 67" replaced it as the template. The enterprise might well have overwhelmed a very young and inexperienced Louis Applebaum — and it would have been understandable if he had avoided its attractions completely, given his domestic complications and the pressures of Juilliard. However, Louis had a friend in New York, Reuben Frank, who, as the son of a newspaper editor, could get free passes to the Fair. As well, Frank had even greater access as a reporter for the *Newark News* and invited Louis to share this opportunity.

For Louis, the World's Fair was a godsend, and for several weeks it became his recreational home. One exhibit particularly drew his attention and he became preoccupied with it — a booth operated by the U.S. Department of Agriculture just inside the main gate. Inside, two films played continuously, both by Petr Lorenz — *The River* and *The City* — and both were in the genre of film art that came to be known as the documentary. These films had a strong thematic base, a commitment to the presentation of actual events, a clear message of despair in the economic system, and a hope that from Roosevelt's New Deal would come a better world. The former film was enhanced by the musical score of Virgil Thomson and the latter, by that of Aaron Copland. Louis saw these films 17 times! He was captivated, entranced and came to the conclusion that this is what he wanted to do — make music that added insight and excitement to the visual presentation of films concerned with real events and living people.

The early war years of the 20th century gave an enormous boost to the art of film-making. Not only did the Spanish-American War, the Boer War and the First World War provide exciting film content, but film-makers realized that if cameras and cameramen were absent from the scene, they could re-create the naval battles and the trench warfare in the studio. Fragments of news became a popular addition to the entertainment expectations of the public in the century's early decades. As a newly literate public had earlier gleaned their news from the newspaper, people in this century were to learn about the world they inhabited from moving images, at first on screens, often in converted vaudeville theatres, and later from boxes they placed in their living rooms and eventually many other rooms in their homes.

Louis perceived, even at this point, that sound, particularly appropriate musical intervention, could give clearer understanding and certainly more intense emotional impact to the depiction of events on film. Aaron Copland, who became America's foremost composer, had been attracted to the role of providing such music, and Louis was already aware that William Walton, Benjamin Britten, and Ralph Vaughan Williams, the music-making giants who had succeeded Edward Elgar in the U.K., were also involved in film projects. Even though Canada had little to offer in film-making in the 1930s, the earliest film of the documentary genre,

Nanook of the North, made by the legendary Robert J. Flaherty, had used the Canadian Arctic as its venue and had created a sensation when it was distributed in 1922.[5] At least there was a tenuous connection for a Canadian to build on.

Roy Harris, the most significant of Louis's mentors at Juilliard, was also fascinated by the possibilities of writing music for film. It provided a challenge to composers in the U.S., Britain, and in several countries outside the English-speaking world. Even in revolutionary Russia, Dziga Vertov was making films about the achievements of the new communist regime: his 1931 production, *Symphony of the Donbas,* was followed by *Three Songs of Lenin.* Even the titles of these works heralded the alliance of film and music.[6] In Sweden and Germany, as early as 1921, Viking Eggeling and Hans Richter began experiments in abstract film which attempted to pattern visual effects to accompany the fugues of J. S. Bach. In fact, Richter's 1928 film was called *Racing Symphony.* In France, Darius Milhaud wrote a score for Jean Painlevé's *Sea Horse.*[7] The New York World's Fair made Louis aware that the documentary film, with a generous focus on music, was going to be an art form that would engage composers in all countries. He decided he wanted to be a part of that development, even though he saw many difficulties and pitfalls for composers in the documentary genre.

Louis was excited not only by the making of music for film, but also by a collective creative experience that he could articulate only after years of active involvement in this genre of film-making. If he had been looking for instant gratification, he would have been better to attach himself to a burgeoning entertainment film company. As well as the process, however, there was the matter of content. Louis had lived through the 1930s as a teenager and had witnessed the effects of the Great Depression on the people around him. He had watched the hopes of young people he had worked with at YMHA and summer camps being dashed by the brutal and insensitive economic system that had dominated that decade. The responses of fascist governments in Europe had included forms of anti-Semitism that had influenced behaviours of young men even in Louis's own neighbourhood of downtown Toronto. In New York he had an opportunity to see what the progressive policies of the Roosevelt years had achieved, and he was impressed. The documentary film movement in that country was driven by a desire to explain the injustices that the economic system had produced and to celebrate the success of the Roosevelt's social reforms — some of which had involved the expansion of the arts and the provision of jobs for artists. Indeed, this connection between reform thinking and documentary film-making in Europe and North America was to bring upon its proponents, indeed upon the entire American film-making community, the suspicion of conservative forces, culminating in the excesses of the Joseph McCarthy era. Louis recognized these links. He commented years later about these films he had seen, mentioning "the way titles speak of living, colourful, and vital issues about which all should be concerned … slum clearance, maternity death rates, rural electrification … the stuff that newspaper editorials were made of … ."[8]

The Canada to which Louis was returning had gone through a decade of joblessness. It had borne all the tragic dislocation that the United States had suffered but had been even less effective in its response. Louis arrived in Toronto, warmly welcomed by a new wife but with no job and no prospects. With the film-making industry in Canada at such a minimal level, there was little hope that Louis's newly acquired interest in film music would have any opportunity to mature and develop — and it was even less likely to provide the means by which he could support a family. To make ends meet he returned to the YMHA and the roles of counsellor, organizer, and social worker, and, as well, to give piano lessons to neighbourhood children and young people. In his role as a teacher he emulated his original mentor Boris Berlin, adopting his methods and insisting that his students "not so much learn to play as learn music" — not just the classics but contemporary music. Berlin had a relative who took lessons from Louis and who reported that his lessons consisted mostly of Louis "playing his own music and encouraging his students to compose their own music." According to Berlin, this former Applebaum student still maintains "an intense commitment to music, even though he is not a professional musician."[9]

Louis's life as a composer had been placed on hold. However, some months after his return he met Godfrey Ridout, another young composer who was also to become a major figure in Canada's music world (though more drawn to the traditional rather than experimental forms of music). Godfrey told him of a new institution that had arrived in Ottawa called the National Film Board. Louis also bumped into another friend, Sydney Newman, who had joined the NFB, and he offered to introduce him to John Grierson, the head of the organization. An Act of Parliament establishing the NFB had just been passed and it was to be a government film-making agency whose genesis was in the event occupying the minds of Canadians in that year — the war in Europe. Within a few months, the crises in Czechoslovakia and Poland had brought Canada into a war. For a young, idealistic Louis Applebaum, the NFB presence in Ottawa solved a number of problems. He needed a job with sufficient income to support a wife and possibly a family. However, he also had other reasons for pursuing work with the NFB. His stay in New York had increased his "Canadianness" and he was anxious to serve his country by applying the knowledge he had acquired and the skills he had honed in the U.S. It was becoming clearer that the war was not just about a badly arranged peace in 1919; a madman had a cause that included the domination of Europe and encompassed the total annihilation of the Jewish people in Germany and any other country he could conquer. The question became: how could Louis — as a musician and, more specifically, as a composer — use his talents in the service of his country, in the defence of the values he held most dear, and on behalf of the Jewish people who were facing the most horrendous slaughter in world history? The National Film Board became the answer to that question in a world that Louis had glimpsed at the New York World's Fair. Just as *The City* and *The River* had justified the Roosevelt New Deal (and the film-maker Lorenz was to follow up these documentaries with one that was even more overtly sociologically based — *The Plow That Broke the Plains*), the mandate of the NFB had to do with helping Canada understand both itself and the war in which it was engaged. Information conveyed through both word and image was a weapon of war even more now than it had been in the early years of the century.

The man who came to epitomize everything the NFB stood for was John Grierson — a charismatic prophet figure, a single-minded preacher, and a passionate social reformer. He believed that film was the greatest hope for democracy, a system of government he perceived to be failing around the world. He saw film as a means by which all people, whatever their language or educational attainment, could become citizens of the world. In his mind, the moving image on film provided the greatest hope for humankind. Grierson was quite clear about his "cause":

> The new world can be felt as so large and so complex that it seems to overwhelm our capacity to find harmonies within it, which the human spirit seeks and must seek. One tendency is to see only the disorder. There may be a certain feeling of hopelessness about finding order within that seeming disorder. You will, therefore, expect some pessimism and even some despair in our remarkable account of this modern dilemma. Waiting for Godot we are, all of us, but what, of course, is hopeful in the situation is that in merely waiting for Godot, we find him.[10]

Greirson had already proven himself as a great documentary film-maker. He had seen what Russian film-makers, like Sergei Eisenstein, had accomplished in making their art form accomplish a social purpose. A Scot, he had been hired by the United Kingdom's Empire Marketing Board to make films, ostensibly to encourage British trade. He had no hesitation in making film statements that served his own progressive purposes. He knew the potential of film as art and his motto was "Art is a hammer, not a mirror."[11] After his film unit was transferred to the U.K.'s Post Office, he had produced the documentary, *Night Mail* — a film Louis perceived as his most important so far. The soundtrack had been the work of Benjamin Britten, a composer with whom Louis was to work later at the Stratford Shakespearean Festival but who had, even at this point, established himself as one of Britain's major musical forces. The soundtrack also included the word rhythms of W.H. Auden, a noted poet and a close collaborator with Britten — another indication of how far the documentary could be stretched with the creative use of sound. The other figure central to the establishment of the National Film Board was, of all people, the Right Honourable William Lyon Mackenzie King, the prime minister of Canada. The amazing aspect of the creation of the NFB is that King and others in the Cabinet recognized the power of a new technology like film to a degree that no Canadian government had before or has since.[12] In King's mind, it was essential that Canadians understand the world and their place in it, and film was the most effective way to make this happen.

The importance of these events for Louis Applebaum cannot be exaggerated. At a symposium some years later, Applebaum described the impact of Grierson and the NFB on his working life:

> The National Film Board is vital to me because it created me. I came to the Film Board out of school, enamoured with film, and Grierson took me and shaped me entirely into what I am. I attribute my whole life to John Grierson. I started living in 1941. The Grierson faith in youth that you've heard about, Grierson's ability to take a bunch of untried, anxious, desperate, passionate youths, and convert them into something else, is what really mattered. That's what happened to me ....He turned us into film-makers, and he turned us into public servants. The idea of contributing to society was something that he instilled in all of us.[13]

Ridout and Newman's news about the creation of the NFB provoked an immediate response — Louis headed for the offices of the NFB and was hired immediately by John Grierson himself who had certain expectations of all those he hired. "Grierson's recruits almost without exception, were socialistically inclined activists inspired by *Drifters* and *Battleship Potemkin* (the ultimate examples of film with a social message)."[14]

It would stretch a point to suggest that Louis Applebaum was a "social-istically inclined activist" but most certainly he fell under the spell of this extraordinary man. When asked how much he expected to be paid, Louis was nonplussed, particularly when Grierson asked how much he was mak-ing in his present employment. Louis blurted out "eighty dollars" — his monthly pay, not the weekly remuneration Grierson was inquiring about. A deal based on this confused information was closed when Grierson offered forty dollars a week and Jan and Louis moved to Ottawa, to 316 Nelson Street, and with the prospect of a family now in sight, to a house situated right beside a schoolyard. The newlyweds were delighted to secure a home in Ottawa after months of having to live with Jan's parents on Louis's return to Toronto from New York. So began a relationship with Canada's capital, a relationship which was to bring them opportunities for becoming involved in developments transforming that city from a cultural desert into, if not a cultural feast, at least a tolerable venue for the nation's artistic expression.

Louis's first task, even before his full-time employment, was to write the music for a film whose title starkly reveals the role for the NFB which had been set out by a country at war: *Call for Volunteers*. Only 10 minutes long, it glorified the women of Winnipeg who were contributing to the war effort through myriad activities, essentially keeping the fabric of society intact. Within a few months of the creation of a Central Volunteer Bureau, 7000 volunteers and a staff of 20 were collecting reading material for the troops, arranging recreation for troops stationed in the area, and collecting salvage that could be recycled. All these activities were visually expressive. The film was to be inspirational and Louis's music would create a sense of occasion with its regal themes and the fragments of enticing melodies. As well, though, there had to be dance music when volunteers were entertain-ing the soldiers and poignant music to accompany efforts to reach out to children in need. The film dramatically exhibited what a community could do both to support the war effort and to carry on essential social services. It was a splendid beginning to Louis's work as a film music composer.

As he had expected, Louis discovered that he had not taken a job, but rather had joined a crusade, an all-consuming activity devoted to one out-come — the winning of a war. He also discovered Grierson's approach to film-making, which he had brought from the U.K. and considered the basis of his success. Films were not made by individual "stars" who were given sole credit and whose word was law on the set, in the studio, or in the editing and cutting rooms. Films were made by teams of artists. Louis found that even though his responsibility might be the soundtrack and the musical score it demanded, he was involved in every aspect of the making of the film. To his surprise, but ultimately to his satisfaction, he soon found he was spending as much time in the cutting room as he was at the piano. And he was learning about every aspect of the art.[15]

Louis was hired in 1941 as an assistant to Ralph Apsey, an American film-maker drawn to the NFB by the Grierson name and reputation. However, before the following year was out, Apsey returned to the U.S. and Louis was put in charge of the entire music department of the Board. It was a major challenge to find competent musicians in a city like Ottawa, which had no symphony orchestra and thus no coterie of professionals who could be hired for particular "gigs." The film industry, at least at the NFB in the 1940s, demanded the services of musicians who could learn their parts quickly, sight-reading accurately and sensitively with virtually no rehearsal. In spite of this disadvantage, Louis ferreted out a number of able instrumentalists. Some were scientists associated with the National Research Council, and he found others in the military bands associated with the armed forces stationed near the nation's capital. In an effort to develop a pool of musicians from which he could draw as the need demanded, he recruited amateurs and brought them together to form an orchestra that rehearsed regularly and became quite proficient.[16]

However, the politics of hiring, remunerating, and firing musicians brought him into inevitable conflict with the American Federation of Musicians and Walter Murdoch, the regional local Toronto Musical Protective Association's determined and aggressive President, whose jurisdiction included Ottawa. In the early 1940s, Murdoch had come to realize that sound films would be a major source of income for musicians, and it was the Federation's strategy to see that adequate compensation was forthcoming to as many union members as it was possible to justify on any particular film job. That meant negotiating for as large an ensemble as possible, at the highest rates, for playing the background music of every film. In Hollywood, the Federation believed that a complement of 50 was a minimum and, as well, that a wage scale should be established high enough to provide a living wage for those musicians so employed. It was Murdoch's belief that "the Queen can afford anything" and that Canada should follow that Hollywood example. However, Louis believed that the NFB was not a giant Hollywood studio with a capacity to make great profits, nor was it an extension of the entertainment industry. It was a government initiative seeking to win a war through the educational process of the documentary film. He was prepared to pay an adequate wage but he wanted to use smaller ensembles that he believed in most cases would provide music more appropriate for a documentary soundtrack. He and Walter Murdoch clashed again and again on this issue and it was not to be the last time that Louis, who, ironically, was to spend a great deal of time assisting his musician colleagues, was to face an intransigent union "boss" who would make his life a misery.

It was not just about labour relations; there was a principle of music creation and performance at stake. Even at this early stage Louis was reacting against the overblown sound produced by large orchestras, and had begun a long struggle of convincing people that, with imaginative composition, smaller numbers of instrumentalists could produce more responsive music on the screen, in the theatre, and on the concert-hall stage. He was attracted even then to lean and flexible musical production with small ensembles of fine musicians. He resisted the unwieldy and expensive source of sound provided by the full late-19th-century symphony orchestra augmented to perform the symphonies of Mahler and Bruckner, and the expansive, imaginative emanations of Berlioz and Richard Strauss (to say nothing of Richard Wagner). In fact, Louis was to produce very few scores for full orchestra throughout a long life of composing.

Seeking out quality sound provided another challenge for Louis in musically unsophisticated Ottawa. Eventually the volume of work and the very limited technology available in the inadequate NFB sound studios forced Louis to record his soundtracks in Toronto and even New York.[17] This expanding need to find recording venues exacerbated the struggle with Murdoch, who worried that the Applebaum pattern for achieving background sound for film might become more widely followed. This tension surfaced regularly over many years as Louis acquired simultaneous roles as composer, conductor, administrator and producer, in the contexts of both film and music theatre.

The most immediate task facing the young 23-year-old musician and composer was that of increasing his skill as a conductor. In the major studios, the musical director of a film would simply hire a career conductor who would be responsible for assuring the quality of musical performance that would enhance the film soundtrack. Not so at the National Film Board. There was no time to work with a professional conductor to produce the sound hurriedly created by the composer, and yet it was vital to instantly achieve the perfect timing for every film segment. It was up to Louis, with stopwatch and baton in hand, to see that the deadlines were met. Because the music was one of the last layers of activity in the making of a film, the deadline was usually not weeks, but days or even hours away from the moment he began to create the soundtrack.[18]

Fortunately, Louis could conduct. He had taken a course from Ettore Mazzoleni, a dedicated music educator and who, for some years, had been assistant conductor of the Toronto Symphony Orchestra. It had been a class which included one of the dominant figures in Canada's musical life,

Howard Cable, a beloved colleague of a lifetime; but at that time conducting was not high on Louis's list of preferred musical activities. He learned quickly at the NFB, however, and it was the launch of a conducting career that developed and expanded with continuous experience, particularly at Stratford and the CBC. Conductors have become media favourites in this century and, with the ease of transportation of contemporary life, a relatively few star maestros may be conductors of several orchestras on more than one continent. (Some would suggest that this is a much abused practice that has lowered the quality of music performance significantly.) Indeed, the 20th century has seen composers such as Leonard Bernstein, John Williams, Aaron Copland, and Igor Stravinsky regularly mounting the podium.

Louis had no interest in this aspect of conducting. He enjoyed conducting as an opportunity to learn a musical score along with colleagues he treated as equals, not as a way of obtaining the public attention and adulation that performance sometime brings. He found joy on the podium in the searching and struggling of rehearsal; not in the applause and "bravos" of audience approval.[19] In Louis's beginnings at the NFB, conducting was simply a "hands-on" task dedicated to the frantic completion of another film — no clapping and cheering, just a silent prayer of thankfulness that another soundtrack was on its way.

Ruth Budd, one of the most proficient string bass players that Canada has produced and a member of the Toronto Symphony for many years, played under Louis's direction on a number of occasions. Her perception was that he had none of the ego needs that wash over "great" and famous conductors. "He knew what he wanted … .he was always serious about the integrity of the score …. you were always learning from him … it was always an experience of working together with the conductor, rather than being pushed … .one was never at odds with Louis Applebaum."[20] Quite an accolade from one working in the back row of the orchestra, but echoed by other musicians who served in the "pit" at Stratford. Ezra Schabas, who, in his role as a celebrated clarinet player was an occasional member of Louis's CBC studio orchestra, explains that Applebaum was not really interested in conducting as a vocation: "it was never an end, only a means to the ultimate expression of the score. In fact, Louis never really cared about conducting … he was a composer!"[21]

Charles Clay, a columnist for the *Montreal Standard* visited the NFB in 1943 and describes the scene and Louis's place in it quite vividly:

> Every room, every department bulges with creative energy … People dash about and everything is geared to the highest level … And strolling around in the midst of this

welter of activity is a nonchalant young man with one of
the friendliest smiles you've ever had aimed at you .... He
is 25 year old Louis Applebaum, senior member of the
music and composing staff ... the man who composes the
background music you hear in *World of Action Canada,
Canada Carries On,* and other Film Board products.[22]

Louis Applebaum was on the front line of the propaganda/information
battle that was part of the total war strategy. By 1941 Hitler's forces had
rolled over western Europe, and it was questionable whether the United
Kingdom could survive after Dunkirk revealed the full extent of Allied
weakness. The NFB saw itself as just as much a part of this determination
to turn the tide as the Allied Command in the U.K. The bosses expected
that films about important matters could be made in days. Louis recounts
times when teams would work non-stop for 72 hours to meet a deadline.
There could be no delay — the films had to be in the hands of distributors
and out in the field with a speed unthinkable in peacetime. The circuit
included schoolhouses in remote farmlands where the entire community
gathered in an evening to view these magical NFB productions that showed
them why their agricultural output was essential to an Allied victory.[23]

Applebaum found himself a member of a very elite group, a combination of seasoned film-making veterans and young, inexperienced, but highly energetic and thoroughly committed professionals who just wanted to
learn everything there was to know about film, particularly documentary
film. The group included James Beveridge, Bob Anderson, Tom Daly,
Sydney Newman, Stuart Legge, and, of course, the incomparable Norman
McLaren, a man whose genius for animation was already world-renowned.
The music and sound team that Louis led included Maurice Blackburn,
Eldon Rathburn, Phyllis Gummer and Robert Fleming — a splendid col-
lection of fine composers who were to be his lifetime friends. Through the
NFB he came to know Lucio Agostini, who, through working for Associated
Screen News in Montreal, became involved in the recording of sound-tracks
and ultimately became a close friend and colleague for many decades after.

The NFB, housed in an old barn on Sussex Avenue, shared its quarters
with the Ministry of Health and the building, even by Ottawa's wartime
standards, was a disgrace as a public building for any purpose. Health staff
conducted experiments on guinea pigs throughout the building, and the
smell of these animals pervaded all the working areas. The NFB's equipment
was of museum vintage, "heavy, ugly stuff" that required constant servicing
and was not easily transportable. A screening room held 20 to 30 people, but
the NFB had neither the funds nor the space for a grand piano and Louis

found that he had to negotiate with the French Embassy nearby which did have such an instrument. However, the Embassy wanted to rid the neighbourhood of this "temporary" structure filled with rodents, some of them in cages, but most on the loose, to say nothing of the human inhabitants — many of whom looked like dangerous revolutionaries. It did not help that this Embassy had had to endure the humiliation of the fall of France and the installation of the Vichy Government. But making these arrangements merely added to the exciting atmosphere of wild experimentation, and of being able to try anything, at any time. To his last days Louis looked back on these experiences as the most exciting highlights of his very full life.

Louis's personal goals at the NFB were quite clear: he wanted to establish the importance of film music ... both within the NFB and beyond, and he wanted to learn about sound and what could be done with it. He realized that on film, music had a physical reality, becoming much more than notes on a page. On film, music could be manipulated. The composer had more control, could indeed be freed from the bonds of traditional musical production with its limitations on the quality of performance for the stage or orchestra pit. No longer was the composer at the mercy of the incompetent or self-indulgent conductor, the inadequate orchestral force, or the unprepared instrumentalist — all of which could contribute to a disastrous performance of the most inspired score.

Sometimes these leaps into new sound creations could create moments of high comedy. Louis remembered the day early in his career when a session was called to record a soundtrack for what NFB literature still refers to as an anti-Japanese propaganda film, *The Mask of Nippon* — a film in the worst tradition of wartime propaganda with no theme beyond that of demonizing the enemy. (On the West Coast, the government confiscated Japanese fishing boats and shipped families to concentration camps in the Rocky Mountains and these actions had to be justified.) The film contrasted the delightful, graceful oriental civilization of the past with the "tribal" society and its accompanying de-humanization. The film required certain unusual instrumentation to produce a clash of charming melody and dissonant percussion. Woodwind themes evoked the past, but Louis wanted relentless percussive interventions to accompany the depiction of militarism that had replaced this idealized society. He had found a small ensemble from Ottawa's Chateau Laurier hotel that played quiet music for the patrons taking afternoon tea, and he hired the players for this "gig." Certain scenes demanded struck strings. However, the ensemble's pianist, who had turned up in black tie, was confronted by the presence of a completely disassembled upright piano and a hammer — this was to be his "instrument." "I'll remember the look on his face for the rest of my life," observed Louis.[24]

"Target Berlin," a 1944 production in the *Canada Carries On* series and a typical NFB effort, was aimed at giving Canadians a sense of pride in their new industrial capacity, in particular, to build the big Lancaster bomber which would bring Germany to its knees through bombing raids on its cities. The challenge of finding workers, particularly toolmakers, to produce the 55,000 parts needed to produce this splendid weapon was integrated with dramatic footage of a raid punctuated by the savage sounds of anti-aircraft guns and exploding bombs. By this point, Louis had learned how to use industrial noise along with the roaring sound of war machines, but his music was mainly martial in nature — a glorious fanfare when the first Lancaster emerged from the hangar, a brass accompaniment as the first plane struggled into the sky, and a string intervention to signal the soaring triumph of successful flight. Louis had learned how to reach the emotional needs of his audience.

A Man and His Job, made in 1943, could have been a simple film outlining the details of the Unemployment Insurance Act. Instead, with Louis's score emphasizing its social message, it was a savage indictment of the events of the depression with such politically charged declarations from a voice-over as "a man has a right to his job, a right to a continuing share in a nation's progress, and a right to expect his skills to be needed."

Strong stuff indeed, particularly when spoken in the context of agitated and dissonant strings. Pizzicato violin themes signal the concerns about fairness, and melodic passages cry out "good times" as discharged employees are supported by courts of referees and appeals to umpires. The film ends in a swirl of enhanced musical expression that promises a future in which these changes promise "a whole new world" and a Canada in which "industrial power will help the worker" as well as the employer.

These statements would be extraordinary in a government-supported film even today; in mid-century North America, they bordered on the revolutionary and, indeed, did not escape the attention of the U.S. House of Representatives' Un-American Activities Committee.

Some films challenged other beliefs. A 1943 film on which Louis worked, *Proudly She Marches*, begins by examining the traditional role of women (with lyrical string music) including the expectation of "modesty" and the emphasis on physical beauty. Suddenly, with a change to martial music, the audience watches a barracks resound to a 6:00 AM bugle call. Then comes a series of vignettes about teachers, salesgirls, librarians, and art students who are now replacing men in the various services and thereby helping win the war. However, the point is also made that women will not be prepared to return to their former roles. To celebrate women's contributions to the war effort, Louis provided bright, positive music, a confidence that this change will benefit both men and women. The film is still used in university programs about social changes in the treatment of gender issues in the last half of the 20th century. A year later, a two-minute short was produced, *The Proudest Girl in the World.* Its soundtrack was a song written by Louis, with words by his old friends Johnny Wayne and Frank Shuster, and sung by a choir of uniformed women. The melody was so catchy that it became a hit in the last months of the war.

Canada owes its reputation in documentary film-making to the NFB, which, even as late as the 1960s, powered the development of film production. Over the past two decades, continuous cutbacks have left it with but a fraction of its previous strength, influence, and reputation.

As the end of the war approached with victory in sight, Louis and Grierson became restless. New opportunities beckoned for making music and experimenting in the burgeoning world of film creation. It was time to look farther afield. The mystery of sound production and the way that sounds could be produced and manipulated had captivated Louis's imagination. Again and again his mind returned to the problems involved in sound production and how they could be overcome through technological invention. At the NFB he had met Osmond "Ken" Kendall,[25] a brilliant electronic engineer whose passion was invention and whose mind Louis admired enormously. Ken Kendall had been brought into the NFB by John Grierson precisely because he had an intellect that relentlessly pursued scientific breakthroughs in the areas that had frustrated and baffled Grierson himself. Louis saw the enormous possibilities that went far beyond fitting music into segments of film action. Advances in science could bring ways for composers to create sounds that went beyond what traditional orchestration would produce, compress and expand music to fill time slots, and do so without changing the pitch. Indeed, a composer might one day be able to manipulate the composition in ways far beyond what was possible with existing equipment. Kendall and Applebaum envisioned an instrument that they called the "Compositron" (later, the "Composer-tron") that would liberate music-makers everywhere.

The purpose behind the machine they began to work on was simple. Louis clearly outlined it in a letter to Arthur Irwin, who had taken over the leadership of the NFB from Ross McLean, who inherited the job from John Grierson in 1944.

> This is not a musical instrument, but a recording console which involves in its structure its own sound generation which can produce complex sounds synthetically.[26]

It would not only provide the means for the "composing and recording of musical works without the participation of any performer other than the operator of the Composer-tron" but would allow the synthetic duplication of any sound — music, sound effect or speech. One could change "the pitch of complete recordings without changing the time factor or the speed" and one could automatically mix sounds in whatever way the film score demanded. The possibilities were endless.[27]

Louis had met Norman McLaren almost on arrival at the NFB and was soon collaborating with him in the making of *Dollar Days*.[28] McLaren was experimenting in the field of animation with sounds that were nothing but squiggles drawn on the film. It could be said that the development of the moving picture had made it possible to see what a sound wave really looked like. With all his experimentation in the making of documentaries, all demanding creative methods of producing a sound track, Louis became convinced that this was the future of music-making for film. He saw both the professional uses of the invention and the entrepreneurial possibilities in the entertainment market, and was determined to find funding for Kendall's efforts both at the NFB and in the private sector. However, the Canadian Marconi Company took little interest at first. Later the company produced a prototype on which Louis and Kendall could experiment. This would become known as a synthesizer, the major electronic intervention in the creation of music in the 20th century. However, in the Canada of 1944, little could be done to spur any interest in either government circles or in the corporate world. Louis decided he would take matters into his own hands. He would seek support for research in the U.S. and he began to make plans to take on the role of inventor and entrepreneur. In spite of the enormous acclaim he was to receive as a feature film composer in these very months that lay ahead, it was to the new process of creating sound that he made his immediate commitment.

The importance of this opportunity cannot be overemphasized. Louis was to engage himself in the very essence of making sound that would revolutionize the future role of composer and performer. When Louis came to resign from the NFB, it was not his plan to write music for film in Hollywood that formed the basis of his reasoning in a letter of resignation in July 1946.

> I am resigning that I might, for a year or two, conduct an experimental project in New York City, concerned with the development of film music techniques in a direction indicated by my work at the Film Board ... It is my intention to return to Canada to the NFB, in order that the

practical results of my experimental work might be incorporated into films made by the organization that sponsored their creation. Hoping that I can at that time be
accepted again into the NFB.[29]

Louis had determined that scientific invention would be his new vocation. And so, in the late 1940s, the Applebaums settled in New Jersey
where the RCA laboratories were located. But RCA had its own engineers
and scientists and had little interest in this Canadian composer with an
enthusiasm for sound research. As well, the expansion of the film industry
as the war ended occupied all of Louis's time and he found that his attention was taken up with film after film as Hollywood, the United Nations,
American Government Departments, and even the NFB sought his considerable talents as a composer, not an inventor.

However, the saga of the Composer-tron continued. As developments
in long-playing records replaced the old 78s and the commercial development of television became a distinct reality, such an invention became
even more attractive. Indeed, there was a sense that a mass market could
be developed from individuals convinced that they might "be their own
composer." While close to New York, Louis continued his intimate association with Kendall, pleading for money from every source he could find
and providing his own expertise to Kendall who, in the beginning, knew
nothing about music or its production. Louis related to Alan Phillips that,
"When I first talked to Ken, he was a musical illiterate. In a couple of
years, he knew all there was to know."[30]

In the mid 1950s the story of the Composer-tron broke upon the
Canadian public. A young reporter, Pierre Berton, tried to inform *Maclean's*
readers about the mechanics of this equipment:

> The compositron contains an oscilloscope to analyze
> sound patterns and a series of tapes or film on reels to
> record sound. Every sound has a pattern and when these
> patterns are played in a certain order on the films and then
> are played together, the required effect will be produced.[31]

Berton could also report that the Canadian government could not
make any commitment to this technology even though "Defence Research
is into it enough to put some of the information about it on the classified
list."[32] The Composer-tron became an item in the long story of Canadian
inventiveness. We were on the edge of leading the world, but without sufficient support from government or business for financing, promotion,

and marketing, we lost sight of a product that might well have burst upon the entertainment scene of the mid-1940s and brought prosperity to Louis and "Ken" Kendall and to the Canadian communications industry.

What the world of technology lost, the world of the arts gained. Louis's accomplishments as a youthful composer were truly staggering: his name appears in numerous credits as "responsible for music;" however, his role as music director meant that he was involved in the production of scores for well over a hundred films — an NFB record that has never been surpassed in volume or quality. His reputation was made. Louis never again applied for another job: one after another, creative projects came to him unsought, and administrative roles followed. Louis's achievements at the NFB formed the basis of an extraordinary career in the arts that defies comparison. Indeed, the National Film Board of Canada could be said to have "made Louis Applebaum."

Chapter Four

An American Interlude

The Dieppe Raid on the French coast on the 19th of August, 1942, had been a disaster. It had shown how difficult an assault on Europe from the sea would be, and had given a new reason for the presence of the National Film Board. The raid had been characterized as a British-American event in the media even though Canada had contributed the most troops (some 5000 officers and men) and had suffered the most casualties (907) and the most troops captured by the enemy (1874). The American involvement had been a mere 50 men and even though Britain had contributed the support of naval and air forces, it had been very much a Canadian affair. How could Canadians be encouraged to sacrifice if the propaganda machines of both the U.S. and the U.K. ignored or trivialized this country's involvement? The NFB became responsible for restoring the balance that had been distorted in the reporting of the event, and for informing Canadians about the very significant involvement of their forces. This was especially important if, as in 1917, the need for troop replacements demanded even more commitment of Canadian youth and if the pledge that Mackenzie King had made to avoid conscription and rely on voluntary enlistment was to be honoured.

Louis Applebaum and his bride, Jan, had moved to Ottawa in 1942 and had quickly become part of the wartime capital's social scene. There was an excitement about the place, a sense of being at the centre of a nation's response to a crisis of civilization. During these years, Louis's contacts with the wider world of documentary film production rapidly extended both nationally and internationally.

One film track from his work in those years had impressed every viewer. In 1943 Louis had written the music for *Action Stations*, a film about the Canadian navy and merchant marine. A cursory note in the NFB files states simply "A Canadian corvette goes on convoy duty in the North Atlantic, sights a submarine and sinks it." The NFB was not in the business of making film "hits," but some productions stood out and the tension and suspense heightened by Louis's score,[1] along with extraordinary visual images, made *Action Stations* the most creative and compelling film of its genre to be completed in that second full year of Louis's NFB employment.

Joris Ivens, an international figure in the making of documentaries, had been brought to Canada by John Grierson to direct and produce *Action Stations* and it soon appeared on screens at the very centre of film production in North America — Hollywood, California. At one screening, members of the invited audience included Lester Cowan, already a renowned producer and director, along with his musician wife, Ann Ronell, a composer of some reputation. Another viewer who had accompanied them to the screening was Aaron Copland, already a composer of recognized stature who had demonstrated his own skill in writing music for film.

Cowan had been approached by the Swedish Merchant Marine to produce a film that would celebrate the exploits of its seamen. As a bizarre sidenote, a particular attraction was the possibility that Greta Garbo could be enticed to return to the screen as the star of this film. Aaron Copland's attention was focussed less on the visual impact than on the impressive music from the soundtrack. The phenomenon of experiencing the increased excitement of watching men at sea facing the challenge of Nazi submarines through both the visuals *and* the sounds attracted the man who was to become the most distinguished 20th-century composer in the U.S. Copland was highly complimentary towards this Canadian called Applebaum, who had been the creator of this music. Ironically, the Swedes did not move ahead with the film they were planning, but United Artists became anxious to produce a very different but more relevant film. Their country needed to understand more clearly the philosophy that had captured the German nation and was creating such havoc. Millions of young Germans had been captured by the rhetoric of Adolf Hitler; they would have to be weaned away from these gross and outrageous ideas and be confronted with the ideals of democracy. As well, the eyes of America had been turned west after Pearl Harbor. The nation had been humiliated as never before. Yet the Allied strategy had become that of winning the war in Europe before turning its full attention to the Pacific. How could this deflection be understood and appreciated by an angry nation already engaged with Japanese forces and anxious to avenge the sneak attack that had brought them into the conflict? It would be a contribution to the American war effort to focus attention on the theories of Aryan supremacy held by Adolf Hitler and his colleagues and their impact on an individual youth, who, in the story line, was to suddenly arrive in the home of an American family. It was not to be a documentary, but a feature film with the plot and character development that had made Hollywood, at its best, the centre of the film world. *Tomorrow the World* was to be the first collaboration between Louis Applebaum and Lester Cowan, who gave him the opportunity to work in a film which would have both a propaganda role and the possibility of a post-war purpose: influencing millions of ideologically inflamed German youth who could pose a threat to a costly peace.

Cowan had secured a splendid script. Originally written for the stage, *Tomorrow the World* had been on Broadway, where the Theatre Club of New York had selected it as the outstanding American play of the season. The star was to be none other than Frederic March, an experienced actor with a following in the United States that assured box-office success. Louis was contacted by Cowan at the NFB and asked if he could take a leave of absence in order to write the music for this important production. Grierson agreed, suggesting that Louis's absence could be explained on the basis of his intense research interests in film-making, in particular the creation of film sound. Ironically, Louis's work on the Composer-tron gave him an excuse to be absent for a few months on the basis that his experience of Hollywood might be valuable for future developments at the NFB itself.

His arrival in Hollywood caused a minor sensation. Lester Cowan was staggered when this handsome but very youthful man arrived and openly admitted that he had never composed a score for a feature film. Cowan questioned his wisdom in hiring such a "boy" for such a major project. Indeed, through his wife, Ann Ronell, he contacted an experienced musician colleague, Max Steiner, who had won an Academy Award for film music and whose task became that of surreptitiously "looking in" on Louis and assuring himself that a competent job was in progress. Impressed by the sketches he saw, Steiner told Cowan that he had nothing to worry about. "This kid really knows what he is doing."[2] The film was completed and released in 1944 to considerable accolades from the critics. Louis experienced the thrill of sharing the credit for a production that received the Hollywood Writer's Mobilization Award, given by a semi-left-wing organization to encourage the film industry to play its part in the battle against fascism.

> This is something of a milestone. A picture has been singled out for an award on the basis of its content. A public meeting has been called [at the Fox Village Theatre] to discuss the picture from the point of view of its ideas. A picture is to be looked at, not with the purpose of finding out whether it is to be liked or disliked but agreed with or disagreed with.[3]

This first major feature film for Louis involved changing people's ideas. Every other feature film with which he was to be associated had a similar intellectual base. Ideas motivated Louis's interest in the art of film-making, and he believed that every film, no matter how "entertaining," should have some kind of informative or educational purpose. This demand for intellectual integrity in film-making remained constant throughout his long career, whether he was commissioned by the NFB, commercial film houses, the United Nations, or government agencies, either in Canada or the U.S. *Tomorrow the World*, designated an educational film in Southern California, was shown in schools across the state as a way of teaching about Nazism and its impact on the youthful mind. In the process of making it Louis had discovered that the feature film with no "documentary" pretensions could address serious subjects and simultaneously give his talents a wider audience. Such productions demanded high drama and excitement but Louis found that, even in such a film, the music of the soundtrack could carry the day when the visual impression was too severe for an audience to contemplate. In one scene of *Tomorrow the World*, Frederic March was depicted choking the Nazi youth with such vigour that the audience invited to view early "takes" broke out in quite inappropriate laughter. Revisions to the film allowed March to be more restrained, letting the music create the desired emotional impact. The scene was saved.

There were other examples of the dramatic use of sound in the film:

> … in *Tomorrow the World*, one of the most dramatic scenes is when a boy, inculcated with Nazi ideology and transplanted to a quiet American college town, makes a murderous attack on his little cousin with a poker. As he creeps up behind her, poker in hand, the audience grows tense. A reverberation, scarcely heard at first, yet mounting in crescendo until the sound fills the entire theatre, crashes to a climax as the boy brings the poker down on the girl's head. Sharp cut-off. The sound ends.
>
> "It was simple," explains composer Lou, "I just recorded a long gong crash, and ran the recording backwards."[4]

The whole feature film experience proved a revelation to a beginning Canadian composer whose career to that point had been with the documentary. On his return Louis regaled his NFB co-workers with the delights of Southern California and the royal treatment he had received. But he also saw Hollywood's limitations.

It's sad to disillusion you, but "down there" they work 18 hours a day too, and they have to swear at moviolas that rip film too, and they lack some facilities too, and they pinch pennies too. [Well, maybe not pennies.] As a matter of fact, and this will hurt, on the lot on which we worked there was not one moviola as good as even the most decrepit at the NFB.[5]

However, Hollywood had made him aware of the advantages of technical riches in producing drama effectively for film. He realized that he could learn a great deal in this centre of the movie world.

But of course they do have magnificent equipment and many great technicians. The scoring stages are acoustical wonders, usually equipped with a streamlined conductor's stand — buttons and coloured lights and pockets and phone and deeply carpeted floor and upholstered chair, etc. [But at the Film Board I never had to conduct for 13-hour stretches. I'll gladly forgo the stand.] And their enormous shooting stages enable them to shoot their "outdoor" stuff in the comfort of a soundproof room. And they have 20-channel dubbing panels, and spray-gun blurping gadgets, and a dozen or so theatres on the lot in which to run their rushes, and they can get 3-hour printing service from their labs, and they don't have to worry about extraneous noises on their sound track, and geniuses are available in droves to solve all problems ... Why then, I wonder, are so many film-makers in Hollywood such tired, nervous, ulcered, cynical people?[6]

Louis's answer to that question ultimately decided where he could work and contribute. His relationship with another composer, Leonard Bernstein, serves as a study in contrast. By chance, Louis found himself in an apartment that looked straight across to the place in which Leonard Bernstein and his colleagues were writing the musical *On the Town*. Indeed, the two composers were geographically so close that it was a wonder that the tunes of *On the Town* did not find their way into the *Tomorrow the World*. Social contacts with the Bernstein clan did happen, usually early in the morning after the Maestro had conducted a concert, but even with all these two had in common in their careers, they never became friends. Indeed, they had widely different personalities and private and public behaviours.[7]

Louis had done more than simply find ingenious ways of heightening the suspense in *Tomorrrow the World.* The thoughtful, effective work of this Canadian "kid" — throughout the entire score — led to another call a year later. Lester Cowan, who had acquired the script for *The Story of G.I. Joe,* and his wife, Ann Ronell, needed a collaborator to assist in the writing of a very complex score.

For Louis's professional development, these invitations to Hollywood arrived at exactly the right time. Though the work of the NFB continued at its frantic pace, even John Grierson had lost his edge and within a year he resigned from the NFB. In his message to his staff, he made it clear that his time in Canada had always been seen as a temporary sojourn and that his ultimate purpose was "to extend still further the economic base for documentary film production and its graphic allies." He reminded his colleagues that from the beginning there had been no money for this genre of film-making except from "the pockets of your friends and relatives if you happened to have friends and relatives with pockets." However, the war had shown that "we could tie what we wanted to do with what government needed."[8] He concluded by making a point about his work that Louis never forgot.

> The proposition that one "leaves the government to go into private enterprise" has no meaning for those of us who have built the documentary movement, because the documentary movement, which is a movement first and last in progressive public enlightenment, is indivisible. It has many allies and associates but only one purpose.
>
> The Film Board's strength depends on its adherence to the principle of the documentary movement and to the courage, ardour, and imagination with which its participants use the film media to serve the Canadian people.[9]

However, Louis could see that, as a government film-making operation, the NFB had a very unsure future. As the end of the war approached, the NFB's focus shifted from winning the war to saving the world, or at least the Canadian nation. Sometimes the film topics focussed on lesser issues, such as safety on the farm, but more often they were concerned with greater matters that would enhance citizens' lives. Louis found this shift quite comfortable. He had already written the music for *Trans-Canada Express* (1944), a 20-minute "tribute to the railroads' contribution to the war effort, but, more important, an historical look at transportation in

Canada, including a short segment on the driving of the last spike to complete the building of the CPR." Louis was to return to this subject in the 1970s when the CBC produced a major television series based on Pierre Berton's *The National Dream*. Themes such as transportation, geography, and nation-building recur throughout Louis's career in film-making.

A year later, in 1945, he wrote the music for *Guests of Honour*, a tribute to all the volunteers who had worked to make the lives of servicemen more pleasant throughout the long war. This film's sub-agenda indicated that such selfless activity could enhance civic life in peacetime as well. Another powerful documentary about social and economic realities, *Mainstreet Canada*, sought to engage citizens in the larger public policy scene that would emerge as peace finally came. However, that peace would be accompanied by the demobilization of hundreds of thousands of Canadians, and Louis composed dramatic scores for *Eyes Front No. 29* and *Good-bye Mr. Gyp* (1945), the latter an animated short warning servicemen and women about the racketeers waiting for them as they left the military for civilian life with their final government cheques.

By the mid-1940s Louis found peacetime issues more compelling than those related to the war. For example, his interest in the visual arts had grown as a result of his wife Jan's commitment to the arts as a talented painter. The NFB's Norman McLaren, now one of the world's finest film animators, had created a three-minute short with a long title, *A Little Phantasy on a 19th Century Painting* (1946), based on Arnold Boecklin's canvas *The Isle of the Dead*. Louis's music created an atmosphere of mystery and apprehension as the film depicted the island appearing and disappearing in the interplay of light and darkness. A year later, Louis returned to the visual arts through the score for a 10-minute film, *Art for Everybody* — an NFB look at what the local art gallery could do to attract adults through its doors, and even more important, to arouse the imagination of children. The music, as inviting as the visuals, with bright, melodic sounds, connected the works on the walls of a gallery with the inspirational and developmental aims of an effective community art gallery. Yet another art form, dance, was given support by a film, *Ballet Festival* (1949). An Ottawa dance company performed *Les Sylphides* to the expected musical accompaniment, but the Volkoff Ballet of Toronto and the Winnipeg Ballet danced *Visages* and *The Red Ear of Corn*, the latter score written by John Weinzweig. The film was the first but not the last that Louis scored for an art form that had little presence in pre-World War II Canada; however, in this case, he played a role in producing a film of a festival that brought Celia Franca to Canada and led directly to her founding the National Ballet of Canada.

In the mid-1940s Louis won great accolades for a 23-minute drama, *The Boy Who Stopped Niagara* (1947), also scored while he was residing in the U.S. In the guise of following the antics of a brother and sister who, while exploring the power generation plant accidentally "turn off the source," thereby literally "stopping Niagara," the film provided an opportunity to understand something of the significance and functioning principles behind hydroelectric power. The whimsical, yet potentially tragic, possibilities of the story line prompted a musical score exuding both delight and foreboding.

A segment of the NFB's *Canada Carries On* series, " Montreal by Night" (1948), gave Louis a splendid opportunity to explore French-Canadian musical themes and styles. It introduced Louis to Montreal and gave him an advantage two decades later when this city became the site of Expo 67, Canada's centennial-year World's Fair. Louis and other composers ensured that Canadian performers and Canadian music had a place in all the national celebrations of that glorious year.

But as peace became a reality, private film companies began complaining about the presence of the NFB, which threatened to dominate the field and take over the important work of commercial film production in both private industry and government ministries and agencies. These productions would provide the basic funding for film-makers hoping to break into the more costly and risky market of both documentary and feature film production. In the light of all these considerations, Louis decided to accept the opportunity to work on Lester Cowan's *The Story of G.I. Joe* in Hollywood. This experience was to change his life.

As Louis prepared to go off to Hollywood again, a happy event took place — but one which he found somewhat disconcerting. Jan became pregnant. Amidst all the questions about his career, Louis now faced the pressure of leaving a wife on the edge of her first childbearing experience. Yes, they had friends in Ottawa, but both their families were in Toronto. Louis returned for short visits, and was present for the birth of his son, David, but was nevertheless absent for those worrying months leading up to the birth, and those frantic weeks that come after a new baby arrives home. For Louis, in the midst of the opportunity of his life, the birth had come at exactly the wrong time and he never ceased to repent his absence. To a question posed at the very end of his life, "Is there anything in your life you particularly regret?" his answer came back without hesitation. "Yes, I should never have left Jan when she most needed me, just when David was on his way and in those disconcerting months which every new mother faces as she arrives home with a child. It was the wrong thing to have done. I should never have gone to Hollywood at that point in our lives." The success of *The Story of G. I. Joe*, the contacts he made in the industry during those crucial months, and the enormous leap in his career that resulted from this work had surely justified such an abandonment, but Louis had only intense remorse.[10]

The Story of G.I. Joe became another of Lester Cowan's triumphs, a classic in war films. The script was based on a best-selling book, *Here Is Your War*, by Ernie Pyle — a book that had won a Pulitzer Prize for Distinguished Correspondence. *The Story of G.I. Joe*, a hit at the box-office, quickly gathered critical accolades. When the Academy Award nominations appeared, *The Story of G.I. Joe* was one of 22 nominations in the category of Best Musical Score for a Dramatic Picture. The ceremony took place on March 7, 1946, in Graumann's Chinese Theatre in Hollywood. Louis and Ann Ronell, Lester Cowan's wife, who had collaborated on the score, faced stiff competition, including the scores for *The Bells of St. Mary's*, *A Song to Remember* (with an impressive percentage of Chopin's entire repertoire as its chief asset), and *Spellbound*, the film that was ultimately declared the winner. For Louis the nomination was a visit to the pinnacle of film music success, and it established his reputation as a film composer. At that time (and for decades after), having excelled in the United States provided the only route to immediate recognition in Canada, in the arts at least. The honour also came at a time when Louis had to face important decisions about his future. He wanted to remain in Canada, but opportunities beyond his imagination beckoned abroad. Cowan had offered him the role of music director for all his films, and he was being courted by Orson Welles to write the music for his upcoming feature film *The Stranger*.

Coincidentally, an article in the Ottawa *Evening Standard* addressed the sudden fame that Louis had achieved even in his own country from his work on *The Story of G.I. Joe*.

> ... he told of his aims and ambitions in the world of music which already has accepted him as one of its most brilliant young composers ... .he is one of Canada's outstanding writers of music and can claim, too, the distinction of being the youngest composer ever to crash Hollywood.[11]

In spite of his hesitations about Hollywood and all it stood for, Louis had been excited by the experience of working on *The Story of G.I. Joe* with Lester Cowan's creative team. From the horror of battle to a poignant love affair, the film stretched Louis's creative forces to the utmost. "Electric in style and idiom is what critics said of his film music."[12]

His success in this film led to a decision to move to the U.S., at least for a time. A year after *G.I. Joe's* successful completion, in 1945, Jan, Louis, and their son, David, moved to a home in New Jersey, surrounded by a large garden in which Jan would be able to play with her new son, enjoy the flowers, and have a sense of security. For Louis, it provided a haven to which he could retreat when not called to Hollywood, Ottawa, or Toronto.

Among the reasons for the move at that time and to that particular site was the opportunity to continue his research interests with Ken Kendall. In an article published just before his move in *Liberty Magazine* just before his move, Louis indicated to the author, Gerald Hawkins, just how important this move was to him.

> But Lou is looking further ahead than whatever fame and fortune he might attain in Hollywood. He is firmly convinced that an entirely new kind of musical language is already in its infancy, born in studios like that of the Film Board which specialize in documentary films. Applebaum wants to develop this language, to add to its vocabulary, to utilize all the potentialities of film as a musical medium.[13]

However, there was a more sinister reason for settling in New Jersey: Louis was having very real difficulty crossing the Canada-U.S. border. He was perceived as tainted by his relationship with the NFB chief, John Grierson, who, after the Gouzenko affair exploded in Ottawa, was under suspicion of communist leanings, particularly in the United States. Indeed, anybody who worked with Grierson shared the guilt by association in the political atmosphere of Washington. Louis reasoned that if he resided in the U.S. while he was learning about writing for film and building on his *G.I. Joe* reputation (as well as making good money), he could avoid this continuing interrogation at American airports. The most important consideration was, however, very personal — in New Jersey he was close to New York, with easy air access to Hollywood and no need to abandon Jan for long periods. Also, he could drive in a day to Toronto or Ottawa, a major advantage for Jan, who hated air travel.

Louis had no intention of remaining permanently in the U.S. Although he had resigned his position at the NFB, he had given every indication that he would return. The late 1940s provided a rich opportunity for a continuing contractual association with the Board as it made the transition to a peacetime film production agency. Ross McLean, a close friend and colleague who had taken over the NFB, recognized Louis's talent.

In a 1946 *Maclean's* article, Elie Abel asked Louis why he was turning down lucrative offers from Hollywood when he could make more money there in a week than he could make in a month at the NFB.

"Three reasons," he said.

(a) "I'm happy here."[referring to the NFB office in which the interview was taking place]

(b) "I think exciting things are ahead in film, radio and television and that Canada is in a position to play a leading part."

(c) "I think money can be made in Canada as well as anywhere else, even in the arts."[14]

Abel identified another reason in his article.

In his first effort Lou shattered more than one tradition. Hollywood is in the habit of hiring a composer to sketch out a piano score, hiring another hand to orchestrate the score and a third to conduct the orchestra at recording sessions. Lou did all these things himself, as a matter of course.[15]

It had to do with workstyle, but, more important, with Louis's philosophy of life — a philosophy he carried into his work with theatre, radio, and television. At the NFB, every film was an exercise in collaboration and synergistic interaction. "One was not merely a film composer, one was a film-maker ... one just brought music to the table, instead of skill with a camera or a capacity to mix or edit. All were involved with the intellectual content, all were directors and producers. Every film was an opportunity to stretch horizontally across a myriad of disciplines."[16] The American style, with complete control by the director, had an obsession with a "big star" system that Louis believed trivialized the art of film-making. As Louis discovered, this style had also become accepted in American documentary film production. Between 1947 and 1949 he scored over 20 films, many reflecting the themes he had explored at the NFB. There were the inevitable travelogues with educational content: *Land of the Midnight Sun* and *Song of Alaska*; but there were also important health issues in *Feeling All Right* and *Rheumatic Fever*. Along with the feature films and the bread-and-butter initiatives, Louis had the luxury of working on the Composer-tron and the benefit it brought to his research into film sound-making.

For Louis, these "American years" were best remembered for his contribution to the feature-film screen. *The Story of G. I. Joe* had scarcely reached the commercial screens before Louis de Rochemont, a former *March of Time* series producer, asked Louis to score his film *Lost Boundaries*. De Rochemont had acquired a script based on a *Reader's Digest* article by W.L. White on blatant racism within the context "of real people who live in a New England town." The story had caused a sensation in print. It was estimated that some 8 million blacks in the U.S. were posing as white citizens, with all the angst, both individual and social, that emanated from this effort to live a lie. The situation provided just the kind of context that Louis had hoped would bring him back to the feature film. The story concerned a doctor, Scott Carter (to be played by Mel Ferrer), a light-skinned black who had successfully hidden his ancestry and been accepted in the northern-state community as a white professional. The issue of race surfaces when Scott joins the armed forces, offers himself as a medical practitioner and thereby automatically qualifies for the status of an officer only to discover that "the Navy does not accept blacks as officers." When his outraged son realizes what has happened he declares to his parents, "I understand it. Dad was a coward. You both were."[17]

De Rochemont's strong ideas communicated his sense of "just cause" to Louis. "The aim of any drama is to give the illusion of real things happening." *Time* magazine described the film (which had cost less than $500,000 to make) as a "first-class social document."[18] *Canadian Film Weekly* said it had enormous impact.[19] The *Toronto Daily Star* headlined its coverage, "*Lost Boundaries* Illustrates the Use of Understatement."[20] Louis's music had to accommodate the theme's explosive nature with de Rochemont's treatment that sought impact through a low-key approach — that of personal hurt, but, more, the loss to a society when it is deprived of the contributions of a substantial minority of its citizens simply because of its intolerance.

Louis himself took great pride in this film and, with growing maturity, he had achieved a remarkable capacity to analyze his own work. In *Film Music Notes*, he published these comments.

> Early in the work on the music for *Lost Boundaries* it became evident that heroics, sweeping statements, and complex thinking would be out of place. A story told with such touching simplicity suggested reticence and comparable simplicity in the composer's work. A forthright score was indicated: one that spoke out unequivocally where necessary, offered unobtrusive support where required, or said nothing.

Where music did not have a specific and pertinent contribution to make, there was no music. This accounts for the presence of several very short musical bridges, the kind that are encountered more frequently in radio plays than in film. The music served to take us from one place to another or to indicate a passage of time, but once that was achieved, no reason was found for prolonging the music under scenes that played well without musical support.

Where the music's role was important, it was given the widest possible scope. For example, there is the scene where Howard, the son, walks through the streets of Harlem. He had run away from home after discovering that he and his family are all negroes and had come to Harlem to learn what it is like to live as a negro among negroes. We see the lonely, frightened boy wandering through the squalor, a stranger in a foreign world. It was found that natural sounds, dialogue or even commentary could contribute little to the mood or understanding of the scene. Music, on the other hand, could penetrate, could reveal the boy's doubts and conflicts and could underline the reaction to his environment. And so the scene was played in two dimensions — the visual and the music — without street noises, footsteps, heart-poundings, traffic or stream-of-consciousness dialogue.[21]

Lan Adomian, an American film composer invited to provide a critique of the score for *Lost Boundaries*, stated appreciatively:

Few composers could have filled the bill as well as Louis Applebaum ... the score makes its effective way from impressive main title, to montages, to cross fades, to bridges and through dozens of situations which could prove traps to a lesser composer ... .at all times a master of technique and style ... .never descends to maudlin sentimentality or to bombast ... Louis Applebaum the film composer does not desert Louis Applebaum the composer of good music.[22]

By the end of the 1940s Louis was approached by Fred Zinnemann, who was preparing to produce a film about an American G.I. who, in the course of the European campaign, falls in love with a beautiful, young Italian woman whose name provides the film's title. *Teresa* offered more than a surface treatment of an age-old problem of newlyweds in conflict with in-laws: it examined the problem of cultural conflict and its damaging effect on relationships. The film introduced a new face to the Hollywood screen — Pier Angeli — but also had familiar names in the cast, Rod Steiger and Patricia Collinge. It became another Applebaum triumph, both artistically and at the box office.

Canadian Film Weekly's headlined article "Praise Applebaum's *Teresa* Score" announced that MGM had decided to use it at a special performance to honour Arthur M. Loew, the head of Loew's International, and referred to it as the "musical score composed by Louis Applebaum, Canada's leading figure in film music."[23] But it was the words of Zinnemann that best conveyed respect for the composer's contribution, though not without a soupçon of criticism.

> I was particularly happy about things like the scene with the girls at the watering trough, the Roman honeymoon, and the wonderful transition you made into the farewell scene — also with the very beautiful guitar solo you had under the wedding night scene. I liked the main themes tremendously and for the most part I was very happy with the way you arranged it for cellos and violas. It gave the whole thing a wonderfully warm quality.
>
> … a few pieces which disturbed me quite a bit — however, I persuaded Arthur Loew to eliminate them. The pieces in question were the scene of the Italian peasants running to get buckets for the distribution of food. Somehow the music struck me as 'cute' and it made the scene feel quaint. This of course I had not intended, because I feel that hungry people just are not quaint. So we more or less buried the music under sound effects ….
> In conclusion, let me say that I feel you made a tremendous contribution to the picture.[24]

As the decade of the 1950s began, two films marked the end of Louis's romance with Hollywood — *Walk East on Beacon* and *Whistle at Eaton Falls* — both de Rochemont productions with themes that justified Louis's involvement. *Walk East on Beacon* looked at the role of the FBI and its use of the new technologies produced by the war, in its efforts to protect the security of the American nation. Although it certainly dealt with a major political issue, it did not bring out Louis's best efforts. *Whistle at Eaton Falls* considered the problem of labour relations in a modern society and how an industrial dispute could destroy the quality of life of those who dwelled in a small town dominated by a single factory. It foretold, as well, the pressure that new technology would create when machines came to replace people. Louis's music did not receive the accolades of his past work in Hollywood, nor did either of the films. And Louis's concentrated attention to commercial feature film came to an end early in the 1950s.

For all Hollywood's "glitz, self-absorption and big spending," Louis came to realize that "There was almost no serious music ....You'd think with all that creative energy there, it would be bubbling out. But it wasn't."[25]

However, he had made important contacts in his American years. Some Canadians working in the broadcast field at the United Nations would become friends and follow Louis back to Canada. Vincent Tovell, who became a brilliant and highly respected CBC producer, and the legendary Mavor Moore, whose various roles in Canada dominated the cultural life of the country, were particularly prominent in Louis's career.

Moore demands special attention. Writing about a job that Louis had worked on in New York, Moore said to the composer that his music was "important, necessary, suitable, brilliantly original and technically praiseworthy ... impressive."[26] Quite a boost to the ego of even a much-praised artist of Louis's dimensions! The relationship with Mavor Moore went on for 50 years more in a host of different roles ... as a producer, arts critic, academic, and finally, as a creative colleague on Louis's final contribution to Canada's musical life — the opera *Erehwon* which opened at Opera Victoria in February 2000, just a few weeks before the composer's death.

In the early 1950s, Louis realized that a change was about to take place. The enormous expansion of newsrooms and the daily "documentaries" that every television network had to produce to fill the endless programming hours engaged the skills of those who might otherwise have followed the path set by John Grierson. The new post-war world wanted information instantly available on the television screen, including film footage of every important happening at all times of the day — but was just as determined to have light entertainment as well. Louis's return to Canada showed a kind of distancing from feature film and its obvious entertainment focus, and a recovery of his beginnings.

He had been attracted to the world of film but mainly to a certain genre — the purposeful educational documentary. Was this what he wanted to do as a composer of "serious" music? Even during the rush of constant work at the NFB he had been discussing the position of the Canadian composer and the need for some kind of organization to give support to the performance of Canadian music, both "live" and on the radio, and to provide assistance to its creators. John Weinzweig, stationed with the RCAF near Ottawa, joined these discussions on Louis's veranda. The NFB conversations were given relevance by the fact that in January 1942, the American League of Composers had presented a concert of Canadian works at the New York Public Library that included compositions by Louis, John Weinzweig, Barbara Pentland, Godfrey Ridout, Hector Gratton and André Mathieu. Characteristically, this proud moment occurred in a foreign country, and it had happened because a foreign organization of contemporary composers sponsored the event.[27] However, that seed finally germinated a decade later when the Canadian League of Composers came into being. Its first priority was to organize concerts of Canadian composers.

When the *Canada Carries On* film series had been launched, an early subject (1945) was the Toronto Symphony Orchestra. The story included significant performances of "a group of contemporary composers selected by Ernest MacMillan and Louis Applebaum, musical director of the NFB."[28] The pieces included MacMillan's "À St. Malo" and Vancouver composer Arthur Benjamin's "Jamaican Rhumba." The NFB promotional notes refer to Louis as a "rising young composer who not only doubled as the conductor" when Sir Ernest was unavailable for shooting, but, as a result of his years as a film-maker, "hummed music from the score to help producers plan scenes." This kind of work satisfied Louis's enthusiasms — a film about a Canadian orchestra, playing contemporary music by Canadian composers, and reaching out to a whole new audience for "serious" music. How could he forsake this kind of opportunity in Canada, even for the delights of Hollywood and New York?

In deciding to live in Canada, Louis had still not firmly faced the basic dilemma of whether composing film music could bring him artistic satisfaction as well as provide him with a living. Most serious composers view writing for film not as an artistic activity, but as a way to pay the bills so one can get on with worthwhile composing for the concert or recital hall. Even today, very few serious music composers in Canada can survive on the commissions they receive from the playing of their music in concert hall, even when these are augmented by broadcast royalties for radio or television.[29] Composers must have other employment to subsidize the hours they spend on composition. Many choose to teach in a Faculty of Music or a Conservatory. (John Weinzweig, Samuel Dolin, and John Beckwith are obvious examples.) Others become church musicians, combining their ecclesiastical duties with composition. (Eleanor Daley, Ruth Watson Henderson, and Derek Holman are in this category.) For many years, Harry Freedman combined composition with his role as an English horn player in the Toronto Symphony Orchestra. In his early years as a composer, Harry Somers was Canada's most famous taxi driver. However, Louis eschewed each of these paths. Although he did teach at York University on a part-time basis in the 1970s and 80s, he received very little remuneration or recognition. Essentially, he composed where he could find immediate recompense, and his other income emerged from administrative and consultative roles. He found a special artistic satisfaction and creative excitement in the process of making music as a member of a team — combining language and sounds to produce intellectual and emotional impact.

In an article on composing for film in a book edited by Sir Ernest MacMillan, Louis quoted the British giant of composers, Ralph Vaughan Williams, who stated early in his career:

> I am only a novice at this art of film music and some of my more practiced colleagues assure me that when I have had all their experience my youthful exuberance will disappear, and I shall look upon film composing not as an art but as a business. At present I still feel a morning blush which has not yet paled into the light of common day. I still believe that film contains potentialities for the combination of all the arts such as Wagner never dreamt of.[30]

Throughout Louis's life, composing for film or broadcast media was an art as well as a business. While still in New Jersey, he was asked to write an analysis of Hugo Friedhofer's music for the film *The Best Years of Our Lives*.

> A reading of the score reveals that Mr. Friedhofer, as many composers do, has chosen to work on the development, juxtaposition and super-imposition of leitmotifs more or less in the Wagnerian tradition. The material itself is definitely not Wagnerian in character but the manner of its handling derives from the Wagner of the Nibelunger Ring. As a result, it is possible in a few short quotations, to list practically all the root material out of which the score as a whole generated.[31]

Louis brought this kind of analysis to his own work. Yet at every stage of his career, he found he had to explain that film music had its own integrity deserving of respect and remuneration. He fought to have film composers considered to be as legitimate in their calling as those who wrote exclusively for public performance. Even fellow composers tended to denigrate his work because it was collaborative and commercially oriented, rather than individually created and artistically pure. He was instrumental in the founding of the Guild of Canadian Film Composers with a small membership, which enjoyed the support of SOCAN, Canada's performing rights organization, in its attempt to seek more appropriate rewards for its members.

Very early in his career Louis had identified the major elements of the art:

> Writing for films is entirely different from other composing. When a composer begins to write for films his musical thought must be completely re-educated … The sound he is to produce must be considered as part of a dramatic conception. The other elements of which are picture, commentary, additional and real sound and the emotional and dramatic movement of the film. It is the artistic correlation of these elements which make good documentary film.[32]

He never ceased reflecting upon this aspect of his work. While working at the CBC in the early 1960s he was able to bring other composers — giants of their time, such as William Walton, Aaron Copland, and David Raksin — into a discussion on a television program devoted to film music. The event was covered by John Kraglund, the long-time music critic of *The Globe and Mail,* who wrote, "It may achieve Mr. Applebaum's aim of demonstrating that some of the most colourful music of today is written for film." However, Kraglund noted considerable hesitation in Walton's mind on this point, even though he had received enormous recognition for his work in *Henry V, Hamlet,* and *Richard III,* by then classics in their imaginative use of music. Walton's view had darkened from his position in the early years. He stated quite bluntly that he did not like writing for film and "There is always too much hurry and one gets quite sick when favourite bits are left out."[33]

Other members of the CBC panel echoed Walton's frustrations. David Raksin, a very close friend and ally of Louis, whose films *Laura, The Bad and the Beautiful,* and *Force of Evil* had received wide acclaim, "confessed he had ceased working in this field." He continued, "I like it very much but it is being treated so badly and the producers don't even inspire one to do good work." Raksin indicated that he "did TV" strictly for the money.[34] Aaron Copland — whose films *The Heiress, The Red Pony, Our Town,* and *Of Mice and Men* had set new standards for film music in the United States — was more accommodating. "You know, writing for film is like having a toy to play with. I enjoy it even more when there are problems to solve. If it is serious enough, it can be inspiring."[35]

Louis was delighted with this comment from a composer whose work he particularly admired. For Louis, film music had to do with intellectual ferment. Indeed he came to see the arts as a way of understanding the world — in stark contrast to the view that the arts were forms of "entertainment." He was coming to see his role as a composer as that of an advocate seeking to create a society that was culturally oriented; whose place for the arts was central, not peripheral; and who saw music as significant, not trivial. This became his overriding life task: his crusade.

Louis had realized that going through the scripts at the NFB had been the greatest learning opportunity one could imagine. Quite often, the knowledge of prime experts in the field of economics, medicine, or political or military strategy was being explored, challenged, and analyzed. He had to discover the patterns of musical thought that would both illuminate and inspire. As a Director of Music at the NFB, writing scores for a dozen films a year on a wide spectrum of subjects and overseeing the hundreds of films on countless topics being scored by his colleagues, he was becoming a highly knowledgeable observer of a world at war and a Canada seeking to find its place in that world. This outlook gave a certain quality to all the films bearing the designation "Music: Louis Applebaum." The most cursory glance through the seemingly endless list of his film credits makes it clear that he was engaged in important matters of the mind and spirit. These film expressions were relevant to the events of the day and the audiences who came to see them. The whole NFB experience, like a graduate program in the liberal arts, became a preparation for the broader role he wished to pursue as a critic of a narrowly conceived society and an advocate of the liberation that the arts represented. There was much to consider as his chosen exile in the United States came to an end.

Chapter Five
Returning Home

In 1949 Louis, Jan, and David Applebaum took up residence in Toronto. The ostensible reason for his return was recounted many years later in an article by Peter Goddard of the *Toronto Star*. Louis had just driven across the George Washington Bridge.

> Applebaum was one of the hot young composers around town, fresh from a stint in Hollywood ....He was part of a brash new generation of classically trained composers adapting their talents to the latest technologies. He felt he was at 'the top of the heap'.
> But his dual career as prolific composer and influential arts administrator ... really got going because of an enormous jam of cars one New York morning. 'That's it.' he told his wife, Jan. 'We're going back.' To Canada, he meant, and to Toronto's then un-jammed roads."[1]

But much more than traffic bothered Louis. He was seeing unpleasant changes in U.S. political life that worried him and forced him to consider the implications of remaining, applying for permanent citizenship, and bringing up David as an American citizen. In the wake of the Roosevelt years the United States had been going through a continuing reconsideration of its progressive behaviour. The country had been forced into World War II by the Pearl Harbor debacle, but had submitted to the Allies' determination to free Europe before turning their attention west. However, this strategy had left the communist Soviet Union as the powerhouse of central Europe. Czechoslovakia and Poland were now in the Soviet Union's sphere of power and influence. Had the U.S.A. sacrificed American lives just to trade one form of dictatorship for another? The loss of influence in Europe, along with the expected loss of power in China as Mao drove Chiang Kai-

Shek's forces off the mainland on to the island of Taiwan. led the conservative forces in the United States to suspect a massive global conspiracy
involving disloyal citizens. Some of those shadowed by suspicion had risen
to the highest levels in the State Department, in the communications
industry, and, most disconcerting of all, in the scientific community. Louis,
still very much a Canadian citizen, with a past that included a close association with John Grierson — an openly left-wing radical — convinced himself that this was not the time to remain in the United States.

There are those who suggest that the discussion of Louis's return to
Canada is merely academic — that mentally he had never left. His
administrative role at the NFB had been taken over by Eugene Kash, an
accomplished violinist who went on to a career as a conductor of
Canadian symphony orchestras and a valued member of the Royal
Conservatory's teaching faculty. This meant that Louis, who continued to
be an NFB consultant, could now do what he most enjoyed — working
with his colleagues directly on the making of films. *The People Between*
offered new professional delights to Louis, as well as political dangers.
The NFB had decided that a film on China — a cooperative venture with
the United Nations Relief and Rehabilitation Agency — could make a
first-rate production. Grant McLean, an experienced film-maker, "was
able to shoot sequences in all parts of the country in spite of the civil strife
that was brewing." The visual materials that he returned with were
unquestionably spectacular. The NFB's publicity department could accurately describe the purpose of its project as that of presenting for the first
time "to western eyes some of the human realities in China today."[2] The
political courage this demanded can be gauged by the fact that, in this
period, *Maclean's,* Canada's major periodical, could not bring itself to
publish a Scott Young article praising the role of Norman Bethune — a
Canadian citizen who was a celebrated martyr to the cause of the communist revolution in mid-century China.[3]

The NFB believed that it had scored a coup by involving Louis, who was
described in its promotional announcement as " Canada's foremost composer of film music." The production of the soundtrack was a real challenge.
Louis wanted to write the score for Chinese instruments, and he found in
New York a man who produced and sold such instruments. Fortunately, this
man was also able to play Louis's music and thereby give an authentic
"Chinese sound" to accompany the remarkable visuals that Grant McLean
had secured. However, Louis discovered that distribution of the film faced a
major problem: American fury over the fact that the most powerful nation in
Asia was falling to the forces of communism. (By 1947 it was clear that
Chiang Kai-Shek was losing. To some American congressional leaders, this

meant that communist agents in the U.S. Government and in society at large were achieving their ends.) A letter from Agnes Fisher of the NFB to Louis indicated how political this film had become. "We finally got the go-ahead signed from External Affairs to proceed with the China film .... We had a screening for Mike Pearson and according to all reports, he liked the shape. So everybody is very happy and work is pushing ahead on it."[4]

With an optimism thankfully missing from most NFB promotional materials, it was predicted, on the basis of the film's revelations, that "Four thousand years of autocratic rule may be at end."[5]

Louis had discovered that film-making and politics went hand in hand. His NFB experience had been one long training process during which every film whose subject matter might impinge on the sensitivities of one part or another of the enormous spectrum of government ministries, departments and agencies, had to be negotiated into existence.[6] Now Louis saw how another nation's sensitivity had to be accommodated at the highest level. Working from the U.S. under this pressure was becoming oppressive, and there was every reason to believe it would only become more so. His NFB work, done while sojourning in New Jersey, was valuable training in political realism. Louis was to spend a lifetime working with governments and their agencies, not only in his continued association with the NFB, but also eventually with the CBC, the Canada Council, the National Arts Centre, the Ontario Arts Council, and as the Chair of a Federal Cultural Policy Review Committee. Even from his then comparatively lowly position in charge of the musical score, *The People Between* project became a lesson in consummate negotiation, a how-to handbook on bringing along nervous politicians and civil servants. The experience certainly influenced his decision about where he was to base his work.

Louis's research on film sound production had not come along as he had hoped. After only a year, he had had received a lukewarm welcome from the RCA and Bell laboratories. Each had its own agenda and these did not include the development of Kendall and Applebaum's Composertron. In an article on Film Music in the *Canadian Review of Music*, Peggy Rooke reported: "He is at present in New York on leave from the Board, studying new technologies. He says he may have to build his own laboratory for his experiments in the field of movie music. This energetic youth's dynamic personality is all directed at producing a Canadian school of film music."[7] However, reality was less positive: producing "a Canadian school of film music" remained an unfulfilled dream.

The overarching reason for Louis's return was, however, an intense national loyalty. He wanted to remain a Canadian and play a part in an expected explosion of arts activity. That, and working on serious films with important messages, meant that he had to come back to Canada. He had known that long before the Manhattan traffic jam.

> From the viewpoint of getting one's message to the widest possible audience, Hollywood is the ultimate answer — except that so few of its films are worthwhile in the respect that they show any awareness of important sociological and political developments. Then, too, I was bothered by the idea of leaving Canada. I owe Canada much for the opportunity she's given me, and I believe the country is just beginning to bubble on the cultural level. There are great chances here for composers to develop ideas and work we've started at the Film Board.[8]

By now, the NFB that Louis had known no longer existed. The Cold War atmosphere he had experienced in New Jersey had infected his professional home, and was exacerbated by the defection of Soviet Embassy employee Igor Gouzenko and revelations about Russian spying activities. Even in 1946, NFB personnel had to submit to the screenings that were being imposed on all government department employees and, by 1949, the NFB had been declared "a vulnerable agency." Surprisingly, Grierson's successor, Ross McLean, had agreed that "until the screening was completed, the Department of National Defence would have its films dealing with classified material produced by outside commercial companies."[9] Opposition critics used this decision to damage the remaining reputation of the Board and mount a barrage of innuendo. They suggested that the NFB was full of unreliable servants of the Crown and that allegation, along with anger over the extraordinary enlargement of the staff to almost 800 persons in the final year of the war, ended any easy path that might have been hoped for in the decade following. Indeed, the Liberal government itself, which had been so anxious to create the agency, now began to see the Board as filled with people who, if they were not communists, were at least unprincipled critics and at best irresponsible free spirits, and who were quite prepared to pass on information to Opposition Members of the House of Commons and other critics of the government. When Ross McLean refused to act on the 30 security risks identified through the screening process, the Liberal government replaced him in 1950 with a loyal friend, Arthur Irwin. Irwin dealt with the communist infiltration threat in short order. Reducing the number of security risks from 30 to 3 cases, he simply requested resignations from the suspects — resignations that were miraculously forthcoming — and the issue ended.

One of the victims of the change in leadership had been the "team process" that Grierson had championed during the honeymoon stage of the Board's development. Irwin had spent two decades working in the Maclean-Hunter publishing empire. He knew hierarchical administrative procedures and distrusted the more democratic but inherently more chaotic mechanisms that had characterized the Board. Irwin saved the NFB from obliteration at the hands of right-wing critics and private film-makers, and he helped it escape continued government interference by engineering a rewrite of the Board's mandate in a new Film Act that recognized its independence. For Louis, as a student of Grierson, full-time employment with the NFB was no longer a promising option.

By 1949, the NFB's main administrative and creative activities were moved from Ottawa to Montreal. The change of location made sense, especially if Montreal was to become a CBC television centre, serving both English- and French-speaking Canadians, which would include a role for the NFB. However, Montreal held no magic for Louis. He was not fluently bilingual and this inadequacy affected his career choices on a number of occasions. Thus, Toronto became the city of choice and #5 Wellwood Avenue became the Applebaums' centre of operations for some years, with nearby Humewood Public School becoming an educational home for David. This was, in many ways, the most important move of Louis's life. By the mid-1950s Toronto — with its concentration of CBC English radio and television, close to Stratford, and with Ottawa easily accessible — became the geographic and creative centre of Louis's professional life.

Within a few months Louis had arranged another kind of relationship with the NFB. The Canadian Film Weekly reported "he will spend four months of each year as consultant to the NFB."[10] Louis would be not just a freelance composer, but would be an advisor on other NFB projects as well. He was pleased. In spite of his concern over the changing nature of the Board, he never ceased to be an enthusiastic supporter of it as a publicly funded institution with a mandate to educate and inform and to support the building of a nation. The NFB, he knew, would never be replicated in any other jurisdiction, certainly not in the U.S., where private interests dominated the film industry. Under the headline "No Place Like Home, Toronto Composer Finds," reporter Lotta Dempsey wrote:

> Louis feels, for one thing, that there is infinitely greater opportunity here than across the border. That's right. Here, in Canada. In his line, anyway. And he referred to the National Film Board, with which he was associated until 1946. He wonders if we in the Dominion know

with what regard and envy it is watched by creative artists
in the United States.[11]

With this arrangement with the NFB, Louis was free to take on
other projects. Norman McLaren, now a world leader in the field of animated film, was commissioned by the British Film Institute to produce
a new work for the Festival of Britain, a veritable explosion of artistic
activity that was to take place in the United Kingdom in 1950. He
immediately thought of his old colleague Louis Applebaum. For Louis it
provided an opportunity to explore another facet of the manipulation of
sound. McLaren was experimenting with the three-dimensional cartoon
feature and the question of an equally experimental sound track became
central to its success.

> McLaren suggested that Applebaum write some three-
> dimensional music for the film. Applebaum became the
> first composer to do this. People, watching McLaren's
> curious figures popping in and out of the screen, became
> aware that the music was doing the same thing. In fact it
> was all around them — coming from behind, from the
> sides, from above. Applebaum did it by using a series of
> filmed sound tracks geared to special speakers placed
> strategically about the theatre.[12]

Louis was well ahead of the recording industry — on the edge of
developing the synthesizer as a means of producing sound and involved in
multiple sources of sound. He knew that stereophonic sound and a battery
of other innovations were about to change the way people made music.
Another great Canadian, pianist Glenn Gould, also became entranced
with the possibilities of modern technology making music more accessible,
but he came to the conclusion that technology would eventually make the
concert hall obsolete. Applebaum could not bring himself to reject the
value of gathering people together as a community to share the magic of
music. He stressed, rather, the opportunity to create enormously exciting
new horizons of sound transmission; even more, he was anxious to see that
such music should empower both composers and their audiences. Louis
was already moving on to even more dramatic implications.

> Why, I wouldn't be surprised if linear direction doesn't
> soon become a tool in the composer's hands as harmony,
> counterpoint and rhythm. The next thing to do, of course,

is to analyze the psychological effects of sounds close at
hand and sounds far away to achieve drama.[13]

Many thousands of Britons who attended the events of the Festival of
Britain saw McClaren's feature, *Around Is Around*, which was one of the hit
presentations. However, Louis found the film industry surprisingly traditional in its understandings. It would take some time before technological
experiments in improved flexibility, quality, and ease in producing music,
as well as the fashioning of multiple sources of sound, would become a
part of the listening life of those who appreciated film and music.

For the Royal Visit to Canada in 1951, Arthur Irwin desperately hoped
to restore confidence in the NFB. He determined that the Board's coverage
should receive the highest priority. The visit of a young Princess Elizabeth
and her new husband, Prince Philip, had all the elements of romance that
could arouse nostalgic patriotism in the hearts of even the most hardened
critics of the monarchy. This rare opportunity would show what the NFB
could do in peacetime, and the event's treatment received attention as no
other production had done before. A new product, Eastman Colour Stock
Film, was to be used and, even though this untried product line was to cause
enormous problems, the visuals would be stunning. The NFB gathered its
very best talent, but there was the problem of timing. The film needed to be
released within a few weeks of the visit's ending, so that *The Royal Journey*
could reach the film screens of the nation while the interest was still high.
On top of this time pressure, Arthur Irwin decided that it was to be a feature film, with a length of five reels, rather than the two customarily required
to document such an event.

This major undertaking required incredible speed. Louis had to find
other composers to write some of the music and he recruited his old
friends, Howard Cable and Morris Surdin, as well as other colleagues, to
work on particular sections even as the Royal couple progressed from
Newfoundland to British Columbia. Louis coordinated and provided
musical bridges that moved the couple from one community to another;
he created fanfares for arrival and departure ceremonies, and even background music for the Royal Winnipeg Ballet's presentation. *The Royal
Journey* proved an extraordinary success, which ironically had much to do
with the survival of the NFB. The film did "more than anything else to
improve the tarnished image of the National Film Board" while simultaneously strengthening Canada's link with the U.K.[14] It became the first in
a long line of "specials" associated with Canadian celebratory events for
which Louis was commissioned to compose music — particularly by his
new client, the CBC.

Having returned to Canada, Louis was now being courted by American film producers. In 1950 the Reorientation Branch of the U.S. Army asked him to write music for a film on adult education. The process of conscripting youth for military service had revealed the disgraceful fact that, in a country proud of its system of universal access to public education, there were an unacceptable number of illiterate or barely literate young people. In view of the armed forces' need for more technically accomplished recruits, and the debt owed to those who had served their country well, adult education had become a major interest. Louis had long since realized that writing scores for documentaries on serious subjects provided a very effective form of adult education for himself. Every note of music demanded research into the film's subject area. This research became the base of his extraordinary command of a broad spectrum of public issues, a command that made him an asset to any role in the cultural sector he chose to pursue. *Adult Education* (1950) offered an opportunity to address this matter directly and Louis was delighted. He provided a score that was scintillating where learning was connected to artistic achievement, and sombre as more serious aspects of adult learning were addressed. One character philosophized, "I was thinking about my farm and the day when I first realized that learning is something that can go on as long as a man lives."[15]

Louis also wrote other musical scores for the American armed forces. An old friend, George Stoney, whom he had known at the NFB in the early 1940s, contacted him in 1957 to write music for two films about the historic background of uniforms worn in the American navy and army. The first, *Jack Tars and White Hats* revealed that navy uniforms had not really changed much in a hundred years and that the history of the force could be explained through an examination of this phenomenon. The significance of this contact reminded Louis of the benefits inherent in working in the U.S. amid the rich budgets of the American Defense Department. After all the financial exigencies Louis had faced at the NFB and, by this time, at the CBC, it was breathtaking when George Stoney related the promise of the U.S. Navy to "supply the recording facilities and the musicians ... so if we need a hundred musicians and three kettle drums we can have them."[16] When, in the same year, Louis undertook a comparable commission for the U.S. Army — *Those New Army Greens* — he found the same liberality. As neither of these films included any ideological stance, he completed the work, provided martial music of considerable quality, and pocketed the generous recompense. His music had animated rather pedestrian themes but, more important, his principles had not been compromised and his serious historical research had revealed meaningful information.

Earlier in the 1950s George Stoney had contacted Louis about another film project: Stoney had returned to the United States after his association with the NFB and had opened the film program at the University of Georgia. Horrified by the conditions of the black community in that state, Stoney seized that opportunity to engage the Georgia health care community in sponsoring a film that came to be called *All My Babies*. Purportedly about midwifery, the film viewed the black communities' despair through the eyes of a midwife, who also happened to be a singer in the choir of the Albany Sanctified Church and who had composed a repertoire of songs about her work. It gave Louis an opportunity to explore the musical culture of the southern U.S. and he was able to include her songs, along with hymns and spirituals sung by her church chorister colleagues. The film, which had become a valuable teaching aid, received a special award from the Robert Flaherty Committee in New York — a group dedicated to rewarding significant films. Stoney reported in 1954 that "almost two years after its release it is being scheduled for special showings at nursing and medical nursing conventions."[17] Louis took particular pride in this film and its score; he hoped it would be a factor in improving the condition of a minority whose outrage was positioned to dominate the domestic policies of the U.S. in the coming decades. He knew something about being a member of a minority and his commitment to the music in the film reflected that sensitivity. As well, *All My Babies* became the first of a number of films on social and medical problems that filled his working life in the mid-1950s.

Hard Brought Up, commissioned by the Mississippi Department of Public Welfare, examined the plight of poor children in a particularly pathetic backwater of the world's most wealthy nation. The film had been "made possible by the voluntary efforts of people of the community and by the cooperation of the Children's Bureau of the U.S. Department of Health, Education and Welfare." For Louis, his own compassion for these children was sufficient to overcome the fact that he did not get paid for his work on the film.[18] Later, the opportunity came to write the music for *None Goes His Way Alone*, a film thematically similar to *Hard Brought Up*.[19] Commissioned by the Television, Radio and Film Commission of the Methodist Church in Nashville, Tennessee, with a script described by director Nicholas Read as "funny and tender," *None Goes His Way Alone* depicted rural disintegration in the wake of new technologies and explored how people could build a sense of community to combat this phenomenon.[20]

Social tensions were not the only subject of Louis's film production during the 1950s. One film of which he was particularly proud was an NFB production that celebrated the work of Canadian artist, Frederick Varley. *Varley* brought him back into Jan's beloved world of visual arts.

Director and writer Allan Wargon had certain ideas on how the music might advance his theme, suggesting the "use of oboe for food ... and body" and the "use of flute for art and spirit." Louis had to compose music that would support Lister Sinclair's commentary, evoking the terrible effects of World War I on Varley's sensitive nature. The artist had seen prisoners of war marching and realized that "victors and vanquished alike plodded the same dirty road; even nature itself seemed caught and torn from her original intention." The experience was a denial of beauty and life, and Varley's depiction of the horrors of battle and the destruction and death left in its wake led to an overwhelming sense of soul-destroying futility. The camera followed Varley's footsteps as he returned to his studio from his sketching session and then moved about the studio selecting various canvasses he had completed as well as documenting his work on new paintings. Louis's music, dark and foreboding, contributed much emotional impact, particularly as it became evident that Varley's personal salvation depended upon his brush and canvas.[21]

Louis had known that residency in Toronto would bring a great advantage to a composer, with a maze of CBC production studios operating in Ontario's capital. This had been part of his reason for choosing that city as his home. However the presence of the CBC meant infinitely more than the convenience of studio work close to home. Louis realized what Canadians are just now coming to understand as they look back over the past century — that the CBC, and especially CBC radio, was crucial to the life of the nation because it could reach into every corner of the land. With floods of immigrants, Canada's story needed to be told in as many ways as possible, and in 1950, radio was the supreme medium for informal education. Louis found producing sound pictures to accompany the human voice to be an exciting challenge — one unmatched in film or television, or on stage.

Canada had built railway lines with unrestrained abandon until the 1920s, but in the 1930s, as the automobile diminished the role of the railway, the new technology of radio seemed to be one of Canada's few hopes for a continued sense of national unity. Yet with the country's small, far-flung population, local commercial radio stations were unable to compete with the powerful broadcasters who were situated just south of the border and connected to massive national networks and rich advertisers. American news and commentary could bury Canada. Cultural understandings in one part of Canada would not be shared with people living elsewhere in this vast land. This led people of all political philosophies to line up behind Alan Plaunt, Graham Spry, and the Canadian Radio League in their efforts to create a national network — indeed a "peoples' network" —that would make it possible for Canadians to communicate with each other across thousands of miles. The CBC, legislated into being in 1935 as a national broadcaster, had a broad mandate that included the saving of a country. Although Louis had been a high-school student at the time, he could remember vividly the hopes that had accompanied the CBC's creation.

When Louis arrived in the last year of the '40s, CBC Radio was in its "golden age" of drama presentation. Producers realized that news dissemination formed only a small part of the way people learned to understand difference, tolerate variety of belief, and gain a commitment to a Canadian culture. The artistic life of the nation had to have some place on the network, and Louis was attracted to the most distinguished programming that Canadian radio broadcasting was ever to mount — the "CBC Wednesday Night" series that had been introduced to Canadian audiences in 1948. The President of the CBC, Davidson Dunton, announced that "at 7:30 EST each Wednesday evening, [beginning on December 3], the facilities of the Trans-Canada Network will be used to broadcast programs that are 'unusual' and 'significant.'"[22] With this evening of programs and other "Stage" series, which both predated and succeeded this development, the CBC became the chief support for a theatre community in Canada and dramatically influenced all that eventually took place — at Stratford, at Niagara-on-the-Lake, and in abandoned warehouses in Toronto. The CBC became the spawning ground of Canadian plays and playwrights. This quality of radio drama presentation provided a new dimension for those nurtured by the amateur community theatre initiatives of the Dominion Drama Festival, Dora Mavor Moore and later, the Davis brothers at the Crest Theatre. During the 1980s and 1990s Toronto became the third-largest English-speaking theatre community in the world — an indication of the CBC's importance to the nation's cultural life.

"CBC Wednesday Night," although blatantly elite programming, lasted until 1963, when it was switched to Sunday evening where it continued to explore the fringe of Canadian culture for several more years. Programming like this did not produce unanimous delight. Some listeners resented the "egg-heads" who seemed to dominate this and other weekly drama series, often expressing radical ideas on how life should be lived and exhibiting ways to make Canada more artistically exciting. But, as always, the world of ideas attracted Louis.

As soon as Louis arrived in Toronto, he was approached to write a score for a special program to be broadcast on a "CBC Wednesday Night" program scheduled for Remembrance Day (November 11, 1949). "The Perilous Dream" was based on an emotionally captivating poem by Hazel Robinson.[23] She drew on her memories of the years from 1939 to 1945 and began the program with a plea: " Let's think no more of war, the world is tired of the carnage and the pain." Indeed the program focussed on how memories of previous wars could help to abort the possibility of another global conflagration — certainly by 1949, not an unlikely event. The U.S.S.R. had detonated its first atomic bomb in August of 1949 and the "balance of terror" between the U.S. and the U.S.S.R. would become the basic reality of international relations for the next four decades. Robinson identified this new face of total war.

> War is not the righting of wrong.
> Modern War has gone far beyond
> The ancient rhythm of revenge for evil done.
> Back in the bloody history of our days
> At least an aim, a brutal callous cause
> Dictated reasons for such genocide.

The CBC brought together a cast that included many legends of the radio waves in the 1940s and 1950s — Lloyd Bochner, Bud Knapp, Mavor Moore, Frank Perry, and the most famous radio voice of Canada's drama broadcasting history, John Drainie. Louis drew on musical ideas from all the war documentaries he had scored and contributed music of enormous power and sensitivity. In a personal letter to Louis, Hazel Robinson wrote about her appreciation for his work:

> I was haunted by the thought that some dreary dirge would be dragged in by the ears, so to speak, which would ruin all the meaning of the piece. But when I knew you were doing the score, I relaxed, and with good reason too. It electrified in the right places and lulled in the right places and all was just 'right'. So many people have spoken to me about the 'grand' musical background and I was so glad to agree with them enthusiastically.[24]

In a country that had little indigenous live theatre, drama on the CBC had become front and centre in the minds of theatre-going enthusiasts who lamented the fact that there was little that was Canadian on the stages across the land. However, the CBC had an even greater role to play. With its mandate and resources, it could celebrate those events which brought Canadians together, whether a royal birthday or journey, a time to mourn the passing of the great national figure, or just as important, a moment to rally the nation around the needs of citizens who faced a terrible catastrophe. The Manitoba Flood of 1950 was just such a disaster — one that demanded a national response. A variety show would raise money as well as consciousness. As Laura Salverson, a Manitoba novelist put it, "We saw houses die across the river ... then wind and rain. Then dead horses ... and broken hearts."[25] The Manitoba Flood Relief Fund Radio Show was an enormous success and it set Louis upon a course of becoming the CBC's special-event composer, a role he assumed with great enthusiasm. Most performers were Canadian, including the Toronto Symphony Orchestra, the Leslie Bell Singers, and vocalists Giselle (a popular performer of ballads) and George Murray (Canada's best known male vocalist). Louis wrote all the "bridge" music connecting the various acts, as well as the background musical accompaniment for John Drainie and John Fisher, familiar voices on the CBC.

Louis was invited to contribute the music for the 1952 program "Queen's Birthday." This demanded all the expected royal accoutrements — the flourish of trumpets, a 48th Highlanders marchpast — all part of Louis's stock-in-trade. In homage to an earlier 1951 visit from the Princess Elizabeth, as she then was, the romantic sound of sleighs bells in the Laurentians captured the ears of listeners and reminded them of magic moments from scarcely a year before.

Radio also provided opportunities elsewhere. Mavor Moore, who had taken note of Louis's film writing efforts, had a role in the commissioning of composers to write for UN radio programming. He asked, "Why are we hiring only American composers ... why not Canadians as well?" He contacted Louis, then living in nearby New Jersey. Mavor wanted Louis to write a score for a major radio feature for which he had contributed the script and was to be the producer. "Year of Decision" had as its theme the challenge to humankind of the presence of atomic power. The script set out the problem succinctly.

> Interviewer: Dr. Einstein, would you say that atomic energy is here to stay?
>
> Dr. Einstein: That, madam, is not the question. The question is: are we?[26]

The program, heard around the world, created a sensation, and Louis's music was crucial in producing just the desired degree of seriousness without seeking to shock, scare, or bludgeon. John Garfield, a famous Hollywood actor, had been hired to do the "voice-over," but it was the music that both relieved the relentless tension engendered by the theme and built to the climax of understanding the possibility that human life could end at any moment. The threat to the species posed by the discovery of this new form of power was to be recurring theme in Louis's work for television and for film as well.

However, the drama department of CBC Radio provided the major focus for Louis during these years. A variety of productions, many of which were radio adaptations of classic dramas — *Juno and the Paycock, Playboy of the Western World,* and *Hamlet* — all demanded original scores.[27] *Antigone,* early in 1953, thoroughly stretched his talent. The themes revolved around "the passionate regard for the sanctity of life" and "belief that moral law exists."[28] Louis described his music as "sombre, fateful … rising to heroic strength … then into a mood of solemn tranquility." At one point "the high pitched voice swells in volume till the tension becomes unbearable. Then it 'uncoils' itself — a musical effect of pulling down to the very depths."[29] The music reflected the intensity of the *Antigone* text and its relentless preoccupation with justice.

Understandably, Canadian plays gave Louis his greatest satisfaction. Harry Boyle, a Canadian novelist and broadcaster, had written a play, *Friends for Christmas,* a drama to be aired on the Christmas Day. About a Canadian family at war within itself, the father philosophized: "Christmas is highly overrated anyhow. It's just developed into a sort of racket for business people to sell other people a lot of junk they don't need."[30] A Polish family recently arrived from a European concentration camp showed their cynical Canadian hosts what Christmas was really all about. In *Friends for Christmas* Louis brought conflict and compassion to a fine balance in the music, using themes that spoke to a victory of decency and humanity over blind, narrow selfishness.

In 1951 Louis came into contact with a drama series which had predated "CBC Wednesday Night" and had established a reputation which was to be unexcelled in the history of the network. "Stage 44" had been launched on January 23, 1944, as a half-hour drama series, and was lengthened to a full hour in 1946. The director became a legend in Canadian theatre history — Andrew Allan, who was quite open about the fact that he was interested in "plays more of the head than the heart." The series, broadcast on Sundays, engaged the most prolific and popular drama writers in the nation — Fletcher Markle, Len Peterson, Lister Sinclair, Joseph Schull, and Alan King. Nathan Cohen, the often acerbic drama critic for the *Toronto Star* wrote on the 25th anniversary of the "Stage" series a veritable paean to its importance to the development of Canadian theatre. Under an exaggerated headline that revealed his own frustration, "After 25 years CBC Stage Once More Is All We Have," Cohen wrote:

The show immediately became compulsory listening in thousands of Canadian homes across the land. We planned our Sunday nights around it. It would be exaggerating things to claim the authors became household words. But the work was listened to and discussed, especially by a rising generation of young men and women with an avid interest in the performing arts.[31]

Louis shared Andrew Allan's view of radio drama and soon became involved in writing music for plays in the "Stage 52" series. Ted Allan, another regular contributor to the "Stage" series, had produced a radio script, *Coloured Buttons,* about a proud Jewish Montrealer, Sam, an inventor and staunch socialist who refused to take money from relatives or friends to develop his ideas. He died penniless and broken-hearted. "I know too much for a man with no education" is how he described his moral plight.[32] Louis, who sometimes described himself as just "a writer of Jewish tunes," used this play to mine his experience of Jewish folk music. For the program — one of the most successful of the series — Samuel Hershenhorn, a CBC conductor with a fine reputation, gave the score a thoughtful and sensitive reading. In the same year, Louis wrote the music for two "Stage 52" productions, a mounting of *Playboy of the Western World* and a drama, *Barrabas,* a Biblical tale about the subsequent life of the thief who was said to have been released in Jesus's place on the eve of the crucifixion. It's difficult to imagine two more contrasting challenges, but Louis had found he could provide music in any idiom that radio drama could present.

The railroad came once again into Louis's sights with a program produced for "Summer Stage 51" (an extension of the regular "Stage" series). *The Paper Railroad* was produced by Esse W. Ljungh — a CBC producer whom Louis regarded as incomparable in the practical day-by-day role of a producer. The theme of the play emphasized the fact that railway safety depended on committed and respected employees "charting the movements of men and machines with life and death a choice in every number and word."[33] Louis's music increased the terrible sense of foreboding as trains moved inexorably towards a dreadful crash, a crash which was averted only by the extraordinary sense of responsibility of an obsessive railroader. Many years later, Louis encountered his greatest challenge in writing music for a television series — *The National Dream* — based on Pierre Berton's book about the building of the Canadian Pacific Railway. *The Paper Railroad* provided a valuable preparation for Louis's involvement in this series about Canada's most important construction project, the one that determined whether there would be a nation at all.

The most ambitious and demanding radio commission Louis received in the early 1950s was a CBC series called *It's a Legend.* It portrayed the stories that have animated the religions and cultures of people around the world over many centuries. Even the titles evoke images of exotic lands: "The True History of H.R.H. Prince Prigio," "The Remarkable Story of the Unpredictable Quern," "Sohrab and Rustum," "How the Toncans Came to Fiji," "The Golden Fleece," "The Vixen and the Viking," "Tyll Eulenspiegel," and "The Girl Queen at World's End." These programs placed a heavy burden on producers and composers, but Louis had the opportunity to explore the musical traditions of countries he had never visited, and indeed would never visit. For Louis, the film furnished a post-graduate course in musicology, intensified by the pressure to produce a score for each week throughout the summer and early fall of 1952. As an offspring of immigrant parents, Louis found it very appealing to examine the central mythical tales that revealed the cultures of both old and new generations of immigrants.

Two years later, Louis was hired to write the music for 13 "Summer Stage" plays written by renowned international authors, but featuring Canadian writers as well. It was Edith Fowke who adapted James Thurber's *The Catbird Seat,* an ironic tale of the battle of the sexes in a corporate setting. Canadian Len Peterson's *Down Payment for a House* described the desperation of a family living in an ugly basement apartment and looking for a solution to their poverty by acquiring a winning a sweepstake ticket. Their winnings, a few dollars hidden in the furnace pipe, accidentally go up in smoke. Louis remembered the sadness of the Depression from his days as a young social worker, and his music captured the sense of despondency and loss evoked by the play. Canadian author Ted Allan contributed two plays to this "Summer Stage" series. One, *For Whom the Horses Run,* was about a bookie who was not only involved in an illegal trade (in the days when even selling a ticket to the Irish Sweepstakes was an offence punishable by fine or incarceration) but also connected to municipal corruption.

Harry Boyle, by now an author very familiar to Louis, was very much like Louis in a few respects — he composed (with words rather than notes) quite a broad range of novels and plays, but also had an amazing genius for administration and a comparable enthusiasm for observing the economic, social and political life around him. His contribution to the "Summer Stage" series in 1954 was a play entitled *Strike,* which showed how such an event brought out the basic philosophies of those who participated on either side of the dispute. On the border of the script are notes that Louis scribbled: the music should be "not too dark" as Boyle's text recognized the glory of work, even the "oily grease that smells kind of good." Such observations had to be accompanied by music which, Louis noted, had to sound both "light" and "defiant," as well as expressing "resentment."[34]

In the "Summer Stage" series of 1954, Charles Brice's *Tidewater Morning* exposed the enormous challenges faced by the United Empire Loyalists. The program reached a considerable Anglo-Saxon audience who, in the midst of massive foreign immigration, needed reassurance that they too had a proud history. The film was also a reminder that their ancestors had once been "displaced persons" and Louis used the opportunity to incorporate the folk music of earlier days in North America.

A Stanley Mann play, *The Strong Man* told a strange tale about a 350-pound giant of a son who eats his family into poverty of both mind and body. The story is an allegory about "difference" — in this case how being physically different could cause a family and society to strike out unfairly against an individual. Once again, the theme spoke to the 1950s when people with varied skin colours, languages, and cultural or religious practices were learning to live together in a country not yet identified as multicultural.

These were the years of the Cold War, and Charles Israel's *Prophecy at Dawn* excited an interest already aroused by Louis's previous work on films about a nuclear holocaust. The Israel play drew its inspiration from another area of Louis's knowledge — Hebrew scripture. The main characters, Harry and Midge, were modern mirrors of the prophet Hosea and his partner Gomer. Harry tried to warn the world of the destructive potential of nuclear weaponry being developed in the American desert. He was confronted by old man who justified the American weapons program with the declaration that "we gotta drop it on them before they drop it on us." Like Hosea, Harry was ultimately silenced.[35]

The subject of weapons surfaced once again in the same series, in a play by Stanley Mann, *Bartholomew Webster, Age 83*. This story revolved around an elderly man who decided to walk from his home to "Gloria," a mythical town some 400 miles away, to convince a professor involved in the American defence industry that he should stop working on a weapon "more powerful than the atomic bomb." Bartholomew's purpose was achieved when his sought-after professor ultimately walked to him, and yet Bartholomew died in the presence of a troubled but inarticulate scientist who could only proclaim, "I don't know."[36] Again Louis faced the problem of making a discussion of the potential annihilation of the human species not just tolerable, but compelling.

Certain critics in the United States considered projects like *Prophecy at Dawn* and *Bartholomew, Age 83* subversive activity. By the mid-1950s, McCarthyism was on the rampage. Indeed, one of the most controversial international interventions at this time came as a result of a CBC Stage production called *The Investigator*. Written by Reuben Ship, it was a clever metaphoric revelation of the real meaning behind the attacks of the notorious Senator Joseph McCarthy. The program was surreptitiously recorded and pirated editions appeared all over the United States. Although Louis had not been involved in that particular production, guilt by even distant association pervaded North America, destroying the careers of countless academics and artists and putting American citizenship out of the question for Louis at a time when opportunities to work in U.S. film and television were expanding exponentially. Louis continued to do single programs for American networks and individual commissions for American film studios, but he had, in these years, burned a bridge that could not be reconstructed. Louis understood the importance of drama to the whole area of public discourse; unfortunately, the anti-communist witch hunters in the American Congress did, too. In Canada, this understanding of the power of drama was shared by the recently formed Canadian Association for Adult Education, led after the war by Roby Kidd. This pro-CBC group concentrated much of its attention on radio, film, and later television drama as well as public affairs broadcasting, because of the educational significance of each to the process of adult learning. If tolerance for debating controversial subjects is greater today in Canadian than in American public life, this is because the presence of CBC Radio drama was an essential factor in shaping this country's cultural response to difficult ideological issues. The major difference in the broadcasting behaviour of the two countries was that the dominant force in Canada was the CBC, a "people's network," funded, at this time through license fees (soon to be removed) and through an annual allocation from Parliament. In the U.S., the commercial advertisers who dominated radio and television outlets resisted, even opposed, controversial subjects, preferring to support the often mindless but safe "situation comedy." Louis had always retained a belief in the right of the people to know, debate, and make judgments about controversial questions. He found the censorship of ideas and beliefs, both official and self-imposed, quite reprehensible in a democratic state.

However, Louis also knew that truth could also be revealed in high comedy. In the same year he was writing music for "CBC Wednesday Night," "Stage," and "Summer Stage," he came into contact with a Canadian legend of humorous prose, W.O. Mitchell. In 1954 Louis composed the music for five, then a year later for six, segments of a program series called "Jake and the Kid." Mitchell, who had spent most of his life in High River, Alberta, knew the Canadian West, and his stories of a young boy on a farm with his mother and a hired man, Jake, were unique vignettes of life on the prairies. Sprinkled through these tales was a bizarre collection of rural western characters that only a Canadian could create. This series formed the Sunday afternoon listening of Canadians from coast to coast as they anticipated the traditional Sunday family dinner. The musical scores for these programs had to be filled with sounds that emphasized the unadulterated high spirits of the inhabitants of Crocus, the mythical western town that provided the setting for "Jake." At the same time, Louis's music expressed the poignancy of difficult times on the prairies. Although Morris Surdin, a composer colleague of Louis, wrote the music for most of the "Jake and the Kid" series, Louis's 11 segments over two years, were a significant contribution to the immediate success of the program. They also meant that, a quarter of a century later, as Louis went from community to community as Chair of the Federal Cultural Policy Review Committee, he could feel right at home in Canada's West.

There could hardly be a greater contrast between of the relaxed relationships of "Jake and the Kid" and the violent ambitions of Shakespeare's *Macbeth*, but both received musical treatment from Louis in 1955. The *Macbeth* production was being prepared especially for school classrooms. With his experience on "CBC Wednesday Night," and by this time, at the Stratford Festival, it was not a huge task; however, it had a lasting influence. Some years later Louis formed a private film production company and remembered his work aimed at the school classroom. One of the projects focussed on providing Shakespearean plays for young people's consumption. *Macbeth* served as the first in a lifelong series of initiatives Louis designed to bring the arts to young audiences.

From 1949 to 1954 Louis wrote most of his music for radio. The pressures of Stratford after 1953 and the opportunities for television after 1954 made it impossible for him to do much more in this medium. One program composed for a "CBC Wednesday Night" production in 1955, and presented again (after a rewrite) in 1957, was a particularly interesting adaptation from the French translation by Maurice Valency of *The Madwoman of Chaillot*. It described the corporate scam being perpetrated by a company that had managed to sell shares to unsuspecting investors even though it had no product line. The corporate position was that the value of the corporate logo was sufficient to outstrip the need for a quality product.

> What we sell is not a share in a business but a view of the Elysian Fields. A financier, my dear sir, is a creative artist. Our function is to stimulate the imagination. We are poets.[37]

When oil is discovered under a café in the centre of Paris, the corporate leadership thinks it quite appropriate to destroy the entire city if necessary to garner as much wealth as possible from the discovery. The "Madwoman" alone proves to be sane, articulate, and convincing about the values that make life worthwhile. With productions like *The Madwoman,* it was little wonder that the CBC was considered by many to be a nest of arrogant intellectuals and a collection of socialist revolutionaries using the Corporation to bring down the prosperity of post-war Canada. Concerned about the music for *The Madwoman,* Louis sent written notes and rough scores of waltzes to Dixie Dean, the director, instructing him to "use one or the other of these you like best." Louis had written two scores for Dean's approval — "a 'bright' and a 'relaxed and simple version.'" Louis's flexibility on such details was a joy to directors who could, with his help, achieve results that escaped them in collaborations with more single-minded composers. *The Madwoman* benefited enormously from this synergy between director and composer and became one of the highlights of the CBC broadcasting season.

Another "CBC Wednesday Night" program, *The Thawing Wind,* was "a mosaic of sight, sounds, music, and impressions of how spring comes to the land." Harry Boyle's script was to be read by the illustrious John Drainie. For this program Louis could hire his favourite choir, Elmer Iseler's Festival Singers (now established as a professional ensemble) and, for this occasion, he had the unusual experience of being able to produce a soundtrack that included his own songs. Thus, "Down From the High," "Sweet Peaks of Evening" and "Happy Now In Childhood" became part of the repertoire of the Festival Singers. The production profiled the reactions of different people — children, farmers, and a shepherd — to the magical arrival of spring. A.Y. Jackson, a distinguished Canadian painter, was quoted: "to me it is the most interesting time to paint." Louis enticed his fellow composer, Harry Somers, to incorporate his orchestral suite, "North Country" as part of the musical score. The cornucopia of sounds and words roused the feelings evoked by nature's coming to life in a northern land.[38] In 1956 Louis made creative use of his now intense commitment to Shakespearean drama by providing the score for Norma Scott Stoddart's *Command Performance,* another "CBC Wednesday Night" offering. She had chosen to present an account of how *Twelfth Night* came to be written — not unlike the genre of film and play that has come to the English-speaking world at the turn of the century with the film *Shakespeare in Love* and Timothy Findley's *Elizabeth Rex.*

Louis's list of credits for "CBC Stage" continued; however, by the mid-1950s, television had taken over the field of drama exactly as predicted, with the attraction of the visual image. Radio still held its own as a public affairs medium, and though the television set had replaced the radio console in the living-room, radio held supremacy in the automobile, particularly for those caught in endless rush. As the role of radio changed, opportunities for, concentrated, reflective listening to drama and social comment declined. As well, it was three times as lucrative to write scripts and music for television as for radio, and Louis was caught up in the economics of supporting his small family. Nonetheless, radio drama had produced an exemplary array of creators and Louis had become Canada's foremost film and radio drama composer. During these years radio drama had created an audience and fostered the careers of a host of able, skilled actors who were to become the base of talent on which the rich, creative Canadian stage was to be built. Louis was to become a part of that live theatre community for the rest of the century.

Though it was regarded almost as an afterthought in a busy career, Louis never abandoned his enthusiasm for experimental film. Upon his return to Canada, Louis found himself taking on a new role — that of a promoter of a particular avant-garde film, *Dreams That Money Can Buy*. It was his only foray into this genre of film-making and it turned out to be a costly venture in terms of his own financial well-being. A German "Dada" artist, Hans Richter, had decided that bringing together the most celebrated experimental visual artists with composers "on the edge of the future" would result in an extraordinary film experience. Indeed, several of the visual and musical participants would become cultural icons in the 20th century, including visual artists Alex Calder, Marcel Duchamp, Fernand Léger, Max Ernst, and Man Ray as well as composers Darius Milhaud, John Cage, David Diamond, Paul Bowles, and Josh White, a popular entertainer. The man Hans Richter chose to compose and co-ordinate the work of these fine composers was Louis Applebaum.

The film was to explore the imaginations of visual artists and musical creators and was produced and directed by Hans Richter himself. It was described as offering "… 7 Dreams Shaped After the Visions of 7 Contemporary Artists"[39] and was an attempt to stretch the imagination, to leap beyond the linear and the rational to the impressionistic, or to be more precise, the surrealistic. As Richter himself put it, "You don't have to understand it to enjoy it." (The film won the Venice Film Award for the Best Original Contribution to the Progress of Cinematography.) The connecting story line for the dream sequences was the desire of a young poet, Joe, who is desperate to fulfil himself and turns to the unique gift he believes himself to have acquired — that of interpreting his dreams through the images of these great artists and composers.

As music director for Richter, Louis found that he had to provide the music for Richter's own filmed dream sequence and write the opening and closing frames as well as the bridges. Bringing continuity to such an array of genius turned out to be a nightmare. As well, he had to hire the musicians to rehearse and record all the music and, as it turned out, pay them out of his own resources. It nearly bankrupted Louis, caught up in all the extra costs of moving back to Toronto, finding new accommodation, and having to build up his reputation in Canadian radio and film. Working with Richter, who knew a good deal less about film than Louis did, was a challenge.[40] In his efforts to deal with the Milhaud sequence he was baffled by the extraordinary orchestration for flute, oboe, saxophone, piano, and percussion. "It seems a very difficult ensemble to balance for recording ... especially with the saxophone." Louis inquired whether Milhaud had demanded this combination of instruments. "Oh no," answered Richter. "I told him to write for that orchestra even though I know nothing of music. I thought it would sound nice." Louis persevered through this fog of musical ignorance and the film became a triumph in American film circles.

Dreams That Money Can Buy was not commercially viable for presentation in normal film venues. Louis had to find groups who would sponsor showings, particularly in major centres such as Toronto and Ottawa. By this time he could promote a film offering that had received at least hesitant acclaim in the *New York Times.* An article by Bosley Crowther that focussed on Alex Calder's work stated that "Many of the image constructions, while obscure, are surprisingly adroit, and the musical score by Louis Applebaum is often more eloquent than the screen."[41] However, there was little interest in art films in mid-century Canada. Louis arranged, through his Ottawa colleagues to have it play at the Glebe Collegiate where it caught the attention of *Saturday Night* magazine and aroused the comment that "the background music is unusually original and resourceful."[42] In a short lecture he gave before a showing at the Museum Theatre in Toronto, Louis encouraged his audience that the viewing would be the "most exciting of your film life" and warned that the film "was an attempt to reach directly to your emotional reaction." Indeed, the audience was advised "You must give of yourself."[43] Those who came were impressed, but it was a small audience that heard Louis's advice.

Lotta Dempsey quotes Louis as stating that the *Dreams* venture had been the most stimulating of his already extensive, though youthful career,[44] but he abandoned the world of avant-garde film after the *Dreams* episode, and to the end of his days, he remembered the cost to his bank balance.

In the 1950s Louis settled into the artistic life of Toronto, writing music for film and CBC radio drama as well as music that was finding its way to the concert hall and the sound studio. It was a pattern that he maintained as the central thrust of his artistic life even when other major administrative roles eroded his time and energy for such composition. The early 1950s had

The Louis Applebaum
family, 1923.

Morris and Fanny standing
with Louis, Ruth (Ootoo) on
her father's knee.

Louis Applebaum at age 10
in 1928.

The Applebaum family, 1942.

Louis Applebaum, working on a score at the National Film Board, 1942.

Louis Applebaum, working on the ancient equipment at the National Film Board, 1942.

Newlyweds Jan and Louis Applebaum, Ottawa, 1944.

Courtesy: Jan Applebaum

Jan Applebaum teaching son David to draw, Muskoka, 1949.

Courtesy: Jan Applebaum

Louis relaxing with his son David in northern Ontario, 1952.

Annual Meeting of the Canadian League of Composers, 1955.
Standing (l to r): Udo Kazemets, Sam Dolin, John Weinzweig, Harry
Freedman, Andy Twa, Jean Papineau-Couture, Barbara Pentland, Louis
Applebaum, John Beckwith. Sitting and kneeling: Helmut Kalman, Leslie
Mann, Harry Somers.

Louis with Tyrone Guthrie, founding Artistic Director of the Stratford
Festival, 1953.

The Concert Hall, a renovated venue for Stratford Music, 1956. It was later to become the Tom Patterson Theatre.

Louis with artists Leonard Rose (cellist), Oscar Shumsky (violinist), who were to be part of the triumvirate to succeed him as directorate of the Stratford Summer School.

Louis conducting the Stratford Festival Orchestra, 1959.

Louis with Jan Rubes, bass, one of the most popular Canadian artists presented by Stratford Summer Music in the 1950s.

The cast of the Tyrone Guthrie production of *H.M.S. Pinafore* at the Greek Theatre in Los Angeles, California. July, 1962.

Louis Applebaum interviewing Aaron Copeland, Sir William Walton, and David Raskin for CBC Television program "Music from the Films," January 21, 1963.

Louis Applebaum working with Igor Stravinsky to produce the CBC
Television Production "Music from the Films," July 14–15, 1962.

Louis Applebaum, Executive Director, Ontario Arts Council, 1971–79.

established him as a national figure in this form of musical contribution. Gerald Pratley, Canada's foremost film observer, could report that "His film scores are highly regarded in London and New York and he has attained the enviable reputation of being one of the finest composers writing for films."[45] However, it was time for a new challenge and, in 1953, this came in the guise of an extraordinary series of events transpiring in the small western Ontario town called Stratford. Louis's response to this challenge would shape his professional musical gifts to the theatre stage for the rest of his life.

Chapter Six
The Stratford Miracle

In 1949 the Liberal Government decided to establish a Royal Commission on National Development in the Arts and Sciences (later to be known as the Massey Commission, after Vincent Massey, its dominant co-chair), which became the most important single event in the history of the cultural development of Canada. The recommendations emerged from a long process of debate and compromise, but they were attuned splendidly to Louis's philosophy — a fact that became even clearer when in 1979 he was given the responsibility of establishing a federal cultural policy for the rest of the century and beyond.

In the midst of this dichotomy of despair (over the erosion of Canadian independence) and elation (that the Massey Commission's recommendations might actually be adopted) came a telephone call to Louis from the renowned British theatre director, Tyrone Guthrie. Would Louis come to Stratford, Ontario, in the summer of 1953 to write the music for two Shakespearean plays that he intended to put on in a tent? The call was not entirely unexpected. Louis had already been approached by a journalist and entrepreneur, Tom Patterson, a native of this modest western Ontario community. In fact, Louis was the first Canadian professional artist from whom Patterson had sought advice on his idea of a summer drama festival in Stratford and, as a result, the first to give him support for this strange venture.[1] When Louis said "yes" to Guthrie's invitation, it turned out to be a call that set him on a lifelong journey. It was fortunate for Guthrie that Louis came on board, as he was one Canadian artist who had been out in the wider world and could understand Guthrie's unique vision and appreciate the strategies that might create a successful Shakespearean Festival in this most unlikely place. From the beginning, Louis saw Stratford as far more than simply an extraordinary Canadian theatre development. In Louis's mind, Stratford would be a symbol of how an artistic expression could become an element in the saving of a nation's independence, an example of how artistic excellence could convince Canadians that anything was possible. Throughout his life, Louis saw going to a play in Stratford not merely as a pleasant evening of theatre but as a pilgrimage to a sacred place of artistic vision.[2]

As one looks back on the events that led to the creation of the Stratford Shakespearean Festival, one marvels at the vision and courage of those who joined Patterson in launching such a venture. Stratford was a quiet, rather dull railway town, a few miles west of Kitchener and east of London. The name of the town was inappropriate in terms of any comparison with its namesake in England. No playwright had ever emerged from this community, nor was there any tradition of theatrical production. Strangely, as inappropriate as the place was, the timing was perfect.[3] It could not have happened in earlier years as the artistic support systems were completely absent in a country with so little professional theatre, and a few years later, there would not have been the euphoric sense of hope that anything was possible in the wake of a Massey Commission Report indicating that support for artistic endeavour was a legitimate role for a nation's government. In every way it was a magic moment, and Tom Patterson had the courage and initiative to seize it.

The story of this one man's astonishing energy, determination, and devotion to what seemed a mad idea is legendary. Tom Patterson could be stopped by no arguments that focussed on financial and human resource limitations. On the advice of Dora Mavor Moore, Canada's first lady of the theatre, he turned to Tyrone Guthrie, already a leading figure in British theatre, who brought along with him Tanya Moiseiwitsch, an outstanding theatrical designer. Together, they would ensure that artistic integrity and world-class quality would characterize the Shakespearean plays to be presented at Stratford.

When Louis finally turned up to discuss with Guthrie his *Richard III* and *All's Well That Ends Well*, Louis met the second major influence of his career. Guthrie was a giant of a man in every way. He stood six feet six inches tall, towering over all the actors, technicians, and administrators, both physically and intellectually. He, too, was a man with a passion. In the case of Shakespeare's work, this included the construction of a thrust stage, the very configuration the Bard himself had known. For Guthrie, Stratford provided a chance to fulfil his dream of re-creating for modern audiences the power of Shakespeare's drama in a way that the proscenium stage, with its restricted movement and preoccupation with sets, could never allow. Guthrie had a vision of what Stratford, Ontario, could contribute to the world's understanding of drama and its social purpose. It was this cause which attracted Louis, who was now ready for another large-scale undertaking that could energize a nation passively failing to reach its potential and perceiving itself as a victim of its geographical position.

Louis's first question to Guthrie on the theatre site was "Where is the orchestra to be?" Guthrie's reply was not reassuring: "Over there, at the side of the stage," he said, pointing to a corner of the site containing at that point an empty space — the construction details formed only in his own mind. Louis's response was, "There is hardly room for a string quartet!" to which Guthrie answered, "We can't destroy the sight lines and we can't lose seats we can sell!" This conversation, vividly remembered by Louis, had enormous implications for music at Stratford for all time. However, in the short term, it meant that only a very small ensemble could be used in the summer of 1953.[4] Neither Louis nor Guthrie could know that a heat wave would coincide with the festival weeks that summer, turning the orchestra "pit" into an inferno. The black gauze hung around the orchestra to hide the players from a curious audience ensured that there was no access to any fresh air in the blistering mid-summer temperatures of a stifling canvas tent.[5]

The summer of 1953 gave Louis his first experience of writing and conducting for live theatre. Fortunately, he knew something about the stage beyond the Wayne and Shuster revues at the University of Toronto. He had also taken part in amateur drama at Hart House in Toronto, where one production had been *The Inspector General*. It had not been an auspicious introduction; Louis had a tendency when on stage to sway as he spoke. His wife, Jan, said that watching him made her seasick. However, at least these experiences helped Louis understand how little he knew, and how much he could learn from a giant like Tyrone Guthrie.[6]

Writing for theatre, Louis discovered, was not unlike composing for film, except that it had to take place in close collaboration with the director throughout — preferably as the play was being rehearsed. Fortunately, Louis had always enjoyed that kind of team approach. Guthrie turned out to be a demanding but intelligent director, although he sometimes reduced actors and technicians to tears in his efforts to make them achieve his ideal production. He realized that this first season would set the standard for the future of the Festival. One decision that had a major effect on Louis's career centred on the question of how to warn people that the play was about to begin and that they should take their seats — in this case, in a tent on a hill in the middle of a field. Louis came up with an idea that has been called a stroke of genius — the audience would be called to their places by a brass quintet (the players were already in the pit orchestra) playing a fanfare. Louis composed three fanfares from which to choose and these fanfares have been played in concerts all over the world. By tradition, for half a century, a fanfare has heralded the commencement of every performance at the Stratford Festival Theatre and another has called the audience back to their seats after an intermission. These fanfares are the most-played compositions of any Canadian composer. Countless audience members have commented that it would not be Stratford if any other method were employed to bring people into the theatre.[7] Elliot Hayes, one of Stratford's most distinguished artistic administrators, has noted the reactions of audiences.

> Each season at Stratford when the first note of Louis Applebaum's famous fanfares sounds in the lobby to announce a performance at the Festival Theatre, one is moved by both the nostalgia and joyful anticipation. What will the performance be like? How will it compare to previous productions? Will it live up to expectations?[8]

The first Festival season was, in many ways, a nightmare for Tom Patterson and the Board of the Festival. The finances were in a state of perpetual crisis. On opening night, Patterson never forgot that as Louis passed him on his way to the makeshift conductor's podium, the composer pressed a cheque into his hand as a contribution to the Festival. Louis reasoned that, as a conductor and musician and member of the Federation of Musicians, he was being paid at the union rate while others on stage and behind it were being remunerated at much reduced levels, if at all. This action speaks to Louis's commitment to an ideal — one he shared with Guthrie, who, after the successful season ended, expressed the belief that "Canada has more to contribute to the wealth and health of the world than its material riches" and compared Canada to a young boy who "so far has not spoken."[9]

Louis conducted every performance of the three-week season and, in the cramped quarters of the orchestra pit, did so virtually on his knees; but he learned much from the claustrophobic corner of the theatre tent. To avoid being bored by conducting repeat performances, Louis analyzed the acting techniques of the two British stars — Alec Guinness and Irene Worth. Louis was transfixed by the way these superb actors developed their roles night by night. Indeed, in Alec Guinness's hands, Richard III was a completely different character by the time the final performance took place. Guinness had added gestures, voice modulations, timing changes — in short, a battery of theatrical tactics that brought incredible richness to his work. He saw less development in the work of the Canadian actors. Louis concluded that both the training opportunities and the limited experience of even the best Canadian actors left them at a disadvantage compared to their foreign contemporaries. Lack of training and experience deprived them of the confi-

dence to experiment and take risks in voice production and body movement. From that time on, Louis placed greater emphasis on the needs of
Canadian artists for training and practical experience. He concluded that
this need was one reason for the low esteem in which Canadian artists were
held, even in their own country.[10]

As opening night approached it became evident that the Festival was
going to be a success. Ticket orders had come from all over North
America. This had not just happened by chance; the person selected to do
the marketing and promotion was Mary Jolliffe, whose lifelong reputation
was established by what transpired in Stratford in the first years of the
Festival. She worked 12 hours a day, 7 days a week to ensure that every
opportunity to secure attention and sell tickets had been explored and
exploited. Her success led to false assumptions on Louis's part about the
size of the audience he could expect for concerts presented during the
three-week span of the Festival. Louis felt that he had every good reason
to try to promote this addition to the schedule of activities: if concerts
were presented, people would come.

> Since it now seemed inevitable that Tyrone Guthrie's
> Stratford enterprise would attract a large, curious, and con-
> cerned audience, the argument was put forward that one
> must not allow to slip by such a fine opportunity to reveal
> to those audiences what Canada could do in the field of
> music, too. The musicians of the country had something to
> offer and, given the opportunity, could provide another
> cause for Stratford pride.[11]

It was a foolhardy idea but, without such an initiative, much that
came later in the decade would never have occurred. Louis was determined
to place music on the agenda of both the administration and the Board of
a just-established theatre festival. He had sought the assistance of Walter
Homburger, Canada's prime arts entrepreneur at that time and the successful manager of the Toronto Symphony Orchestra for many decades.
With his help, Canadian musical talent was identified. However, in the
1950s, even the names Glenn Gould, Jan Rubes, and Lois Marshall held
insufficient drawing power. Promotional efforts were pathetic. Mary
Jolliffe, who knew little about music but loved Louis for not patronizing
her, was too busy selling the Shakespeare Festival. Indeed, there was scarcely time to arrange the concerts, let alone promote them.

Looking back, one is left breathless by the quality of the offerings at
these concerts. On such short notice no international figures were avail-

able (even if Louis, with no budget, could have afforded their fees). However, outstanding Canadian artists were ready and willing to perform. Louis began the Music Festival on July 21 with a recital by Jan Rubes, a Canadian bass, who had already achieved international notice before leaving his native Czechoslovakia. His two recitals were followed by two with Lois Marshall, and then by a performance from violinists Gerhard Kander and Albert Pratz. The last offering in July presented a Festival Trio — Albert Pratz, Isaac Mammot, and a young pianist just launching his international career, Glenn Gould. Chamber music as a basis for a music festival was a revolutionary idea in 1950s Ontario, but Louis expanded on this idea as the decade proceeded. He believed, both in his own composing and in the concerts he wished to see at Stratford, that music performed by a small ensemble had a unique quality and flexibility. Louis continued this direction in later years with the Festival Singers — a chamber choir led by Elmer Iseler — and the National Festival Orchestra — a small but stellar ensemble of first-class instrumentalists from which various quartets and trios could be drawn. The Orchestra also provided incomparable performances for Stratford productions of Offenbach and Gilbert and Sullivan.

In August, the offerings of the Music Festival included two further recitals by Glenn Gould and one featuring a popular tenor of the day heard regularly on CBC, Jimmy Shields. However, of all the concerts, the one which most reflected Louis's own interests took place on August 7. The work of Canadian composers was played by Hyman Goodman, Marian Grudeff, and Leo Barkin and sung by Barbara Franklin. The performance included contributions from Harry Somers, Harry Freedman, Oskar Morawetz, Jean Papineau Couture, Robert Fleming, and Lorne Betts. Presented in cooperation with the newly established Canadian League of Composers, this concert was the culmination of a long series of events.

Louis's preoccupation with the problems of being a composer in Canada could be traced back to his days with the National Film Board. Since then he had worked with colleagues who shared his concern about the invisibility of Canadian contemporary music on the programs of the country's symphony orchestras, chamber ensembles, or even recitals of individual artists. In a 1954 talk for the CBC on "This Week," Louis spoke of those days: "There was naturally some talk about the status of native music … and also the possibility of banding together for common purposes …. to form a Canadian branch of the American League of Composers."[12]

Everyone had agreed for years on the need for such action if music was to play a role in the development of Canada's cultural future, but nothing had happened.[13]

In 1951 Canadian composers took an important step. One winter Sunday afternoon, John Weinzweig, Harry Somers, and Sam Dolin met and created a Canadian League of Composers. Louis had not been at the initial meeting, but was soon drawn in and became the first Vice-President of the League.[14] The President was, predictably, John Weinzweig, certainly the leading figure of the new wave of contemporary composers. The Massey Commission, completing its work, encouraged the League's establishment and members of the Commission offered their patronage. Louis's analysis was that the timing was everything that it had not been in 1942, as "things were different ... the composer in Canada was finding himself an almost full-fledged citizen who sometimes managed to make himself heard."[15]

A major role the League undertook was organizing concerts of Canadian music. The 1953 Stratford concert was an early effort, but not the first that the League had put together. With extraordinary energy, by March, 1952, the League had already hired the Toronto Symphony to play a program of Canadian music under the baton of Geoffrey Waddington. By October, Leopold Stokowski had been convinced that he should present a concert of Canadian works in New York. Both of these extraordinary events made it easier for Louis to convince the Stratford Festival board members that such a concert had a place in their schedule.[16] Thus, Canadian contemporary music became as important a cause to Louis as the presentation of Canadian performers when the Music Festival was officially launched in 1955.

The first summer of music at Stratford included 14 concerts, all given by Canadian artists, and, as well, a range of Canadian compositions had been heard — an amazing expression of artistic achievement, accomplished in only a few weeks. Yet it was a disaster from every other point of view. With meagre audiences, the box office failed to cover the costs, producing a deficit and a series of embarrassments. The most serious of these involved the visit of Governor General Vincent Massey. He had come to a Gerhard Kander recital with his entire entourage. As it turned out, they made up more than half the audience of a dozen or two in a tent large enough to accommodate hundreds.

Louis's efforts bore little fruit in that first season but there were many reasons for the disappointing response. With little help possible from the Festival administration, he found that he was left to his own devices to provide promotion and sell tickets. He did want people to know about the existence of the music program, so "a number of singularly unattractive brochures were printed and distributed (the music budget was understandably less than tiny), a few ads were placed, and snippets of publicity were extracted from the barrage that flowed out of the office."[17] The "barrage" had included well over 60 press releases before the opening performance but there was scarcely a word about music in any one of them. It was a hopeless task.[18] "With Guthrie, Alec Guinness, and Irene Worth as centrepieces, who would care to devote space to unknown youngsters like Glenn Gould and Lois Marshall?"[19]

Only a few of those who did come returned for a second or third musical experience. Even the most enthusiastic listener had to strain to hear violin or voice; the canvas of the Festival tent structure absorbed rather than reflected sound. There was even a mechanical defect in the piano acquired as the accompanying instrument for all the programs. Yet Louis certainly had the support of Guthrie in developing these concerts.

> Tyrone Guthrie with Tanya Moiseiwitsch (Stratford's brilliant designer) on his arm, both enthusiastic concert-goers, insisted on paying their $1 admissions to join the handful of others who had come to hear Jan Rubes (a splendid bass soloist and the first performing artist) and John Newmark (his accompanist) in recital.[20]

Perhaps the most savage deterrent to concertgoers was the devastating heat in the tent. A Stratford benefactor tried to assist by delivering hundreds of pounds of ice and half a dozen fans. His strategy was that there could be some relief from the 90 degree temperatures by playing air over the blocks of ice. The effort, however, produced equatorial rainforest conditions. Then there was the final affront — an impending federal election commanded the attention both of the Stratford Beacon-Herald and the people of the town.

Louis was deeply disappointed by the failure of this first major venture to make music a central and integral feature of the programming of the Stratford Shakespearian Festival. No Music Festival took place in the summer of 1954 — it became a planning year when the only music heard was that which accompanied the plays on the main stage. When the Festival announced the 1955 season of concerts, they called it the "Inaugural Season" of the Stratford Music Festival, drowning memories of 1953 in the euphoria of a glorious new venture.

Louis had learned much. For the Music Festival to succeed, he must find internationally known performers, just as Guthrie had done. Louis, however, was determined that Canadian soloists and ensembles should be seen as the *raison d'être* of the program. Also, the necessary continuity could be achieved by repeated involvement of musical ensembles that would contribute to a series of concerts and, in some cases accompany international figures. Perhaps most important of all, the Music Festival demanded some kind of centrepiece — an opera, for instance, or an unusual orchestral presentation that would capture the attention of the music critics. Finally, a more inviting venue had to be found.

With the exception of the Music Festival, the Stratford Shakespearian Festival did well in its first year. Crowds came to see Guinness and Worth and were enthralled by the Canadian actors who joined them on stage. Even the critics were suitably impressed — especially those who had come from other countries.

In 1954 Stratford brought in another British star, James Mason, to draw audiences to the Festival. Although most people conceded that the artistic standards of the previous season had not been equalled, the season had gone well.[21] During that summer, Louis composed music, conducted for the performances of *The Taming of the Shrew* and *Oedipus Rex*, and prepared for the summer of 1955. That included a great deal of "name-dropping" of possible stars who might appear, and inviting Ezra Schabas and Geoffrey Waddington to form an advisory committee from which he could seek advice, and whose presence might impress the Festival's Governors. By now, the Applebaums had moved to a larger house on Windley Avenue and this became the Toronto office of Stratford Music. Louis enticed various performers to come to Stratford, often for reduced fees, with the promise of lunch in Toronto. Jan became the volunteer cook — not a task she relished but one which she loyally carried out with skill and efficiency.[22]

By spring of 1955, Louis started his assault on the seemingly impenetrable disinterest of Stratford and Toronto audiences. He shamelessly courted the administrative staff (now augmented, through Mary Jolliffe's effort, by music teacher Barbara Reid) to ensure publicity for the forthcoming season — optimistically named "The Annual Stratford Shakespearean Festival of Drama and Music." Louis worked assiduously to develop a program that would place music in the spotlight during what would now be a four-week Music Festival in a new venue, the "Casino."[23] It was in terrible condition, both filthy and in need of repair. A stage had to be built, along with a small administrative office at the back of the building. However, Louis now had a structure of a more appropriate size that could be used when the main stage was occupied for rehearsal or performance.

By 1955, Louis knew that the audience should feel "they are participating in a momentous occasion."[24] He had also convinced the Festival's Governors and administration that simultaneous performances of drama and music would not diminish theatre audiences, but would bring in a whole new clientele to see Shakespeare, and listen to Bach and Britten. The argument carried the day in 1955, but there were still Governors who saw the music program as a road to financial ruin.[25]

Perhaps the most important asset that Louis commanded was the continued support of Tyrone Guthrie. He wrote Louis encouragingly:

> My feeling is that the Stratford Committee should not be unduly scared by the prospects of a $10,000 deficit the first year (1955) if:
>
> 1. the figure includes work done on the Casino — non-recurring expense
> 2. the results are artistically creditable
> 3. the results are financially promising
>
> This is the first year. For a year or two, the Shakespeare plays may have to carry the music. Later, I suspect that the boot will be on the other foot.[26]

Louis began his search for musical groups who would commit to a four-week residence, participate in several concerts, and agree to be perceived as in-house Festival ensembles. By this time he had developed a close relationship with Ezra Schabas, who was in charge of public relations for the Royal Conservatory and a fine clarinetist. Louis and Ezra heard about a choral group gathering to rehearse at the "Central Tech," a secondary school in Toronto, working under a young Healey-Willan-trained conductor, Elmer Iseler.[27] Overwhelmed by the sound and musicality of these singers, Louis and Schabas immediately engaged the group as the "Festival Singers" for the 1955 season.

The search for a comparable orchestral ensemble was less successful. Boyd Neel had been invited by the Royal Conservatory to come to Canada from the U.K. As an amateur conductor with his own chamber orchestra, he had been encouraged to create a comparable ensemble to be associated with the University of Toronto. Though Louis and Schabas were somewhat hesitant, they did approach Neel to come to Stratford. He refused to call his ensemble the "Festival Orchestra," but retained the Hart House designation, wishing to draw on the reputation of that institution's famous String Quartet. Neel came to Stratford but did not "lift off" as did the Festival Singers.[28] Nevertheless, this orchestra made possible the major presentation of Stravinsky's *A Soldier's Tale,* directed by Douglas Campbell, with Alexander Schneider as solo violinist and with William Needles, a fine Canadian actor, as the narrator.[29] Stravinsky's work was too short to fill an entire evening; however, Jan Applebaum had watched the mime artist Marcel Marceau on a television program and thought his presentation skills were astounding. She felt that the visual effect of his performance would complement the "The Soldier's Tale." Louis contacted Marceau and the production launched his considerable North American career.

Louis knew he had to find "names" to draw crowds. Elisabeth Schwarzkopf was one of the most renowned sopranos in the recital and opera world of the 1950s. Louis approached her after a concert in Toronto, indicating the importance of this Festival to the musical life of Canada. She had contractual obligations that would make Stratford quite impossible; however, drawn by Louis's appeal, her response was, "make me an offer." She came between her European engagements at a reduced fee and agreed not only to perform in two recitals and make a concert appearance with the Hart House Orchestra, but also to give master classes for students of the Royal Conservatory.[30] The artists Louis had gathered now included violinist Isaac Stern, soprano Lois Marshall, contralto Maureen Forrester, cellist Zara Nelsova, bass Jan Rubes, violinists Eugene Kash and Albert Pratz, and oboist Perry Bauman. Louis commented, "You wonder at the generosity of these people!"[31]

Altogether, there were 22 concerts planned, with programs including a repertoire that challenged even the most sophisticated audiences.[32] John Kraglund, the music critic for *The Globe and Mail*, wrote approvingly of the approaching season: "The year of planning has paid off and this season Stratford has come up with a Music Festival which for us, is more exciting than the dramatic presentation."[33] Dr. Leslie Bell, a noted choral conductor and journalist, viewed the upcoming season of the Stratford Music Festival with some apprehension, as well as with admiration for its founder who, in 1955, had officially been appointed Music Director.

> This new music festival is a gamble, however, and needs for its assured success the guiding hand of someone who is a combination of idealist, artist, and business expert. The newly appointed director Louis Applebaum is just that type of person. Indeed, without Applebaum's vision and stubborn tenacity, the Stratford music festival would probably never have come about.[34]

Still, to Louis's chagrin, the crowds did not come. Even the first Elisabeth Schwarzkopf and Isaac Stern recitals did not fill the "Casino." The Hart House Orchestra concerts were sparsely attended. Part of the problem is explained by the University's "in-house" publication.

This was truly a massive task for so young a group and that they undertook it at all, and carried it bravely, even if sometimes unsteadily, must always be remembered to their credit and to that of their distinguished leader.[35]

In his Report on the 1955 Stratford Music Festival, Louis saw this major weakness: "The complete failure of the Hart House Orchestra concert that had no name guest artists seems to indicate that audiences are not attracted by musical work alone."[36]

Appropriate repertoire posed another problem. Louis had insisted on the inclusion of Canadian works. Healey Willan's *Song of Welcome,* Somers's *Suite for Harp and Strings,* John Weinzweig's *Interlude in an Artist's Life,* Godfrey Ridout's *Two Études,* and Oscar Morawetz's *Divertimento* had all been programmed at concerts largely as a result of Louis's pressure. But these compositions had not enticed audiences. This disappointed Louis, who wanted the Festival to be a showcase for Canadian composers as well as performers.

However, in his report, he made it plain that he would not abandon his plans to present Canadian works.[37] He would continue to explore the possibility of opera — of all things — at Stratford. Opera was surely the most expensive of all the performing art forms; but Louis made a point that he was to build on for the next 20 years. He was not considering the introduction of "Grand Opera;" rather, his attention was drawn to operas like those by Benjamin Britten — operas that required a small orchestra, a small chorus (or none at all) and a handful of soloists. He believed that great music and the effective communication of important ideas could take place within a genre that did not overwhelm music and text with costumes, sets, movement, and excessive numbers of performers. Louis was even more conscious of the financial implications; yet somehow, he had to find a focus that could attract larger numbers of people.

His report also stressed the importance of continued partnerships with outside groups, such as the Royal Conservatory and the National Council of Christians and Jews. In addition to opera, Louis was also considering the inclusion of dance on the Stratford program. He was looking to new audiences and dance seemed a natural way to broaden the appeal of Stratford Music. Modern dance could be performed on small stages with minimal set and orchestral accompaniment,[38] and ideally with Canadian music.

To carry out his plans, Louis would need improved publicity and promotion and, perhaps most important of all, staff assistance. He had been a one-man operation long enough, as his report made clear. In 1956 Gordon Jocelyn assumed the duties of Assistant to the Director.

Finally, Louis dropped the hint that he was considering adding jazz to the program. Its emphasis on small ensemble work, its connection to creative presentation, its flexibility and popularity, all seemed relevant to what the Shakespearian Festival was seeking to achieve in theatre. However, when Louis decided to experiment with jazz as a component of his 1956 season, even though he promised the finest musicians — Dave Brubeck, Art Tatum, and Cal Jackson being the headline artists — he unleashed a tirade of abuse; not only from those who resisted having music at Stratford at all, but also from classical music purists who saw in this addition the dilution of the quality of offerings they had now come to expect.[39]

In 1956 Stratford Music was finally "getting itself together." Louis's program showed what he had learned in both 1953 and 1955. With Benjamin Britten's *The Rape of Lucretia* on the Festival stage, he had an opera of appropriate dimensions that could serve as an attraction, and whose appeal was heightened by the inclusion of Regina Resnick and Jennie Tourel in the cast. As well, he had Jon Vickers — on his way to a stellar career — and his reliable and personable bass, Jan Rubes. Herman Geiger-Torel from the Conservatory's Opera School directed the production, bringing with him access to all the talent in that institution and, as a result, making *The Rape of Lucretia* into a truly Canadian production. John Kraglund's review, written under the headline "Stratford Opera is a Triumph," declared: "It was the finest example we have seen of Canada's ability to produce first-class opera."[40] George Kidd, reviewing the production for the *Toronto Telegram,* described the reaction of the audience: "A capacity audience of more than 1000 spontaneously rose to its feet as the first Canadian presentation of the 10-year-old opera came to its conclusion. Applause and shouts greeted the performers as they lined across the many-leveled scenery-bare stage ...."[41]

Louis had been right. An enticing opera with outstanding singers would draw the crowds. He was ecstatic. *Lucretia,* with its exciting cast, had made the difference; but Louis had also given attention to the quality of sound emanating from the pit, creating a Festival Orchestra of fine musicians who could cope with the demanding score.[42] This attention to orchestral sound led to the formation of a National Festival Orchestra, a major contributor to the success of later seasons of the Festival.

Jazz did appear on the 1956 program, in spite of protests on all sides. Oscar Peterson replaced the legendary Art Tatum, and Oscar's appearance turned out to be a sensation. Jazz fans were thrilled, but it was Phil Nimmons, appearing with his ensemble, whose reputation soared. In 1956 Nimmons was Canada's leading jazz exponent and an adviser to Louis. A recording contract ensued and Nimmons's career as Canada's foremost jazz performer, composer, and scholar was assured. John Kraglund exclaimed that "any doubts about the right of jazz to be part of a music festival had been expelled by the fresh exhilaration."[43] Louis made a habit of introducing the more serious performers to the jazz musicians who had so often been seen as beyond the pale. Nimmons's artistry staggered Claudio Arrau — "Zees Nimmons group ees fab-ulous … fab-ulous, simply fabulous."[44] Duke Ellington, the most illustrious jazz musician on the American music scene, also came to Stratford at Louis's request, along with his 15-piece band. A close friendship with "the Duke" resulted, lasting over many years. Louis realized that many in the audiences would be hearing jazz for the first time and he took care to provide hosts who could interpret the nature of this genre. And once again, Canadian music benefited when Duke Ellington quite uncharacteristically included the work of Canadian composer Norm Symonds in his performance. Louis, in one stroke, had legitimized jazz in Canada as a respectable art form.

Much to Louis's delight, his suggestion to include a film festival had been picked up. Tyrone Guthrie had a close friend, Leonid Kipnis, a film producer in the U.S. Anticipating that he might someday film Stratford's *Oedipus Rex* and possibly a complete set of the Shakespeare productions staged at Stratford, Kipnis agreed to take on the initial film festival for a fee of $1. With Tom Patterson's supervision the Festival presented such international film classics as *Citizen Kane* (American), *Alexander Nevsky* (Russian), *Romeo and Juliet* (French), and *Odd Man Out* (British). Astonishingly, the film festival actually made money, much to Louis's surprise and satisfaction.[45]

There were disappointments. Two splendid vocalists, Inge Borkh and Alexander Welitsch, produced disappointing attendance. Even more disastrous, Borkh's Royal Conservatory master class attracted only a single student — quite a decline from Elisabeth Schwarzkopf's previous enrolment of 35. The future of music in a Festival devoted to large-scale theatre presentation still remained tenuous. A new building (replacing the tent) for the 1957 season had increased the deficit, and a disastrous loss resulting from a lush but luckless *Tamburlaine the Great* production sent to New York on tour produced a financial crisis. Governors and administrators were becoming nervous and, though the costs of music presentations were now under control, there was no chance that the season would become a moneymaker. Indeed, the old complaint that theatre audiences were reduced by the inclusion of music began to be heard again.[46] The possibility of a cancellation of the Music Festival loomed large, even as the number of accolades grew. Robertson Davies, whose interest was essentially that of a player and playwright, wrote in a "summing-up" column for *Saturday Night*: "I am told on good authority that Claudio Arrau, after his experience this year, counts Stratford one of the six really significant artistic festivals in the world, which, from such a source, is the highest praise."[47]

Outside Canada, critics were taking notice. Barry Ulanov, in a column of *Downbeat*, a popular American arts publication, enthusiastically reported:

> Now this is what I call a festival, this Stratford Festival in Stratford, Ontario …. My enthusiasm traces to several sources but most of all to the conviction that has animated the preparation and presentation of music at Stratford … the central and basic one that a summer festival should be festive, fertile, and directed at different aims from those of a night club or a stage show, or even of a winter concert hall. And in this, Louis Applebaum, the director of music at Stratford, has succeeded where other festival producers have failed.[48]

Just at this point, Louis decided to resign. He had worked with no staff or inadequate staff, without a realistic budget, and without sufficient support from the Festival's promotion and publicity department, in venues that were inappropriate at best and impossible at worst. Although Tyrone Guthrie and Cecil Clark had been supportive, the new Artistic Director, Michael Langham, had difficulty following in Guthrie's footsteps and was less able to garner support for the music program. The ultimate determinant of success, the full house for every performance, had eluded Louis. The 1955 season had lost $23,000 but, although the loss in 1956 would be considerably less, there was little chance of ever being in the black.

As well, questions regarding personnel issues, working conditions, and remuneration began to surface. The Stratford theatrical activities had filled a vacuum. There were no professional actors, technicians, or designers being displaced by people coming to Stratford from outside. The case was somewhat different for music. There had been a small establishment of working music professionals — from military and community bands (even the Canadian National Railway employees had such an ensemble) and local hotels. These musicians saw the arrival of the Music Festival as an opportunity to increase their incomes. However, both Louis and Tyrone Guthrie recognized the considerable inadequacies of some local musicians and Guthrie encouraged Louis to look outside of Stratford and its environs for the calibre of musician he required. The locals resented this behaviour. They saw these attitudes as just another example of small-town Ontario being dominated by big-city Toronto.

As well there had been an ugly incident. To honour the founding Artistic Director, the Tyrone Guthrie Awards had been inaugurated in 1954 and a benefit concert was organized to raise money for these awards to Festival participants who had distinguished themselves. Musicians were, on the average, paid more than actors and it was expected that they would voluntarily hand back their cheques for playing at this benefit performance. After the event, a number of musicians refused to donate their stipends and this soured Louis's relationship with some of his orchestral colleagues.

In the midst of this, Louis met with the local executive of the Musician's Union over disputes involving wages and working conditions. At one point, hostile members asked that a tape recorder be employed to assure an accurate account of what was being said. Louis agreed, as long as the tapes would be used only for private and official purposes. In the context of the confidential discussion Louis made it quite clear that, in some cases, local musicians did not meet international standards of accomplishment and he had no intention of hiring them, either for his "pit" orchestra or for Festival orchestral concerts. To Louis's anger and embarrassment, this private discussion was made public and the union threatened Louis with expulsion. Though the threat never materialized, it left a residue of bitterness. More important, this outrageous behaviour became a factor in Louis's decision not to continue as the Music Festival administrator, even though a breakthrough had resolved the issue of remuneration in 1954.[49]

> The chief problem, one which was to recur almost annually, causing much strain and occupying much time involved the local musicians' union. This season, the local wanted weekly rates fifty percent higher than those in Toronto and insisted that the Board hire nine musicians, although only four were required ....The board dug in its heels and sent four people to Cleveland to meet the Executive Board of the Musicians' Union. That group proved reasonable, and the local settled for a compromise closer to the Board's wishes than its own.[50]

Louis's expectations that the Hart House Orchestra would become the Stratford Orchestra were not working out. That meant that he would have to hire musicians for an independent Festival Orchestra from the group with whom he had come into conflict. Also, Louis was exhausted. His job involved contacting dozens of artists, negotiating their contracts, seeing to their travel and accommodation arrangements, and assuring himself that every performance venue, however primitive, was properly bedecked. In short, looking after the endless list of duties for every concert as well as conducting night after night in the Festival Theatre had simply worn him out. The situation was not helped when, in 1956, he attempted to bring in another outside composer and conductor, John Cook, to share his duties, especially the nightly presence in the pit. The union local demanded a contribution for a "stand-in." This, to Louis, was unbelievable. These unpleasant confrontations had another important impact. Louis began thinking about how orchestral playing at Stratford could be seen as a learning opportunity for musicians at the height of their capacity and ambition. Could he find a way to engage the best professional musicians he could muster from orchestras across the entire continent? What would excite their attention, capture their love of making music, and, at the same time, provide him with the finest orchestra for both Stratford productions and the concerts? That was the problem, and its solution would bring something unique to the musical life of Canada. However, at the end of the summer of 1956, that answer had not come and Louis prepared to leave.

There was another concern even more central to Louis's discontent: he had set out to be a composer and he had become an administrator. He put it quite directly to Lenore Crawford of the London Free Press.

> I'm supposed to be a composer .... That's how I hold a job as music consultant to the National Film Board, why I'm on the CBC staff, and why I am in film, radio and television work in New York. I haven't written anything big for two and a half years. It is time I did.[51]

Not true. He had not written any "big" works for the concert stage but then "bigness" was never a high priority in his creative thrust. He was never to write symphonies, concertos, requiem masses, or oratorios; only in his final years did he tackle an opera and that was in the nature of a chamber opera. Nevertheless, he had made a major contribution to radio productions at the CBC and he had most certainly launched his career in television drama during these Stratford years.

Even beyond radio, film, and television, major projects engaged his genius. For example, in 1954 he had responded to an unusual request from the Jesuit Order to write the music for a Marian Year Pageant. For a practising member of the Jewish faith, this was quite a challenge. Slated for performance at the Coliseum of the Canadian National Exhibition, the music had to be on a grand scale, with 23 musical numbers. The producer, David Lord, asked for "simple melodies ... strong bagpipes, drum effects, a sentimental Irish waltz and an English folk dance." In spite of these bizarre suggestions, the event came off well, as G.S. Sherry wrote in a letter thinking Louis for having "so generously devoted your time and talents to make the music of the show 'a thing to remember.'"[52]

For the summer of 1957, Gordon Jocelyn took over the work of administration, but Louis continued to compose for Stratford. He simply couldn't abandon the vision of collegiality and dedication to excellence in the Canadian music scene. By the summer of 1958 Louis was back, not only composing the scores for *Much Ado About Nothing* and *Two Gentlemen of Verona,* but also as Music Director of the Stratford Music Festival.

Chapter Seven

Return to Stratford

In 1951 the Massey Commission had set out clear lines for the artistic and scholarly enhancement of the nation, recommending, in particular, the creation of the Canada Council. But implementation of that Report happened only in 1957, thanks to a windfall of financial resources from the succession duties of two prominent prosperous estates and without any real commitment of regular support from the Federal Government. It was not an auspicious beginning. The Liberals had completely failed to recognize a burgeoning Canadian nationalism. Many citizens resented the increased power of the U.S. over Canadian affairs and wanted to reverse this assault on the nation's independence. Louis became convinced that Canada's survival depended on an explosion of its arts.

In the House of Commons, in the spring of 1955, the word "arrogance" took on new meaning as the debacle surrounding the passage of the Trans-Canada Pipeline Bill dominated the days leading up to the 1957 election. Louis Applebaum — temporarily relieved of administrative duties, yet still composing for the Stratford's stage and serving other clients in film, radio, and television — watched the election of that year produce a powerful champion who led a Conservative Party to power. Though the Conservatives had achieved only a minority position, they were dedicated, at least in hustings rhetoric, to a new vision of Canada that included the strengthening of Canada's independence from American economic domination. Louis believed that Stratford's Festival could only benefit from government attention to this problem, even though John Diefenbaker had shown little interest in the arts.

Diefenbaker, having proved himself to be a brilliant campaigner, called a second election within a year and, by the time Louis returned to Stratford in the summer of 1958, victory had given the Conservatives a majority government of a dimension never before seen in Canada. In the context of this Conservative vision, Louis, though never partisan, saw an opportunity to gain support for the arts.

As Louis reconsidered his future within the Stratford context, he had been approached to do something he had never before attempted — the writing of a musical comedy. At that time, American musical comedy was sweeping back into fashion, indeed, saturating the theatre scene in North America. Characteristically, Louis wondered: was it possible to say anything worthwhile through this medium? Stratford had prepared him for the technical problems. He had demonstrated a genius for using music to create an atmosphere and for bridging the action from one scene to another, as well as providing lyrical moments of mirth and poignancy. But would his talent for writing music help him produce ballads that audiences would hum on their way out of the theatre? That seemed to be the essential hallmark of a successful Broadway musical. When Donald Davis and the Crest Theatre decided to mount a Canadian musical, Louis agreed to provide the musical score, particularly after he had read the book by John Gray upon which the plot was to be based and had surveyed the lyrics of the songs.[1]

John Gray's work raised important issues. *Ride a Pink Horse* is an intellectual musical comedy whose story line is pregnant with meaning. A mythical animal, a centaur, is discovered alive by archaeologists and prepares to seek entry into Canada. Having no living relatives, the centaur finds approval difficult to obtain under existing immigration regulations. Eventually, the centaur attracts the love of a woman who wishes to marry him. There are issues of acceptance of difference and tolerance of, in this case, a new species. Ultimately, all is lost when the centaur dies from overexposure to the public's attention. The plot provided an opportunity for both rich and trivial commentary on the ills of Canadian society, but the production received mixed reviews. Harry Freedman, Louis's composer colleague who had assisted in providing the orchestration, actually did leave the theatre whistling tunes from the musical[2] but Alex Barris, the CBC critic, described the music as "glacial and unmelodic." Mavor Moore took a different view, writing in his review that *Ride a Pink Horse* contained "a cerebral score by Louis Applebaum" and making the point that "his only peer today in subtlety and invention is Leonard Bernstein."[3] The advertisement for the musical in the *Toronto Daily Star* quoted Moore's invitation to attend the Crest and enjoy this "exotic musical comedy with promises that … many delights await you. I had a fascinating ride."[4] Scott Young, writing for *The Globe and Mail*, gave the production a mixed review. " I thought there were two hours of excellent entertainment in *Ride a Pink Horse* at the Crest. The play, when I saw it, ran about a half an hour longer than that. The ending also seemed to me to spell out unnecessarily the symbolism of the centaur — the unattainable that man always is, or should be, seeking."[5]

Perhaps the most significant controversy surrounding *Ride a Pink Horse* was the apparent willingness of the newly formed Canada Council to fund such a project. The outcome would not only affect Louis's beloved Stratford, but would have implications for future decades during which Louis was to play a number of roles — adviser to the Canada Council, chief executive officer of the Ontario Arts Council, and recipient of grants (either as an individual or as an associate of a host of arts organizations.) The issue arose over the perception that only truly serious (i.e., classical) music should benefit from the largesse of the Council. As the presenter, Donald Davis had received the grant. True, the musical was based on a Canadian literary work and the music had been composed by the very Canadian Louis Applebaum; but could a musical comedy be seen as an appropriate recipient of public support? Donald Davis refused to address the universal issue but was quoted as saying: "*Ride a Pink Horse* is not just a string of tunes with some dramatic interludes. If you peel away the veneer of comedy and satire, you find that he [John Gray] really has something to say."[6] Critic Herbert Whittaker wrote:

> *Ride a Pink Horse* is certainly not what anybody would have thought the Canada Council would foster when that body loomed over our cultural horizons. There will undoubtedly be people who think the august spenders have wasted their money — our money — whoever's money it is. But there will be others who will be thankful to find that the Council can encourage the frivolous, the witty, the gay, and the whimsical, as well as the weight-worthy.
>
> Mr. Applebaum has supported Mr. Gray wittily and well in musical accompaniments, which run to endless recitative, and some pleasant, delicate tunes. He does not supply a major theme, however, and we long for a strong line to thread the delicacy and wit.[7]

Ironically, the very rationale used to argue for public financial support provided the reason for the production's lack of success at the box office. This was obviously not Rodgers and Hammerstein. It was meant to be, in part, a thoughtful experience and not just trivial titillation. Looking back over the years, Louis commented that, "it was the worst musical ever mounted."[8] But that was the personal reaction of a disappointed artist — and one whose eye was already turning to other things. Understandably, though, Louis never again composed a musical comedy.

In Louis's absence as music director for the 1957 season at Stratford, Gordon Jocelyn invited Benjamin Britten's English Opera Group, including the composer himself as conductor, to perform his chamber opera, *The Turn of the Screw*. Peter Pears, Britten's companion and inspiration, played the leading role, along with other experienced soloists brought from England. For the small orchestra required, the best Canadian players that could be found were in the pit, impressing even the composer with their quality of performance. Louis's belief that a chamber opera could draw crowds proved correct and *The Turn of the Screw*, enhanced by the presence of such distinguished international artists as Britten and Pears, filled the house.

The Festival Singers also returned to Stratford to provide splendid choral programs. The CBC Symphony Orchestra, arguably the best ensemble in the country, took up residence for four weeks, and the much-beloved Lois Marshall returned as a soloist. Perhaps the most satisfying addition to the roster of artists was John Boyden, a citizen of Stratford who had enrolled in Elisabeth Schwarzkopf's master class in the summer of 1955. Schwarzkopf, highly impressed with his voice and his obvious musicality, expressed an interest in his future to Tom Patterson. To Patterson's question, "Are you really serious about Boyden's potential?" Schwarzkopf replied, "Get him to London … I'll take him under my wing." Patterson raised the money from Stratford citizens help Boyden cross the Atlantic, but ill health was to intervene, forestalling what would, no doubt, have been a long and successful career. Louis regarded the Boyden episode as a vindication of his enthusiasm for regarding the Festival as an educational mechanism for training Canadian performers for national and international careers.

Louis had indicated his plans at the time of his resignation in August 1956. He wanted to get back to composing, which included, among other projects, a 12-hour documentary for the NFB on the modern Commonwealth.[9] As well, he wanted to continue freelancing with the CBC. However, the break from Stratford's administrative duties did not preclude his composing music for any Festival plays that might interest him. However, this task brought him little glory — very rarely did a review do more than list the name of the composer responsible for the music. Louis could do little to change the critics' understanding, but he was determined that original music would be commissioned for every production on the Festival stage. This was to be the case even when the Festival had a musical score filed from a previous season. In most North American theatre companies, music was less honoured — classical and popular selections were available on record or tape for adaptation, or old scores could be recycled to negate the need for new composition. In many theatres, sound scarcely entered the directors' minds beyond the most obvious interventions demanded by the text. Louis regarded increased acceptance of contemporary music and quality sound as one of his greatest contributions to the excellence of the Stratford Festival, which, by the late 1950s, was gaining some reputation around the world.

On occasion, the music of a particular Stratford production would receive more attention. The 1957 season included a production of *Hamlet* that led music critic and choir director Leslie Bell to comment that — even though Louis's incidental music for the play consisted of "a few short pieces scored for a small instrumental group hidden off-stage" — he felt that Stratford "should give [music] a more vital role." He was sure that "Louis Applebaum's genius allowed more scope, could make an outstanding contribution to any Stratford production."[10] Even Robertson Davies, although overwhelmed by the acting and overall impact of the *Hamlet* production, commented: "It is appropriate at this point to mention also the fine musical score, unobtrusive but complementary, composed by Louis Applebaum."[11]

Louis was only involved in writing for the Festival stage in the summer of 1957, but he also set aside time for the filming and recording of Britten's *The Turn of the Screw* — a project that was ultimately aborted due to complications. These and other matters diverted Louis from the non-Stratford composing he had planned, and he found he was still caught up in the excitement of the Festival. He went through constant sessions of soul-searching, particularly as he drove between Toronto and Stratford. The result was a proposal that he believed would truly make a difference, not only to the Stratford Music Festival itself, but as an example to be followed across the nation. On September 16, 1957, he circulated his document, "A Proposal."

> The Canadian musician has, paradoxically, begun to suffer from his own success. Leading orchestral players in Toronto and Montreal are busier than their counterparts in almost any place in the world. This busy Canadian performer plays not only in the symphony orchestra. He is forced, by economic pressure, to find work in Radio and TV, in film recordings, in popular music ensembles and commercial jingles. While such activity might lead one to comment "Good for him, he must be making a good living out of music," it is not difficult to see the drawbacks of this state of affairs.[12]

The paradox: in spite of the comparative well-being of the frantic few musicians in Toronto and Montreal, "symphony orchestras everywhere are deeply concerned with the problems of finding able string players." In the expanding musical scene of the early 1950s, this phenomenon led to a strange situation — a "handful of good ones" in Toronto and Montreal were kept very busy, indeed too busy for their own professional good, while the rest, in outlying communities, were "hard put to make a living from music." One result of this dichotomy was that "arguments for youth to devote themselves to hard musical study cannot be real or convincing." But Louis's proposal had other implications. Even in Canada's major cities, there was not "a fine string quartet" in spite of the talent that was technically available. Unfortunately, the devastating schedule of the talented players left no time for rehearsal, creating "a compromise in quality" and "a consequent loss of respect for the musicians' craft." For a composer who exulted in music written for smaller ensembles, this was a tragedy. Louis stated, with perhaps some diplomatic exaggeration, that "Stratford, almost in spite of itself, has become not only a leader in the realm of the arts, but a symbol of quality. With the attention of the nation and of the world on its activities, Stratford is forced to assume the responsibility of directing and inspiring by its example and vision."

Louis's work had already made a difference to the musical life of the nation. Far beyond simply presenting concerts, the Music Festival had "helped create musical groups that later assumed independent careers (the Festival Chorus, the Hart House Orchestra). The Stratford platform commanded wide attention — it put Canadian artists into close contact, for a brief period, with some of the world's musical leaders." Most important of all, in Louis's view, the Stratford Music Festival had "helped underline the error of the attitude that apologizes for Canadian inadequacy in the realm of musical achievement." Indeed, Louis, in his argument, discounted the Stratford Music program as a "sort of miscellany of concerts" and concluded ominously "that they have no real relationship to the spirit of growth upon which the well-being of the Festival, and the arts it is encouraging, depend."[13]

The alternative Louis suggested was a new concept: "The creation, in Stratford, of a resident community of Canadian musicians" who would come together for eight weeks in order "to make music together; to make it better than anyone thought they could. Out of their work together would emerge a series of public concerts that could earn the admiration of the world."[14]

But the concerts would not be the ultimate purpose.

> "The next phase of work in the cause of Canada's musical future would seem to consist of receiving or creating the essential attitude of respect and dedication that the 'art' of music demands. Unless sufficient numbers of our

ablest musicians can be imbued with this attitude, little of value can be expected from the future."[15]

The "resident community" would be made up of the finest musicians in Canada, under the leadership of a composer-conductor. The names Stravinsky, Bernstein, Britten, and Hindemith were put forward. Suggestions for string players included Casals, Oistrakh, Menuhin, Schneider. Possible singers were Schwarzkopf, Flagstaff, de los Angeles, and Fischer-Dieskau; and pianists included Serkin, Hess, Moiseiwitsch, Arrau and, to the surprise of many, Glenn Gould.[16]

Louis included his special interest — the Canadian contemporary composer. He foresaw concerts that would not only include orchestral presentations — "small ensembles and solo events" — but, even more important, "special works for special ensembles, commissioned from leading composers and writers, requiring unique staging that would emerge from the particular facilities and techniques of the community." Not only would the less able or less fortunate performer be attracted, but also the group upon whom the future of Canadian music depended — the music teachers and school supervisors. Louis realized that this phase might involve the Royal Conservatory as a partner.

The proposal was well received and formed the basis for Louis's return as Stratford's Director of Music for the 1958 season. He now had a cause. In December, 1957, Stratford announced that the Music Festival (from July 14th to August 16th) would include opera, orchestral concerts, jazz, and recitals by outstanding artists.[17] This was soon followed by the announcement of Louis Applebaum as General Music Director and of Ezra Schabas as Manager.[18] A great deal did hang on the 1958 season — there had to be some indication that what was being referred to as the "annual" deficit could be turned around.[19] This meant full houses.

The season opener, *Le Roi David*, by Honegger, was preceded by an opening fanfare and anthem written by Louis especially for the Festival Singers and the opening concert. Both were enthusiastically received.[20] Yet even with all this preparation, the production did not draw a capacity audience. Still, those who did attend were wildly enthusiastic.

> Long after the work had come to a conclusion promptly at 10 PM to fit within the confines of a one-hour CBC broadcast, the 500 persons applauded the work of conductor Elmer Iseler, his 31 singers, Mary Morrison, Patricia Rideout, Jean Paul Jeannotte and narrator, Rabbi Reuben Slonim.[21]

The season's major production, *The Beggar's Opera*, had a relatively unknown Robert Goulet in the lead role, but was still expected to draw a strong audience response. The production's impressive artistic merit prompted Herbert Whittaker to write:

> Mr. Applebaum has linked the musical genes together into a fashion that is almost operatic. It has kept them part of the action. He conducts with fine awareness of the humble origins of such tunes, so that the musical support is never pretentious but always light and melodious.[22]

For the 1958 summer, the CBC Symphony Orchestra returned for four concerts with four different conductors: Heinz Unger, Walter Susskind, Geoffrey Waddington, and Uri Mayer. Hometown artist John Boyden and the ever-popular Lois Marshall were back. Responsibility for the jazz segment had fallen to Gordon Jocelyn, and crowds came to hear Dizzy Gillespie, Count Basie, Billie Holliday, the Teddy Wilson duo, Gerry Milligan, and Ron Collier and his quintet. Louis's decision to extend his music program to include jazz was paying off, both artistically and financially. Now he was ready to try another experiment — folk music with Richard Dyer-Bennet as the featured artist.[23]

Louis kept to his original programming concept of excellence and variety, realizing that his ambitious proposal could not be implemented for the summer of 1958. Nevertheless, he brought dance to the Stratford stage once again with the Little Carib Dancers, a West Indian group who had been popular the previous season. As well, Louis introduced the New York Pro Musica — just the kind of ensemble he thought would fit into his proposed pattern of a residential program emphasizing chamber works. Unfortunately, in the latter case, "the public stayed away in droves."[24]

Jacob Siskind analyzed the state of the Stratford Music Festival as "in decline," describing the programs of the past couple of years in the same terms as Louis had in his proposal.

> For the past two seasons [the Festival] has been little more than a collection of unassorted performances, all usually of some artistic calibre but lacking any central theme ….The Music Festival has not succeeded in building up a loyal and adventurous following largely, I feel, because of the inconsistency in the programs actually presented. After the disappointing initial season the musical public has tended to shy away and little has been done to entice them back.[25]

Louis agreed with these observations but believed he had solutions that he could launch in 1959. In the meantime, another intervention was bringing him delight. His music for the theatre in 1958 was a main-stage production of *Much Ado About Nothing*.

It was the custom to play "God Save The Queen" on opening night. On this occasion, the audience dutifully rose to its feet only to discover this was a rendition they had never heard before — performed as an 18th century minuet, scored for flute, oboe, harp and bassoon. It brought the house down. A few die-hard monarchists reacted with horror, but it became an anticipated introduction to every performance of *Much Ado*, and a perfect way of recognizing that season's visit of Queen Elizabeth.[26]

Though the Stratford International Film Festival was not technically a part of Stratford Music, in 1958 Louis was accorded the role of Film Festival Director. The Film Festival was becoming a money-maker able, at least in Louis's mind if not in the formal budget calculations, to carry his less popular music programs.

To bring off his proposal for 1959, Louis had to entice major figures to accept roles as musician leaders. He wanted Glenn Gould as one of the resident master artists, as he knew Gould's name would draw others. Also, having one prominent Canadian in this position was crucial. Gould, as Canada's most illustrious hypochondriac, felt he must decline the invitation, saying he was "too ill and must rest" that summer. However, "he still wanted to work at Stratford … and wanted to talk."[27]

This was a disappointment, as the 1959 season would be the first opportunity to bring together outstanding soloists with Louis's assembly of first-rate orchestral players for his proposed purpose — spending each day rehearsing and exchanging knowledge and skill in a variety of instrumental combinations. Though he had failed to attract Gould for 1959, he *had* been successful in bringing Leonard Rose (cello), Oscar Shumsky (violin), Julius Baker (flute), and Robert Bloom (oboe). Louis's commitment to this scheme had long-term implications, but in the short term he also wanted a scintillating orchestra to play the operatic offering of the season — Offenbach's *Orpheus in the Underworld*. This was a production based on an English translation by Robert Fulford and James Knight. Louis thought the work guaranteed an audience, but knew that the orchestral score was boring for instrumentalists and he would not find good players clamoring to join him in the pit now to be found at the Avon Theatre.[28] The new ensemble, called the National Festival Orchestra, graced the pit with extraordinary enthusiasm. One critic commented "that the composer himself would have been envious. They played Offenbach as if it was a challenge to their professional competence and the sound was unique."[29]

The players were well rehearsed from playing the demanding chamber and concert music repertoires that Louis had chosen, and the Orchestra had already been performing as an ensemble in concerts that formed Louis's Festival program. Indeed, the Stratford Music Opening Concert had been a triumph. Eric McLean of the *Montreal Star* stated unequivocally that the *Haydn G Major Symphony* was given the best reading I have ever heard." The *Variations on a Rococo Theme* had been turned into chamber music with a tone and clarity and an exchange between the soloist, Leonard Rose, and the Orchestra that was more characteristic of that more intimate genre. It led McLean to comment:

> The bulk of the credit must go to Stratford's Music Director Louis Applebaum. This was not an assemblage to provide Stratford theatre-goers with something to listen to during their off-nights this year. Applebaum is experimenting with a musicians' workshop. A score of professional instrumentalists have been engaged from several Canadian and American orchestras .... These musicians are not only paid to give chamber and orchestral concerts but, equally important, they were offered the opportunity of studying and playing together with a completely informal exchange of ideas.[30]

By early August, the orchestra was honed to previously unimagined heights. Louis had scheduled an all-Bach concert, once again challenging a summer theatre audience. Then, disaster struck and an ailing Lois Marshall, the guest soloist, had to withdraw. However, the concert went on with Oscar Shumsky playing an unaccompanied Bach *Sonata in G.* His playing produced an artistic and technical listening experience that stunned his audience, and the reaction to the entire concert was a vote of confidence for Louis's strategy of programming demanding repertoire.

> Not only was the evening a great personal triumph for Mr. Shumsky, who has never played better, but it was the culmination of the weeks of work that have been going on here ... the beauty and grandeur of Bach ... with all its intricacies of form ... must be lived before it can be performed ... In the past weeks, the members of the orchestra ... having been 'living' music.[31]

Later in the week members of the National Festival Orchestra, after providing a number of Saturday morning concerts, gave an evening performance of Mendelssohn's *Octet* and Mozart's *Clarinet Quintet*. The enthusiasm was even greater: "the ovation was not only applause and calls of 'bravo' but also included a number of whistles — possibly the first time a chamber music concert has been whistled at as a tribute."[32]

The orchestral players — who had worked 12 hours a day rehearsing chamber music morning and afternoon and playing in the pit orchestra for *Orpheus* at night — also expressed their enthusiasm. At a meeting they were unanimous in their thanks to "Mr. Applebaum," whose idea it had been to bring musicians and soloists together for concerts and workshops — a vindication for Louis. Even 40 years later, musicians who participated look back to those halcyon days when making music took on new meaning.

Perhaps the most flattering assessment came from one of the musical "giants" Louis had brought in, Oscar Shumsky.

> If you want my opinion, on what has been happening in Stratford during the past weeks, it will all be in superlatives. Professional musicians are pictured as rushing from one appointment to another with an instrument case in one hand and a union card in the hip pocket. But there was nothing like that here in Stratford. These boys would be rehearsing or playing at night and then be around early next morning wanting to get at it again.[33]

It was Shumsky's view that "there was nowhere else it could have happened like this." Ralph Thomas, writing some years later, could see the impact of this workshop process on Canadian music-making.

> One of the boons to Canadian music lovers was the establishment, five years ago, of the Stratford Festival Orchestra workshop. The workshop has not been noticed yet; but its effects are being felt across the nation. Musicians are playing with greater excellence and spirit; orchestras are improving apace, chamber groups are springing up; a new feeling has begun to invade Canada's impoverished musical scene.[34]

The value of this experiment — coming just as a major expansion in the number of orchestras was about to take place in Canada, along with the "professionalization" of many existing amateur ensembles during the 1960s and 1970s — will never be accurately measured. Louis himself, writing his 1959 Music Festival Report for the Stratford board, expressed a terrible ambiguity. "The completion of the Fifth Music Season has left the Festival reason for pride and disappointment." Once again, the concerts that were unusual had attracted very few listeners.

One of Louis's most hopeful experiments in joining drama and music was the presentation of a program of music with Shakespeare's poetry — programming Louis thought would excite playgoers and simultaneously delight music lovers. The concert, another of Louis's efforts to meld more than one art form, had the participation of Michael Langham (later the Stratford Festival's Artistic Director) as narrator. Yet the program "played three times to small houses." Louis had no doubts about the Orchestral Workshop: "the fondest hopes for the enterprise were realized ... so dedicated were leaders and players, so joyful were the results, so powerful and valuable its potential influence that the need to carry on and develop the plan is beyond question."[35] However, the Festival's Board was neither fully aware of the importance of, nor particularly sympathetic to, the ideals of Louis's workshop program. They may also have grown tired of indulging the musical ambitions of Louis Applebaum, particularly when the costs increased annually. Altogether, these offerings had drawn an average audience of just 36% of capacity — a figure so discouraging that it led Louis to consider, once again, resigning his directorship. One thing kept him for another year — his plans for an international conference of composers. Louis had tried to bring this off in 1959 but lacked sufficient time. He had even gone to Russia in hopes of attracting Shostakovich, but his efforts had failed.[36] With or without Shostakovich, he wanted to make a major contribution to the writing of serious music in Canada in 1960.

In the midst of this struggle, Leslie Bell, the music columnist for the *Toronto Daily Star*, launched a Toronto Music Festival. With its light and popular repertoire and a large urban music audience to draw on, Bell conceded that the two music festivals had little in common. He recognized that Stratford presented seldom-heard music, as well as commissioning and premiering new Canadian works. Bell's solution was simple — bring the Stratford Music Festival to Toronto where "it would be welcomed." Louis had no intention of cooperating in such a move. In Toronto, his Music Festival would be buried in a plethora of non-arts activities. Ironically, with all its accessibility to a large market and its patently unchallenging repertoire, it was the Toronto Music Festival that disappeared.

Then again, Louis had another reason for keeping music at Stratford. He had just heard from Tyrone Guthrie that the D'Oyly Carte "monopoly" on interpretive rights to Gilbert and Sullivan operettas had run out. Guthrie now wanted to mount Gilbert and Sullivan operettas that would truly capture their genius after so many years of productions hobbled by tired conformity. For *H.M.S. Pinafore*, he would scrape a half-century of barnacles off the work and he promised that "Gilbert and Sullivan will be given the respect due a Mozart opera."[37] Guthrie also saw this initiative as a commercial venture. He wanted to tour this production and perhaps even put it on film. There would be ample time for rehearsal, and the production would have an opening run at Stratford of some 24 performances as a part of the Festival, all with Louis Applebaum conducting. Thus began the *Pinafore* project — an extraordinary showcase of Canada's talented performers, but also a presentation of the design and technical capabilities that Stratford had now gathered unto itself.

When the 1960 Music Festival was announced, the International Composers' Conference received top billing. "Shostakovich Ousts Jazz" was the rather embarrassing headline in the *Toronto Daily Star*, putting the spotlight on the one composer who failed to turn up. However, the Stratford promotion material promised a series of five or six concerts featuring works of the world's most prestigious composers, performed by Canadian musicians, but unfortunately "leaving no time in the schedule for jazz and folk music."[38]

In Louis's opinion, the Composers' Conference became the crowning achievement of his work at Stratford. Many music lovers would, of course, remember the thrilling concerts. Orchestral players would stress the value of the Workshop — and that would certainly have been another source of pride for Louis.[39] Indeed, Stratford, a theatre festival, had become an important testing ground for musicians at the highest level. It had also attracted other musical groups. The Pan-American String Congress and a Civic Orchestral Workshop both decided to hold their meetings in the Festival city in the summer of 1960. More important by far, in the long run, was an initiative from Walter Susskind, conductor of the Toronto Symphony Orchestra. He had come to believe that Canada's orchestral future depended upon the creation of a National Youth Orchestra and determined that the perfect place and time to launch the idea was Stratford in the summer of 1960.[40] In a letter to Louis he made his point.

> I am convinced that a National Youth Orchestra of Canada is a necessity and I sincerely believe that the Stratford Workshop is the logical place to launch this project. Your affiliation with the venture would be of tremendous value in guaranteeing its ultimate success and I am therefore inviting you to lend your name and support.[41]

Louis supported Susskind but felt that Stratford could not take on the NYO. As an alternative, a private company, with Susskind's blessing, ran an instrumental workshop for young people and adult amateurs in Stratford. This was called the "preliminary session of the National Youth Orchestra." A group of spirited citizens founded the actual NYO corporation in the fall and appointed Susskind as musical director. Thus began the distinguished role of the NYO in the preparation of orchestral players for Canadian symphony orchestras. Louis took no credit for this development but there is little doubt that without the Stratford Music Orchestral Workshop, there would have been neither the inspiration for nor the possibility of a successful establishment of a youth orchestra.

That year, the International Composers' Conference commanded Louis's most intense attention. With his own international reputation, Louis could approach composers around the world. He had already worked with many major figures in the world of film music, and was convinced that Canadian composers were as good as any he had met. He believed that Canadian composers needed only the confidence that came from interacting with composers from other lands, hearing about their problems and frustrations, listening and responding to their music, and hearing their responses to Canadian compositions. According to Graham George, he was right:

> It [the Composers' Conference], like last year's orchestral workshop, began in Louis Applebaum's fertile imagination. Many doubted … it could result in anything but a consolidation of prejudice. Yet, despite such reservations, the conference was a huge success and, as Mr. Louis Applebaum said at the closing gathering, something that Canada at this stage of her musical development had to have.[42]

This conference, organized in cooperation with the Canadian League of Composers, changed the very nature of composing music in Canada. The number of composers increased dramatically in the 1960s and 1970s, and their reputations in other countries finally became established. Literally to his dying day, Louis was convinced that this Conference had made a singular difference in the role of the Canadian composer in the last decades of the 20th century.[43] His belief is substantiated by the contemporary reaction of Alfred Frankenstein, the music and art critic of the *San Francisco Chronicle*:

> In 30 years' activity as music critic for U.S. newspapers, the only Canadian composer I had ever heard of was Healey Willan, whose choral works are often performed in the

U.S. That there was a Canadian League of Composers was complete news to me when I was invited to the Stratford festival, and that these composers practice all manner of styles and media was an even more striking revelation.

It was Frankenstein's view that the conference had put Canada on the map, and

As a result of it, I have no doubt but what Canadian orchestral and chamber music will figure more prominently on international programs and Canadian music will take its proper place in the international scheme of things. It is obviously past high time for such development.[44]

At the end of the summer of 1960, Louis resigned as Music Director, this time leaving his administrative role behind for good. His leaving was a considerable blow to Stratford Music. He had been the one remaining Festival artist-founder still actively engaged there. Tyrone Guthrie and Tanya Moiseiwitsch had long gone and Louis was a source of strength to Langham and others who had joined later. As well, he was the only Canadian in that original group of artistic founders.

Louis had returned, summer after summer, staying — sometimes for a whole season and at other times only for a few days — in the homes of local Stratford citizens. Stories abound of his warmth and affability, his humility, and his good humour. Laura Pogson, then a child of ten, remembers Louis renting a room in her parents' house on the Avon River across from the Theatre. She vividly recalls finding Louis in the living room, dancing alone, while composing the music for *A Midsummer Night's Dream* — a behaviour she found entrancing in an adult. Her father, Ed Smith, worked for the Bell Telephone Company in a technical capacity. Laura remembers long conversations between Louis and her father as Louis continued to consider the future of the "Composer-tron" — the invention that he and Ken Kendall had worked on for over a decade. Through the 1950s, as theatre people came and moved on, Louis had continued to make music and organize presentations that had astonished people from around the world. Upon his resignation, the citizens of Stratford honoured him at a banquet. They knew he would be missed.[45]

Louis had hoped that someone else would take on the artistic directorship of the Music Festival, but no one was available. Ezra Schabas was willing to play a role, but not take on full responsibility. So a triumvirate was formed by three musicians who had made a great contribution to the musical leadership of the Festival and particularly to the orchestral work-shop — Leonard Rose, Oscar Shumsky, and Glenn Gould. The idea was a dreadful mistake. Leonard Rose was just not interested in administrative decisions and Gould had none of the skills of patience and diplomacy that were needed. Only Shumsky had both the interest and the capacity for the task. The end of the triumvirate was assured when Gould, in a fit of anger, screamed at Schabas during an open rehearsal. Schabas wisely decided that he had had enough and, without his contribution, the triumvirate became completely dysfunctional.[46]

The momentum of the Applebaum years ensured that music would con-tinue to be a significant part of the Festival's activities throughout most of the 1960s. The National Festival Orchestra contributed to the programming, and chamber music performed by its members continued to delight increas-ing audiences. Even the Saturday morning chamber music series became a box-office success.[47] Canadian contemporary works and other challenging repertoire continued to be played.[48] Louis supported these efforts, not least because they gave him a great asset — a first-rate orchestra to elevate the somewhat pedestrian music of the Gilbert and Sullivan operettas.[49]

Louis's continuing involvement is witnessed by the fact that, in 1962, he was engaged in discussions about the possibility of a new Music Building which would include an opera house, a concert hall, and a motion picture house, as well as rehearsal rooms for orchestral workshops, dressing rooms, a music library, and management offices. The dream never materialized.

By the end of that summer of 1962, Udo Kasemets concluded a review of Stratford Music with the comments that the Festival "lacks firm leader-ship" and that the "three-man directorate created after Louis Applebaum's resignation two years ago has outlived its purpose and should give way to a strong one-man directorate."[50] Writing eight years later, Lenore Crawford summed up the situation: "It took 10 years for the dream of music at the Stratford Festival that was Louis Applebaum's to be shattered."[51]

Stratford Music in the 1960s deserves a more balanced analysis. Louis's successors did produce some noteworthy concert seasons. Certainly 1961 and 1962 saw a diminution of musical activity, but in 1963, the National Youth Orchestra and Rudolf Serkin, along with Gould and Shumsky, provided artistic excitement and a new initiative, a Festival Choral Workshop. This resurgence continued in 1964 and 1965, and, in 1965, under Oscar Shumsky's leadership, Mozart's *Marriage of Figaro* was performed under Mario Bernardi while Louis was providing a dramatic counterbalance on another stage by directing the music for Kurt Weill and Bertoldt Brecht's *Rise and Fall of the City of Mahagonny*. That same year saw Benny Goodman and Dave Brubeck delight jazz audiences, while members of the National Festival Orchestra continued to give Saturday-morning chamber concerts hosted by Douglas Campbell, Peter Donat, Frances Hyland, Leo Ciceri, and Tony Van Bridge. In addition, The Festival Singers excelled themselves with an offering of Handel's *Solomon*.

As time went by, music became less central in the activities of the Stratford Festival. Major figures in the Canadian musical world — Raffi Armenian, conductor of the Kitchener-Waterloo Symphony Orchestra for many years, and Mario Bernardi, the first and most successful conductor of the National Arts Centre Orchestra — tried to make it work. Neither artist could gather the resources needed to restore the Music Festival to its former heights. However, the pattern of Saturday and Sunday concerts was holding firm, still with outstanding soloists and ensembles, including the Orford String Quartet and the Beaux Arts Quartet. Sunday recitals by Louis Quilico, Lois Marshall, Claudio Arrau, the National Youth Orchestra, Itzhak Perlman and, for more modern tastes, Gordon Lightfoot, all contributed to the hope that Stratford Music would continue to be a force in the musical life of the nation. Eventually, though, Stratford Music was to be overshadowed by Stratford musicals — Gilbert and Sullivan productions and Broadway revivals that brought audiences and filled the Stratford coffers.

By 1973, the centrepiece of Stratford Music was the appearance of the New York Philharmonic under Michael Tilson-Thomas, and, later that season, the Chicago Symphony Orchestra. These appearances represented the triumph of marketing over music. This was precisely the bloated kind of programming that Louis found inappropriate. By the mid-1970s the National Festival Orchestra — a name resounding with country-wide purpose — had been more modestly identified as the Stratford Festival Ensemble. The number of evening concerts had fallen to a handful and were mainly built around prestigious soloists — Paul Tortellier, Janos Starker, Alexander Lagoya, and Philippe Entrement — with a sprinkling of Canadian performers.

By 1970, Louis was having serious personal doubts about a continuing Stratford Music Festival. In the 1970s the Guelph Spring Festival was launched, followed some years later by the Elora Festival. Both were excellent in quality and showed a commitment to Canadian contemporary music and Canadian performers. The Toronto Symphony Orchestra was playing two or three times a week at Ontario Place on the Toronto waterfront. No one, however, would even consider the Orchestral Workshop and the special attention to the specific needs of Canadian composers that had distinguished Stratford Music's earlier contributions.

Louis saw other roles for the Festival. The National Youth Orchestra had not found a permanent home and Stratford, he was sure, would be a perfect setting. He never gave up his dream that the Stratford Shakespearian Festival was the obvious place for providing training for performers of lyric theatre, perhaps linked with a university music faculty presenting an academic program that stressed contemporary composition in that genre. However, he was becoming increasingly philosophical about all institutionalized artistic expressions, gradually coming to the view that they all had a certain lifespan and could remain vital only for a few years. His advice to the Festival in 1970:

> If you are not going to do anything for a purpose, then don't do it. Maybe Stratford doesn't need music and this would have been a great year to have the Festival Theatre empty. Stratford wouldn't have lost an audience ... when Stratford is ready to spring something new, the audience will come. It always has.[52]

Stratford did not heed his advice and the music program continued through the 1970s. Despite Louis's misgivings, there were highlights that delighted him. In 1975 Harry Somers's opera, *The Fool*, and Jean Vallerand's *The Magician*, two unusual Canadian works, were produced. However, by the 1980s, the Stratford Music Festival was no more. Boris Brott revived the concept of Canadian artists making music in conjunction with the Festival, not on-site but at the Stratford City Hall, but the Brott experiment also ultimately succumbed.

The Stratford Music Festival has never been forgotten, even though its full impact on Canadian music-making has never been recognized. It was much more than a "blip" on the musical performing scene of the 1950s, and its influence on the development of audiences for future festivals was considerable. Yet nothing that happened on stage compares with the effect the Festival had on the future of Canadian music composition and the excellence of orchestral performance throughout the 20th century.

Chapter Eight

On the Road with Gilbert and Sullivan

T he decade of the 1960s would bring a period of frantic frag-mentation to Louis's career. Gone were the years with a strong central focus around which he could continue his freelance work in film, radio, and television — the NFB in the 1940s, and Stratford in the 1950s. Although Louis had rejected any idea of return-ing to New York or Hollywood and was very much a Canadian nation-alist, that enthusiasm was not shared by his son David, who looked longingly to the more exciting opportunities that he sensed could be found south of the border.

David was now a teenager, discontented at school and dissatisfied with the prospect of spending July and August in a dull western Ontario setting — a problem his parents settled by arranging for him to attend a good music camp. However there was no simple solution to the negative attitude that he had developed, not only towards school, but also towards Canadian society as a whole. David resolved to drop out of high school and leave Canada, and, in 1962, he headed for Southern California where he hoped to attend classes in an American university. There, David believed, he would find academic courses that would bet-ter fit his vocational interests. However, in the first few months after his arrival, David met several young men his own age and decided to join them in sharing a large apartment in Los Angeles. All thought of attend-ing university had vanished, and concerns about David's proximity to various dangers were high in the minds of both his parents. David was entranced with the bright lights of Hollywood and, although he realized that he had none of his father's talent for making music, he believed — accurately, as it eventually turned out — that he could find work in the field of sound production.

With his only son living in California, Louis developed an intense interest in American political and social affairs. His attention was captured by the idealism of the Kennedy Administration — committed to address-ing the deterioration of the American social fabric and determined to halt the erosion of good will and civility on which America's survival depend-ed in a world with nuclear capability. Kennedy's challenge to the "bright-est and the best" to conquer space was to bring focus and rapid improve-ment to the nation's technological skills.

This age of renewal was an exciting time for artists who joined the new generation of Harvard-prepared intellectuals, journalists, historians, and economists with access to the White House. A parade of actors, musi-cians, dancers, and playwrights began to find themselves quite at home with the President and his First Lady. Kennedy demonstrated his own sol-idarity with artists and their values when, on a visit to Amherst, Massachussetts, in October, 1963, he stated: "It may be different else-where. But democratic society — in it, the highest duty of the writer, the composer, the artist is to remain true to himself and to let the chips fall where they may."[1]

Kennedy's vision and values provided a stark contrast to Ottawa's efforts. From the pathetic drift of a totally divided Diefenbaker Cabinet to the sordid series of scandals that beset a newly elected Liberal minority Government in 1962, it seemed that these years were passing the Canadian nation by. Yet, ironically, before the end of the 1960s, the triumphant celebrations of Canada's Centennial Year and the immense success of Montreal's "Expo 67" would fill Canadian hearts with pride.

Within three weeks of the celebrated Amherst speech, President Kennedy was dead — struck by an assassin's bullet as he drove through the streets of Dallas. Much of the rest of this decade in the United States would be characterized by sad stories of alienated youth and racial strife. Eventually the pressure built until the hot summers of the mid-1960s when the centres of dozens of American cities were burned, and rioting in the streets became a regular event. By the late 1960s, the discontent had moved to the nation's university campuses where anger at civil rights violations became exacerbated by opposition to the Vietnam War.[2]

Some spillover of this dissent certainly influenced Canadian young people — particularly those who were meeting and conversing with the considerable number of young Americans who arrived in Canada seeking refuge from forced military service in a war they opposed, supported by an Administration they detested. This discontent infected young people in at least two major Canadian centres.

And the young were increasingly unhappy as the years
after 1957 went on. On the streets of Yorkville in
Toronto and Kitsilano in Vancouver they were unhappy about Canada's close ties to the United States
through the North American Air Defence Command
and NATO links that the Vietnam War brought home
to them. They were unhappy at the prospect of dying
in a nuclear Holocaust, a possibility that that few could
dismiss after Soviet-American confrontation over Cuba
in 1962.[3]

Canada had its own problems, different from those that beset the
U.S. There was a growing dissatisfaction on the part of French-speaking
Canadians with their place in the nation's political and economic life.
This movement gained ground with the Quiet Revolution in 1960, and
became noisier and more violent as the decade of the 1960s proceeded.
Louis found this an issue that would come to dominate the affairs of
every federal agency with which he was associated. It was to influence his
work at the CBC, his involvement with the Canada Council and his part
in the planning of Ottawa's National Arts Centre — an initiative that
would become the federal government's major centennial project in the
nation's capital.

Through a private film company he was to form in the early 1960s —
Group Four Productions — Louis would be ready to act on a broad scale
to deal with language issues — particularly through the introduction of an
educational television program called "En France." But the Government
was slower to move, and this lack of commitment — at least until Pierre
Elliot Trudeau arrived on the scene — had serious implications for Louis's
aspirations as a corporate executive.

By 1960, the Diefenbaker Government, which had promised so
much in its bid to attract the support of Canadians from coast to coast,
was in a state of paralysis. A recession had brought rising levels of unemployment and there was resentment over a fiscal policy that appeared to
be using high interest rates to stop the major perceived threat to Canada's
well-being — rampant inflation. All federal agencies were at risk in this
economic context, but the CBC, to which Louis had given his commitment, was in dire straits. It was threatened not only by cutbacks, but also
by Government policies that weakened the national broadcaster in favour
of private broadcasters who deeply resented the predominance of the
Corporation and its Board over all other radio and television transmis-
sions in the country.

Along with most Canadians, Louis welcomed a new nationalist strategy for keeping Canada independent, but was disappointed by the inability of the government to administer the country with some confidence and effectiveness. The strength of the Canadian dollar and the stability of the economy were of particular concern as he launched his private-sector initiative, Group Four Productions.

Louis was not a "political animal," caught up in the partisan political struggles that characterized this decade on Parliament Hill. He realized that policies that could benefit Canada must be welcomed from whatever source they came. His long-term political interest was in the development of a society that would esteem the arts and respect the creativity of artists. However, he quickly came to realize how party ideology might have an immediate and severe impact on public enterprises, such as the CBC, the NFB, the Canada Council, and, later in the decade, the National Arts Centre. Ultimately, the survival of arts organizations depended on public support — a fact that gave a terrible relevance to debates that raged in the House and ultimately produced potentially damaging legislation.

Even by the mid-1960s, with only a few years to plan the celebration of Canada's 100th birthday, no commitments had been made — a matter of deep concern to artists and arts organizations who looked forward to playing a part in events that would increase their activities and enlarge their revenues. For Louis, whose Group Four operation was in place to respond not only to film production but also federal initiatives involving public celebrations of any kind, it was a terrible setback.

The Canadian polity was reeling from a divided and indecisive Conservative government under John Diefenbaker to an accident-prone minority Liberal administration under Lester Pearson. Although the Liberals hoped to return the country to sane, rational, predictable government, the newcomers stumbled badly in their first few months. At the same time, the economic maelstrom that afflicted Louis's efforts in both the public and private sectors cast him into doubt about the future. Even more depressing was the atmosphere on Parliament Hill, where Pearson's and Diefenbaker's complete lack of respect for each other soured the political life of the country for most of the decade and, in the context of a minority government, made solutions to the nation's ills seem quite impossible.

The only ray of light in all this gloom was cast by bright hopes for the upcoming centennial — hopes that gradually dimmed as people began to wonder whether there would be anything left to celebrate by the time 1967 arrived. However, before all hope was lost, the Liberals secured a near-majority and proceeded to promulgate legislation that gave Canada its flag, put the Canada Pension Plan into place, and even took on the unpopular but courageous task of unifying the armed forces. The economy rallied and unemployment levels fell. When Centennial Year finally broke upon the nation, the Canadian people were ready to celebrate. Pierre Berton described it as "a psychedelic year, a McLuhanesque year, a crazy mixed up year," and called his book on the subject *1967: The Last Good Year.*[4]

Louis Applebaum's career mirrored the triumphs and failures that characterized the national scene during these dramatic years. He had left the administrative duties of the Stratford Music Festival behind him in the summer of 1960 and had subsequently been appointed as an assistant to Geoffrey Waddington, CBC Television's Director of Music. He was now "on staff" and he thought this would provide a base for all his other activities — composing, consulting, and conducting. He saw an opportunity for a change in lifestyle and worried about his teenage son, David, on the verge of departing for California. Louis realized that he had been absent for much of David's childhood, with Jan looking after the home front while he was in London, Moscow, Hollywood, New York, or wherever work beckoned. Although Jan accompanied him on as many trips as possible — particularly to Ottawa and Stratford — there were long periods of absence.[5]

Now, Louis believed, he could centre his activities in Toronto and, except for the *Pinafore* project which was forming in Guthrie's mind — a commitment that might take him across the continent for a number of weeks a year — he would remain in his home town. Indeed, in the summer of 1961, he allowed himself to be nominated for membership in the Island Yacht Club — a beautiful facility on the Toronto Islands overlooking the magnificent cityscape. Louis and Jan introduced themselves to the Club by having dinner there one night. It was a great occasion — but also a singular experience. They even looked at some yachts that they thought might provide them with good times. As it turned out, they never returned to the Club and Louis successfully claimed back his initiation fee. The dream of being a "normal" couple, perhaps with a modest vessel moored in the Centre Island marina, was a fantasy. The time it took to cross Toronto's bay and the hours needed to look after the social and marine responsibilities inherent in such a membership were simply beyond Louis's capacity. There was no leisure time in the pastiche of frenetic activity to which he had devoted himself and his talent. The schedule of CBC Television administration demanded an extraordinary amount of weekly conducting — this was the era of "live" as opposed to "taped" television

— and the pressure of responsibilities with Group Four Productions required time and energy. Then the *Pinafore* project was rapidly succeeded by the *Penzance* project, *The Gondoliers, The Mikado,* and *The Yeomen of the Guard.* With a Festival presentation at Stratford, a television production, and extensive touring, Louis's enterprises filled every moment of his schedule. As the decade matured, the Canada Council and the planning of a new arts complex in Ottawa needed his expertise, to say nothing of a new provincial agency for grants to the arts that was just being launched in Ontario. And he continued to compose. Recreation on Toronto's waterfront? Impossible.

Tyrone Guthrie's decision to mount and tour a Stratford production of Gilbert and Sullivan had come to fruition in 1959. An entrepreneur as well as a director, Guthrie immediately saw the long-term potential for Gilbert and Sullivan ("G & S") operettas — several of these were available for tours in subsequent years and *Pinafore* would show that touring productions could be made to work both artistically and financially. *Pinafore* drew on all of Louis's background as an "on the spot" organizing genius. The program would be mounted first as a Stratford Music Festival offering, and would be scored for small orchestra and designed to use easily transportable sets. Once the Stratford season ended, another short period of rehearsal in another theatre would prepare the production for several weeks, even months, on the road. There would be some new voices — both solo and in the chorus — but essentially, it would be a Stratford experience for people across the continent. At the time, Louis and Guthrie could not have foreseen how successful the touring would be. Its success meant that there were, on occasion, two Stratford G & S productions in process — one performing, or preparing to perform, at the Festival, and another performing, or preparing to perform, on tour. The tour would not involve the Festival administration, but would be carried out by a private company headed by Leonid Kipnis, a friend of both Guthrie and Louis. Guthrie, at least, believed that the venture could actually make money. In any case, the Stratford Festival would be at no risk financially.

For Guthrie, and for Louis too, there was an artistic challenge involved in all this. From their beginning in the 19th century, the Gilbert and Sullivan operettas had been monopolized by the D'Oyly Carte Company at the Savoy Theatre in London, England. By 1960, these works had come into the public domain. This meant that the old-fashioned, nineteenth-century hand of the D'Oyly Carte tradition would no long be an impediment to more contemporary treatment — allowing changes that would brighten and enliven. *H.M.S. Pinafore* —

very popular and filled with light music — would be a test case. Guthrie was well aware of the outrage that would ensue if he in some way spoiled the *Pinafore* experience for the army of faithful G & S devotees. In an article in the *New York Herald Tribune*, Guthrie wrote, "my production will make no attempt to be revolutionary." The setting would still be the deck of a sailing ship in Her Majesty's navy, and the cast would be costumed in naval uniforms and 19th-century dresses. However, he promised a younger chorus, with "freshness and charm" — a commitment that Louis took seriously. Guthrie went on to promise that his production would be respectful, maybe even too much so, in its attempt to interpret a work which "light and unpretentious though it may be, we regard as a Victorian relic to be preserved in mothballs rather than as a classic which every epoch has a right to re-examine and express in contemporary terms."[6] Guthrie's confidence in the face of reinventing Gilbert and Sullivan is quite staggering. By his own admission, he had not even seen a high-school production — much less a professional presentation — of Gilbert and Sullivan's work. On that score at least, Louis, with his Harbord Collegiate experience, was considerably ahead of the renowned director. On the other hand, Guthrie claimed that this lack of contact with these paragons of the musical stage had left his mind free to be creative and innovative, completely undefiled by whatever follies previous productions had perpetrated on these musical gems.

Throughout the late winter and early spring of 1960, Louis spent weeks auditioning actors and singers for the summer production. By *Pinafore*'s opening night in Stratford, he was able to assure Guthrie that not only were there New York agencies waiting to take the production to Broadway, but two companies were vying for a contract to record the entire work. In a letter to Guthrie, Louis noted the talents of two stellar Canadian actors: "Bob Christie ... hasn't much of a voice, but he's anxious to work with you and Millie [Amelia] Hall ... again, no voice, therefore the question, can we spare the opportunity to assemble good singers for the sake of having good actors?" That problem would face every director casting a musical at Stratford (or anywhere else, for that matter) in a century that came to demand some semblance of realism in even the grandest of operas or the most trivial of operettas. It is a measure of Louis's commitment to the quality of the drama in this production that, as musical director, he was prepared to submit the question to Guthrie for his advice.[7]

A memorable, rejuvenated *Pinafore* certainly depended on splendid actors who could sing but, as well, on an orchestra that could play a somewhat tepid orchestral score with musical intelligence and enthusiasm. Fortunately, Louis could still count on his formula from the *Orpheus* production of the year before. The *New York Times* correspondent identified the strategy with complete accuracy:

> The National Festival Orchestra of 22, conducted by Mr. Applebaum, gave a sparkling account of the score .... To tempt the very best musicians into what might otherwise be found a rather dowdy assignment, Mr. Applebaum, a Toronto composer and director of music for the Festival, has made membership in the orchestra a passport to a chamber music workshop.[8]

On opening night, a handwritten note arrived at Louis's dressing room minutes before he was to lift his baton. It was addressed to "Captain Louis Applebaum R.N." and expressed the following sentiment: "Keep good time dear Lou and good luck to all aboard, with best wishes," signed, Tanya Moiseiwitsch.[9] Louis certainly needed the encouragement. It was terribly hot that evening — so much so that it threatened the quality of his performance.

The opening night performance was a triumph in every way. Clifford Hulme, writing in the Brantford *Expositor*, was effusive in his praise:

> To repeated storms of applause throughout the evening and a thunderous five minutes of near delirium, Gilbert and Sullivan's *H.M.S. Pinafore* set sail last night on a three-week cruise that will add a notable chapter to Stratford Festival history.[10]

Needless to say, the *Pinafore* run at the Festival was quickly sold out. Jacob Siskind of *The London Free Press* put it more succinctly: "It's simply insane – but it's magnificent."[11]

Pinafore was well received in Stratford, but the Phoenix Theatre in New York was a different sort of venue and Louis and Tyrone Guthrie approached their first stop on the tour with some trepidation. The cast was largely Canadian, and this was a long time before it would be considered quite safe to "originate" major musical productions in Toronto, even though Toronto eventually offered an array of Canadian dancers and singers trained by music, dance, and drama faculties at Sheridan College, Ryerson Polytechnic Institute, George Brown College, York University, the Opera School at the Royal Conservatory, and other such institutions in southern Ontario. In short, there was every reason for such fears, and the rehearsals at the Phoenix Theatre were filled with apprehension. However, the New York critics were ecstatic. In fact, in a special report, *The Globe and Mail* featured a collection of their responses that were deemed "superlative." Frank Aston of the *World Telegram-Sun* wanted to keep *Pinafore* in New York all winter. Walter Kerr of the *Herald Tribune* described *Pinafore* as "quaint and thoroughly delightful. I am sure that Sir Arthur Sullivan would have loved what Mr. Guthrie has done." Howard Taubman, in a *New York Times Service* piece dated September 7th, had given his comments under a headline expressing all that Louis and Tyrone Guthrie could have hoped for: "Guthrie, Applebaum Brush Off the Barnacles."[12] In a later column in the *New York Times*, Taubman wrote that "Louis Applebaum deserves an extra large helping of grog for the tact and sensibility of his musical preparation and his conducting."[13] John Chapman, writing in the *New York Daily News*, concluded that Louis Applebaum's orchestra "is just right – never assertive but always there."[14] It was a short moment of triumph — Louis had to return to Toronto the day after the New York opening to take up his new duties at the CBC. Louis had enjoyed the process of launching the first touring production of *Pinafore* — one that was still on the road four years later. These accolades were a welcome experience for him. Normally, his composing and his conducting for theatre brought little attention and few mentions in rave reviews. His work was supportive rather than "assertive" and it was the performers, directors, and even the designers and lighting technicians whose work was recognized. In this regard, the *Pinafore* experience was a satisfying aspect of his Stratford work, and he welcomed the opportunity to establish himself as a freelance associate rather than as an employee. The production was sufficiently impressive that the CBC decided to film *Pinafore* and present it as a special program on its national network.

Ironically, Gilbert and Sullivan, not Shakespeare, became the first Stratford production so honoured by Canada's broadcasting system. The producer of the CBC presentation was Norman Campbell, a man who would become a world figure in the creation of such spectacles involving future Stratford offerings, but would become even better known for his work with the National Ballet of Canada and the Canadian Opera Company. *Pinafore* was taped for a national network on its way to New York's Phoenix Theatre. The program guaranteed the best sound by ensuring that "a full orchestra of top Canadian musicians, directed as at Stratford by Louis Applebaum, was right in the studio instead of in a separate studio as in most large scale TV productions."[15]

Pinafore was remounted, and toured Canada and the United States once again in 1962. However, the real test for *Pinafore* came in the winter of 1962 when the production was taken where it all began — London, England. Though not at the Savoy Theatre, it would be performed at the Haymarket Theatre, equally prestigious in the eyes of London audiences and critics. Not only were the theatre and its English context threatening, but the First Performance was to take place in the presence of Queen Elizabeth at a charitable event in aid of King George's Pension Fund for Actors and Actresses. On this occasion, a most bizarre review, headlined "Voyage of Discovery," was penned by Alan Brien, writing in the *Sunday Telegraph*. He opened his piece with an admission that this *Pinafore* was "the first G & S I have ever seen" and after effusive accolades, concluded with the unassailable statement that it was "the best performance of *H.M.S. Pinafore* I have ever seen."[16] However, the production predictably aroused the anger of the traditionalists, as well as those who were outraged by the effrontery of a colonial shadow of England's Stratford-on-Avon Theatre presenting a new interpretation of their beloved Gilbert and Sullivan. Neither group was in the least amused. Andrew Porter, in the *Financial Times*, representing both critical views, assailed the production as "a coarse, third-rate presentation of *H.M.S Pinafore*, for all that it bears the legend, 'directed by Tyrone Guthrie.'"[17] Porter was supported by Noel Goodwin in the *Daily Express* who referred to the Canadian *Pinafore* as a "burlesque."[18] However, the *Evening Standard's* review was totally positive and certainly mirrored the reaction of the audience which was entirely enthusiastic in its response.

> *H.M.S. Pinafore* at Her Majesty's Haymarket Theatre, is more than just a first-rate piece of entertainment. It is an historic act of resuscitation performed on the trussed but still breathing corpse of a famous partnership.[19]

By early August 1962, *Pinafore* was back in North America and in San Francisco. Stanley Eichebaum's review in that city's *Examiner* bore the headline, "Guthrie's Bouncing Jovial Pinafore" and commented that "the orchestra under Louis Applebaum is crisp and frothy as it should be for Gilbert and Sullivan."[20] Theresa Loeb Cone in the *Oakland Tribune* found Louis's work particularly praiseworthy. "Louis Applebaum's musical direction is first-rate, one should add, and altogether Guthrie has provided theatre-goers with a new dimension of appreciation of G & S …. It's a show that simply should not be missed."[21]

By August 10th, *Pinafore* had reached Vancouver and, once again, it was greeted with enthusiasm both by audiences and critics. Vancouver's acceptance of the production pinpoints the importance of these years of touring the Stratford productions of Gilbert and Sullivan — they carried the image of this new Festival, ensconced in a small Ontario municipality, across the country and beyond. The Festival had begun as a local initiative, had hoped to be perceived as a national institution, and ultimately had come to be seen as a national treasure. The fact that this and subsequent touring productions were the creations of a private company that had taken on the responsibilities of organizing the tour was of no interest beyond the boardrooms of the Festival. So far as people across Canada and beyond were concerned, this was a Stratford Festival triumph.

One Vancouver critic was particularly conscious of Louis's role in the artistic success of the venture: "Louis Applebaum held the orchestra and singers with authoritative leadership. The instrumental playing had a wide range of colour with some of the lyrical passages beautifully phrased."[22]

Although the production was receiving, on the whole, artistic adulation, the financial aspects of touring a large company of actors, along with technicians, sets, et al., were challenging. This was a completely commercial venture. There was no subsidy from any government's granting agency. Even with full houses, the expenses threatened to bring the entire enterprise down. Leonid Kipnis was looking after these arrangements and was concerned that the cost of the London tour could be disastrous, especially in view of losses on the U.S. tour. He could only hope that the longer four-week runs in San Francisco and Vancouver might reduce travel costs, bringing the 1962 tour back into the black. Meanwhile, Louis was doing his part to find extra revenue by trying to convince RCA that recordings, both of *Pinafore* and its successor on the Stratford stage, *The Pirates of Penzance*, should be made and sold as quickly as possible. This was not to be; RCA was interested only if there was a tape already available, but could see no point in bearing the expense of a recording session.[23]

Unbelievably, *Pinafore* was still on the boards as late as 1964 and, by that time, other Gilbert and Sullivan tours had been arranged, involving Louis in rehearsing the new show and conducting for at least the opening night in each city on the tour. Louis arranged to begin rehearsals in Los Angeles in 1962, in spite of the fact that Guthrie, who was still keeping his hand in the process, hated California. Louis insisted. He and Jan had personal reasons for wanting to be in that part of the world. Their son David was sharing an apartment in Los Angeles with a rather restless group of teenagers; he still had no job or prospects and was certainly not forwarding his education or his career. Louis was determined to talk with David, and, if possible, lure him back to Canada.

When Louis and Jan arrived in California they found that nearly all David's clothing had disappeared and he looked destitute. Jan's strategy was to give David enough money to allow him to find other accommodation, so that he would not be dependent on his friends, and issuing an invitation to him to stay at their hotel whenever he wished.

In the meantime, Louis found the rehearsals more demanding than he had expected. New cast members had arrived as old "hands" had moved on, and the tour was to be very intensive — opening in Los Angeles in September, and then on to San Francisco in early October, and then Salt Lake City, Dallas, New Orleans, Kansas City, Chicago, Columbia, and eventually Montreal, Ottawa, and a final performance in Albany, New York. Yet Louis's mind was very much on his son's well-being. The youth culture of the 1960s, which was now in its early, formative stages, had descended upon the Applebaums, and it included a strong resentment against parental advice or interference. After a particularly exhausting day, Louis and Jan, returning to their hotel, were relieved to find that, for reasons that were never fully explained, David had moved into their suite.[24] He returned with them to Canada and Louis found him a low-level "gofer" job at the NFB.[25] It was just makeshift employment , but it was related to sound production and that soon captured David's attention. For Louis, the fact that he was back in Canada was a great comfort; but David continued to see his future across the border, in a country that held more opportunity in the field where he hoped to find a career one day.

The 1964 tour of *Pinafore* was going well, even though the cost of the tour was a source of great consternation. In July, Louis had been warned by Michael Parver, now employed by Leonid Kipnis to take responsibility for the financial health of the tour, that "the big problem as of this moment is the fact there are not sufficient monies to pay the transportation for the musicians."[26] Parver's solution? Let the musicians find their way to Los Angeles at their own expense! Louis was outraged and protested, but the budget problem remained. As a last resort, he would have to use local musicians in his orchestra. Louis was reluctant to reduce the size of the orchestra from the 16 instrumentalists he felt were a minimal requirement.[27] In San Francisco, disaster struck. Alfred Frankenstein brutally described his angry reaction to the opening performance: "… each and every member of the orchestra should be hanged by the neck from the yardarm until good and dead." A more fitting solution would have been to hang Mr. A. Doolittle, the local manager of the theatre, who thought he could hire members of the San Francisco Symphony Orchestra and put them in *Pinafore* without rehearsal. The review ended with a reference to the conductor, Louis Applebaum, "one of the best musicians of Canada" and "we apologize for the mess he got into in our town."[28] A catastrophe like this did not happen a second time and the tour finished in December — soon enough for all to return home for Christmas. It was a reasonable success, but it was to be the last tour. *Pinafore* had taken its final transcontinental journey.

The succeeding tours of Festival G & S productions were similar in both their moments of triumph and the presence of the odd disaster. The 1960 *Pinafore* production and tour had been so satisfying that Louis was able to entice Guthrie to take on his second G & S production in the summer of 1961 — *The Pirates of Penzance*. It too was scheduled, after its Festival run, "for a television production at the CBC where there was every expectation of a large audience and foreign sales of the program. Then, there would be a tour of the United States in the fall. The pattern was now established."[29] The difficulty in casting *Penzance* was that there would be two Stratford G & S touring companies operating simultaneously in the fall of 1961— each demanding its own cast.

It was left to Louis to solve this problem and he spent many days in the winter finding actors for both productions. He did not have to look far. He was deluged with letters, telegrams, and telephone calls as young performers from across the country and abroad saw the Stratford musical experience as a door to a stunning future. Every telephone call, indeed, every telegram and every letter, was answered personally by Louis, a task that took enormous time and energy from all his other pursuits of the 1960s. In some cases, the circumstances were quite heartbreaking. A Mrs. Elston, of Kingston, was prepared to give up her husband and children in order to join the Stratford Gilbert and Sullivan enterprise, justifying the abandonment with the argument that "she mustn't have her children grow up under the shadow of a mother who gave up a brilliant career." She was even prepared to go to Ireland to see Guthrie if that would help. Louis dissuaded her on both counts.[30]

When *The Pirates of Penzance* opened on July 7, 1961, it was met with the same enthusiasm that had greeted *Pinafore*. Under a headline "Better than Pinafore," Lenore Crawford of *The London Free Press* wrote: "Guthrie, Applebaum, and Brian Jackson who designed the costumes and sets, again proved themselves an unbeatable team.[31] She recognized Louis's role as a "fine collaborator" with Tyrone Guthrie was equally important as his role "as music director, and this year, more than last, this is important for the music has much more subtlety than the music of *Pinafore* and demands more of the singers in every role." Ron Evans, by the next decade a close associate of Louis at the Province of Ontario Council for the Arts was at that time the arts correspondent for the *Toronto Telegram*. He was complimentary in his review of the *Penzance* opening night.

> Louis Applebaum is again, happily, in the pit for this generally sound reading and last night he led his orchestra through its musical paces with a strong sense of authority and an over-all control that helped ease some of the dullness of the overture and underlined the action on stage without infringing on the rights of the singers.[32]

Blaik Kirby wrote in the *Toronto Daily Star*: "The show was even better than last year's *Pinafore*.... From beginning to end, the operetta is full of delightful Guthrie invention." Herbert Whittaker, in *The Globe and Mail*, thought that "never has one heard such singing." After 45 performances at the Stratford Festival, playing to nearly 50,000 people with an average of 92% capacity for all performances, *Penzance*, like *Pinafore* before it, went off to New York. Ron Evans went along and was able to report with a good deal of national pride that "Last night's capacity crowd of 1,200 whooped and hurrahed for this Canadian show from curtain to curtain," but noted that Louis Applebaum, was "here to conduct for the opening and then went off to resume his duties as director of music at the CBC."[33]

While the fall tour of "Penzance" was proceeding as scheduled, the television special was aired and was an unqualified success. It had been produced by the CBC's Norman Campbell, who had discovered a year earlier how to overcome Tyrone Guthrie's dislike of certain aspects of the electronic media — particularly the television director's penchant for close-up shots during moments of intense drama. During rehearsal, Campbell simply presented a splendid shot of the action on stage and allowed Guthrie to exclaim, "That's it! That's what I want!" It happened to be the kind of close-up that Campbell himself wanted and, from that point on, he had his way on matters of visual expression.[34] Indeed, Guthrie became so impressed with Campbell's work that he hired him to take on the direction of the touring company of *Penzance*. The general opinion was that the television version of *Penzance* was even better than *Pinafore* had been the year before.

The touring of *Penzance* began in January, 1962, and, once again, it was decided to take the production to the U.K. — beginning with a run in Brighton and then moving on to London in February. The pattern was now predictable, but the honeymoon with the critics was over and they were more negative than previously. Like *Pinafore*, the Stratford Festival production of *Penzance* received a mixed response. However, it was now more difficult to reach the standard that had been set previously because of financial restraints. As well, Guthrie had largely lost interest; other projects on both sides of the Atlantic were demanding his time. From this point on, he took only sporadic interest in the G & S productions, leaving the artistic decisions to Louis and financial matters to Kipnis and his hired help.

Louis continued as the major figure in the Gilbert and Sullivan project, conveniently "on hand" in nearby Toronto. For the 1962 season it was *The Gondoliers* that he chose for the Festival production. Once again, G & S drew large audiences. The director on this occasion was a rising star in the Canadian artistic firmament, Leon Major. *Variety Magazine* commented ungenerously that "*The Gondoliers* adds nothing to Major's stature," but did add that "the only outstanding assets of the show are the musical direction of Louis Applebaum and the singing of the mixed chorus."[35]

The most thoughtful review of the production came from John Kraglund in a commentary headlined "Direction, Costumes Disappointing but Music a Success in Gondoliers." Kraglund observed:

> By now it should be clear that *The Gondoliers* was essentially a resounding success on a musical basis. True, the success was not an unqualified one, for the production was decidedly slow to come to life. Mr. Applebaum allowed many of the slower numbers to drag and it was not until the lively fandango, choreographed by Alan Lund, that the entire cast appeared to come to life.[36]

However, it was becoming clear that the Gilbert and Sullivan phase of Stratford's work was coming to an end. George Kidd, in his review of *The Gondoliers*, made this point: "It is to be hoped that Stratford and Gilbert and Sullivan will also part company, at least for a few seasons. This production is bright and sparkling throughout but the novelty has worn off ...."[37] It was still the music that held the attention of *The Hamilton Spectator's* Ed Hocura. "The music for *The Gondoliers* is in the expert hands of Louis Applebaum and his is an applaudable contribution. Whether he is backing a duet or a chorus of 30 voices, Applebaum is there to give a needed lift to the oft-times ponderous proceedings."[38]

Ignoring the hints of critics that the time had come to move in another direction, the next year at Stratford brought a production of the *The Mikado*, directed by Norman Campbell — his first original production of G & S, although his television work on *Pinafore* and subsequent offerings had provided him with all the experience he needed. Indeed, *The Mikado* revived interest in Gilbert and Sullivan with its enormous energy and creative initiative. It was Campbell's idea to have Louis write a version of "God Save the Queen" in a Japanese musical idiom that included gongs to open each show, much to the delight of Stratford audiences who were now used to such in-jokes. The critics were more effusive than they had been about *The Gondoliers*, but there was still an undertone of disappointment that their advice of restraint about "too much of a good thing" had been ignored. Ted Miller, in the Guelph *Guardian*, wrote:

> Louis Applebaum has done his usual good work in supplying a well trained orchestra though doesn't seem to have the chorus entrances perfect yet – and he has to combat a tendency for the chorus to run away at times. Still he copes well.[39]

W.J. Pitcher, writing in the *Kitchener-Waterloo Record*, was more appreciative of Louis's role, commenting on the "good chorus singing and splendid work by the crack orchestra led by Louis Applebaum" which he felt had led to the success of the *Mikado* production.[40] John Kraglund of *The Globe and Mail* also perceived the strength of Louis's involvement:

> Credit for general music achievements must go to conductor Louis Applebaum under whose direction the national festival orchestra managed to give an effectively stylish interpretation despite the customary problems of making allowances for unexpected rhythm changes on stage.[41]

The Mikado followed the now familiar pattern, but this time Norman Campbell was able to take his own production into the studio and CBC aired it on October 2, 1963, to accolades across the country.

The Yeoman of the Guard, in the 1964 Stratford season, was to be the last G & S production for several years. It was a disappointment on all sides. It had been necessary to find a director at the last minute. An American, William Ball, was brought to Stratford, but it simply did not work out well. The opening night proved to be a dismal effort and the entire production had to be revised, hastened, and brightened up. Even then, it did not add to the reputation of the Stratford Festival productions of previous years. Guthrie's influence was long gone, and Louis had most definitely cut back on his commitment as other enterprises demanded his time and attention. The experiment was played out. The mainspring of the initiative had been to show that Canadians could put on classic operetta with the same elegance — and a good deal more energy — than the best companies in the United States, and with perhaps even more excitement than the original D'Oyly Carte purveyors of G & S in the U.K. In expressing sentiments that related to the *Gondoliers* production, Louis could have been referring to any of the first four Stratford seasons of G & S:

> My last experience with D'Oyly Carte Co. was in London a year ago, at which time I had the most doubtful pleasure of seeing their production of *The Gondoliers*. I speak so snobbishly because I felt that our Stratford production would, in most respects, turn out to be superior and I think I am right.[42]

Louis had certainly given the Stratford Festival a template for enhancing future seasons with music that did more than pay its way. Even more important, Stratford had broken in upon the consciousness of the English-speaking world, not just through touring, but especially through the medium of television. There would be other tours of Stratford dramatic productions, but as the century wore on, the financial costs of travel and accommodation became prohibitive except in the most extraordinary cases. For reasons that are obscure, neither the CBC nor any other network took up the challenge of providing the country with representative offerings from the Stratford season on any continuing basis. There were particular plays that caught the interest of the network, but these were regarded as "specials" — not instalments in an enduring series of stellar productions that had graced the Stratford Festival stage.

The Gilbert and Sullivan initiative had been a unique example of Canadian enterprise and it was Louis's administrative capacity, his enormous energy, his unfailing eye for talent, and his total commitment to an ideal that made it work. Indeed, Louis Applebaum had come a long way from the back row of the chorus at Harbord Collegiate.

Chapter Nine

Television Beckons

L ouis had left his post as Music Director at Stratford in the summer of 1960, in hopes of making a contribution to the rapidly expanding world of Canadian television. He had joined the staff of the CBC Television on a consulting basis to work as an assistant to Geoffrey Waddington, the CBC's Director of Music.[1] Waddington was an able and popular figure who had played a major role as a producer and conductor of music programs from the Corporation's earliest days of radio broadcasting. With only eight years of broadcasting experience, Louis's role was to encourage and promote the performance of "serious" music. As a freelance composer who had been with CBC Television since its inception, Louis knew the network had been "under construction" throughout the 1950s. Although programming in Toronto had begun in 1952, the budget and the energy of the Corporation, for its first six years, had been directed more towards initiatives that would allow it to reach every Canadian home than towards its programming. In spite of that reality, there was no subsequent period in the Corporation's history when it did broadcast — on both radio and television — such a range of serious music, and certainly no period when Canadian composers were so royally treated. These "birthing" years prepared Louis for his next venture.

There was every reason to have great expectations for CBC Television when CBC Radio was such a national treasure. Indeed, Louis's own Stratford Music Festival had received a warm welcome from CBC Radio. In 1957 fifteen broadcasts had come from Stratford and, by 1958, the CBC Symphony had become almost the resident orchestra. Even more impressive, in the very summer that Louis decided to leave Stratford, CBC Radio covered concerts associated with the International Conference of Composers, giving Canadians a taste of the music of world-renowned composers — and even some exposure to the esoteric genre of electronic music. The work of John Cage, an American leader in experimental trends in composition, was on the menu, along with the works of Canadians John Weinzweig and István Anhalt. By 1960, Louis and Tyrone Guthrie's first Gilbert and Sullivan production had attracted the attention of CBC Television. This was the decade when CBC Television became more conscious of what CBC Radio had accomplished — that is, effectively raising the cultural consciousness of the nation — and sought to emulate its splendid example. Later, the influence of American private-sector television would come to set the standards by which Canadian broadcasters judged themselves and their work.

However, Louis's relatively short stay at the CBC (1960-1963) was not his happiest career interlude. Frantically busy with the touring Gilbert and Sullivan productions, Louis also had to be attentive to new interests in arts funding that were stirring in Ottawa, and also lead a private company in carrying out political and artistic objectives impossible to imagine in a public agency. This was more than enough to occupy his time. That, combined with disappointments brought on by political squabbles and funding cuts, ultimately led Louis to return to freelancing. Still, he never lost his respect for the Corporation, and particularly for its mandate and the best expressions of the role that, on occasion, resulted in superb and memorable programming. Louis never lost touch with the fine artists who were his colleagues, but by 1963 he knew all there was to know about the CBC's "warts" and limitations and he had had enough of dealing with them on a daily basis.

It was difficult for CBC Television to share a border with a country that had pioneered the development and wide distribution of television, placing enormous pressure on Canadians "to keep up." This challenge would stretch the CBC's resources to the breaking point. It was a miracle that CBC Radio, launched only in 1935 and facing the stringent budgets of the Depression and the difficult years of World War II, had achieved such heights of excellence. However, there was little reason to expect that the Corporation could achieve the same results with television broadcasting. Television was incredibly expensive if Canadians were to match the costly production standards of the American networks, but there were those who were determined to make it happen. Indeed, it *had* to happen if Canadian audiences were to be attracted back from watching shows produced by stations south of the border and were to gain some pride in their own artists and innovators. Yet it could be stated quite openly and ominously in the 1955-1956 CBC Annual Report that " the CBC found itself responsible for one of the largest and perhaps of necessity the most complex broadcasting systems in the world, with diminishing financial means in sight."[2] This statement held no surprises for Louis. He realized that it would take almost a wartime commitment from the government to pay for the technical developmental costs and support sufficient programming to make CBC Television worth the effort.

In the shadow of these financial pressures, questions had arisen about who would control this new form of communication. The Massey Commission had made it quite clear that the triumphs of public radio broadcasting of the 1930s must be reinvented for television in the 1950s.

> The Commission therefore recommended that the control of the national broadcasting system continue to be invested in a single body [the CBC] responsible to Parliament; but that the present board of governors be enlarged to be made widely representative. No private networks should operate without the permission of the CBC.[3]

In typical Canadian fashion, neither the private network pattern of American culture nor the entirely public system of the British Broadcasting Corporation in the U.K. were to be slavishly copied. Through the years, a unique amalgam would be forged in the northern latitudes of the continent. With extraordinary prescience, the Massey Commission outlined the basic nature of the tension that would bedevil the CBC throughout the 20th century. With the enormous cost of producing pictures to accompany sound, "the pressure on uncontrolled private operators to become mere channels for American commercial material would become almost irresistible."[4] The Commission did not know that the economics of television broadcasting would place special pressure on American networks to sell their productions abroad after their airing in the United States. In fact it eventually turned out that the foreign purchase could pay most of the cost of an original production. Later in the decade, the CBC and Canadian private broadcasters found they could buy American programs for one tenth of the cost of producing comparable programming in Canada. Even without this knowledge, the Commission could insist that, left to its own natural development, television consumption would operate on a north/south, rather than east/west pattern, ending any hope that this new medium could be a unifying factor in the Canadian polity. Therefore, the Commission advised, no commercial television stations should be licensed until the CBC had its own service available to Canadian citizens — just as local stations had been described in their radio role by Davidson Dunton, the CBC President who had pronounced that, "the prime functions of the CBC and the private stations were different and therefore, not competitive; their functions were complementary in the whole Canadian system."[5]

Louis knew that, in the context of restrained national budgets, there would be every possibility that successive Governments funding the Corporation would have enormous power over the annual financial allocations. Through this financial control, the policy and program decisions of the CBC could be influenced. Louis had a lifelong faith in the importance of "arm's-length" relationships between governments and their agencies, even when the latter were at risk financially, and particularly when creative activities were involved. He believed this mechanism could protect public agencies from the worst kinds of interference. In 1960 not even Louis could have predicted the extent to which a government could punish an agency like the CBC that might be perceived as too critical or politically assertive. Indeed, he could not have predicted that the government's fiscal policies would ultimately terminate his own relationship with the Corporation.

With his belief that Canadian television, like Canadian film and radio, should promote the interests of Canadian artists, he was in complete agreement with the objectives of the Massey Commission. When, in September, 1952, the first programs struggled out of the Toronto studios, they did so with the highest purposes and principles. They were intended to give the country a sense of its own history, thereby assuring its survival as a nation, and to advance the cultural hopes and expectations of Canadians who saw a new era before them. Immediately, Canadian private interests clamoured to compete. By 1960 they were in full cry. "It seemed to be an important [some said indispensable] part of the capitalist system on the North American continent,"[6] where the struggle against worldwide communism was still making it quite acceptable, even in Canada, to spout ideological hyperbole on behalf of private broadcasting. Very soon, the threat that private popular broadcasting would overwhelm the CBC had the effect of diluting the program content quality in an attempt to achieve higher audience ratings. Louis had to fight this pressure at every level as he sought to find a place for music, particularly Canadian music, on the network.

Equally, he was convinced that the issues of individual and collective identity were the stuff of great historic drama of the ages — Shakespeare, Molière, Sophocles, and Ibsen. All of these authors were given the Applebaum musical score treatment in television offerings in these years, and were regarded as legitimate television fare. However, Louis was also convinced that important issues could be addressed even more appropriately by Canadian playwrights. At the time, there was virtually no professional theatre in the country — the CBC was the only stage available to actors and directors who might share Louis's views about the role of drama in informing people about vital issues. The tensions around peace and war, the pressures created by mass immigration, the enormous dislocation of a fast-changing economic system, the issue of Canadian identity on a continent dominated by a giant neighbour — all were subjects that Louis felt a national broadcaster must address. This belief in drama drew Louis's interest, as a composer, to programs which featured the theatrical, even as he worked on documentary programming in the public-affairs realm of CBC Television. Supporting Canadian authors who told stories of Canadian people through drama eventually became the pinnacle of Louis's contribution to the Corporation.

Although Louis had begun by writing music for distinguished radio programming already in place, he was prepared to address television production, when it beckoned, with the same intense commitment. From 1955 to the 1980s, most of Louis's professional work as a freelance composer was concentrated on television, and by far most of his writing was for CBC productions. Even before he had joined the CBC TV staff in 1960, he had been commissioned on many occasions as a free-lance composer. Composing in the heat of preparing a score — usually at the last minute and almost always dealing with revisions — was still a challenge. Pressure increased when the directors and producers were themselves learning the craft of television production, and showed little sensitivity to, or understanding of, the role of music in theatrical productions or public affairs programs. This was a repeat Louis's experiences in film and radio, but it was also the source of his excitement and sense of accomplishment as his talent grew more mature and he began to set higher standards for himself.

For Louis, the most important point about Canada's national broadcasting system was its legislated responsibility as an educational institution. However, that view was expressed less and less often in the swirl of excitement created by television. The world was losing its post-war collective idealism and was now more dominated by individual economic hopes and expectations. As a result, Louis was to have little interest in radio's continuous transmission of popular song and insignificant patter, or the sitcom-dominated television that had quickly become the standard fare of entertainment television south of the border. Instead, serious drama and important events were to be the stuff of his new involvement in composing music for Canadian radio and television.

Louis knew that he could be consumed, not only by the politics of broadcasting, but also by economics. To support the kind of quality work he was interested in doing, the CBC had to be a well-funded network. If radio, with its relatively modest production costs, demanded a Canadian public system of broadcasting — television made it imperative.[7]

It was in 1954, when he was heavily involved in planning the music program for the Stratford Music Festival, that he had been approached to write the music for his first television program. Ironically, this was in the same year that his radio work had increased and, indeed, the year that "Summer Stage" and "Jake and the Kid" — both series with many program demands — filled his composing time. Still, Louis's previous film work was perfect preparation for dealing with another visual medium, and he found the immediacy of television compelling. He also found that working with a visual image stretched his capacity to use music to increase the impact of the total experience.

Louis liked the short, fast-moving style of television production, and his experiences had led him to appreciate the thrill of working to often frantic schedules and moving rapidly from project to project. As well, Louis enjoyed working with a team, and television fulfilled his social needs in the workplace. In essence, television was such a powerful medium for communication that radio and film took second and third places in his composing life from the mid-1950s on.

Louis had been fortunate that the first program, in 1955, was a brilliant play by Eric Nicol and that it was directed by Norman Campbell, who was to become a close friend and associate during the Gilbert and Sullivan phase of his career. "The Big Dig," described as an "autopsy on the recently departed year nineteen hundred and fifty-four," was written from the perspective of archaeologists unearthing the site "of the ancient Canadian city of Toronto" in the year 6155. The play was full of the humour for which Nicol was to become famous, and his sense of irony was directed at events on the contemporary Canadian scene. For example, the scholars found evidence from their digging that

> They [the Government] couldn't afford to keep up their Maritime fleet, yet they heaped wealth upon a girl who swam Lake Ontario. [a reference to Marilyn Bell, a young marathon swimmer who in 1954 had thrilled the citizens of Toronto with her feats of endurance and courage].[8]

It was not only the excesses of the sporting community that suffered the sting of Nicol's wit. The archaeological dig also unearthed a copy of "The Report of the Royal Commission on the Art, Sciences and Humanities" (the recently released Massey Report). The tantalizing dialogue surrounding its exposure reveals the blank incomprehension of the finders. "Curious, I don't remember a film with that title. Possibly it was one of those stories they were unable to adapt."

Louis survived his initiation into television with flying colours[9] and soon moved on to his next challenge — W.O. Mitchell's *The Black Bonspiel of Willie McKrimmon.*

The Black Bonspeil — a treatment of the Faust legend embellished with an incredible blend of curling-rink commentary and mystic meandering — challenged Louis's creative instincts. The main character, Willie McKrimmon, made a bargain with the Devil; he agreed to trade his soul for the chance to skip a team in the MacDonald Brier, the most prestigious competition in his chosen sport. The incomparable John Drainie played Willie and such stellar colleagues as Bud Knapp, Bill Needles, Frank Peddie, Tommy Tweed, and Eric Christmas joined him in their roles as colourful citizens and insatiable "rink-rats." Ron Poulton, in the *Toronto Telegram*, commented on the program's "pure delight" and suggested that the CBC "can repeat it every year from now to doomsday." Indeed, *The Black Bonspeil* would be repeated on a number of occasions, and would become a standard-setting example of how a Canadian television program on a Canadian theme can delight and inspire, while still revealing an aspect of the country's unique character.

In that same year, 1955, Louis had worked on another show in the "Scope" series. "The Family of Man" was essentially a dramatic examination of links shared by all humankind on a planet seeking peace and harmony. The program tapped Louis's extraordinary command of the repertoire of the great music of the ages, baroque and romantic, classical and contemporary. The score included the works of Bartok, Shostakovich, Britten, Barber, Elgar, Harrison, Hindemith, Prokofiev, and Walton — all 20th-century composers — but also drew on much earlier music from Purcell, Mozart, Corelli, Vivaldi, Handel, and Bach. By this stage in his life, Louis had become thoroughly familiar with the compositions of all the major western composers in virtually every genre of music. A program whose scope was the entire experience of humankind demanded a proportional musical response, and Louis had the giants of western composition at his fingertips.

A month later, "Scope" aired a production of *Hamlet* produced by Franz Kraemer. Kraemer was not only the creative force behind some of the stellar "specials" of opera, theatre, and concert programming at the CBC, but, more than any other figure, he was to awaken Toronto audiences to chamber music in the 1980s with his entrepreneurial work at the St. Lawrence Centre. Louis knew the play very well indeed and his notes on his personal copy of the script indicated the frame of mind he brought to every scene. The opening must exude "cobwebs, expectancy" and must be "tense, sinister." The line "O, that this too solid flesh might melt" should be accompanied by music which concludes with a long discord, and the text "My thoughts be bloody or nothing worth ..." must be shared with chords that are "intense, taut."[10]

The year also brought another special television program called "Seven Days to Victory," which was produced to celebrate the tenth anniversary of the Allied victory in Europe. It included film clips — many familiar to Louis from his work at the NFB — and it featured the voice of Lorne Greene, describing, as he had done in 1945, the final week of the war. But perhaps the most poignant voice was that of a survivor of Auschwitz. Louis was able to draw on his musical contributions to the war effort in the 1940s to give this program a documentary atmosphere that would arouse the memories and emotions of those who were now a decade away from the most significant event of their lives.

While engaged in this task, Louis also became involved in his first TV series. The mission of "Tabloid" was to bring subjects of importance to the attention of Canadians. It was built around its hostess, Elaine Grande. In one segment, Elaine took her audience to Lyndhurst Lodge, where they could learn about the problems facing paraplegics and the role that a facility like Lyndhurst could play in bringing people "back to a full life" as workers and family members. Louis produced a score for this program that expressed triumph rather than despair, loss, and deprivation.

In 1956 Louis became as familiar a figure in the halls and studios of the CBC as he was in the rehearsal spaces of Stratford. He took on the responsibility for a 37-week series of programs under the title of "Graphic" — CBC's answer to Edward R. Murrow's very popular interview program, "Person to Person," aired weekly in the U.S. on CBS. Murrow was a hero to every public-affairs broadcaster in the world; he had taken on the destructive communist-hunter, Senator Joseph McCarthy, and, despite much personal risk, had successfully brought him down. "Graphic" was to be broadcast in prime time (Friday evening at 9 p.m.) and, although Murrow's program was perceived as a lineup of famous American figures from the political and entertainment worlds, the Canadian version was to be much more inclusive of lesser lights from all the nation's regions. The host, surprisingly, was not a media person with a recognizable voice and face. Rather, the CBC decided to invite Joe McCulley to play the "Murrow" role. Joe was a familiar figure in educational circles, being at that time the Warden of Hart House — the cultural and athletic centre for men on the campus of the University of Toronto. McCulley was a tall, angular, out-going man with both a warm personality and a fine intellect. Providing the music for such a program would extend even the experienced Louis Applebaum. The *CBC Times* of March 11-17, 1956, described Louis as "a 37-year-old Toronto composer-conductor with a brilliant career in film, radio and TV work already behind him." The description of his new role was revealing.

> Composing and conducting the music for "Graphic" will be one of the toughest jobs he has tackled, for it will be a new experience – as he says, "it will be like writing music

in the dark." Often he will be scoring for something he hasn't seen.

To do this job he will have to call on a knowledge of his previous experience – from radio, a knowledge of musical bridges; from TV, facility in working with visual elements and the scoring of opening and closing sequences; from film, knowledge of scoring for complete and self-contained film clips.

Finally, it will involve a great deal of nervous strain. In working on film, Lou was often given two weeks to score one reel for a ten-minute film. On "Graphic" he will be lucky to get two days to accomplish the same task.[11]

It was a formidable task. Not only was Louis composing all the music for each program, he was in the studio conducting a small orchestra every Friday night as the program went out "live to air." It was complicated. "While Joe McCulley talks in the Toronto TV building to people in Ottawa or Montreal, the musical background is played by Louis Applebaum and an orchestra from Studio G of the radio building. Anybody for ulcers?" asked media reporter Alex Barris.[12] In spite of the expressed desire to be different from its CBS counterpart, the names of the guests on the program did include some stellar figures from the field of arts and letters – Christopher Plummer, Herman Geiger-Torel, Clyde Gilmour, W.O. Mitchell, Thomas Costain, and politicians such as Charlotte Whitton, the controversial mayor of Ottawa who appeared on an early program. Even the scholarly Claude Bissell, then President of the University of Toronto, was a welcome guest. A segment entitled "Square Dance, Bop, and the Classics" included Canada's distinguished jazz musician, Phil Nimmons, along with Mr. and Mrs. Frank Masella — the parents of eight sons who were classical musicians in a variety of ensembles. But the common folk with a story to tell turned up as well. On one program, steelworker Reg Harris appeared, along with "Lord" Athol Layton, a professional wrestler identified as a "bad guy" even in his bizarre profession. The producers were looking for variety and most certainly achieved their aim. As well, the show presented an extraordinary spectrum of Canadian citizens who added colour and excitement to a public life that was often cast in the media as dull and grey. But for Louis, composing and conducting the music each week was often a nightmare. Every program concealed pitfalls that could bring the production to a dishevelled conclusion. Indeed, with Louis as conductor giving signals to musicians like a first-base coach of the New York Yankees, it was never certain whether a precise entrance could be injected and indeed, on occasion, a whole musical interlude fell apart.

Yet despite these moments, Louis not only successfully completed his first television public-affairs series, but was re-engaged as composer-conductor for the "Graphic" series for another 29 weeks the following year. For any other man, this task would have been a major threat to health and sanity; for Louis, it was simply a job that made his life as a full-time composer financially possible and psychologically attractive.

Louis was intrigued by any program that enabled Canadians to tell their stories to each other. Stories were Louis's abiding interest; whether in a drama series or a simple interview, he knew that storytelling was a way for Canadians to come to understand themselves and each other. Particularly for Canadians, inundated by stories from another country to the south, broadcasting played an essential role that made possible the life of a nation. There were film clips available for each program that helped Louis provide appropriate musical accompaniment, but much of the music had to be based on his conjectures about the probable nature of the interviews and the subject matter likely to be covered. Each Friday night, Louis occupied Studio G, headphones in place and baton poised, ready to cue his orchestra — a band of superb musicians who, even with little opportunity to rehearse, could rely on Louis's sensitive scoring to help them sound like a string quartet or a full symphony orchestra. For two years, this engagement prevented Louis from participating in the services of his synagogue and required his presence at his piano from Saturday morning until the following Thursday. If he was at a Stratford opening of a production to which he had contributed, he had to return to Toronto in time for Friday evening's "Graphic."

In spite of this continuous pressure, "Graphic," more than any other experience, was to prepare him for the next stage of his career — a more participatory consultative role on the administrative side at CBC. In this role, Louis became familiar with many people at the Corporation who became lifelong friends. Most importantly, he came to know what the CBC could be at its best. He saw that Canadian "serious" music could benefit significantly from the work of this productive programming machine; indeed, the CBC could help Canadian artists and composers become known and respected. Louis also became aware that broadcasting Canadian recorded music, particularly on the radio, was essential. If television took more and more of the attention and budgets of the Corporation, fewer and fewer live broadcasts would be possible and radio would become dominated by recorded music. If there were no Canadian artists and no Canadian music available, program hosts would turn to British and American sources. Louis devoted much of his time to this problem in the later years of the 1960s and this was, in part, because the "Graphic" program had brought these issues to his attention.

In 1956 CBC Television, desperately trying to achieve the quality of drama that had given such distinction to radio, had engaged Louis to write the music for four plays in a "First Performance" series sponsored by Canada Savings Bonds. Louis was the common thread, along with the host, Joel Aldred. "First Performance" was described as "four specially selected Canadian dramas that have not been presented on television."[13] This was a major effort by the Corporation and had been in preparation for a full year by the time Louis became involved. Four well-known Canadian authors had been approached to submit scripts — Arthur Hailey, Joseph Schull, Max Rosenfeld, and Leslie McFarlane. The first presentation, "Black of the Moon," by Joseph Schull, was about the Riel Rebellion. The theme was summarized succinctly as, "A white man's promise, a rebel's lie, a war chief's hatred, the safety of a man and his innocent daughters … all these elements held in balance."[14] The drama focussed on the human side of the Rebellion as the federal government's plans for their newly acquired land receded in the horror of frontier warfare. The music included Métis themes as well as British ones and reflected the battle of will and rifle in the remote Canadian west. However, of all these new presentations, the most gripping was Arthur Hailey's "Time Lock" — a story about a little boy who becomes trapped in a bank vault that will not open for 63 hours. The suspense is unbearable as technical experts seek to find some way to reach the boy before his oxygen runs out. The music revealed Louis's capacity to build tension as background sounds evoked the terror of the youngster, and captured the emotions of those behind the frantic efforts to save him.[15] For Louis, the series was about using the work of Canadian writers and artists to tell about events that had, or could have, taken place in Canada. It was a perfect example of the standard Canadian television had to maintain if it was to carry out its mandate.

Just as with radio, television "specials" seemed to gravitate to Louis's pen and piano, particularly, with some irony for Louis, at the Yuletide season. The Christmas Eve production in 1955 was "Our Lady's Tumbler," a retelling of the old story of "Le Jongleur de Nôtre Dame, who offered the Statue of the Virgin Mary the best thing that he had – his skill in acrobatic tumbling." His gift brought him the insight that "the supreme humility of his gift is sufficient to achieve a miracle"[16] The production allowed Louis to use the Stratford Festival Singers, who provided appropriate anthems to accompany the dramatic movements of the acrobatic performance. The CBC had found a story in the French tradition that could be perceived as universal and appropriate for the celebrations of all Canadians of the Christian faith on that sacred night.

For Christmas 1956, a program was conceived that would awaken Canadians to the wide variety of sights and sounds of a multicultural

Christmas in Canada. Based on a script by Len Peterson, the program's mission was to visit as many communities as possible across the country. The camera and the sound equipment took viewers from quiet moments in Montreal's Chapel of the Grande Seminaire to a skating rink in Winnipeg, a performance of Quebec singers, and a telephone conversation in Toronto between a father recently dispatched to keep the peace in the Middle East and the family that sadly missed his presence as the festive season approached. There were other voices ... a carol sung superbly by Kitchener's Mennonite community, Inuit from the far north, recently arrived Hungarian refugees ... in short, a representation of a broad spectrum of Canadian celebratory life. Louis's task was to create music that would bridge these varied images and sounds. It was a magnificent challenge, and one that was crowned with considerable success as new technology showed its capacity to bring together the increasingly different cultures of Canada to celebrate a common theme. These were the years when the identity of Canada was under stress in many communities. Wave after wave of immigrants brought increasing demographic differentiation that left some older citizens uncomfortable and confused. These were also the years leading up to what came to be known as the Quiet Revolution — a period of rapid change in Quebec that began with the election of a Liberal government in 1960. But for such multicultural programming, the inevitable eruption of tension in Quebec might have been much worse. Nevertheless, the role of Quebec became the problem that would dominate the nation's politics in the 1960s.[17]

Louis's increased responsibilities at Stratford in the late 1950s made the task of composing for television particularly onerous. However, two "specials" were particularly appropriate for Louis, in light of his interest in CBC Television. These programs celebrated the final stages in the linking up of broadcast regions that would join Canada from coast to coast. On February 2, 1958, an hour-long "Tower Trail to the Sea" documented the joining of the communities east of Quebec City with those in the central network that stretched all the way to Calgary. For the first time, Maritimers would be able "to see live performances instead of film-recordings of all the main evening network shows." The special telecast that Louis was to work on was intended as a showcase of Atlantic Canada. Canada's most loved and laughed-with morning radio host, Max Ferguson, was to headline the program, and the show was to take advantage of 17 cameras posted at the most recognizable sites in the eastern provinces. These included the Confederation Chambers at Charlottetown, the choir loft of Nôtre Dame d'Acadie in Moncton, the gun emplacements on Citadel Hill in Halifax, and at the bottom of that city's harbour where frogmen were swimming in the icy waters – a veritable panoply of sights and sounds from the east coast. Louis composed the music and conducted a 25-piece orchestra of Halifax musicians, providing the bridges between the events, creating a background for the many voices of people interviewed, and adding to the sense of occasion.[18]

Even Gordon Sinclair, often a critic of CBC and its elitist tendencies, noted that the program "showed few towers, little sea and no trails. But it showed a lot people of the type we're glad to know." Even on that level, the show was a fine example of the CBC at its best — providing a basis of respect for the citizens of one region by those of another.

The second program of this nature, broadcast on July 1, Dominion Day, did not fare as well. It was to honour "the last spike" — the opening of the coast-to-coast television web that was now the largest in the world. The title, "Memo to Champlain," was possibly a bit pretentious and the program was extended to 90 minutes in hopes that it would excite Canadians with its visual images from across the land. For commentary, the director sought out both prestigious figures — such as the Right Honourable John Diefenbaker and Senator James Gladstone, Canada's first Native Senator — and ordinary citizens, including a native logging foreman and crew members of the RCMP schooner St. Roche, moored in Vancouver. Louis's role was as one of the composers of the "background and bridging" music. Unfortunately, the entire enterprise was something of a disaster. Ron Poulton commented:

> This 90-minute program signaling the opening of CBC's coast-to-coast TV network should have called for the best of scripts, direction, and narration.
>
> Instead, it got a heavy-handed and lacklustre treatment marred almost beyond belief by a gravel-voiced narrator named René Lévesque, with occasional interruptions from Joyce Davidson.[19]

Poulton's critique was an echo of what Sandra Lock had said earlier in the *Toronto Telegram*. She lamented that the program was like "an amateur movie" and "if any other nations see this they will think we are hicks."[20]

Also in 1958, a weekly children's program was launched by the CBC. This program was to play a large part in Louis's work at the CBC. Called simply *Junior Magazine*, it was clearly intended as an "educational" series and Fred Rainsberry — the head of children's programming at the CBC — was quite open in aggressively pursuing educational goals through superlative productions. An offering of this type a few years earlier had been mainly a "vehicle for short, informative films" — an exploration of the St. Lawrence Seaway, for example.[21] However, by 1958, the host, John Clark, and a sports expert, Doug Maxwell, had decided to provide a half-hour live section. In 1960, when Louis arrived at the CBC in his official capacity as the "serious music man," this series was the first to draw his attention.

Louis's actual job as "Consultant" was never formally described or officially established. Technically he was an assistant to Geoffrey Waddington, but, in fact, Louis's continued presence at corporate headquarters was neither required nor desired. There were already others assigned to specific roles in music programming and they perceived themselves to have this function well in hand. Louis, in the words of Norman Campbell, was in the business of advocacy. Going from department to department, he harangued every person at the CBC within hearing distance "to think MUSIC!"[22] Louis was building on a short but proud tradition of good music on CBC television that was in some need of expansion. There was a "Pied Piper" cachet to this task, and with Louis's charm and persuasive skills, things could and did happen. In bad times, however, there was a danger that Louis had not foreseen.

He had accepted the task of promoting serious music on television because he felt that this was where audiences would be found in the days ahead. At the same time, he did not want to run a "special department" with its own financial allocation. He believed that every sector of CBC television could be inspired by his enthusiasm for good music, particularly Canadian music. Indeed, drama, public affairs, children's programming, even sports and news, were open to influence. Louis wanted neither an executive office nor a separate budget line — a decision he was later to regret. *Junior Magazine* was a perfect place to start, with exactly the audience he felt was crucial to the success of serious music in the future.

In the complex world of television production there are no individual heroes, and although the role of producer Paddy Sampson must be given its due, Louis's arrival at the CBC heralded a new direction for the program. In the fall of 1960, Louis scheduled three *Junior Magazine* concerts — beginning with Ronald Turini, a splendid young pianist supported by a 45-piece orchestra led by Mario Bernardi. The program also included selections from a CBC Youth Choir conducted by Elmer Iseler. A second program had Teresa Stratas as the main attraction, accompanied by a 12-year-old harpist, Erica Goodman. A third was a recital by 14-year-old pianist Arthur Ozolins, who was already perceived as a prodigy and was to have an illustrious international career. Louis believed that excellent programming, with performers who were young themselves, could catch the attention of a youthful audience and make good television for all ages. For the first program, he commissioned his friend Godfrey Ridout to write a piece for chorus and orchestra that would excite the young people in the choir, and "The Dance" did exactly that. Turini, part of the same program, played the last movement of Liszt's "Piano Concerto #1" with all the considerable energy and dynamism he could muster. Louis even brought in a classical guitarist to play a few selections, realizing that this artist's presence would have special meaning for young people whose folk-singing heroes brandished just such an instrument.

Louis was the on-air host for the opening program. In his description of the series, he stated:

> We are not preaching and not teaching. These are concerts we hope the young viewers will enjoy. The concerts will present a variety of music, new and old, with a little more emphasis on the new. We think it is more communicative and reaches youth more directly than classical music. We hope Canadian music will find its way into nearly all the programs.[23]

The music programs lasted for two years. In the 1961–1962 *Junior Magazine* series, Louis played the host and, once again, Elmer Iseler had a CBC Youth Choir. These 12 boys and 12 girls worked with professional singers who provided training and leadership for each section. Promotional releases noted that "Iseler's ambition is to revive choral music in Canada." As a high school teacher and a musician, Iseler could inspire the young people he conducted, as well as those in the audience.[24] That same season of Youth Concerts included a world premiere of Harry Somers's "Abstract for Television" — a commission that encouraged Somers to continue as a composer when his main source of income at the time came from music-copying tasks found for him by Louis at the CBC. The program was, by every measure, a successful venture. It compared favourably with the "Young Peoples' Concert" that Leonard Bernstein and the New York Philharmonic had initiated in the U.S., and was a thoughtful approach to introducing the joy of good music through the newly established national television network. Still, it did cost more than the "packaged" programs that had preceded Louis's intervention in the *Junior Magazine* series, and was deemed too expensive — especially in view of the restraints that would soon be imposed on the CBC by the besieged Diefenbaker Government.

There were, however, other victories. Louis "coordinated a Sunday afternoon series which began in January, 1962, with 'Portrait of an Orchestra.'" The subject of exploration was the CBC Symphony Orchestra and the list of conductors included Geoffrey Waddington, who had established the ensemble in the early 1950s, as well as Wilfrid Pelletier and Victor Feldbrill. There was some poignancy to this since, a mere two seasons later, the orchestra was disbanded as a result of CBC budget pressures.[25] It was nevertheless a splendid program, and was followed by a production of Vaughan

Williams's Riders to the Sea, and then a public performance from Vancouver of American composer Elliot Carter's Quartet for Flute, Oboe, Cello and Harpsichord that included a discussion with the composer — a process that was becoming a hallmark of an Applebaum presentation. This was followed, in turn, by a Feldbrill-led performance of John Weinzweig's *Edge of the World,* performed by the Winnipeg Symphony, and even *An Evening with Gilbert and Sullivan,* which drew on Louis's Stratford experience to the advantage of both artists and audience.

Another outgrowth of Louis's Stratford experience was a 1961 presentation by Glenn Gould, "The Subject is Beethoven," a hilarious romp through Beethoven's contributions to the world of music. After playing the "Eroica Variations," Gould joined Leonard Rose in presenting the Sonata for Piano and Cello, Op. 69, continuing the collaboration that by this time had led to their relationship as two of the "troika" of artistic directors replacing Louis at Stratford Music. Finally, when CBC Television decided, with Louis's assistance, to emulate CBC Radio in honouring Igor Stravinsky in the "Festival" series of 1962, it was "L'Histoire du Soldat" that was presented to illustrate the composer's genius — the very work that Louis had used to introduce Stratford audiences to this giant of 20th-century music

The most prolific CBC series of programs of fine music emanated from Montreal. The track record of "L'Heure du Concert" stood unequalled anywhere on the network. In December of 1963, the CBC presented a documentary produced by Norman Campbell — "The Looking Glass People" — a very lush look at the National Ballet Company and Celia Franca's vital role in its development. The program placed a special emphasis on the role of the National Ballet School, where Principal Betty Oliphant was producing dancers of extraordinary quality. It was a joy for Louis to be involved with this project as a composer; his musical output had actually diminished during his years as a consultant to CBC Television. "The Looking Glass People" provided an experience with the relentless commitment of young dancers that led Louis to an important decision about the next phase of his career. He began to realize that, rather than spending time arguing with fellow administrators about production money for music programming, he really wanted to compose — to take a more active part in the creative aspect of television.

It became apparent, particularly after 1962, that the Diefenbaker Government did not view the CBC as its highest priority. Indeed, the Prime Minister believed the Corporation to be filled with recalcitrant Liberals and subversive socialists. The CBC Television coverage of the Coyne Affair and the other failings of the Government had been altogether too enthusiastic. In spite of the presence of George Nowlan — the Minister responsible for the CBC in the Conservative Cabinet and one of the finest protectors and advocates the CBC was ever to have — the Corporation felt very threatened throughout the entire Diefenbaker sojourn at 24 Sussex Drive. As the economy faltered in the early 1960s, the cuts came down heavily on the Corporation. Now Louis discovered a truth he was never to forget: in a corporation of great size and complexity, one must maintain control over one's own budget. Louis had opted for the route of persuasion and cajoling, rather than the more traditional route of gathering resources and using them to encourage, or even co-opt, the cooperation he needed to mount the music programs he wanted so much to present. When the cuts came, CBC departments simply dropped anything that involved costs emanating from other sources, and money for Louis Applebaum's initiatives evaporated rapidly. The extent of the impact of government cutbacks can be summed up by one example. In April, 1960, CBC Radio had established an experimental bilingual FM Network involving three cities — Montreal, Ottawa, and Toronto. Just two years later, and in spite of pressure from francophone Canadians, that network was gone. It had fallen "victim to austerity measures prescribed by the government."[26]

Undoubtedly, those working fulltime in the production of music programs felt that great music had been part of the television programming from the outset and needed no "consultation" — just increased resources. Yet, in 1961, Louis's presence had resulted in 90 hours of music on CBC television. By 1963, the various departments had dropped his initiatives and his work was essentially at an end.[27]

There were other reasons for Louis to consider a change. Life was becoming altogether too hectic. His home life had virtually disappeared and Stratford's demands were erratic. Not only did the preparation and touring of Stratford productions of Gilbert and Sullivan impose hugely upon his time, but Michael Langham also took other Festival productions on tour. In 1955 the tour of *Tamburlaine The Great* had nearly brought the Festival to its knees. Still, in 1957, Langham proposed to tour *Two Gentlemen of Verona*, along with a short play by Don Harron — *The Broken Jug*. *Two Gentlemen* had an outstanding cast, including Lloyd Bochner, Bruno Gerussi, Douglas Campbell, Douglas Rain, Roberta Maxwell, Amelia Hall, Eric House, and Powys Thomas. These productions would tour London, Toronto, New York, and Montreal in what turned out to be a relatively successful effort, though one not without its difficulties.[28]

By 1961, Langham was preparing to take another Stratford Festival production, *Much Ado About Nothing*, to the very home of the Bard — Stratford-on-Avon, England. Louis had already been informed by Patrick Donnell, General Manager of the Royal Shakespearian Company, that he must reduce his orchestral forces as there was no pool of local musicians to be found there. Even more shocking, he learned that the RSC could pay only £150 for his services as composer, although they assured him that "this is the highest fee we have paid to any composer for incidental music at this theatre."[29] Louis concluded that the whole affair was "a cock-up. It's going to be tough, this remote operation." His letter to Langham on CBC letterhead revealed Louis's level of tension:

> For me, life has been more frantic than ever. After Stratford [the summer of 1960'], I was blitzed into finishing the Ballet that I should have been working on all summer … then getting to know this outfit [CBC]. What a thing that is! … then writing and appearing in a series of TV shows [no doubt, "Junior Magazine"] … Youth concerts, they are … then a few things in NY … and *Pinafore* involvements … and CBC involvements … and moving to a new home (you'll have to come out to see all the grass) … and David growing to frightening heights … and trips to Ottawa and Montreal … and Jan doing marvels with flowers … and David not practicing or studying and will he pass his exams?… and on and on life has flitted …[30]

By 1961, Louis's increased activity with the Canada Council, along with heightened expectations from that group, added to his sense of horrendous over-extension. In that same year, a new challenge appeared on the horizon that he could not turn down — Group Four Productions — a private-sector venture that would take more time and energy than he could, at the outset, have imagined. By 1962, the CBC had lost its place in his schedule. It was easy to leave; he simply stopped "consulting," and, in 1963, he and the CBC went back to the relationship they had enjoyed when he was a freelance composer and the CBC was simply one of his clients. He continued to write music for television productions for the next 30 years, including some of the most popular compositions of his career.

However, 15 years later, Louis was invited to chair a committee charged with the task of reviewing the cultural policy of the federal government. The CBC became a central subject of debate in that process, and Louis had the unenviable task of supporting, not uncritically but at least positively, the nation's public broadcaster. Ironically, when the Report was released in 1982, he was reviled by those who believed that the recommendations of the Report of the Federal Cultural Review Committee would destroy the Corporation and its effectiveness as the binding force of the nation.

Chapter Ten

The Making of a Culture

In 1957, after more than half a decade of delay since the Massey Commission Report had made its recommendations, a federal arts funding agency was finally legislated into existence. The Canada Council was given a grant of one hundred million dollars, with half to be used for capital grants to Canada's expanding university system, and the other half as an Endowment Fund whose income would support not only the arts, but the humanities and social sciences as well.

There was considerable angst among some politicians that governments were venturing into a region of public "subsidization" of a volatile and potentially embarrassing field of endeavour. On the other hand, one could look abroad and see that Canada was far behind other jurisdictions in providing government support to the work of artists and the organizations that nourished their efforts. For a nation preoccupied with its identity in the shadow of the "elephant" of American cultural expression, this was a reasonable defensive measure that the "mouse" could take to survive. Artists like Louis, who had seen the way things were done in Britain and Europe, could bring the successful measures of other countries to the attention of advocates such as Arnold Walter, Dean of the University of Toronto's Faculty of Music and Principal of the Royal Conservatory. Walter wrote:

> Of course state patronage is nothing new in itself. It would be easy to cite figures from Switzerland, Austria or Holland, from Italy, Denmark, Hungary, Poland, to say nothing of France, Germany or the Soviet Union ... the point is that Britain, Canada and the United States had long been disinclined to follow continental examples. By 1945, they were the only countries of the West to leave the arts to the tender mercies of the private sector.[1]

When the United Kingdom established the Arts Council of Great Britain in 1945, the die was cast for Canada, which tended to follow the lead of the former mother county in cultural matters.

Louis had watched the long process of the Canada Council's gestation from his position of financial responsibility for music at the Stratford Festival, an organization which had almost been submerged by financial pressures during those years of delay. He knew the significance of the mandate statement that the Canada Council would "create a climate in which the arts might eventually flourish." Needless to say, he became a strong supporter and enthusiastic partner of those employed by the Canada Council as it wended a tortuous path towards the granting programs that would bring a new era of cultural expansion.

The Council had scarcely gathered its small staff before Louis received a letter from the Council's first Director, A.W. Trueman, inviting him to attend a conference in Kingston, Ontario, between December 27th and December 29th, 1957.[2] In spite of the inconvenience — on the 29th he had to leave early to conduct the music for a CBC–Stratford production of *Peer Gynt* — Louis accepted enthusiastically and his connection with the Canada Council was now secure. The Kingston Conference turned out to be a review of the many issues faced by the establishment of any funding agency. How, specifically, does one assist the arts community most effectively, when in fact there can never be enough money to satisfy the ambitions of a country's creative artists? How does one assure the public that its money is being well used without creating a barrage of paper and monitoring operations that would stifle all creativity?[3] With its inadequate staff and total lack of experience, the Canada Council turned to an organization which already had a structure in place for evaluating funding requests from charitable organizations — the Canada Foundation. The Foundation had for some years been accepting and evaluating applications for funding of good causes and Louis was immediately engaged by this operation to provide "peer assessment" — a process of providing judgement not by civil servants, but by fellow artists. This was a process that Louis was to defend vociferously throughout his career, not only during his work with the granting programs of the Canada Council, but even more when he became Executive Director of the Ontario Arts Council some years later. Louis's success in providing evaluation can be gauged by a letter from the Foundation's Director, W.B. Herbert.

> I am ashamed of how hard I have been working some of my judges: but it is their own fault. I quickly learned which adjudicators are conscientious and helpful and I find myself tending to send more and more applications

to them for consideration. So; if you were clever enough
to be a poor judge you would not be worked so hard.[4]

Out of this constant struggle to be just to individual and organizational applications during these early years with the Canada Council,
Louis developed the set of values that served Canada's, and particularly
Ontario's, artists well. It was not easy work. Some wanted to give money
only to established arts organizations, such as the Montreal Symphony or
the National Ballet. Louis was convinced that only courageous efforts to
place resources in the hands of individual artists would make a difference
to the cultural life of the nation. Others felt that only the established performing and visual arts disciplines should be funded. Louis knew from his
own experience that unless there was an effort to reach out to individual
artists and to address new media arts, the Council would soon become
irrelevant to a large sector of the creative community.

He was soon thrust into an evaluation that would test another of his
beliefs about public funding. Crawley Films was led by an extraordinary pio-
neer in Canadian film-making, Budge Crawley. Louis knew him well and
this placed increased pressure on the integrity of his decision-making.
Crawley wanted money to produce instructional films about the playing of
musical instruments — a worthy project of value to music teachers across
the land, and one that Louis found attractive. But the means of production,
the intended market, and the distribution process were not, in Louis's view,
acceptable. Should the Canada Council, he asked, invest $35,000 "in a proj-
ect that could conceivably be profitable to the recipient, that involves U.S.
personnel, that is directed at the U.S. market and that features a U.S. institution, its director, orchestra, staff and student body?"[5] Louis advised that
the request be denied. He was anxious to see film-making be perceived as an
appropriate recipient of Canada Council support, and Crawley had certainly shown that he could make effective and accountable use of public money,
but it seemed to Louis that "Canadian-ness" should be one of the highest
priorities of the Canada Council, and that the question of whether
Canadian artists would be employed should be paramount.

Other issues arose. One was the arm's-length principle. In his attempt
to lure Shostakovich to his International Composers' Conference at
Stratford, Louis had seen the stultifying effect of a smothering state influence in cultural affairs. It had destroyed the expectations of Soviet audiences
for new and creative expression and produced both a docile clientele and a
listless artistic community. Politics and politicians must be kept away from
the granting process, but how, Louis wondered, could this be done? In a
political system that emphasized, in the name of democracy — certainly less

blatantly than south of the border but nonetheless openly — the principle that to the electoral victors belong the spoils, it was not immediately obvious. Nothing pleases politicians more than the opportunity to present a cheque to an artist-constituent or a local arts organization, preferably in the full view the media.

This was not the only issue facing the Council as it took its first steps. There was growing tension between the English- and French-speaking Canadians, and a flood of immigrants were gradually transforming this country's cultural expressions. Also, artists and arts organizations tend to concentrate in cities where there is inspirational contact and audiences to support their activities. How does a government funding system benefit all regions, and all cultural groups, with an egalitarian spirit? In addition, there was the inevitable tension between arts disciplines competing for resources. If one accepted a policy of inclusiveness for the various arts expressions, how did one divide the money for program support among music, drama, dance, visual arts, and new technologically oriented arts such as film production — an art form that Louis found most deserving? Finding a balance that would provide a dynamic arts presence was especially difficult as every artist, in every discipline, believed that he or she was personally saving the world.

Even within particular disciplines the competition was understandably fierce and unrelenting — for example, between the Toronto Symphony and the Montreal Symphony. And this was just one of hundreds of similar situations from every region across the land! How did one balance the institutional needs of such major organizations against the needs of individual artists? In the fields of creative literature and visual arts, creators were alone and isolated. How could the Council help them in a way that would be seen to be fair? Louis's interest was obviously concentrated on "serious" music, but what call did popular music have on the resources of a national funding agency? With his experience with jazz and folk music at Stratford, Louis was more responsive to popular idioms than most of his colleagues; yet artists in the field of popular music had, by far, the greatest opportunity to prosper. Was that a reason to reject their claims? And what of the amateur artists, whose quality of work was of the highest order but who, for practical reasons, could never be professional in the sense of living off the income from their artistic activities? In some rural areas, grants might provide the only path to professionalism. These crucial issues influenced the Council's response to every request for funding.

Of all the values that Louis applied in his assessment of applications, one out-ranked all others — a demand for excellence. While parts of the country were in a state of relative deprivation, and lowering its standards might extend the Council's influence, Louis knew that fiscal irresponsibility would rouse the enemies of public subsidization and lead to the collapse of support.

The issue of excellence came into question in 1964 over grant requests from the increasing numbers of symphony orchestras that were appearing on the Canadian scene. In North America, where the symphony orchestra (not, as in Europe, the opera company) is seen to be the basic foundation on which the musical culture of a community can be built, the question of "opening up" funding was a hot issue. There was much at stake. Increasing the size of the audience could have implications for the economy of an entire city, especially when the orchestra could attract tourists. With many musicians involved, an ensemble could be the source of musical experience for school audiences and provide private instruction to gifted students. Orchestras in both Toronto and Montreal had benefited from the generosity of the Council, and now every city of any size wanted to emulate their success. In August of 1964, Louis stated his position clearly in a letter to Peter Dwyer, then Associate Director of the Council. Louis's thesis was that the only way to react was through the rewarding of musical performance "in areas of greatest achievement, thereby maintaining high standards." He expanded on his reasons for rejecting applications of musical organizations that were obviously inferior in quality:

> I cannot see justification for Canada Council grants to an orchestra like Calgary [Symphony] or even in New Brunswick. This does not belittle their existence nor does it deny that they should persist in their good work ....I am aware that, should these orchestras go under as a result of being denied aid by the Council, a few professionals would be done out of present employment, Canadian artists would have fewer outlets, and the odd Canadian composition that such orchestras play would remain silent in that area.[6]

Louis's solution was to encourage towns and cities to seek more effective alternatives to funding that would lead to long-term improvement. It would be better to have "an arrangement with a top orchestra than to persist in maintaining an inferior orchestra of their own."[7] That orchestra could then give master classes when it came through the community on tour. Alternatively, the community could establish smaller ensembles in pursuit of the "smaller is better" option. The level of performance of a chamber group could be improved on the same budget required to maintain an inferior symphony. This was not popular advice and did not result in the Canada Council terminating support for mediocrity, but it did encourage restraint in funding of the most obvious examples of incompetence, and put pressure for excellence on those ensembles that were clearly less able and more at risk.

If there was one other value that Louis espoused with comparable determination, it was the creative spirit. The highest call on a national granting agency, Louis believed, must be from those who were seeking to understand and communicate their insights into the contemporary problems facing every Canadian. In 1967 Alan Neil, a Vancouver artist, approached the Canada Council with a grant request for sound equipment that would enable him to record voices, piano, and percussion and to inject these sounds into his own musical compositions. That Neil was a jazz player of some reputation did not strengthen his case. His application failed. In Neil's view, the rejection indicated that while contemporary poets and visual artists were treated with some understanding, "the music division has yet to enter the twentieth century."[8] When David Silcox asked for advice,[9] Louis staunchly took Neil's side.

> I find his ideas intriguing …. Perfectly valid … the search for valid and interesting sound combinations in his compositions is very commendable …. Mr. Neil deserves encouragement.[10]

In 1965 Peter Dwyer invited Louis to join the Advisory Arts Panel where he would work with other distinguished Canadians to develop and present the principles upon which artists should receive assistance, and upon which it could be determined that arts organizations merited public support.[11] In so doing, Dwyer was indicating the degree to which Louis was far more than simply an evaluator; he was a source of wisdom on the total process of arts support. Louis served with distinction until, by the end of the decade, his attention was drawn to the provincial level, to the Province of Ontario Council for the Arts. This shift initiated another major phase of his career.

The very first Canada Council conference at Kingston had been followed shortly afterwards by a gathering in May, 1961, at the O'Keefe Centre in Toronto. This assembly was organized by the Canadian Conference for the Arts — the voluntary body representing all the arts disciplines in the country, particularly in their approach to the federal government. In fact, the centennial decade produced a series of conferences, called, sometimes by the Canada Council, but at other times by the Canadian Council for the Arts. With a new granting agency just now finding its way, and a celebration in the offing, it was essential to have artists in a position to influence what was transpiring in Ottawa. Louis became very much a part of this process, a process that ultimately produced the policies that carried the arts through much of the later 20th century. It was not only a matter of useful discussion and debate; these events led to the writing of reports that found their way to the desks of politicians and Ministers of the Crown. Ultimately, all of this activity led to an explosion of the arts in the 1970s and 1980s that surprised even Canadians themselves.

For the O'Keefe Centre conference, Louis chaired a panel on "The Composer and the Public" — one which provided a forum for discussing the frustrations that musical creators felt in their isolation from the mainstream of the nation's cultural life. This was a topic that Louis, composer colleague Barbara Pentland, arts writer Ken Winters, and arts entrepreneur Walter Homburger had no difficulty in addressing. As well, Louis had been asked by Council Director A.W. Trueman to gather some of his colleagues for an informal discussion of Canada Council policies, now very much "in the making."[12] It was apparent that Louis was becoming a "host" of Canada Council gatherings, such as the "meeting of musicians" that Peter Dwyer organized in New Brunswick, in 1963, at Stanley House — a delightful venue acquired by the Canada Council for workshops and small conferences. Not only was Dwyer anxious to have Louis at the meeting in a leadership role, but he also asked Louis to make suggestions about who else should be invited.[13] At the Stanley House meeting Louis, now coming to the end of his formal employment at the CBC, warned participants that "a serious situation had arisen" in the area of CBC broadcasting. For his colleagues in music composition, it was a real crisis. The costs of television production, combined with government restraints in funding, could mean "that CBC planners may be pressed into large-scale reduction of its AM radio service, very seriously affecting the field of Canadian music."[14] A sense of despair led Louis to follow up on the Stanley House conference with a typical intervention. In a letter to Peter Dwyer, written in August, 1963, Louis suggested that what was needed was "a full-scale investigation into future musical needs of our society."[15] Dwyer responded immediately, asking whether the Canadian Music Council could take on the investigation, and pointing out that such studies could not be funded through the Canada Council's music granting process. Sir Ernest MacMillan, by all measures Canada's most prominent orchestral conductor and arts educator, and the head of the Canadian Music Council, replied that the Council had no resources to carry out such a function.[16]

Louis suggested another source — one with money at its disposal. He had recently been elected Chair of a Committee of CAPAC (a performing rights organization representing composers and music publishers) and the CAB (Canadian Association of Broadcasters). The mandate of the committee was to promote Canadian music. Though its interest was understandably focussed on the recording of Canadian works for broadcast, Louis was unable to secure the funding and the study was not carried out. Still, the idea remained a force and resulted in other studies, notably Louis's work on orchestral development both in Ottawa and Toronto. What is apparent from all this negotiation is that, by the mid-1960s, Louis was becoming a major force in the field of arts administration. His experience bridged a wide array of arts organizations — the Canada Council, CAPAC, the CBC, the Canadian League of Composers, and the Canadian Conference of the Arts. Undoubtedly, these were the reasons for Dwyer's determination to secure Louis's participation on the Advisory Arts Panel and in every gathering of music people he could organize. Louis was also a member of an advisory council to assist the Canadian National Commission for UNESCO and, by 1964, he had become a member of another advisory council to determine Canada's role in the 1965 Commonwealth Festival. All this international attention stemmed directly from interest created abroad by the International Composers' Conference Louis had organized in 1960 at the Stratford Festival. These interactions spurred on another interest that was to engage him during the last years of the 1960s: the recording of Canadian works not only for a domestic market, but for distribution around the world.

In 1965 the Canadian Conference for the Arts took centre stage once again. This time it was the result of a request of the Hon. Maurice Lamontagne, Secretary of State in the Pearson Government. Lamontagne wanted to meet with arts professionals in anticipation of the centennial celebrations that would soon envelop the country. It was the first occasion that such a request had ever been made by a Minister of the Crown, and the CCA was determined to put its best foot forward. Partly, this was due to the fact that Lamontagne had taken the initiative. He was close to Prime Minister Lester Pearson, and was a suave, cultured academic. As a leading figure in the French-speaking contingent in Cabinet, he recognized clearly the importance of the centennial in the context of the Quiet Revolution. He stated to the participants at the conference, Louis among them, that "1967, as well as marking a century of building Confederation, may well prove to be the year of its true completion ... if the culture of a country may be likened to an arch, then surely the keystone is the arts."[17] Louis found this view most comfortable and he soon became a member of the "Seminar '65" Conference Committee, along with Dwyer, Jean Gascon, Tom Hendry, Peter Jarvis, William Kilbourn, John Parkin, Jean-Louis Roux, David Silcox, Vincent Tovell, and Toronto businessman and arts supporter Arthur Gelber. They saw the event simply as a "working party asked by the Secretary of State to enquire and make recommendations concerning the many pressing problems which face all the arts in Canada at the present time."[18] However, as the only professional musician on the Committee, Louis was determined that the agenda of the proposed Seminar would reflect his presence, and, indeed, it did. Considerable attention was given to music — particularly the training and development of musicians, with special emphasis on the shortage of able teachers at every level. In the same year, Louis was writing a report that would encourage the University of Ottawa to set up a Faculty of Music. He had come to realize the inadequacy of school music teachers, in terms of both numbers and quality.

"Everybody we spoke to was unanimously appalled by the over-all low level of elementary music education,"[19] noted Louis on his agenda for the "Seminar '65" Conference. The university sector was also completely unprepared to address the problems of creating a musically sophisticated citizenry. There were not enough schools of music of high calibre, and a lack of national standards for post-secondary study, few library resources, little graduate work, and no organizational structure did little to improve the situation.[20] As well, the plight of the composer, a crisis that had become Louis's clarion call as the centennial approached, received appropriate attention. The CBC was becoming less able to give support.[21] The private television networks were "hopeless" — content simply to import foreign programming that guaranteed no Canadian music and no royalties to Canadian composers. Canadian orchestras could "make only polite gestures," and the newly launched Canadian Music Centre could provide only limited support.

"Seminar '65," perceived as the most important intervention on cultural matters since the Massey Commission, had an immediate impact. Within three months the federal government increased the support of the Canada Council by $11 million. The arguments presented had much to do with the fact that during the centennial year, some $91 million would be spent on commissioning music, touring arts organizations, and supporting countless centennial projects at the local level. Not one word of criticism about this apparent excess emerged from the House of Commons. "Seminar '65" gave hope for continued support to such organizations as the Canadian Music Centre, the Jeunesse Musicales — an organization that provided performance opportunities for young artists — and the National Youth Orchestra. Louis had mixed feeling about the plans for centennial year, plans that were driving a sudden largesse from the Government of Canada to the Canada Council and, through that agency, to hundreds of arts clients. There were welcome opportunities for artists to be involved in a great moment in the nation's history, but there were also potential dangers. In his personal notes on his agenda, Louis expressed excitement about the possibilities of festivals in every provincial capital in 1967, about national touring of arts organizations, and about the provision of a central booking agency to ensure balance and avoid schedule conflicts in arts presentations. However, he was also one of the few to realize that this sudden expansion would inflate the budgets of all arts organizations, and that if there was no momentum in 1968 to maintain this activity across the country, these organizations would soon face serious financial difficulties.[22]

"Seminar '65" was followed by "Seminar '66," which produced a report with the grandiose title "Building the Kind of World We Want to Live In." "Seminar '66" was more modest in its content, reflecting, to a large extent, Louis's work with the University of Ottawa. No solutions could be found in the schools in the United States, where the treatment of the arts was "little better than abysmal." Arts professionals had to become involved in the schools, and even in the teachers' colleges devoted to the preparation of the classroom professionals. Louis would return to this issue when he joined the Ontario Arts Council in the 1970s.[23]

Peter Dwyer had no sooner invited Louis to join the Advisory Arts Panel than he was suggesting that Louis undertake the first in a series of studies, a "survey of the professional musician in the Canadian community."[24] Louis accepted, but not without real reservations about the availability and accuracy of the statistics available.

He reasoned that this survey must leave aside professional musicians engaged in popular music, as well as those engaged essentially in arts education, and that it would ignore amateur music makers completely. He would focus entirely on professional instrumentalists and vocalists in ensembles, and on solo performers or concert artists. To assess the financial viability of a career as a professional musician, he would have to consider the arts organizations on which the artist depended and the quality of the musical life in the community he served. Even the unions that assisted and protected the musicians from exploitative situations would have to be examined.[25]

It soon became obvious that Louis's vision was not going to be accepted by the Board of the Canada Council, nor was the "elephantine" survey that Peter Dwyer had envisioned (the assessment of audiences and the sociological impact of music on a community). Nor was the Board prepared to devote its time to developing a philosophy of artist subsidy and its effect on the community. After several months of delay, Louis proposed a survey that he thought would be "do-able," in terms of the Council's concerns over both content and financial costs. The survey would emphasize two areas:

> (a) the collection of data that accurately reflects the status [mostly economic] of the professional musician in our society

(b) the circulating of the results of the study, via publication or other means, to all who might be able to use the information in developing plans for music in Canada.[26]

This survey, as soon became evident, was still beyond the interests and financial resources of the Council. However, an issue was about to arise that would demand just the kind of data that Louis was preparing. It was the writing of a response to a dispute between the Toronto Symphony Orchestra and the CBC that raised the issue of the distribution of City of Toronto's orchestral resources. The CBC had created its own symphony orchestra (with largely TSO personnel) in the mid-1950s. Now, integrating the schedules of the two institutions seemed impossible. The nature of the CBC made it difficult to plan for its needs far in advance. Trouble arose with a plan to present a series of public summer concerts in Toronto — concerts that would conflict with the plans of the TSO for a summer extension of its performing season. Louis set out to place the CBC-TSO confrontation in a larger context: he wanted to find a way to help professional musicians in Toronto make a decent living, and he planned to write a report with recommendations that might serve other communities and their artists. He recognized that, in Toronto, there were three major arts institutions — a ballet company, an opera company, and a symphony orchestra — all needing the services of first-class professional instrumentalists. The TSO, with its fine reputation, could offer its members work and remuneration for only 40 weeks a year. Louis's report on "Toronto's Orchestral Resources"[27] attempted to discover how Toronto's musical resources could be organized so that each of the arts bodies could expand and improve its musical offerings while, at the same time, the musicians could be more adequately compensated. It was certainly a matter of scheduling; each institution wanted access to the finest instrumentalists. However, Louis discovered that the institutions had little interest in cooperation. There was disciplinary competition as well, with each institution believing its own art form to be of paramount importance to the cultural life of the city and, in the case of the CBC, the entire nation. Louis recommended the creation of a "service" orchestra of about 65 players which could look after the needs of the CBC, the National Ballet and the Canadian Opera Company, under a Board which would have representatives from all three organizations and could ensure the quality of the musical product.[28]

That recommendation and most of the others were ignored, but the report did provide a basis for encouraging collaboration. Louis was more anxious to promote the expansion of music performance in Toronto than to provide scheduling patterns that would ultimately reduce musical activities and produce less work for musicians. His document signaled a new era for the arts in Toronto, outlining opportunities for greater public enjoyment and a concern for the prosperity of the professional musician. Written amidst all the excitement of the centennial year, the report documented new attitudes among Canadians. People had enjoyed their access to a new level of arts performance, and the tours across Canada had been a success. The TSO had always engaged in modest touring each year, but with little enthusiasm, as the players resented the discomfort of travelling, disliked being separated from their families, and regretted the income they lost from other performing or teaching activities. Louis reported:

> A remarkable reaction however, was prompted by the Centennial tour of Ontario in the fall of 1967. This proved to be a thrilling morale-building event not only for those communities the orchestra visited, but especially for the players in the orchestra. A sense of purpose and achievement seemed to be experienced by each player returning from the tour. The oft-repeated argument that the Toronto Symphony has a responsibility to other communities especially those in its own province now seemed to ring truer.[29]

Louis wanted to encourage touring. Many communities had constructed performing arts venues — like the National Arts Centre in Ottawa — as centennial projects. These beckoned as attractive spaces for large cultural organizations. Even more important, Louis observed that new developments in arts education were now within the reach of the TSO. The Junior Women's Committee had organized local in-school musical events and Louis wanted to encourage the expansion of this enterprise to the hundreds of schools not yet touched by the program.[30] These observations were taken seriously; the performing season of the TSO expanded and more resources were directed to youth concerts and programs in the schools. With a sharp increase in the number of gifted musicians, both the COC and the National Ballet Orchestras improved immeasurably, even though they were now deprived of the presence of the TSO members. (Indeed, under the guidance of Richard Bradshaw, the splendid COC Orchestra now presents several orchestral concerts a year in the Toronto area, often accompanying young Canadians who have made their mark on the opera stage.)

Louis's four-year contribution to the Council was substantial, both as a member of the Advisory Arts Panel and as an assessor of applications for grants. These were the years when the very basic questions of public support for the arts had to be worked out. Even in the years of enthusiasm for "less government" and "privatization," the arts and arts-funding agencies have survived. Louis had a great deal to do with that survival.

He also endured his defeats. By the late 1960s, Louis had become obsessed with the idea that recording might be the salvation of Canadian contemporary music. When he sought support from his Advisory Arts Panel, his colleagues decided that, as the Canada Council had already decided not to become involved in film, "it ought not to become involved in the question of recording" either.[31] Louis saw himself as a representative of the music community and celebrated the music that had been commissioned for the centennial year, reporting that "many significant musical compositions had been produced, and that the relative amount of money spent on commissions had been small." He encouraged his panel members to consider grants to support the extra rehearsal time that contemporary music inevitably demanded.[32] He was also aware that most music commissions were played only once and then forgotten, before there was any opportunity to achieve familiarization either on the part of audience or performer. He observed the need for support of second and third performances of new works.[33]

As the 1960s came to an end, so did Louis's deep involvement with the Canada Council. Still, his influence continued to be felt and successive Directors, Staff, and Board Chairs sought his advice. Vincent Tovell, who chaired the Advisory Arts Panel during its first years, observes that Louis's greatest and most lasting contribution was his focus on the creative artist. Yet in spite of that focus, he never lost sight of the "big picture" that was needed to sustain the artistic community. His work in film, dance, and drama, as well as with music of many kinds, had given him a breadth of experience and understanding that was awe-inspiring. He also demonstrated an impressive knowledge and experience of Canadian regions and their people.[34]

David Silcox, the main organizer of the O'Keefe Centre Conference, felt that, by the time Louis came to the Council, he had developed a great deal of political "savvy" and was conscious of the complexity of organizational processes. This had been an extraordinary advantage. Most of all, Silcox came to respect "an uncanny sense of what the priority should be" that Louis exhibited on every issue.[35]

Louis's legacy has helped the Council, even when ungenerous governments have made it difficult to nurture the arts. Most important of all,

Louis was always a reminder to the Council's Board and Staff to be staunch and fearless allies of the country's artists.[36] Canada needed that exemplary model if the arts were to create a more decent society, indeed if the arts were to influence the way Canadians treat each other and the environment that sustains them.

Chapter Eleven

A Performing Arts Centre for a Nation

By the early 1960s, Canada Council meetings were bringing Louis back to Ottawa on a regular basis. The Ottawa to which Louis drove from Toronto or Stratford every few weeks had not changed much from the nation's capital he remembered from the wartime years, when he and Jan had made their home there. Indeed, still standing were the "temporary" wooden structures built to house the extra military personnel and civilians who had arrived to serve their country.

For a post-war national capital of a developed country, the city's cultural life was a scandal. A Tremblay Series of musical programs at the Capital Theatre, the result of the entrepreneurial spirit of a local Ottawa citizen, Earl Crowe, and a concert or two from a touring Montreal or Toronto Symphony Orchestra — these were the highlights of the season. A semi-professional symphony orchestra, the Ottawa Philharmonic, had developed from Louis's efforts to find musicians for NFB soundtracks in the 1940s, and the choirs of Ottawa's churches had developed a proud choral tradition. However, there was no adequate performing venue anywhere in the entire region. The situation was as desperate in the visual and dramatic arts. The National Gallery's collection was housed in a drab office building, and a small, courageous theatre company performed Canadian plays in an obscure warehouse, far from the centre of the city.

People came to Ottawa from other countries, often establishing embassies and consulates, only to discover that in order to enjoy great music and theatre, to see the works of Canadian artists presented effectively, or even to have a good meal, they had to travel to Montreal. As a result Ottawa residents, including those who had roles in making policies that governed the nation, were left bereft of the insight and inspiration that would have been offered by the arts in any other capital city in the industrialized world. If Canada at mid-century could be called a cultural desert, Ottawa was certainly no oasis. Yet it was from Ottawa that the idea of an arts granting agency, a Canada Council, had emerged with resources to assist musicians, actors, dancers, and even painters.

A few years later, a group of influential women in the city, understandably distressed by the lack of cultural expression to be found in the nation's capital, determined to change that "art-less" world. In 1962 these highly motivated and energetic women, led by Faye Loeb, found exactly the right man to champion their cause in the halls of political power. Hamilton Southam, a career diplomat, had grown up in Ottawa as a member of a prestigious family with a history of interest in the performing arts. Both his father, after World War I, and his uncle, in the 1920s, had attempted to initiate a campaign to secure an appropriate venue for theatrical presentations.

By the time Southam became involved, there was another factor to advance the cause. Surely Lester Pearson, an academic and a student of history, and the Liberal Party would wish to celebrate Canada's centennial year in grand fashion. Some of these celebrations would have to take place in Ottawa, and a proper venue for the performing arts would be essential. As well, these supporters of the arts believed that an annual arts festival should become a continuing part of the life of the nation's capital — another reason why a performing arts centre was crucial. Their arguments were compelling. In a rash moment, Southam agreed to find someone, within two weeks, who would lead the crusade, or, he said, he would do it himself. The Ottawa women were in luck. Southam's search failed and he took on the role that he had never sought, but that he had somehow had been born to assume and had spent a good part of his life preparing for — leading a campaign to provide a great performing arts centre for a nation's capital.[1]

The year 1963 was spent consolidating alliances and completing studies and briefs, all of which focussed on a newly elected Liberal Government. Southam described the process some years later in a speech to the annual meeting of the Canadian Music Council. The concept of the National Arts Centre, he said, had come from "a group of Ottawa and Hull citizens, some of them theatre or music lovers, some of them (imagine!) theatre- and music-loving civil servants who banded together in 1963 to form the National Capital Arts Alliance."[2] Southam, as a member of the External Affairs elite, knew Lester Pearson very well. As Southam had expected, Pearson was drawn to the idea of a grand edifice devoted to the arts in the centre of the nation's capital, to be established by the federal government for the centennial, and expressed his support.

Southam was wise enough to know that he needed advice, and a great deal of it. He knew nothing of the intricacies of building a national arts centre and little about what should happen in one. He called upon Peter

Dwyer at the Canada Council for the names of artists who had the respect of the arts community, but who also had management and administrative experience and might be willing to chair an advisory committee associated with music performance. Dwyer had just the right person — Louis Applebaum — and a luncheon in Toronto decided the issue. Louis would work with Southam to plan a performing arts centre that would be the pride of the nation's capital. So began a relationship that was far more than an opportunity to work together on a good cause; it became a friendship that lasted for the duration of the century. Early in 1964, a formal letter from Southam to Louis invited him to chair the Centre's Advisory Committee on Music, Opera, and Ballet for a fee of $100 a day plus expenses — a welcome addition to the Applebaum income, badly damaged by Louis's efforts to keep the Group Four enterprise solvent. The Gilbert and Sullivan touring was ending and Louis's administrative role at the CBC was about to come to an end.[3] In addition to the income, Louis wanted the challenge. Even more compelling was the chance to work with a driven, idealistic, uncompromising figure like Hamilton Southam. Louis had had little to do with Southam before the 1960s, but Southam fit the pattern of leadership established by both Grierson and Guthrie, and Louis was immediately attracted to the prospect of working with him in Ottawa — work Louis hoped to structure around his activities with the Canada Council.

The pressure was on. With only three years until centennial year, nothing had been planned. However, by the end of February, 1964, Lester Pearson announced that the City of Ottawa had agreed to donate a site for the arts centre on the Rideau Canal, almost in the shadow of the Parliament Buildings, and that Hamilton Southam had agreed to act as coordinator of the project. Immediately, the basic question arose. What kind of place was this arts centre to be? Louis was determined that it was crucial to have the acceptance of the local community and the enthusiastic backing of the people who would be the patrons and financial supporters long after the centennial celebrations. The centre also needed to be connected to the rich spectrum of educational institutions that served the Ottawa region, particularly the two universities. Louis was very conscious of the challenge that a large performing arts venue, with three theatres to fill every evening, would pose to the Centre's administration, even in a capital city the size of Ottawa.

Secondly, because of its location in the nation's capital, the centre should take a hand in fostering Canada's artistic life — perhaps playing a role as a showcase venue for the best productions of music, theatre, and dance from across the country. Lastly, in order to draw crowds week by week, it must have an artistic life of its own, and develop its own productions that could not only attract Ottawa residents and visitors to the capital but also go on tour to show the nation's creative potential. He put forward these ideas, along with an appropriate management strategy, to a Steering Committee comprised of the Chairs of four Advisory Committees that Southam had created. From the discussion within these committees, there was soon some sense that there should be orchestral and operatic events as well as theatre productions in both of Canada's official languages, and that someone would have to arrange these performances. At this Steering Committee meeting,

> ... discussion turned on Mr. Applebaum's conviction, fully supported by Mr. Langham [Stratford's Artistic Director], that the Board should engage in artistic productions at least to the extent of assuming complete artistic and financial responsibility for the resident professional companies, such as the orchestra, the English and French repertory companies and the national festival organization.[4]

Louis was able to count on members of the Advisory Committee on Theatre to join Langham in supporting his position, and received particular support from John Hirsch and Jean Gascon, each of whom was later to become an Artistic Director of the Stratford Festival. The draft memorandum to the Secretary of State, "A Proposal for a Canadian Centre for the Performing Arts," stated, in rather grandiose terms, that "the centre should have a soul as well as a body." Only the "Stratford" model could accomplish that goal by providing a philosophy, a direction, and an assurance of artistic quality. The document was even more specific:

> The facilities should be used, not merely for the entertainment of the people of Ottawa, but to raise standards of artistic performance and refine public taste in the national capital and throughout the country, and to secure for the performing arts their due place and influence in national affairs.[5]

A month later, Southam reported to the Steering Committee that, in his discussion with the Secretary of State, he had "outlined the concepts being studied by the Committee — the Brussels concept of an organization limited to management functions, and the Stratford concept outlined by Mr. Applebaum's letter of July 17, of an organization which would also engage in artistic production."[6] Secretary of State Maurice Lamontagne indicated that the Brussels concept "would, of course, be easier for the cabinet and Parliament to accept." The Committee was undeterred and was heartened by the support of Nicholas Goldschmidt — by now the key person in developing performing arts activities for the centennial year. Goldschmidt expressed the hope that resident companies would "be included in the trans-Canada touring which was envisaged."[7] Lamontagne, however, was easily convinced by Louis's arguments and became a supporter of the "Stratford" model. Southam was to remember Lamontagne's instructions decades later:

> He told me to model the Centre on the state-supported opera houses and national theatres of Europe rather than on Broadway. Sol Hurok, whose dream was of course an O'Keefe Centre in every North American city to book his shows, said we were mad when I told him what we were planning to do.[8]

Louis felt he was winning the battle, but he made a further appeal, putting forward the point that "it is essential that artistic efforts of the highest quality fill its halls." He warned that "(a) a community of Ottawa's size could not be expected to create musical and theatrical ensembles of the calibre and size required and (b) the Centre and its ensembles would necessarily fulfil functions directly related to other Arts Centres." Louis realized that this was the more costly course to take but if the Centre was to be a shining jewel in the artistic holdings of the nation, the federal government would have to make a commitment to its operating expenses. It also meant that other levels of government, and major public enterprises, would have to participate, even to the extent of being included on the Board of Trustees that would become responsible for the Centre's policies and operations. Thus, when the Centre formally came into being, the Mayor of the City of Ottawa, the President of the CBC and the Chair of the Canada Council would all be included in the Board's membership. This inclusiveness, Louis was convinced, would lead to a greater access to the highest quality of music, theatre, and dance being developed throughout the country, as well as a broader base for assuring the financial well-being of the Centre. Even the annual arts festival, which had been a part of the original concept, would not be lost as the Centre's Board would take on that responsibility as well.

Louis had the full support of Hamilton Southam, who had visited the sites of the Lincoln and Kennedy Centres in the United States, both also in the process of being prepared for openings. These trips had convinced Southam that he wanted no "national shrine" rental house. He and many others had, at least in their minds, taken the Centre far from the Brussels and Broadway models, in which the Board administered the plant and left artistic matters to the private sector.[9]

Though no final decision could be made until the Centre had legal reality, even by 1964 unanimity developed that a "resident" orchestra would be the major musical ensemble in the Canadian Centre for the Performing Arts. Then the main question became "what kind of orchestra?" The answer had serious ramifications in terms of the support the Centre needed from the government. Both the Toronto and Montreal Symphony Orchestras opposed the introduction of another orchestra in Great Lakes-St. Lawrence-Ottawa River region. Both appeared each year in the capital city and another orchestra would, in their view, end that tradition, as well as have a negative impact on their budgets. In addition, the presence of a competitor for Canada Council support, CBC broadcasting revenues, and even private sector donations was not at all welcome. Louis advised Southam and his colleagues on the Advisory Committees that it would be wise to plan, not a full 19th-century symphony orchestra, but an enlarged chamber ensemble. For Louis, now Music Adviser to the Centre as well as Chair of an Advisory Committee, it was not just a matter of cost and competition, but also a matter of philosophy. A smaller ensemble would help to develop a mature musical appreciation in the nation's capital city in a way that would appropriately reflect Canada's population and resources. He put this opinion in a letter two years later:

> ... but mainly I would like to see the status and influence
> of the government focussing the attention of the nation
> on refined music-making instead of the grandiose. I'll
> lose the battle, I know, but it's fun at the moment.[10]

As it turned out, he did not lose the battle — other artistic and financial considerations would ultimately bring victory. Louis, with all his experience of small ensembles, had concluded that a small, less-expensive orchestra could develop a quality that a large orchestra could never achieve. Even in the matter of repertoire, there were only a few 19th-century composers who could not be played by such an ensemble — Berlioz, Mahler, Bruckner, and Wagner — and for these, extra players could be hired. As well, a resident orchestra should highlight the work of 20th-century Canadian composers, and such composers often demanded less in terms of orchestral force.

The issue of orchestra size was to divide those associated with the Centre for the next two years. Ezra Schabas, Louis's colleague from his Stratford days, wrote a helpful letter proposing a 40-piece chamber orchestra "which would be a community venture," but of "high calibre, capable of performing many roles."[11] Louis, with his knowledge of Ottawa, was not convinced that local "community" players would be easy to find. He wanted first-class musicians for a small orchestra, and he preferred not to call it a "chamber" orchestra simply because this term raised images of a precious ensemble playing only Handel, Haydn, Bach, and Mozart.

Louis harboured serious misgivings about the future of the Centre that went far beyond his disappointment that it could not be established before 1969. His concern was mainly for what might happen in the years after the excitement of the opening had passed. His time in Ottawa had convinced him that there was no considerable segment of the population "trained" to support concerts, opera, or dance performances, either by attendance at performances or through charitable giving. His nightmare was: "What would happen if the Centre opened ... .and nobody came ... or cared?" Out of this anxiety, Louis determined that the Centre and its orchestra, large or small, should be regarded as the pinnacle of Ottawa's cultural life. The place to begin to reach the people, he soon realized, was in the local schools and universities.[12] In the winter of 1965, Louis took a survey of the local music education scene and was appalled to discover that Ottawa's only semi-professional symphony, the Ottawa Philharmonic, was silent due to a labour dispute. In addition, there was scarcely an embryo of a music department at Carleton and Ottawa universities, there was no Conservatory of Music in the city, and there were no special schools for gifted arts students in the public education sector. In his document, "A Proposal for the Musical Development of the Capital Region," which contained his argument for a modest-sized orchestra, Louis also set out a vision of the kind of community which would, both immediately and in the distant future, produce audiences and supporters for music performance at the Centre. This document had an enormous effect on what the National Arts Centre ultimately became — and stood as warning about what would happen if succeeding governments failed to provide appropriate funding.

The Schabas letter had included the possibilities, from a music educator's point of view, of "first-desk players becoming a first-class orchestral instrumental faculty" in music faculties at one or other of Ottawa's universities. As well, he had foreseen how "reaching down" in the orchestra could help provide high-calibre teachers for young people. Schabas felt this all could come together "in the relatively quiet context of Ottawa, where musicians would be looking for work, unlike the Toronto scene, where musicians flitted from the TSO to the television studio and the countless 'gigs' in a communication centre of that size."[13]

The condition of the Ottawa Philharmonic was especially troubling. It had been a modest ensemble, partly professional but mainly amateur. Now it was silent, the professional members caught up in a labour dispute with the orchestra's Board. Surprisingly, both musicians and Board members seemed content to watch what was happening at the proposed Centre. When Louis turned up to examine the situation, someone suggested that he might act as an "implementer" and thereby help to resuscitate the Philharmonic. Louis declined, realizing that his involvement in the ruckus over the Ottawa Philharmonic would not advance the interests of the Canadian Centre for the Performing Arts and its musical program.

By this time, Louis knew that the role and the size of the Centre's orchestra had to be determined before he could give advice on the musical-education needs of the community. The opening sentence of his Proposal confirms his interest in both areas.

> This proposal, though dealing with the prospect for the establishment of an important orchestra in the Capital Region especially as it relates to the Canadian Centre for the Performing Arts, will, it will be noted, examine other areas at some length, especially those dealing with music education.[14]

Louis expressed his views about the educational role of performing ensembles with some frankness and much experience on the front line.

> Orchestral musicians who come to or emerge from a community must continually and thoroughly involve themselves in the community's life and especially with the education of its youth. Orchestral players should teach and participate in ensembles of all kinds and sizes to provide a variety of musical experiences to many groups in the community – to schools, universities, clubs, study groups, whoever is or should be interested in what they have to offer.[15]

Louis appealed to those obsessed with financial concerns, indicating that there were savings to be found in "utilizing the services of orchestral musicians beyond their role as members of an orchestra." He knew audience development was a key factor in the survival of the Centre, but he saved his most eloquent salvos for the beneficial effects of a community-conscious orchestra on the lives of the Region's children.

> A thriving musical life can have other salutary, though less apparent and virtually unmeasurable effects on a community. How do we estimate the value of having in our midst a large number of dedicated, able, enthusiastic musicians who can inspire and lead us, who can open the eyes of our children to new attitudes and aspirations? How do we assess their effect, over the years, on educational and community institutions, on a city's plans and hopes, on a child's development, on our "culture," in effect?[16]

Through his own experience, Louis realized that exposure to music, and the discipline of learning to sing and play instruments, could change the lives of children. Certainly his Proposal was about audience development in a city that had scarcely any performing arts life, but its scope was really much greater. He felt quite comfortable asking Hamilton Southam and other readers of his Proposal to imagine a future Capital Region with its own fully professional orchestra on a 52-week contract, providing every musician with "security and support that enables him to assume the role of the dignified and respected artist." He continued by projecting his image of such an orchestra.

> The orchestra is unique also in its size; it numbers about 45 players. It does not aspire to becoming a "grand" orchestra of 100 or so, but intends to be and to remain a highly refined, polished, precision tool, an instrument of jewel-like appeal, a "concert orchestra" of special attainment.[17]

He foresaw the orchestra being led by a conductor of "wide renown," with the assistance of two or three associates. It would give several series of concerts at the Centre and a "great number" of school concerts, but would also visit "a dozen or so communities on a fairly regular basis and tour other parts of Canada and other countries." When not engaged in playing concerts, the members of the ensemble would teach at a University School of Music or Music Faculty — possibly at the newly proposed Conservatory of Music or even at an institution that was Louis's most unlikely fantasy, a special school for musically gifted teenagers from across the nation. No doubt spurred on by his contact with the National Youth Orchestra and even more by the success of the National Ballet School established by Betty Oliphant, Louis was convinced that Canada had an enormous potential if it would just make available proper training for its youth. Finally he envisioned a full program of adult education supported by the Centre, the universities, and the Board of Education.

Louis planned for all this to begin in the following year, 1966, so the planning of the Centre would be driven by community expectation and the orchestra members would come ready to take on responsibilities beyond simply accepting a busy performance schedule. The possibilities were infinite, if only the leadership of Ottawa and its Region could be convinced to make a commitment.

> If it does, the Region will have taken a huge and remarkable step into the realm of miracle making. It will have transformed a city which has traditionally presented a rather forbidding face to the Gods who would "culture" it, into a vital, aggressive, exciting haven for the musical art. The CCPA would be providing a home for at least one "tenant" deserving the magnificent facilities it so magnanimously offers. The Capital of our country could with pride, show off the musical accomplishment of its own home. Most of all, our children could grow up with the insights and relationship with music to which they are entitled.[18]

The Proposal received wide circulation. Louis obtained considerable help and advice from Arnold Walter, associated as he was with both the Faculty of Music and the Royal Conservatory at the University of Toronto, and also from Ezra Schabas, who had been asked by the Ontario Federation of Symphony Orchestras to do a study of the province's community orchestras. Schabas's Report and recommendations — particularly his recommendation in favour of the establishment of regional orchestras — supported Louis's work in Ottawa. Schabas's ideas coincided with Louis's vision of an orchestra that would serve several communities in Eastern Ontario and become heavily involved in the educational systems of each one.[19]

While the Proposal was being researched and written, Louis was already in contact with the two local universities — both very different, both expanding, and both on the edge of some kind of development in music education. By April 1965, he had met with Father Guindon, the Rector of the University of Ottawa — a French-language university across the canal from the site of the Centre — and Bill Boss, the university's Director of Public Relations. Louis was impressed with the prospect of working with the University of Ottawa, since it "was about to achieve greater financial resources [that would put it] in a better position to undertake ambitious plans."[20]

In May, Louis met with Davidson Dunton who, as President of Carleton University, expressed some interest in expanding the music options within the school's Faculty of Arts. However, he had no interest in a full-scale Faculty or School of Music and certainly not one emphasizing instrumental instruction, although he thought there might be some basis for cooperation in addressing that need with the University of Ottawa. He certainly had no interest in sponsoring a Conservatory.[21]

Within three weeks Louis had returned to the University of Ottawa, where Bill Boss made it quite clear that the cooperative model with Carleton University would not work. However, Louis was heartened to know that the University of Ottawa was indeed interested in building on its own meagre music offerings, and that the establishment of a Faculty, School, or Department of Music was a distinct possibility.[22] Louis himself would be hired to write a report to outline the implications of such an academic direction. In November — some months after the public distribution of Louis's Proposal — a letter from Bill Boss informed Louis that, in a presentation to the Senate, " a special committee had been set up to study the project" and "the Board of Governors had been asked to make a provisional allocation ... in the 1965 budget for a start in 1966."[23]

By that time, Louis had already prepared another report, "A Plan for a School of Music at the University of Ottawa." In the world of university decision-making, things were happening at breakneck speed. Louis, in his plan, gave an overview of the situation in post-secondary music studies. He concluded:

> Obviously, Ottawa is in an ideal position to fill a clearly defined need. It can and should become the university in Eastern Ontario to satisfy the new high (and welcome) standards of the provincial Department of Education. It can relate to the growth of music education in the school system of Quebec. Its position in the Capital of the county, its proximity to the new and magnificent Arts Centre, its probable close working contact with the emerging

university, its bilingual philosophy, its enterprise and spirited growth, are all conditions that cannot be duplicated elsewhere. Further, they reveal the prospect that a new, energetic, superior School of Music at this university can rapidly establish an enviable reputation both nationally and internationally.[24]

Louis stressed particularly the enormous need for qualified teachers that "in this area alone would justify the decision to launch such a school."

The report is an extraordinary document, particularly since it was written by someone unfamiliar with the byzantine traditions of universities, the proclivity of faculties to protect their turf, and the preoccupation of administrative officers to keep as far from controversy as possible. Its directness was a collective cold shower for the University of Ottawa community and its laborious, careful processes. However, the detailed description of programs and courses and the careful budget projections that accompanied every recommendation reassured the entire University. Even the specifications for an adequate capital expansion, along with the likely costs of construction and estimates for properly equipping the new facilities, were included. Louis added his recommendation that appropriate extension programs for area adults should included as a responsibility for the new Faculty or School of Music.

By February 1966, Father Guindon informed Hamilton Southam that Louis's report had been approved in principle by the Senate and that the Board of Governors had indeed put money in the budget and, finally, had forwarded the necessary information to the Department of University Affairs in Toronto. Guindon was optimistic "that the money would be forthcoming." Needless to say, Louis's hope that 1966 could be the launch year for a school of music was hopelessly optimistic. However, a Department of Music was indeed established, and it would have strong links with the NAC Orchestra, particularly in its early years.

Louis's plans for a Conservatory and the "special school" for artistically gifted children proved an unattainable ideal. However, his vision did have an impact on many Boards of Education.[25] In the decade to follow, the North York and Etobicoke Boards in Louis's own municipality of Toronto would establish schools that were to become a source of pride, and that would provide a constant flow of applications to the Fine Arts Departments of universities across the nation. Louis's hopes for a Conservatory were never fulfilled. Although an institution called the Ottawa Conservatory was established in 1972, it had no formal connection to either the university or what was now called the National Arts Centre — an institution whose capacity to provide cultural leadership had been starkly reduced by parsi-monious funding. This was far from the vision Louis had shared with Hamilton Southam when the Arts Centre had been nothing but a dream on the Rideau Canal.[26]

Still, Louis's wish that a National Arts Centre would be an inspiration for excellence in making music for the entire city, and par-ticularly for its young people, did come true. One can measure the impact of Louis's advocacy through the eyes of one artist-teacher, Barbara Clark, who was to become the Director of the Ottawa Board's Central Choir, In 1967 the Choir participated in the National Arts Centre's "sod-turning." In the years that followed, the NAC Orchestra often turned to this choir when a chorus was needed. Clark recalled "having the honour of singing some of the finest music under the baton of the most distinguished conductors: *Carmina Burana, Midsummer Night's Dream, War Requiem, Missa Gaia,* and *St. Matthew Passion* with directors such as Mario Bernardi, Franz-Paul Decker, and Trevor Pinnock."[27]

In 1965 Brian Law had appeared on the scene, bringing with him new standards of excellence for Ottawa choirs. Law was "a very crucial factor in the linking of the community choral scene and the NAC in its early years." He would eventually become the conductor of a revived Ottawa Philharmonic Orchestra — the ensemble whose early beginnings could be traced back to Louis's need for an orchestra to play music to accompany NFB films in the 1940s. The National Arts Centre was not to be as inte-grally involved in these developments as Louis would have wanted but Clark could write, some 30 years later, that:

> ... choral music is alive and well in the Ottawa region and we must thank the NAC for its support and interest not only in its own programmes but also those in the community in which it exists. Its young peoples' concerts are sold out by subscription annually. It holds very suc-cessful student matinees throughout the year which often include student choir involvement ....[28]

At the time of the National Arts Centre's sod-turning, Louis was one of two Canadian composers (Clermont Pepin being the other) commis-sioned to provide both a fanfare and a choral selection for the event. Louis chose a poem by a Canadian poet, Earle Birney, and with the admonition to conductor and singers that the music was to be "brisk" and "vigorous," the "Song for the National Arts Centre" rang out on the slopes of the Rideau Canal, sung by the Ottawa Central Choir.[29] Despite the optimism of the moment, it would take some effort to open the Centre by 1969. The costs of construction escalated from an original estimate of $9 million to an eventual $46 million, partly because the site was located on solid rock.

Meanwhile, debate about the orchestra continued. Louis engaged the interest of another ally, his old friend Tyrone Guthrie, who became an advisor to those engaged in the planning of an annual arts festival. Southam, too, had been proclaiming the significance of the NAC's educational role to anyone who would listen. In April 1966, he regaled the Annual Conference of the Canadian Music Council with the uniqueness of the role of "resident" orchestra and the proposed relationship it was to have with Ottawa's educational system.

> I wish I could tell you something of the fascinating proposal for the orchestra, worked out by Professor Schabas and Mr. Louis Applebaum with its relationship to the University of Ottawa and the Ottawa School system, which altogether would offer year-round employment to musicians for the first time, I believe, in any Canadian community.[30]

Two months later, the National Arts Centre bill had been given Second Reading in the House of Commons. The Bill, presented by the Secretary of State, Judy LaMarsh, went far beyond normal expectations for a federally-sponsored cultural facility, affirming the government's responsibility "to develop the performing arts in the national capital region" and "to assist the Canada Council in the development of the performing arts elsewhere in Canada."[31]

But the size of the orchestra remained undecided. Advice from Leonard Bernstein in New York and Charles Munch in Boston fuelled the promotion of a full-scale symphony orchestra. In October 1967, Southam produced a Feasibility Study for the Board of Trustees that set out a good deal of statistical information justifying the establishment of a "National Symphony Orchestra."[32]

In the previous February, Southam had asked Louis to set out the arguments for a full symphony orchestra and for a smaller orchestra respectively. In a three-page response Louis listed 10 points in favour of a full symphony orchestra, and 14 in favour of a smaller orchestra, along with a "special plea" for the smaller orchestra that he felt would better serve the Centre. He concluded with the statement that "future development of the musical arts in Canada lies principally in the direction of the fine, the refined, the intimate, the economically manageable smaller ensemble."[33]

By now, new factors had intervened: the CBC could give no guarantee that its programming would bring substantial support to the orchestra's budget, and rumours of post-centennial restraint were filling the air. Neither the Toronto nor the Montreal Symphony Orchestra could be brought to support an Ottawa-based orchestra of any size, and, in the end, Southam's only option was to recommend the establishment of the smaller orchestra Louis preferred.[34]

Louis had won his battle for the wrong reasons — the decision had been made for financial rather than philosophic considerations — but he had won nevertheless. The National Arts Centre Orchestra, originally under conductor Mario Bernardi, became a national treasure, known throughout the world for the quality of its performance both in concert hall and on recordings. There was an immediate recognition that the nation's capital had "pulled off a real coup." Joseph Siskind, writing in the *Montreal Gazette*, declared: "it was not merely one of the best orchestras in Canada, but it is easily one of the best of its kind in the world."[35]

Over the years the National Arts Centre has suffered setbacks. It never became as integral a part of the community and its schools and universities as Louis had envisaged. Nor did the orchestra develop a network of concert series in nearby smaller cities (although after the Schabas Report of 1966 there was a surge of orchestral development in Ontario that led to the funding of more community orchestras). The NAC Orchestra reached its nadir in the late 1990s when two labour disputes soured relations and affected the artistic quality of the ensemble. However, as the new millennium arrived, it brought with it the welcome presence of a new NAC Director-General — Peter Herndorff — whose reputation for dealing with troubled arts institutions has been the source of marvel to Canadians. Herndorff, along with David Leighton, a respected corporate leader who made an incomparable contribution to the development of the Banff Centre and is now the new Board Chair, has promised a new future for the NAC and its orchestra. By attracting world-famous violinist and conductor Pinchas Zukerman to the Centre and by sending the orchestra on an extended and successful tour, this new management team has provided evidence of a return to the National Arts Centre's original mandate.

In April 2000, on the occasion of the tribute to Louis's historic role at the National Arts Centre, Hamilton Southam spoke of those who had worked with him, this "band of brothers" who had created this magnificent performing-arts space. Southam singled out Jean Gascon, who had wished "to give the Centre a heart that beats," and Louis Applebaum, who "gave us that heart in our superb orchestra."[36] Few citizens have the satisfaction of knowing that they have improved the cultural life of their nation's capital. Louis knew his work had made a difference.

Chapter Twelve

A Venture Into the Market

John Ralston Saul described the Canada of the 19th century as "complex," "contradictory," "incomplete" and "conceived in permanent motion."[1] In the 1960s, Louis could have described mid-20th century Canada in identical terms. But through all his ventures, he found ways to express his true passion — writing music which, when animated by the talent of his colleagues, could bring new meaning to voices and visual images.

As Louis assessed the "incomplete" Canada of the early 1960s, he found problems whose solutions lay beyond the reach of governments and their agencies. CBC Television was seeking to attract Canadian audiences who had been seduced into watching American stations. Every Canadian cityscape was decorated with a forest of ugly aerials — installed on almost every roof and doing a fine job of "pulling in" American stations. Canadian private networks and stations, while willing to join the competitive game of audience-finding, had virtually no production capacities and little intent to produce Canadian programs. What did not exist in Canada, in spite of the influence of the NFB over so many years, was a vibrant feature-film industry that could produce not only full-length productions but also a spectrum of programming to satisfy the voracious appetite of television.

In 1961 Louis set about the task of creating a film production company — Group Four Productions. Unless production facilities and the potential of Canadian artists could be developed, Canadian television would simply be an outlet for American programming. Louis had long since realized the importance of Canadian music and drama in enabling Canadians to tell each other their stories, and he was not prepared to lose the battle for a Canadian television presence without making an effort to address the issue of credible, creative content. Both his freelance work at the CBC and his Gilbert and Sullivan experience with Guthrie and Kipnis had convinced him that his goal of creating a vibrant Canadian film industry could only be accomplished in the private sector.

There were, as well, immediate and specific matters of public interest that captured Louis's attention, and that could be addressed through his venture. It took most of the decade of the 1960s, and the election of the Trudeau government, to fully apprise Canadians of the unity issue that was brewing in Quebec and elsewhere, and to convince them to take steps to address it. Soon after their election in 1963, the Liberals appointed a Royal Commission on Bilingualism and Biculturalism, chaired by two outstanding Canadians, Davidson Dunton and Andre Laurendeau. This soon became known as the "bi-and-bi Commission." The Commission sought to make recommendations that, when implemented, would improve the position of francophones across the nation. Louis himself could not converse with any ease in the French language, and he was, in the future, to be overlooked for positions in Ottawa, even those that obviously matched his strengths and talents, simply because of this lack.

There was also a third issue behind the launch of Group Four Productions. Teaching the arts was not considered a priority in most elementary schools, and, by the time students reached the secondary school level, Shakespeare was being presented as "great literature," not "great theatre." To be fair to the teaching profession, there was a dearth of good materials from which students might catch the spirit and joy of live theatre. Louis came to believe that this lack might be the window of opportunity whereby a newly created private company could intervene to improve the learning of young people.

To launch his enterprise, Louis gathered a group of men who would share his concerns. He contacted Leo Clavier, an old friend with markedly left-wing political tendencies who had, surprisingly, close contacts with Dominion Stores. Dominion's corporate interests in promotion included game shows, and Clavier foresaw that money might also be directed to more culturally significant and educationally valid enterprises. Harry Verner, another member of the group, had experience in the complex, far-flung world of publishing. A third colleague, Ed Rollins, had financial and accounting skills that were crucial to the success of any company. There were four men in the group — Louis, Clavier, Verner, and Rollins — and this occasioned the name of the new enterprise, Group Four Productions.

They hired a small staff, mainly secretarial and technical, and the operation was launched with little fanfare but great expectations. It was apparent that, as President, Louis was to be the "idea" man as well as the contact with the artistic and technical services Group Four Productions would require. The goal of the company was twofold: to address the critical issues Louis had identified and, at the same time, to make a profit. With only the limited personal resources of the four principals, the enterprise was massively undercapitalized. However, high hopes were place on the potential cash flow from Dominion Stores and its promotional budget. Fortunately, none of the partners depended on the company for his livelihood, least of all Louis, who was now on staff at the CBC, touring G & S, and accepting commissions to compose music from any source that served his own intellectual interests.[2]

"My father should never have gone into the marketplace."[3] This opinion, expressed by Louis's son, David, is largely supported by his wife Jan.[4] Louis's motivation for moving into the business world had little to do with money, profits, or bottom lines. "He simply had no interest in money," David and Jan Applebaum state quite categorically. Louis entered the private sector because he believed he could make a contribution, support a process to make Canada a bilingual nation, arouse an interest in the arts among young people, and find employment for Canadian artists. Such altruistic and unrealistic pursuits ultimately brought disaster. Although Louis and his colleagues fully recognized the laws of economics and the imperatives of fiscal responsibility, the company began with a reliance on federal political will that failed to materialize, and Louis's visions demanded a quantity of time and resources that Group Four Productions was never able to realize.

The Dominion Stores promotional venture centred on a bingo game played with cards customers could obtain by shopping at their stores. The game was played in the context of a television show, "Domino," for which Group Four productions took responsibility. From the profits of this enterprise, Dominion made money available to Group Four to produce educational materials — forging a relationship that was both commercial and charitable.[5] The other main profit source for the Group was to be the production of more popular television fare — soap operas, no less. But in 1960 there were relatively few Canadian buyers for such a product, and the purchase of American programming was relatively so cheap that Group Four had to reduce its prices to compete. Profits were slim — certainly insufficient to undertake any major programming initiatives or to allow the company to break into the costly feature-film industry. The company was only viable as long as extra revenues, such as the proceeds from bingo games, were available to subsidize its activities. On a strictly business basis, Group Four was unsustainable.

Louis was accurate in his analysis that Canadian television would have a desperate need for new materials. With a wealth of artistic talent at hand, he thought that he and his colleagues could do the job. What he failed to take into account was that the development of a new technology takes place slowly. As well, he failed to see the extent to which this new technology had already been dominated by existing market forces, resulting in a television culture with little interest in national unity or artistic expression. Those insights came only during Canada's centennial year, and they arrived quite unexpectedly. Even after the explosion of creative energy that took place in Canada in 1967, Canadians still need to be reminded, year after year, that the stories of our beginnings and our survival really are the stuff of self-awareness and tolerance. Unfortunately for Louis, the Canadian film industry began to flourish only after tax advantages made private investment in filmmaking relatively advantageous and generous public granting programs were developed.

In a way, Louis's own commitment to excellence worked against him. Production values in the North American broadcasting industry, though extremely high in technical terms, emphasized technique over the quality of the content. Group Four's offerings were generally socially relevant and high-quality projects that failed to find a sufficiently wide market to justify the costs of production, promotion, and marketing. Eventually, the subsidy from Dominion Stores would vanish and Group Four would disintegrate, causing considerable angst and, for Louis, personal and family disruption.

However, hopes were high in 1961 when Group Four was launched. As President, Louis was quoted some months later in a "Perspective" column in the *Toronto Daily Star* about his hopes for the new enterprise: "I want to see Group Four become a founding part of the feature film industry that is building slowly."[6] The operative word in this projection is "slowly." Louis hoped to fill a vacuum, but the timing was not right. In the meantime, Group Four's immediate energies centred on producing the "Domino" game.[7] More artistically satisfying was Louis's contact with Canada's leading bass voice and dramatic personality from Stratford days, Jan Rubes. Rubes's participation enabled Group Four to initiate a children's show, which was picked up on television and became quite popular. Indeed, it ran on a Hamilton television station for many years. It combined learning with joyous music and Rubes was a superb host for such a venture. At the outset, things looked rosy. In fact, Group Four created a series of five-minute "fillers" called "Guess What?" with Jan Rubes and made them available to television stations across the country. That series, and the production of a splendid short film, *In Search of Medea,* about the work of Canadian artist, Sylvia Lefkovitz (whose sculptures had received worldwide attention culminating in an exhibition in Milan, Italy), gave Louis hope that the film industry of his imagination was within his grasp. However, *In Search of Medea* attracted a limited audience, and a series of programs about Canadian artists was never initiated.

Louis and his Group Four colleagues turned their eyes to the question of Canada's bilingualism almost a decade before Ottawa's efforts. The company set about developing a program to teach anglophones about the

French language in a way that would be painless and non-threatening. It would not be an easy sell. Through school, most English Canadians had acquired only an academic interest in French literature and a slight capacity for the written word. The idea of training children to converse fluently in French had not been an objective of any province's French curriculum. As a result, even educated English-speaking Canadians were far from being functionally bilingual. Even more depressing, their schooling experience had left them with little appreciation for the delights of language studies. In spite of this, Louis saw an opportunity to make first-rate education accessible through television, to make it entertaining, and at the same time, to address a recognized national crisis.

"En France" was Group Four's multi-media response to the challenge of making language learning a comfortable, even enjoyable experience. As a comprehensive French language course, it combined the most modern audio-visual techniques of television, records, and books into an effective whole that could actually make it attractive to the whole family. This was Group Four's argument for proposing that the program be broadcast on at least one station serving every community. "En France" could also be adapted for target audiences — Louis's company made a proposal for providing language training to the federal Civil Service Commission, but with no success.

Louis was convinced that "the ability to converse, write, and read French is assuming greater importance to businessmen, officials, and even their wives as biculturalism becomes more widely accepted as a vital cornerstone of Confederation."[8] As the pressure for bilingualism increased, Louis thought that these programs might be made available to some 800,000 secondary-school classrooms across the nation. Indeed, they would be valuable even to tourists intending to visit France or other francophone destinations.

The production values of "En France" were of the highest quality. The series included 26 half-hour programs produced in France but adapted 100% for the Canadian market. There was considerable initial success: "En France" showed three times a week on 20 television stations, at one point reaching 20 million people. The host of the presentation was an international personality, Dawn Addam, and the on-air instruction, bolstered by both books and records, was virtually an "at-home" immersion course in a language spoken with authentic French dialects in recognizable French settings. One of the valuable elements of the program was the use of various performers with a wide variety of accents, intonations, and rates of speech articulation, few of which could be emulated in normal classroom instruction. Group Four was essentially the broker, pulling together the production talents and the business capacities of a host of enterprises. *Time* magazine described the program in laudatory terms declaring "it makes most educational TV look like home movies." The program also received a boost from the University of Toronto when "En France" was chosen for use in the University's French Summer School on St. Pierre-Miquelon.

Some might claim that it was the "content-starved" stations looking for daytime programming that picked up "En France." Nevertheless, in 1962 it was the only independent television program that had played on both English and French CBC networks, largely, no doubt as a result of Louis's connections within the Corporation. The costs were very high. The program itself was produced in Paris, while books and other printed materials, along with records, were produced by other publishers and recording companies. Even the cost for storage and distribution was astronomical. At one point, Group Four attempted to forge an alliance with *Canadian Weekly* magazine for distribution. The company hoped that this exposure, along with weekly television programming, would allow "En France" to reach a mass audience. Unfortunately, Louis couldn't convince the magazine to join this crusade to save the nation.

There was no lack of accolades. In 1963, C.D. Rouillard, Head of the Department of French at the University of Toronto, wrote: "the series will set a new high in combined language instruction and entertainment. The scenes are authentic in atmosphere and acted with zest." Bernard Goulet, who was a full-time member of Canada's regulatory agency for broadcasting — the Board of Broadcast Governors — stated that "As a Frenchman having been brought up in English, I must say that this is by far the best method I have come across — including the Berlitz system." Even more surprising support came from Jan-Marc Leger, Le Directeur de l'Office de la Langue Française in the Province of Quebec. "I am happy to tell you I was very favourably impressed [with] the substance of the dialogue, the judicious choice of centres of interest, the direct and living quality of the vocabulary."[9] Little wonder that, in his announcement of the extension of the program to Kitchener, Barrie, and 17 other stations, Louis claimed that "we could do more to make Canada bilingual than the whole bi-and-bi commission"[10] — a commission which by this time was touring around the country holding public meetings, and inviting briefs.

By 1964, "En France" seemed to be doing well. The University of Toronto reported excellent results from its use of the program at its Summer School. In 1965, in the context of wider realization that the question of language was crucial, Louis approached the CBC. Could this program not be a feature of Canada's national broadcaster; a kind of extended public service announcement in the context of a nation facing breakup? In a brief letter from Bruce Raymond, Assistant TV Program Director,

English Network, CBC, Louis was informed that it was "unlikely we can place it [En France] in the schedule."[11]

By this time it was clear that "En France" would never be accepted as the nation's answer to the dual problems of bilingualism and national survival. Neither television executives nor government officials could see this new medium as an educational tool, even though universities were beginning to adopt television technology. In North America the word "Entertainment" had been stamped on television's brow and mainstream networks have never been ready to include much in the way of purposeful learning within their programming. The emergence of dozens of specialty channels in the last years of the century finally showed that television could respond successfully to people's particular needs and interests. Even so, little attention has been paid to finding appropriate fare for purposeful adult learners.

For Louis, "En France" was a financial disaster. Although employment at the CBC had given him some assured income for a while, he depended for most of the Group Four years on his commissions from the CBC and the NFB, with small infusions coming from his Stratford commissions and his involvement with G & S tours. For a freelancer, time was indeed money. Because it was Louis who had the contacts at CBC and the colleagues associated with private stations and film production, it was mainly his time that had been taken up with Group Four's endless negotiations. The administrative costs of the venture had been substantial and the revenues had been spent on promotion and production of materials. Richard Rosenberg, who had become an associate of Group Four in its last years, declared as early as 1965 that "Every possible means of exploiting "En France" has been attempted and all with notable lack of success. Presently we are on only a few television stations and the book sales are absolutely nil. We consider the whole deal and our tremendous investment lost." Rosenberg pointed out that the principals at Group Four had invested their own money in the enterprise and "our personal lives suffered greatly."[12] Several projects were responsible for the ultimate fall of Group Four, but the most ambitious and the most costly failure was that of "En France."

Contemporary with the "En France" debacle was another Group Four project introduced with high hopes for success — *Living Shakespeare*. It was aimed at introducing the Bard's plays to viewers across North America, with a special emphasis on young Canadians. This was a double-pronged initiative — a comprehensive presentation of Shakespeare to young audiences and the production of materials designed for people of all ages. An educational kit would be created around each play and would include a complete and thoughtfully annotated text, as well as essays and studies. However, the main feature would be pictures and film sequences from recent productions. Louis intended to use not only the Shakespearean plays mounted by the Stratford Festival, but also productions of the Royal Shakespeare Theatre in England and the Shakespeare Festival in Connecticut. Louis secured the support of Tyrone Guthrie, now Sir Tyrone, even convincing him that he should act as artistic adviser, along with another distinguished English director, Peter Hall. Included in the school kits would be a filmstrip and an organized series of lessons, teachers' guides, instructional aids, and, of course, a film of important scenes from new productions. Louis believed it would be possible for the company to complete three or four of these kits each year until all the major Shakespeare plays were in place.[13]

The major problem was distribution — the company lacked an infrastructure that could carry the product into the marketplace. They approached Encyclopedia Britannica and Louis and his colleagues were received initially with moderate enthusiasm. In a letter to Louis, Milan Herzog described the Shakespeare project as a "new venture," the main problem being "how to gauge the speed of acceptance for such materials in the high schools of America." However, he said, the company wanted to proceed.

> We fought a bloody battle around your proposal. Shakespeare would have written quite a scene about the 'passions' displayed in the Management meeting. The reason for the 'passion' was mainly that everybody here wants your materials, but no one knows exactly how to go about getting there satisfying your and our needs.[14]

Nevertheless, Encyclopedia Britannica was ready to move ahead with three plays, the first being *Macbeth* at the Royal Shakespeare Company in the fall of 1962.

Trouble surfaced immediately. Louis had no sooner made a cost estimate — using *The Taming of the Shrew* as an example and finding the "public package economically feasible" — when he received a brochure in the mail advertising a "Living Shakespeare L.P." A recording of a play, with a copy of the text [later discovered to have been substantially condensed] was being sold off the store shelf for $1.98. Louis was outraged. Not only had Group Four's series title been "stolen," but through low-quality production and substantial "hacking and hewing" of the text, the cost had been slashed. This cast into doubt the success of the "public package" — a part of the plan that was crucial, as the school marketing "could not carry it financially."[15]

Encyclopedia Britannica quickly lost its first rush of enthusiasm and Louis tried frantically to find a lever he could use to make the project happen. He even tried to approach Capitol Records, RCA, and Angel Records to see if he could lower costs by having them record upcoming productions at Stratford, but not one was interested in trying to sell recordings of the spoken word. Then Encyclopedia Britannica decided to move cautiously ahead, preparing school packages of two productions in the winters of 1963 and 1964. Shortly after that, the roof fell in. The Group Four partners were called to Chicago for an emergency meeting with Encyclopedia Britannica staff. The company would only agree to market the packages in return for 90% of the selling price. It was all over. "I couldn't believe the attitude of that corporation," was Louis's reaction. Group Four had put all its hopes in one basket and now the months of work, the lining up of productions for presentation, and the mountains of correspondence had resulted in nothing.[16]

There were lesser projects, none of which carried the high expectations that Louis had for "En France" and *Living Shakespeare*. In 1963 Louis enticed Susan Rubes, an accomplished actor and arts entrepreneur, to head the cast for a dramatic series, or more accurately a soap opera, called "The Bridge of Love."[17] He assembled a fine team of writers and producers but had no luck in finding buyers; private and public television were cutting back on commitments to new productions. "The Bridge of Love" was another financial failure.

In 1964 Group Four hoped to launch a publication that would replace the American *TV Guide*. This was the year when Canadian periodical publishers thought they had convinced the Canadian Government that the extended lower-cost Canadian runs of American periodicals, such as *Life*, *Time*, and *Reader's Digest*, were unfairly advantaged in competition with similar Canadian publications. To placate Canadian publishers, the O'Leary Commission had recommended the end of income tax relief to companies advertising in American periodicals. There was also some hope for a Canada Customs regulation that would ban the entry of foreign publications if more than 5% of advertising was deemed to be aimed at the Canadian market. Even in the highly nationalistic 1960s, the Canadian Government stopped short of incurring the ire of the American publishing industry, and gave only a token gesture of relief to Canadian periodical publishers. *TV Guide* was left untouched and Group Four's hopes were dashed, along with Louis's dream of a way to bring Canadian talent to the attention of Canadians. Unfortunately, Canadian television programs and Canadian artists received little attention in the American media. Canadian broadcasting was producing some good, even excellent, television programming with Canadian artists who were every bit as appealing as those appearing on American networks. A truly Canadian-produced television guide would have benefited both the industry and the nation.[18]

Despite its problems, Group Four had not lost its hope of producing full-length feature films. Louis's old friends Johnny Wayne and Frank Shuster, had done very well in the entertainment industry. By the 1960s they were indisputably Canada's most prestigious comedy team and had appeared on American television on North America's most-watched variety program, the Ed Sullivan Show. Louis believed they had the potential to carry a full-length feature movie.[19] However, financing could not be found and Group Four was forced to abandon yet another idea that might have given encouragement to the Canadian film industry.[20]

The overall theme for Expo 67 was "Man and His World." This leap in imagination was an inspiration to many artists, and was the genesis for yet another Group Four project. Louis was contacted by David Bairstow, a film-maker he had met at the NFB. Bairstow wanted to produce a film about the great arctic explorer, Vilhjalmur Stefansson, whose widow was willing to cooperate in the venture. Bairstow hoped to forge a partnership with Group Four. He wanted Louis to meet Mrs. Stefansson and convince her that a feature film — possibly as a co-production with Russian film-makers — would make a great contribution to the Polar Pavilion, and would be a fitting tribute to her husband.[21] There was some suggestion that a television series on the North-West Company might ultimately emerge, and that it might be featured on a Canadian television network.[22] However, the planners at Expo decided, perhaps with some good reason, that a film about a particular Arctic explorer did not fit their image of the pavilion as a place that would foster people's understanding of the Arctic, capture its beauty and fragility, and help people see how it might be protected. The demise of both the film and the potential for a related television series proved to be another setback for Louis.

Other proposals emerged. One TV series under development was to be devoted to the contribution of "Canadian actors, producers, directors, writers and camera-men to the motion picture industry in the English language world" — certainly a theme to which Louis felt he could personally contribute much. Canadians, although they had no feature film industry of their own, had become a resource from which other countries could draw talent and creativity. Louis's own experiences in the U.S. bore witness to this. In fact, Canadian film artists almost seemed to be involved in an international conspiracy to dominate the entire film industry outside Canada's borders. To develop a film to explore this extraordinary situation seemed an exciting prospect, but it too came to nothing.[23]

As well, there was a proposal to develop travel shows. One planned for the U.K. would have Sir Tyrone Guthrie as host. It would have followed a format — aerial views followed by focussed visits to particularly important sites. Many years later, this style of program was to become a very popular feature on television, and on the American network PBS in particular. From the travel-show idea came the notion to develop programs that would feature travelling Canadian artists as they made their way from coast to coast during the centennial year's touring program.[24] Connected to this project was a proposal from Group Four to the Centennial Commission to produce a five-minute radio series, to be aired twice a week, that would describe all the events taking place through that year.[25] By 1963, Louis, in his role as a composer and arts administrator, had become enmeshed in the preparations for the centennial year and was serving on a committee chaired by Hamilton Southam. Other committee members included Vincent Tovell, Jean Gascon, Mavor Moore, Gilles Lefebvre (of Jeunesses Musicales fame), and Alan Jarvis, from the National Gallery. The committee was "to consider special events in the Canadian Government pavilion at the World Exhibition in Montreal, 1967." Venues for these events included the bandshell area, which would hold two or three thousand people, and a nearby theatre to be used for smaller presentations. By 1964, Louis had been asked by the Centennial Commissioner, John Fisher (who was to emerge from the Centennial process bearing the designation "Mr. Canada"), to join the Performing Arts Sub-Committee for a National Conference on the Centennial, along with Doris Anderson, John Pratt, and Leon Kossar. But even being on the "inside track" in the centennial-planning process seemed to give Louis and Group Four no advantage.[26] In fact, none of Group Four's centennial-related projects were to come to fruition.

The time finally came when bankruptcy threatened. Group Four Productions had achieved minor successes but the development of feature-film opportunities had eluded Louis and his colleagues. The company was forced to reduce its operating costs until the office was staffed by one single individual, desperately trying to keep track of all the projects that were in various stages of development and disintegration. Finally, the affairs of the company reached crisis proportions. Jan Applebaum remembers vividly the occasion when she was "set up" in the recreation room of their home. All the directors of Group Four were gathered about her, Louis included. The purpose of the meeting soon became clear. Group Four Productions was close to bankruptcy and an infusion of cash from all the directors was essential if Group Four was to continue to exist. For his part, Louis had no ready cash, but there was the Applebaum home which could be used as collateral to secure immediate funds to keep the company alive. However, Jan was a co-owner of the property and, without her signature, the deal could not be concluded. All the directors pleaded with Jan to allow her home to be put at risk for money that would "save" the company. Jan was adamant. "This is all we have … we have no bank account. If this goes, we are on the street." The directors continued to plead. Finally, she had to tell them what she truly believed — "that the company was going bankrupt anyway."[27]

Jan was right. Group Four Productions continued to limp along as a legal entity for another couple of years, hoping that the great project would emerge, and then it quietly died. Its loss went unlamented. Even Louis, its President, scarcely noticed its demise. By this time, in Ottawa, the NAC and the Canada Council had become his focus and, in Toronto, the CBC was still his artistic home. His performing rights society, CAPAC, was capturing more of his attention, vying for his time with Stratford each spring and summer. By the 1970s, the disappointments and frustrations of Group Four Productions had become nothing but a memory.

Financial crises were the order of the day for the Applebaums in the 1960s. Jan, the careful organizer of the family resources, had come to know poverty during her childhood and youth, and she had no intention of allowing Louis's generosity to individuals and causes to bring them to ruin. Louis's salary kept them well housed and Louis always drove a good car and was perceived as well dressed. They were not in want, but cash flow for a composer dependent on commissions was often unreliable and, on occasion, when Louis was between jobs, demanded some restrictions. Jan did work intermittently as an interior decorator and as a dress designer. She pursued her interest in visual arts but was never under pressure to sell works in order to keep the family afloat. Although Louis had sustained a huge workload in the varied salaried roles he had played throughout the 1950s and 1960s, his income was not substantial. His output in terms of radio and television was enormous, but a $50 fee for a radio program was the going rate. A television program might provide a couple of hundred dollars, and that was one of the reasons why Louis's attention shifted from radio to television in the late 1950s and early 1960s. The career he had chosen was not a lucrative one, and he received little income from royalties as his composing for the public concert and recital performance repertoire was quite limited.[28]

By the later years of the decade, the Applebaums faced the most traumatic event of their married life. It concerned their son David. He had returned to Canada in the mid-1960s and had done well at the job Louis had arranged at the NFB, eventually moving to Montreal. He was fascinated by the techniques of producing sound and was very good at what he did. The NFB had been the perfect place for David to hone his considerable skills. He had gone from being a "gofer" to a music tape splicer and eventually a music editor. He knew he lacked his father's skills for composing original music, conducting it, and fitting each musical segment into the appropriate time allotment, down to a fraction of a second. David had tried to learn to play the piano under the tutelage of the same person who had inspired Louis, Boris Berlin, but with no success. He came to hate every moment of his time rehearsing at the keyboard. Then he turned to the trumpet. He showed some talent but it was clear that he would be neither a performer nor a composer. However, just like his father, he was drawn to the world of communications media. In particular, he was hypnotized by the wonder of sound, in all its many expressions. Yet David had little formal academic background. In fact, after a short time at Toronto's Vaughan Road and York Mills Collegiates, he had dropped out of secondary school without graduating and had left home. He loved both his parents but, like most teenagers, he felt misunderstood. He was aware of how much his mother loved him, but he had resented her over-protectiveness and had used that as his reason for fleeing to California.

David remembers affectionately, "I had a good father." David knew that Louis cared deeply for him, even though he was not at home much during David's early years, and even though Louis "was not the kind of Dad who played catch in the backyard." David realized that his father worried about his preoccupation with girls, cars, and motorcycles, and recognized that Louis would have liked him to follow in his footsteps.[29] Eventually, feeling that the NFB and Montreal had no more to teach him, David returned to Toronto and to a job at CTV *Newsmagazine*. He had come to realize that he was what his father was not — an entrepreneur who felt more at home in the private sector than in the halls of government or its agencies. As well, unlike his father, David was drawn to the world of popular music and entertainment. Long before film production became a major industry in Canada, David built and equipped a "sound effects" library and, through shrewd manipulation, gathered under his control a wide collection of "sound effect" materials. By the late 1960s he could say with some confidence that he was "involved in virtually every film produced in Canada." David possessed at least one attribute bequeathed to him by his father — he was a man of vision, perhaps even more practical than his father, who was too far ahead of his time to realize the profits which might have come when the market he sought to serve developed through the expansion of a Canadian film industry during and after the 1970s.[30]

David married Frances Messinger, whom he had known from early childhood and on November 28, 1969, a son, Jordan, was born to the couple. Jan and Louis were pleased. They loved their new daughter-in-law and were delighted to have their first grandson. Sadly, David's marriage to Frances did not last. Within 2 years of Jordan's birth, the break-up occurred.

Jan and Louis were deeply disappointed. Such a break-up was not only an affront to the sanctity of marriage and the importance of sustaining the family that their religion emphasized, but they had opened their arms to Frances and come to regard her very much as one of their family. Louis and Jan were both heartbroken at the prospect of losing their closeness with the little boy, Jordan, who had captured their love. Although the divorce was amicable, both David and Frances naturally wanted access to Jordan, who has vivid memories of an occasion when two determined grandfathers, both anxious not to lose touch with their beloved grandson, came near to physically tearing him apart. Jordan remembers that it was Jan who stepped in and said to Louis, very quietly and simply, "Let go. He goes to his mother."[31] That wise move ensured that Frances and Jordan would continue to be part of the Applebaum family.

Jordan believes that, from the moment Jan first saw him in his crib, she pledged that nothing would be allowed to damage that baby's future. At a time when Louis's income was modest she decided that they would support Frances, who faced enormous difficulties as a single mother. Not only did Jan and Louis contribute to Jordan's support, ensuring he would never have to go without and that the costs of his education would be covered, but every weekend, Frances, as a working mother, was given a break from the time-consuming task of single parenting while Jordan came to the Applebaum household.

By the time the 21st century dawned, Jordan was to have an MBA in finance and marketing. Now a mature, successful businessman, Jordan has no doubt about who made a difference to his life. He has no sense of being deprived as a result of having come from a broken family. Jan, even more than Louis, shines forth in Jordan's mind as his salvation and he looks after her financial affairs as a token of his love for her. "They reared me," he says forthrightly.[32]

In so many ways, this misfortune did end happily. David remarried and his new wife, Sandra, a young Canadian mother with a daughter, Jennifer, has brought joy to both Louis and Jan. Another daughter, Carrie, soon arrived to enlarge David's new family. Although David returned to the United States, the Applebaums made frequent pilgrimages to Gainesville, Georgia, to visit David, Sandra, and their children. At the same time, Jan and Frances remained as close as a mother and daughter and their love for each other never faded, despite the trauma of the broken marriage.

As Group Four Productions was gradually disappearing from the horizon, Louis turned his attention to a different professional challenge. This had to do, once again, with the task of encouraging Canadian composers and music. New technologies had resulted in an enormous expansion of the selection of recordings available not only to individuals but also for broadcast on radio. This was an unparalleled opportunity for composers and musicians. With radio now almost entirely dependent on recordings as the basis for programming — and with new recording formats and increased quality of sound production becoming more available — music was everywhere. Yet little of this was having any impact upon the status or remuneration of music creators, and particularly of Canadian contemporary composers. Ironically, the more music there was available, the less support there seemed to be for its creators. Collecting the strength of composers and addressing ways and means of securing a fairer share of the proceeds of a lucrative music industry became Louis's preoccupation in the mid- and late 1960s.

Chapter Thirteen

The Composer's Champion

L ouis's interest in the issue of performing rights began when he composed music for *Tomorrow the World* and *The Story of G.I. Joe.* Over the
years, he devoted much consideration to the well-being of his fellow
composers — particularly those whose financial survival depended on performances of their music in the concert or recital hall, or on radio broadcasts.
Louis, himself, was never in that position. He wrote in return for commissions that were paid "up front," mainly by the NFB, CBC Television, and the
Stratford Festival. As well, he secured a substantial portion of his income from
his work with various arts-related institutions. During the 1960s, this was a
varied collection — the CBC, the National Arts Centre, Ottawa University,
the Canada Council, and CAPAC (Canadian Association of Publishers,
Authors and Composers), the performing rights society that would entice
him to join their ranks before the end of the decade.

Victor Feldbrill, a Canadian conductor, stated at an award ceremony
for Louis held at a Roy Thomson Hall a few months before his death that
he was unique in the degree to which he supported his composer-colleagues
through acts of generosity and self-sacrifice, a behaviour that too rarely
occurred in the ranks of artistic creators. Phil Nimmons echoed that perception: "He championed us all ... he enhanced the entire community."[1]

By tracing and billing those who were using Canadian music, CAPAC
ensured that composers would be paid whenever their music was played,
whether live, over the airwaves, or accompanying action on a movie screen.
Later, and partly as a result of Louis's involvement in the late 1980s, CAPAC
would merge with a second performing-rights body, BMI Canada (Broadcast
Music Incorporated Canada, by then renamed PROCAN), to become
SOCAN (Society of Composers, Authors and Music Publishers of Canada).
It was no small task in a far-flung land to trace those who should be charged
for such usage, and CAPAC was bedevilled on all sides long before the ter-
minology "intellectual property" was in wide use. Some critics felt that any

music that was merely played or sung was public property. At the same time, as John Weinzweig explained, there were many composers who wrote music "for a million dollars or a nickel" and cared little for recompense; some didn't even bother to establish copyright for their works. Louis, whose royalties formed an insignificant fraction of his income, nonetheless supported CAPAC's initiative to ensure that Canadian composers would achieve respect for their valued work.[2] For Louis, it became a full-time crusade.

Another of Louis's longtime commitments was to the Canadian League of Composers, an organization that encouraged the public performance of Canadian music. Few listeners in Canada, or, in fact, around the world, seemed to care much about contemporary music. In a century in which human affairs have become "dissonant," composers have turned to atonal, harsh, and often "tuneless" musical expressions. The resulting styles are difficult to appreciate, especially by those who believe all music should be a source of pleasure and delight. As visual arts tended to become less representational, so music became less lyrical. But audiences were not attracted. They found refuge in the past — in the music of Bach, Mozart, and Beethoven — and this attachment was fuelled by the rapid development of recordings, tapes, and CDs, and the omnipresence of radio music in the kitchen, the car, the elevator, and the office. The League had the enormous task of persuading music listeners to be open and receptive to music that was "different" and more "challenging." As Harry Freedman points out, contemporary composers are in competition with every composer who has ever lived. Shortly after its creation in 1951, the League received a letter from J.B. Salsberg, a member of the Ontario Legislature. That letter included an excerpt from Hansard regarding an intervention he had made in the Legislative Assembly during a debate on the budget estimates of the Department of Education — the source of any provincial funds which might be consigned to cultural institutions. Salsberg had been moved by the appeals of the Toronto Symphony Orchestra and the newly formed National Ballet. As well, the plight of a Canadian composer, Harry Somers, had come to his attention.

> We read in the papers of symphony orchestras going around pleading for contributions to maintain themselves. We read about a young composer having to drive a taxi in order to support himself and yet he is considered one of the most promising of the younger composers.[3]

Salsberg recommended the establishment of a cultural branch within the Department with a budget of half a million dollars. But Louis, the League's vice-president, knew better than to celebrate this sudden attention to the arts. Salsberg was one of only two Communist members ever elected to the Ontario Legislature. From his experience at the NFB and the ideological difficulties that had ensued, Louis recognized the disadvantages of any support emanating from that source. Salsberg's assistance to the League would be "the kiss of death," and the letter was ignored.

Throughout the 1950s and 1960s, the League focussed on one objective — getting Canadian music played as often as possible. John Weinzweig, the League's president, had landed a job at the University of Toronto's Faculty of Music in 1952 (somewhat miraculously, in the light of the Faculty's commitment to traditional modes of music composition). Weinzweig's campus office became the centre of the League's activities, with Louis often present as vice-president and Harry Freedman as secretary. They had set out to build a mailing list to boost financial support as well as attendance at the concerts they proposed to mount — both essential for the League's survival.

Almost as soon as it came into being, the League became a point of contact for similar organizations in other countries wanting contemporary Canadian works for concerts and recitals they were presenting. The League asked members to submit compositions for possible inclusion in a Los Angeles concert in 1953 and, a year later, for one at the Haifa Concert of International Music (at which Jean Coulthard's piano sonata was played). Then came a notice for a series of radio broadcasts in London, Rome, and Copenhagen, and a request for Canadian works. Louis had the task of collecting and submitting scores to foreign festivals and music organizations. By 1954, the CBC had become aware of the League, and Louis, along with Jean Coulthard in Vancouver and Jean Vallerand in Montreal, was invited to take part in a program explaining the League's purpose and activities.[4] Surprisingly, the League was commanding some attention.

The League's primary objective was to produce opportunities for Canadians to hear the work of their own composers. A concert series in Toronto went well during the League's first few years. The 1953–54 season included two concerts in Eaton Auditorium (still a prestige venue in the city, although nearing its demise) and two film nights for films with musical scores composed by Canadians. The film nights were organized and presented by Louis at the Towne Cinema, a theatre in the heart of the city.[5] Other events included a single Massey Hall concert (a TSO concert conducted by Sir Ernest MacMillan that attracted 1400 people), a concert Louis presented at Stratford in 1955, and concerts in Montreal and Vancouver. Together, these gave an amazing kick-start to the work of the League. In 1958, when Louis was in Russia attempting to woo Shostakovich for his International Composers' Conference, he carried a letter from the League, introducing him to the Association of Soviet

Composers and stating that he was bringing the League's greetings and "was authorized to initiate exchanges of recent works."

However, there was a downside. The composers' wives, realizing that their husbands were spending too much time organizing concerts and not enough time composing, set up the "Concert Committee of the Canadian League of Composers," later known as the "Canadian Music Association." Thus, Helen Weinzweig, Ruth Somers, Jan Applebaum, and Noreen Nimmons became the fundraising and concert-promotion wing of the League. Being the wife of a composer was a sufficient burden to bear, but this was often exacerbated by the financial difficulties that dogged the everyday lives of many families. Now the wives implored corporate heads and friends and associates alike to contribute money and attend concerts. For Jan, who was shy, this was a considerable challenge. Even Noreen Nimmons, a talented and trained concert pianist, found it difficult to approach E.P. Taylor, Canada's corporate icon, for funds.[6]

To facilitate the involvement of composers, and particularly those who spoke French, the League adopted a brave measure. They decided that the administration of the League should alternate between Toronto and Montreal every 2 years (later extended to 3 years). This meant that Montreal composers had to form the executive and run the organization during the years of its presence in their city. This idea ensured a long future for the League, but reduced its momentum in Toronto, even though the amount of activity continued to be prodigious. It also allowed Louis to work more effectively with the composers, their concert programs, and his own film nights. Years later, Louis would recognize that he and his associates had encouraged a discernible growth in the numbers of French-speaking composers from Quebec when other national organizations were irrevocably splitting along a language fault line in the wake of growing unrest in that province.[7]

When the League, represented by both Louis and John Weinzweig, presented its first brief to the newly-created Canada Council, it requested $10,000 to assist in presenting a more broadly representative repertoire of works — symphony, solo, chamber, and choral selections — from the League members. The brief stated: "It is the aim of the Canadian Music Associates [the concert committee of the League] to break the chain that frustrates the composer — a chain of indifference, ignorance, and neglect."[8]

The application was successful and brought new energy to the League. As it received more and more requests for Canadian contemporary music, from within Canada and from abroad, for live performance or broadcast, the League needed an agency to collect and store the scores of Canadian composers.[9] If the scores were difficult to secure, they would not be played. If not stored carefully, they could disappear into an attic, basement, or trash can. The League also needed an organization that would collect information about the composing of music in Canada. There was an abysmal dearth of knowledge about that subject across the entire nation. The League had neither the funds nor the human resources for this; someone else would have to take on the responsibility.

Louis persuaded the Canada Council to retain Kenneth Le M. Carter to inquire into the desirability of a Music Centre for Canada.[10] Such an agency could handle all the requests for information about Canadian music composition — and, more important, the cataloguing, filing, storing, restoration, and lending of such scores could be efficiently centralized. By the mid-1950s, the League itself had 70 scores, but there were hundreds, probably thousands, more in the hands of composers and, in a few cases, their publishers.

As the 1960s dawned, Louis could be proud of the League's efforts, and of his role as one of the founders of the Canadian Music Centre. The CMC — soon funded by federal and provincial arts funding agencies as well as performing arts societies and private donors — increased the amount of music available for performance gradually and consistently.[11] Since its founding, it has become the most effective promoter of Canadian music and has provided a spiritual home for Canadian musical creation, as well as being a source of significant national influence.[12]

In the 1960s, Louis and the League could over their work of the previous decade with considerable pride. In spite of his Stratford duties, Louis had been able to be a part of the "moving of mountains," as John Weinzweig characterized the League's achievements in its first decade. In spite of his CBC role, his Group Four responsibilities, and his growing involvement in Ottawa's affairs, Louis stood for a seat on the 1962-63 Executive of the League and remained active throughout the decade.[13] However, by the early 1960s, the white heat of commitment that had characterized the League in its first years was dissipating. Although there was still a concert series, the support for it was eroding, as it was reported to the annual meeting in Montreal.

> The members observed with regret that League members themselves were not always fully in support of the concerts despite the fact that this season a total of 24 members were represented on the programs. It was morally difficult to understand the non-support by composers of a common project by which all stood to benefit.[14]

By 1965, it was difficult to get sufficient members to the League's annual meeting in Montreal. The reality remained that composing is, in essence, a lonely business and composers are not by nature "joiners." As orchestras, choirs, and smaller ensembles increased their attention to Canadian works, the League's role as a presenter became increasingly redundant. Nevertheless it weathered these difficult years and its membership continued to grow.

In the mid-1960s, the League faced another challenge: composers were becoming aware of the possibilities offered by the upcoming centennial year. The League created a tough resolution that would influence presentations on the stage at the Canadian Pavilion, the most prestigious venue at Expo 67. It stated quite directly that "Each performer must be willing to include one piece of Canadian music in each proposed performance." The Canadian Music Centre now had a stock of Canadian repertoire that was readily accessible to any performing artist or ensemble. The principle was to be strictly enforced. "If a performer will not play at least one piece of Canadian music, he or she will not perform at the Canadian Pavilion."[15] In a normal context, Louis did not perceive legislated Canadian content as the solution to having Canadian works performed. In this case, however, there was every justification to ensure that Canadians and visitors would have an opportunity, at least in this venue, to hear the works of the host country's composers.

By now, Louis's role in the Canadian League of Composers was diminishing and a new wave of composers (Fleming, Garant, Morel, Mather) were joining and sometimes replacing the league's founders and early supporters (Weinzweig, Beckwith, Nimmons, Freedman, Somers, and Applebaum) in key positions. However, at the 1966 Annual Meeting, Louis put forward a resolution on a topic that was to consume his interest for the next five years — the recording of the repertoire of Canadian composers. It was a simple resolution: "that the new executive take up the matter of recordings of Canadian music in that there will be from 30 to 50 LPs made of Canadian music in 1967."[16] Louis believed that recordings had to be made available for every kind of Canadian music — popular music, obviously, but more important and more difficult to achieve, "serious" composition. Developing the taste of the country's audiences could be achieved by the familiarity that recording made possible. Audience members would then insist on having Canadian offerings on the programs of solo musicians and ensembles — from the string trio to the full symphony orchestra. Radio had changed the nature of music listening, but now, with television taking a larger portion of society's discretionary time and advertising resources, radio stations were turning increasingly to recordings. Music was now fundamental to the economics of radio broadcasting, and was the key to survival for myriad small stations boasting little more than a recording studio, a turntable, and a collection of discs. The well-being of the Canadian composer depended on whether Louis could persuade the music community to take up the battle for the production of Canadian recordings. Louis had realized, even before his initiative, that the

League did not have the financial resources to take the lead on this issue. It was to CAPAC, his performing rights society, that he turned for results.

After a particularly bitter dispute, CAPAC and CAB (Canadian Association of Broadcasters), had arranged a truce in 1963, and had marked the occasion with a pledge to jointly donate a quarter of a million dollars to "encourage creation, development, and use of Canadian music." The money, to be released over a five-year period, was to be administered by a Committee. Louis, along with an old friend, Howard Cable, and a third member, Cyril Devereux, would represent CAPAC. The Committee decided that this development could be achieved most efficiently through commercial recording companies, and almost immediately, five recordings were launched.[17] A report in the *Canadian Composer*, a periodical circulated by the Canadian Music Council, indicated that the Committee "has encountered both success and disappointment. But an encouraging atmosphere about the Canadian music scene generally would seem to indicate that the Committee has done its work well."[18]

In 1966 the Committee established an office under Louis's direction "to assess the results of the initial recordings and direct the production of further recordings recognizing that more concentrated effort was needed than the Canadian Music Centre could provide."[19] By September 1967, Louis had produced another album of extracts from popular Canadian musical shows, including *Anne of Green Gables, The Navy Show, Turvey, The Pied Piper,* and *Wild Rose*. In that same year, Louis conducted the music of Eldon Rathburn, a fellow composer at the NFB, for a recording of his work. He also produced a recording called *Labyrinth,* made especially for Expo 67 in the NFB sound studios. Only someone with Louis's obsession with the mysteries of sound could have succeeded. Clyde Gilmour, broadcaster of the widest selection of music to grace the Canadian airwaves for many decades, described the complicated triumph in uncharacteristically enthusiastic language: "The different tracks feeding 858 speakers had to be accommodated in the complex audio system devised for the recording. Heard at home on a good stereo rig, it's a disc for which the adjective "sensational" is not excessive in describing the sonic qualities."[20]

Louis's efforts had encouraged other developments, notably a joint release of Canadian music discs by RCA Victor and the CBC's International Service. These included 42 compositions by 32 Canadian composers, to be followed in 1967 by a further 11 recordings. Obviously, the promotion of Canadian music through recordings was an idea whose time had come. In that same year, Louis received increased public attention for his work on producing recordings, particularly for a project that involved the Toronto Symphony Orchestra. Blaik Kirby, writing in *The Globe and Mail,* reported that the TSO was "making recording history. The players were creating something never before heard in North America – a sponsored, sold-in-advance, guaranteed mass market disc of Canadian classical compositions."[21] The recording was part of a promotional scheme to celebrate the opening of the St. Laurent Shopping Centre in Ottawa (a welcome byproduct of Louis's presence in the nation's capital as he worked on the affairs of the Canada Council, NAC, and Ottawa University.) Louis was referred to in Kirby's article as "the spark-plug of the Canadian recording industry."

Although Louis had achieved some success in having recordings made, he had not made any breakthroughs in securing effective distribution — a job that rightly belonged to the record companies. The economic challenge was typical of every Canadian artistic project — the costs of recording in Canada were the same as in the United States, but there was only a fraction of the market. There was little mystery to the reaction Louis received when he approached the Canadian Record Manufacturing Association and asked them to set up a "native Canadian recording industry." Not even the threat that foreign, mostly American, recording companies might be faced with a Canadian content ruling had attracted their support.[22]

With this rejection, Louis launched a full-scale assault in April 1967 at the Annual Meeting and Conference of the Canadian Music Council. His statement at the meeting received wide distribution, and the timing could not have been better. The country was in the midst of a nationalistic euphoria, with Montreal's Expo 67 in place, and with Canadian arts organizations and artists touring the land. Louis felt that his Canadian colleagues were not "cashing in on the record bonanza" that had exploded in the 1960s — Canadian recording sales totalled $56,000,000 in 1966! Though all these recordings had been manufactured in Canada, "all creative aspects had been imported." The major problem facing the Canadian creator appeared to Louis to be "that we, together with much of the world, seem content to play and hear non-Canadian products." The fifty record companies operating in Canada "exist to represent the *imported* product." Conceding that this was not unlike the situation facing the film, periodical, and book-publishing industries, he opined: "We end up with a standard of living and attitudes toward life that are virtually identical with those of our affluent and dynamic American neighbours." Yet Louis believed there was proof in the successful creativity exhibited by the CBC, and particularly by the Stratford Festival, that Canadian creative talent was superb when given an opportunity to flourish. Even more important, in the centennial year, "the *biggest* achievement ... will be the psychological one .... Expo will really prove to us in a dramatic way that we can match, and even excel, the rest of the world." There was, then, no reason why the recording of Canadian artists singing and playing Canadian music should not be equally successful.

Louis pointed out how important recordings had become in radio broadcasting. He illustrated his argument by describing the breakthrough that had taken place in Quebec. "The Quebec phenomenon" was a healthy record industry, which Louis realized had developed behind the "protective wall" of a distinctive language. However, he insisted that "In Quebec, the music industry is successful because it has found a common chord in the emotional life of the province." In practical terms, his work with the CAPAC-CAB Committee had convinced him that the essential factor in the creation of a strong recording industry was distribution. "The real problem is to get Canadians ... to want Canadian artists and music on records. The problem is that simple: the solution less so." He recognized that there were many players involved in the game — manufacturers, broadcasters, record retailers, writers, performers, and the arts councils. His solution:

> I propose that a number of such interested parties get together to create a new, and *independent* agency to serve their *collective* interests in the field of Canadian creation and performance; that one additional partner be brought into the agency – the federal government; that together they set out to conduct a multi-pronged program consisting of (1) research and analysis, (2) promotion, or education, or whatever you call it, (3) recording and (4) distribution in Canada and abroad. The purpose of agency would be to make Canadians and the rest of the world aware of Canadian achievement through the medium of recordings."[23]

The proposal was now public. In September, Louis placed a resolution before the Canada Council's Advisory Arts Panel suggesting that the Council should take a lead role in developing an agency with almost identical purposes as the one he proposed to the Canadian Music Council. Peter Dwyer's response was cautious, suggesting that the proposal should be discussed with the Director. However, when Dwyer "told the panel that funds could be set up for a committee with an agency to explore the situation," Louis received the Panel's endorsement.[24] Even with all this support, nothing happened. There was a sense that culture had been given a major boost in the budgets both before and during the centennial, and that now the federal government needed to turn to other areas. The delays and the dreadful overrun in construction expenditures for the

National Arts Centre was also an influence. It was a mindless reaction, but it seemed to many as if the artistic community had somehow shown how financially irresponsible it could be. Also, there was a changing of the guard in Ottawa with the leadership contest which — although it resulted in the election of Pierre Trudeau, the most "cultured" prime minister the country was ever to have — nonetheless slowed the flow of funds for arts-related enterprises.

By 1968, Louis had taken on another staff position. CAPAC had shown considerable interest in the recording project and wanted him to continue with this initiative, and possibly others as they surfaced. Besides, CAPAC found it now had serious competition from BMI Canada, the other performing rights society operating across the country. Louis was the perfect diplomat — a respected composer, an unusual figure who had been involved with popular, folk, and jazz music as well as 'serious' composition, and a musician whose track record with a number of arts organizations was widely recognized. Here was a man who could entice artists to the ranks of CAPAC, even from the broadcasting segment of the composing community that had hitherto been attracted to BMI Canada. It was a perfect alliance. For Louis, CAPAC was much more than an agency collecting royalties for its members and ensuring that arts entrepreneurs and broadcasters were paying their appropriate fees. The organization had the resources to do the things that neither government agencies nor organizations like the League of Composers could hope to accomplish. William Littler caught the sense of a mission in an article in the *Toronto Daily Star* headed "Louis Applebaum the Music Booster." Reporting on an interview with Louis, Littler gave expression to Louis's perception of his CAPAC role, which was "to help Canadian music achieve recognition... unofficially he has been doing the same thing most of his life."

> This country, says Louis Applebaum, is sitting on the edge of an explosion. It could happen within the next 10 years. If it does, don't be surprised if Louis Applebaum turns out to be the man who lit the fuse.[25]

Louis continued to support the Canadian recording industry, and certainly in the popular field the impact has been monumental. In that broad genre, Canadian artists and songwriters have not only survived but are dominating several categories of music production on the North American continent. Unfortunately, for reasons that have nothing to do with quality or accessibility, these heights have not been scaled by composers of "serious" music.

Louis's immediate role at CAPAC was that of assuring the continued health of CAPAC in its continuing competition with BMI Canada. Although institutional rivalry was not Louis's deep concern, he did realize the extent of the inroads that BMI had made when, in the spring of 1970, he was sent on a tour of the west, visiting Vancouver, Edmonton, and Calgary, where he began to understand how CAPAC had been badly served by its representatives in the past. The Vancouver CBC chief librarian informed him that "CAPAC used to have a representative here who was terrible," whereas now "BMI provides quick and obliging service for nothing." On the whole, he found Vancouver a very active centre, "living in a sense of isolation from the 'East', busily developing a musical world of its own …." He discovered a "pressure towards independent action, almost as intense as Quebec's" and perceived the beginnings of an alienation that was to develop during the 1970s and would be a hallmark of Canada's political life for the rest of the century. He was distressed to learn that the recording industry in the west had "a very strong BMI bias" and that "opening the BMI office made the music business blossom." One firm associated with CAPAC was inactive and a second "has very fancy offices, has spent a lot of money, but has produced little substance." He was particularly troubled by the "degree of ignorance about the business, performing rights, etc." Apparently the managers and bookers were as "ill-informed" as the artists, and he found that the "mythology, misinformation, lack of information and unreality about the music business is hard to believe."[26] All in all, it was a depressing experience, even though he had some success in arousing new interest in CAPAC and its work.

When William St. Clair Low, the man who had been the CAPAC's CEO, had suffered a heart attack and resigned in 1966, Louis had been given some hope that he would eventually succeed him, or at least be a joint holder of power and influence at CAPAC. To everyone's surprise, early in 1971, Louis announced his resignation. In a letter to his friend and mentor William St. Clair Low, Louis wrote: "I have been offered and I have accepted the post of Executive Director of the Ontario Arts Council." He felt he must provide an explanation.

> If the CAPAC assignment had worked out as you had visualized it and I had hoped, there would have been no question of my accepting any other position, even one as attractive as this one. I think we both had envisioned an exciting and worthwhile program of growth and pertinence for CAPAC in respect to the creators, to the place of music in society, to CAPAC's relations with government, artists and public. There was an excitement about the project and one

that seemed to make use of my background and talents in a full and meaningful way. It was not to be … in most matters functions have been circumscribed so that the rate and kind of growth that I had expected was not happening."[27]

In a warm letter of congratulation on his new appointment, Low responded to Louis's letter:

> After my second heart attack when my doctors said I simply had to give up the strain under which I was working, I recognized, and in fact had discussions with John Mills as to his unwillingness to do and be involved as much as I was with Canadian authors and composers and the Canadian cultural scene. That is why, before retiring, I asked the Board to appoint you to do that part of my work and assumed that after my retirement they would naturally appoint John Mills to do the other portion of my work. I viewed these two appointments as being equal but totally different. When I returned from Europe I was amazed to find that you had been forced off the Board and had been given no title and as time went by I realized from various sources just how restricted your activities had been. I am truly sorry for this, as I felt certain that not only with your great ability and talents but by such a person as you devoting his whole time to what I was trying to do along with everything else at CAPAC tremendous success would have resulted."[28]

Possibly, Louis had been misled. More likely, close work with Louis was, perhaps, too much of a challenge for CAPAC's Board of Directors. Louis was a man with a cause. He had one proposal after another for projects that would ensure the success of the organization and connect it with the larger community, but each one cost money. The more that was spent, the less there was to send out to composers and writers. Louis's philosophy was that CAPAC should enlarge its mandate, play an active role in expanding, not only their membership, but also their influence on the way that music might become a part of the way of life for all Canadians.[29] John Mills was CAPAC's skilled legal counsel, and his promotion was reassuring to those who had a stake in the status quo. As well, he had the proven capacity to carry out the narrower definition of the central role of the society — to navigate through the murky waters of performing rights legislation and get the fairest deal for composers and artists alike.[30] Less than two years had gone by since Louis had joined CAPAC as a regular employee, and now all his hopes for a major role were dashed.[31]

Even more to his disadvantage, Louis did not share the enthusiasm for competition with BMI Canada that John Mills and some of the Board thought necessary. Louis felt that ongoing disputes and games of "one-upmanship" between BMI Canada and CAPAC were self-defeating. It would be another 20 years before he would be in a position to deal with that issue.

Given Louis's wide range of activities, the 1960s were not his most prolific period of music composition. There were years when there was not a single commission, but looking at the total list of his 1960s involvement in television, film, and even radio, one is left breathless. Only on a comparative scale with the flood of works in the 1950s and the 1970s can one see any diminution of his "normal" output.

The 1950s had ended with Louis's agreement to score a number of programs for CBS's *Twentieth Century* series, and in 1961 Louis wrote the score for "The Siege of Malta." He was working with Isaac Kleinerman, who was anxious to have Louis write at least one more segment of the series. Kleinerman knew that Louis was not enamoured with the glorification of war that characterized these programs. In an attempt to convince Louis to continue, Kleinerman was most complimentary about "The Week That Shook The World," the first program to be completed and Louis's initial contribution: "... very seldom has a mix gone so smoothly. The way the music worked with the picture and narration made life easy for us."[32]

Louis, however, was anxious to end his part in the war series. The quality of the work was of the highest order and the remuneration was generous, but Louis saw no advantage in further engagement, particularly in the context of the Cuban missile crisis that took place during the writing of this series. The "Patton and the Third Army" program in the series had particularly sickened him, and Louis insisted that "Target: North Africa" would be his final contribution to this film genre. Kleinerman wanted to keep the door open for further collaboration. "I shall make an unequivocal promise. When I next call on you, it will not be a score for a war picture."[33]

In spite of that commitment, Louis's work for CBS came to an end, and except for programs on Canada's regions for CTV, a newly-licensed Canadian private network, all of Louis's television work for the rest of the decade would be with the CBC. Of course, Louis's freelance composer status had come to an end when he took a position with the Corporation in 1961. Two radio programs — both produced by Keith MacMillan, who was juggling his CBC contribution with his role as the Executive Director of the Canadian Music Centre — particularly pleased Louis. Each, in a different way, was a CBC effort to open the minds of Canadians to the world beyond North America. The first, "Gift of the Young," examined the roles that young people were playing around the world in "teaching, exploring, developing and healing, scouting, and soldiering." From Alert Bay, at the tip of Ellesmere Island, to the heights of Kilimanjaro; from Christian Island to Gibraltar; from New Zealand to Pakistan; the voices of youth flooded the planet with the sound of their energy and enthusiasm.

"The Commonwealth of Sound," produced a year later, was once again an effort to mirror the world beyond Canada's borders. This time it included sounds of nature — the animals and birds in the depths of a Malayan jungle, a loon calling its mate on a northern Canadian Lake, natives pounding drums in Ghana, the uproar of debate in Hyde Park, London, and the song of the native people of Botswana at the killing of a lion — all laced together with Louis's musical thread. It was a singular challenge to make some sense of this apparent cacophony.[34]

"It's All Yours" was a light-hearted celebration of CBC Radio's "new network, an integrated and expanded service ... which can now reach 90% of homes ... and reach through no less than seven of the world's twenty-four time zones." Max Ferguson set the tone of the program, exclaiming that "CBC radio is gettin' like a giant octopus, which is slowly chokin' us with Canadian culture." The entire panoply of radio programming — music, religion, public affairs, sports — received Louis's attention. He had to provide the musical introduction for each segment.[35]

There were highlights in Louis's television work as well. "Affectionately Hockey," based on a script by sportswriter Scott Young, focussed on the experiences of Billy, a boy living on a farm west of Winnipeg, Manitoba, who built his own rink and practised hours every day in his determination to become a professional player. Johnny Wayne brings Billy to Toronto to be a part of a documentary film on hockey. He meets his sports heroes — Frank Mahovlich, Eddie Shack, Johnny Bower, Bert Olmstead, and other Leaf players. Hockey was not one of Louis's enthusiasms, but his interest was aroused because the program was sparked by a comment in an American magazine that the reason Canadians made better hockey players was that they were anxious to get out of the "hick towns" in which they were unlucky enough to be born. It was a gratuitous observation and the program was a celebration of "hick towns" that had produced famous hockey players — Floral, Saskatchewan (Gordie Howe), Shawinigan Falls, Quebec (Jacques Plante), and Belleville, Ontario (Bobby Hull). Louis's score reflected the rhythm of the game, the exuberance of the fans, and the physicality of the players.[36]

The 1963 broadcast season's "Looking Glass People" brought Louis back to an earlier love, ballet, and in particular the National Ballet of Canada. The program "shows the workaday world of ballet dancers, day-in-day-out rehearsals, endless warming up, hurried cups of coffee, jangling alarm clocks, tour buses, first night nerves, camaraderie and team work." Though responsible for the music and acting as musical director, Louis worked in a collaborative relationship with George Crum, the Ballet's permanent conductor, and the program received warm praise across the continent and abroad.[37]

In that same year, CBC aired a children's series that Louis had worked on two years earlier during his involvement with administrative and promotional responsibilities at the Corporation. A Canadian opera singer, Alan Crofoot, played the role of the lead character, Mr. Piper. Thirty half-hour weekly episodes wove together three elements: a fairy tale segment; a travel film segment ("Port of Call") showing children's activities in other countries; and a miniature set sequence involving animals in various adventures. Louis was "to take over fine-cut work and voice tracks and cutting in the music effects tracks and to supervise the final mix" making it possible to "turn over the completed negative sound track of high quality" as well as compose the bridges to hold the program together. These activities pleased Louis. He had a strong belief that arts programming for children should be just as quality-oriented as adult programming — not a view shared by many involved in broadcasting in the 1960s, or, for that matter, in the mainstream performing arts community. Every week there were new sounds to create and new challenges to overcome in a short half hour divided into minute-long "bites" of visual impact. An additional wrinkle was that the music had to be composed to attract and retain the attention of a very young audience while skirting the edge of chaos at all times.[38]

One of Louis's most satisfying projects of this era was a centennial program called "And Then We Wrote," in which Louis played a role as both composer and conductor. A review called it "a smashing variety show" directed by Norman Campbell, and with the inimitable Max Ferguson as the host. It was "a light look at Canadian music over the past one hundred years." It covered ballet, light opera, and musicals that had been written in Canada, including *Peg o' My Heart* and *The World Is Waiting for the Sunrise* — as well as the deservedly less-well-known offerings, *Brave General Wolfe* and *I Didn't Raise My Boy To Be a Soldier*. In more serious moments, John Weinzweig's "Round Dance" and Gilles Vigneault's "Mon Pays" shared time with Robert Fleming's "Ballet Introduction." For Louis, the program celebrated Canadian creativity and musicianship, and he joyfully composed the introductory and concluding passages as well as the links between compositions that gave the program momentum and focus.[39] The program featured Louis bedecked in formal "tails" — a rare sight on TV — conducting the orchestra in full sight of both studio and television audience. This was a far cry from his usual place — leading his ensemble from the depths of a dingy basement studio hundreds of yards away from the TV cameras and the brilliantly lighted main stage.

There was also continued contact with classic theatre, with a CBC excursion into a classic anti-war drama, Bertoldt Brecht's *Mother Courage.* Based on the events of the Thirty Years' War in Europe, it depicted the experiences of a woman surviving in the midst of meaningless violence and societal mayhem. It suited Louis's philosophy of war as a poor solution to humanity's problems, but providing the music was a special challenge.[40]

> Paul Dessau's original incidental music and song settings have been adapted and arranged for the CBC Festival Production by Louis Applebaum, who conducts a five piece ensemble consisting of piano, drums, piano-accordion, guitar and trumpet.[41]

The Canadian Composer wrote of another of Louis's successes: "Louis Applebaum is in the news and will be regularly now that his composition is being played as a new theme for the CBC's national news telecasts." In time, this theme was to become the most-heard piece of music that Louis wrote in the entire decade. Many composers had submitted scores, but Louis had won the competition. For several years, these notes rang out every evening across the land, drawing Canadians to their living rooms to find out about the events of the day.

During the 1960s, Louis experienced success in film as well as on television. One early venture was an avant-garde film, *The Mask*, produced by Warner Brothers in Canada. *The Mask* was called a low-brow surrealist exploration of dark fantasy. A reviewer in *Canadian Film Weekly* perceived that the film:

> throws a hypnotic light on an ancient ritual mask that brings black and magical fantasies to anyone wearing it. In many respects the motion picture is unlike any seen before and as such should provoke a strong response at the box office. Special glasses are given for use during these sequences in which fantasies take place. The picture, shot in Canada, is the product of the talented producer-director Julian Roffman.[42]

The film reached New York in October 1961, and Variety Magazine commented that "Louis Applebaum's music, into which electronic sounds have been incorporated, nicely complements the desired mood."[43] Clyde Gilmour, then a columnist for the *Toronto Telegram*, indicated the importance of this experiment in terms of the nation's film-making community, referring to *The Mask* as:

> the first Canadian-made, Canadian financed feature film ever to get international marketing by a major company ... a gallery of three-dimensional phantoms that might just as well have originated in Hollywood or London: a haunted forest, a mammoth serpent and a skull with flame-throwing eyes ... a fantasy thriller in the horror category. [44]

Another film that Louis found tantalizing was *Athabaska*, commissioned by the Sun Oil Company. For his work, Louis won an Etrog Award for "the Best Original Score" at the annual Canadian Film Awards celebration in 1968. The soundtrack was scored for both large orchestra and smaller instrumental groups and Louis was particularly delighted that his son, David, had produced the special sound effects.[45]

The Red Kite — a very intimate story of a man who builds his daughter a kite that becomes the basis for a relationship with a host of very different neighbours — was another film commissioned by the National Film Board. It was very successful, receiving awards at film festivals in Columbus, Ohio, and New York City. *The Red Kite* was perceived as a treasured source of understanding about how people create a civil society through common interests and qualitative interactions.

Perhaps the most celebrated documentary film of Louis's entire career was a modestly titled production, *Paddle to the Sea*, based on an acclaimed children's book by Holling Clancy Holling. The screenplay was written and narrated for the NFB by Bill Mason, a Canadian legend in the eyes of outdoors enthusiasts, canoeists and environmentalists. The story line was simple. A hand-carved canoe, a few inches in length, containing a human figure with a paddle, enters the water near Sault Ste. Marie and gradually makes its way to the St. Lawrence River and finally the Atlantic Ocean. It would be described as "a children's odyssey." On the journey the traveller encounters and overcomes a series of potentially destructive obstacles — rapids, towering waves, Niagara Falls, forest fires, polluting tankers, and spectacular climatic conditions ranging from glorious sunlight to blizzards and ice-storms, to say nothing of a panoply of animal and bird life. The little canoe and its occupant survive to reach the ocean — and that is the miracle. Presented as a series of simple images, the story is a metaphor for the struggle of the individual who overcomes all odds and ultimately triumphs.

At the same time, it is a glorious tribute to nature and the Canadian land-scape, and a warning about the importance of caring for its environmental health and natural beauty. The music is magnificently evocative. As the canoe is placed in the surf, the music is minimal, just woodwinds and a soaring violin solo. Flutes echo bird calls and strings accompany the scurrying of squirrels. The accompaniment becomes darker as gulls attack and a forest fire threatens the canoe's destruction. Ominous sounds emerge from a fuller orchestra as tankers plough through the water, leaving a wake of pollution to sully the clear, blue water. The music enhances a central message that the universe is one. *Paddle to the Sea* won an Academy Award nomination and a host of awards at film festivals around the world.

Bill Mason fully recognized the role that Louis had played: "I was thrilled with your music. The paddle theme is just the sort of thing I had hoped you would create. Your music effects for the danger sequences are hair-raising. In other words, your music has fulfilled my wildest expectations."[46]

Paul McIntyre, head of the Music Department at the University of Windsor, wrote some years later: "I recently had occasion to see *Paddle to the Sea* again for the 45th time and only now realized how much the musical score contributed to the effect of this beautiful film."[47]

Another important part of Louis's creative life continued to be the composition of music for plays at the Stratford Festival. As a freelance composer, Louis provided original music for one or two of the plays being presented every summer during the 1960s. There were moments of great delight, eclipsing the frustrations of his work with Group Four Productions and his administrative role at the CBC. The 1963 Opening Night offering at Stratford was a rather dark play, *Troilus and Cressida*, and Louis decided, once again, to provide a little drama before the curtain went up. In the Canada of the early 1960s, it was still considered appropriate to play "God Save the Queen" before any important event and this year, once again, the Stratford Festival received a royal visit. For the occasion, Louis orchestrated the traditional salute to the sovereign in a way that produced some unsuitably strange "un-royal" sounds. Even the critics were caught off guard. Nathan Cohen took the whole joke seriously and commented on the rendition of "The Queen" as "strained and shapeless." With wit and humility, Cohen made amends in a later column.

> "What was unknown to me, and most of the audience, was that a different arrangement of the anthem had been worked out for each of the productions, consistent with and slightly satirical of the play and its period. i.e., martial and whimpering for *Troilus and Cressida*, elegant and swaggering for

Cyrano de Bergerac (both by Mr. Applebaum) and frivolous for *Comedy of Errors* (by Gabriel Charpentier). For what it is worth, the device is amusing and rather successful.[48]

Another of Louis's triumphs at Stratford in the 1960s was *Twelfth Night*, directed by David William (his first production for the Festival). The show became the hit of the 1966 season. Louis, as the composer for this play, had to bring the "new boy" along. Williams wanted to use the traditional numbers associated with the play and Louis had to inform him that: "Since the Festival's inception we have managed to compose *new* musical material for each production." To assuage any nervousness Williams might have, Louis indicated that he would offer the director a choice. He would compose the new songs and, if Williams didn't like them, Louis would agree to use the traditional tunes. Williams and Louis were to become very close friends and this initial sensitive response by Louis was a key factor in this relationship. It also revealed the extent to which Louis could set aside his own creative judgement when required.[49]

1966 also saw an effort to bring to life a new play at Stratford — *Nicholas Romanov* by William Kinsolving. Michael Langham, the director, had agreed to launch the play at the Manitoba Theatre Centre. The score was to be filled with chants from the tradition of the Eastern Orthodox Church and a small choir was to be an essential element of the accompaniment. On the script of the play, Louis made notes to himself about the nature of the score and the ideas to be expressed: "... longing for God... Holy Ghost among us ...." There was an extraordinary lavishness about the play's production but the reviews were devastatingly negative. Critic Heather Robertson described the impression of feeling "as if Dr. Zhivago, Ben Hur, and Cleopatra [all celebrated 'hyped' films of that era] suddenly moved into three dimensions. [The play] lacks spontaneity." Robertson continued, "Even when they [the Romanovs] were shot to death by the Soviets, the members of the royal family reclined in a graceful heap."[50]

Stratford cancelled the play and replaced it with *The Last of the Czars* by Michael Bawtree. It had the same theme — the assassination of Czar Nicholas and his family in 1917 — framed by the dramatic device of a play about a play about an assassination. A fine cast was assembled and Louis was commissioned to write the music. With his busy schedule, he was able to draw on much of the work he had produced for *Nicholas Romanov*. Herbert Whittaker, after commenting on the Leslie Hurry design, wrote that "Louis Applebaum's musical contribution is equally helpful with the "Russian Anthem," the "Internationale" and "La Marseillaise" to match Mr. Hurry's 'iconery.'"[51]

In the following year, 1967, the Festival mounted *Antony and Cleopatra* with British actress Maggie Smith in the lead role and Louis provided the music. Now Louis was working with Robin Phillips who had become one of Louis's favourites. The two would collaborate on a number of Stratford productions.[52]

The first decade of his absence from the day-to-day operation of the Stratford Festival produced a pattern that Louis came to enjoy. With whatever administrative challenges he pursued, he hoped he could keep his creative spirit alive by writing the music for at least one Stratford production. This expectation was to be fulfilled for nearly a half-century, with the exception of one year when no commission appeared in the confusion of a change of artistic directorship.

Before the 1960s ended, Louis encountered a new opportunity — an invitation to contribute to the Shaw Festival in Niagara-on-the-Lake, Ontario. Founded shortly after the Stratford Festival, the Shaw program had grown to be quite mature and artistically satisfying. However, rather than to accompany a play, Louis was commissioned to write music for special program celebrating George Bernard Shaw's connection to music as a critic — a portrayal of the playwright intended to complement another production, Part I of *Back to Methuselah*. The production, entitled *Four Variations for Corno Di Bassetto* — Corno Di Bassetto being the *nom de plume* of Shaw in his role of music critic — was described as "a musical entertainment" and was arranged by Louis and Ronald Hambleton.[53] In addition, Louis gave a lecture on "Shaw and Music" at the Festival on July 21. There was lots of material; as William Littler pointed out, "in his brief tenure, he [Shaw] turned out some of the wittiest, cleverest and most devastating critiques ever penned in the English language."[54]

Four Variations was Louis's only foray into Shaw territory. As much as he enjoyed the experience, he remained wedded to the drama of Shakespeare and the Festival in Stratford. This "blip" in Louis's loyalty to Stratford somehow seemed an appropriate conclusion to a decade of many contrasts. At no point was there a crisis of despair (with the exception of Group Four Productions) over the many directions in which his work was taking him, and the frustrations besetting him in his efforts on all fronts. He continued to compose throughout the decade, as witnessed by his work in film, television and stage. The 1960s found Louis Applebaum enjoying an array of activities with much apparent delight, quite prepared to face disappointment and frustration in the course of following his own star. Little did he know that the decade of the 1970s would bring with it challenges and triumphs unlike any he had ever experienced.

Chapter Fourteen
A Troubled Arts Council

For Louis Applebaum, the 1970s were consumed by his commitment to an arts funding agency — the Ontario Arts Council. His goal was to help the Council stabilize its support, expand its mandate, and, most important, establish trust and confidence in its integrity. The entire decade was personified for many Canadians by one man, Pierre Elliott Trudeau. His style and intellect both reassured and exasperated Canadians, who had only to look across the border to see how a nation's confidence could be eroded by crises in its leadership — the Kennedy assassinations, the humiliation of Vietnam, and, most damaging of all, the Watergate scandal, which brought into question the central issues of public morality and behaviour and shook the very foundations of the American system of governance.

During these years, Louis was at the height of his power. He exuded an energy and focus that came from 30 years of achievement, along with a maturity that had been honed by the disappointments and failures of the Group Four Productions bankruptcy and expressed in his retreat from the CAPAC battles. In the final years of the 1960s, from his Ottawa-NAC vantage point, Louis had come to know Trudeau, whose agenda — fashioning a truly bilingual country and welcoming an enormous variety of cultures — would soon become a nation's.

Trudeau was rowing against a societal tide that was carrying Canadians in the direction of increased power at the local or regional level. He was motivated to oppose those forces that sought to fragment Canada — the separatist movement in Quebec and eastern resentment of the generous share of energy resources in the western provinces, particularly Alberta. Later, the repatriation of the Canadian Constitution would become the battleground on which these issues were to be addressed. Louis, involved in the development of the National Arts Centre, saw Trudeau as a Prime Minister who was knowledgeable about Canada's culture and prepared to make use of this cultural asset, the NAC, whenever he needed a venue to entertain foreign dignitaries.[1] Louis hoped that the presence of this articulate, sophisticated figure on the national scene would influence the development of the nation's cultural expression, not only in Ottawa, but also in provincial capitals across the land. In this hope, Louis was to meet with both inspiration and disappointment.

Trudeau's popularity was palpable in the early years of his tenure as Prime Minister, particularly with artists who felt that the Kennedy "Camelot" had moved north. The image was there.[2] Here was a man who loved the arts, indeed attended music, dance, and theatre performances at the new NAC and, moreover, had actively participated in the "letters" of his country, writing extensively on the politics of his province of Quebec for many years before he was attracted to federal politics.[3] Yet, in spite of all this, the money to maintain the momentum of the centennial year did not materialize.

Trudeau's attention was on societal and constitutional issues, but rising energy costs soon became a vital area of concern. With oil and gas in greatest abundance in Alberta, that province expected to benefit from the high world oil prices. Other provinces, particularly those less well endowed with such riches, tended to see natural resources as national treasures and resented being taken advantage of by fellow Canadians with the good fortune to be resource-rich. Trudeau's intervention aroused the fury of Alberta, and thus began a trend of western outrage.

At the time, inflation was rampant, sending interest rates to unconscionable heights, bankrupting small businessmen, and increasing the costs faced by arts organizations, almost always on the edge of financial disaster. The arts organizations responded by raising admission prices — a strategy that in some cases led to reduced audiences and even more financial pressure. Canadian cultural institutions — orchestras, ballet companies, and theatre companies — had not yet learned to seek private sector funding. Louis's response to this crisis in the arts took two forms: haranguing governments at every level about the importance of the arts, and encouraging the subsidized arts to seek more alternative funding from the private sector.

The federal government did move on the cultural front with a spate of initiatives that has led many observers of these years to refer to the period as a "golden age." In 1968 the Canadian Radio-Television Commission — now the Canadian Radio-television and Telecommunications Commission but still known as the CRTC — came into being. A new Broadcasting Act was passed, and, in the light of new technologies on the horizon, a federal government "White Paper on Satellite Communications" was produced. That same year brought a National Museums of Canada Act and, a year later, it was followed by an Import-

Export Cultural Control Act. Gerard Pelletier — the Minister directing all these initiatives — had established the guidelines for a Canadian cultural policy that would dominate throughout the rest of the century, emphasizing such values as pluralism, democratization, decentralization, federal-provincial relations, and international cooperation.

By 1972, federal policies had been developed not only for museums and publishing, but for film as well.[4] As Louis watched all this focus on culture, he was led to believe he would find opportunity in the activities of an arts funding agency — in this case, the Province of Ontario Council for the Arts. (In 1971 the name changed to Ontario Arts Council.) Louis could never have guessed that all this attention to the creation of cultural infrastructure would result in a need to sort out the roles and responsibilities of all these agencies, and *that* would lead in turn, only a decade later, to a federal cultural policy review by a committee that he would be invited to chair.

The Liberal Government in Ottawa was anxious both to strengthen internal unifying forces — including those considered "cultural," thus keeping Canadians together — and simultaneously to contain the power of a neighbour whose combined friendliness and isolationism could undermine the capacity of Canada to survive at all.[5] Louis's experience had convinced him that strengthening the arts was the most important defence strategy available to any national jurisdiction, but especially to Canada. John Kenneth Galbraith, a Canadian-born economist of international renown, when asked about how the country could maintain its political integrity in the wake of these threats, had good advice.

> I would be much more concerned about maintaining the cultural integrity of the broadcasting system and with making sure that Canada had an active, independent theatre, book publishing industry, newspapers, magazines and schools of poets and painters ... these are the things that count.[6]

In 1971 — and in this economic and political climate — Louis Applebaum became Executive Director of the Ontario Arts Council, and he centred his attention on this organization throughout the decade. The Council had already come through a relatively short but active history as the province's arts funding agency. Arts granting agencies usually receive little or no attention unless there is a dramatic cut in their annual appropriation. If a disgruntled ballerina takes a dance company to court over perceived wrongs, if the conductor of a symphony orchestra fails to draw audiences or hold the confidence of his colleagues, if an opera company finds itself at war with various levels of governments around its obvious need for a proper venue in which to perform — these situations invariably find their way into the pages of the mainstream press, often on the front page of at least the Entertainment Section. However, rarely is there any concern over the workings of an arts council except in the context of a self-interested complaint by an aggrieved artist or arts organization. Part of the problem is that arts councils try to maintain a low profile, hoping that their work behind the scenes will pay off in increased resources for their clients. They usually leave the high visibility and media recognition to their clients (who need that attention in order to survive) and to the governments (who provide the annual appropriation and who hope to be re-elected). Yet the effectiveness of the staff, the sympathetic responses of the Council members, and, most important, the relationship of this arm's-length body to the government which has created it and funds it, can have dramatic implications for the entire arts scene. An arts council's actions must be based on an accurate analysis of the government's expectations, since serious miscalculations can erode the level of grant appropriation. In Canada, at a time when government allocations might constitute 20% or 30% of the budget of an arts organization, these factors could decide their fate. In 1971 the future of the OAC as a funding body was definitely in question. Those who maintain that the arrival of Louis Applebaum and his effectiveness as a leader saved the OAC from extinction have a strong argument, even when the efforts of Arthur Gelber, Frank MacEachern, Anthony Adamson, and other major figures on the Council are factored into the equation.

Nearly a decade earlier, in 1963, Arthur Gelber, a Toronto real-estate businessman and arts enthusiast, had taken Floyd Chalmers and Trevor Moore — both business associates in the field of publishing and oil but also involved with major arts organizations — to meet with John Robarts, the newly elected Premier of Ontario. They had made the point to Robarts that Toronto, as the capital of Ontario, was the English-speaking cultural centre of the country. They had put forward the idea that an arm's-length arts funding agency like the Canada Council in Ontario could relieve the Government of the responsibility of assuring the economic health of the province's large arts organizations, in particular, the ones they themselves represented. As well, they had argued, through such a mechanism the politically unpleasant task of saying "no" to unreasonable expectations could be avoided and, ultimately, the Government would be able to take credit for producing a better society, even though individual grants would not be seen to have come as the result of a particular act of political largesse. Robarts had agreed, and within a few months, the Province of Ontario Council for the Arts (the POCA) had been created. The Chairman was J. Keiller Mackay, who had just retired as Ontario's Lieutenant-Governor. The Council was appointed by the Government largely from representatives of boards of major arts organizations that had initiated the process (National Ballet of Canada, Canadian Opera Company, and Toronto Symphony), along with the representation from the Stratford Shakespearean Festival, which in a few short years was to dominate the theatre life of the country. The new Council was given a modest budget of $300,000, certainly adequate to carry out what was perceived as its main purpose — to keep these large institutions from bankruptcy and to protect the Ontario Government from harassment on their behalf. However, when Bill 162, the legislation establishing the Council, was drafted, its mandate was found to be substantially more generous than its appropriation. The Council was "to promote the study and enjoyment of, and production of, works in the arts."[7] This mandate, patterned on the mandates of the Arts Council of Great Britain and the Canada Council, was the foundation for an extremely innovative funding body that could respond to an exploding cultural scene and encourage development in areas, both territorial and artistic, where there was a need. It was this mandate, years before Louis's arrival at the Council, that had become focus of conflict and dispute between staff and Council, and between staff and the Government of Ontario. The view of Government leaders and civil servants that the role of the OAC was to assist large arts organizations, such as the National Ballet and the TSO, was shared by most Council members and Ministers of the Crown. The staff, on the other hand, saw the mandate as a legitimate mechanism for encouraging artistic expansion across the entire province. Just as his predecessor had done, Louis was able to interpret this mandate in such a way that the demands of the new post-centennial era could be addressed with considerable effectiveness.

Louis's first major contact with the POCA had come in 1966, a mere three years after its creation. The first Executive Director had been Milton Carman, an imaginative journalist with an intense interest in the arts, and particularly in musical theatre. Carman saw immediately the opportunities that could be extended far beyond the mere placating of the "majors" — not just the opera and ballet companies and the symphony in Toronto, but the Stratford Festival and, not long after, the Shaw Festival in Niagara-on-the-Lake. He perceived the fast-increasing range of arts needs, a growing army of artists, and expanding discipline fields that also deserved attention and financial support. With a small initial budget in the Council's first years, Carman saw that much could be achieved by building up the external pressure of expectations through broad consultation with artists and arts organizations across the entire province. Carman, a most engaging visionary, organized a series of conferences on particular arts disciplines that galvanized the various arts communities and encouraged a willing, but somewhat nervous, government to see how more money could benefit both the arts and their potential audiences. It was at this point, in the mid-1960s, that Louis's name first appeared in the records of the new Council as an advisor and a consultant

The POCA staff was small but highly competent and, in 1966, Louis was enlisted, along with Elmer Iseler, his choral conductor associate from Stratford, and Arnold Walter from the University of Toronto, to plan a conference on the subject of Music in Ontario. Louis participated in the planning and also agreed to prepare a paper for one of the five workshops, "The Professional Musician."[8] The Conference had come at the right moment for Louis; he had been giving a great deal of thought to the question of music education. He had worked his way through the basic tenets that must be included in any quality program designed to shape the professional musician as well as create a committed audience for good music. In his conference paper, Louis set out the prospects for the professional instrumentalist in post-war Canada and the limited opportunities there were for employment outside the major centres of population.

Louis then turned to the problems that beset the concert soloist. His solutions for the City of Ottawa seemed relevant to the entire province. A process must be initiated to bring professional musicians into the schools, even if this demanded devoting a portion of the mill rate to the support of schools in every jurisdiction. Also, Louis put before the Conference the proposals he was preparing for the CAPAC-CAB Committee, suggesting an expanded Canadian recording industry as a solution to the many problems facing Canadian musicians. Even the ways in which the contemporary composer could be used in the classrooms of the province were placed before the most prestigious gathering of music advocates and educational leaders ever assembled in Ontario.

At the beginning of the Conference, Robert Secord — a prominent civil servant devoted to community recreational needs in Ontario, and the opening dinner speaker — stressed that this was to be a "decision-making" event, thereby encouraging a series of resolutions that were to animate the teaching of music for years to come.[9] Louis's impact on the Conference was quite apparent. One recommendation expressed the view that a composer-in-residence program should be established in the elementary and secondary schools, as well as the universities, along with a program of involving professional musicians in the teaching of music throughout the system. At the conclusion of the Conference, Louis was included in the POCA Music Committee that was created to follow up and achieve some level of implementation — a role that meant confronting the Ministry of Education about its lack of attention to the needs of the arts. Louis was adamant that research into the music curriculum should be maintained. In the report of the proceedings a revolutionary idea had emerged — that the teaching of music should be integrated with regular subjects within the school system, such as literature and history, and should not be isolated and trivialized as a "frill." Louis pushed the idea that this goal might be better accomplished if a pilot project were undertaken for the integration in a school (or in several schools) of high-calibre academic and musical development.[10]

This was not an easily accepted concept in the 1960s; few of Louis's colleagues would have been enthused by the dilution of pure musical instruction with other more established academic disciplines. However, even in the new millennium there are few examples of such integration. The power of the individual discipline and the subject specialist within the educational system has been too great to overcome. For Louis, because of his personal experience, the value of connecting and thereby enriching all knowledge to achieve understanding — and a capacity to cope with the multi-disciplinary problems of a complex world — was crucial. But he had few allies.

The timing of the Conference recommendations was key; they reached out to the post-secondary community just as teacher education was to be transferred from separate teachers' colleges to faculties of education in the province's universities. There, single disciplines reigned supreme and the arts had neither the status nor the resources to support the experimentation that the Conference had recommended. Fortunately, in spite of the opposition his recommendations were soon to arouse, Louis's first involvement with the POCA had been entirely positive.

By 1968, the most controversial document on education in the province's history had arrived — the infamous Hall-Dennis Report — and educational debate in the province for the next 20 years revolved around the ideas it contained. Hall-Dennis was either magnificently humanistic and exciting, or anti-intellectual and destructive, depending on the philosophic stance of the reader. The Hall-Dennis Report was very much a sixties document that saw formal education, particularly at the elementary level, not as a preparation for a working career but as a process of personal liberation and an opportunity for individual expression. Soon a second report, "The Learning Society," was generated by a Committee chaired by

Dr. Douglas Wright (who was later to become an Ontario Deputy Minister of Culture and Recreation and then the President of the University of Waterloo). This report suggested that the school was only one of many community resources for human development and that libraries, museums, concert halls, and galleries were also major educational venues that *must* be available to every citizen.

However, the hard realities of the 1970s were just around the corner, and many perceived these reports as the emanations of maudlin idealists. Society, now engaged with harder and more materialistic ambitions, was beginning to view the competitive nature of the marketplace as the model for solving problems. As well, political realities were at work behind the scenes. Premier Robarts had seen the POCA as a mechanism to release the government from the unwanted task of providing support to large arts institutions. But something of an invisible conspiracy had led to a legislated mandate of "promotion of the arts" being added to the POCA's role. This diverged considerably from the intent of the Conservative government.

The POCA had been set up as an arm's-length agency, but during its first decade questions continually revolved around which ministry it should report to and from whom it should receive its yearly allocation. The obvious choice was the Ministry of Education, with its huge and expanding budget — a ministry so prominent that it was regarded as a launching pad for those who aspired to the premiership. As the 1960s came to an end, there were at least two Ministers of the Crown with legitimate ambitions to lead the province — Education Minister William G. Davis and Robert Welch, the articulate and personable Member from the Niagara region.

In the gathering storm that led up to this change in Conservative party leadership, the POCA did meet with Davis about the matters discussed at the Ontario Music Conference. The outcome of the meeting was a sense of general disillusionment on the part of the POCA staff. Davis had understood completely what would happen if these recommendations were accepted. In the near future, if there were a shuffle of responsibilities, the POCA's recommendations could shift an important aspect of curriculum planning and development away from the Ministry of Education. Davis saw valid reasons for not allowing a diminution of his Ministry, particularly as regarded his personal ambition to be the next premier. As well, a massive community college system had to be established at an enormous initial cost, and Davis was fighting for large budget increases to cope with university expansion and the continuing need to accommodate the baby-boomers in the elementary and secondary schools. And so the POCA was told that these recommendations were simply "not on." The Council was warned that it should return its original role as an arts funding agency rather than striving to become a mechanism for educational and social changes that would rock the world. For Louis, the experience was chastening, but invaluable. He had witnessed his first, but not his last, confrontation between an aggressive government ministry, led by an able but ambitious politician, and a threatened arm's-length agency.

These tensions were mirrored within the Council itself. Its members, appointees of the Government of the day, were inundated with requests from theatre companies and musical ensembles they had never heard of and knew little about. Milton Carman, captivated with the excitement of using the arts to intervene in the lives of his fellow citizens, had already begun the process of proaction that led to a dramatic expansion of the role of the Council. "Carman was not merely trying to exercise power for its own sake. He had ideas about society, about the humanizing influence that the enjoyment of the arts could have on people."[11]

Meanwhile, as the federal Prime Minister, Trudeau was promising new commitments to youth programs and the POCA soon became the Ontario Government's agency for providing summer job experiences for young people. Ron Evans, a newly acquired staff member from the *Toronto Telegram*'s coterie of fine journalists, took on the provincial response to this federal initiative. He quickly became involved in the POCA, providing young people with projects that would lead them to make music and theatre and use the camera to explore various social realities. The process was disorganized, frenetic, and in some ways self-defeating. Enormous problems of control and accountability were never resolved. Yet the attempt revealed opportunities beyond the traditional arts activities, and Evans, imaginative and energetic, turned out to be the right person to cope with the chaos.[12]

During the early years of the Council's life, Carman's determination had inspired his small staff. However, they soon realized that there was a dichotomy at work in the functioning of the Council. On the one hand, the Ontario government was not anxious to engage in a broad range of arts-support activities; on the other hand, the 1960s had produced a community of artists with a sizeable number of people who were now real and potential audiences. And they were citizens and voters. Even if the aggressive stance of the Council made the government uncomfortable, someone would have to address this growing need, and if it was not the POCA, who would it be? Initially, the staff felt that Carman was both "politically astute" and "filled with creative ideas."[13]

By the end of the 1960s, Carman's expansive ideas had come into conflict with the more traditional concepts held by members of the Council and the politicians with whom they conversed. Carman, so much entwined in the philosophy of the 1960s, found it increasingly difficult to deal with the inability of the POCA's staff and Council to accept the more outrageous of his innovations. With his unconventional behaviour and intemperate utterances criticizing the Government threatening the very life of the Council, the intervention of Arthur Gelber was to become crucial.[14]

Louis had come to know Gelber rather well. Gelber had been an active participant in the work of the Canadian Conference on the Arts, the National Arts Centre, and the St. Lawrence Centre — all institutions with which Louis had been associated. As the instigator of the POCA's creation and a member of it from the outset, he had played a central role in maintaining its well-being. But Gelber had been Carman's father figure and ally in his efforts to reach beyond the POCA's initial focus. Gelber was also a knowledgeable music and theatre devotee who regularly visited New York, the U.K., France, and elsewhere to savour the best of world-class arts experiences.

Over time, it became obvious to Gelber that Carman had to go. The entire staff was leaderless, the Council felt demeaned, and the Ministers of the Crown were outraged. Fortunately, before Gelber faced him with an ultimatum, Carman submitted his resignation. The Council found it possible to go on record "as deeply appreciative of the outstanding role which Mr. Carman has performed for the Council."[15]

Gelber knew he had to find a new leader for the Council who had the respectability and experience that would give reassurance to the government. Also, the new Director would have to exhibit expertise and flexibility in order to inspire a discouraged staff. First, though, there needed to be a selection process. A retreat for both staff and Council was organized at Niagara-on-the-Lake. The future of the Council was to be the theme but the task of finding the right Executive Director monopolized the attention of every participant. Both the staff and the Council drew up lists of their choices. Louis's name topped both lists.[16] Now it was a matter of enticing Louis to join the POCA.

Louis was anxious to leave CAPAC, but he wanted to compose music full time. Gelber began a personal campaign, making telephone call after telephone call. He pleaded with Louis as a friend to see the Arts Council as a place where his talents could be used to greatest effect. Louis was hesitant. His administrative work at CAPAC had not been positive, and his experience at the Canada Council had acquainted him with all the pressures he would be forced to face as the Director of the POCA. In the course of their POCA work together, he and Carman had had extended conversations — Louis was well aware that the POCA would consume his time, energy, and creativity. This was a multi-year commitment. However, Louis had come to know and respect the staff of the Council, and eventually agreed to take on the role of Executive Director.[17] Arthur Gelber was triumphant.

In a period of dynamic expansion in every art form and at a time of continuing double-digit inflation, the annual appropriation had increased by only 4.4%. During the previous six years, the increases in appropriations had ranged from 16% to 66%, with an overall average of 40%, admittedly on a very small base, but impressive nonetheless. Louis was faced with the task of convincing a reluctant government that now, even in the period of restraint that loomed, special allocations to the arts were essential. Thus, securing more resources became the major focus of his first year as Executive Director. Within a few months Louis had initiated "several successful attempts to improve communications between the POCA (soon to be renamed the Ontario Arts Council) and the Minister responsible for Youth and Recreation, the Department of Tourism, the Provincial Secretary, the Minister of Citizenship, University Affairs, the Provincial Treasurer's Office, and the Ontario Institute for Studies in Education" — all areas of government activity which had some connection with the arts.[18]

However, Louis was not about to lower the pressure on the Government to raise the appropriation. Only a few weeks after his arrival, in a speech to the Annual Meeting of the St. Lawrence Centre — a project to which he had given advice some years before — he commented on the immediate crisis that this institution faced and presented it as an example of the problems facing all such organizations.

> ... behind the scenes at the St. Lawrence Centre ... there is much agony, mostly about living up to the potential envisioned by the artistic leadership ... agonies caused by the lack of funds ... not enough to let Leon Major [the Centre's first Artistic Director] do his job properly ... politicians talk of the "quality of life" ... yet we allow our cultural organisms to go on living in starvation and frustration ... to become psychotic through living under attack and abuse, and even worse, neglect.[19]

Raising the allocation from the government became Louis's "magnificent obsession" — an obsession that, in the midst of a new societal commitment to fiscal restraint, produced results. The Government showed its confidence in his leadership and Ministers of the Crown, notably Robert Welch, connived to find more money. From the meagre 4.4% increase that Louis had had to accept in his first year, allocation increases rose to over 38% in 1972-73, 49% in 1973-74, and 38% in 1974-1975.[20] Louis articulated arguments that became the mantra of every succeeding Ontario Arts Council (OAC) Executive Director: every dollar invested in the arts returned nine dollars in revenue to the Government through prosperity engineered by increased tourism and hospitality industries, as well as an increase in employment which produced tax-paying citizens. However, Louis's most basic reason for arts support was the creation of a decent and humane society. And he found allies within the government. John White, the Minister of University Affairs to whom the OAC's reporting responsibility was moved in 1971, "called for Ontario to reorganize the arts activity perhaps by interrelationships not now existing which could create greater effect than now. He called for Ontario to lead the world in a Renaissance."[21]

When, in 1972, the Ontario Government mounted a consideration of the problem of Canada's survival as a nation in the shadow of the economic and cultural American dominance that pervaded the province's life, Louis was invited to appear before a Select Committee on Economic and Cultural Nationalism. He began his comments by saying: "I think what we are to talk about this morning is what we do about conserving our soul, conserving our spirit." This shocked the Select Committee members, but it made the point that, essentially, the arts were about the spiritual, not the economic concerns of society.[22]

A flood of requests for support continued to arrive at the Council. In the very month when Louis's appointment was announced, Nathan Cohen asked his *Toronto Daily Star* column readers why the COC, the Festival Singers, the Toronto Mendelssohn Choir, the National Ballet, the Shaw and Stratford Festivals, the TSO, and even the Young Peoples' Theatre were being favoured when the Toronto Dance Theatre, an exciting new "Martha Graham-inspired" troupe, and George Luscombe's experimental Toronto Workshop Players were being ignored.[23] Louis did not have any breathing room. His strategy was to downplay the competing rights of arts organizations and to exploit the question of appropriations, sharpening his argument for more total resources. Years later, while stating with some pride that during his time the allocation had risen from just over $2 million to over $9 million, his observation to journalist Janice Dineen revealed what was uppermost in his mind. "I can easily demonstrate to you the need for $50 million."[24] By the fall of

1971 Louis had been successful in restoring the confidence of the Council and had rebuilt a level of trust between the Executive Director and the Council and staff.

The one question about this work was how it would affect his life as a composer. In an article in the London Free Press, "Volpone Score is Applebaum's Swan Song," Louis was interviewed by a reporter and quoted extensively: "as director of the POCA, he feels committed to be a nonparticipant in any institution, organization, or project which does, or might, receive POCA grants." He stated categorically, "I could not recommend a grant for something from which I would receive benefit." He had only been in office four months, he pointed out, and "the Volpone commission had been arranged many months before."[25]

A few months later, Louis received a letter from Stratford's David William with a pertinent question. "Now is it irrevocable – that pronunciamento you made in Washington D.C.[at a conference of American State Arts Councils] – i.e. that your executive Ontario hat must displace your Stratford Maestro Hat? I ask because Stratford has invited me to direct *Lear* [which is just about my favourite play]; naturally I would like you to do the music, storms and atmosphere and everything."[26]

Louis was delighted but not sure what to do. He wanted to compose and his music was now receiving increased attention. However, he had taken on this major public role. In a return letter some months later he recounted to David William that he was "pleased and excited." He had "asked many members of the Ontario Arts Council whether they thought it would be unethical of me to work for Stratford. To my pleasure, they all urged me to work on *Lear* with you. In deference to their wishes ...." Louis wrote the music for William's production of *Lear* — a production that was most successfully toured — and also for at least one Stratford Festival production every year he was at the OAC.[27] In 1973 he wrote the score for a controversial production of *Othello*, providing "echoing trumpets and a throbbing beat ... notably suitable for dark deeds."[28] Louis's relationship with David William had warmed to the point that William felt confident in giving considerable advice on the music. In a letter of March 10, 1973, he declared that *Othello* is "the most musical of all Shakespeare's plays." He noted two jobs to be done — "the functional ... .fanfares, et al.," and "the pointing up of various elements/nuances in the play that might help a modern audience more easily sense its climate and connection, e.g., the distinction between Venice and Cyprus." In Act I, scene iii, William wanted "a brief majestic fanfare; Venice incarnate in brass: order, power and grace." From that scene into Act II, scene i (up to line 82), he had more expectations, "Possibly begin with a furtive, stealthy statement of an atavism theme, rising into the storm .... Perhaps a storm mixing music with 'scales'/ Applebaum technological bit of glory – something dangerous running under the text but resolving and purging and ending with Desdemona's entrance. Goodness has triumphed for the time being!" In Act II, "Othello's entrance. A magnificent fanfare." For Act II, scene ii to scene iii, "Festive music to greet the herald's proclamation, 'streety', popular, something to dance to, local in flavour, rather improvised, and coming from all around," and in Act II, scene iii, "Like all your good drinking songs it should be boisterous with, here and there, a sentimental undertow."[29]

In 1977 Louis was asked to compose the score for *All's Well that Ends Well*, described by McKenzie Porter as "the most thrilling, most chilling play ever staged at the Stratford Festival." Porter continued even more effusively: "In 40 years of first-nighting on both sides of the Atlantic, this reviewer has never seen better Shakespeare acting ..." and chose to single out Brian Bedford's contribution. However, he went on to other elements of that splendid production: "Louis Applebaum's music and Gil Wexler's lighting thicken the atmosphere of baronial intrigue and bloodshed ...."[30] A year later, the same reviewer, under the headline "Winter's Tale a Smash Hit," not only singled out Louis's music for special mention but also gave the Festival administration some advice.

> Campbell's song "Jog on, Jog on" like the peasant dances in the sheep shearing festival is set by composer Applebaum to intoxicating eastern European gypsy rhythms and melodies. All of these should be recorded for sale in the lobby because they represent an important milestone on the highway to Robin Phillips' ambition – plays with a stronger element of music and dance.[31]

Porter believed that Robin Phillips was serious in his desire to enhance music at the Stratford Festival. In 1975, the year he assumed the mantle of Artistic Director, Phillips was quoted in an interview: "It is, I believe, possible in the future that we will revolutionize opera in the same way as the thrust stage revolutionized theatre. It takes time and it takes money."[32] Throughout the years after his departure from the Festival's administration, Louis had tried to encourage Stratford to increase its commitment to music, particularly music theatre. Just two years after Robin Phillips' prediction, Louis took up the theme once again. The annual Stratford *Beacon Herald's* Special Festival Edition contained an article entitled "Louis Applebaum: The Festival's first music man." The article opened with

Louis's expression of pleasure that, with all its financial problems, Stratford was "one of the few theatres in North America that continues to have original scores for all its plays." However, he soon turned to his favourite area of hope and expectation of the Festival and its direction. "What I think could have been, and still could be established here is close contact between singers and actors. This always struck me as an ideal centre for a lyric stage, where actors could learn musical phrasing and singers could gain some insight into acting."[33]

Louis had taken on the executive directorship of the OAC with great reluctance because he, like every composer, harboured the belief, illusory or real, that full-time composing would result in a greater flowering of important composition. The late 1960s had been a time of trial for Louis. He felt caught between the proverbial rock and hard place. He needed the money to look after his small family — now expanded to include a daughter-in-law and grandson. Jan remembers this as a very tough time, when they had to measure every expenditure.[34] In the 1970s, the OAC provided a job with a good salary. Once the question of permission to compose at Stratford had been settled, the next question became the re-establishment of Louis's role as a composer for television — a role that had been for many years not only a source of income but also a matter of great personal satisfaction.

Louis was now ensconced in Toronto, in close reach of the centre of CBC production, yet the directorship of the OAC was very much a full-time job. With the discipline he had developed as far back as his time at the NFB, he knew he could use his weekends and the odd evening to do the creative work he craved. The advantage was that he had no "conflict of interest" problem with the CBC — the Corporation was not a client of the OAC. Once that bridge had been crossed, his own reluctance broke and a flood of music-making began. Louis remembered the next few years as perhaps the most satisfying of his career. He renewed his relationship with the CBC in 1971 with a modest beginning, "The Journals of Susanna Moody." He achieved, through musical intervention, a balance of attention that shifted between the efforts of a cultured woman seeking to keep her mind alive in the Canadian wilderness and the depiction of the terrible conditions that existed in the forest. "Susanna Moody" was followed by two CBC productions in a series called *Images of Canada*, for which Louis both provided the music and conducted the studio instrumentalists. The programs were entitled "Heroic Beginnings" and "Folly on the Hill." Vincent Tovell, Louis's friend from New Jersey days of the 1940s, was the producer, and promised Louis that "the music shares equal importance with the visual and spoken word." Tovell provided clear advice on the music he wanted. "I hear the odd bagpipe, fyfe, fiddle, drum, etc .... I hear a quiet ending, thoughtful, evocative. I would like to talk instruments and logistics with you as soon as you can spare the time."[35] "Folly on the Hill" was enormously successful, winning, like *Paddle to the Sea*, a Wilderness Award. Then came an opportunity to return, through the medium of television, to the place Louis had felt most at home. "Stratford, 20 Years Young" celebrated the Festival's success. Louis used excerpts from the scores of many productions he had been a part of, and, in essence, the program built on the extraordinary "Stratford Adventure" — the CBC production that had heralded the arrival of a major theatre presence in a country with little to boast of in the area of theatrical performance.

In 1972 Louis was invited to participate in a major series of programs based on Pierre Berton's two popular and expansive books on the building of the CPR. The series took its title from Berton's first volume, *The National Dream*. Eight hours of program time would require a great deal of filming on-site in the Canadian Rockies. The CBC knew it needed a consummate professional writer of musical scores to produce music that would complement such breath-taking visuals. They chose Louis Applebaum.

The stellar cast of *The National Dream* included Stratford actors: William Hutt would play Sir John A. Macdonald, with John Colicos as William Van Horne, Joseph Shaw as George Stephens, and Tony Van Bridge as Sir Sandford Fleming. The series had the most generous budget ever projected for such a program and, in a promotional booklet produced by the Corporation, Knowlton Nash, Director of TV Information Programs, described *The National Dream* as a further example of the CBC's commitment to Canadian history. It was to be a "block-buster" and it certainly was the most impressive piece of work ever presented on Canadian television to date. Nash was unrestrained in his description of both the content and presentation: "And there is no more majestic success story in Canadian history than the building of the Canadian Pacific Railway ... the CBC has presented these programs as the most exciting most popular Canadian history course ever known."[36]

A 1973 promotion document heralded the fact that "Louis Applebaum, one of Canada's most versatile and talented musicians, has been contracted to do the original score for *The National Dream*." The announcement quoted Louis as observing that, although the series was still in production, he had viewed some of the rushes, which he termed "remarkably impressive." He added, "It's only in recent years that Canadian television has begun to offer major programs based on our historical heritage and I'm excited about being a part of such a series."[37] Louis spent considerable time and effort on the production, realizing its importance to the CBC. As well, in spite of what seemed a large budget, it was clear that the money would go mainly to the expensive task of on-site production. Louis commented after the series' completion:

> The trick here is to give a proper sense of the period and not over-romanticize. This is the kind of project where the music must synthesize with the actual sounds in the pictures and it has to be done with modest resources. Composers don't like having economy thrust upon them but in this case it serves a good purpose. Television needs lighter textured scoring than larger screen features and the composer is forced to use his imagination rather than fall back on lush orchestration."[38]

It was almost a holiday for Louis to be asked, in the midst of such a serious project, to write the score for a series of eight Victorian melodramas called, collectively, *The Purple Playhouse*. Each week, the eminent author, playwright, newspaper publisher, and raconteur of chilling ghost stories, Robertson Davies, was the host of the program. It was intended to be good, but not necessarily clean, fun. Executive producer Paddy Sampson made the point clearly: "We will in no way do a send-up of these plays. We will do them absolutely straight. Our purpose is to entertain, to expose contemporary audience to plots that thrill in a style of a different era."[39]

For Louis, these programs provided comic relief from the serious job of writing the music for *The National Dream*. He provided the music for episodes ranging from "Sweeney Todd, The Demon Barber of Fleet Street" (a story that was to inspire a musical by Stephen Sondheim) to a more serious drama, "The Bells," to a classic horror tale, "Dracula." Although the dialogue was punctuated with one climactic moment after another, Louis's music had to make it clear when it was time for the normal reaction of booing and cheering in a 19th-century theatre. Louis had all the tricks at his fingertips. John Beckwith, a composer-colleague of distinction, observed on more than one occasion that Louis "had a bank filled with musical sounds in his head." Just a year before, in 1972, an important partnership had been forged. It was to last for several years and would be the basis for a series of television programs that graced CBC Channels for two decades as one after another received repeated airings. Harry Rasky had begun his career as a journalist and had founded the news-documentary department at the CBC in the 1950s. He had gone on to a series of careers, but his passion was always for film-making, and by the 1970s he had won awards from major film festivals around the world. Louis and Rasky were the perfect team to address major literary and visual-arts figures of the 20th century, including George Bernard Shaw, Tennessee Williams, Arthur Miller, Marc Chagall, and Henry Moore. The productions they made together were to gather many awards and honours.

"The Wit and Wisdom of GBS" proved a splendid start to this CBC series. The script was written by Harry Rasky, in consultation with scholar and University of Toronto President Claude Bissell. The cast included such stalwarts of the stage as Christopher Plummer, Barry Morse, Paxton Whitehead, John Colicos, and Genevieve Bujold. With Shaw's writings to draw from, it was a wonderful celebration of an extraordinary mind, but it gave Louis less to do than he might have wanted — for this production, the spoken word was everything.[40] If the Shaw production minimized Louis's talents, then the next offering did just the opposite. A special hour-and-a-half-long program profiled the state of Israel on its 30th anniversary. "Next Year in Jerusalem," with Sam Jaffe and Canadians John Colicos, Barry Morse, Joseph Shaw, and Toby Robins, brought an intensity rarely seen on the small screen. Louis was anxious to make this film relevant not just to a Jewish audience, but to people of all faiths and national backgrounds. Louis conducted his original score with a full orchestra and an eight-voice choir, but, with a surprising twist that turned religious expectations on their toes, he brought the magnificent voice of Maureen Forrester to the soundtrack, singing a solo from Bach's "St. Matthew Passion" as well as a touching rendition of the traditional Hebrew chant "Kol Nidre." There were even popular songs, including an Israeli hit tune for the opening titles of the film as well as a new song for the closing titles — "Next Year in Jerusalem," written by Louis Applebaum with words by Harry Rasky. The music filled a full 50 minutes of the 90-minute feature. "Next Year in Jerusalem" won an ACTRA Award in 1974 as the Best Program of the Year. The musical score exudes a warmth and compassion for the state of Israel and deals sensitively with memories of the holocaust that so many of Israel's citizens had endured. It should be a source of pride to Canadians that this program was shown around the world in theatres, as well as on the television networks of many countries.[41]

Louis's next year brought a major figure to the screen — Canadian humourist and economist Stephen Leacock. Christopher Plummer brought Leacock back to life in what was essentially a one-man show, afterwards referring to this as his "most personal performance." Though the presentation was largely filmed on a train retracing routes that Leacock himself had traveled, Louis "went to old McGill University song books for some of the themes" and incorporated one of the university songs intact, "as sung by a choir, into the sound track."[42] *Leacock* was well received and won a nomination from the Writer's Guild as Best Film of the Year.

It was 1977 that produced the most highly honoured Rasky-Applebaum collaboration, *Homage to Chagall, The Colours of Love* — a stunning retrospective of the artist's work with footage of interviews with Chagall that no other journalist or documentary film-maker had been able to secure. The visuals were, in the language of Judith Crist of the *Saturday Review*, "rare and wonderful … simply dazzling." The music that Louis brought to the film was lyrical and subdued. It reflected perfectly the sublimity and humility of an aged artist looking back over his life's work. Although Rasky had engaged James Mason to do the narration, it was the voice of Chagall himself that captured audience attention and it was the music that flowed with the artist's colours and spiritually imaginative forms that made the work so utterly unique. The work toured the art film venues of the world and "four of New York's leading film critics chose it for inclusion in the top ten best films of the year."[43]

The last Rasky-Applebaum effort came at the end of the decade when the two collaborated in the making of a 90-minute portrait of Arthur Miller, whose contribution to the 20th-century English-speaking stage has been monumental. Louis's music for *Arthur Miller on Home Ground* received less attention than his work in many other Rasky films, but it did win an award nomination from the Writers' Guild of America in the category "Documentary, Other Than Current Events."[44]

The film was made at Miller's home in Connecticut and included a number of clips from many of his plays, with parts acted by Lee J. Cobb, Colleen Dewhurst, Faye Dunaway, Clark Gable, Burt Lancaster, Marilyn Monroe, Christopher Plummer, and Edward G. Robinson. The problem for Louis was that of bridging the numerous scenes from Miller's plays to the Rasky interviews and to a continuing commentary on the author's life. Louis was struck by one interjection by Miller that "Each man pays a price for being what he is." Rasky asked pointedly, "Has Arthur Miller paid the price?" Miller replied "Yes, the price is that you are stuck at a task that never leaves you. You're never satisfied. A lot of people are satisfied. They feel they have accomplished great things. I never do. I don't know the writer who does." This spoke to Louis on a very personal level. As a music writer he had paid the price, perhaps more than most composers. He had written music throughout a long career, yet he had never had the luxury of casual composing, with weeks or months to create, revise, and revise again a large work that might become his magnum opus. He too could point to a massive oeuvre of musical composition, but he wondered, both alone and with colleagues, what it all meant.

In the midst of these productions celebrating the contributions of world-renowned writers and artists came a more modest commission from, once again, Vincent Tovell at the CBC. Tovell had devised a program that would feature Northrop Frye and would bear the intriguing title, "Journey Without Arrival." The program was billed as an opportunity for the nation's most respected intellectual "to muse out loud about Canada, Canadian attitudes – and what makes Canadians the way they are."[45] Louis's music on this occasion was written for both orchestra and voices, and provided a splendid background for the Gordon Pinsent's assertive narration, as well as the quiet reflective tones emanating from Frye himself. "Journey Without Arrival" was well received. In a letter, CBC President Al Johnson congratulated Louis "for another of your unique contributions" and indicated that he was "extremely pleased that the jury at the recent Prix Amik Awards presentations singled out your special contribution to the music component in 'Journey Without Arrival.'"[46] Louis's contacts with the formidable Al Johnson a few years later would be of a different nature, focussing on the criticisms that his examination of the CBC was eliciting (as an aspect of his federal cultural policy review), and there would be an unpleasant confrontation with the CBC's President in the context of Louis's C-Channel's application to secure a pay-TV license.

During the OAC years, Louis also wrote the music for three very different CBC productions with two elements in common – a woman's name as title and a woman's life as theme. "Nellie McClung" was based on the life a Canadian political icon, the country's most illustrious suffragette. Kate Reid, one of Canada's most respected actors, played the lead role with a combination of toughness and compassion that revealed why this historical figure infuriated both her adversaries and her supporters. And Louis's music did not cloy or obscure her single-mindedness.[47]

"Sarah" could not have been a greater contrast to Nellie. Sarah Bernhardt was a flamboyant, totally self-possessed actor, who burst upon the international stage and fashioned an unequalled reputation as a great artist. Louis's music was highly dramatic and drew attention to the points at which Zoe Caldwell, playing the lead role, depicted Bernhardt engaged in the self-destructive behaviour that could only end in pain and tragedy. The program received the Best Non-Fiction Television Program of the Year nomination at the International Emmys, the first ever received by the CBC in that category. Though not singled out for special mention for its music, the quality of the film was enhanced by Louis's contribution and his efforts both as composer and conductor were recognized as a major element in the success of the production.[48]

Louis's final musical contribution to the trilogy was to "Stacey," a fictional character in Margaret Laurence's book, *The Fire-Dwellers*. The program focussed on the pressures of modern life, in particular, marital isolation. Louis had met Margaret Laurence and knew of the autobiographical elements that the play explores and exposes, and his music had a gentleness and tenderness that gave poignancy to the expression of these elements on television.[49]

"The Masseys" was an examination of Canada's most famous family. Vincent Tovell, the producer, had divided the production into two segments — "Early Times" and "Modern Times." David Fox, a regular on the Canadian stage, and Janet Amos, a considerable force in Canadian theatre as artistic director of the Blythe Theatre and Theatre New Brunswick, played Hart and Eliza Massey respectively. On this occasion, Louis was assisted by a man who was to become his close collaborator in later years — Glenn Morley. The music conveyed the promise and the realization of the Massey contribution to Canadian economic, political, and artistic history. Louis received the Canadian Music Council Award in 1979 for the music he composed for this production.[50]

Louis's experience with Jewish life and faith came into play in a production called "The Making of the President" — the title a take-off on books devoted to the choosing of the American chief executive. This was in no way a story about the U.S. presidency, but rather a humorous and entertaining account of the search for a president of a synagogue situated in Sault Ste. Marie, Ontario. The music emerged from recollections of the many hours Louis had spent immersed in the wide-ranging culture of Judaic music and the program was a scintillating expression of Jewish life, with Paul Kligman and Paul Soles taking major acting roles. The reputation of the synagogue was in question and the issue was just as serious to the congregants as the issue of choosing a president is to the Americans. Louis had to inject themes of light Jewish song literature without losing the tension that gave meaning to the drama.[51]

Another project, "The Peking Man Mystery," must have reminded Louis of his very first excursion into the world of making music for television, "The Big Dig," produced a quarter of a century before. That production had been about fantasy archaeology, but the Peking Man was a very real mystery involving the disappearance of excavated bones from "at that time the oldest record of homo sapiens"[52] — a being who inhabited the earth some half million years ago. This was another Harry Rasky production, with Christopher Plummer as narrator. The bones had been uncovered by a Canadian paleontologist from Toronto, Davidson Black. In the chaos of World War II, these bones had disappeared only to resurface again and again. The story was indeed a "real-life tale of intrigue involving a priceless relic, a mysterious woman in black, eminent scholars, and exotic locations."

How Louis could have written the music for so many theatrical presentations and so many television productions in his years of administrative leadership of a major arts funding agency is a mystery to all those with whom he associated. For Louis, however, writing music was as essential as breathing. Good administration was a different form of creativity, and Louis found that his work in assisting artists across the province injected energy and purpose into his composing. He had taken on the OAC reluctantly and he knew that he might stay three, four, or five years. He had not expected to remain for eight years and then go on to *another* non-music-making role. The 1970s brought him conflict and accommodation, challenge and frustration; but his music-making brought him release and satisfaction, making him an even more effective OAC Executive Director. To artists approaching the Council, he was very much "one of them." His work as a prolific composer through these years contributed an incomparable legacy that is a far greater treasure than anything a job in administration could possibly leave to future generations.

Chapter Fifteen
Cultural Czar

What made Louis Applebaum such a superb administrator for the OAC? Artistic prowess and administrative efficiency are not necessarily allied attributes, and as Executive Director, Louis was answerable both to his Board and to the various artistic communities. Though a compassionate advocate and colleague of artists, Louis brought a certain business toughness to his decision-making. Yet he never lost the respect, and even the affection, of either his own staff or the Council members. He had to provide bad news about rejected applications to many artists, yet he never lost the love of the community he served. The answer to his success lies in part with a lifetime of professional experience with people involved in many art forms. This gave each arts discipline good reason to maintain confidence in his commitment. Louis didn't show favour to his own discipline and didn't emphasize the contemporary at the expense of the traditional. He successfully maintained a balance that both challenged and reassured his OAC Board members.

Louis's great strength was that he brought to the OAC a clear sense of what culture, particularly Canadian culture, was all about. It transcended the performing arts, and most certainly the individual disciplines that made up the granting programs of the Council. Louis had come to understand what his colleague Paul Schafer has described as a "cultural world-view." He recognized the full significance of artistic creativity and its relationship to every aspect of the good life.[1] Indeed, this "cultural world-view" elevates the work of an arts-funding agency to a level above the mere granting, or not granting, of money to particular artists or arts organizations.

Louis's years at the OAC sent him on a continuous search for new possibilities that the Council might address. At no point did he believe that the existing programs were the final word in the support of a cultural world-view. In 1968 the Keiller MacKay Five-Year Plan had stated that it was "anxious to undertake over the next 5 years, programs designed to alleviate cultural deprivation in Ontario. Some of these programs will involve bringing people to the arts, ticket subsidization schemes, and subsidized transportation from remote areas to cultural events."[2] This statement recognized the full importance of the artistic life of a country and the importance of every citizen having access to it. But Louis had to shift the institution's understanding of culture, and make an expanded vision attractive to Board members still very loyal to specific arts forms and the major arts organizations that expressed them. In one debate at a Council meeting, Louis contrasted his inclusive view with the narrower traditional perception of the role of the arts council:

> Mr Applebaum pointed out that Council was created to "promote the arts". How do we promote the arts except through the total life of a person? How do we promote the arts if we start only at a certain point? He agreed that Council cannot give up the search for excellence; that has to be held up as a good to everyone. But, Council is searching also for a way to promote and make it possible for more people to take advantage of the arts. It has to start with people, old and young.[3]

Already an increasing emphasis on arts education indicated the changing philosophy of the Council, with the MacKay Plan pointing out that "one of the most effective ways of realizing the vast and abundant artistic potential in Ontario today is through the educational system." This tied the Plan to the Hall-Dennis Commission's "Living and Learning," which had just been released. Indeed, the OAC had developed a Centre for Arts Research in Education under Paul Schafer, and from here would emerge the successful "artist in the classroom" programs featuring composers Harry Somers and R. Murray Schafer and actor Araby Lockhart.

Louis realized that this broader vision would arouse opposition and resentment. He had a biting sense of humour that he used to counter the criticisms on the editorial page of *The Globe and Mail,* where it was sometimes suggested that OAC involvement in educational experimentation was inappropriate. Before Louis's arrival, the OAC had cooperated with the recently created Ontario Institute for Studies in Education in designing and producing a "Music Box" — a treasure trove of materials that could be used to make music and could be delivered to classrooms across the province. Although such kits were rapidly accepted in progressive circles, some regarded them as an assault on the traditional teaching of music, which relied on well established formal methods. Louis's open letter to editor Richard J. Doyle, just a few months after his arrival at the OAC, was a counter-attack and indicated very clearly the direction that the Council would take under his leadership:

> Curses, foiled again. Just when we were going to sneak a little subversive imagination, innovation and [shhh] creativity into music education, the vigilant *Globe and Mail* steps in and unmasks our devilish 'plot to raise the roof'. You've caught us red-handed: we admit responsibility along with several hundred consultant educators, composers, musicians, parent and school teachers and school children – for developing that sinister 'cacophonous package', the Music Box. Actually, though, it's a gentle silent weapon until it falls into the hands of a classroom of children ... those kids respond to the discovery that all the world's people make music in their own ways and that they can, too.[4]

The editorial bemoaned the cost of this innovative teaching tool to the public purse and Louis reminded Doyle that "Boards have to ... choose other important tools like football uniforms, electric typewriters and the like." From the beginning Louis was prepared to take on anyone who revered the status quo, particularly when this view was expressed in Canada's most powerful newspaper. He was fearless in supporting his view that the OAC had a higher purpose — and this purpose included a duty to introduce young people to a cultural milieu they could seek to understand and celebrate. It was revealing that Louis sought immediate policy from the Council in two areas — more support for touring artists around the province and a working definition of creativity which would become guiding star of those making grant decisions. In Louis's view, the individual artist, particularly the one in literature (a novelist or playwright), in music composition, or in the visual arts, who worked in isolation, had no institutional support systems comparable to what was available for the artist involved in orchestral music, dance, or opera. Louis was determined that individual artists, too, should be assisted.[5]

By November, 1971, Louis had made his point to the Council and, by the next year, when the OAC held a Policy Meeting, "It was unanimously agreed that there be very much stronger emphasis on creativity and accessibility in the future."[6] Louis saw the work of the OAC, in the long term, as an intervention that would challenge the very nature of society. In a speech to the Art Liaison Committee of the Metro Toronto School Board in the winter of 1972, he took the argument to another level.

> ... the big pressure for change seems to come from forces that are common to most of the world. It has become a cliché to remark on the need to replace the drive to acquire material things in this, our highly industrialized and science-oriented life, with a drive to acquire spiritual and self-revealing things and to use them and express them in a self-fulfilling way.[7]

In his tenure at the OAC, Louis had many other issues to confront. The Council had been set up to help solve the problems of arts organizations, but what about the problems of individual artists? Somehow there had to be a way of putting resources in the hands of individual creators without drawing them into the toils of an administrative system so complex and time-consuming that it would erode their imagination and energy. At the same time, some kind of accountability was needed to allay the concerns of those who would perceive even modest grants as a giant pork-barrel devoted to subsidizing artists bent on shocking or even on overturning accepted social values. Louis put it succinctly: "I think it's our duty to help the creative person to create. It's as simple as that ... and we have tried to free ourselves from that 'jury system bind' that the Canada Council finds itself in."[8] With his associate Ron Evans, Louis worked out a process that became a major innovation for the OAC. This process maintained the peer-evaluation system that inspired confidence in the excellence of those chosen to receive rewards, but at the same time recognized the reality described in the MacKay Plan that "artistic activity and creativity are spontaneous, combustible and unpredictable." The introduction of third-party recommendors (such as publishers, gallery curators, and theatre administrators) would ensure that those who were familiar with the nature of artistic activity and who, by definition, would want the best artists to be rewarded with support, would become a part of the decision-making process.[9]

A matter which required Louis's immediate attention was an analysis of the best aspects of the process of collegial decision-making that Milton Carman had first put into place. Based on the 1960s mores of shared power, this meant that every decision was the result of all the officers' input, rather than the outcome of the expertise of one particular staff member whose client's work was being adjudicated. It also meant that decisions were often fraught with arguments as the Council moved from the initial client request to formal approval or denial. Indeed, the most demanding point in the process was the meeting the staff referred to as "the dry run" at which every application received the scrutiny of every member of staff. This collegial approach could be a very positive way of ensuring fairness, equity, and adherence to the Council mandate, but it also became a time-consuming process that was frustrating and inevitably led to internecine battles between discipline officers and offices. Louis, who believed in efficient decision-making, was understandably horrified by this exercise. However, he was wise enough to listen to others and ultimately came to see the advantages of engaging in debate, and the importance of this process to people's perception of the Council's integrity.[10] While Louis was prepared to concede the legitimacy of collegiality, he didn't want individual staff members to be stifled and deflected by incessant discussion and accommodation. He expected professionalism and measurable results without constant handholding, overseeing, and interference from above. The formerly obligatory annual review of subordinates' work was given short shrift. James Norcop, who was developing a program to encourage artist tours, was staggered when his first yearly interview with the new Executive Director took about 30 seconds. Louis simply said "create platforms for artists ... you're doing it right and get on with it." The review was over![11]

While Louis brought calm to the Council, he used these still waters to plan a barrage of new approaches, all based on a holistic sense of the importance of a culturally motivated society and the centrality of the individual creative artist. And preparatory research showed the appropriate way to respond to the needs outside Toronto. Louis was a Toronto man and he understood that artistic inspiration tends to concentrate in cities where there are people to offer appreciation and criticism. But the resentment over the percentage of the budget that came to be spent in the province's capital never completely died down, even when it was explained that the impact of this expenditure on urban interaction benefited the cultural life of the entire province. The distribution of financial resources to remote areas of the province gave Louis some difficulty. He was anxious to hold to the highest standards of excellence, standards that were difficult to attain in Sudbury or Thunder Bay. He listened to the arguments of Lightbourn and Norcop — officers whose knowledge and understanding of various regions in Ontario exceeded his own — and he was prepared to accede to some of their requests. He came to appreciate that, even though the Peterborough Symphony would never sound like the New York Philharmonic, there was good reason to reward groups that were obviously striving for quality.[12] During Louis's first years with the Council, regional offices were established in northern Ontario and the Niagara regions, and, by 1975, Louis was able to report that the rate of increased activity in the more rural regions of the province "is many times greater than the rate of growth in the Toronto area."[13]

The long and tortuous process in reaching out to the Franco-Ontarian community took longer. Franco-Ontarians were, on the whole, not enthusiastic about joining various "umbrella" organizations, such as the Ontario Choral Federation and the Ontario Federation of Symphony Orchestras. They often felt that these organizations had no inkling of their particular culture. Even before Louis's arrival at the OAC, a Franco-Ontarian Office of the Council had been established and it came to make an enormous contribution to this far-flung minority population. Louis's policy saw to it that this aspect of the Council's work thrived.

As well, the heady recommendations of the POCA Music Conference eventually became the inspiration for an Arts Education Office at the OAC. Its major focus was something Louis fought hard to retain — the involvement of professional artists in the classroom working with teachers and students, providing them with an example of excellence. Louis's enduring commitment to arts education can be gauged by excerpts from a speech he made in Oshawa.

> ... the arts are not a subject – they are the road to education ... not divorced from mathematics or history or science but part of them ... not separate from life, but integrated into what we see and feel and react to....
>
> To engage in artistic experience is to open new vistas — to arouse new interests, to ask questions, to create an awareness of the world as it is worth knowing.....With this kind of involvement the arts can provide ... learning is inevitable — without it learning is probably impossible.[14]

Finally, Louis ensured that Norcop's report on increased touring of Canadian artists was given strong support, since artist tours could give a much needed burst of momentum to local musical efforts. A unique event called "Contact," initiated by Norcop, brought artists and sponsors together from all over the province for a huge conference — with booths and presentation opportunities for artists and arts organizations who hoped to organize tours. This translated to more and more Canadian artists finding their way to stages in smaller centres across Ontario.

Some of the most difficult moments of Louis's tenure at the OAC involved two related developments initiated by the Ontario government in the mid-1970s. One was a move to support cultural activities through lottery funds, reducing the dependence of arts and other cultural organizations on tax revenues. The other was a decision to establish a Ministry of Culture that would be directly responsible for cultural issues. In a few short years, the government had moved from a position of assisting cultural activities invisibly — through discretionary grants to major arts organization that could be buried in the budgets of individual ministries and the premier's office — to open support of the arts through a Ministry explicitly devoted to the health and well-being of a host of cultural enterprises. A government that, just a few years before, had to be pressured to form an arm's-length granting agency now began to recognize that cultural activities were central to the lifestyle of Ontarians, and that there was a political advantage to offering support for these activities.

As early as 1972, Frank McEachren warned fellow Council members that a Ministry of Culture was on the horizon, and "indicated that if that was the case then he wanted the OAC to be responsible for creativity and regional artistic activity."[15] Another member of Council, Elizabeth Murray, commented that "if the Council opted for the status quo, government might disband that Arts Council for a more effective organization."[16] Louis was at the meeting and heard the interchange, but was not concerned. He had, by this time, developed a positive relationship with the Minister of Citizenship, Robert Welch, and with the premier, Bill Davis. As well, Louis had reported to the Council just two months before that "a great deal of activity has been taking place within government regarding the cultural sector, the most significant being the establishment of an Interdepartmental Committee to review cultural policy." The purpose of the committee was to "discuss such intergovernmental issues, fiscal, and jurisdictional issues as will arise in this area of talks with the federal government and possibly other governments."[17] Behind this Welch initiative was a recognition of the multicultural reality emerging, particularly in Ontario. No mention of a special cultural ministry was made when Louis, accompanied by Anthony Adamson, Frank McEachren, and Ron Evans, appeared before the Committee and set out the OAC's position on a number of points. The hearing appeared to go well and Robert Sirman, Welch's closest adviser, reported to Louis that Cabinet Ministers D'Arcy McKeough and René Brunelle, neither considered particular friends of the OAC, had indicated "the need to re-focus from economic issues to those of cultural issues." This unwonted expression of interest in cultural issues, however, was a danger sign that Louis should have caught.

When an informal meeting involving Louis and Premier William Davis did take place, it was about medals to honour achievements in the arts. Now that culture was producing heroes, it was becoming a political asset.[18] Louis suggested an alternative to medals: use government revenues to purchase works of arts or commission works from composers or writers. Needless to say, this was not a response that a politician seeking public opportunities to reward artists found particularly attractive.

However, behind these public events, there had been forces at work since the late 1960s that would ultimately drive the government inexorably towards the creation of a Ministry of Culture. When John Robarts had stepped down, both Davis and Welch had been obvious contenders for the premiership. While Davis had occupied the high-profile Ministry of Education, Welch had become Minister of Citizenship. Welch realized that the concept of citizenship rights could be expanded to include access to recreation, access to the arts, indeed access to a broad range of cultural activities that were possible within the context of the multicultural society. This broad concept of citizenship created a platform on which Welch could stand in the leadership race and, although his bid was unsuccessful, he brought to culture and the arts a prominence that could have been achieved in no other way in so short a time. Welch, though disappointed in his defeat, was not prepared to allow this enthusiasm to fade.

The next phase of Ontario's political development was a short-lived experiment that involved clustering newly-created ministries around particular strands of government policy and appointing super-ministers to coordinate the clusters. For Welch, one of the super-ministers, these new arrangements meant another opportunity to address his "total citizenship" concept. However, Welch soon discovered that he was politically neutralized by the fact that the programs and budgets were in the hands of the individual ministries and essentially beyond his direct control.

As well, additional resources were needed to fund these ministries, and there was talk of using a financial strategy that had succeeded elsewhere — government-run lotteries. The idea of lotteries represented a window of opportunity for the government, but there was a moral problem. Welch, a good Anglican churchman, indeed a lay preacher, opposed the introduction of lotteries. Davis, though more flexible personally, was influenced by a grandparent who was very much against this source of funding. By 1974, however, Welch had become the lone advocate of taking the moral "high road" even as Davis was prepared to bow to what he had come to believe was inevitable in the North American context of opposition to increased direct taxation. The premier hoped that Welch might be won over if he could pursue his ideal of "total citizenship" in a new ministry, over which Welch would truly be the operative minister.

The result of all these machinations was the establishment of the Ministry of Culture and Recreation which included the wider cultural and recreational field as well as the arts. Louis was devastated. In spite of his close relationship with all the "players," he had not been consulted or even warned in advance about this decision. The experience revealed the extent to which Louis was outside the political loop. Now Louis was confronted by the proposition of working with a new ministry and reporting to a new minister whose cultural and multicultural agenda would dominate everything the OAC had developed. With a strong minister at the cabinet table who had access to seemingly inexhaustible sources of lottery money, the Council could become obsolete! At best, the arts would be in direct head-to-head competition with sports — surely the most popular form of "cultural" entertainment. Robert Secord, leading the sports side of the ministry, had grand plans for facilities that would be used for training Olympic athletes. As well, such a ministry would no doubt contain a platoon of ambitious civil servants who would have agendas more attuned to pleasing and flattering politicians than to maintaining a supportive relationship with artists and arts organizations. Members of the Provincial Legislature would be driven in the direction of equalizing support for the arts across the province, rather than rewarding excellence. In short, the arrival of this cultural ministry threatened everything Louis held dear.[19] He saw his precious principle of keeping an "arm's-length" relationship between government and the arts disappearing before his eyes!

At the first OAC meeting following the announcement of the new ministry, in February 1975, there was a storm of question and comment. "Mme. Rivard asked Mr. Applebaum if the cultural agencies had been informed of the government's decision to form a new Ministry of Culture and Recreation." Louis was forced to speculate that the agencies had been deliberately left out of the consultation process, "since this would have delayed or even prevented a quick enactment of the government's intention to create the Ministry."[20] And although Chairman McEachren reported that, at his meeting with the Minister, he had been assured that "the Ministry had no intention of interference with [the OAC's] independent policy-making status" there was general consternation. Even more disconcerting was Welch's announcement of the formation of the Ontario Lottery Corporation and his expectation that the OAC would participate. Arthur Gelber recognized immediately that the OAC "will have to fight harder for dollars"[21] but it was apparent that the Minister's abhorrence for lottery funds had been overcome, largely because of assurances that the

revenues from this questionable operation would be devoted to good causes, particularly in the arts and culture area of his ministry. Welch had not
counted on Louis's own unwillingness to see the arts in a position of
dependence on the gambling instincts of Ontario citizens. Louis's argument was simple. If the arts were to be the basis for a new cultural age,
they must not be dependent on games of chance, but rather they must be
at the centre of the government budgeting process. In a democratic society, Louis felt that the arts could make a convincing case for "real" money
collected from the pockets of the taxpayers.

Other provincial arts councils, like Manitoba's, gladly accepted the
increased support provided by the lotteries. However, in rebuffing the offer
of lottery funds, the OAC had won the respect of Robert Welch and tweaked
his own conscience. Louis had counted on the fact that Welch was a man of
generous spirit and he was right. The new Minister of Culture and Recreation
was able to funnel money for the OAC through his own programs.

Indeed, Welch did all that was in his power to ensure that the annual
appropriation would exceed the level of inflation, allowing the OAC to
expand its activities and its client base. The Council's annual percentage
increase after 1975 was reduced from previous heights — an experience
shared by every other government agency during this decade — but by
1977 the base level of support had reached well over $10 million, a signif-
icant increase over the $2 million base that had been in place when Louis
arrived. Roy MacSkimming quotes Louis in the 1975-76 annual report:
"The commitment of the government to develop and promote the arts in
an on-going way through tax-based funds should not be compromised by
Wintario."[22] Obviously, it wasn't. Louis had taken a gamble that the OAC
would be fairly treated and it was. Tax dollars continued to flow into the
coffers of the OAC.

Time proved that ministry officials and politicians were content to
leave granting to individual artists to the OAC. They wanted no part of a
process they could not control and that led, in the majority of cases, to a
negative response. The Ministry tended to take on the funding of service
organizations and arts institutions — grants that demanded little artistic
judgement— and leave those that required some assessment of artistic
merit with the OAC. However, if the Ministry began to hand out massive
one-time capital or project grants from its unlimited lottery-based sources
of income, Louis realized that OAC would then be expected to sustain
whatever new levels of activity were achieved as a result. For this reason, the
Council staff wanted to be consulted about any large grants in the offing.

In the new milieu, Louis became the mediator between the Ministry
and the Council. He was determined that the arm's-length principle

should not be undermined and that politically motivated grants would not destroy the integrity of the entire grant process. Constant vigilance and continued questioning became his stance — not one that he found particularly attractive.[23] He began to look beyond his OAC administrative role, and even beyond composing for television and theatre, to find another way to use his energy. But first, the next assault on his Council had to be contained.

It was just a few months before a crisis brought the Ministry and Council together in a way that no internal pressure could have achieved. Maxwell Henderson, the Auditor-General of Canada, knew how to ferret out waste in government operations. The Davis Government, confronted with the burgeoning expectations of every sector of the bureaucracy, turned to Henderson as a restraining influence on expenditures. A Special Committee was formed with an impressive cast of characters: Eric Winkler (Chair of the Management Board of Cabinet), D'Arcy McKeough (Provincial Treasurer), A. Randall Dick (Deputy-Treasurer and Deputy Minister of Economics and Intergovernmental Affairs), James Fleck (Deputy Minister of Industry and Tourism), and some distinguished citizens from outside Queen's Park — broadcaster Betty Kennedy and Robert S. Hurlbut, President of General Foods. It was clear that this was a serious effort, not to be taken lightly by any ministry or government agency.

When the Henderson Report was released in November 1975, one of the areas singled out for significant savings was the new Ministry of Culture and Recreation. Now the OAC itself was at risk. The report recommended that the whole Ministry be limited to a 5% increase, that no new program initiatives be launched for three years, that any Wintario Lottery funds devoted to cultural or recreational pursuits be included in the 5% limitation on annual increase, and that there be a moratorium on the funding of community recreation grants until criteria could be developed for controlling the level of funding. The OAC and its clients were in a state of panic. Suddenly, the arts had dropped to the bottom of the government's agenda. Louis's success in raising the OAC's allocation over the previous few years now worked against him. In response, Louis and his Council members mounted a campaign to undermine the recommendations of the Henderson Report. They found an ally in the Minister of Culture and Recreation and were given additional support from the civil servants in his Ministry. Welch was able to use his power in Cabinet to stop the proposed cuts in the cultural development of the province. Every one of the recommendations was rejected, either in whole or in part, and the crisis was averted. Louis's role in strengthening the OAC in the four years of his tenure had paid off.[24]

Sobered by this "close call," Louis never stopped his relentless advocacy on behalf of the arts. In 1976, just a few months after the uproar of the Henderson Report, Louis was invited to give the Dunning Foundation Lecture. He reminded his audience that 25 years ago, the Massey Commission Report had stated, "One measure of the degree of civilization attained by a nation might fairly be the extent to which the nation's creative artists are supported, encouraged and esteemed by the nation as a whole." Louis picked up a theme that deserved repetition: "We should reassign our creative people from their present status as social misfits to their rightful place...at the hub of our lives."[25]

Some months later he was to extend this argument to the development of a culture of "esteem" for artists and their work in a popular opinion column, "The Mermaid Inn," that the Globe and Mail opened for contributions from its readers.

> Vincent Massey urged esteem. We should have listened. Can we now? We just don't seem to care about ourselves … about self-fulfillment, about our heritage and, strangely for a young country, about our future …. We, in English-speaking Canada have been content to float along in a benign state of ignorant complacency.[26]

Louis saw a vital first step — "putting money in the hands of artists." But that was only the beginning. He wanted artists to be working in a supportive environment of respect and "esteem." In 1978, he attempted a preemptive strike, designed to bring attention to the artistic community.

> Mr. Applebaum unveiled his proposal [for] "Arts Manifestation Day," which would be a province-wide celebration of the arts and their impact on the daily lives of Ontarians during a 24-hour period in the spring. Because union and business support will be required, preliminary discussions have begun. Initial reaction to the proposal has been favourable and talks will continue. To be held under the aegis of the OAC, the "Celebration" would also require substantial media exposure. Mr. Applebaum will keep the members abreast of developments.[27]

Arts Manifestation Day was not to be. There was not enough time. Only a few months after his arrival at the OAC, Louis had written a letter to Lan Adomian — a composer friend from his days of working in the

American film industry — in which he had expressed considerable discontent about his life.

> I have been caught up in "administration" for two or
> three years now so that my own output has dropped considerably. I still do something at the Stratford Festival
> each year and the odd – very odd television show. A couple of years ago there was an important documentary
> which won for me a Canadian Film Award but beyond
> that it has become a question of attending meetings and
> drawing up plans.[28]

It was apparent that Louis was reacting to the final years with CAPAC,
as well as his first at the OAC. However, a letter written in 1978 to Reuben
Frank, a New York colleague, reveals a very different frame of mind.

> For seven years now I have been the Executive Director
> of a big governmental agency [but arm's-length ... no
> political interference] I have built confidence by the government in the operation, have raised the appropriation
> from 2 million to about 14 million in that time and have
> got a nice solid operation going, etc. This, as you know,
> from a life of total independence for some 30 years.[29]

Another passage from the same letter made it obvious that Louis's creative life was also active and healthy.

> So I learned to write with great speed ... which really
> means only that you go with whatever idea comes to mind
> ... no time for weighing and discarding. So recently there
> has been ... Stratford [2 plays ... now for each of 25
> years] and a test piece for voice and the Montreal
> Symphony for a competition, 2 TV documentaries, etc.
> ... within about 6 weeks.[30]

But Louis was continually driven to look for new challenges and, in the
spring of 1978, he initiated a series of events that ultimately brought him
down, along with many of his closest friends and colleagues. The cause of this
downfall was the notorious C-Channel — the first Canadian network dedicated to showcasing the nation's arts triumphs on the television screens of its
citizens. Events were set in motion at a dinner in Stratford with Robin

Phillips, who was still the Artistic Director of the Stratford Festival. Discussion revolved around the marketing of the arts in Canada, and Stratford, in particular. Louis believed that Canada's artists stood up to any in the world. However, in his view, the arts organizations had not given sufficient attention to marketing. There was another element to the problem: there were now "spin-offs" in communication technology, such as videotapes, satellites, and pay-TV that could provide extra revenue to the organization and bring Stratford productions into homes and classrooms and abroad. Today the word "branding" describes, sometimes in a derogatory way, how major corporations invest in a host of products and services that seem peripherally linked, in order to create a global market dominance that will result in huge profits and command the attention of millions of people. It was the embryo of this marketing strategy that Louis brought to Robin Phillips. Louis, with all his respect for the public service, wanted Canadians to be instigators, developers, and entrepreneurs, rather than "hangers-on, gofers, and apprentices to big-time operations in New York and Los Angeles."[31]

Robin Phillips was convinced, and Louis had found a valuable ally.

> Such a long-standing favourite theme of mine found a relatively sympathetic response in the dynamic and imaginative character of Robin Phillips and the 4-hour dinner led to a promise of mine to prepare and submit a plan to set up a marketing operation that would serve not only the Stratford Festival but a group of other major Canadian companies that shared such marketing deficiencies ... the National Ballet, the Canadian Opera Company and the National Arts Centre.[32]

Also in the spring of 1978, Robert Anderson — a former NFB colleague and now a semi-retired film-maker — had approached Donald McSween — Hamilton Southam's successor as Director-General of the National Arts Centre — with a plan for outreach that would bring the Centre closer to its goal of becoming a national arts institution. Anderson contacted Louis and was surprised to discover that Louis's mind was on a similar track. Anderson's paper, "New Audiences, New Dollars," mirrored exactly what Louis had been thinking.

> Canada's major performing organizations are in a position to reach out to new audiences, new earnings, new forms of expression, new ways to test and expand themselves. They need effective thrusts into the worlds of film,

TV [network, syndication, domestic and international], recordings, video-discs, pay-TV, audio and video cassettes, books and other publications, and all the other communications systems, existing and emerging.[33]

Within days, Louis was surprised to receive a call from Hamilton Southam, asking him to lunch. Louis was speechless when Southam presented him with a paper expressing concerns about and responses to the marketing needs of the NAC. Louis had brought his own "Stratford" plan and the two exchanged papers. With a great faith in the validity of magically shared visions, Louis came to believe that Lively Arts Management Builders (LAMB) — the name given to the proposed vehicle for recording and circulating arts productions that emerged from these conversations — had been the result of inspiration from above. The emphasis in his discussion shifted from the co-operative model to "an independent service organization with major companies as clients; though it was to be a solid business venture, profit-making was almost ancillary to the good to be achieved by such business."[34] Anderson wanted Louis to head up the enterprise but Louis was reluctant, even though plans for his departure from the OAC were already beginning to take shape.[35] He had already indicated to Robin Phillips that administering another organization was not in his future: "I wish I were about 25 years younger, but at my point in life I decided it wiser to look ahead to writing music rather than setting the world on fire."[36]

There is room for speculation about what might have transpired if Louis had been able to remain associated with LAMB throughout these years. He was certainly the only member of the Board whose close links with television production and with the artistic community would have benefited the enterprise in its initial planning and development phase.

By 1979, an array of prominent Canadians had been gathered to form the LAMB Board. Along with Arthur Gelber from Toronto, Douglas Fullerton, formerly Chairman of the National Capital Commission, and Howard Beck, a leading Ottawa lawyer who had assisted with the incorporation, had joined Louis, Southam, and Anderson. Southam became the President, Anderson the Vice President, and Beck the Secretary. Though Louis had provided the impetus for the corporation, he was still the Executive Director of the OAC and realized that a conflict of interest would be perceived if LAMB began interacting with Council clients. Louis agreed to remain as an investor and advisor. Immediately, LAMB issued preferred shares to raise money for the first two years and set about promoting its first project, the popular Canadian play *Billy Bishop Goes to War*. By seeking venues in the U.S., they hoped to give the play the international reputation it deserved. By October, 1979, Ed Cowan, a former publisher of *Saturday Night* magazine, had been contacted by Arthur Gelber and hired as LAMB's operational head. An office was established in Toronto's Park Plaza Hotel.

There was, however, an inexorable process afoot that was to entrap LAMB and sidetrack its efforts to serve the marketing needs of Canadian arts organizations and artists. The subject of pay-TV had arrived on the public agenda, having been successfully launched in the United States. The CRTC, Canada's regulatory body, had considered providing pay-TV access to the public twice in the 1970s and had held off, preferring to protect the major networks, including the CBC, from audience and advertiser fragmentation. Now commercial interests had added their voices to the public outcry for access. When the CRTC gave in and indicated that they would hold hearings on the feasibility of encouraging pay-TV in Canada, LAMB was faced with a dilemma. The organization's birth had been in response to a marketing need, but Cowan realized that, even if LAMB could develop successful productions, it had no distribution system. A bold notion occurred. What if it was possible to establish a national network totally devoted to the arts? Certainly the struggle to bring cable companies and television networks onside could be avoided if LAMB actually had a license to broadcast Canadian productions and then sell them to other regular or pay-TV channels, both at home and around the world. It seemed too much to hope for, and Louis had no illusions about how difficult it would be to convince the CRTC that LAMB's proposal was reasonable, would appeal to audiences, and would be financially viable.

Before LAMB would be ready to face the CRTC, there were many hurdles to leap. First and foremost, financial resources had to be found to support the concept of an arts channel. Such a channel would be infinitely more expensive than one devoted to old movies, especially at the outset. If LAMB were to commission the National Ballet or the Toronto Symphony to mount a production that would appeal to a television audience, there were bound to be special costs involved in bringing it to the screen. Pay-TV depended to some extent on the willingness of cable companies to carry the network at reasonable cost, and this willingness was rather dependent on whether the cable company itself was allowed to own a pay-TV license. The cable companies, such as Rogers and Maclean Hunter, saw the potential for huge profits in having their own pay-TV licenses, essentially for low-cost movie channels. But once the CRTC closed that window of opportunity, they had little interest in adding the cost of additional channels to their customers' monthly bills. Nor were they interested in making the technological adjustments that might have enabled them to add a few stations at virtually no cost. This lack of co-operation by cable companies meant that the vast majority of customers could not receive pay-TV signals even *after* the licences were finally granted by the CRTC.

In the midst of all this confusion, the CBC proposed to launch a second network, CBC-2, whose purpose was to carry the very kind of quality arts programming that LAMB intended for its audiences. Then there was the overriding question: Would Canadians, who had come to see television as a free service, subscribe to pay-TV channels in sufficient numbers? If so, how long would it take for enthusiastic supporters of the arts to realize that the quality programs LAMB planned to offer would be worth the added expenditure? There were already a host of corporations with deep pockets, ready to make a substantial investment to secure a private channel. Until a subscriber base could be built up, C-Channel would have only the resources of the LAMB supporters — a few individuals with some personal wealth, but with nothing like the capacity to cope with major capital needs, to say nothing of the above-average programming cost. Even more disconcerting was the fact that C-Channel had made commitments to Canadian arts organizations that original productions would be a hallmark of its enterprise. This was in marked contrast to competitors who would be largely importing films from the U.S. It would be a costly business, requiring not only more investors, but also a considerably larger subscriber base. Louis estimated that a movie channel would need only 150,000 subscribers to survive, but C-Channel, with all its commitments to original Canadian production, would need at least 450,000.

Louis thought that LAMB could benefit from working more closely with the CBC and used his long friendship with Bob Sunter — a former colleague at the OAC and now Director of Radio Music at the CBC — to bring this about. He knew that the marketing and distribution of recordings was a source of embarrassment to the Corporation, and put forward a proposal on behalf of LAMB. He thought he had an agreement.

> In a sentence, LAMB can take over the CBC recording and
> distribution activities and potentials, become their vehicle
> for the manufacture and distribution of virtually all their
> recordings and other materials and could become a major
> Canadian record distribution and production company.[37]

This was a grand plan, but it came to nothing in the end. It soon became evident that the CBC was determined to "go it alone" in promoting and distributing its recordings, but much more important, and would not be dissuaded from its plan to secure another basic network, CBC-2. Recordings were not going to be a bridge to CBC/C–Channel

cooperation. The editorial writer for *The Globe and Mail* put it succinctly when commenting about television regulation: "You can't legis-
late the effects of an explosion." In the context of the scramble now
promised by the CRTC's determination to open up the system, circumstances became confrontational and LAMB found itself appearing before
the CRTC in opposition to the CBC-2 proposal. At the hearing, LAMB
indicated that it would be facing unfair competition, and if the CBC
received a license for CBC-2, LAMB would withdraw its proposal.[38]
Fortunately for C-Channel, or in the long run perhaps not so fortunately, the CBC's proposal could not go ahead without the government's
support in the form of a $35 million increase to the Corporation's budg-
et. This increase was not forthcoming. When the CRTC also rejected the
cable company proposals to secure pay-TV licenses, it seemed that there
was some hope for the LAMB initiative. By this time, Louis had left the
OAC, and was absolutely overwhelmed with his work in Ottawa as
Chairman of the Federal Cultural Policy Review Committee (FCPRC).
LAMB might be in the midst of an explosion but Louis was in the midst
of a hurricane. He could scarcely read the flood of letters, memoranda,
and financial sheets that continued to arrive from Ed Cowan's office. In
fact, Louis had little confidence that LAMB would secure a license in
view of the competition from some very powerful interests that were lining up to await the pay-TV hearings.

One thing was sure: if LAMB could provide the channel, the arts
community could certainly provide the programming. The main problem was financing. The money from the original LAMB investors had to
be supplemented by investments from other arts enthusiasts, and finally, the Toronto-Dominion Bank came in with a substantial loan. The up-
front cost would be enormous. Cowan estimated that C–Channel would
need substantial funding in its first year: $8 million for producing new
programs, $2 million for the purchase of existing quality programs, and
a further $2 million for seed money to encourage arts bodies to experi-
ment with television production, as well as to support basic administrative needs and provide a small profit for investors. Success would require
many subscribers, but Louis and his LAMB colleagues believed they
were out there. In April of 1980, after a four-hour meeting with CRTC
officials, Southam could report "that we came away from that hearing
with the feeling that we had been as well received as possible in this highly tentative stage of our planning."[39] John Meisel — the distinguished
professor from Queens University who now chaired the CRTC — was a
strong supporter of the performing arts, and he and his staff were taken
with the idealism of the LAMB group.

By June 1980, Bill Teron, Jim Coutts, and Maurice Strong — all prominent Canadians — had joined the ranks of LAMB investors. At this point Cowan was made President of the company with Southam as Chairman of the Board. Then came more months of delay as the CRTC prepared itself for the formal hearings on the appropriateness of pay-TV in the Canadian context and the technical obstacles that had to be overcome before any of the proposals submitted by the television community could be addressed. The applicants hoped that by May of 1981, the hearings would be completed and decisions made on the proposals, so start-ups could be scheduled for September. This timetable soon proved to be hopelessly optimistic. In the meantime, every delay was costing C-Channel money — money that, for LAMB, was in very short supply. It was not until March 26, 1982, that Cowan could inform the LAMB Board that their patience had been rewarded.

> Congratulations everyone. We have been granted a
> license to operate an English-language specialty program-
> ming service for pay-television. The license is a good one
> and is the cleanest of licenses granted in terms of special
> conditions. But we are not alone.[40]

Indeed, LAMB was not alone. In its enthusiasm for enlarging the horizons of Canadians, the CRTC had opened the gates for several new channels, all of which would be competing for subscribers in a relatively small market. Not only that, but the market was composed of people accustomed to receiving their television entertainment for no cost. Despite these challenges, C–Channel was now licensed to broadcast "7 days a week for 4 hours each evening in prime time [and] to market the service through affiliated retailers, licensed cable operators, and licensed satellites." Louis had now left the Ontario Arts Council, but the question of conflict of interest was still in the air. As Chair of the FCPRC, Louis had been forced to resign from the LAMB Board and his shares had been put in trust.[41] Nevertheless, he continued to assist his LAMB colleagues in areas in which he alone had expertise and experience.

The truly important question hinged on the potential audience for C-Channel. As this was an area of Louis's interest, he read the figures — in his capacity as advisor — with mounting dismay. Little could be gained from U.S. experience where television broadcasting was a commercial operation and the idea of payment for service had wide acceptance. As well, the U.S. market was ten times as large as the Canadian market. There were great expectations. Subscribers could be expected to sign up in droves. After all, there were 5.2 million theatre-goers, 2.1 million orchestra afficionados, 740,000 dance lovers, and 400,000 opera attendees in Canada. Of course these were aggregate figures of total attendance in a single year at all events, and the total of 8.4 million represented several times the number of people who actually attended. When it came down to estimates of individual subscribers, the numbers were more modest — an estimated 95,000 in 1983, rising to 243,800 in 1986, and jumping to 413,400 in 1987.[42] Obviously success depended on holding tight through the first years and awaiting the time when the customer base would provide an adequate cash flow.

With the FCPRC winding down by late 1982, Louis felt he could participate more fully in the C-Channel enterprise. Cowan was hiring a staff capable of completing all the work which needed to be done before the launch in February 1983. In July, Louis was appointed Chairman of the Program Advisory Committee.

Already Board members were afraid the programming plans were placing too much emphasis on blockbuster movies and not enough on arts presentation, and Louis's involvement was expected to restore the balance. A cursory review of the program schedule of C-Channel reveals a richness and variety that speaks to Louis's influence. Cowan had hired Ann Coles to look after the programming and the results bear witness to her competence and hard work. When C-Channel finally became available in February 1983, there was a cultural feast for every subscriber,[43] but there were too few subscribers to carry even a fraction of the mounting costs. Louis found himself being told by his many friends that live arts-dominated pay-TV was "mad" or, at best, an idea that was before its time.

By the time the launch had taken place, Louis's role had expanded. A month before the launch, Gelber had insisted that Louis be put on salary and he signed a Memorandum of Agreement which made him Consultant on a half-time basis for $37,500 a year, with particular responsibility for programming, long-term strategic planning, and seeking out business opportunities. His role was soon increased to include monitoring the operation and "reporting to the President on a day-to-day basis on the fulfillment of C-Channel's programming aims and principles."[44] He would have special responsibility for liaisons with the artistic community — a role that was perfect for him. However, Louis had arrived too late. Many in the artistic community were already upset that C-Channel had not provided immediate access to both new resources and audiences. Lotfi Mansouri, Artistic Director of the COC, was furious because he had given support to the LAMB application for C-Channel and had heard nothing since. The programming continued to improve. For March, C-Channel included in its schedule the Royal Shakespeare Company's *Nicholas Nickleby* — a production of monumental proportions and incomparable quality. Even this was not enough to bring the desperately-needed subscribers in droves.

By May, the programming could be described as sensational and accolades were coming from all sides.[45] There were plans for a 24-hour Charlie Chaplin comedy celebration. Opera lovers could revel in both *La Bohême* and *Samson and Delilah*. Canadian programming included *Ticket to Heaven*, the best Canadian film of 1982, and a program featuring Liona Boyd, one of Canada's most accomplished classical guitarists. But the subscriptions still failed to materialize. At the end of February, C-Channel had reported only 30,882 members, and even a "Survival" campaign later in the spring did not bring substantially more.

Essentially, though, it was the failure of the financial side of C-Channel that ended its short but glorious existence. Efforts to raise the resources from a wider investment community failed. The apparent chaos of the pay-TV environment and the unwillingness of the CRTC to monitor and supervise the process, particularly in relation to forcing the cable operators to carry out their responsibilities in the best interests of the public, discouraged potential investors.

It is somewhat ironic that C-Channel, devoted to the broadcast of Canadian arts, ceased to exist on June 30, 1983 — the night before Canada Day. LAMB had gone into voluntary receivership. The TD Bank called the loan, paid virtually nothing for the shares that were held, but did propose to sell the remaining assets to the highest bidder. The station was acquired by Rogers, but the transaction fell through when the CRTC refused to allow the transfer. As Louis put it, "we all lost a lot of money." He had responded to the call for cash ($5,000) three times, even borrowing from his wife Jan, but Hamilton Southam had lost many times that amount. Louis had only 28,000 shares but Southam had acquired 905,000 shares and even Arthur Gelber, with 77,000, faced a considerable loss.

The failure of C-Channel was one of Canada's most dramatic techno-cultural events of the late 20th century and there were many reasons for it. In spite of the plethora of pay channels licensed by the CRTC, people were only interested in buying movie channels. Most television watchers were confused by the sudden "explosion" of new services and were waiting to see how things sorted out. Within these few months, three other channels also went bankrupt. The uproar around "Playboy" programming reduced the respectability of the entire enterprise. As well, C-Channel's decision to provide only four hours of programming each day seemed to be a disadvantage in selling the product, especially when repeat broadcasts filled some evenings and other pay-channels were offering a full 12 hours. Wide availability of similar motion picture programming, including home video rentals, posed a distinct problem in a highly competitive entertainment market.

The rapid demise of C-Channel surprised Louis, but not Jan.[46] She saw that C-Channel's expenses were rising rapidly as it hired additional staff (nearly 50 in number at the end) but revenues were not keeping pace. Louis was convinced that Arthur Gelber and Hamilton Southam, who had much more to lose, knew what they were doing.

In the end, it was left up to Cowan and Price-Waterhouse to tell the employees it was all over and then to clean up the mess. Cowan's assessment of Louis's role is most laudatory. He "was always there when I needed him, unlike many directors who abandoned the sinking ship as it went down." Louis remained "on board" until the last moment, even trying to make last-minute arrangements with the CBC that might have saved C-Channel. "He was personally decimated by what happened."[47]

Could Louis have saved C-Channel if he had not been occupied with OAC and the FCPRC from late 1979 to late 1982? Louis did not think so. Two reasons shaped his response to the question. Although Louis knew more about television than all the other members of the Board combined, he could not have overcome the massive under-capitalization for such an enterprise. The leap into a full-scale national pay-TV service, with all LAMB's commitments to the arts community, meant a "sea-change" in terms of financial resources. Secondly, the CRTC would not force cable operators — who showed little interest in accommodating the technical and financial needs of pay-TV licensees — to carry out their public responsibilities. With all his experience and management skills, even Louis could not have overcome these challenges.

But he never lost interest in the possibility of an arts channel and, in 1993, when the CRTC was once again calling for applications for broadcast licenses, Louis intervened with characteristic frankness with a letter to the then Minister of Heritage about the behaviour of his own agencies

> May I again draw your attention to the anomalous situation briefly mentioned when we met last week. It concerns a display of arrogance and silliness that is hard to believe, let alone condone.
>
> In the context of the CRTC call for applications for new cable channels some four ventures have applied for licenses for "culture channels." As someone closely

involved with the late [and lamented] "C-Channel" I heartily applaud the prospect; we desperately need such a channel now. Canadian audiences, performers and creators need that outlet, given the failure of the CBC to adequately fulfil the needs of the arts sector.

What is preposterous and probably self-defeating, is that two agencies within your ministry, the National Arts Centre and the CBC have each filed for such a channel, describing similar goals, expecting the same audience to respond to their programming concepts. Each agency, in competition with the other, is spending considerable amounts of money and executive effort in wooing needy and hungry arts companies all across Canada, in preparing their own promotional materials and selling their own views.

This foolish and unnecessary duel must cease. The misguided self-interest being flaunted by both agencies could well jeopardize this unique opportunity, one unlikely to be repeated for decades. The two agencies must merge their ambitions and plans into a single effort. The CRTC must hear a clear and strong voice enunciating a comprehensive vision, one that the CRTC dare not refuse. Otherwise, this divisive struggle could lead the CRTC to respond with "a plague on both your houses" and give the license to someone else.[48]

Louis was proven to be absolutely correct. Neither the CBC nor the NAC application was successful.

The Minister of Heritage was not the only government representative to benefit from Louis's wisdom and experience. On October 1978, several members of the federal Conservative Party, led by MP David MacDonald, had come to see Louis and several OAC colleagues about federal cultural policy.[49] MacDonald could not have known that a year later, as a Minister of the Crown, he would be seeking out the man he met that night, who had impressed him with his knowledge and insight. As the new Secretary of State, MacDonald invited Louis to head up a cultural policy review. This offer was made at just the right time. Reuben Baetz had replaced Robert Welch as Minister of Culture and Recreation and Louis was witness to the development of a whole new dynamic in Ministry-OAC relations that he did not wish to address. Most of all, he was aching to get back to his role as a composer. MacDonald offered an opportunity to perform a short-term service to artists and the Canadian people that would allow Louis, after a few months, to return to his first love, making music. It was a proposal that was too difficult to resist, and Louis's days as the OAC's Executive Director came to an end. Louis's expectation of a short-term commitment and a return to "composing and other ventures" is revealed in his letter of resignation to Arthur Gelber.

> This is to inform you and your colleagues on the Council that I will be terminating my work as Executive Director of the Ontario Arts Council. I have agreed to serve, on a part-time basis, as chairman of a new Advisory Committee on Cultural Affairs being established this week by the Secretary of State. I hope, in this way, to find time for composing and for other ventures.[50]

In his speech to the January 1980 meeting of the Council, Louis was emotionally stirred and members of the Council were overcome.

> Since this is my last Council meeting I want to be able to say not only farewell but all good luck, good wishes and good deliberations in the future …..I just want to be able to say 'thank-you' very much for allowing me to have nine years of such thrilling, all-encompassing involvement ….[51]

A new challenge had arrived and Louis was ready, but he could look back over the previous nine years with considerable satisfaction. According to Ezra Schabas, Louis's intense commitment to the economic and psychological well-being of artists, and his devotion to promoting Canadian art, were driving forces during his leadership at the OAC.[52] Another focus of Louis's leadership had been education. He had established what became known as the TKO Committee (the name being taken from T.H.B. Symons's report on Canadian Studies in Canada's universities, "To Know Ourselves"). Symons himself was a member of the Council and conversations with him gave Louis an opportunity to stress the importance of the arts as an essential way of "knowing ourselves" as Canadians. Sonia Keorner was appointed to lead the Committee, and Louis knew exactly what he hoped would happen. He wanted to "mainline the arts," particularly in Ontario's post-secondary institutions, by encouraging "the exploration by non-artists of the meaning of the arts; the integration of the essence of music or painting into the process of learning in non-arts faculties …. We were looking for ways to make it possible for universities to experiment along these lines."[53]

The TKO Committee did make a number of grants to universities in hopes that the concept of integration would take off. Although a number of exciting projects were initiated, the idea did not capture the interest of the university community as Louis had expected, because of the conservative nature of the institutions. However, the OAC's commitment to the integration of the arts and the traditional forms of learning, as well as to Canada's future, had been established. Symons himself has made the point that, even if Louis's leadership were to be judged solely on this initiative, he would still have to be seen as one of Canada's significant mid-century nation-builders.[54]

Others who were close at hand during this time add their praise to Symons'. Paul Schafer,[55] James Norcop[56] and Ron Evans stress the enormous intelligence he brought to the job. Ron Evans was impressed by the extent to which Louis worked from a basis of reason in all his work, in contrast to the tendency of creative artists to be emotionally motivated.[57] Charlotte Holmes[58] and Naomi Lightbourn[59] believed that his scrupulous honesty gave him an advantage on the slippery slopes of political decision-making. Louis's ability to manage conflicting responsibilities was never seriously questioned.[60] Both Holmes and Lightbourn saw his integrity as the saving grace for the effectiveness of the Council.

Along with Louis's enthusiasm about the role an arts council could play came a healthy suspicion of what all government ministries and agencies could impose on the fragile and economically threatened artist. Whenever the desire of Council to intervene, direct, control, manipulate, develop, or design became too strong, Louis would emphasize the "responsive" nature of the process and advise his staff, Council members, and ministerial colleagues of the dangers that awaited bureaucratically influenced and publicly dictated artistic values. On his return from Russia Louis had stated: "To me the whole situation is unhealthy. A true artist must be a leader, not a follower as the Russian composer has become … with little chance to assert his individuality." This comment stemmed partly from a visit to the Russian Ballet, where Louis had found the music to be "pure drivel."[61] He was determined that no such interference should be ventured by any art council or ministry with which he was to be associated.

The Arts Council years saw Louis in his most collegial role. Many projects were initiated by other officers, with Louis's encouragement and support. He never took personal credit for a collegial effort. And there were many successes. One can look in vain for any jurisdiction that experienced a comparable flowering of its culture in such a short time. There was an expansion of artistic endeavour, audience response, and private support across an enormous jurisdiction as never before or since. There were many reasons for this, but one is surely Louis's tireless work at the OAC. He encouraged individual artists to create and have pride in their creations, and he influenced the way millions of dollars were directed to both artists and arts organizations. Louis put his stamp on an institution and challenged every succeeding Executive Director and every staff member to maintain his ideals, even through the periods of disinterested and penurious treatment that would follow the golden decade of the 1970s and challenge even Louis's faith in the positive influence of government on people's lives.

Chapter Sixteen

A Cultural Policy for a Nation

I n the 1970s Canada belonged to Trudeau's Liberals. This was a decade of reaching out to people with needs and disabilities; to people who had arrived from other lands; to the people of Quebec, with hopes for greater social and economic opportunity; and to seniors who felt that they no longer had a place in a society devoted to youth. It was also an era of spending. The national debt continued to rise, and, each year, there was a troubling deficit in the national accounts. The Province of Quebec's demands for greater control over its affairs had dominated these years, but "la belle province" had not been assuaged and the rest of the country had become tired of federal accommodation to the demands.

As the decade progressed, people sensed that the economy had gone seriously wrong — inexplicably, there was both high inflation and bloated unemployment. Not only was Quebec dissatisfied, but the western provinces, particularly Alberta, were convinced that their economic hopes were being hampered by the Liberal determination to assure a supply of cheap energy for Ontario and Quebec. As well, the nation had become impatient with Trudeau's obsession with constitutional reform, including the repatriation and amendment of the British North America Act. In the 1979 election, the Liberal defeat did not surprise any serious observer. Trudeau, who had been the object of such adulation in the late 1960s, had now become unpopular. His perceived arrogance, his lack of concern for real suffering, even the bizarre elements of his personal life — all were grist for the mill of electoral defeat. The prospect of Conservative leadership by the virtually unknown Joe Clark excited neither Clark's allies or his enemies. However, the vitriolic fury of Canadians at the Liberal Government's lack of action in the face of economic turmoil made a change of government inevitable.

Like everyone else, the arts organizations had suffered in the economic climate leading up to the election. Theatres, music and dance organizations, museums, and art galleries had all seen their budgets devastated by inflationary pressures that, from 1975 to 1978, totalled 35%. Arnold Edinborough, now heading a newly formed "Business and the Arts" organization, wrote a column in the *Financial Post* as early as 1976 under the headline "Now Time for a New Royal Commission in the Arts." Edinborough foresaw that serious structural problems would emerge if financial pressures continued to mount. In addition, he saw problems with the overlapping of authority between a host of cultural agencies; a lack of training opportunities in a number of fields; and a shortfall in exports that that was occurring despite the high-quality work produced by Canadian artists. Most important in the short term, however, was the problem of financial difficulties.

> Such an enquiry might also serve to curb that chauvinis-
> tic spirit that has become apparent in some sectors of the
> arts, and to guide us toward a new and fuller appreciation
> of our true national identity which can best be formulat-
> ed and expressed by devoted, dedicated, debt-free artists
> and performers.[1]

Nearly three decades earlier, the Massey-Lévesque Commission had found a vacuum in the area of cultural policy and a dearth of artistic activity. Now it seemed that a veritable forest of federal agencies had joined the CBC and the NFB, and dozens of choirs, orchestras, dance companies, galleries, and museums — many of which had emerged in the centennial year — all needed some public support to survive. A new cultural review would also have to give definition and order to the cultural infrastructure as well as provide a vision for the future.

By 1978, another complication had arrived. A group of artists had cre-
ated a full-scale lobby with active participants from across the land. Calling itself "The 1812 Committee," this group chose a name that linked the arts-funding crisis with a previous threat to Canadian survival, the War of 1812. Now the battleground was Canadian culture. Trudeau, at the Juno Awards celebrations the following year, acknowledged that the arts were "big busi-
ness," but added, "We realize that they also express their own soul, their own feelings, their own interior strengths. But they also sing the song of Canada — they sing from the heart of Canada. And for this reason they deserve our support."[2] Even with the last-ditch support engendered by rhetoric like this, it was too late to rescue the Liberals. Within weeks of Trudeau's speech, more than a decade of Liberal domination came to an end. Still, the Conservatives had not gained a majority, and this fact played a major role in Louis's future.

Although cultural matters had played a small part in the 1979 campaign, there was a crisis to be faced in this area, and Clark chose one of his most experienced followers as Secretary of State — David MacDonald from PEI. Not partisan in his expression of political views, MacDonald was nonetheless left of centre — a stance that gathered respect from Red Tories, progressive Liberals, and even the members of the NDP. Louis had spent most of the 1970s working with the Conservative Government, which had created the Ontario Arts Council and increased its support during his tenure as Executive Director. When MacDonald called on him for help, Louis had no reservations.

In an article entitled "Will MacDonald Do It All for Our Arts?" Toronto arts critic Gina Mallet expressed the expectation that the new minister would bring hope to an arts community battered by a decade of financial woes. She quoted MacDonald: "We are very much committed to expanding the arts ... our sense of objectives relates to our intellectual health ... [ ] inundated with the largest amount of foreign cultural material of any country and my commitment is to getting maximum exposure in all media for both Canadian artists and Canadian audiences."[3] MacDonald had prepared himself well for his role as Secretary of State. In the late 1970s MacDonald had been the member of Joe Clark's shadow cabinet responsible for "all things cultural." He had toured Canada with other members of the caucus and met with representatives of arts organizations and cultural industries as well as those engaged in funding artistic activities. He had responded as an Opposition member to the 1812 Committee's demands for help by suggesting a 100% tax write-off for investment in film, and tax incentives for investment in Canadian publishing and sound recording. One of his exploratory, fact-finding trips had been to Toronto, to see Louis Applebaum and his colleagues at the OAC, and it was clear to Louis that he and MacDonald were very much on the same wave length in matters of arts funding and support. When Conservative electoral victory came in 1979, MacDonald knew exactly what he wanted to do. First, he accepted the Secretary of State role and, as well, the Ministry of Communications. Together, these gave him control over the entire cultural field. Secondly, he revealed his seriousness by accepting two strong deputy ministers, Pierre Juneau and Bernard Ostry, even though they were closely associated with the defeated Liberals. Finally, he was determined to have the cultural life of Canada examined, and to do it in such a way that government legislation and financial support could be justified — through a Joint Committee of the Senate and the House of Commons.[4]

Now MacDonald had to find someone to chair a small working group that would prepare a "blue paper" on cultural policy for the consideration of this Committee. This review of the nation's cultural health would consider every aspect and every institution involved. The Chair would need unquestioned credentials, would have to be comfortable in the many fields the study would encompass, and would have to win the confidence of MPs and Senators from all parties. T.H.B. Symons, the founding President of Trent University and a respected contributor to national policy, looked like just the man to initiate a review of federal cultural policies, particularly in view of the large number of federal agencies whose roles and functions were coming under fire. Symons declined, since he was already overloaded with work and was serving on several federal agencies that would be under scrutiny in such a review. However, he did agree to become a Committee member and suggested another a candidate for the Chair: Louis Applebaum at the Ontario Arts Council. MacDonald agreed and the invitation went out. For Louis, the timing was perfect. He was ready to move on, and he welcomed the prospect of a short-term, part-time role at the federal level, especially one that would provide some income while he shifted his energy to writing music.

MacDonald wanted the Advisory Committee on Cultural Policy to be small, and Louis hoped it would remain so. He was delighted to hear of Tom Symon's interest in serving on the Committee; in the process of working together they had become firm friends.[5] Louis also knew that Juneau saw the Advisory Committee as very much an in-house operation, tied closely to the Ministry.[6] He therefore thought it wise to have the Assistant Undersecretary, Leo Dorais, on the Committee, as there would be times when Juneau's other duties would call him away. Another Committee member was Albert Breton — a respected economist and a member of the faculty of the University of Toronto — a former adviser to Trudeau and someone whom Louis would come to trust implicitly.[7] It was a high-powered quintet: two distinguished civil servants, two highly respected academics who were thoroughly familiar with the workings of government, and a Chair whose experience in the cultural life of Canada was unequalled.

However, the fantasy of a small advisory committee that could act quickly and efficiently soon evaporated and the politics of representation took over. Louis dreaded both the enlargement, and, at that level, the tendency to make political appointments. However, the additions proved to be distinguished ones. They included: Joy Cohnstaedt, Director of the Manitoba Arts Council; Alex Colville, a noted Maritime realist painter; John Dayton, an architect; Shirley Gibson, a noted poet; Denis Heroux, a filmmaker; Elizabeth Lane, a former President of the Canadian Conference of the Arts; and Guy Robert, a respected writer from Quebec.[8] The Committee had grown to include 15 members and, with later additions, would become even larger — much larger than Louis had ever wanted. By December, all the members of the Parliamentary Joint Committee (which the Advisory Committee would be "advising") would be in place.[9] In the meantime, the Advisory Committee commenced its work, beginning with the goal of creating a global context for its work. Louis contacted Paul Schafer, the country's major scholar in the field of international culture.

A second goal of the Committee was to make the government aware of the economic impact of arts activities. It took only a few weeks for Louis to realize what a treasure he had in Albert Breton and, even though Breton was a member of the Committee, he was commissioned to present a paper on the topic.[10] Parliamentarians need economic justifications and Louis set out to ensure that they would have the best advice at their fingertips. The Committee seemed to be off to a good start, but something was about to happen that Louis never expected.

On the morning of December 12, 1979, David MacDonald turned up at the second meeting of the Advisory Committee with an ominous warning: his Conservative Government was in danger of being defeated in the House of Commons that night on a vote of confidence on the budget. Such a development would place the entire process of developing a cultural policy in jeopardy.[11] For Louis this was a disaster. If the Conservatives lost the confidence motion, there would be another election and, even though the production of the "blue paper" setting out the directions of the review could go on apace, the entire project might be either aborted or distorted beyond recognition.

In spite of the Minister's announcement, the Advisory Committee used the December Meeting to "get on with it." Already, in Louis's mind, the main theme of the "blue paper" was emerging. There is a handwritten note, almost unintelligible, on his copy of the agenda of that meeting — a personal reminder that he must "find a way of establishing attitudes, to establish 'creation,' ... to provide products and systems as yet unimaginable."[12] This theme came to dominate both Louis's thinking and the final document. By the December meeting, the Committee had also determined what the "blue paper" would not include. Science and technology were "pervasive and unavoidable," but its examination would distort the inquiry. Sports, though accepted as an important aspect of culture, was receiving sufficient attention already, as was the daily press. Education was a peculiar problem. Educational responsibility was a provincial matter, and yet every area that would be studied by this federal committee would have an educational extension. In the interests of expediency, these extensions would have to be set aside for now. Louis, whose concerns about arts education had dominated his thinking since the 1960s, was disappointed, but he recognized that it would only lead to confusion and ultimate disaster if education became a specific topic of concern for the committee and led to an increase in federal-provincial tension.[13]

As David MacDonald had feared, the Conservative government fell in the very midst of the Committee's December meeting. In a miscalculation that stunned the nation, Joe Clark had ended one of the shortest administrations in the country's history. He had not believed that the other parties would vote him out of office after only a few months. The electorate had wanted to give the Liberals a message and that had been done. Now they were prepared to judge the Conservatives on their short tenure. The Conservatives had promised to "fix" the economy, but they had shown no more talent for solving its mysteries than had the Liberals. Interest rates had gone up four times in the few months since the Conservatives had taken office. As well, Clark quickly realized that his Government would have to back down on its promise to reduce the tax load on Canada's citizens. These and other policy misadventures had made the Conservatives highly vulnerable.

However, it was the budget that the Treasurer, the Hon. John Crosbie, brought down before the House of Commons in mid-December that provided the opportunity for the NDP to unite with the Liberals behind a motion of non-confidence. Although the Liberals had seemed leaderless in the wake of Trudeau's November post-1979 election resignation, the party believed that Trudeau could and would come back and would win once more. They were right.

The election campaign of January and February 1980 certainly did not turn on cultural considerations, though there were indications that Canadians were more aware than ever before that the economy was not the sole issue on the hustings. In "Politicians are Wooing the Arts," an article by Sol Littman published in the *Toronto Star* on the day before the election, Littman observed:

> This is possibly the first election campaign in Canadian history in which political leaders of parties are wooing the people who go to symphony concerts, the ballet, the theatre .... In recent years, however, federal, provincial and municipal politicians have been unable to ignore the rapid growth of interest in the arts"[14]

Littman went on to analyze the reasons for this new interest and to give early warning signals.

> When recently completed government surveys reveal attendance at concerts, museums, art galleries, plays, and

> dance recitals growing faster than television viewing,
> movie attendance, newspaper readership, and magazine
> circulation, politicians are bound to pay attention ... but
> this new recognition of votes to be gained by wooing those
> interests carries with it not only the possibility of increased
> funding but also the threat of increased interference.[15]

After many years of working with both the Canada Council and the Ontario Arts Council, Louis fully appreciated that warning and he ensured that the "arm's-length" principle of arts funding found its way into the final report of the Federal Cultural Policy Review Committee, which was to carry on the work of the Advisory Committee under the new Liberal regime.

Louis and his Committee colleagues had been committed to a particular advisory process and assumed that David MacDonald, who had appointed them and whose vision they found attractive, would be the Minister. On February 18, when the new Liberal Government took its place and the make-up of the Cabinet was announced, Louis did not know Francis Fox, the new Secretary of State. He feared that things might unravel quickly.

Just ten days after the election, Juneau, Dorais, Breton, Symons, and Louis met over lunch. In an *aide-mémoire* composed just hours after the event, Louis outlined the discussion that had taken place. It was agreed that everything had changed and that it was time to take a look at what the Advisory Committee had learned in the three months of its existence. Assuming that the process was still "on," "the time had come for a re-examination of the operations of the work of the Advisory Committee, perhaps to re-focus and regroup, ... overcome the sense of bafflement, and to achieve better understanding of role and process"[16] Leaving behind the political maelstrom, Louis opined that "public expectations are high, the attention is on the Committee and misunderstanding of its present role is widespread." Indeed, "there is a growing feeling that the original plan for a comprehensive Review is unworkable: it is too large to encompass within the time frame available even if that were stretched somewhat."[17] It was an accurate analysis, but the process was too far advanced to profoundly shift its focus and procedures.

This inner group — Applebaum, Symons, Breton, Juneau, and Dorais — decided they needed a Steering Committee, perhaps to be called the "Chairman's Committee," made up of themselves with the possible addition of Guy Robert. If the Review was to continue, it would have to assume an executive function. It was obvious that a "writer," really a director of research, needed to be appointed immediately. The first step in reaching the public would be to go to "leading thinkers" for their opinions. (Northop Frye was the first choice on all sides.) There was general consensus that the idea of a "Joint Parliamentary Committee with a mandate to deal with all areas of culture within 12 months or so, is probably unworkable; the issues are far too complex, if the job were not done well, the public disappointment would be severe."[18] Louis and his colleagues were aware of the pitfalls that would face a Joint Parliamentary Committee but, ironically, did not yet know that these would be precisely the obstacles that they themselves would face as they moved in subsequent months from being an Advisory Committee to a Joint Parliamentary Committee, to a Cultural Policy Review Committee that would produce a Report with recommendations for Parliament and the Secretary of State. The members of the new Chairman's Committee had watched a particularly vitriolic election campaign and had even come to the conclusion that "the forum of the Joint Parliamentary Committee would be used for partisan bickering and struggling" and were quite prepared to advise the Minister that it would not work as a forum for examining the nation's arts and culture.

On March 3, the "Chairman's Committee" met once again. The attitude of Francis Fox to this Review was still undetermined. The Committee decided "the Minister should be advised to take a 'cool', globally integrative approach to the review" and that it might take about three years to put together a White Paper on Federal Cultural Policy "which is what the public really expects."[19] Now they thought it wise to form a group of lay panels of "personalities" — Northrop Frye was mentioned again as a possibility — and hoped that the Minister himself might agree to chair one of them. Thus, the Advisory Committee would "assume the guiding and assessing role for the whole process ... and the Minister would have assumed responsibility for the Review Process in his own way, putting his stamp on it." The special Joint Parliamentary Committee could be abandoned and the Minister could consider alternatives, including a group of Task Forces. There was a realization that "the pressure for quick results had militated against organizing a proper Review process that included orderly planning, discussion and 'thoughtful' examination through a well-operated synthesizing mechanism."[20] This "pressure for quick results" affected every stage of the process, even when the advisory role to a Joint Parliamentary Committee stage was abandoned.

By the spring of 1980 it was essential that the role of the Advisory Committee be clarified. Louis encouraged his Committee to send a Memorandum to Francis Fox asking some very basic questions. By this time, there had been eight meetings of the Advisory Committee, and it "had reviewed the plans and programs of the Federal Departments and Agencies." Monographs had been commissioned on "various aspects of the arts and culture." The first question on everyone's mind was: "Does the Minister intend to review the membership of the Advisory Committee?"[21] This matter had to be resolved. Was the Committee now to have a more politically friendly membership? Would it be restructured to represent specific interests? The new Minister had announced at the Juno Award celebrations at the O'Keefe Centre in Toronto that he was appointing Sam Sniderman — the popular and loquacious "Sam the Record Man" — to the Committee to represent the recording industry. Louis was outraged. He had feared a flood of Liberal Party advocates, but did he also have to cope with a Committee made up of individuals who saw their roles as opportunities to "flog" for specific cultural industry interests? Sniderman was an old and valued friend from elementary and high school days, but the implications of such appointments were horrendous in the light of this review process.[22] Instead of receiving an answer to their question, the Committee was merely told that the Minister would announce additional appointments. This aroused Louis's greatest fear — a large, politically-oriented Committee articulating only narrow personal and professional interests rather than a broad vision of the cultural scene that the Massey-Lévesque Commission had modeled so many years before.

In the light of subsequent events, the most important issue brought before the Minister concerned the future of the CBC and NFB. The Committee asked him whether he favoured both these institutions contracting out more production to the private sector. The Minister replied that "both agencies ... are putting out more formerly 'in-house' production in private hands" and that the Government's position was that of "continuing consultation" on the matter. In Louis's view, this left the field open for the Committee to formulate specific recommendations. As it turned out, this issue would become the dominant battleground during the preparation of the final Report.

The Minister had publicly promised help to arts organizations and the Committee questioned whether, in fact, the review was necessary at all. Francis Fox's reply simply reminded the Committee that the government's response to crises could not come to a standstill while everyone waited for a report still some years from completion, and that "a long view was necessary." Finally the Committee sought the opinion of the Minister on "whether deficit reduction programs for arts organizations will encourage mismanagement."[23] The reply came back that these deficits had come, not as a result of mismanagement, but from spiraling costs spurred by the economic situation. This generous response left open an opportunity for the Committee to argue in favour of more resources for the Canada Council — a funding agency whose budget had been frozen for some five years.

There was a bizarre element to the whole interchange between the Advisory Committee and the Secretary of State. The Minister's Deputy, Pierre Juneau, the man responsible for the reply of the Secretary of State, was sitting on the Advisory Committee and taking an active part in its activities. Nevertheless, the Minister had confirmed that the review was to go forward and, on a number of issues, had indicated a positive attitude towards the arts. This formalized in writing the perceptions the members had received from Juneau and was now a basis for the Committee's confidence in the next phase of the proceedings.

At this time, Louis's chairmanship came into question. He had been appointed by a Conservative Government, and now the Liberals were in power. It soon became apparent that Francis Fox was willing to accept Louis's presence, but wanted a co-chair, possibly a woman, and certainly a prominent figure — someone who came from Quebec. The Minister selected Jacques Hébert, a distinguished publisher and author. Hébert was a close personal associate of the Prime Minister and a passionate man who, as Founder and President of Katimavik and Canada World Youth, had made a great contribution. There was no question of Hébert's qualifications, but his partisanship and the effect this would have on the integrity of the process bothered Louis. Fox held his ground: Louis could remain as Chair, but Hébert would be Co-chair. This had enormous implications for the future. From this point forward, Louis would be sharing the leadership with a man who had the ear of the PM and who could use his considerable political connections to advance his own ideas and position. The final Report of the FCPRC was to be called the Applebaum-Hébert Report, or perhaps even the "Applebert" Report. Louis's considered opinion many years later was "I should have resigned at that point."[24] However, he did not resign. Partly, this was due to his commitment to the cause of a cultural policy that would rescue beleaguered arts organizations and artists. Louis also realized the enormous impact of the Massey-Lévesque Report that had led to the creation of the Canada Council and a host of other changes to the cultural life of the country. As well, he had established a close relationship with a number of the Committee members, some new acquaintances like Albert Breton, but others who were old friends like Tom Symons and Joy Cohnstaedt. Although the Advisory Committee was still in place during the winter and spring of 1980, and would remain so until the Minister made the formal announcement of its demise and the birth of a new body (the Federal Cultural Policy Review Committee) in August 1980, there was the problem of maintaining both energy and integrity for the duration. Louis's presence or absence would make a crucial difference, so he stayed.

While the Advisory Committee waited for the official announcement of its demise, there was much to do. The arts community had to be assured that the review process was still "on." Both Louis and Juneau set about the task of reducing the frustrations of all who contacted the Committee.

However, when the full Advisory Committee met in March 1980, it was informed that "the Secretary of State does not necessarily regard the establishment of a Joint Parliamentary Committee as the appropriate mechanism for conducting the cultural policy review."[25]

Louis kept up the morale of the Committee (and his own) by assuring the members that, during the interregnum, research would go on and discussions of the major issues would continue. Louis himself devoted special attention to keeping in touch with the deputy cultural ministers in the provinces. This was not an easy task, since the country was preoccupied with the separation referendum launched by Quebec Premier René Lévesque, and all provincial and federal politicians had this crisis on their minds. Louis also used this time to establish a close association with John Hobday, the National Director of the Canadian Conference of the Arts — a body that was preparing a major document. "A Strategy for Culture" was being prepared, in part, as a presentation to the Committee, but its main role was as a clarion call to all those who cared about the arts and the problems they faced.

The "business as usual" stance that Louis took can be gauged by the fact that at the Review Committee's fifth meeting in April, a "Draft Summary of a Broadcast Review" (no identifiable author) was introduced for Committee consideration. As the issue of broadcasting was at the top of the Secretary of State's agenda at that moment, moving ahead was paramount. Louis and his Committee members were unaware that broadcasting would soon become the *cause célèbre* and that recommendations regarding the CBC would dominate the public reaction to the entire review process. The paper set out the challenge succinctly but dramatically:

> Broadcasting is the greatest disseminator of culture the world has ever seen ... the Canadian broadcasting system has reached the worst crisis of the past fifty years. It is over-Americanized and under-Canadianized. ... Canadian television is no longer Canadian. We are swamped with imports, largely American. Two-thirds of all available English television is foreign...74% of viewing time of English-speaking Canadians is spent watching foreign programs ....[26]

By the spring of 1980, concern mounted about the cultural review. The problems facing the arts had not disappeared in the midst of either the election confusion or the Minister's indecision and delay. The arts community, which just two years before had established the 1812 Committee, remained militant and John Hobday had made use of this spontaneous expression of anger and frustration to galvanize the Canadian Conference of the Arts. This pressure had made it possible for MacDonald to move quickly, and the same pressure now forced the hand of the new Minister, Francis Fox. Hobday, who had contacted Louis as soon as he became Chair of the Committee, was offering the assistance of the CCA and promises of cooperation, even to the extent of organizing any hearings that might seem helpful. However, Louis felt that the official review had to be done at arm's length from any perceived interest group that might be seen to benefit from the Committee's recommendations and their implementation. He was, however, not beyond using Hobday as a lever to achieve an arm's-length distance from the Undersecretary of State, Pierre Juneau, the man originally responsible for the review process and whose connections with the ruling party were strong and varied. In a memorandum to Juneau, Louis set out the CCA's expectations (which were to be presented at the annual meeting of the conference — a meeting at which Francis Fox had agreed to speak, but from which he had to withdraw in order to engage in the referendum battle in Quebec).

> I had a talk with John Hobday. It seems the CCA resolution (or several) is being prepared re: the Review process. It will ask that the Committee/Commission (whatever will be carrying out the review) should be seen to be "independent" of the department, that the present structure does not have credibility in the eyes of the "community." It will ask: that the Review be provided with adequate resources and a good secretariat, again "independent" of the Department; that there be systematic consultations with the arts community and the public. It would ask that the "Commission's" final report be completed by the end of 1981 and that the report be made public.[27]

A week earlier Fox had responded on the floor of the House of Commons to a question posed by MP Mark Rose: "Can the Minister tell the House whether that Committee [the Advisory Committee on Cultural Policy] is still active?" Fox replied that indeed the Committee was active but it was "not in a position to present its Report." He added to his response the fact that he had changed his mind about the review. "I intend to encourage the Committee to hold public meetings throughout the country."[28]

A week later Rose questioned the Hon. Francis Fox on the reasons for his absence from the annual meeting of the Canadian Conference of the Arts. Fox replied sharply that he had been involved in the referendum campaign and "the future of the country is at stake and if there is to be a conference of the arts next year, there will have to be a country." Rose asked a supplementary question. "Can he tell the House whether he intends to follow the commitment of the previous government and follow the Applebaum preliminary Blue Paper with a parliamentary committee?" Rose received no answer.[29]

By this time, the Committee was being assured that public hearings would occur and that the Blue Paper was being transformed into a questionnaire format that the Chairman's Committee realized "must be based on a solid, accepted framework including all key issues." An Action Plan was developed that might assist the Minister to "issue a clear statement about what the public might expect" and form a basis for the Advisory Committee's advice to the Minister on "appropriate and relevant items." [30]

It was really no surprise when, at the end of August 1980, the Minister finally announced the formation of the Federal Cultural Policy Review Committee — not just a renaming of the Advisory Committee on Cultural Policy, but a designation that signified a major change. The Committee would now be responsible for reaching out to the public and for making specific recommendations to the Government and the representatives of the people. However, Louis had initially bought into a part-time advisory committee process. Now this was to become a full-scale policy formation exercise that would take at least two or three years. The job would involve extensive consultation, both in public hearings and private conversations, a large staff which would have to be managed, and possibly a different kind of Committee with a membership more acceptable to a Liberal minister. The issue of Committee membership bothered Louis constantly. He had wanted a small committee of experts, but now there would be even more pressure to make it more representative of regions and of specific arts disciplines. Once again, under the guise of a populist approach, the possibility of political appointments would be opened up — appointments that might dramatically diminish the quality of the Committee and create a forum for endless wrangling between competing interests. This concern, at least, would prove to be unfounded. Indeed, an announcement from the Minister advised both Parliament and public that the Advisory Committee roster would remain in place. (Surprisingly, both Pierre Juneau and Leo Dorais were still included.) The FCPRC now had a Co-Chair, Jacques Hébert, and more important, a new function – that of meeting the people of Canada through hearings in 18 different cities in the spring of 1981. The Committee had already made progress on the production of a Discussion Guide, "Speaking of Our Culture," which would provide a format for the cross-country discussion that would take place in a few months. The Guide was rushed into publication by January 1981 and thousands of copies went out to arts organizations and were made available to every citizen who requested a copy. [31]

As the hearings approached, Louis found himself carrying an enormous public relations burden. He was hearing criticism on all sides. He was told there was total apathy on the one hand, and on the other, an intense interest fuelled by a massive distrust of the Liberal Government. That party had failed to rescue the arts community in the late 1970s and was now back in power with a minister who seemed little committed or involved and who was simply carrying forward a process initiated by his predecessor. John Hobday, pressing hard on behalf of his Conference of the Arts, told Louis quite directly that "nobody trusts the Secretary of State." As long as the review was seen as part of that Ministry's responsibility (and with Juneau and Dorais still ensconced as Committee members there was ample evidence that this was the case), there was little hope for any effective outcome in either the long or the short term. Hobday's advice was, as Lister Sinclair (President of the CCA) had put it, the arts community "doesn't like the Committee ... it should be scrapped and an independent review launched." However, Louis soldiered on, determined to bring something out of the maelstrom. His hope rested with the hearings. If there was sufficient national interest, and lively debate about the issues received both press and media attention, no minister could ignore the Committee. In fact, the Committee itself would be spurred on to greater efforts to write a report that gave support to the arts and encouraged federal leadership in solving its many problems. Louis encouraged Rogers Cable to give full coverage to the hearings, to increase public awareness and ensure there would be a complete visual record available to the Committee. Meanwhile, another crisis had been simmering and had finally erupted. One of the immediate tasks identified by the "Chairman's Committee" early in 1980 had been to procure a "writer," really a research director. Tom Symons had spoken highly of Ralph Heintzman, and he had been brought on board the following summer. Heintzman immediately found himself caught up in the chaos the Committee was facing. He began to pull together the research that needed to be done to bring about a substantive paper, "blue" or "white" as it might be, but soon found that everyone's energy and attention was being poured into creating a Discussion Guide for the upcoming hearings. When hired by Pierre Juneau, Heintzman had been assured that he would have an adequate staff and budget to carry out the research activity, and that he himself would have full authority to hire that staff. Moreover, he had insisted on an arm's-length status with the ministry (which already had a staff of researchers in place). In spite of the formal hiring arrangements, he would be an employee of the FCPRC answering to the Chair. By the fall of 1980,

Heintzman was complaining bitterly that none of his initial agreements with Juneau were being honoured — he had no adequate budget and the Executive Committee (the "Chairman's Committee"), under the influence of Juneau, had obstructed his plans to hire a staff. Furthermore, the Committee was holding *in camera* meetings, creating a distance between the Committee and the FCPRC staff. It was Heintzman's perception that all his expectations were being frustrated by Pierre Juneau, who, as Undersecretary of State, was really in charge. He believed that Juneau was reluctant to have outside eyes observing the internal affairs of his jurisdiction, and that this was the basic reason for the difficulties he was enduring. By the fall of 1980, after only a few months on the job, Heintzman had already resigned, but had withdrawn his resignation on assurances that all would be well eventually. The Committee authorized a budget and he was able to assemble a staff. He found, however, that outside research was being commissioned by the Committee and, on the occasion of a dispute with an Executive Committee member, he resigned once again. In spite of the latter incident, his resignation had really come about as a result of Juneau's unwillingness to carry out his original agreement, a reluctance that, in Heintzman's view, was frustrating the whole research effort.[32]

At this point Heintzman sent a formal letter of resignation to Louis as Chairman, which was ultimately accepted. However, there was a basic strategy issue behind the resignation that was never resolved. The prospect of the hearings was delaying substantive policy discussion by the members of the Committee. Such discussions had failed to take place before the hearings, and afterwards, would be seriously constrained by the rush to consolidate the results and deliver a final report. Heintzman had not been replaced, and many of the research papers that might have provided ample evidence to support the recommendations of the FCPRC would never be commissioned and completed.

With Heintzman's resignation, his work was transferred to Louis and his closest colleagues, Tom Symons and Albert Breton. Other Committee members had to take on specific tasks that needed attention, and a whole phalanx of staff members had to be assembled to organize the cross-country hearings. In the end, the hearings and the submitted briefs, along with the personal experiences of the Committee members, loomed large as the main sources of information that steered the Committee's deliberations leading to the final report. The loss of Heintzman and that balance of research meant that Louis had few levers with which to moderate the particular prejudices of individual members when it came to assembling the recommendations. This situation put special pressure on Louis to restore the balance he was seeking to achieve, at great personal cost.[33]

The public hearings of the FCPRC took place between April and June 1981. There were actually 56 presentation days and nearly all Committee members tried to get to every hearing, although, on occasion, in larger centres, the overwhelming number of sponsors of briefs demanded the formation of two panels. It was an exhausting but exhilarating experience that Louis never forgot.[34] He had an opportunity to meet people in Montreal, Ottawa, and Toronto, where the major federal institutions — the CBC, the NFB, the National Library, and the National Museums of Canada — as well as representatives of all the major arts institutions — the Canadian Opera Company, the National Ballet, the Toronto Symphony Orchestra, Stratford, and Shaw — all appeared before the Committee. Even more important was the opportunity to meet thousands of Canadian citizens who had a profound concern for the health of the arts that Louis, in the midst of all the havoc surrounding the review process, could never have predicted.

The original deadline for the submission of briefs had been February 9, 1981, but a postal strike and the appeals of artists and arts organizations for more time led to an extension to March 9. Louis had been staggered by the response. "By the week of the postal deadline, briefs were arriving from every part of the country at an average rate of about 100 a day."[35] The Committee had been able to schedule 521 presentations in the 18 centres. These hearings, along with all the travelling, had consumed three months of the Committee's time and came to dominate the life of the FCPRC, to the detriment of research and discussion by the Committee members themselves. David Ellis, who was to be the coordinator of the final report believes that, in spite of the importance of listening to artists and supporters of the arts, "the hearings diverted the process" and that, in fact, the Committee had found it a "tempting diversion" from the tough task of debating differences and finding agreement. The loss of discussion time was a serious blow to the work of the Committee, especially when there was pressure to have records of both the hearings and the submitted briefs published so the final report of the Committee could be the hands of the government within just a few months.[36] The whole situation gives poignancy to Louis's assertion that "in the winter of 1980, when the issue of my chairmanship arose, I should have resigned." Louis chaired nearly all the meetings, although he did ask Tom Symons to replace him in northern communities where the briefs would contain issues concerning native people and their particular cultural challenges. For Albert Breton, the hearings and, even more, the late-evening informal discussions with artists and arts administrators were a revelation. He credits Louis with opening up "a whole new world .... I was guided by someone who knew what the arts were about and who loved them so much and who communicated his love so well. I have not been the same since. I would now defend the arts to my death."[37] Symons watched one Committee member, Sam Sniderman, leave behind his initial role as an advocate of his own commercial interests to become a thoughtful, concerned Canadian, deeply troubled about the state of his nation.[38] Sniderman himself felt that these hearings represented the essence of the Committee's work.[39] Joy Cohnstaedt, with all her experience as the director of a provincial arts council, was still "amazed at the determination of artists to be heard."[40] Mary Pratt had a distinguished reputation as a visual artist but recounted to Louis the extent to which she felt she had been hidden away in Newfoundland and how the experience of meeting so many people had changed her artistic vision. Now she wanted to paint people and the splendid figures that emerged from her brush in the 1990s reveal that influence.[41] Even the very sophisticated Jean-Louis Roux came to describe the process as both "moving " and "energizing." He had never visited the Northwest Territories and the Yukon before and suddenly his vision of Canada enlarged exponentially.[42] Louis was completely at home in every locale and he met old friends at every meeting. He was with his favourite people — the artists he had championed for four decades. Roux felt he gave "marvelous" leadership to the entire process. "It was amazing that an administrator could care so deeply about artists."[43]

To a large extent, the hearings emphasized the complex problems the arts community was facing at the end of the lean 1970s. In Saskatoon there was the advice to the Committee "that the immediate need is to establish a clear national policy for the support and development of visual and performing arts in this country" and there were detailed recommendations on how this support should be forthcoming:

(a) all three levels must participate
(b) funding should be over the life of the project and to the same degree as the initial grants
(c) the multicultural composition must be seen as an incredible opportunity [44]

In the smaller communities, there was the fear that support for the arts was becoming concentrated in the large cities and the warning that "the policy should not be structured so that three or four cultural meccas are created."[45] Louis found that one topic surfaced at virtually every hearing and it was one that the Committee had decided could not be part of its agenda — arts education. In spite of the Discussion Guide's exclusion of "formal education" as a topic for debate, it came up both in submitted briefs and in open discussion at the end of each session. As Chair, Louis had the option of closing off discussion, or allowing it to continue, with the record of the proceedings then being available to the provincial ministries of education. He chose the latter course. In the Ottawa meeting, an arts organization, "All About Us," stressed the importance of "encouraging creativity in young people from 6 to 18 years old" and proposed "that a Young Canadians Creative Centre be set up."[46] Also in Ottawa, the Board of Education Instrumental Music Association presented a brief that comprehensively outlined the value of the arts — a value that is understood by few even today, as school boards across the country divert resources from arts education to buy more computers and provide more courses in science, mathematics, and technology. Music, the document stated, "develops co-ordination in auditory awareness; can be used to teach almost everything; gives each child a chance to achieve and reach his own level; and provides relaxation."[47] The Association asked "the federal government to support and enrich music education in the schools." At the Quebec City hearing a month later, there was a populist plea that "all art galleries be available without charge."[48] Louis responded positively. He had become deeply concerned about how the rising costs were forcing up admission prices at institutions housing Canada's artistic treasures.[49]

Louis's friend Vincent Tovell, then involved with the CBC's coverage of the FCPRC's hearings, had the opportunity to watch Louis chair many of the meetings and was enormously impressed by Louis's warmth, his patience, and his sensitivity. With consummate diplomacy, Louis could allay the fury of disappointed artists and angry citizens. He would even recognize individuals who had made great contributions to the cultural life of the nation sitting in the audience — and never in a perfunctory way. For example, when he saw that Norman Mackenzie had appeared in Vancouver, he knew he had before him a former university president and a man who had given much of his life to his country. Louis left his chair on the platform and walked down the aisle to greet him.[50] This gesture left both FCPRC members and the audience at the hearing with the realization that there were great Canadians who had contributed much, and who deserved to be honoured. In his own way, Louis was making an important cultural statement. The characteristic that both Committee members and presenters admired most was Louis's infinite patience as Chairman of the hearings. Mary Pratt speaks of the contrast in Toronto, where it was necessary to set up two panels in order to hear all the briefs. The hearing chaired by Jacques Hébert was over before suppertime, but Louis's hearing went on until 10 o'clock at night.[51] Louis refused to see these interactions as "hearings" … they were conversations between artists and Committee members and Louis insisted on seeing that every presenter had not only been "heard," but also understood and appreciated. It made each session long and demanding for all, but Louis was determined that, by the end, artists and the public at large would be satisfied that they had indeed been "heard."

The hearings also forced Louis to recognize that his Review was in some trouble. No "glue" was emerging that would bring unity or consensus to the deliberations of the Committee. After the Ottawa hearing he wrote in his personal journal:

> The need to pull it all together is more difficult than ever — the committee is big and diffuse and the issues are, too. Maybe in time we can find the connections and sift out the big issues. The briefs were important — need careful study for what they are saying and <u>do not say</u>. So we mustn't depend on verbal exchanges only. Also, if we can get the information out (ex., TV etc. & better press), it may give clients a sense of what others have said about their issues.[52]

There was one aspect of Louis experience at the hearings he could not have anticipated. It was expressed in a letter to Ian Morrison, Director of the Canadian Association of Adult Education:

> In the public hearings which this committee conducted last summer, we heard from all corners of Canada an almost palpable desire, almost a demand with a voice, for participation in the cultural future of Canada, for a place in the decision-making processes. People wanted to be able to reach out, to exchange views with their neighbours in all other regions. It occurred to me that the needs today, as expressed during the public hearings, could be paralleled with needs of 30 to 40 years ago.
>
> These days are quite different from the earlier period, and the trappings of our lives are quite different. Our potential for communication is infinitely more sophisticated and, in fact, we are on the edge of a period when two-way video exchanges will be commonplace. At the same time our urbanized "information" society seems to generate in individuals a sense of isolation, of uninvolvement, of being a passive receiver of messages, especially via TV. This is now developing a pressure for change, just as the conditions that prevailed in the 1940s demanded action. We need, once again, to give the people of Canada a sense of being part of their governing system, to give them a role to

play in our cultural development, an opportunity to be engrossed in, not alienated from, the qualities that will shape our country. Many now argue that our future is more likely to be shaped by cultural considerations than economic or political ones.[53]

The Canadian Association for Adult Education was an organization with deep concerns about national cultural agencies. In another comment to Ian Morrison, Louis identified what was to become the most characteristic element of Canada's political scene – the fragmentation of the nation.

As I have listened to people who have become before our Committee in all parts of Canada, particularly beyond the Montreal, Toronto, Ottawa triangle, I have heard a common theme: people are feeling disconnected from their country; their sense of belonging is fragile and they don't consider that those in authority are listening to them, or even care what they think. My sense is that this is a widespread new phenomenon, and decision-makers are oblivious to the strength of this sentiment.[54]

Louis had known and experienced the impact of the informal conspiracy of people, from myriad of organizations, who had enabled Canada to survive a Depression, win a war, and create a post-war nation of decent pensions, unemployment insurance, and universal health care. This was why Canada drew Louis back after his flirtation with prosperity and fame in the U.S. during the 1950s. The hearings convinced Louis that this society was gone. Now television and a shift in values towards personal ambition and individual wellbeing had eroded the "social capital" on which the old Canada had been based. The hearings had "charged up" and changed members of the Committee, but they had also saddened its Chairman. However, Louis came to believe in the creative spirit of Canadians and its capacity to solve society's problems, and he was determine to highlight this confidence in human creativity in the final report of his Committee.

Chapter Seventeen

The Report:
Achievement and Disappointment

When Louis accepted the Chairmanship of the Advisory Committee on Cultural Policy, he and Jan had left their Toronto townhouse near the corner of Bayview Avenue and York Mills Road — a bright spacious home that had served Louis well during his Ontario Arts Council years. There had been adequate room for a studio for Jan and a place for Louis to work as well. It had been a happy arrangement: it was convenient to OAC's offices at Bloor and Avenue Road and, just as important, close to the synagogue they attended — and close to a playground and outdoor pool to which Louis could take grandson Jordan when he came to them on the weekends.

They moved to Ottawa without trepidation; they knew the city well and had many friends there from NFB days. With no expectation that it would be a permanent move, they chose to rent a downtown apartment just steps away from the Committee's offices. As Louis's role on the Committee had begun as a part-time task, they kept a little *pied-à-terre* on Balliol Street in Toronto, not far from the various CBC properties that ranged across the city south of Bloor Street. Louis had every intention of devoting more of his time to musical composition, and the Corporation was the likeliest client. As well, he expected that the LAMB enterprise would take up any remaining hours he had in his week. Having launched the idea, he wanted to be both a partner and an expert consultant. These expectations were effectively destroyed by the policy review. For a few months in 1979, when the Advisory Committee was in place under a Conservative Government, things went according to plan. Still, Louis found that he had to spend more time in Ottawa than he had expected, mainly meeting people and taking the measure of the job. Then, in January and early February of 1980, the review was essentially put on hold until it was determined whether there would be a new Government and/or a new Secretary of

State. This period of indecision was followed by a complete change in the review process under the Hon. Francis Fox, and Louis and Jan frequently travelled back and forth from Toronto to Ottawa.

When things finally fell into place, the clarification of Louis's role and the enlarged mandate for the Committee — now the Federal Cultural Policy Review Committee — ended any hope that Louis could be in Toronto very often for the next two years. It was a difficult time for Jan, and Louis worried about her constantly. Her painting had thrived in those years when OAC responsibilities had kept Louis in Toronto most of the time, even though the spring and summer meant inevitable pilgrimages to Stratford while Louis consulted on his music for one Festival play at least. Louis had been busy at the CBC, but he could handle much of his work at home during the evenings and weekends, when he was not off at some OAC affair or appearing at a performance or gallery opening. During the Committee hearings, though, Jan was left alone most of the time, sometimes in Toronto and sometimes in Ottawa. Louis recognized that the peripatetic life was not one that she cherished, particularly when her own work in her studio was left undone.

With the hearings over, the summer and fall of 1981 were occupied with developing a summary of the presentations the Committee had heard, and analyzing briefs provided by individuals and groups who had not been involved in the hearings, or whose briefs had arrived too late to be heard. There were predictable themes, but now, the concerns of unhappy artists and angry citizens had a sharp edge of crisis about them that the Committee hoped would secure the Government's attention.[1] This was certainly Louis's hope. He was determined that the summary would bring the many hardships borne by the artistic community to the attention of the Secretary of State and his ministerial colleagues before the full report of the Committee was presented. In listening to stories told at the hearings, Louis had faced the disillusioning experience of discovering that his decades-long advocacy had failed to make much difference. For example, Louis was understandably pained to hear that, as the brief of the Canadian League of Composers put it, "it is possible that the creators of music are only slightly better off [in 1981] than they were in 1951."[2] All that voluntary effort by Louis and his colleagues had apparently produced only minimal improvement.

Again and again, the subject of arts education arose, and the Committee included these observations in the summary as a signal that something had to be done, obviously at the provincial level, but possibly by the local boards of education as well. Louis's colleagues from the Canadian League of Composers put that case most convincingly:

Ways must be found to introduce more Canadian music, new or existing, into schools for performance and more studies of Canadian musical life. Although education is primarily a provincial responsibility, the Government of Canada must do something to redress this shocking situation that exists in respect to the ignorance of Canadian composers and their music in the schools.[3]

The advice that the federal government should "do something" about the schools was proffered by a plethora of organizations whose representatives addressed the Committee. The Canadian Music Centre, another of Louis's enthusiasms, made several recommendations regarding music education. One of these suggested "commissioning missing-link works from Canadian composers in areas where none or few are available for school children to perform [and] conducting workshops with Canadian composers and school supervisors and teachers."[4] These initiatives were outside the jurisdiction of the federal government, but their presence in the document satisfied Louis's hopes that the Review process would bring to light major problems that those in provincial or local jurisdictions might be animated to solve.

There were even recommendations in some briefs that involved the nature of an art form itself. Louis had always been critical of "grand opera" in the Canadian context of a small population with limited resources for the arts. Michael Bawtree warmed Louis's heart with the recommendation that "although we should not exclude totally all Canadian activity in the field of opera, we should concentrate our efforts on developing an art form which, though not opera, ... has thematic content which says something to us in this country.[5] Even the Canadian Opera Company, dedicated to the performance of the traditional standard repertoire, told the Committee "of its desire to establish opera as a native Canadian art form, an expression of the Canadian people."[6]

Louis had for many years taken a view expressed by the League of Composers: "If the composer is denied access to recording, he surely does not exist, just as he would not have existed had he not been in print in the 19th century." Louis could report — through the expressions of industry representatives contained in the summary — that "the cultural importance of the Canadian recording industry had not been adequately recognized, with frustrating consequences for all the elements in the musical life of the country."[7] For Louis, who had tried and failed during the 1960s to secure a commitment to recordings by any level of government, it was *déjà vu*. For the Government and the public, the summary provided arguments for intervention in the unexplored territory of the recording industry. Indeed, the summary gave a picture of the intricacies of an industry whose nature was almost unknown, in spite of the attention it received in the market-place. Fortunately, the Committee had, in Sam Sniderman, an expert adviser. The summary revealed, through the eyes of both artists and recording company executives, opportunities that the country had forgone in its lack of interest in this particular cultural industry — unfortunately made up of branch-plant extensions of American corporations of little interest to the government.[8]

The "Summary of briefs and hearings" publication was greeted with general approval and appreciation by a discouraged artistic community who, having now been heard, were impatient and anxious to see the FCPRC recommendations, and infinitely more important, the government's response. This placed even more pressure on Louis and his colleagues to bring forth a full report with recommendations as quickly as possible — in weeks or months, rather than years. Part of the success of the hearings, and of the document that summarized their proceedings, had come as a result of the efforts of John Hobday who had, by the end of 1980, produced the Canadian Conference of the Art's own "Strategy for Culture."[9] Louis had kept in close touch with Hobday and welcomed the pressure that the CCA had mounted. He had been thankful for the steps the CCA took to ensure that the Committee received many briefs and requests to appear, and that the hearings were well attended.

The hearings and the subsequent publishing of the summary had highlighted the major stumbling block faced by the FCPRC in establishing its integrity as an independent inquiry — the presence on the Committee roster of the Undersecretary of State, Pierre Juneau, and his departmental colleague Leo Dorais. These two had remained in place even after the Advisory Committee — originally devised as an "inside body" to help provide an agenda for a Joint Parliamentary Committee — had been succeeded by a completely new body, the FCPRC. For several months the position of the FCPRC was in severe jeopardy as the presence of Juneau and Dorais aroused criticism from the entire artistic community. Along with the uproar surrounding Ralph Heintzman's resignation, the pressure of preparation for hearings, the hearings themselves, and the frenzied efforts to complete the summary had conspired to push this issue to the back of Louis's mind. However, once it became clear that the names of FCPRC members would be published in the summary, Louis knew the matter had to be resolved.[10] He had to secure the resignation of both men — not an easy task in view of the fact that the entire review process had been the initiative of Juneau as Undersecretary to a previous Minister. Louis wrote himself an *aide-*

mémoire after meeting with Juneau on October 21, 1981. Under a heading "Re: Signing the Hearings Report," Louis recorded that, in his conversation, he had discovered "that Mr. Juneau wants to sign the Report." However, Louis had secured Juneau's agreement that both he and Dorais would leave when the summary report was released. The issue was now whether the Minister would agree to a plan to "integrate the announcement of the withdrawal of Juneau and Dorais [with the tabling of] the 'Summary of briefs and hearings' in the House of Commons."[11] At the October 29th meeting of the Planning Committee of the FCPRC, the issue of the method of passing on the summary to the Minister and the House of Commons came up and Louis had to report that there had been no resolution of that question. "The Committee discussed the possible withdrawal of Mssrs. Juneau and Dorais and examined both the way in which it might be announced and the possible reactions on the part of the cultural community." Pursuing the question was left, as was proper, to Louis, but it was plain that there was unanimous agreement that the FCPRC's position would be untenable if the signatures of Juneau and Dorais were attached to a subsequent report containing the Committee's arguments and recommendations to the Minister and the House of Commons. At the same meeting, the Committee planned a dinner to which the Minister would be invited — obviously a farewell occasion involving the attendance of the full Committee "in honour of the two deputies."[12]

At the full FCPRC meeting in November, Louis was able to report that "Pierre Juneau and Leo Dorais have decided to resign." In a handwritten note with Louis's copy of the Agenda, obviously directed to members of the Committee, Louis gave a complete statement.

> The decision was a most difficult one. As the deliberations of the Committee continued during the public hearings phase it became more and more evident that fundamental changes in many aspects of Canada's cultural life were being requested by the public, many of which will be reflected in the committee's recommendations.
>
> The final recommendations will be presented to the minister in 1982(?). Following that time, both Juneau and Dorais, in their senior capacities in the dep't of communications will be called upon to advise the minister on the recommendations and have therefore determined that they would leave the committee prior to the formation of the committee's recommendations.[13]

The long wait was over. Juneau and Dorais would sign the "Summary of briefs and hearings" and then immediately resign. Now the Committee members could develop the recommendations from what they had heard from the hearings, from the briefs, and from their own discussions and their own life experience without the oppressive presence of the very department heads whose actions or lack of action were being criticized.

However, irony won out. Within a short time, Juneau moved from his Undersecretary role to a position as President and CEO of the CBC — the very agency that was to receive the most critical attention of the Committee. As members of the FCPRC were to learn when the final report was released, they had not heard the last of Pierre Juneau.

In the midst of all this drama and besieged with tasks for the FCPRC, Louis was spending virtually all his time in Ottawa now. The pressure to have the final report of the FCPRC out before the end of 1982 was unrelenting, in part because of the demands of the arts community. Just before the release of the summary, the Canadian Conference of the Arts published another volume, "More Strategy for Culture." The preface to this document made it clear that, although things were happening at Secretariat of State — the Arts and Culture Branch had been transferred to the Department of Communications, for example — there had been no addressing of the major issues. At the forefront of these were the problems faced by the CBC at a time when plans for new private networks and stations were being announced almost daily. There was a clarion call for response: "We are convinced this is a time for action, that we have debated our problems long enough and should now start to solve them."[14]

By 1982, the Government itself was becoming quite concerned about the complexities of broadcasting and the CRTC's continuing delays in resolving issues about its role in the midst of technological innovations that were about to transform the entire broadcasting environment. Joined with this concern was a need to address the Pay-TV expectations — a matter that affected Louis's personal interests in the LAMB operation, which had tendered its application for C-Channel just a year before.

The writing of the report in just a few months, while discussion of the recommendations continued at every meeting of the FCPRC, was an incredible feat of creativity and energy. There had been pressure from the beginning to write a report that would examine all the federal departments and agencies involved in cultural activity, and how they might respond to the expectations of the arts community for a new vision of the arts and increased federal financial support. Now, after the hearings, the size of the Committee began to take its toll as members struggled to resolve the conflicts between these two groups. Amidst the frenzy of consideration and composition, many members of the Committee concluded that they could best help by representing the cultural area or discipline they knew the most about. Inevitably, the quality of the "big picture" discussion eroded. There was little that Louis could do to restrain the understandable predisposition of individual Committee members to solve the problems one by one, with a separate resolution for each.[15] There were occasions when members of the Committee felt that time pressures were depriving them of the opportunity to criticize. Jean-Louis Roux, for example, felt that he had been taken advantage of when the perception of film production as private enterprise was allowed to diminish the role of the venerable NFB.[16] As it turned out, the NFB was outraged by the recommendation that it should withdraw from production and become a training institute. A major part of the revolt against the final report of the FCPRC was organized by the NFB, hand in hand with CBC advocates. Louis was less disappointed about the NFB than he came to be about the CBC recommendation; he believed the NFB had already become the major Canadian training facility for film-makers and that it should be proud of the role it had played for half a century.[17]

Ultimately, there were 101 recommendations — a fact that baffled most observers and left the Committee open to ridicule by the media, who saw confused priorities and a lack of research support. Tom Symons, an invaluable source of strength for Louis from the outset, realized that he could best provide assistance in two areas — Heritage and International Cultural Relations — and Louis welcomed his willingness to oversee the writing of those chapters. Albert Breton, as well as focussing on the practical fiscal and financial implications of proposals, concerned himself with the broad understandings that were essential if the recommendations were to make any sense. It was Breton who insisted that there should be a unifying theme that would give intellectual meaning and force to the report. He had convinced Louis that the justification for increased arts funding should not be based on the argument that the nation would automatically benefit from its presence in any unique way — that there would be more jobs or an increase in economic well-being. The reason for this was that pumping money into many other activities would have precisely the same beneficial effects on society — sports being an obvious alternative object for public investment. Breton convinced Louis that the theme that had carried Louis throughout his life — the central importance of human creativity — should be the overriding justification for the Committee's recommendations.[18]

Louis took his advice, and thus creativity became the theme of the report. Every recommendation was expected to pass the test of explaining how this characteristic was enhanced in a particular area of Canada's culture and could be strengthened and assured by federal action.

For the report to be concluded within the time allowed by the Secretary of State, it was necessary for different individuals on the Committee to take responsibility for much of the writing and editing in chapters that concerned their areas of personal expertise. For example, Jean-Louis Roux, an experienced actor and director, was given the task of bringing the chapter on the performing arts into focus. Sam Sniderman was assigned the section on sound recording, but things did not go smoothly. Sniderman was adamant that recommendations concerning the recording industry could not be completed by the deadline. He was aware that there was a deep chasm between his views and Louis's on how best to support the industry. Louis, from his own experience, thought that distribution was the problem. Sniderman wanted to ensure that recording artists — both popular and serious — would receive as much government support as could be made available. In the end, an altercation took place. Sniderman was convinced that industry would not be pleased with the recommendations that were going forward, but Louis felt that there was no time for further discussion. To Louis's demand that "It must be finished!" came Sniderman's "It can't be done!" Louis had the final word: "I'll have to finish it myself." As Louis wrote those pages for the report, he was well aware that his expert in the field was not "on board." Yet Sniderman's respect for Louis did not allow him to openly indicate his disappointment through any "Minority Comment" when the final report was tabled.[19]

Even without the Sniderman episode, Louis himself would have to write much of the report, although he would do so with the help of senior writers, consultants, and editors who had been gathered to complete the job. One contributor stands out — a man who had been a staff member with the Committee from the beginning. Frank Milligan worked tirelessly and his extraordinary ability and commitment made an enormous difference to the report, both in the quality of the prose and the timing of the release. Throughout the final stages of writing, it was Louis who never lost sight of the "big picture." At a time when governments were adopting a policy of intervention in the name of accountability, and were simultaneously withdrawing financial support in the name of fiscal responsibility, Louis felt some things had to be said loudly and clearly. He was determined that the government's support for the Canada Council should be reinforced and the Council's budget increased. More than any other institution, the Canada Council had been at the centre of the cultural explosion that had taken place in the past three decades. At this point the Ministry of Culture had not yet been established, but Louis had become aware of rumours of a Ministry that would effectively co-opt the role of the Canada Council, and he felt that it must be stopped. However, the FCPRC's support for the Canada Council came with serious expectations about change and future commitment. The federal government was advised that it should "regard the Canada Council as a primary instrument of support to the arts" and that the Council should "initiate a program of incentive grants related to the presentation of new Canadian works in the performing arts." Even the rather amorphous role of the Council toward educational activities was redefined in a direct and specific recommendation that the Council "should continue to be a source of federal funding to the National Theatre School of Canada and the National Ballet School."[20]

The strong recommendations of the FCPRC advised the Government to increase the budget of the Canada Council and rejected the mechanism of a Ministry of Culture. Their position was based on what the Committee had heard during the hearings, and had the unanimous support of the Committee members. Although these recommendations received little attention when the Report was first made public, they had a valuable impact on the development of public policy in the long run. The 1980s could have been a ripe time for a diminution of the Canada Council. Margaret Thatcher's United Kingdom and Ronald Reagan's America were to fracture and trivialize both the Arts Council of Great Britain and the National Endowment for the Arts in Washington, D.C. This was an unforgiving decade in Canada that saw two major federal advisory bodies disappear without a trace — the Science Council of Canada and the Economic Council of Canada. Despite all its crises and financial restraints, Canada Council Directors Tim Porteous and Joyce Zemans, along with Chairs Mavor Moore and Maureen Forrester, had the support of Report recommendations that celebrated the presence of the Council. From that base, they fought to maintain the Council's status and integrity in its role as the nation's essential arts funding body.

Over the decades, Louis had fought a tireless battle to save arm's-length funding for the arts, and this principle was recognized and emphasized in the Report. It was to become an issue that led to a heroic resignation on the part of Tim Porteous when he felt the principle was being violated. The Report validated arm's-length funding, unpolluted by political favouritism, as a special necessity if the freedom of artistic expression was to be retained. The Report came to support the public funding policies, not only of the Canada Council, but of provincial and municipal arts councils as well.

It was the plight of the CBC that engaged the Committee most intensely, and it was the CBC recommendations that caused a barrage of criticism when the Final Report was released in November 1982. This was to be expected. The recommended changes were dramatic. Most debated was Recommendation 67: "With the exception of its news operations, the CBC should relinquish all television production activities and facilities in favour of acquiring its television program materials from independent producers."[21] The Committee could not have discovered a more effective way to outrage the entire Corporation and all its supporters.

Recommendation 67 occasioned a red-flag controversy from coast to coast. The annual federal contribution to the Corporation was over $700 million — more than was granted to all the other federal cultural agencies combined. The CBC was the one agency to which every Canadian was connected daily, by either radio or television. As well, the country was situated next to a nation in which private interests provided nearly all the television programming, and seemed to do it very well indeed. The fact that the development of the recommendations began in the midst of the referendum campaign in Quebec, and continued in its wake, posed special difficulties. The referendum was a direct challenge to Canada's unity. What should be the role of the CBC under such circumstances? Should it report on the Quebec situation in a completely dispassionate way? If so, how could the Corporation justify its approach in light of a mandate which was interpreted by many people as an obligation to support national unity?

Finally, the CBC, like all broadcasters, was caught up in a maelstrom of technological change. Some of these changes would threaten the very validity of the CBC's continuance as a public service, particularly in the context of a growing opposition to taxpayer funding for public agencies whose responsibilities could be fulfilled by the private sector. As early as August 1981, while the "Summary of briefs and hearings" report had still been in preparation, Louis had set out his views in a two-page document called "Notes on a TV Broadcasting Policy." While Louis conjured with the Corporation's future, members of one of several unions withdrew their services at the CBC. Intriguingly, one of the points at issue was the CBC's insistence on its rights to use independent producers and other freelance personnel. The union response was that the CBC was moving into an overall policy of eliminating staff employees in order to use freelance technicians — a course of action, in the union's view,

that would turn the Corporation into a mere distributor of outside programming rather than a producer of its own material. Thus, one major
CBC issue was already on the public's mind, even before the Committee
began to consider its recommendations. Louis's "Notes" set out the background for the Committee's consideration in the midst of this union-
management confrontation. There was no preamble indicating the
essential role the CBC played as the major influence on Canada's capacity to survive as a nation. The Committee members had listened to the
CBC, as well its opponents, at the hearings and needed no further
nationalistic rhetoric. Louis took the same attitude toward the CBC that
he was encouraging the Committee to adopt toward all the other federal agencies — a "coolness" to self-justification and a focus on the objective the Committee wished to achieve, one which he articulated succinctly: "We want to preserve, develop, and increase our unique, independent, multi-faceted cultural life (character) and broadcasting is a vital
element in achieving that goal." Louis reminded the Committee that the
"present operational conditions are breaking down very quickly, with
numbers of outlets and choices multiplying for the whole country." The
expectation of access to hundreds of channels and the inability to
restrain access to imported programming had to be faced. Louis's solution was not tied to institutional territoriality but rather to the idea of
making "it possible for Canadian creative talent to manufacture programs that are attractive enough to win Canadian audiences" and "win
audiences away from U.S 'blockbuster' programming," as well as "function in world markets." However, that strategy was "limited" and "in
addition must be supplemented [by encouraging] smaller, more dis-
cretely-aimed productions." Louis was anxious that "experimentation
and the development of new ideas and talent must be maintained [and]
technological developments must be made available to those able to use
them ... the training of future broadcast creators and operators must be
built into the system." Broadcast policy, Louis wrote, must be aimed at
"promoting program production of excellence; the people to make the
programs, and their acceptance at all levels." These were to be the criteria that any broadcasting policy must measured by and it is noteworthy
that the CBC, its internal institutional troubles, and its perceived or real
inadequacies were not even mentioned in Louis's "Notes."[22]

Early in the new year, Louis met over lunch with CBC President, Al
Johnson. Johnson began by making the point that "the CBC is the most
efficient public broadcasting system in the world," as proven in a recently completed management study the Corporation had commissioned. In
spite of a 50% cost increase to the Corporation, "all 'incremental' pro-

duction within the CBC would now go to private producers."[23] Addressing the total picture, Johnson predicted that there would not be such a proliferation of channels as had been predicted. Programming would be very expensive and, of course, audiences would be fragmented. As a result, television networks would be unable to bring to advertisers the critical mass of potential customers that would make their commercial advocacy through this medium advantageous. Johnson was quite aware that private producers were anxious to see the CBC "getting out of production," but questioned how many of them could succeed in a broadcast industry with such a small population base to serve. Louis never stopped searching for ways to understand the CBC dilemma. As late as April 14, Louis met with the strongest supporters of the CBC in the country — the Canadian Broadcast League — the very body that had fought the successful battle for a national public broadcasting system in the 1930s. His journal entry records his disillusionment: "Graham Spry and the Broadcast League were rather pathetic — 4 Senior Citizens — Spry hadn't even read the brief. Best they could do was plead for saving the system but could offer no help in doing it."[24]

Louis was now encountering the arguments that would be mounted when the CBC recommendations were made public in the final FCPRC Report. It was, however Jacques Hébert's "Notes on the CBC," distributed to the Committee members in April 1982, that signaled the fact that the broadcasting issue would override all other aspects of the Report.

Hébert's role as Co-Chair of the FCPRC was central. He not only appeared to speak for the government but, particularly after Juneau and Dorais left the Committee's ranks, he seemed to command the socio-political arguments that would move the government to act. Louis, though far from being naïve politically, tended to make the arguments he thought were intrinsically valid — arguments that supported artists and celebrated the country's cultural expression.[25] Hébert remained focussed on institutional legitimacy, conceding the importance of the role the CBC had played in "contributing to the spread of culture [and] promoting Canadian artists." He added further that, "In the area of information and public affairs, the CBC has consistently been the leader." However, he warned his FCPRC colleagues that even the parliamentary committee to which the CBC reported was "ill-equipped to exercise effective control over the Corporation's complex operations."[26] He then reminded his colleagues that, even in 1981, the CBC was down to 29% of the English-speaking television audience and 34% of the French-speaking. By 1990, he predicted, these already very small percentages would be even smaller and Canadians would no doubt wonder if the government would be justified under these circumstances in spending perhaps a billion dollars to serve such a tiny share of the audience. Hébert argued that the CBC "must offer a different type of service" as its only hope; that "there are things the private stations in Canada now do and could do better without competition from the CBC." This would demand a new mandate, freeing the Corporation from its "obligation to be all things to all people" and could provide Canada with an improved public affairs and news service. He advised that the CBC should get out of commercial advertising entirely — and that became the basis for a FCPRC recommendation to that effect in the final Report. Hébert argued that the CBC broadcast day should be restricted to only 5% of programming produced in foreign countries. Finally, he demanded that the CBC phase out its in-house programming and depend on private producers.

> Today, the abundance of independent producers throughout the country makes in-house production unnecessary and actually detrimental to the well-being of the private production houses, which could develop in a more normal fashion if they were able to count on the CBC as a client.[27]

Hébert went on to say that the entire purpose of the proposal "would be seriously undermined if the CBC continued to produce even 10% of its programming." From this Hébert paper came the infamous Recommendation 67 — "that the CBC should relinquish all television production activities and facilities in favour of acquiring its television program materials from independent producers."[28] Hébert predicted, with considerable prescience, that "In today's climate of austerity ... a climate that will probably continue for some time to come," there would be a reduction of financial support from the government. In that prediction, Hébert proved to be absolutely right. He and Louis were also aware that Canada in 1981 was a different land than the one the Massey-Lévesque Commission had addressed. There was now a bevy of private producers who, with public subsidy, were quite confident they could supply the film and video products that would fill the needs of the CBC.

By August of 1982, Pierre Juneau had been appointed the new President of the CBC and was hearing rumours that his former colleagues on the FCPRC were considering major structural changes in his recently acquired place of employment. Juneau met with Louis and expressed himself with disarming candour. In an *aide-mémoire*, Louis recorded Juneau's warning:

He feels that the CBC should assign more production
outside but that recommendations that they get out of
production or other structurally motivated moves
would generate all the defences that are natural within
the CBC and would divert CBC energy, government
energy, and public attention from the real problems. ...
He would fight such moves with every fibre and had let
it be known when he took the job that he had no intention of spending five years in such a fight. He wants to
move ahead and not spend all his energy on a fight of
that kind.[29]

Jacques Hébert played a paramount role in developing the CBC recommendations of the FCPRC, although there were others on the
Committee who shared his distaste for the institution.[30] The FCPRC's
considerations were going on in the midst of the separatist referendum
campaign and Hébert, as a loyal Liberal, had been much involved on the
side of continued unity. His perception (although, to be fair, it was not
just his) was that the French-speaking CBC community in Montreal,
and particularly in outlying areas of the Province of Quebec, had not
only exhibited separatist tendencies themselves, but also had used their
positions in the CBC structure to assist their separatist friends. Although
the anti-separatist forces had won the day, the vote had been too close,
with the federalist cause gaining a healthy, though not overwhelming,
59% of the referendum voters. René Lévesque, Quebec's premier, had
had to accept the defeat but promised there would be another opportunity in the future.

Hébert was determined that the CBC should be suitably diminished in
the affairs of the nation, and a healthy cut in its budget, a more restrained
mandate, and a substantial reduction in its number of employees would
accomplish that mission. The issue was highly charged. Joy Cohnstaedt
remembers one occasion in a Committee meeting when Jacques Hébert "let
loose at the CBC," excoriating particularly the journalists associated with the
Corporation with such intensity and ferocity that one staff member from
Quebec, Linda Gaboriau, burst into tears. When Cohnstaedt tried to intervene, cautioning the Committee to take a "freedom of speech" position, she
in turn was attacked and became "that woman" in Hébert's descriptive ter-
minology from that point.[31]

Louis, who had spent many decades with the CBC, wished only to
make the Corporation a leaner, tighter operation, capable of providing
Canadian artists and creators with opportunities to reach Canadian

audiences. However, in the face of such an articulate Co-Chairman espousing what appeared to be Liberal Government policy, Louis felt incapable of restraining Hébert. The ensuing recommendations and the accompanying text were to outrage not only CBC executives and employees, but also a significant number of Canadians. They saw in the Report a bludgeon that threatened a vital defence mechanism for thwarting the American entertainment interests who sought to swamp the country's culture.[32]

There was one last area that the FCPRC was concerned to address: copyright. This was a complex issue that baffled both creators and legislators, but Louis knew that Canada's culture would be crippled unless the matter was tackled and wrestled to the ground. He was also aware that this was one area in which he had the support of Francis Fox, who wanted to move swiftly in the direction of rewarding authors whose books were being read through library distribution, but whose income was not increased as a result. As late as September, Louis presented a paper to the FCPRC meeting, advocating changes in an Act that had not been revised since 1928. At the time, he warned members of the limitations of this solution to the problem of the niggardly rewards Canada was according the vast majority of its authors and composers.

> At the same time, nobody should be under the delusion that Copyright legislation, by itself, will solve either the economic or the social problems of all authors … it serves best [creators] whose work manages to appeal to large segments of the public. It cannot solve the social and economic problems of those authors whose works, though they may have great aesthetic value, will earn very little because they appeal to a relatively small number of users.[33]

The Report *did* focus public attention on the Copyright Act, but Louis realized that it was essential to mount a massive campaign to change public attitudes toward the importance of the arts and to increase public recognition of the significance of the presence of artists. However, this was outside the mandate of the FCPRC, although a recommendation supporting the assistance of artists — particularly dancers, who have short professional careers — did find its way into the Report. As well, Joy Cohnstaedt was able to see that the equity issue pertaining to women's roles in the arts was included, much to the dismay of some journalists. In his own field of music, Louis had watched two organizations (CAPAC and PROCAN, formerly BMI Canada) appear before the FCPRC to advocate on behalf of music creators. It was his view that the presence of two competing performing rights organizations had weakened the case for strong action. This lack of solidarity led Louis, in the months and years that followed the Report's publication, to take on another initiative on behalf of his artist colleagues — the creation of a new entity, SOCAN, which would unit both existing performing rights organizations.

The other institutional support system for serious music that Louis had helped establish, the Canadian Music Centre, was addressed in Recommendation 42. It was recommended that the Centre "should be given adequate financial and other support to enable it to carry out its functions on behalf of Canadian music, including the promotion and dissemination of the works of Canadian composers and the employment of new technologies for the storage and use of musical compositions."[34] That recommendation would become an anchor to which this crucial organization could hold in subsequent storms of grant-cutting.

Even Louis's beloved National Arts Centre, as a federally supported agency, found itself being encouraged to "adopt a policy of showcasing the best available Canadian talent and productions in all performing arts." With words that pained Louis, but in the name of financial responsibility, one Recommendation advised the NAC to "forgo in-house production of theatrical and operatic works in favour of co-productions with other Canadian companies." To Louis's satisfaction, though, the Committee concluded the Recommendation with the assurance that "the National Arts Centre Orchestra, however, should remain as a resident and touring organization."[35]

On February 15, 1982, Louis informed the Committee by memorandum that he hoped to have the Final Report in one language completed by June 30 and delivered to the Minister and the House of Commons by October. This meant that the discussion and debate of the issues and the formulation of recommendations had to be completed by the end of May. These months were filled with the writing of drafts by Committee members with the help of members of the staff — drafts which were often "savaged" and rejected by some Committee members and subjected to aggressive interventions by others. The size of the Committee and the obvious conflicts within it created a kind of mob scene that frustrated everyone. Despite the heroic efforts of the Committee's Chairman, there was simply was not time to resolve disputes in a calm, thoughtful and reflective manner. By this time the Committee had become infected by cynicism — a loss of confidence that anything would come of it all. Even Louis was losing hope that the government of the day had any real commitment that would lead to change. When Mary Pratt — a comparatively young Newfoundland visual artist with a world reputation but little experience of such a process — expressed her own disillusion with the Committee's proceedings to Louis, he could only confide that she should have some hope that "things would evolve."[36] Louis fought constantly to restore the amicable relationships between members of the committee and staff that were being frayed by a relentless process.[37]

In July, Louis informed members that the meeting of the FCPRC on August 16 and 17 would be "probably the most important of our long and fruitful association .... In fact, this will be the last meeting at which we will be able to make substantial changes in the chapters which are new or which were not fully approved by the Committee at previous meetings."[38] That the Report was completed by September 2nd, and published by November, can only be described as a minor miracle. Only Louis, "as a consummate 'dance-master,' as a patient, deliberate, and determined Chair," could have made it happen.[39]

Having diverted the Minister from his plan for an early "confidential" release of the Report, which would have led to complete chaos,[40] Louis was determined that the Report should be released in a way that would present the ideas of the Committee as effectively as possible. On November 1, the Report was in the hands of every Committee member on a confidential basis, and on the evening of November 15, a briefing session was held for the FCPRC. At 11:00 on November 16, the press conference was held in the National Press Building Theatre. The materials for Committee members, prepared under Louis's supervision, outlined the main messages he wanted the public to hear, including excerpts from the Report itself. The News Release made the point succinctly: "If we fail to make the stimulation of our creative imagination the heart of our cultural policies, we will continue to live in a country dependent on the products of other cultures."[41]

That, in essence, was the proposition that the FCPRC placed before the Canadian people. Of course, examples of the 101 recommendations demanding federal response were dangled before the press. One of the many presented, and one that received little attention at the time, expressed the Committee's support for a new federal agency that would engage the marketplace. It suggested that "the promotion and marketing of Canadian cultural products should be pursued by a new non-government organization. Its task would be to improve public access to artistic performances, records, magazines, books, and films through increased awareness and incentive measures."[42]

Here was the solution Louis had first proposed in the 1960s to address the lack of recordings of Canadian music, except that it had now been broadened to include other forms of expression and their products. There were many other recommendations which received little attention, but that were nonetheless highlighted in the news release — an enlarged role for the Canadian Film Development Corporation, the creation of a new Contemporary Arts Centre, and the revamped Design Council, now to be called the Council for Design and Applied Arts. There were also, very significantly, new arm's-length agencies — a Canadian Heritage Council and a Canadian International Cultural Relations Agency, the latter to be associated with the Department of External Affairs. These had emerged from years of committed work by Tom Symons in his many advisory roles to the federal government. Well down the list of emphasized recommendations in the press release came the outline of the FCPRC's treatment of the CBC; but these recommendations buried all the others in the stories filed by the press, particularly those stories carried on radio and television. Needless to say, an understandably defensive self-interest was evident in the CBC's coverage of the event, but it was unfortunate that this story eclipsed all others. Even the Committee's balanced demand that the CRTC be more rigorous in its expectations of quality for Canadian programs produced by private networks was little reported. Sadly, the initial coverage was pathetically inadequate, and almost entirely negative. Not even the Committee's call for immediate action "to prevent the demise of endangered performing arts groups" and the plea for a society that would provide an adequate living for its professional artists made any great impact. Tragically, the load of 101 recommendations — so many dealing with particular federal agencies — seemed to deprive the journalists of vision and, as a result, little of the Report's splendid articulation of support for artists and their creative contribution sifted through the barrage of disappointed expectations.

Louis and Jacques Hébert had to be seen to have one message. In their joint statement, the main theme was directly stated — that contemporary Canadian creativity must have the highest priority.

> We hope to set in motion a chain of events which, over the course of the next thirty years will lead to an outburst of artistic activity. This should be the objective of cultural policy.[43]

The Globe and Mail, in its self-appointed role as Canada's national newspaper, gave several days of coverage to the Report. Under the headline

"Applebert Report laudable but impractical," columnists Adele Freedman and William Johnson assessed the initial reaction of the media.

> The flood of pre-publication publicity which greeted the release of the Federal Cultural Policy Review Committee Report yesterday seemed to suggest the Report would consist of only one chapter – on broadcasting.[44]

The response of Pierre Juneau was given special attention, in recognition of his unique role as instigator of the cultural review some three years earlier as Undersecretary of State and a participant in the Committee until the final phase of drafting the Report and its recommendations. Juneau, now CBC President, was unrestrained. Under a headline, "Juneau says the report goes too far" came the charge that

> The Report is not balanced...The Committee has gone too far. Their proposals are so radical that they imply a dismantling of the CBC, a selling of our facilities ... proposals to end in-house production and discontinue selling air time for commercial advertising are dogmatic and simplistic.[45]

Supporters of the CBC, and there were many, came to the Corporation's defence. People in remote areas who saw CBC Radio as their lifeline to intellectual excitement were furious. Louis was deeply disappointed in both the coverage the Committee's Report received and the "spin" that seemed to dominate the media's commentary. He felt that the central message of the Report — about the crucial importance of creativity and the many ways of strengthening its place in Canadian public life — was almost completely missed. Mary Pratt, the Committee member from Newfoundland, could understand people's anger over the criticism of the CBC and their seeming unwillingness to differentiate between television and radio broadcasting in the Committee's assessment.[46] One defender of the Corporation was certainly not a disinterested on-looker. Harry Rasky was perhaps the most celebrated Canadian creator of quality television specials that the country had ever produced — one whose work was being shown to great acclaim around the world. In a letter to *The Globe and Mail,* he expressed his pain and disappointment.

> My friend and teacher, the late great Marshall McLuhan, used to talk of what he called the Canadian disease of

going through the garden and cutting off the heads of the largest tulips. He would be amused to read the Applebert Report, which suggests, in my view, killing the entire garden.

In suggesting the CBC get out of the production business it would in fact destroy the possibility of making the kind of films I do, which have won some 100 international prizes for Canada .... It is naïve to consider that the private sector would take on such subjects as Next Year in Jerusalem, Tennessee William's South, Travels Through Life With Leacock, [and] Homage to Chagall:The Colours of Love. It is more ironic that the composer for all these was Lou Applebaum, co-author of the Report.

My great documentary predecessors, Flaherty and Grierson, would be turning in their graves at the Report. We are in danger of having a country without tulips.[47]

Michael Valpy, a respected columnist with a very wide readership, warned that the reduction of the CBC's advertising revenues would mean that its programming would have to be sold to foreign countries and, that this in turn would require the programs to be less Canadian in style and content. Referring back to when CBC radio had been "a moribund, shabby corner of the broadcast world," he reminded his readers that resurrection was possible and the Applebert Committee had simply "given up."[48]

Louis found himself in an impossible position. He did not agree with every recommendation of the FCPRC but he knew that, as Chairman, he would have to defend the Final Report at meetings, conferences, workshops, and citizens' forums across the nation. Louis composed two contributions for the "Mermaid Inn" column — a space offered to independent contributors by *The Globe and Mail.* In neither of these articles was he prepared to confront his critics. In the first, after a short reference to his own career as a professional artist, he tried to emphasize the essential message of the FCPRC as simply as he could:

Our intention has been to create conditions which would allow our artistically-talented fellow citizens to contribute to Canadian society in the best way they know how. It should not be, as it was with me, merely a matter of luck. If there is one clear message from our

Report that I would like to come through loud and
clear, that is the one.[49]

His second effort was less successful, attempting in a few paragraphs
to prepare Canadians for the wonders of the new world of broadcasting
technology and the opportunities it had in store for Canadian creators.

Other members of the Committee did engage the press. Albert Breton,
a Committee Vice-Chair, wrote in defence of the FCPRC's CBC position:

> There have been some who have interpreted the
> broadcasting recommendations [as implying] the
> demise of the CBC. This is hard to understand. The
> committee's CBC would be an efficient body that
> would have a budget no smaller than the one the
> CBC now has, and hopefully larger, that would be
> designing programs, inventing shows, searching for
> new talent, eliciting ideas, and coming up with a win-
> ning schedule that would entertain, educate, inform,
> and lead to reflection.[50]

In one bright moment in an otherwise dark time, it was announced
by the Royal Conservatory of Music that Louis Applebaum was to
become the "first recipient of an honorary Associateship at the spring
convocation." Of all the honours Louis was to receive — honourary doctorates from the University of Windsor and York University, and
Fellowships from the Ontario Institute for Studies in Education and the
Ontario College for Art and Design — he valued none more than this
recognition of his professional contribution that had come during the
most difficult time of his life. Ironically, the most complimentary reaction
to the Report came from an American cultural writer, Christopher Mark.
He wrote enthusiastically:

> The Applebert Report is to be admired because it exists.
> The exercise of spending more than two years taking testi-
> mony from one and all across Canada with a bipartisan
> committee has the effect of keeping an arm's-length
> arrangement with other aspects of government and poli-
> tics. Having a written guidebook that essentially spells out
> the priorities along with suggested solutions beats the hell
> out of our system .... The Report sums it up this way: " ...
> the essential task of government is to remove obstacles and

enlarge opportunities without seeking to direct cultural activities ...." Amen to that.[51]

For Louis, the opportunity to present a review of Canada's cultural policy should have been the culmination of his lifetime of contribution to the arts of his country. No other person in Canada could have brought such a wealth of experience to the task. The table of contents of the Report of the FCPRC could have doubled as a commentary on the structure of his whole career. There were eleven chapters and Louis had been involved, in one way or another, in the issues covered in every one. As well, he had been associated with many of the federal institutions and agencies mentioned throughout the volume, particularly, of course, the Canada Council, the CBC, the NAC, and the NFB. As well, he had been engaged in private-sector enterprises associated with both film and television; he knew the performing arts intimately; he had written for theatre, dance, and the concert stage; he had worked on sound recordings; and he had been central in having Canadian composers recorded. His work in making films was now legendary. His broadcasting experience had included both the creative and administrative roles, and his initiative in establishing an International Composers' Conference at Stratford in 1960 had given him a unique insight into how other countries supported their creative artists. Finally, his participation in extensive touring in the 1960s had provided him with a great deal of knowledge about the workings of the commercial sector of the cultural scene.

What had happened? The environment had changed. Both an election and a key referendum had taken place during the process of developing the Report. Perhaps the internal shifts in the cultural policy review process had created trauma. Members had moved from an expectation of a small committee to the reality of a much larger one; from serving on an advisory committee to acting as part of a recommending body; and from a committee prepared to gather research and statistical evidence to one charged with organizing, holding and reporting on hearings that would involve briefs from thousands of citizens from coast to coast.

In the huge Federal Cultural Policy Review Committee that had been gathered, a host of agendas surfaced, largely on the basis of professional expertise, but in some cases as a result of prejudices. The Committee, rushed beyond belief, had become infected with disappointment at the nature of the process. The Report lost its capacity to inspire and degenerated into a list of concerns about particular problems, a compendium of ills, a fragmented attempt to resolve real or perceived federal institutional inadequacies. No matter that the driving force of respect and celebration of creativity had shaped the Report and given it a theme – the resulting list of 101 resolutions, seemingly in no order but one imposed by chance timing, was overwhelming rather than convincing.

It was the wrong time for such a Report. In a way, the Committee knew this. The "Background Notes" prepared for the FCPRC members who might face the press made it clear that the authors of the Report realized the importance of economic pressures on all governments. It was conceded that at the time of the Report's release, there was high unemployment, high inflation, and unprecedented levels of federal deficit. However, it was also recorded that the Recommendations would reduce or redistribute federal spending on cultural agencies, create private sector jobs, promote Canadian cultural products abroad, and make it possible for artists to find work and thereby contribute to the economy. Unfortunately, the Report was mistimed. The 1960s and 1970s were over. Outside forces related to broadcasting were preoccupying the Government and its agency, the CRTC, as well as the general public, diverting attention from everything else.

Is a longer-term judgement possible? In nearly every area covered by the Committee, changes have taken place, and, in most cases, in the direction recommended by the Committee. The CBC now concedes the value of productions that take place beyond its walls. The greater role of outside producers has made it possible for the NFB to do more with the limited resources at its disposal. The judgement of Jean-Louis Roux, now ensconced as the Chair of the Canada Council, deserves attention and consideration. In his view, a great many of the changes that have taken place slowly but continuously over the years originated with the Federal Cultural Policy Review Committee's work in the early 1980s. These changes have strengthened the position of art galleries and museums, theatre and dance companies, and musical ensembles large and small, and made it possible for this cultural community to survive the unfriendly years of recent decades.[52]

In the short term, Louis had every reason to feel badly used. The months following the Report's release were a living hell as he tramped from meeting to meeting, trying to justify a Report that had been declared a failure.[53] Yet, years after, Louis was able to see that the Report had indeed made a difference. Certainly members of the Committee were unanimous that his role had been crucial in every success the process had achieved. Tom Symons called the Report, with all its failings, a "blue-ribbon effort" and a few months later wrote to Francis Fox that "while much of the Committee's Report had proven controversial, I think it is a solid piece of work that will be of help to both governments and the cultural community for many years."[54] Symons, along with Joy Cohnstaedt, who believed the Report was a "turning point" in Canada's cultural development, agreed that Louis's work had made the difference in the quality of the document that had emerged.[55] Albert Breton felt that Louis, in recognition of his enormous contribution, should have been appointed to a seat in Canada's Senate Chamber.[56] Instead that honour went to Co-Chair Jacques Hébert.

Chapter Eighteen
Aftermath and Renewal

The press conference that launched the Report of the FCPRC took place on November 16, 1982, and the Federal Cultural Policy Review Committee ceased to exist. It was all over. Louis and Jan moved back to Toronto permanently that same month, shifting from the apartment they had kept on Balliol Street to one on Walmer Road. At this point, Louis and Jan no longer needed a house and felt that a condominium would serve them well. Louis also maintained a studio near the corner of Yonge and Church Streets. This provided a place for him to compose without bothering Jan. The studio was only a short drive from home; it was a small bachelor apartment with just a kitchenette, a living room, even a solarium, which came to be used for storage, and a bedroom into which he could fit his piano and all his electronic equipment. Louis hoped that now he would finally be able to devote his time to composing the music that he hadn't had time for during the "survival" years. As well, he expected he would be able to resume his part-time teaching role at York University. There was just cloud on the horizon — C-Channel — and the first few months in Toronto were taken up with the last gasps of that doomed project. More quickly than Louis could have believed, by the summer of 1983, it too was "all over."

In reality, the fallout from the Cultural Policy Review went on for months before it was truly over for Louis. Nearly 14,000 copies of the English-language version of the Report, and another 6,000 in French, had flooded the country in the last weeks of 1982. People who, up to that point, had depended on media accounts and commentary were now able to read the document themselves. Louis was deluged with invitations to address meetings, conferences, and forums across the nation. What was at an end, however, was the presence of any secretarial or organizational help to cope with the flood. The period in Ottawa had not been a happy time and the last months of 1982 and most of 1983 — taken up with what was essentially the FCPRC aftermath — were even worse.

What worries me is that the essential statement we made in our report — the one we all believe to be profound and affecting — about the centrality of creativity — has been all but ignored in public discussion. Is it that people don't want to understand its implications?[1]

The Report had been immediately referred to the Standing Committee on Communications and Culture, chaired by Mr. Robert Gourd, the Member for Argenteuil-Papineau. That Committee was encouraged by all the controversy in the press to discount the recommendations. The process they adopted trivialized the extensive materials emanating from the FCPRC's hearings on its tour across the country. Even though every session had been videotaped, and the account of the "Summary of briefs and hearings" had been published, all this material was treated as irrelevant. Robert Gourd wrote to every presenter to the FCPRC indicating that:

The Standing Committee would like to hear your reaction to the Report...It would not be useful to re-do your brief, as we have it. Rather we would like you to indicate, briefly, how comfortable you feel with the conclusions of the Review Committee regarding your field of interest.[2]

A copy of this letter fell into the hands of Mary Pratt, who shared with Louis her understandable outrage that the FCPRC's work with the artistic community was to be repeated by the Standing Committee, and that the resolutions in the Report were not going to be considered until after yet another interaction with all the parties "in order to have their opinions of our opinions." Pratt informed Louis "I wrote him [the Standing Committee's Chair] a tart letter in which I told him how committed and scrupulous and, indeed, nit-picking we'd been and suggested the country needed our recommendations more than it needs his questions. I hope you approve."[3]

Louis had equally ungenerous feelings about the follow-up process of the Standing Committee. He appeared before the Standing Committee and stated the Review Committee's views as cogently as they could be expressed. He also read the Standing Committee's collection of all the responses collected from the arts community and his rejoinder was restrained but filled with disappointment.

I read the compendium with great interest. It is fascinating to see how many of the readers [skimmers] of our Report either do not understand what we said or deliberately choose to ignore or change what we said into something they can refute. As you say, it is unfortunate that so much interpretation has replaced reason in discussing our comments on film and broadcasting. I am most anxious that what we have established as basic principles and goals be understood and absorbed. As I said at the Committee hearing, I hope that all decisions in the cultural field in the future will use as a benchmark against which to measure their aptness, a question like 'are we in this way doing all we can to activate creativity?' Clearly all recommendations in our Report are motivated by that thought.[4]

In addition to meetings to attend and speeches to make, Louis had a mountain of correspondence to answer. All the frustrations of those with dashed expectations were targeted at Louis. He had to explain not only the reason for the Committee's apparent disregard for their opinions, but also the fact that the FCPRC no longer existed, and thus he could do nothing. One example of the kind of response that troubled Louis came from Forrest Nickerson, Executive Director of the Canadian Cultural Society for the Deaf. "We must say that the Report is now void and we find it grievously disappointing that your Committee has carried their discrimination and insensitivity to the extreme by leaving out our concerns." But the decision had been made that responding to "special interests," even those with special implications where the arts were concerned, was impossible within the mandate of the Committee. Louis knew there was nothing he could do.[5]

There was anger at other perceived forms of neglect as well. Guy Sylvestre, the National Librarian, wrote "I was naturally disappointed that there should not have been any recommendation in the Report regarding the future of the National Library."[6] It seemed somewhat bizarre that, in a Report containing 101 recommendations on cultural policy, there was not one that dealt with so important an institution as this federal agency, even though the general area of heritage needs had been addressed. Louis could only agree and express his sympathy.

Another interest group angered by the lack of specific reference in the Report was the multicultural community, which felt that the marginalization of its contribution by a cultural policy review was particularly unacceptable. It confirmed in the minds of those who were not English- or French-speaking that the total preoccupation of the federal government and all its agencies was on the two founding nations, to the exclusion of everyone else. There was another reason for the seriousness of this issue. One of the areas of disagreement that had arisen in the Committee was the seeming unfairness of the federal granting agency, the Canada Council, in refusing to fund dance, theatre, and music performed by the vast array of high-quality presenters who were outside the mainstream of English- and French-speaking society. The issue for the Canada Council was not the low quality of Ukrainian and Scottish dance troupes, but the fact that these arts organizations were amateur, not professional. With limited funds available, only the latter category could be considered for support. This was a dispute that Louis had already faced at the Ontario Arts Council. He had found no financially viable solution and there seemed to be none that the Cultural Policy Review Committee could put forward. He could do nothing to soften the negative position the Committee had ultimately taken on the extension of Canada Council funding to amateur activity. Unfortunately, a scarcity of resources had characterized the previous decade and would likely continue into the future.

A more pointed response to the Report came from the Social Science Federation, which issued a press release complaining of the "scanty research base," and making the point that research for this Report had been less comprehensive than for the one commissioned from the Massey-Lévesque Commission so many decades before. Even more important, the FCPRC was criticized for its inappropriate definition of culture, focussing as it did on "the culture of the humanists — the writers and artists who cater to the 'cultured' public, [and] leaving little room for creative contributions by the Canadian people generally, and not much more for those of the academic community." The release went on to judge the recommendations, declaring the chapters on publishing and broadcasting "hugely disappointing."[7] Louis was not unsympathetic to these criticisms. He had been conscious of the lack of research and was aware of the fact that, after Ralph Heintzman's resignation, he had been dependent on federal government researchers, some quite committed, who had been released to the Review Committee for the duration. However, the Committee had never had access to a fully developed research arm with a "big picture" understanding of the evidence that would be needed to support the recommendations.

One area receiving little attention was the role of women in the arts, but even a minor reference was a source of some concern to at least one critic, Robert Fulford, then editor of *Saturday Night*. Fulford had termed the very meagre commentary in the Report (included mainly as the result of member Joy Cohnstaedt's urging) as "stuff and nonsense." However, Jane Martin, a researcher who had written a report on the matter, citing as an example the small number of women's art works that had been acquired by the Canada Council's Art Bank, sent Louis a copy of her letter to Fulford. In it, she presented statistical evidence that connected the number of women on any Canada Council jury to the chances of women artists receiving grants from that particular jury. It seemed obvious there was a very meaningful relationship between the presence of women on a jury and the likelihood that female applicants would receive grants. Since this presence could not be guaranteed on every jury, female applicants were held to be disadvantaged. Such a charge demanded attention and response. Louis wrote to Martin: "I understand your views and I hope that your continuing battle with past and present attitudes and operations continues and bears fruit." Although gratifying to Martin, this was scarcely enough to allay disappointment over the Review Committee's inability to change the culture of a nation in this substantial area of injustice.[8]

There were other positive moments in Louis's correspondence. Joy Cohnstaedt, in a "Season's Greetings" card, could report that her Winnipeg community "is now taking time to read and understand the Report. More and more people are telling me of their support."[9] Mary Pratt, some months later, raised Louis's morale with a report of her own experience: "The new work is about people, not things. All those people and you people and all the conversation and all the ideas — after 20 years in the wilderness shocked me into thinking people. ... The individual response to the world is the most important response."[10]

The winter had been taken up with a round of appearances before arts groups and university forums. By spring, Louis had had enough. His reply to Pratt reveals the ennui he felt. Even his own professional affairs had not gone well. By the time he had found time to focus on C-Channel, all the programming decisions had been made and, by mid-winter, it was clear that C-Channel was simply not going to reach financial viability in time to be saved.

> As for my own work — I still haven't found the energy, drive, momentum to work. I've written the music for Richard II at Stratford but that's pure craftmanship — no thought, no demands. I have three works I'm supposed to be hooked into — big ones — but I'm nowhere on them. Am I scared? Worried about failing to match expectations? Or just resting? — or just incapable? I'll have to get over this period of finding excuses not to work.
>
> I spend a good deal of my time here at C-Channel but that intensity, total dedication to one thing [the Committee for about three years] is certainly not persisting. I feel so loose, casual, relatively uninvolved — things

don't seem to matter nearly so much, even though we are living through a very different period — financially .

I am speaking in Guelph this week, Waterloo next week and Vancouver the following week — all on the Report but I hope the process will stop. I expect not because in June/July the Austin Committee will come out with something — in Sep't — the CCA will come out with another strategy — and in between Fox is likely to issue new policies on this and that. I wish I could feel more strongly about such developments but they somehow brush by me without stirring up violent reactions. Maybe I'm just getting old."[11]

Indeed, a "different period" had fallen upon the Report and its authors. The Austin Committee, a committee of cabinet chaired by Jack Austin, had taken on the study of the Report and its recommendations at the same time as the Standing Committee was carrying on its task of re-inventing a consultation with the cultural community. Having come to the political process of Parliament and Cabinet in late November, the Report was buried during the Christmas recess and very quickly the momentum was lost. As a young scholar, John Elvidge, stated:

> The media pegged it as a lame duck report, Parliament only partially examined it, a cabinet committee that was set up to dissect it vanished from public attention and many of its most prominent recommendations were disregarded without apology in government policies.[12]

The world had changed. The Trudeau Government of the early 1980s was not one that had much interest in cultural matters. The state of the economy was its obsession, and the rate of unemployment had reached a 50-year high. Disaffection in Quebec was still rampant after the 1980 referendum, and now a serious breach with Alberta over energy policy was creating another centre of opposition. Throughout these years it was clear that Trudeau wanted to leave politics. The question of leadership became central to the Liberal Party, delaying long-term solutions to any problem that could safely be put off until a successor could be found. Almost a "lame-duck" PM, Trudeau set out on a personal crusade to save the world from the increasing confrontation of East and West, and to put an end to the proliferation of weapons that could make any conflagration an end to human civilization. Although this personal effort to build a peace had the support of

the artistic community, it did nothing to solve its immediate problems. In 1984 John Turner replaced Trudeau, who had decided, after his renowned "walk in the snow," to retire from politics. Turner's tenure as prime minister was short-lived and even though he, and particularly his wife, had an intense interest in drama and the visual arts, there was no time to revive the Review Committee's work.

The paradox is that, during the Liberal years, the Report never quite lost its designation as a Conservative initiative, but when the Conservatives did return under the leadership of Brian Mulroney in 1984, the Report was regarded as a leftover Liberal document. Concerns about the arts sank quietly in a sea of other issues that were topics for parliamentary committee study and discussion — foreign ownership, the needs of the handicapped, the voluntary sector, nuclear energy, and the prevention of over-runs in government financing. In his undergraduate thesis, "A Study of the Influence of Advice on Cultural Policy Making," John Elvidge concluded: "Clearly from the day Pierre Trudeau resigned until the September 1984 election, very little attention was paid to policy, cultural or otherwise [and the federal commitment was] further reduced in the election of the Conservatives."[13] This fairly describes the context for Louis's futile endeavours to ensure that the Review Committee's recommendations would not be forgotten during the early and mid-1980s.

There was one direct link between the work of the Federal Cultural Policy Review Committee and what was to become Louis's major contribution to his fellow composers in the late 1980s and early 1990s — the creation of a single performing rights society in Canada. His efforts to create such an entity had come directly from the experience of watching the two organizations he knew so well — CAPAC and PROCAN — appearing before his FCPRC. But his pursuit to establish a single body capable of protecting his composer colleagues was really the culmination of all his efforts to found a Canadian League of Composers and a Canadian Music Centre, to strengthen CAPAC, and to enlarge CAPAC's commitment to the recording of Canadian "serious" music. He could trace his involvement in this issue all the way back to 1944, when, having written the music for *The Story of G.I. Joe* in the United States, he sought out the performing rights society in his native Canada.

In an age of burgeoning technological change and widespread activity in the arts, it was essential to make the case again and again that fair payment for music usage was in the best interest of the entire country, its creative artists, and its culture. As well as the pressure of coping with changing technology, CAPAC would be responding to the more powerful and influential corporate interests that were increasingly coming to dominate broadcasting, films, and record production. The issue was no longer that of forcing the small radio station to pay its proper music license fees, or of harassing the would-be entrepreneur presenting Canadian music in a high school auditorium to acknowledge his modest responsibility to the creator. Now the battle was with massive, multi-purpose operations that would regard the Canadian music scene as an insignificant speck on the horizon of global mass entertainment.

As well, Louis knew that performing rights organizations in foreign countries not only protected their membership, they also subsidized the development of composers and authors through generous grants taken "off the top" of the money they collected. Louis foresaw a single strong organization in Canada with the capacity to emulate the policies and behaviours of similar organizations in other countries.[14]

All members of CAPAC had been delighted to have their colleague in a position (on the FPRCP) to bring some understanding to bear on the complex and controversial subject of performing rights. Little did they realize that this appointment would have significant consequences for their own performing rights society.

After the Committee had begun its hearings across the country, both CAPAC and PROCAN (Performing Rights Organization of Canada, formerly called BMI Canada), had presented briefs. As Louis listened to their presentations, he recognized as never before the degree to which the presence of two competing organizations was weakening the cause espoused by both. At the PROCAN appearance, a discussion ensued about the inappropriateness of such competition, the wastefulness of having two administrations, and the degree to which the rivalry of the two organizations played into the hands of their common "enemies" — the presenters and broadcasters who tended to see paying royalties to writers and composers as a diminution of their profits. After the discussion, Louis received a letter from Jan Matacjek, PROCAN's Managing Director.

> PROCAN's belief that the existence of two societies in Canada is an asset rather than a liability is simply based on the premise that competition in the interest of music creators and publishers, and freedom of choice resulting from this competition in our North American context, is more desirable than a monopoly.[15]

The discussion with PROCAN at the FCPRC hearing legitimately aroused the chagrin of CAPAC officers, particularly its General Manager, John Mills. A few weeks later, Louis received a letter from

Mills that set out CAPAC's disappointment in the treatment they had received from the Committee.

> At the CAPAC hearing with the FCPRC, the "question of multiplicity of performing rights agencies" was not raised. However, immediately following CAPAC's presentation, an in-depth discussion occurred between the Committee and PROCAN as to the advisability of multiplicity of societies functioning within one country ... CAPAC did not have a chance to reply to the statements ... the time limitations did not allow for any so-called "rebuttal" presentation.[16]

The reason for this seeming slight was undoubtedly the fact that Louis was conscious of CAPAC's long-term understanding that one performing rights society was sufficient, at the same time as he was most certainly aware of PROCAN's reluctance to engage in any process that might lead to that result. There was no way to rectify this seeming injustice, since the hearings were shortly to come to an end. But by the end of the 1980s, Louis was even more convinced that a merger of the two organizations was absolutely essential. The Review Committee had been guided through the likely patterns of technological development of the next decades and it was patently clear that there would have to be enormous changes monitoring practices to accommodate new ways to record and present music.

Louis knew there were risks in any institutional change. The two organizations had very different origins and very different cultures. For example, the Board of CAPAC was elected by its members, while the PROCAN Board was appointed by the corporate owners of the organization. There had been an effort as far back as the 1960s to have PROCAN's predecessor, BMI Canada, "rolled into" CAPAC, but that effort had failed. As well, Louis had no confidence that there was widespread understanding about the importance of copyright legislation even after all these decades of debate. However, he knew many people who agreed with him that, when the time and opportunity arose, there could be a successful merger. He never abandoned this cause.

Louis had already been involved in the kinds of battles that were waged less effectively because of the presence of two performing rights bodies. In 1972, he had been part of a campaign to force the National Film Board to give royalties to various organizations in foreign countries, largely through the offices of the Department of External Affairs. Here, the federal agency made the argument that "all rights of producers, composers, authors ... are waived by the head office." This lack of responsi-

bility was quite staggering and had led to a letter from John Mills to
Freeman M. Tovell of the Cultural Agencies Division of the Department
of External Affairs:

> I am particularly disturbed at this situation which has
> arisen inasmuch as I have difficulty in understanding on
> the one hand, the Canadian Government undertaking
> the expenditure of maintaining cultural affairs personnel
> abroad in order to promote Canadian creativity, and on
> the other hand that they should take a position which
> would deprive Canadians of a just return for the use of
> their music in those countries.[17]

Louis knew that such issues would rise again and again. He worked
constantly to support John Mills, CAPAC's Director, who had come to
realize that the adage "in unity there is strength" had relevance to the copyright arena. John Mills would be of an age to retire from his CAPAC duties
in 1984, and Louis could be confident that his successors at CAPAC
would also be open to merger talks. Indeed, while Louis was still at the
FCPRC, Mills had put forward a very surprising proposal:

> CAPAC would suggest that an independent body such as
> your Committee might well be the focal point for a ref-
> erendum of all Canadian composers, lyric writers, and
> publishers, in order to ascertain their wishes as to the
> administration of their rights in Canada and for its part,
> CAPAC would be more than willing to forward to its
> members any ballot that might be independently drawn
> up to ascertain the direct wishes of each and all of its
> membership and, if PRO-Canada would do the same
> thing with respect to those who have assigned their rights
> to PRO-Canada, then clearly, at least the views of the
> people most affected could be ascertained.[18]

This was not a process that the FCPRC would undertake, but it did
indicate there was some hope for merger talks being initiated in the future.

Fortunately, Jan Matacjek — a man whom Louis had met at his
Stratford Composers' Conference in the 1960s and whom he had helped
immigrate to Canada — was now the Managing Director at PROCAN.
Matacjec gradually came to share Louis's view that having two competing
performing rights organizations in Canada, when every other country had

one unified voice, was unwise. As well, on the PROCAN Board was a colleague Louis valued highly — his York University teaching partner, Paul Hoffert. Centred around Louis was a developing coterie of people who understood the issue and who were prepared for change. Indeed, during the entire process, Hoffert acted as a "Trojan horse," acting on behalf of his PROCAN colleagues by carrying on informal discussions with Louis that would enable the Boards of both organizations to better understand each other.[19] Finally, in 1986, while still acting as CAPAC's vice-president, Louis brought the question of a merger to the fore.

> The Board had agreed, in principle, to an investigation into a possible cooperation between CAPAC and PRO CANADA and to that end it was moved by Mr. Louis Applebaum and seconded by Neil Chotem that (a) the Board authorize its officers to look into this possibility and (b) CAPAC's President request that PROCAN establish a group from its Board for that purpose. The motion was approved unanimously.[20]

By 1988, a notice to all CAPAC and PROCAN members went out indicating that discussions had begun. The greatest initial argument was that there would be a savings of $5 million as a result of having one tariff, one logging system, and a single administrative office. Not only would this arrangement benefit all, but the money saved could go out as royalty payments to composers. Louis knew there were formidable hurdles to clear. There was no groundswell of support from the members whose only real interest was in CAPAC and PROCAN as collecting agencies. There were also some distinguished "serious" composers who had made special arrangements with PROCAN for a guaranteed fee distribution, not related to actual performances, and any integration would reveal the realities of this subsidization and throw the entire system into a new realignment. This situation had clouded the relationship of "pop" and "serious" composers for many years and had been an issue for both PROCAN and CAPAC.

There was one common reality. Most of the payments that came into CAPAC and PROCAN were from the work of popular composers. However, there had been an air of willingness to accept that "serious" composers were a cultural asset with a commitment to teaching the basics of music creation to generation after generation, and that their support should therefore be perceived to be more important than the money they actually generated from performance. Thus, the system was aligned to ensure that serious composers received more from both organizations than they could have expected on the strict basis of the units of broadcast or public performance they submitted for compensation. Now, in a negotiation of every aspect of the work of both performing rights organizations, all the historic adjustments would be revealed and would be open for realignment.[21]

Finally, there were members of both organizations who had a high level of attachment to and respect for staff in their respective organizations, as well as a commitment to the style and peculiar attraction of one or the other. Louis, with all his organizational experience, knew there would be difficulties and recognized that the consolidation would have to happen quickly. Any delay would initiate a process of recrimination ending in disaster. Simply put, the organizations had two very different cultures that had to be respected, but an extended negotiation process would simply bring the entire structure of both entities to the ground.[22]

Fortunately, the leader of the PROCAN forces was Hagood Hardy, a strong supporter of the merger and a very able composer of popular music. Louis and Hardy would alternate as Chairs of the Merger Negotiating Committee. However, as CAPAC was already favourably disposed to a merger, a special burden of advocacy and promotion at the negotiating table came to rest on Louis's shoulders. The greatest challenge for both sides was to produce a governing structure that would effectively represent all the interests of those who received remuneration for the performance of their creative work, as well as those who paid for the use of this work. Composers, lyricists, songwriters, and publishers all had to have a place on the executive council and the committees. There was also the need to ensure that both English- and French-speaking members were adequately represented. For years, there had been the constant threat that French-speaking participants would leave and form a separate organization.[23] Finally, in a nation of Canada's size, every region had to be represented at the table. Balancing all these factors to produce an electoral system that was not a nightmare to administer, and a Board that was not a mob, became the toughest job that Louis and his colleagues faced.

Louis was the perfect advocate. Along with his superb administrative skills, there was his long history in the movement. He was aware that there had been a delicate balancing of all these factors within both the merging agencies. He was also aware of the overriding desire of an unsophisticated public to have access, at little or no cost, to the creative products of CAPAC and PROCAN members, and particularly the American repertoire that these societies administered, all in the name of the democratic distribution of information. Louis wanted people of all incomes to experience great music and literature, but realized that, without proper remuneration for creators and publishers, there would be no contemporary arts to experience. In no area of economic life was there more contrast between the rich corporate interests in the broadcasting industry and the poor artists at the bottom of the ladder. Even among composers themselves there was a perceived, and in some cases real, differentiation of wealth due to the success of a few popular music composers — performers who made millions of dollars. Their financial success was in sharp contrast to the state of the "serious" composers whose work brought miniscule rewards from royalty payments, but whose cultural contribution and devotion to music education was beyond monetary valuation. There was even a tension between the "academic" composers in the Faculty of Music classrooms — who depended less on royalties and so were less threatened by change — and the independent, freelance, non-academic creators who depended on every cent that could be directed their way. Louis, with his focus on radio, film, and television, earned little from royalties for public concert performance. Also, because he was essentially a freelance composer, he was not seen as one of the elite academics. To some extent, he could be perceived as a personification of neutral ground.

Certainly, the most serious issue became that of assuring an appropriate representation to the majority of CAPAC and PROCAN members, "pop" composers who contributed by far the most money to the coffers of both organizations. A trend was already developing, one which was worldwide and societal in its expression, that power should be in proportion to money contributed. This change in values from the idealism of the 1960s propelled public and private policy toward a more self-interested stance. In this case, if the "pop" music and its composers and publishers were paying the bills, then the new Board should reflect this reality. Louis hoped that the music creators could stand against the wind of attitudinal change and devise a system of just rewards that would please all. He was wrong. Perhaps because his attention had been centred on the FCPRC in the early and mid-1980s, Louis had not realized the extent to which every element of Canadian society had been influenced by this change of direction.

Louis *had* noticed what he regarded as a trend in the diminishing of CAPAC's attention to the "serious" composer as early as 1979. After perusing CAPAC's periodical *The Canadian Composer*, he wrote to its editor to complain: "I think it is worth noting that the April '79 issue of *The Canadian Composer* devotes *all* of its 48 pages, including both covers, to "pop" music, with the only exception being three small items in the 'CAPAC Members in the News' column.... I don't think it is reasonable or balanced...."[24] The issue of the predominance of "pop" would finally drive Louis, after only two years, to decline to stand for the Presidency of the new organization he had helped to found, SOCAN. However, at the time of the CAPAC-PROCAN talks, it did not restrain him from putting his energies toward a merger he saw as the only alternative if composers' interests were to be effectively supported.[25]

At the first meeting of the Merger Negotiating Committee in September 1988, it became apparent that a long list of problems would have to be resolved before the two organizations could become one. What did it mean to be a "member?" How one could find a place on a Board of Directors? What would determine the difference between a "pop" composer and a "serious" one? Other questions dealt with how one qualified to be a "francophone" composer, the length of term a Director should have, and how the administrative arrangements were to be integrated. Discussions took over a full year, during which Louis's famous patience was stretched beyond description. However, by October of 1989, an Information Bulletin sent to all CAPAC and PROCAN members was able to report that regional representation had been sorted out and election procedures had been defined, with two-year terms for all Directors. There would be offices in Vancouver, Edmonton, Halifax, and Montreal, with the head office in Toronto. Committees had been struck to deal with elections and distributions of royalties. Even a Writer-Publisher Communications Committee had been established. By that same date, Louis was able to propose to a Joint Executive Committee of PROCAN and CAPAC that the name of the new organization should be SOCAN (Society of Composers, Authors and Music Publishers of Canada). Most important, it was announced that there would be an election in the spring of 1990 that would produce the first Board of Directors.

Regional distribution was a particular problem for a performing rights organization. Canada was becoming more regionally self-conscious, yet the greatest concentration of composers and publishers was most certainly to be found in Ontario and Quebec. There had to be a sense in the West, along the West Coast, and in the Atlantic provinces, that this new organization would have the interest of all creative Canadians at heart. Louis's work on the FCRPC had made him particularly sensitive to this issue and it was left to him to draw up the regional representation pattern. At the same time, addressing the interests of francophone composers, writers, and publishers might lead to a Board of as many as 26 members — obviously too large to be effective. Louis and his colleagues finally came down to a slate of 18, with nine writers/composers and nine publishers. One third of the Board members would be francophone, and at least three composer/writers and one publisher would represent "serious" music.[26] Now the challenge would be to devise an electoral system that would provide those results.

Of particular significance in a bilingual organization was the problem of communications. In CAPAC's case, a very effective bilingual publication, *The Canadian Composer*, had been established 25 years earlier by

Allister Grosart. (Grosart had also been the major figure in the election-planning that led to the victory of John Diefenbaker in the late 1950s, and he had been rewarded with a seat in the Canadian Senate.) At the time of the establishment of *The Canadian Composer*, there were only 1000 com-posers-members of CAPAC. As time passed and this number grew, the quality of the periodical increased. Eventually, SOCAN would establish two periodicals — one in English, with a circulation of 20,000, and another in French, with a circulation of 6,000. In spite of his criticism of particular issues of *The Canadian Composer*, Louis was anxious that this publication be strengthened as a way of informing a wider public of the contribution of composers to the life of the nation. That, of course, was Louis's perception of the role that CAPAC and PROCAN, at their best, had performed. He was determined that SOCAN would continue to cel-ebrate the work of both "serious" and "pop" creators.

It was essential that old commitments, such as support of the Canadian Music Centre, be continued. There was also a commitment to such essential ensembles as the Esprit Orchestra, devoted to the playing of contemporary Canadian music composition. But there were other commitments, prizes, and awards for excellence that both merging organizations had nurtured. Louis was determined that more, not less, of such activity would be a part of the new society, and that SOCAN should not become totally preoccupied with the task of ensuring that composers receive remuneration for the per-formance of their works. By 1990, the Communications Committee had become Louis's particular interest. It was this Committee, transformed into the Board of a SOCAN Foundation, that was to be Louis's pride throughout the last decade of the century. He saw this Foundation as a mechanism for supporting the Canadian "serious" composer; as a kind of replica of the European system whereby performing rights organizations generously sup-ported their own composers. Indeed, by July 1990, he was instrumental in having the SOCAN Communications Committee pass this motion: "The main goal of SOCAN's financing in the area of promotion should be to stim-ulate performances of Canadian music, both nationally and internationally."[27] Even before the Foundation was officially launched, Louis was able to estab-lish a granting program that would channel resources to the Canadian Music Centre at a time of extreme financial exigency, when government funding in the new decade became more stringent. As well, grants went to the Canadian League of Composers, the National Youth Orchestra, and the Kiwanis Festival. Louis also wanted SOCAN awards for young composers and con-tinued to press the issue at the Communications Committee even before the Foundation had been put in place. As the number of requests increased, the Communications Committee turned to Louis, asking him to "prepare for the next meeting a preamble or mission to introduce the Guidelines" for future funding. And it was Louis and Jan Matacjek who met to arrange for the funding of recording programs that would bring Canadian music to the attention of the music-loving public.[28] During these crucial months of SOCAN's infancy, Louis never stopped stoking the fires of the broader role he saw for this new and stronger society. By the time the SOCAN Foundation had finally been established, a commitment to advancing the cause of Canadian music had been made in the minds of all involved in the task of creating a single performing rights society in Canada.

It was fortunate that there was this idealistic and totally altruistic element in the merger. "Serious" composers were quickly losing confidence in the process. By the 1990s, Canadian composers had fallen far behind their colleagues in European countries.[29] A letter to Louis from a disgruntled composer stated the case quite boldly: "Royalties to composers of serious music have plummeted in the past few years."[30] This was true not only on a collective basis, but on an individual basis as well. More "serious" composers were submitting compositions and, of course, the special treatment of certain "serious" composers had been terminated. In any case, the litany of reduced income attached itself unfairly to the creation of SOCAN for many of Louis's colleagues.

In 1990 Louis was elected to the first Board of Directors of SOCAN and became the new Society's first President. By this time, however, things were going badly. In the election process, the overwhelming numbers of "pop" composers had made a difference. Even efforts on the part of "serious" composers to increase their voting power by casting ballots only for their own kind could not change the final result. The "pop" composers simply outnumbered the rest by at least three to one, in spite of the weighting that had resulted from the negotiations. More important was the change in the generosity of spirit. Composers who were contributing the most in the way of financial support — the "pop" composers — wanted to benefit from the process of basing distribution of rewards on performance. In short, they suggested that SOCAN's system of subsidizing "serious" composers should change in order to reflect the reality of music performance, and arguments about the educational, cultural, and developmental roles of the "serious" composers should be discounted or ignored. The former acceptance of the need to ensure the presence of a contingent of "serious" composers began to erode, and now the "pop" composers had the power to ensure that their views would prevail. Although members were delighted to have Louis as President — his presence added to the prestige of the new organization — they were not prepared to accept his perception of the need for a balance of royalty payments that would help his "serious" colleagues. Louis felt betrayed. There are even indications that he momentarily came to regret his part in the merger. The "follow the dollar" cry had triumphed. By December 1989, "serious" composers outlined their anger: "Composers representing serious music expressed serious reservations concerning the new schedules proposed for credits to be allocated that considerably change the existing schedule contained in Rule 12 of CAPAC's by-laws."[31]

Obviously "serious" composers were no longer to be prestige members. PROCAN had proclaimed its cultural significance by pointing to Harry Somers and R. Murray Schafer, while CAPAC had celebrated the presence of John Weinzweig and Harry Freedman. In the monopoly position that SOCAN commanded, there was now no alternative organization to which "prestige" composers could turn.

In a letter to composer Murray Adaskin, Louis outlined the battle that was to take place:

> I'm sure that in the end it will be better for us all. I must say though, that we are in the throes of a big campaign by the pop music world (which brings in and takes out most of the society's income) to downgrade the place of "serious" music in the distribution scheme of things, remove any sense of special acknowledgement of the fact that we composers may not be a significant economic factor but we have a vital role in the musical firmament for other good reasons. "Follow the dollar" is their battle cry ... so I dare not miss a meeting for fear of an end-run somewhere.[32]

By the spring of 1991, Louis was successful in devising a strategy for rescuing the organization from a course of obliterating his segment of the composer community. A Serious Music Sub-Committee was added to the organizational roster of SOCAN, with Louis as Chair, and John Weinzweig and George Ullman as members. The confrontation of "pop" and "serious" composers was at its height. Board meetings were characterized by heated arguments and confrontation. In the SOCAN Communications Committee, Louis had to derail a resolution that might have led to a grant allocation structure more nearly reflecting the contribution levels of the two groups, rather than the needs of the applicants. The plan would have assured a 75-25 split for "pop" versus "serious," even in the programs of support for musical development projects. Such a step would have put at risk Louis's cherished allocations to the Canadian Music Centre and other essential institutions. Louis was frantic to ensure that these organizations survived.[33]

In the late fall of 1991, to the surprise of his colleagues, Louis announced that he would not be a candidate for election to the 1992 SOCAN Board. It was a shock. Louis had given enormous time and energy to the formation of SOCAN over a period of almost four years. His reason for not standing was simple. He had given enough to the struggle and the battles were becoming too unpleasant and debilitating. His life had become meeting after meeting. As well, there were countless hours spent in private meetings and on staff negotiations about the compensation that was rightly due as the difficult transition to becoming one organization worked its way out. Louis even had to address architectural problems involved in the construction of a new building for SOCAN's head office. He was tired and, as far as he could allow himself, he was disillusioned, in part because of many people's negative reactions to his efforts. A typical letter made the observation that "the payments are and continue to be an unfair treatment to the dignity of trying to be an active composer in this country. The amounts are simply unacceptable. They are not even close to the amounts received for the same and similar work from PROCAN."[34]

In the fall of 1991, Louis received a letter from Bill Houghton, who had been both a supporter and a critic of the merger process. The letter indicated his regret that Louis was not standing for re-election to the SOCAN Board. Houghton's comments reflected Louis's own attitude toward the state of affairs: "Certainly, a we/they condition did evolve between 'serious' and 'pop' writers. Many of the areas have been resolved and certainly the wounds heal. I have never given up on the idea that out of all this would come a situation that is fair for all and that good will prevail."[35] Houghton went on, drawing a parallel between the previous three years and "a rehearsal for a new musical." He asked Louis, "Are you surprised there are revisions?"

Louis responded, obviously pleased by Houghton's reference to the world of theatre.

> I like your analogy to "music theatre." But now that the rehearsal period is over, and the opening night behind us, we cannot afford to settle down to a nice, long, comfortable, complacent run. We face such serious problems, and I'm not referring to internal organizational ones, that will demand everyone's full energies and capacities.
>
> To use another metaphor, now that the conception, pregnancy and birthing brought forth an assumedly healthy baby, the services of an obstetrical team need to be replaced by another and different kind of expertise and practitioners. The top management is about to be

transformed, a second Board is about to elected, and I'm convinced that a new leadership at the Board level can only be helpful.[36]

Louis departed the Board but was immediately invited to participate in the new granting agency — the SOCAN Foundation. Through the Communications Committee of CAPAC, he had prepared the way for a very broad spectrum of grant policies that would include The Royal Conservatory and the MacMillan Lecture series — Louis had himself been central to its revival and the invitation to Stephen Sondheim to be the first lecturer in a renewed series — as well as the New Music Concerts, Chamber Concerts, and the Banff Centre. Of particular joy to Louis personally was the opportunity to contribute to the long-term success of "Music at Sharon," presented by Lawrence Cherney, a major entrepreneur with whom Louis was now working professionally.[37] It would be here, through the SOCAN Foundation, that Louis would build a Canadian funding mechanism that would offer a level of support to composers comparable with those in France, Germany, and the U.K.

The battle over the direction of SOCAN had continued throughout Louis's tenure as its first president, and included in the ranks of the discontented were some of his closest friends and associates. John Weinzweig was quoted by *The Globe and Mail's* Kate Taylor: "I am concerned by what I call 'pop power.'" Gary Kulesha, a rising star composer of "serious" music (a term he dislikes, preferring 'classical' as his designation), pointed out his concern in the same article: "The thing most serious composers bemoan is Mulroney-think, bottom-line think. ... serious music cannot simply be viewed as potentially lucrative entertainment."[38]

By March of 1992, R. Murray Schafer, Harry Somers, and Patrick Cardy appeared before SOCAN's Distribution and Tariff Committee to point out that there was a significant diminution in royalties received by "serious" music composers and publishers for domestic performances, even though the earnings for foreign performances appeared to be increasing. R. Murray Schafer was particularly incensed about the different levels of payment in Canada and the rest of the world, noting that the Canadian fee was ridiculously lower. Harry Somers commented on the fact that the "contributions of the serious music community over the years [were] not being given due credit."[39]

Louis's decision not to run again for the SOCAN Board was as much an act of defiance in the face of a society unwilling to accord reward for creative services as it was an effort to shock SOCAN Board members into bringing an end to their conflicts.[40] As President and Chair of the Board,

Louis was bitterly disappointed in the slow progress SOCAN was making towards the goals of justice and higher rewards — goals that had been behind the merger in the first place. Instead, the organization had exacerbated the division between "pop" and "serious" composers and made meetings of the Board a battleground. During these years, Alexina Louie spent a great deal of time on committees with Louis, not only at CAPAC and then SOCAN, but also on the Board of Roy Thomson Hall — the newly built concert hall in which the Toronto Symphony Orchestra was to play. She was a brilliant young composer who had trained in the United States, returned to Canada, and achieved immediate success. Her assessment of Louis's work at this time was "that Louis suffered greatly during these negotiations and the first years of SOCAN's existence." He was "one of the smartest men I have ever worked beside. He painstakingly weighed every decision when it was not enough to know you were right, but [you also] had to mould the discussion until everyone else knew it was right." Louis was a mentor to Alexina, who had a tendency, in her words, "to blurt out her own thoughts." But for her and for Louis, the first Board of SOCAN was a painful experience — everybody was "yelling at each other." Yet, Louis never lost his "naive faith in the essential decency and civility of all creators."[41]

Perhaps the most eloquent (and angry) description of the pain suffered during these years was penned by Gary Kulesha in the Canadian League of Composers' *Bulletin* of March 1993. This literary diatribe is a reminder that, for most composers, committee work of this sort is an unwelcome interruption to their thought processes and their creative drive. Administrators may thrill to the thrust of confrontational decision-making; writers may find the drama of human interaction at a board table a tableau in which men and women reveal themselves in unique ways that later emerge in their novels and plays; but composers write in another language with a much different pace and rhythm. Sonatas and symphonies are not conceived sitting around in a meeting, particularly if the topic involves the crass reality of remuneration within copyright legislation and complex schedules of payment. Kulesha describes his experience dramatically:

> In the seven or eight months during which I have served as one of the two "serious music" representatives on the Board of SOCAN, I have come to realize that there is virtually nothing in the musical community of Canada that inspires more anger and frustration, and which is more misunderstood, than the process of the collection of payment of performance rights. I myself am still swamped in information and subtly interlocked pieces of a puzzle which no one

seems to understand fully. The complexities of performance rights extend far beyond the visible boundaries of 'fee collected, rights paid'… I would like to add, on a personal note, that being on the SOCAN Board is the most unpleasant job I have ever done in my life. May I say on behalf of Alexina Louie, John Weinzweig, and Lou Applebaum that no one can imagine how Byzantine, labyrinthine, and acrimonious Board duty is. Why do I do it? It has to be done.[42]

In only four years (from 1988 to 1992) — an extraordinarily short time as measured in the annals of institutional development — Louis had been able to create a single performing rights society, albeit with certain faults and limitations. Such an achievement would not have been possible without the assistance of a number of colleagues — Michael Rock, Jan Matacjek, and members of both PROCAN and CAPAC.

Louis had been nearly 70 years of age when the negotiations began, and he continued to serve the Foundation nearly to the end of his seventh decade. His patience and diplomatic skills were essential to the success of the process. Michael Rock had given strong leadership to CAPAC and was to become the General Manager of SOCAN. Jan Matacjek at PROCAN had faced even stormier seas, but nevertheless guided his organization safely into the harbour of the joint organization. Glenn Morley states of Louis's role, "No one else could have performed the miracle."[43] Louis had successfully reversed decades of public and private acrimony — and raiding of each other's territory — and had ended the mythology that the leadership of that "other" organization was made up of knaves or fools.

For Louis, this was the culmination of a series of major interventions in the artistic life of the nation. He knew that the timing of the merger coincided with sinking financial returns on performed music, and that this would bring criticism, as it most certainly did. But Louis knew there was no alternative. Without a stronger organization, Canadian creators would be at even greater risk. Bringing together two such organizations resulted in inevitable mistakes and administrative glitches, but Louis weathered each storm, always keeping a careful eye on his destination.

Another beneficiary of Louis's energy and inspiration was the Guild of Canadian Film Composers, which had been established in the early 1980s with CAPAC's financial support. Composers like Glenn Morley and Ben McPeek, who, like Louis, worked with films and television, had needs that differed from those of other composers. For example, in 1994, a dispute between the CBC and its composers broke out over the publishing rights for music, with the CBC insisting that the composers must give over these rights as a condition of employment. It took a year, but the battle once again was won through collective action of creators led by a man with vision and determination. The Guild, supported by SOCAN, became another defensive bulwark protecting Canadian composers. Today, SOCAN stands as a strong performing rights society that continues to work on behalf of composers, writers, and publishers in a world that rarely celebrates their contributions.

Just as the informal initial discussions about a merger were taking place at CAPAC and PROCAN, Louis was swept up into what would become a wonderful experience. He was asked to take over the role of Artistic Director of the Guelph Spring Festival — an event that transpired every May in this beautiful town on the Speed River in western Ontario. By 1988, the Guelph Festival had achieved 20 years of success under the guidance of Nicholas Goldschmidt, and now occupied an important place in the musical life of the country. When "Niki" resigned as Artistic Director, the Festival Board knew it was the end of an era — no one else could possibly replace him in the sense of continuing the programming he had initiated. Instead, a decision was made to change direction and to appoint a very different kind of person, with different strengths, as Artistic Director. They chose Billie Bridgman, who had given leadership to Comus Music Theatre in Toronto and had also developed a fund-raising capacity through her own company in Toronto.

Two years before Goldschmidt was scheduled to take his leave, Terry Crowley, the President of the Edward Johnson Music Foundation (the sponsor of the Festival), invited Louis to be the facilitator at a retreat to be held at the nearby Millcroft Inn. Louis "agreed without hesitation."[44] He did so because, over his many years as Director of the Ontario Arts Council, he had come to know the unusual group of volunteers who had gathered around this event, and whose efforts had made a jewel among the many small music festivals that were springing up across the province. Although the Guelph Festival had been started modestly in the mid-1960s, before Louis's arrival at the Council, he had come to appreciate that, like his beloved Stratford, this community had decided on an ambitious experiment — the creation of a major music festival in a small town only an hour's drive from Toronto. As well, Guelph was an educational centre, with an agricultural college that was moving towards being a full university. In the beginning, it was from the academic community that both financial resources and leadership for the Festival came. The founding figures were Murdo MacKinnon, Eugene Benson, and Leonard Conolly and their spouses. The Festival was founded in 1968 with the help of the Edward Johnson Music Foundation. Edward Johnson, a native of Guelph had become a renowned a world-renowned tenor and the General Director of the Metropolitan Opera in New York. He had established the Edward

Johnson Music Foundation in 1957, in order to bring high-quality music to the people of his home town, and to provide a musical education for their children. The Festival was a natural outgrowth of these aspirations.

Louis never lost his expectation that the arts and intellectual pursuits could, hand in hand, change society, and a university was an obvious place to bring these forces together. He quickly came to realize that Guelph was spinning magic in music; that fine Canadian artists were gaining exposure; that Canadian music was being commissioned; and that the Festival was achieving excellence through smaller recitals and opera and concert presentations. Like his beloved Stratford Music, these presentations often featured the musical drama of Benjamin Britten, as well as solo recitals and smaller ensembles that Louis believed could speak to the hearts of people living in a sparsely populated land.

The Festival Board discussions at the Millcroft Inn were expected to lead to a five-year plan for the period 1988-1992, and to determine the goals that should be established. Louis wisely allowed the Directors to range far and wide, remembering past successes, but recognizing as well that audiences were becoming more difficult to attract. Crowley insisted on asking the basic question: "Should we have a Guelph Spring Festival?"— indicating the real potential for it to become nothing more than a booking agency.[45] The Artistic Director Designate, Billie Bridgman, was there and received a great deal of valuable advice. There was a need for a more focussed, coherent program, perhaps with fewer events over a shorter period. The Festival should remain focussed on music, but also needed to recognize that younger audiences had to be attracted with different kinds of events.

Louis stressed the importance of finances, pointing out that, in the previous season, $72,000 had been devoted to publicity expenses while box office revenue had returned only $77,000. This meant that nearly all the other costs of the Festival were being borne through donations or grants — sources that might become less generous in the future. He also raised the flag of society's new focus on business-oriented values. His final piece of advice was contained in his summary: "Program what you believe in and find a way to market it."[46]

A year later, in the fall of 1987, Louis was called on once again to act as facilitator at a second Millcroft Inn retreat. By this time Bridgman was prepared to present her vision. Her goal was a major international festival of music theatre, with a longer season and more events. Much of the festival "would take place out-of-doors," with "small cabaret evenings contrasted with large events." With a later opening, the Guelph Festival would be "on a circuit tour with Stratford and Shaw Festivals."[47] It was heady stuff and the Board was divided in its response. The die was cast and the planning for the

1988 season was well underway. It turned out to be an exciting program. The central presentation was a world premiere of *Saint Carmen of the Main,* a musical version of Michel Tremblay's play. However, this event was fraught with disaster. It was controversial in its subject matter — relationships in the underworld of a Montreal populated by prostitutes and criminals — but the main difficulties stemmed from the financial costs. The transformation of a hockey rink into a theatre venue, as well as the need for a generous cast , sent the budget soaring and conflicts in the production team led the technical director to resign in disgust. The Board lost control of the budget and, when the dust cleared, the Festival was facing a frightening deficit. Although the deficit was mainly the result of *Saint Carmen of the Main,* it could also be attributed, in part, to the fallout from ticket sales for many events that fell far below expectations. The staff of the Festival felt distraught and disillusioned. When Billie Bridgman resigned in the wake of the disaster, there was only one person they could turn to — Louis Applebaum. Louis agreed to be, not Artistic Director, but Artistic Advisor, and only for one year, until they found a successor to Bridgman. Murdo MacKinnon, the Festival's prime supporter from its inception, states simply: "He [Louis] had always been a friend of the festival, always praising us." MacKinnon cited the contribution Louis had made to a Guelph conference of community arts councils as far back as 1974, as well as a meeting of composers he had chosen to bring to the city in the 1980s, and, of course, his role at the Millcroft Inn Board retreats. Louis was the only one who could "pick up the pieces."[48] As Nancy Coates (who was the Festival President that year) put it "He saved our bacon." Even more, "he restored our confidence in ourselves." He did it by treating the battered volunteers "as colleagues."[49] It was made clear that this was "their Festival," that decisions would be ones that "they felt comfortable with." With Louis's geniality and warmth in evidence, the shell-shocked survivors found new energy and commitment.

The 1989 program was artistically satisfying but, at the same time, was innovative and broad enough to satisfy a wide range of tastes and expectations. Before Louis had arrived, the Festival had commissioned Canadians John Beckwith and James Reaney to write a mystery opera, *Crazy to Kill.* This would be presented with a minimal cast and orchestra, but with the cast augmented by fifteen puppets and taped music to enhance the sound. It was a brilliant solution to the problem of maintaining the Festival's role as a place where Canadian creativity could thrive — but at reduced cost. It worked, although not without some tension, and Louis emerged as the figure who "calmed things down" when Beckwith and Reaney chafed against the reduced support system of the Festival. Louis's "great sense of theatre" gave them confidence in the outcome.[50] Along with *Crazy to Kill,* The

Manitoba Chamber Orchestra returned to play a number of concerts. This was just the size of ensemble the Festival had sought from its outset, and one concert was presented in conjunction with the Guelph Youth Orchestra. This combination pledged a continued commitment to the music education and development that the Edward Johnson Foundation, now a main Festival sponsor, saw as its central *raison d'être.*

Louis knew that for many patrons the Festival *was* Niki Goldschmidt. He arranged to bring Niki back to host the opening concert, "A Night of Glorious Singing," that featured an array of Canadian vocalists, including Heather Thomson, Richard Margison, Allan Monk, and others, many of whom had filled Festival stages in past seasons. In short, "Applebaum did not hesitate to acknowledge that the Festival was returning to its traditional formula."[51]

A key part of this formula was the inclusion of events designed to appeal to families with children. The Festival offered specially reduced children's tickets to a number of events. One of these was a "magical, mystical, musical play for children," *The First Fable*, written by Timothy Findley and with music by John Hawkins. Families were also given special ticket prices for outdoor performances, including "A Day in the Park" with a cornucopia of local talent. Events like this were particular delights, and seemed to exhibit the values of small-town Ontario without losing any of the excitement and innovation that had given the Festival a unique status.

There were also typically Applebaum touches — an evening with Colin Fox portraying Tyrone Guthrie in *Guthrie on Guthrie*, and a world debut of a trio featuring Steven Staryk, Tsuyoshi Tsutsumi and John Perry playing Beethoven, Shostakovich, and Brahms. Not unexpectedly, there was also to be a film festival — a direct result of Louis's long-time personal interest in this form of creativity.

Even Louis Applebaum could not turn around the financial situation in a single year. Costs were still higher than revenues and a deficit continued to be a burden for the future Festival Boards. Yet there is a unanimous refrain one hears from Guelph Festival enthusiasts — "Lou saved the Guelph Spring Festival" — that no amount of grumbling about revenues or expenses can dissipate. Even the immediate response was positive. Kathryn Elton, Director of Marketing and Publicity, wrote to Louis a month after the last concert that "though the attendance and box office figures were not what you'd hoped for," nonetheless, "this season is being considered a success." She revealed that there had been a "60% increase over last year in number of seats sold and box office dollars," which was being seen as "a good showing in the light of competition."[52]

One of the most moving tributes to Louis, after his death, would take place in the new River Run Centre, the splendid performing space the Festival had made essential to the well-being of the community, on Saturday, June 3, 2000. It would reflect the love affair between Louis and the Festival volunteers that was so important to him and to them. In an insert to the program, Eleanor Ewing assesses Louis's year as Artistic Advisor:

> Initially, we may have thought he would be an artistic miracle worker, who single-handedly would create an instant music festival. As he worked with our Board it became plain that Lou's view of his role was that of a colleague who could devise with us a season in which we could all take ownership and pride. Eventually, the 1989 Festival rejoiced in 24 concerts and 23 educational events.[53]

This intimate experience of working to save a troubled Festival was a source of enormous pleasure to Louis at a time when his working life was slowing down, his future was unclear, and his mind was preoccupied with the difficult negotiations required to create an effective performing rights organization. Throughout his involvement in the Festival in 1988 and 1989, he was able to convey his vision that this was not just a series of concerts to fill two or three weeks each spring; instead, music was the "means of enhancing the country's cultural life."[54] In many ways, the Guelph Spring Festival was an expression of Louis's Canadian nationalism. It would be no surprise to him to hear that the Festival would recover its financial stability and continue into the new millennium as a source of pride to the people of Ontario, and even to the rest of Canada.

Chapter Nineteen

"I want to be remembered as a composer."

The title for this chapter came from Louis's own lips, as a response to a question about his own personal hopes and expectations of remembrance. It was not a completely satisfying answer. Louis made an enormous contribution to the cultural life of this nation through his work with a plethora of organizations, through reports, studies, speeches, and general writings, and through his personal interaction with several generations of artists and arts administrators. To focus on just one role seemed to unfairly diminish the rest. Indeed, Louis's breadth of involvement in so many areas makes it difficult to discover a single thread woven through the tapestry of a 60-year career. Yet, throughout these decades, there was one constant — Louis never lost his desire to compose music. It was the passion that that dominated his life and, indeed, gives his wish to be remembered as a composer legitimacy and integrity.

Louis did not fit the stereotypical image of the "composer." Fellow music-maker John Beckwith quotes Keith Bissell, a colleague, who characterized the true composer as a person totally consumed by the need to write music, driven by an inner demon that could never be restrained. The composer is like the novelist who must write whether his work published or not, or the visual artist who paints with no thought about whether the completed canvas will ever be seen by the public. Lister Sinclair, the CBC's resident renaissance man, describes this concentrated attention to creativity as a total commitment to the expression of a single body of work, and expressed through a variety of genres – symphonies, concertos, suites, operas, et al. There may be hundreds of opus numbers and a broad array of styles, but the composer's work is, in a true sense, a single oeuvre of many parts. This is what makes it possible for the listener to hear an unidentified piece of music on the radio and know immediately that it is a work of Bach, or Mozart, or Mahler.

But Louis Applebaum was different. There was an all-consuming commitment to music, but his compositions were almost always written in response to the particular needs of the director of a play, or the producer of a film or television program. Louis referred to himself as a "functional composer." His genius lay in perceiving each individual situation with unique sensitivity and finding a way to use music to spark in his listeners a moment of clearer understanding and warmer appreciation. He was driven by the particular challenge of the stage or film production, but not by any personal need to write music that would stand as a monument after he died.

Robert Sirman remembers being shocked by the response to his proposal to Louis that he write a specific composition that might express his ideas of the moment. Louis's reaction was: "Why would I do that? Who would pay me to write that piece?" For Sirman, who shared the collective image of composers as creatures driven by internal forces to write whatever the inspiration of the moment dictated, this was a revelation.

Louis's repertoire, based on the compilation of the scores of films, radio and television programs, and stage productions, is truly monumental. Taken together, the extent of his musical composition would stand comparison with the output of any contemporary — even with that of the most prolific baroque, classical, or romantic composer. Yet only a very small amount of it is accessible to the listener except through the process of discovering prints or tapes of films and radio and television programs in the few media archival collections to be found throughout the world. Most of his music is not to be found on the shelves of the Canadian Music Centre, but rather in his own archival materials at York University, or in the collections of the CBC or the NFB. On the whole, most of this kind of music has been ignored by musicologists, and yet some of the most illustrious composers of the twentieth century have produced music for film drama. These include Aaron Copland, Sergey Prokofiev, Dmitri Shostakovich, and William Walton, along with others whose work has been concentrated in this area, such as Erich Korngold, David Raksin, and Elmer Bernstein.

Now there is a revival of interest in music written for the electronic media. Tapes and CDs have become an integral aspect of the marketing for every film production, and there is already a movement to mine older film scores for the treasures they most certainly contain.[1] The implications of this development for the future understanding and appreciation of Louis Applebaum's music are quite significant.

Louis did not write a large amount of music for the concert and recital hall — still the basis on which a composer's output is normally measured — and yet a number of his pieces are and will continue to be played often. The choral tradition of the synagogue has been enhanced by the addition of Louis's "The Last Words of David" and "Two Nostalgic Yiddish Folk Songs," written in 1989 and 1987 respectively. His name can also be found on choral programs for the most attractive arrangements of Christmas carols; both his "Carols of French Canada" for chorus and orchestra and his "Four English Carols" are often performed. Orchestras will continue to play his "Concertante for Small Orchestra," a composition commissioned by the Edmonton Little Symphony Orchestra in Canada's centennial year, and one that has been played by most major orchestras in the nation, including several performances by the NAC Orchestra.[2] Louis's latest work for orchestra, "Five Snapshots for Horn and Strings" (1999), is a virtuoso concerto for English horn based on themes from the opera, *Erehwon*, which he was writing shortly before his death.[3] His "Suite of Miniature Dances" from *All's Well That Ends Well* (1958) as well as his "Three Greek Dances," a piece uncharacteristically drawn from the soundtracks of two NFB films, have received broad attention from across Canada and beyond. Similar attention has been accorded to an orchestral suite, "Action Stations," based on background music Louis wrote for his breakthrough film at the NFB and adapted for concert performance in 1958.

In the 1980s, the brass band as an ensemble attracted Louis to write two fine compositions: "High Spirits: A Short Overture for Concert Band" and in the same year, 1986, "Passacaglia & Toccata," the latter commissioned by Wilfrid Laurier University. There were smaller works which Louis identified in 1968 as high points in his composing career, namely, "Cry of the Prophet" for baritone and piano, and "Variations on an Original Theme" for piano, oboe, violin, viola, and cello. These, along with String Quartet no. 2, were pieces he felt had been among his best work in the early years of his composing.

For Louis, music for public performance was often tied to a single occasion. He was called on for major compositions when, for example, the National Arts Centre was opened[4] and when music was required for the installation of a new Governor-General. Ceremonies for Jeanne Sauvé, Ed Schreyer, and Ray Hnatyshyn were all graced with the music of Louis Applebaum. The opening of a major performing space, Hamilton Place, occasioned the writing of an orchestral piece, "Place Settings." Although the title associates the work with this particular event, the suite has been played beyond Hamilton's borders on several occasions. That was not to be the case for another fine piece, "Terre des Hommes, a Fanfare for the Opening of Expo 67." Like so much of Louis's work, this piece was not transferable and could never find a place on the concert programs of Canadian orchestras and ensembles. Such pieces were heard by hundreds of thousands of people, in some cases even millions, but their purpose was to bring glory to a moment, and when the moment ended, they receded into memory.[5]

Louis was always very drawn to the idea of providing music for special moments. He enormously enjoyed the opportunity to take part in unique events, where his music could add to the sense of occasion. He not only contributed songs for the anniversary celebrations of the schools he had attended, Clinton Public School and Harbord Collegiate, but he also delighted in writing a "Graydon Overture" for the opening of Gordon Graydon Memorial Secondary School in Mississauga — an occasion for honouring the contributions of a prominent local politician.[6] Even more precious was a 1999 commission from David Silcox and his wife Linda Intaschi whose close friends, Shanitha Kachan and Gerald Sheff, were about to be married and to whom they wished to present a very meaningful gift. Carl Sandberg's poem "Counting" was selected as the text, the rights for its use assured, and Louis composed a song for the wedding.[7] Composing for such an occasion gave Louis enormous pleasure and it was one of the last songs he was to write. However, there was to be one more wedding song, written for an event that Louis enjoyed beyond description. Jordan, his special grandson, married a dancer, Andrea Burridge, and Louis was delighted to present them with a musical tribute to their love. For someone like Louis, making music for family events was only natural. In fact, over the last years of their lives together, Jan received a song on every anniversary of their wedding, These remain in her hands as precious manuscripts that, to this point, have not received public performance.

The fact remains that the vast majority of Louis's work was written for stage and the electronic media. Yet he was largely unsympathetic to the idea of separating his music from the work for which it had been composed, except in the case of a handful of compositions, and he rejected the suggestion that he should arrange "suites" from his many soundtracks.[8] He felt strongly that the integrity of his music was compromised when it was wrenched from its dramatic context.

In the 21st century, entertainment may be more given to multi-sensory experience than in previous epochs. As audiences for the traditional symphonic concert or recital hall experience dwindle, it may be that older films will be re-released with enhanced musical soundtracks, revived in live shows with orchestral and choral components, or accessible on Web sites. If so, Louis's music will be available to the listener in the new millennium, perhaps more so than that of many of his contemporaries. Louis's work may well receive considerable attention in the future, but this attention will be nothing new. Louis's first public recognition came early, in 1949, when Lazare Saminsky came from the U.S. to research Canada's music for a book called *Living Music of the Americas*. In one section, he chose to concentrate his attention on three composers he felt were outstanding examples of "Young Men of Toronto:" Godfrey Ridout, John Weinzweig, and Louis Applebaum. He referred to them as a "gifted trio." His response to Louis's music was most positive:

> "In the opening movement of his best work so far, the "Second String Quartet," we find this fine creative talent still in the prison of atonal thought, but there is something keenly his own in both emotion and thematic curve. The lively second movement of the quartet is fresh, individual, spurred on by an attractive rhythmic energy.[9]

Not long afterward, in 1953, the newly created National Ballet of Canada commissioned a young Louis to write music for a ballet based on "the sensational American folk narrative of Barbara Allen, object of the fundamentalist preacher's desire, whose love for a mysterious Witch Boy turns her mountain community into a lynch mob."[10] Celia Franca had been very impressed by music Louis had written for an NFB film about the ballet festival that brought her to Canada for the first time. The ballet was given the title *Dark of the Moon* and was choreographed by Joey Harris. The work was taken on tour in 1953, 1954, and 1955 to generally wide acclaim. S. Roy Malley, writing in the *Winnipeg Tribune*, commented: "Mr. Applebaum's music is starkly realistic and dynamic, with dissonant episodes, highlighting highly dramatic sequences."[11] The critic writing for the *Detroit News* commented that "the music, again reduced to keyboard skimpiness, is by Louis Applebaum, a Canadian composer of obvious gifts."[12] Not all comments were as appreciative of the sounds of Louis's music. The *Windsor Star* critic thought it was "weird, untuneful and cacophonous," but conceded that it was "right in the groove for *Dark of the Moon*."[13]

The broadest and most profound observations about the significance of the *Dark of the Moon* score came from John Kraglund, who was later to become one of the country's most distinguished music critics. The theme of his critique was the general complaint that "Music by Canadian composers has attracted little attention on the Canadian concert stage" and that "music by Louis Applebaum did attract considerable attention at the

Royal Alexandra Theatre [in Toronto]." Kraglund was impressed with Applebaum's work and its appropriateness for the dance:

> "It speaks well for both the composer and the choreographer that on first hearing and seeing the music and the dance became a single unit. But this makes an attempt to analyze the music rather difficult .... Like much modern music — and it is modern although not in the sense that it appears to strive for strange tonal effects — there is an element of starkness in the score. Mr. Applebaum has used sufficient melody to indicate that he would be quite capable of composing a happier, more melodic setting if the case should warrant."[14]

Kraglund points out that there is "something of the qualities of film music, a medium in which Mr. Applebaum has had considerable success." The memories of Louis's triumph in Hollywood and his youthful achievements at the NFB and CBC, while contributing to the familiarity of his name, were conspiring to make his success as a "serious" composer all the more difficult.[15]

Kraglund was particularly intrigued as he saw this score as a leap towards what most Canadian composers perceived as ultimate success — the opportunity to write an extended work in which there could be some development of theme and variation, and in which the composer's genius for complex creation could be fulfilled. "Perhaps a step to the theatre, one that has been taken by Canadian musicians (although it is questionable that they have been as successful as Mr. Applebaum), may be a step nearer the concert hall." This commentary was an encouraging vote of confidence in a young composer just returned from the United States, and who had been surviving to this point by writing music for film and CBC radio. However, the possibilities of becoming primarily a composer for dance presentation had little promise in economic terms. There were few dance companies in the 1950s, and even fewer who could afford to hire a composer to write scores for newly conceived works. Later in the century, the increase in the number of modern dance companies would mean that a few composers would eventually be able to make writing music for dance a recognizable part of their income. For ballet, there was another problem. Even today, the box-office revenue for most ballet companies comes mainly from performance of the great traditional repertoire of Russia and Western Europe. These are the works that draw audiences and "sold-out" performances. The music of

Tchaikovsky tends to become the standard fare. The economics of being a composer for live performance in the Canada of the mid-1950s propelled Louis toward the Stratford Festival. In the same year that *Dark of the Moon* was launched, Tyrone Guthrie enticed Louis to make music for the stage and, as well, to bring Canadian musicians and composers to a special music initiative at the Shakespearean Festival. For the most part, dance was abandoned. This was to be the first of a number of "roads not taken" in Louis's long career.

Even so, Louis had not heard the last of the music for *Dark of the Moon*. In 1961 the National Ballet decided to mount another ballet based on the Barbara Allen story, but using the name of the familiar folk song as the ballet's title. Thus, *Barbara Allen*, choreographed by David Adams, became a commission for Louis to revise his *Dark of the Moon* score. There was some drawing on the previous production, so that critic Nathan Cohen referred to the work as "a score from a previous ballet of faintly similar nature."[16] However, Cohen also noted that this rendition was not as successful as its predecessor: "[The work] is so full of incongruous ideas and devices that aesthetic shapelessness soon sets in."[17] Herbert Whittaker, characteristically more charitable, pointed out that "Louis Applebaum's ominous music, reiterating the theme of the familiar folk song, promises us more than Mr. Adams gives up."[18] *Barbara Allen* was a prominent feature in the National Ballet's repertoire in 1961 but never became a recurring work.

The years between *Dark of the Moon* and *Barbara Allen* were frantic for Louis, with Stratford drama and Stratford Music to contend with, along with increasing work in radio, film, and television. Louis realized that an opportunity to compose an extended work was one to be treasured, but he also understood that present-day survival tactics had to precede long-term career strategies that might include dance.[19] However, he did write a number of dance sequences for films, and particularly for plays, and he took the opportunity on rare occasions to put a collection of dances into a suite that was often repeated on orchestral programs, both live and on radio. "Miniature Dances," for example, from the Stratford production of *All's Well That Ends Well*, became one of Louis's most popular concert offerings.

For Louis, the advantages of living and working in Canada far outweighed the disadvantages. However, a rich country like the United States, with large foundations or corporate donation programs for "new" music, is more likely to support its composers as they fulfill their dreams for extended compositions. In Canada, private support and the generosity of government granting agencies seldom cover the costs of the extra rehearsals that new repertoire demands, and will certainly not compensate for the box-office losses that too often accompany the presentation of a new work. Thus, shorter pieces become the order of the day, and most of Louis's compositions can be accommodated as one of several pieces in a concert program.

As well, composers in post-World War II Canada depended heavily on the willingness of CBC Radio to commission contemporary works. Even more flexible programs devoted to classical music found it difficult to accommodate symphonies, concertos, and extended suites of orchestral music. Orchestras, aware of the unpopularity of "new" works — Canadian or not — preferred to use short pieces as a kind of warm-up before turning to the more familiar long works of established composers. R. Murray Schafer drew attention to this problem by calling one of his TSO commissions "No Longer Than Ten [10] Minutes." The audience was invited to respond by applauding intermittently, effectively lengthening the piece. As it turned out, the "10-minute" composition took 23 minutes to play. Schafer used his marvelous sense of humour to expose the fact that Canadian composers were being kept from creating music with complex ideas and emotions that took time to work out — the very kinds of music that might become known internationally and establish a lasting legacy. While at the CBC in the early 1960s, Louis made attempts to address the situation. However, his responsibility was in the area of television programming — a medium known to be unkind and unforgiving to "serious" music — and he remained at the Corporation only two years.

Although atonal elements are very much part of Louis's music, he was essentially a traditional classical composer. His enormous respect for the skill and creativity of the masters and his principal need to find the right sound for hundreds of radio and television productions forced him to be familiar with the work of virtually every composer. With his emphasis on the role of music as communication, he searched for the common elements of human experience — ugliness and violence as well as beauty and joy — that allowed composers in every century to create music relevant to people's lives. Thus, although his work was connected to the latest technology of film, radio, and television, he was also working in the tradition of the great composers of the 20th century. To the question "Which composer has influenced you most in your musical composition?" Louis responded, without hesitation, "Igor Stravinsky, and to a lesser, though important degree, Aaron Copland."[20] When asked to name the Canadian composer to whom he felt closest, Louis immediately responded "John Weinzweig." It was not only Weinzweig's music which touched Louis, but also the man's commitment to his profession and to the entire music-making community, as indicated by his role in creating the Canadian League of Composers and the Canadian Music Centre.[21] In analyzing his own musical style, Louis conceded that his desire to write music with recognizable structure and lyrical content — and his anxiety that his music encourage the listener to think and understand the message it was conveying — had kept him from experimenting too enthusiastically with twelve-tone composition. "I did write some pieces in the twelve-tone format, but they tended to sound like all the rest of my output."[22] Although Louis respected the greater freedom for innovation that composing such music allowed, he was not drawn to the discordance and the "angular sound ... the big leaps ... with no melodic structure." He, like Leonard Bernstein, tried to write both a film score and concert pieces within the confines of this genre of composition, but he found that his music came out "more lyrical than could be accommodated within that style."

There was another composer who exerted a surprising influence on Louis — Healey Willan. Willan had been one of Louis's teachers and his very British 19th-century style, more pre-Elgar than 20th-century in its form, was devoted to high-Anglican Church music. He was not appreciated and respected by many contemporary composers, who tended to be one another's severest critics. However, Louis's admiration for Willan could be traced back to his teenage years when he had, with Willan's daughter, Mary, been a member of the "Junior" extension of the Vogt Society — a group of young people devoted to the promotion of Canadian music, with Willan as a prominent recipient of their adulation.[23]

Louis may have adopted a somewhat conservative compositional style, but he refused to be contained within the traditional walls of form as expressed in such designations as "symphony," "concerto," "sonata," "quartet," "suite," or "tone poem."[24] He preferred titles that were more descriptive and did not confine the listener's expectation to any particular form — "Dialogue with footnotes for jazz band and symphony orchestra;"[25] "Algoma Central" for soprano, harp and flute; "Notions" for violin and piano; "Diversions," for flute and piano; "Nightscape" for harp; and "Duologue" for harp and oboe. With his obsession for music as the supreme mode of communication, Louis felt that these titles would prepare the listener to accept sounds that did not slavishly follow the "sonata" form or the "fast-slow-fast" series of movements, or exhibit the limitations that older formats inevitably forced on contemporary composers.

In one area Louis was the supreme master: the fanfare. He was Canada's master of the fanfare and, although this may seem a modest source of reputation for a superficial form of composition, Louis brought enormous variety, harmonic complexity, and effective vigour to this particular form of musical expression. The "Stratford Fanfares" were a beginning and Louis placed them in a suite that has been played by orchestras and brass bands all over the world, particularly for ceremonial occasions.

Louis would not allow other theatres to use them to summon audiences to a performance as he insisted these were "Stratford [Ontario] Fanfares." In a country largely devoid of ceremony, people regarded the fanfares as an element of theatre they could find nowhere else — and Louis was determined to give Festival audiences that thrill. However, his commissions for fanfares were endless. The Stratford fanfares aroused an appetite that ranged from the Opening of Expo 67 to the occasion of the visit of Queen Elizabeth, to the ceremonial fanfares for President Reagan's visit to Ottawa in 1981, to a Scarborough Festival "Festive Fanfare" in 1984,[26] to Louis's famous CBC fanfare, which introduced the CBC Television News for many years. He successfully raised the level of the quality of this musical flourish, giving each occasion an air of both joy and dignity.

Louis reveled in the many variations he could create for fanfares. In 1987, in Andrew Davis' final season with the Toronto Symphony, the group toured Canada. There was a reason for celebration when this great orchestra had the opportunity to play in such distant communities as Whitehorse, many of whose citizens had never experienced such a concert before. Davis wanted to use Godfrey Ridout's "Fanfare" — one that he had also used at Ontario Place at the Toronto International Festival. Since Ridout had passed away, Louis was called upon to re-score the original, written for 12 valveless trumpets, so it could be played by three standard-valved trumpets. "Not that the music appeared to have lost much of its declamatory effect, as the brassy opening phrases came out, tumbling over each other in whole tone progression before the full, organ-re-enforced orchestra declared itself."[27]

Louis's talents were superbly suited to writing music for special occasions. One such occasion was a "gala" held in 1987 to honour the centennial of the Royal Conservatory. It was a glorious affair — a concert that brought together "stars" of the RCM from many decades. These guests included Victor Feldbrill, Zara Nelsova, Corey Cerovsek, Arthur Ozolins, Robert Aitken, Steven Staryk, Glynn Evans, Janet Stubbs, Sandra Graham, Lois Marshall, Greta Kraus, Don Garrard, Rosemary Landry, Jon Vickers, and many others, all of whom had shared the experience of being either a student or faculty member at the Conservatory. The evening concluded with Louis's "Play On," a musical entrance vehicle for the arrival on stage of a huge birthday cake, wheeled in by cultural ministers (Lily Munro and Flora MacDonald) from the provincial and federal governments. A capacity audience at Roy Thomson Hall joined the performers for the singing of "Happy Birthday."[28] "Play On" became another example of an item in Louis's repertoire that had served its purpose and would never be heard again. It was occasion-specific, demanding the talents of a full symphony orchestra, the Mendelssohn and Orpheus Choirs, several of the soloists who had already performed in the program, additional instrumentalists, and a quartet of young artists on two pianos, all conducted by the composer. Even if new lyrics could have been devised, a repeat performance would have been impossible. Most certainly the contribution of Jon Vickers — "Get on with it … I beg you do get on with it...please do get on with it" — spoken in his best "Peter Grimes" voice, could never be replicated.

Louis composed a different oratorio for the 150th anniversary of the incorporation of the City of Toronto in 1984. It was called "Ode to a Birthday City." The composition, commissioned by the Toronto Mendelssohn Youth Choir under the direction of Robert Cooper, was a demanding offering. It provided for celebration, but was perhaps not as melodic or harmonically satisfying as a group of young choristers might have expected. However, it did give them a sense of the dynamic of their own city, and how its qualities could be expressed in musical terms. "Ode to a Birthday City" is another example of an item in Louis's repertoire that was performed only once, pending the occasion of another birthday celebration. Lister Sinclair's lyrics, referring to the "Blue Jays" and "Argonauts" (Toronto's baseball and football teams), ensure that, without substantial changes, the piece will never be used to mark the birthday of any other city.[29]

By the mid-1950s Louis had made a commitment to the Stratford Shakespearean Festival that would end only with his death. He wrote the incidental music for the first two productions of the first season and then for 57 subsequent offerings from 1953 to 1999. Although each season brought other playwrights to the stage of the Festival, Shakespeare attracted his interest consistently, with a total of 45 commissions. There were, of course, repeats of the Bard's most popular plays; indeed, four productions of *Hamlet* were scored during those years. But there were other classics he worked on with equal enthusiasm – *The Cherry Orchard, Volpone, The Way of the World, Three Sisters, Oedipus Rex,* and *A School for Scandal* being the best known and most popular. Still, Shakespeare was Louis's passion. In July of 1963, he was asked to give the "President's Lecture" at Convocation Hall at the University of Toronto. His called his talk "Shakespeare on Stage." Coming ten years after he had scored his first production at the Opening Season at Stratford, this was an opportunity for reflection on and analysis of his commitment. Louis began by providing a contrast between the modern theatre and that of the Bard. "In Shakespeare's day, music was an essential theatrical ingredient …. As a self-respecting playwright, Shakespeare naturally had a thorough and accurate knowledge of music and his frequent and sometimes detailed musical metaphors were no problem, it seems, to *his* audience." Louis recognized how fortunate it was that he had been invited to participate in the design of the orchestra pit at the Stratford Festival, both in the tent and the permanent structure that followed. In each case, the pit had an architectural presence that supported the musicians' contributions to events on stage.[30]

Louis was proud to be able to state, "In Stratford, every play has its own original musical score .... Not only the orchestral music but all the songs and vocal music have been recently composed for that show." This was the reason why, when asked if his music could be used in another theatre's production, Louis could only reply in the negative.

> That's why I was rather surprised, almost shocked, last year when I received a spate of enquiries, all from U.S. Colleges, some in the east, others in the west or south, all unrelated, all of whose drama departments seemed to be staging *Hamlet* and all of whose drama directors asked whether they could borrow from me or Stratford the musical score to *Hamlet.* Which *Hamlet?* What kind of *Hamlet?*[31]

He was forced to inform his correspondents that

> I have composed *Hamlet* music four separate times...and each one completely different. Not a single element on one *Hamlet* score could be used in any of the other *Hamlet* Productions... four absolutely new scores were required....[32]

For Louis, the music for each presentation was absolutely non-transferable, as "all aspects of a musical score (the concept, the style, even the cueing and instrumentation) grow out of the director's attitude to the play in question."[33]

Over the previous ten years, Louis had learned a full battery of devices for providing musical support, and he was able to provide his Convocation Hall audience with many examples. He made it clear that he did not regard his role as merely subordinate and responsive to the peculiar whims and predilections of a particular director. Rather he saw himself as a full member of an artistic team devoted to the proposition that Shakespeare had something to say to every age and that his own role was that of clarifying and enhancing that message.

Louis had the satisfaction of knowing that he was the composer laureate for classical theatre in North America. In the last days of the 1990s, Louis worked hard to organize the production of a compact disc of music from Stratford plays from the previous half-century. Although the music was not exclusively his own, the disc came to be largely through Louis's pressure and insistence. After Louis's death, Glenn Morley produced another recording with the appropriate title, "Fanfare." This was entirely made up of Louis's music, beginning with his initial fanfares but drawing on songs from eight of the Bard's plays. It is a splendid collection.

Louis's theatrical genius could cause laughter or tense moments. On several occasions, he transformed the regal "God Save the Queen" or the Canadian national anthem into a joyous and appropriate introduction to the particular play to be enjoyed. In 1966, his rendition of "O Canada" was aptly described by Sydney Johnson: "It was delicate, sweet, exquisite and subtly humorous and the audience first chuckled and then gave it a pro-longed ovation before they sat down again to await the opening lines of the play."[34] The next year, "O Canada" became the introduction to *The Merry Wives of Windsor*, at which time critic Nathan Cohen took the opportuni-ty to congratulate Louis, but also to make an acerbic comment about the play. "Louis Applebaum is not required to contribute much music, but his perky arrangement of "O Canada" is one of the few felicities of the inter-minable evening."[35] Louis could be quite self-deprecatory about his com-posing if he thought there was a chance of provoking a smile. When approached by Pat Sykes, who was commissioned to provide an article for the annual special Festival edition of the Stratford *Beacon Herald*, he announced that he wrote "instant music." To the question of how long it took to provide the score for that summer's production of *Romeo and Juliet*, he answered with another question. "Do you want me to tell the truth or should I make it sound impressive?" He gave her both responses: "It takes a few hours ... but say a couple of weeks."[36]

The Applebaum hallmark for theatre music was its unobtrusiveness — thus the very quality that made it successful as an element of the total production also allowed his music to be dismissed and forgotten. Except when the action of the play allowed for dances and songs that could stand alone, the music rarely drew comment. Yet over the several decades of his Stratford work, newspapers and periodicals carried hundreds of single-line accolades, usually in the last paragraph of the review. To give but one example, the 1961 production of *Coriolanus* occasioned a review in the Stratford *Beacon Herald*: "and the music for the play by Louis Applebaum was, as usual, an appropriate contribution to the mood, without being obtrusive."[37] Yet Louis's music for the Festival became the standard of qual-ity that every other Stratford composer sought to emulate. However, being a "standard" does not necessarily bring appreciation for musical genius. Too often, his contribution was taken for granted by critics and audiences alike, as well as by his fellow artists and composers.

Perhaps Louis describes his own intense commitment most clearly in a reply to a letter from John Corigliano, an American composer who, by the end of the century was to achieve a substantial international reputation. Corigliano wished to build a rental library for incidental music and wanted to know whether Louis would like to have a company called Music for the Theatre handle his work.[38] Louis replied, indicating the limitations that his style of composing for theatre would place on such "handling."

> The scores I write are very carefully integrated into and a part of the specific production as conceived by that director for the occasion. For example, though I have made settings of the songs in Shakespearean plays, even these are treated according to the needs of that production, sometimes with vocal support, sometimes instrumental, etc.[39]

Louis's work for film, radio and television drama was voluminous and often just as "occasion-specific." He received many awards but, too often, "incidental" came to mean "invisible." It is unconscionable that the commercial value of time encourages the trivialization of the creators of television drama, in particular, by running the list of credits at such speed that they cannot be read by the audience. The composer looks in vain for any strong message of appreciation or understanding. Louis was not alone. Virtually all composers shared this sense of being exploited, manipulated, and under-valued in this genre of musical composition. The irony is that the performer's name often becomes a household word, while the creator remains unknown and unheralded.

Louis learned very early that if he was to ply his craft in this field of endeavour, anonymity would often be his fate. Another area unkind to creators has been that of music or drama for children. There is a general perception that such work is, by definition, lesser in quality than what would be produced for adults. In literature, Canada has achieved international prominence for its splendid children's books. But Canadians are also well served by the theatre companies that produce plays for young audiences — and the composers who provide music for them. Louis had no hesitation in accepting commissions for children's productions. Indeed, with his belief in the necessity of first-class arts education, he welcomed the opportunity. His old friend Lawrence Cherney, a superb woodwind artist and now an arts entrepreneur, conceived the idea of a special series of newly created works for children and their families, "Musical Mondays." He asked Louis to write the music for a ghost story.

A potential author for the story came immediately to mind. For years, Robertson Davies had been writing ghost stories for adults, often presented at Massey College where he was Master. However, these were very much "adult" offerings. Would he write one for children? It turned out that Davies was delighted. Cherney had engaged another prestigious pair, author/dramatist James Reaney and composer John Beckwith, to write another piece that would precede the ghost story on the program. Called "All the Bees and all the Keys," it was to be a romp that would both entertain and inform. Cherney gathered a small orchestra of the finest musicians and enlisted Richard Greenblatt, a talented actor and director, to ensure that the productions would be of the highest quality. These children's evenings are still remembered by adults who might initially have been dragooned into an evening at the Young People's Theatre, only to find that they were as enthralled by the performance as their offspring. Davies proposed to tell a very personal story, *The Harper of the Stones*, purporting to be about the large stones on the border of his retreat property in the Caledon Hills. It was a perfect setting for the author to meet a "very dirty, old man dressed in clothes so worn and stained, I could not tell whether they were cloth or leather." He was found to be playing a harp, "not *to* the stones but *for* them," in order that they might dance. Louis had to use every musical trick at his disposal to convince his young audience that those stones were really dancing. Though restrained by the size of the orchestra that John Beckwith had gathered for the first piece on the evening's program (flute, clarinet, violin, viola, cello, and percussion), Louis added, in order to "extract a variety of harp-sounding colourations," a synthesizer. This was an instrument that he himself had become familiar with, and one his young audience would recognize immediately. Robertson Davies' text created an atmosphere of both fun and foreboding; the description of the past witnessed by these stones informed the audience of the rich heritage of Norse, French, English, and Irish traditions Canada possessed. Louis's music created the rhythmic expectation that would inspire the stones to dance, and a lyrical delight that would engage the children's interest. *The Harper of the Stones* was greeted with warm enthusiasm by both children and their parents.[40]

Four years later, Cherney invited Louis to work with the imaginative humorist Paul Quarrington on a short play with the intriguing title, *So You Think You Are Mozart*. The plot was outlined in a column authored by Ron Hambleton.

> When the ghost of 13-year-old Mozart kibitzes in hockey-loving Jeremiah Danby's piano lesson, which he finds sheer torture under the tart comments of Mr. Pachter, his

nit-picking teacher, the two boys have intelligent fun making music together, while they poke fun at Pachter to whom Mozart is invisible.[41]

Hambleton found the play "musically charming," enjoyed Louis's "opening overture...with its variation on Mozart themes," and declared it "typical of Applebaum's competently animated music." Louis had a small orchestra led by Lawrence Cherney on oboe and English horn. There were also two violins, a viola, a cello, and a double bass. One might have expected Louis to have made liberal use of Mozart's music, but except for excerpts from the "Sonata in C, Opus 112" and the "Minuet in F," all the music was composed by Louis himself.[42] The only other piece of "outside" music he used was the theme for CBC television's "Hockey Night in Canada" — a piece of music Louis used, with variations, to buoy up Jeremiah's efforts to help Mozart's ghost understand Canada's national winter pastime.

These scores were written for children but were given the same amount of working time and creative energy as the most solemn offering for church or synagogue. There was no "composing down for kids" in the works of Louis Applebaum. He demanded the highest standards of himself and of those with whom he was collaborating. Fortunately, in Davies and Quarrington he had associates who were as devoted to works for children as he was, and in Cherney he had a presenter with an equal commitment.

He was to have other artistic collaborations with Robertson Davies. In 1980 Louis was commissioned to write "A Holly Wreath" for the Christmas "Gaudy" at Massey College, to be sung by the Massey College Choir under Giles Bryant. The libretto was a collection of very modern and purposefully irreverent carols, written or adapted by the college's Master, Davies. The first, "Wot ye, Churl" included a melody line sung by women's voices and supported by tenor and bass chanting of "Alcan, Xerox," and later "Postum, Nabisco, and Domtar" as the rhythm changed. The selection concluded with a culmination by full chorus of this paean to Canadian corporate power. The second carol, "Cold Blows the Wind," was a reverie, not only evoking the unpleasant climate of the country, but also the irritation felt by citizens who had to rise early in the morning to face it. The music sought to match the expression of distaste captured in the lyrics. The third carol had as its main theme "Luckless King Henry VIII," married "thrice to Catherine, twice to Anne, and once to Jane Seymour." "Swift to adore" and "so swift to scorn" summed up each relationship and the music had a remarkable Elizabethan ring to it. Finally, "A College Noel" contained a greeting that only an institution of higher learning could have expressed, and the music rocked with celebratory rhythm. It was all a glorious romp to be enjoyed by singers and their audience of somewhat inebriated scholars.[43]

Even while Louis was prepared to contribute his gift of music to all sorts of occasions and projects meant to evoke laughter and gaiety, he took the task of composing very seriously. There was little likelihood that his music would capture the interest of recording companies, yet he worked for decades to find the resources that would encourage the production of recordings of Canadian music. His royalties for performances of his music, either live or on radio, were quite minimal, and yet he worked assiduously to strengthen the performing rights organizations for the benefit of those composers who depended upon their royalties. Most important of all, Louis was a continuing advocate for contemporary "serious" music, convinced by his experience with the International Conference of Composers at Stratford in 1960, as well as own travels, that Canadian composers were the equal of any to be found in the world.

Louis used his Federal Cultural Policy Review role in the early 1980s as a platform to proclaim the quality of Canadian composition within the context of his theme of support for creativity and creators. However, he was troubled by the fact that, in contrast to the mass-market appeal of pop music and Hollywood film, "public attention [in the area of serious musical expression] is focussed on the past to the almost total neglect of both the output of today and those responsible for it." In particular, he opined "Attention to new music is uncomfortably close to zero." In a document he wrote for the FCPRC, he asked the question, "What explains the large gap, especially in music, between what creators are currently authoring and what the public is ready to accept"? He responded by positing that, for 50 years, "artists have grasped at new ideas, sounds, visions, concepts, and theories for their own sake and in order to stay abreast of peers in other parts of the world ... and the public seems to have been pushed aside and, finding itself out of the mainstream, has in turn turned its back on those who seem to live and operate in a little world of their own." Ultimately, he argued, the audience for "serious music" could now be divided into "two publics:" a large one for "the safe, acceptable, comprehensible music of the classical, romantic periods and a very tiny one for today's music." Louis asked his colleagues on the Federal Cultural Policy Review Committee, "What can we, or should we do about turning an audience that is indifferent, if not antagonistic, into one that is involved and participatory?" He recognized how public broadcasting around the world had given air time to new music, and even commissioned new works. He saw new music festivals as a focus opportunity and the strengthening of copyright legislation that supported creators as part of the solution; however, he was driven to the despairing observation that "It may be true that if we were to stop composing … such works, hardly anyone would notice." And yet he knew that, if that happened, "we would be depriving ourselves of the essence of our future heritage." This was the ultimate truth, in Louis's eyes. He believed that encouraging the educational system to provide residencies, not only at the university and college level, but also at the elementary level and in community settings, was essential. "Giving artists grants to buy time, the commissioning of works" were all worthwhile strategies. However, "in a society engaged in breathless change, we need to be able to sort out the useful from the worthless, the valuable from the wasteful." His conclusion: "Perhaps the most useful in the long run would be to evoke in Canadians greater respect for inventiveness, to help them recognize and appreciate innovation." In the wake of such a change in societal values would come new opportunities for contemporary music. In this context, the composer would become a "player" involved completely in the mainstream of Canadian life.[44]

And Louis continued to compose music. Within a few months after his work on the Federal Cultural Policy Review Committee was completed, he was contacted by Harry Rasky to compose the score for a film about Raymond Massey, designated in this production as the "Actor of the Century." In spite of Louis's feeling that his skills were rusty from the years of attending committee meetings, making speeches, writing reports, and coping with conflict on all sides, Louis's music for the film turned out to be a triumph. Rasky had spent four days filming conversations with an aged and very fragile Massey who, unfortunately, died the day after the process was completed. In the midst of all the drama of the occasion, Louis found new energy and composed one of his finest offerings. When Rasky was asked by Mike Boone of the *Ottawa Citizen* why he was so interested in artists as subjects of his documentaries, this man who had, in the past decade, completed films on Bernard Shaw, Henry Moore, Marc Chagall, Tennessee Williams, and Arthur Miller put into words what could have served as an epilogue to Louis's Federal Cultural Policy Review Report: "I have to sound a little religious.... I think the act of creation is the closest you can come to godliness. It is fascinating to look at the struggle to create."[45]

Mike Boone was most adulatory about Louis's supporting role in the Massey production. "Louis Applebaum composed a marvelous music score for the film; and Maureen Forrester's rendition of 'Try to Remember,' heard over the introductory and closing credit sequences, is absolutely spine-tingling."[46] Indeed, the film became a "fitting memorial to a great Canadian artist."

In 1988, at the age of 70 and in the midst of the CAPAC-PROCAN merger, Louis took on a major project, a CBC two-part, four-hour miniseries, "Glory Enough for All." With one of Canada's finest actors, R.H. Thomson, in the central role as Dr. Frederick Banting, the program told the story of the discovery of insulin — a discovery that had saved millions of lives and brought Canada its first Nobel Prize in 1923. The script, based on Michael Bliss's biography of Banting, was described by Michael Bawden as "Canadian drama that makes history live." The spellbinding series was, for Louis, an opportunity to write music that would attract audiences to a story — sometimes unpleasant — about medical research that had been one of the major triumphs of the 20th century. "Glory Enough for All" was a fine production that Bawden concluded " is Good Enough for a new category: the Canadian historical drama." The presentation not only depicted the actual discovery, but also the ambitious desire for exclusive accolade craved by both Banting and Best, as well as some of their lesser-known colleagues. It was a compelling documentary about human pride and vulnerability — made more poignant by its focus on a little girl who whose life was saved by the miraculous cure for diabetes. Louis captured the despair of failure and the triumph of success, but, even more, the myriad conflicting human emotions that permeated a fine script.[47]

It was perhaps fitting that Louis's career as a freelance television drama composer should draw near to a close with two CBC Television productions of Stratford Festival summer offerings, *Much Ado About Nothing* in 1987, and *The Taming of the Shrew* in 1988. *Much Ado* had a cast that included Richard Monette, Tandy Cronyn, and William Hutt. Peter Moss, the director, had set the play in Victorian England and the theme of the suffragette movement came to dominate in what Ray Conlogue of the Globe and Mail called "a sober tack." In this guise the play lost its lightness, humour, and joy and "so it is that the famous verbal dueling matches between the two [principals], all those wonderful insults and brilliant repartée, come out with something of a dull clunk." Even Louis's music received a barbed response. "Louis Applebaum's musical settings of the play's songs are saccharine in the extreme, even if he does try to save one with a barber-shop quartet ending. A little more irreverence would have gone a long way with this production."[48] As might be expected the television production did not prove any more successful than the stage version.

On the other hand, the television production of *The Taming of the Shrew* was well received by the critics. To quote the headline to Robert Crew's critique: "Stratford's Shrew shines on CBC-TV." The summer production had been a debut success for Richard Monette as director of a major production. In his review, Crew expressed his approval of the fact that "the characters break into voluble Italian and sing Italian songs (actually translations of Shakespeare)."[49] This was a very satisfying conclusion to all the work

Louis had done to put Stratford productions on the CBC, and he was rewarded with the special treat of having Norman Campbell produce this final broadcast offering.

The final Applebaum contribution at the CBC was a score for Harry Rasky's program on Yousuf Karsh, "The Searching Eye." The film showed how the famed photographer "searches for the inner power of his subjects..." and, to Louis's delight, it received an Emmy nomination.[50] For Louis, this marked the end of over four decades of composing for radio and television. In particular, it was his final contribution in a career devoted to a medium that exposed every inadequacy, but had nevertheless brought immense satisfaction to Louis.

However, Louis's role as a composer was still not over. He continued to accept commissions from musicians and musical organizations. In the early 1990s, with his health now in a state of some jeopardy, he began the task of writing his most ambitious composition, an opera, *Erewhon*, with Mavor Moore as librettist. "*Erewhon* gave me two extra years of life," Louis contended. From the point of view of his doctor, who had predicted his death some years earlier, this was an accurate observation.[51]

Mavor Moore had contacted Louis in Toronto from his home in Victoria, British Columbia, in 1995, reminding Louis of their pledge to write an opera together. Moore had been at the United Nations in the 1940s and had hired Louis to write the music for a radio feature, "Year of Decision," featuring the opinions of Albert Einstein on the challenge to humankind represented by the presence of atomic power. On that occasion they had enjoyed working together and, at the end, Moore had suggested that the two should write an opera together. "And we drank to that!" said Moore, describing the incident many years later.[52] Now, nearly half a century later, it was time. Both were now septuagenarians, in rather poor health (both had undergone lung operations) and as Moore put it to Louis: "The best news is the successful lung surgery. You and I and our lungs, kiddo. How were we to know they'd get back at us like this, just for taking them for granted? If my doctors are correct, we'll just have to learn to live with part-time breathing."[53]

Moore had become interested in utopian literature back in the 1950s, having adapted Voltaire's *Candide* for CBC Radio. The result was the first musical produced on the network and was called "The Best of All Possible Worlds." Although Moore had been interested in producing Voltaire's work for the stage, another version of *Candide*, composed by a young American composer named Leonard Bernstein, promised severe competition.[54] Instead, Moore turned to a late 19th-century author, Samuel Butler, who had written two utopian novels, *Erewhon* and *Erewhon Revisited.* Now

Moore reminded Louis of their projected collaboration and directed him to the Butler works. Louis reacted positively. "I'm glad you enjoyed the Butler epic. I felt sure its cutting edge would appeal to you. Who was it said a librettist's main role is to inspire the composer?" It was at that point that Moore, who had no intention of writing an opera with anyone else, revealed his plans in more detail.

> You are quite right in supposing that I have an unconven-
> tional work in mind — possibly akin to *The Rakes Progress*
> or even *Candide* than to traditional European opera seria or
> bouffa, but possibly also quite original. I see many of
> Butler's intellectual points made by visual means — the
> museum, the colleges, the court, the banks are marvelous
> challenges to ingenious set and costume design — with
> only essential verbal/vocal helmsmanship.[55]

This opera was to be much more than a dramatization of a rather intellectual novel about a world that never existed. As it developed, it became a commentary on the inanities of 20th-century morality and social behaviour. The sets and costumes became a problem, rather than a solution. Louis, with his unfailing sense of the dramatic, saw the central issue quite clearly:

> The tricky part comes from making the satire obvious to
> the audience realizing that what seems to be perverse and
> up-side-down Erehwon justice and social behaviour is real-
> ly what our society is living in the 1990s. How subtle dare
> we get? Or how obvious before we're accused of Kitsch?
> But those are questions you can deal with off-hand.[56]

By mid-July of 1997, Moore had made an important decision: the hero, Higgs, should be a Canadian. This focussed the irony of every situation squarely on the beloved homeland of both creators. Not only did this ensure that the social comment of the dialogue would have obvious connections to political events in Canada, it gave an even greater reason for the interest of one of the possible venues for the world premiere, the National Arts Centre in Ottawa. Louis was delighted.

> I have just had the unique thrill of reading your first three
> scenes of our epic. I am driven eagerly to the score paper.
> I must say that I am awed by your ability to treat theatri-
> cal problems so effectively. I can get to work with the

material exactly as it is. I think the idea of making our hero Canadian is brilliant. It leads inevitably to the exposure of our inherent foolishness and strengths.[57]

Louis was thrilled to be involved in making an opera. His work at CBC had dried up and, except for the Danny Grossman commission to write the music for a production of "The Nutcracker," there was nothing on his desk. He was anxious about whether the style of his music would be appropriate for the 19th-century visionary novel that Mavor Moore was adapting. As he began to write music to Moore's text, he warned his librettist of possible reactions.

> Herewith a rough sketch of Scene 2 ... to give you an idea of the idiom in which I think. As you see, it is rather tonal ... with touches of discord. I'm sure the 'modern' thinkers and critics will dismiss it out of hand, but even when I write on a 12-tone base, the figures seem to come out this way.[58]

Louis, as always, was determined that this opera enterprise should be more than just fun for the creators. He wanted to see the opera staged, if possible, in his own lifetime. There were a number of possibilities. Moore had a close relationship with the Charlottetown Festival and Louis, of course, was still composing for the Stratford Festival, but these were unlikely prospects. The Canadian Opera Company, under Richard Bradshaw, was committing itself to Canadian opera with a production of Randolph Peters and Robertson Davies's *The Golden Ass*, so it was unlikely that a second contemporary offering could to be considered in the short term. Louis still had connections with the National Arts Centre and this looked promising in view of the positive response of John Cripton, the NAC's director. It turned out to be the wrong choice.

Louis knew there was money available. The irrepressible Niki Goldschmidt had yet another project underway. Called "Music Canada Musique 2000," its purpose was to celebrate the millennium year by supporting the commissioning of new music works by Canadian composers. In short, it was to honour Canadian creativity, a goal close to Louis's heart. Though Goldschmidt had asked him to be an advisor, Louis had declined, not wishing to "advise" on the quality of his colleagues' work, but also realizing that he himself might wish to be an applicant. He secured Goldschmidt's interest immediately.

> Niki: You asked about the opera Mavor Moore and I are developing. Mavor had proposed a work based on Samuel Butler's *Erehwon* and *Erehwon Revisited.* Though written in the 1870s this brilliant satire speaks eloquently to the 1990s. Just as the title, read backwards, says "Nowhere," the society that emerges in this hidden land discovered by our hero is topsy-turvy in all its social structures and attitudes: machinery, including clocks have been banned and relegated to museums; illness and poverty are severely punished as crimes, while what we call crimes are treated as illnesses by the equivalent of our medical practitioners. Banks do their business to music; the university is "the College of Unreason"; hospitals treat boredom and on it goes ....[59]

Niki, whose adulation of Louis's cultural contribution was unbounded, was to be both a source of revenue and an active supporter of the opera's production in the year 2000. Obviously Louis could do little composing until Moore had written the libretto. Thus, though there were a few flurries of interchange during 1996, a storm mostly of e-mails ensued in the next three years, backed up by a few telephone calls, faxes, and large packages sent by courier. On occasion, a speaking engagement brought Moore to Toronto, and a rare opportunity for face-to-face collaboration occurred. But the circumstances produced a rare phenomenon — an opera written with librettist and composer thousands of miles apart. Perhaps *Erehwon* is the first opera written through the extensive use of e-mail — hundreds of such messages crossed the country, adjusting the score and the libretto often down to the tiniest detail. The result of this process is that posterity has a complete record of the creation of a major work by two cultural icons of 20th-century Canada.

One wishes that the production of *Erehwon* could have gone as smoothly and collegially as the writing, but that was not to be. Once the National Arts Centre agreed to house the production, it took some of the pressure off. For example, the NAC was prepared to support (with the assistance of Music Canada Musique 2000) the cost of workshops, and Louis and Mavor Moore began to organize these in Toronto. The elation of having found a presenter was short lived; just when the arrangements for scheduling and producing were to be made, an uproar erupted around John Cripton's leadership at the NAC and occasioned his departure. Another venue had to be found. Fortunately, with Niki

Goldschmidt's help, Pacific Opera Victoria took up the challenge. The artistic director and conductor, Timothy Vernon, was successful in attracting the interest of Brian Macdonald — a choreographer and director of major renown well known to both Louis and Mavor Moore. However, danger signs emerged early in the relationship as Macdonald seemed reluctant to engage in any preliminary planning sessions with the authors. This lack of contact unleashed a series of events that led eventually to a limited success on stage, and a disastrous financial loss to Pacific Opera Victoria.

Even before the conclusion of the NAC's involvement, Louis and Mavor Moore were putting their time into the task of organizing the first workshop in Toronto in 1998. Louis was aware of the importance of fine, articulate singers and made his point in a characteristically modest fashion.

> As our work emerges, I feel that we need singers blessed not only with fine voices, but, almost more vitally, with real dramatic insight and talent. The music is not original enough in style to lead audiences into new areas of response, but, combined with the words and story we can generate the kind of reaction we are aiming for. That means the words must be heard clearly and their implications interpreted clearly by the cast, calling for special care in casting the workshop, don't you think?[60]

The workshop went well. The invited audience was enthusiastic and there were congratulations on all sides. As Louis and Mavor Moore had hoped, there were criticisms and welcome advice. John Brotman, then the Music Officer at the OAC and soon to become its Executive Director, commented that "the work needs more musical moments like the 'love duet' — very moving." This gave Louis and Moore the energy to carry on and, by the end of 1998, Moore was feeling confident that the work was coming together.

> I've just been through the new score and congratulate you on the sensitivity and invention with which you have spruced it up. The arias and duets work splendidly and throughout you have caught every little nuance, and neatly re-tied every problematic knot. My notes are really more like grace notes than real notes.[61]

Another workshop on the second act of the opera a year later was received with comparable enthusiasm, though, by this time, Louis was too ill to attend.

In the meantime, events surrounding the production at Pacific Opera Victoria were not going well. Brian Macdonald felt overwhelmed by the storm of e-mails flying back and forth between the authors. (Louis and Mavor Moore had added his address to their e-mail loop.) Feeling that he was being given no creative leeway, he resigned, with the parting comment to Moore that the last memo "was one memo too many" and he "couldn't face ten more weeks of that." Moore's comment was that "we have more confidence in you than you seem to have in us."[62] Timothy Vernon, at Pacific Opera, was shaken and worked assiduously to bring Brian Macdonald back. He succeeded, but at a price. From that point, there would be no direct contact between the director and the authors of the opera. All communication would be through Vernon himself. It was not a happy arrangement and no further meetings arranged to patch things up were successful.[63] Moore's perception was clear:

> My instinct tells me that to keep Brian aboard Tim has already caved in and sold us down the river. That is he has agreed to the arrangement whereby Brian will be freed of all contact with us ... This means in effect that Brian will have carte blanche, and we will be shut out of the production from here in.[64]

Moore's prediction proved to be accurate. Moore, who was raising money from generous benefactors, was stung when the Manager of Pacific Opera commented that "just because you raised money doesn't mean you have a right to interfere in artistic decisions." At this point, Moore had to remind the administrator that he was one of the writers of the work to be performed. In the end it came down to a situation in which Moore, the only creator on site, had no part in the designs of costumes or sets. What had been conceived almost as a chamber opera became "grand" in design, at enormous cost. This extravagance significantly buried the intellectual content and, at the same time, the effectiveness of Louis's music. Mavor Moore, and particularly Louis, were experts in copyright and had every right within the contractual arrangements with Pacific Opera to be consulted on changes in the original concept and script, but it would have meant that they would have had to threaten to withdraw the production. Mavor Moore was anxious that Louis hear his work before he died, and chose to step back. The opera went on in February 2000 and Pacific Opera Victoria lost $250,000.

Erehwon was Louis's most extensive composition and it is tragic that the production was not up to the expectations of the creators. Louis believed this opera to be his most important work. It is difficult to believe that this opus was composed by a man in his 80s, suffering through the last debilitating stages of cancer. The music was lyrical, joyous, and highly evocative. The orchestration supported the singers and the text magnificently. With all the ironic commentary of Butler's novels intact, the story had romantic interest that was well served by the lush beauty of composition that enhanced Moore's expressive lines. Louis's philosophy of music-making is described in the program notes he wrote to provide a description of the collaborative process that had brought the work about.

> The music for *Erehwon* is bound intimately to the words with which Mavor Moore built his libretto. That he has been able to convert what is in fact a satirical essay by Butler, into flesh-and-blood theatre, is remarkable and noteworthy. The musical goal has been to provide for the all-important goal, settings that could enhance their meaning and their context, clarify the sub-text and assist in probing the characters. The collaboration between this librettist and this composer has been exceptional. Since any verbal phrase can be turned into music in dozens of different ways, there has been a continuous exchange of ideas and understandings, using all available mans of communication.
>
> For over 30 months both have been totally devoted to this work, all day every day. Throughout there has not been a hint of tension or misunderstanding. Scenes have been written and then cut out; characters have been excised and others drastically rethought. The score and the libretto have thus gone through several versions but always on the basis of complete respect for the integrity of each other's work. The precision and concern for significant detail have been key elements in the evolution of this opera.[65]

The ultimate disappointment for Louis was that his doctor strongly advised him not to go to Victoria for the Opening Night of *Erehwon* on February 17, 2000. He was devastated, having looked forward to this occasion for many months. The reviews were not entirely positive, although Alan Boss's special coverage for *The Globe and Mail* caught some of the main strengths of the work:

> Mavor Moore and Louis Applebaum have proven again their status as Canadian cultural icons with a new opera that transports its audience to another world.
>
> *Erehwon*, which debuted at Pacific Opera Victoria on Saturday, tells the story of a man who goes in search of his fortune to Erehwon: a land where values and morals take second place to wealth and position. In Erehwon, it is illegal to be unlucky, victims are sent to prison and criminals receive therapy. Sound familiar?
>
> In many ways, this opera is an ironic parallel to today's society, where injustices happen all too frequently. The right people get punished and the wrong people win the day .... Applebaum's music, conducted by Timothy Vernon, works to enhance the drama in every scene. When the text calls for love, sweet melodies drift out of the pit and land in our ears. Dramatic scenes are created instantly by his notes.[66]

Erehwon was a splendid effort. A reading of Butler's novel and its successor, *Erehwon Revisited*, leaves one amazed that any librettist and composer would seek to create an opera from these volumes. *Erehwon* is almost entirely a philosophical treatise. At one point, Mavor Moore and Louis were considering whether it might be called *An Opera Adventure* or *A Fantastical Opera*. This might have provided some helpful distance between *Erehwon* and the plot-laden operas of Verdi and Puccini. The richness of the irony and the singular relevance of the subject matter was clarified by what Louis believed to be his most accessible music. The production, which emphasized the development of the characters and the tension inherent in their relationships, as well as the elaborate sets and costumes, overwhelmed the creators' intentions. The text was "the thing," but it was buried in production decisions that would have been more appropriate for a different tradition of operatic work. The references to a "Board of Cultural Propriety" and a "Royal Commission on Worldly Wisdom" were lost, to say nothing of the "Colleges of Unreason," all overflowing with messages for Canadians. The final words written by Mavor Moore were set to a hymn-like tune and exhibited the Canadian nationalism of both of *Erehwon*'s creators, much of it tongue in cheek, but also expressing their hopes for the future of their beloved land.

> How fortunate we are …
> How smiled upon we are!
> How happy to be living here and now!
> How lovely to be strong and beautifully made!
> How very radiant we are.
> Here in Erehwon.
> How virtuous and pure,
> How decent and humane … .
> How honest and spontaneous we are!
> So peaceful! so polite,
> So tolerant and wise …
> Here in Erehwon!
> How well endowed we are,
>   how modest, how refined and morally inferior to none,
> How wonderful to know how wonderful we are,
> so gifted, so able, so clever, so stable, so wonderful we are,
> Here in Erehwon!

Fortunately, CBC Radio had taped the production for presentation on its "Saturday Afternoon at the Opera" program and Mavor Moore, through the efforts of Executive Producer Robert Cooper, was able to convey a prerelease tape to Louis before he died. In many ways, radio's concentration on sound gave Louis a sense of accomplishment and a confidence that this last composition was a worthy example of his art.

While *Erehwon* was being written, a celebration of Louis's life as a composer —and his 80th birthday — came on the night of April 6, 1998, in the Jane Mallett Theatre at the St. Lawrence Centre for the Arts. The celebration was presented by Soundstreams Canada, the company established by Lawrence Cherney, Louis's long-time friend and artistic collaborator, whose entire family had known Louis since the boys' teenage days selling magazine subscriptions in Eastern Ontario.[67]

It was a glorious occasion. All his friends were present from across the continent, and particularly from Toronto and environs. Although the celebration was a sufficient reason for the gathering, the event was also the initial step in procuring financing for a Composers' Fund to be administered by the Ontario Arts Council. The Fund would recognize the excellence of Ontario composers — a cause close to Louis's heart. The Laidlaw Foundation and a host of Louis's friends had ensured that the financial results of the evening would be bounteous. To Louis's utmost satisfaction, the program was given over almost entirely to musical works drawn from various periods in his composing life. The only diversion from this musical program would be an appeal for funds from Hal Jackman, the OAC's Chair, along with a delightful musical tribute from his composer friends from the earliest days — Harry Freedman, Phil Nimmons, Harry Somers and John Weinzweig — who provided a series of variations on his theme from *All's Well That Ends Well*. There was in place a phalanx of actors, musicians, and vocalists, all of whom had donated their services. The host for the evening was Louis's Stratford colleague, Douglas Campbell, along with his son, Benedict — now almost as distinguished an actor as his father — and Billie Mae Richards. The Canadian Brass and the Elmer Iseler Singers (now, after Iseler's death, conducted by Lydia Adams and with Peter Tiefenbach accompanying) were all on stage. Soprano Monica Whicher and tenor Mark Dubois were present as were Robert Cram, a close friend from Ottawa who was on flute, and composer Gary Kulesha, who was at the piano. On the harp was Erica Goodman, who would commission one more piece from Louis in the last year of his life — a piece he was never able to complete. Rounding out the group was Louis's closest collaborator, Glenn Morley at the keyboard.

It was an assembly of friends committed to a demonstration of this man's genius as a composer. The program opened with *A Holly Wreath,* a collection of songs with words written by Robertson Davies. These were followed by songs written by Louis in the mid-1990s, witness to the fact that the muse had remained with the composer, even as time and illness advanced. Then followed "Algoma Central," an appropriate selection that Louis had written in 1976, on commission from the Algoma Spring Festival in Sault Ste. Marie, emphasizing the inspiration of Canada's north along with the importance of the railway in opening up the lands to settlers and thus creating a nation. There was humour and relevance in the titles of the movements — "Baggage," "Timetable," and "Fugue" — all promising a delightful musical journey. The second part of the program began with the songs from Louis's productions at Stratford, introduced by the famous Stratford fanfares. Louis's music for W.O. Mitchell's "Jake and the Kid's Christmas" was delightfully narrated by Billie Mae Richards, but the Applebaum touch in scoring for radio drama was palpable. The evening ended with Louis's setting of a poem by Rabbi Alvin Fine, "Life's Journey." No piece of music, no enhancement of text, could have ended the evening with so much poignancy and satisfaction. Louis had written the music in 1994, just two years after his lung operation, and at a time when both his doctors and his own body were letting him know that his time was coming to an end.[68] Larry Howe, a colleague from the University of Saskatchewan, expressed the view of everyone present when he wrote to Louis a few days later that "everyone had such a happy time, the music was wonderfully played and sung, there was a glow of goodwill over the hall throughout the night … the Composer's Fund is well launched."[69]

When his funeral was being planned two years later, his family knew he wanted no eulogies. On the evening of the celebration, his friends, both on stage and in the audience, had paid him their tributes through the performance of his own music. That was enough. People would remember him as a composer, and this was the legacy Louis wanted most.

Louis with Sir Ernest MacMillan, Rosa Ponselle, and Gordon Kushner on the occasion of the first MacMillan Lectures, 1970.

Louis Applebaum with James Westaway (a former chorister of the Mendelssohn Choir and Chair of the Board), bidding farewell to Elmer and Jessie Iseler as they are about to set off on the Choir's tour of Europe in 1972.

A British Council sponsored visit to the United Kingdom. Left to right: Gilles Lefebvre (Director-General, International Cultural Relations, Department of External Affairs, Canada); D. Paul Schafer (Arts Consultant, Canada); Louis Julé (Executive Director, Department of Youth, Saskatchewan); Warren Langford (Director-General for Culture, Department of the Secretary of State, Canada); Lord Donaldson of Knightbridge (Minister for the Arts, U.K.); Louis Applebaum (Executive Director, Ontario Arts Council); Tim Porteous (Associate Director, Canada Council); John Hobday (Executive Director, Canada Council for the Arts). January 11, 1979.

Louis Applebaum with Robertson Davies in collaboration for the production of "Harper of the Stones," 1987.

Louis Applebaum with Timothy Findley on his right and William Whitehead on his left, working on the CBC production of "The National Dream," 1976.

Louis and Jan Applebaum at Rideau Hall on the occasion of his appointment as an Officer of the Order of Canada, 1976.

Louis Applebaum, Chair, and Jacques Hebert, Co-chair of the Federal
Cultural Policy Review Committee, 1981.

Jan and Louis Applebaum with grandson Jordan on the day of his graduation from York University, 1992.

Louis Applebaum flanked by his grandson Jordan and his son David at the 1994 University of Windsor Convocation. Jordan graduated with an MBA, and Louis received an Honourary Degree.

Courtesy: Jan Applebaum

Jan and Louis Applebaum at the University of Windsor
Graduation, 1994.

Louis and Jan with their granddaughters, Jennifer and Carrie, 1990.

Louis (Artistic Advisor, Guelph Spring Festival) in conversation with author James Reaney and composer John Beckwith, both creators of the 1994 Festival production "Crazy to Kill," a musical mystery.

Louis Applebaum (Artistic Advisor), Nicholas Goldschmidt (Founding Artistic Director), and William Lord (a succeeding Artistic Director). Guelph Spring Festival, 1994.

The Great Celebration:
Louis Applebaum's eightieth birthday, St. Lawrence Centre, April 6, 1998.

Louis Applebaum with Gwen Setterfield — a successor as Director of the OAC.

Louis Applebaum speaking with Victor Feldbrill, conductor, as sister Ruth looks on.

Louis Applebaum, greeted by David Silcox, a close friend and colleague.

Louis Applebaum in conversation with the Dean of Canadian composers, John Weinzweig.

Chapter Twenty
The Sage

The Federal Cultural Policy Review Committee had imposed a serious change on one aspect of Louis's life — his role as an academic. In 1975, while at the Ontario Art Council, Louis had embarked on a journey of some importance. He had been approached by the Fine Arts Department of York University and invited to teach a course that would blend music, film, and theatre arts. Louis was delighted. In spite of the pressures of OAC administration and a very busy schedule of composing music, this invitation was not just welcomed, it was celebrated! Through four decades, Louis had envied the benefits of academic positions enjoyed by colleagues such as John Weinzweig, the Adaskins, John Beckwith, and Phil Nimmons. They were privileged to spend a part of their lives thinking about music, studying the work of other composers, and best of all, passing on to future generations the knowledge they had gained from their own experiences. As well, this invitation was an indication that Louis's creative specialty — bringing music to screen and stage — was receiving serious attention, even in the halls of higher learning.

Louis had no Canadian competitors in his areas of expertise. In theatre, he had 20 years of writing music for Stratford under his belt; his work for radio was prolific; he had pioneered the field of film music at the NFB; he had experienced the "mecca" of Hollywood; he had visited, on occasion, the world of the "art film;" and he had successfully made the transition to composing for television. Moreover, he had already tried his hand at teaching through single lectures and seminars he had presented at various universities and colleges. As far back as 1947, before he was 30 years old, he had been asked to contribute to "the first series on film music ... at the New School's Dramatic Workshop Film Department in New York City." On that occasion, the teachers and students had wanted to hear about the music for *Tomorrow the World* and *The Story of G.I. Joe.*[1]

Louis had experienced the enormous satisfaction of meeting students who were intrigued by his philosophy of film music, and who found his exploration of the film genre exciting. In his York University course, he made use of his own films to illustrate how music could bring clarity and excitement to a text. His classes were not for the mildly interested or scarcely motivated. He geared his lectures and laboratory sessions to serve the truly involved student. Unfortunately, in the late 1970s, the class size tended to be too large for suitable concentration on the needs of individual aspirants to a career in writing music for theatre or film. His teaching did, however, give Louis the opportunity to give "the Big Picture" of the arts of music, theatre, and film to students who were really interested. He taught by the project method. For example, he would provide a scenario of action that could appear in any drama and the student would produce musical sounds that might accompany such visual expression in such a way that the scene would be enhanced. One student remembers writing music to accompany the washing of hands.[2] Louis was patient and understanding about any technical shortcomings that students exhibited, but he did want the composition of music for theatre and film to be taken very seriously. Louis cared little for the pass-fail game. Very often he brought guests to the class. Vincent Tovell and Harry Rasky came often, year after year. Although Louis's was a general course, there were aspiring composers in the class and Louis wanted those students to meet individuals who had made a great contribution to the art of film-making.[3] He was not sure that one could teach music composition — a function he felt to be a very personal expression — to anyone else. Later in life, he was asked, "What advice would you give today's young composers?" His response summed up his teaching philosophy:

> There's an axiom that has always pertained: Develop your craft! A technique that gives you fluidity and ease of creation, and the ability to handle your material. Today, with computers and synthesizers, it's very easy to generate musical sounds for hours on end, but it can't be done without the understanding of what it is that makes music – the shapes and balances that are required in a musical work. There aren't any easy ways out![4]

Louis enjoyed his years of teaching; however, when he took on the Chairmanship of the Federal Cultural Policy Review Committee in 1980, he had to withdraw from his teaching responsibility. He found this interruption disappointing, and told officials at York that he was looking forward to resuming his teaching as soon as his work in Ottawa ended. However, on his return to Toronto in 1983, he found that the University was not prepared to restore his course in the Music Division of the Fine Arts Department. By the early 1980s, the universities were experiencing serious funding cuts and seized every opportunity to reduce teaching costs.

Fortunately, there was a way out of the difficulty. Paul Hoffert was a fine, innovative musician Louis had met years before. (In the mid 1990s, he was to become Chair of the Ontario Arts Council.) Hoffert was presenting a course on music in film and television in the Film Division of York's Faculty of Fine Arts. He invited Louis to become his teaching partner. Louis and Paul Hoffert split the teaching, each taking the class on alternative weeks, but sometimes giving a class together. As Louis tended to adopt the "touchy-feely" or "creative-impulse" style of instructing, and Paul was very much in the "technical excellence" school, their differing pedagogical styles enhanced the presentation of the course. Both brought films they had worked on into the classroom, much to the delight of their students. Hoffert had put a cap on the numbers of students who could be accepted, so classes would be no larger than 15 or 20 students. This meant that individual students could be better served. In describing Louis as a teacher, Hoffert, who regards Louis as his mentor, uses the word "giving." He was totally "flexible" in his attitude to the process of learning. Hoffert found Louis's capacity to size up and address the needs of students quite extraordinary.[5]

This teaching arrangement served for the rest of the 1980s, but 1991 brought further financial restraints to the operation of universities in Ontario. As Louis explained to a friend, the Applebaum-Hoffert course had to be withdrawn "as the university couldn't afford the $3000 they were paying him because the tenured staff had to be sustained during a 1% cut in the faculty salary budget."[6] The loss of this position may not have had a very serious impact on Louis's financial situation, but it did disappoint him deeply, even though, by the 1990s, he was well past the age of retirement for regular York faculty members.

Louis's interest in higher education went far beyond teaching. His experience in convincing the University of Ottawa to establish a School of Music at the time of the founding of the National Arts Centre had drawn his interest to the issues in post-secondary curriculum development and the relationship of music offerings within the entire university community. In March 1980, he was invited to the University of Calgary, where a symposium was being presented on the place of music in higher learning. Although his paper was titled "Some Thoughts About Graduate Programs in Music," he pointed out that his own academic credentials were limited — he had a diploma in Grade 2 theory from the Hambourg Conservatory;

a framed document that proved his graduation graced the wall of his studio. He outlined his work, through the Ontario Arts Council, with postsecondary institutions that had been concentrated on "mainlining the arts." As a result, his interest lay in "the exploration by non-artists, of the meaning of the arts; the integration of the essence of music or painting into the process of learning in non-arts faculties." This had been the major goal of the "To Know Ourselves" project at the OAC — and grants had been made to several universities in order to advance it. Louis explained, "We were looking for ways to make it possible for universities to experiment along these lines." He had long been aware of the limitations imposed by a society that isolated and trivialized the arts as entertainment. Anticipating the major theme of his FCPRC Report, he said: "We have been slow to realize that creativity must be the basis for cultural planning." He believed that the university was the perfect setting for experiments in both integrating and enhancing the role of the arts in society.[7]

In 1985, Louis was asked by the Principal of the University of Windsor, Richard Householder, to assess the university's School of Music. After Louis's experiences over the years with the inadequacies of teacher preparation, particularly at the elementary level, he was impressed by the fact that the University was shifting its courses in the direction of supporting the placement of first-rate teachers in elementary-school classrooms. Louis emphasized the need for a degree-stream program that would attract those "who lack extensive background in performance but who could be provided a background that would allow [them to become] outstanding teachers." He was anxious to ensure that the problem of "inadequate physical facilities" would be resolved. It was his belief that appropriate space stocked with the necessary equipment was essential for excellence in performance.

In one area of the University of Windsor's music program development, Louis was quite critical. The University was offering a Bachelor of Fine Arts in Music Theatre. Louis's enthusiasm for this form of expression had been lavished upon Stratford and beyond. He was upset that Canada had so few opportunities for training young people in a genre he felt had such an enormous potential in the future. However, at the University of Windsor he was disappointed to find "that this enterprising venture seems to be floating in a doldrum even as it should be sailing ahead."[8] In spite of this criticism, he was largely supportive of the directions that the University of Windsor was pursuing. Louis's relationship with the University of Windsor reached its zenith in 1995, when he received an Honorary Doctorate at the same Convocation where his grandson, Jordan, received his Master of Business Administration degree. There can scarcely have been a closer relationship among grandfather, grandmother, and grandson and this occasion was a red-letter day in the life of the entire Applebaum family.

The University of Saskatchewan's Faculty of Music, on the Saskatoon campus, was to receive a less generous treatment from Louis in an external evaluation. David Elliott, a leading music educator at the University of Toronto's Faculty of Music, was the other assessor. While conceding that students graduating from the Faculty "have succeeded in becoming performers and composers," Louis and his colleague excoriated the Faculty, stating that "the University of Saskatchewan does not have a music department in the normal sense of the term." They made the point that unconnected classrooms and offices in one corner of a standard campus do not provide for even the most basic needs of a music faculty, namely, "proper performance space, appropriate music practice facilities and, of course, a central library." All of these were absent in this case.[9] With a candour rarely found in such reports, the authors stated "that it would take us pages to document the shortcomings of the University of Saskatchewan in this regard." Moving to the academic program, the criticisms were equally blunt. The curriculum for the Music Degree was acceptable in certain areas, but "the authors deem the present curriculum to be a failure in the preparation of string players ... [and] the failure to develop a cadre of choral music educators for the elementary and secondary schools of Saskatchewan is tragic."[10]

One would look in vain to find a more savage evaluation of a music department and its program. However, the criticisms came from within the university, as well as from outside. Both disappointed students and disaffected faculty clearly outlined areas for improvement in sessions staged to give them an opportunity to express their feelings about the failings of the music program.[11]

The authors saved their most severe criticism for the graduate program: "Unfortunately, our present finding is that the graduate program is in administrative disarray. Put bluntly, 'there's nobody home.'" This was certainly a devastating assessment; but its target was not so much the faculty's efforts as the university administration and its lack of concern for music education, or, indeed, the arts in general. This document conveys the anger and frustration of an eminent composer and musician, along with that of a distinguished academic colleague, at the degree of disinterest that universities as a whole, and certainly this university, had displayed towards the performing arts in comparison with their treatment of the literary arts, languages, and social and physical sciences. Louis recognized that restrained financial resources had diminished the all university functions, but the fine arts seemed to take much heavier cuts than business, engineering, or medicine — or even the traditional liberal arts.

Louis and his colleague, David Elliott, were also making a statement about the role of the university in general. They saw universities as vitally important because, in most provinces, universities had acquired the prime responsibility for the training of teachers. Their Saskatchewan report was one step along the road to improvements which did, eventually, come about in this University's program, and in the programs at other insitutions.[12]

Many forms of voluntary service consumed Louis's time and energy in the century's last decade. In every case, he sought an advisory role so that his experience in the arts could be used to greatest effect. At the end of the 1980s, Louis had been approached by the Laidlaw Foundation to join its Performing Arts Advisory Committee. It was an inauspicious time for such an invitation — the CAPAC-PROCAN negotiations were in full swing, the Guelph Spring Festival was fraught with problems, and Louis was at work on his last major drama for CBC television, "Glory Enough for All." Still, Laidlaw represented a unique opportunity to influence a modest, but extremely arts-oriented, foundation which had taken up the challenge of supporting creativity in Canadian music and theatre. The organization worked in a very different political environment from the one Louis had known in the 1960s and 1970s. He accepted Laidlaw's invitation, but not before he had thought through his plans for the next decade.

By the early 1980s, all seemed right with the world as Louis sought time for composing. To the question: "When do you expect to retire?" — not an inappropriate query to a man of 70 — Louis would reply "Retire to what?" His head was still full of the sounds he wanted to express in his music, and the idea of lying on a beach or plodding about on a golf course never entered his mind. Even at the height of his career, Louis rarely took a holiday. If he and Jan drove south to Georgia see son David and his family, they often stopped along the way in a city or town that took their interest. Otherwise, a few days at a resort in northern Ontario, perhaps canoeing or motor-boating, was a sufficient change in routine that he returned with renewed vigour for composing or administration. For Louis, a trip to Stratford was a holiday even though it meant hours of late night rehearsals. As the 1980s progressed, Louis wanted very much to understand a world that seemed to be in the throes of rapid change. He knew he wanted to compose music that would help him interpret that world.

Louis's FCPRC Report had not recommended huge increases in federal cultural spending, but there was an assumption that arts and culture would continue to receive sufficient, if restrained, levels of support. With the election of the Mulroney Government in 1984, that assumption was proven to be unrealistic, and Louis had redoubled his efforts in his role as the consummate advocate. His comments invariably focussed on the theme of the

Report — only by supporting arts organizations through generous funding would it be possible to ensure appropriate remuneration for the nation's creators. Louis's was an uphill struggle, and one that he believed he could continue effectively through the Laidlaw Foundation. His role there would allow him to intervene in the funding of cultural activities in ways that would both supplement and, in some cases, strike a contrast with the initiatives of government funding agencies. Louis knew that there was an ebb and flow in the way that society moved from collective to individual response to its needs and problems. He had learned to weave his way through times of preoccupation with fiscal responsibility, reminding himself that in the public realm, overreaction was the inevitable style of operation.

Nick Laidlaw, a warm, rather eccentric entrepreneur, had set up the Foundation in 1949. The organization was very much a family affair, although Nick was certainly the chief figure in the success of its efforts. In its early days, social services and social sciences had been the major focus of its donations. However, Nick's interest in the arts — an interest shared by other family members — had broadened this focus and, by 1968, a substantial share of the Foundation's annual granting budget was being allocated to the arts and educational projects. Obviously, this turn of events required some expert advice, and David Silcox, whose knowledge of the granting process both at the federal and provincial levels was incomparable, had been brought in to write a "strategy paper." The guiding principles he identified, with few adjustments, have served the Foundation well. First, he advised that the Laidlaw Foundation should concentrate its resources, which were not infinite, on arts funding and, in particular, on the performing arts. Secondly, he was adamant that the transcending criteria for funding should be quality. The success of an application for support should depend on the excellence of the applicant's work. Finally, to build a national representation, the Foundation would have to adopt a particular focus — the support and nurture of artistic innovation.[13] For Louis, these principles were a clear commitment to artistic creativity and to creators.

Now, some 10 years after Silcox had made his recommendations, the Laidlaw invitation was an opportunity for Louis to join distinguished colleagues in the pursuit of a mandate he strongly supported. By 1986, the Foundation had formed a Performing Arts Committee with David Silcox, William Littler, the *Toronto Star*'s prestigious music critic, and Gerry Eldred, whose work at Stratford and later, Harbourfront, was to place him at the forefront of arts-management advisors in the country. Two years after the Committee had been formed, Nathan Gilbert was brought on as the Foundation's Executive Director.[14]

Louis was approached by the Committee in 1989, joining at the same time as Tim Porteous, a former Director of the Canada Council. By now, over 25% of the Foundation's total granting budget was allocated to the performing arts. From the outset, the Laidlaw support to arts organizations was perceived to be complementary to Government funding, and Louis's knowledge and experience added much to what Porteous and others could bring to the Committee's deliberations. Also, by the new decade, government funding agencies were feeling the full impact of budget cuts, and judicious evaluation became the order of the day. Every application, whether accepted by the Canada Council, the OAC, or a local municipal funding agency, had to be given full attention in order to assess whether it met the Foundation's eligibility expectations. Already, the Foundation had put forward as its goal "to enrich the quality, vitality, and diversity of Canadian cultural expression and communication." Thus, to Louis's satisfaction, the concepts of "creativity" and "Canada's cultural expression" were merged.

Louis's work on the Laidlaw Foundation's Performing Arts Advisory Committee was significant. He pushed and cajoled to get support for the "new and experimental," but did so with grace and elegance. The main challenge facing the arts was certainly economic but there was an added sting that came from a change in national policy. With the North American Free Trade Agreement, the artistic community feared, with good reason, that Canada's arts industries would not be able to fend off the enormous cultural power that fuelled the most powerful entertainment industries the world had ever seen. Louis saw, during the early 1990s, a role that foundations could play — fostering the creative urge that he saw as the only defence against the otherwise inevitable move towards integration with the U.S. In his life since the 1940s, Louis had been on a mission to help citizens see the arts and their creators as a front-line defence against foreign cultural invasion, and a major mechanism for building a strong and viable nation. Now he came to see the arts as the only refuge from a tidal wave of free-trade intrusion and globalization that was sweeping into Canada and threatening everything that was Canadian. Louis believed that Canadian foundations in general, and the Laidlaw Foundation in particular, could be his allies in what he came to see as the major threat to the Canada he loved.

By 1994, Louis's colleagues on the Laidlaw Foundation's Performing Arts Advisory Committee had elected him as Chair. By this time, some new members had joined the Committee. One was Robert Wallace, a highly respected professor of theatre at York University, and an author and director who was on the cusp of the innovations that would arrive during the 1990s. Don Himes was a prominent Toronto musician, and Joyce Zemans was another York academic, now ascending to leadership at the

Laidlaw Board level. She had been a Director of the Canada Council and knew more about the world of arts funding in the latter part of the century than any other person in Canada.

The Laidlaw Foundation's Annual Report of 1994 refers to "special efforts made to encourage applications from organizations whose work is reaching young audiences."[15] One of the first of these grants went to a new organization, the Ontario Arts Education Institute. This was a body created by both arts teachers and artists involved in classroom programs in Ontario. The emphasis was on preparing teachers to deal with a curriculum that emphasized the integration of arts disciplines in the early years of elementary school. The first step was to empower these professionals to find their own artistic "centre." The Institute provided a summer course, with weekend extensions in the following autumn and winter, for working teachers anxious to develop their skills in all the areas of arts education — skills that their own preparation in the Faculties of Education in the universities of the province had failed to furnish. At a time when the educational authorities were dismantling arts education, this intervention proved to be crucial, and the Foundation's generous support of the OAEI continued during these years in spite of the change of curriculum direction.

By 1997, when Louis was ready to retire as Chair of that Committee, the Annual Report would record that by this time "the dollars being given through the arts envelope surpassed the funds for any other programme area at the Foundation."[16] By then, the Foundation had a whole new coterie of recipients and, indeed, arts funding had become connected to another Laidlaw enterprise — "Children at Risk" projects. Louis's tenure as Chair had strengthened the mandate and influenced the style of the Committee. He was determined that the artists should feel comfortable approaching the Foundation and that, in fact, the Foundation could help to encourage young artists to follow their stars. Louis believed that this encouragement was worth far more than its cost in dollars.[17]

Robert Wallace, who was to succeed Louis in later years, "could hear Lou's voice in the room" at tense moments when basic principles were at issue, even years after he had left.[18] This was far more than a spiritual presence, it was the direct result of a "modus operandi" that Louis had encouraged. His commitment went far beyond simply providing order at meetings and influencing the granting behaviour of the Committee. He maintained constant contact with artists, encouraging them and urging them to apply and to carry out their dreams and visions. Robert Wallace sums up Louis's enthusiasm: "He simply enjoyed the company of artists talking about the arts."[19] Nathan Gilbert observed that it was a "wise, gentle, kind treatment to hopeful artists that characterized his leadership. He was always available."[20]

Louis was particularly anxious to see artists assess the true costs of their works, since they were invariably the main subsidizers of their own art. Even for a successful Laidlaw applicant, the Foundation grant covered only a portion of the cost of the project. Artists might expend several times the value of a project through their own time and energy. Louis tried to reduce the gap between expenditure and return. To do so he had to teach creators to respect the value of their own work and to develop the ability to calculate the real costs of creation as they planned their applications. For example, he had to explain to a choreographer who "rented" dancers in order to develop a dance piece that the cost of the dancers should be detailed in the request for funds. Gilbert stated that he had only seen Louis angry once in all the years he spent in the offices and boardroom of the Foundation. A dancer had arrived on his doorstep with a contract to do a dance for Bravo! — a television network with a special interest in the arts. She was about to sell her copyright in the dance for ludicrously inadequate remuneration. Louis exclaimed that the contract was "an outrage" and explained his loss of temper in the exchange by explaining to Gilbert "we have to educate her to know her own worth" and "educate Bravo! to stop exploiting artists."[21] Before he left the Foundation, Louis was made an Honorary Member of the Foundation — a tribute to his enormous influence not only on members of the Board, its Advisory Committees and its staff, but also on all the artists and managers of arts organizations who had requested assistance.

The early 1980s brought a new performing arts venue to Toronto — Roy Thomson Hall. Massey Hall had served the city well throughout most of the century and still stood proudly on Shuter Street, perhaps a little shabby and threadbare, but still filled with the memories of many great performances. (These memories, along with the Massey name and the heritage role it had assumed as a consequence, ensured its survival.) The decision was made to create a single corporation that would guide the fortunes of both institutions. Community representation was needed on the board, along with a strong artistic presence. Louis was a natural choice. The quality of a city's life, Louis knew, was the result of many factors. There had to be creators, composers, and gifted musicians; and there had to be educational opportunities to develop these artists, along with intelligent audiences. The artists and technicians would not come without adequate incentive, so success also depended on astute union leadership to ensure fair remuneration and employment practices. Effective arts administrators, supported by loyal and generous Boards, would ensure the presence of audiences. And there had to be venues — attractive and welcoming places with policies that would invite and encourage Canadian performers and creators. Without these factors, musical performance in any city would be in jeopardy — and Toronto was no exception.

Louis had enjoyed many years as a music presenter. He knew that quality of performance was a crucial factor in animating a city's musical life, but not the only factor. He was also aware of a growing tendency on the part of audiences to expect exciting visual images. As early as 1962, Louis was quoted in a newspaper article: "There is not enough show business in our concerts. They should be presented in an exciting way for those who derive part of their musical pleasure from what they see."[22]

Pricing and booking policies influenced what took place on the stages of both Roy Thomson Hall and Massey Hall, and, as a member of the program committee, Louis continually pushed an agenda of excitement. As well, he was able to give his support to a Founders Fund that donated $10,000 each year to provide placements to university and college students in programs of arts administration. This Fund also provided $10,000 worth of free concert tickets at both halls, to be given to music students at the Royal Conservatory and the University of Toronto's Faculty of Music. Once again, Louis could feel comfortable being part of a process with an outcome near to his heart — the provision of practical experience to young, aspiring musicians.

One problem came to dominate the affairs of the Committee — the acoustics of the new Roy Thomson Hall. Music lovers came to revile the acoustics, and there was a shared perception that this hall, with so much space to fill with music, with so much concrete (instead of wood), and with its peculiar round configuration (instead of the familiar shoe-box) was an embarrassment. The increased difficulty of building a TSO audience was blamed on the "dead spaces" and the loss of dynamic impact that particularly disappointed young people with sophisticated knowledge of sound and its projection. Louis's colleague, Alexina Louie, fought year after year to have the acoustics problem addressed — as other performance venues on the continent were successfully addressing similar problems — but to little avail. Suzanne Bradshaw, one of Toronto's most admired and knowledgeable music supporters, had by this time become the Chair of the Corporation. She found it difficult to get complete agreement that acoustical repair of Roy Thomson Hall was the highest priority, especially when the cost would be over $20 million. However, Alexina Louie, supported by Louis, ultimately prevailed, winning the support of the other Board members, and the renovation of the Hall finally took place in 2002.[23]

Louis's work for the Board was much appreciated and applauded. On a joyous occasion in the late 1990s, Louis was presented with the Roy Thomson Hall Award for his services not only to the City of Toronto's two major concert halls, but, as well, to the enhancement of the musical tradition of the entire community.

The second Board that Louis joined in the 1980s was that of the Stratford Festival. Richard Monette, now Artistic Director, wanted Louis badly. He knew Louis had the respect of every person on staff, and was still fondly remembered in the Stratford community for all his work. Monette had known Louis professionally for many years, acting in plays for which Louis had provided the music; but more important, Louis had been responsible for the music in the first major production that Monette had directed, the 1988 presentation of Shakespeare's *The Taming of the Shrew.*[24]

Stratford had come to realize that one problem — the training of young actors — could only be addressed on-site. There had been attempts in the past to deal with the problem, but none had survived the changes in directorship. In the early 1990s, when the Stratford Festival was facing the same financial pressures as all the other arts organizations, Monette brought forward his idea of a "Conservatory." This program that would pay young actors, many of them graduates from theatre programs in universities and colleges, to engage in a program of "Classical Theatre Training" for a 15-week period in the fall and winter before the opening of the regular Festival season. They would have the benefit of instruction and, even more important, close association with the veterans of North America's most prestigious Shakespearean theatre. At the end of the training program, they would join the company on-stage for the ensuing season. Monette brought the expensive concept to the Board with some reluctance — and there was certainly a coolness that could have ended the project. Louis, however, was ecstatic. His support was unbounded. He never let up. From that point, Monette found that the normal roles of artistic director and board member had been reversed. Now he was feeling pressure from Louis to move ahead with the project. In view of the respect that Louis had already won from his colleagues, no one could oppose him on such an issue. Monette is quite adamant, both in public — at the "Tribute to Louis Applebaum" held in the Festival Theatre on August 21, 2000, just months after his death — and in private conversation, that "without Louis's support, we could not have established it." When the tenure of Richard Monette ends, his success in providing both many fine seasons of artistic triumph and financial stability will be celebrated. However, in terms of Stratford's long-term success, it will be the "Conservatory" that will fill the stage with successors to William Hutt and Martha Henry. Louis's role in making this happen will assuredly be remembered.

Louis served two terms on the Stratford Board. Throughout his entire stay, he never stopped advocating for a resumption of the commitment to music presentation that he had initiated in the 1950s. In spite of the centrality of drama and the expansion of music festivals in the decades since Stratford Music, Louis felt that the Festival still had a role to play in advancing Canadian music, Canadian musicians, and Canadian composers, and he never let up on that crusade.[25]

In 1994, the Stratford Festival established an Award in Music Theatre in Louis's name. This award "helps cover the expenses for an aspiring composer to audit Festival activities." The hope is that a young composer might discover the thrill of writing for the theatre, and decide to follow in Louis's footsteps. Louis, for whom the Festival was an artistic home, never stopped his advocacy on behalf of Canada's Stratford. To him, Stratford was where the best theatre in the world could be seen, and where Canadians could learn that excellence was possible, even in a land with a small population and limited resources, if there was sufficient vision and commitment. He was fêted with a banquet when he retired from the Board, and the entire season that followed his death (in 2000) was dedicated in his honour. One man who keenly felt Louis's loss was Bert Carriere, the Music Director at the Stratford Festival over many years, who regards Louis Applebaum as his mentor as well as his close friend.[26] As Music Director since 1973, Carriere has been well aware of Louis's strongly held principle that every play should have its own musical score, and that music should play an integrative role. On Carriere's first day at the Festival, "Louis took me under his wing and taught me every trick he knew about creating a dramatic score. [He] always wanted you to learn something." When Louis was writing a score for *Cymbeline*, the dance that he had composed for the play just didn't work, and Carriere suggested that a tango might go well. "So, you think it should be a tango? O.K. Use the tune I've got and make it into a tango!" was Louis's reaction. The two composers developed quite a rapport over a quarter century of collaboration, to the point where Carriere would often step in to add a cue when a commitment of Louis's meant there was no time to complete the musical phrase. When this happened, Louis would present Carriere with a penny if it was 4 bars, and two pennies if it was 8 bars that had to be composed. "More bars of music meant a nickel … but never more than a nickel." It was Louis's way of reminding both of them in a light-hearted way that every musical creation should be paid for.[27] More important by far, Louis always ensured that Carriere was given credit for his contribution in the Festival Program.

Louis left the Stratford Board in 1996. By then, attendance at meetings often meant discomfort and attempts to bravely disguise his constant coughing. The late 1990s were filled with pain and physical weakness — not a welcome condition for a man who had always enjoyed exceptional strength and vigour. Even in the late 1980s, he had been often "under the weather" and had been highly susceptible to colds and congestion in his chest. In 1988, doctors had given him an X-ray, but all seemed well. By 1992, however, Jan insisted that he see a doctor once again. Claiming "I'm all right," he delayed.

Finally, late one night, his insistent coughing led her to call a doctor for some respite. Along with medication, the doctor demanded that Louis be in his office the next morning where, once again, an X-ray was ordered. This time there was a spot on his lung, not large or seemingly life-threatening, but significantly larger than anything that had appeared on the previous X-ray. Louis was referred to a specialist at the Toronto General Hospital, who diagnosed the spot as a tumor on Louis's lung, likely to be cancerous. The diagnosis proved correct. When Louis asked about his chances, he was told, "Without an operation, about 6 months. With an operation and radiation, about 6 years." Those years were to be filled with medication and chemotherapy – but the cough never fully disappeared. Yet Louis kept up his busy schedule, going to meetings at Stratford, at the SOCAN Foundation, and at Roy Thomson Hall. He spent time at his office, composing music for various events, and appeared annually at the Festival to compose for at least one offering in the summer. He continued his work on *Erehwon* and he answered a mountain of correspondence.

A good part of Louis's working day, throughout his entire career but particularly in the 1990s, was taken up with answering a deluge of letters and cards from people he had encountered in the varied venues in which he worked, and from friends and colleagues. This private correspondence reveals his constant care for individuals, something that was sometimes overshadowed by the monumental achievements of his public life. It was this quieter aspect of Louis that revealed his decency and humanity and led to a respect and affection that few artists could have inspired. For example, James Parr had been a Deputy Minister of Colleges and Universities at Queen's Park during the Davis years. He had gone on to become Director-General of the Ontario Science Centre and ultimately, CEO of TVOntario, before his retirement in the early 1990s. Both Louis and Parr were members of the Arts and Letters Club in Toronto — a refuge for artists in the centre of the city, and housed in a grand old building on Elm Street. Parr, a proficient photographer and poet, decided in his post-retirement years that he wanted to write music. He took a couple of courses at the Royal Conservatory, with students young enough to be his grandchildren, and proceeded to compose songs. He soon contacted his old friend Louis and met with him regularly, presenting his work and seeking advice. Louis was delighted to act as a mentor to an amateur who had no ambitions to become a professional music-maker, but who simply enjoyed setting to music the poems he loved. Exhortations to "Jim" to be "more adventurous" were met with a modest response. "If I only had the wit to act upon 10% of your gentle and generous suggestions. As it is, thanks to you I've enjoyed a pleasure I'd never have imagined."[28]

In the last years of his life Louis heard from one after another of the artists with whom he had worked over many decades; musicians like Erica Goodman who wrote with appreciation "for all the support you have given me, both directly and indirectly, through all the sometimes frustrating but always fascinating years of music-making."[29] Michael Wood, a percussionist, wrote "You, Lou, have touched me in so many ways through your music, but it is your spirit given so freely that passes [through] my mind when your name is mentioned in conversation."[30]

Throughout the 1990s Louis was to be the recipient of many public honours. These would lead him to realize that, even though the cultural age he had fought to create had not come to pass, the battle had not been in vain. But there were also less publicized tributes from his closest colleagues that pleased him just as much. In 1997, he opened a letter that informed him that he had been made an honorary member of the Canadian Music Centre. With obvious pleasure and gratitude he replied to Simone Augur, its CEO, that "composers continue to champion the CMC because you have never lost sight of your goals and sense of purpose." A month later, another missive informed him that his work had been recognized by the Eaton Centre, which, in a "Salute to the City" [of Toronto] gave $250 to each of 100 citizens who had made a great contribution to the well-being of the community. The recipients were invited to pass the financial award along to the charity of their choice. Not surprisingly, Louis gave his cheque to the Stratford Festival.

There were times when he used his letters to old friends to express a despair that he never allowed to appear in his public utterances. In a holiday message to "the Adaskins," a noted composer family in Vancouver, Louis lamented "We've battled for 50 years (longer by several decades if you've read Ezra Schabas's fine biography of Ernest MacMillan) ... and yet how little progress we have made. The public is still interested in only the superficial, especially in music."[31] However, there was one cause that never failed to move him — an effort to reach out to children through the arts. In his written reply to Susan Habkirk's request for a testimonial that would help her seek funds for her "Prologue for the Performing Arts" — an agency devoted to bringing the best of the arts to young people — he fashioned a response that reflected this lifelong commitment:

> It should be understood that opening young people to
> the riches that our artists can expose and bring to life is
> the only sure way to generate arts attenders, participants,
> and supporters .... Almost all creative and performing
> artists can pinpoint some performance, some personality,

an experience during their school years, that changed their lives, their ambitions, and that pulled them into a life dedicated to the arts. No child should be denied that moment, its attendant joy and motivation. Anything less is self-destructive to Canada as a nation.[32]

These were years in which Louis's life was filled honours and awards that gave him the satisfaction of knowing that his contribution was fully recognized, not only by his colleagues, but by Canadians as a whole. He had been the recipient of the Centennial Medal back in 1967, and many of the media productions that he had been a part of had won Emmys and Wildlife Awards for their quality and, in particular, for the excellence of his music. As Director at the Ontario Arts Council in 1976, he had been particularly honoured by being made an Officer of the Order of Canada. There were also honorary degrees and fellowships: an LL.D. (honoris causa) from York University, where he had been teaching for a few years as a part-time instructor, and another from the University of Windsor, and Honorary Fellowships from the Ontario College of Art (later the Ontario College of Art and Design) and from the Ontario Institute for Studies in Education. Louis found all these academic awards somewhat bizarre, in light of the fact that, in his early years, he had failed to graduate from the University of Toronto. Yet of all the awards from Canada's educational community, it was the Honorary ARCT he received from the Royal Conservatory of Music in 1982 that held a special place in his memory. He was the first person to be so honoured, and this had great meaning in terms of his work and his contribution to music and music performance in Canada. In addition, the award had come at the point in his Chairmanship of the Federal Cultural Policy Review Committee when he was most disillusioned and distraught.

One award that particularly moved him came at the end of the 1970s as he left his OAC post. The Toronto Theatre Alliance presented him with a Silver Ticket — a free admission for him and Jan to enjoy any of the productions put on by the theatre companies that made up the Alliance. This was a particularly fitting way for the Toronto theatre community to celebrate all the ways in which Louis had served them during his term as the OAC's Executive Director, and it reflected Louis's ability to put aside his passion for music in the service of the other performance arts.

In 1989 Louis received the Order of Ontario, an indication that as a citizen of both Toronto and Ottawa he had served his native province well. However the pinnacle of all his work as a Canadian citizen came in 1995, when his role as an Officer in the Order of Canada was elevated to that of "Companion," the highest level, and one that can be held by a maximum of 165 living Canadians at any time. Of all the general awards, this one most appropriately recognized his life experience; his choice to work in Canada; his devotion to enhancing and strengthening Canadian culture; and his commitment to the artistic community from coast to coast. It is the nation's most prestigious award and Louis wore the insignia with great pride. The award symbolized, as did no other, his intense nationalism: a fierce pride of country that had led him to make sacrifices that could never be justified on economic grounds; to take risks that were sometimes to his personal and professional disadvantage; and to dedicate his talent and energy to causes that he believed would make Canada a better nation.

Because Louis considered himself primarily a composer and creative artist, honours bestowed by his peers brought immense satisfaction. In 1998, the Canadian Conference of the Arts awarded him the Diplome d'honneur, the highest mark of achievement in its area of interest, the cultural richness of the country. The first recipient had been Vincent Massey, who had ushered in the decades of cultural activity in which Louis had been so heavily involved. Many of Louis's associates had also been so honoured — Tom Patterson, Floyd Chalmers, Esse W. Ljungh, Tanya Moiseiwitsch, Glenn Gould, Arthur Gelber, Mavor Moore, Robertson Davies, Niki Goldschmidt, John Beckwith, Maureen Forrester, and others with whom he had worked over the years. It was a stellar occasion, and though he was then in the latter stages of his fight with cancer, he reveled in the opportunity to join such a broad spectrum of Canadian artistic stars. There were, of course, special awards he received from the organizations he had sought to serve and enhance. Of all these, SOCAN, which in large part owed its existence to his efforts, brought him great joy by awarding him the Special Achievement Award in 1998, and the SOCAN Serious Music Award in 1999. These were fitting tributes to his roles as a volunteer administrator and as an artist, as was the Roy Thomson Hall Award of the same year.

At the end of the 1990s, as Louis's illness advanced, there was a realization that there was little time left in which to express the appreciation of the community. Toronto celebrated his contribution with a Lifetime Achievement Award in the late 1990s. He had lived most of his life in the city and his influence in the arts community had been pervasive. The jury's citation on that occasion made the point that the year 1998 "marks the birthday (the 80th) of Louis Applebaum, who has perhaps done more than any living Canadian to foster music and the arts in Canada." It was a special time for Louis. His closest colleague over so many years, John Weinzweig, received the Toronto Arts Music Award at the same ceremony. Significantly, in 1991, the city's Jewish community had already named him the "Arts Man of the Year," for all the leadership he had given to a long list of Jewish cultural organizations, as well as for the significant body of music he had contributed to the repertoire of the synagogue. There had been a special poignancy to this recognition from his closest friends as this last decade of his life began.

The Jewish community has been very cognizant of the centrality of culture as the "engine" of a society. But there is also a magnificent tradition that explains the extraordinary contributions that certain members of the Jewish community make to the common good. "According to the Jewish Tradition, there are just 36 men and women – *tzaddikim* – alive at any one time. They are the pillars of society, holding it up. No one knows who they are. Not even the *tzaddikim* themselves." If any individual could be perceived to be such a "pillar," most certainly Louis would fit the description.[33]

Early in 1998, a tragedy struck Louis with extraordinary impact — the death of Arthur Gelber. Gelber had been in poor health for some years, but this did not relieve the shock and sense of loss Louis felt. He and Gelber had worked closely together over the years, particularly during the 1970s when Louis had been at the Ontario Arts Council, and their collaboration and friendship had lasted and matured. Louis visited Gelber every few weeks and it was Gelber who nominated Louis for the Companion of the Order of Canada. For Gelber, who had four very accomplished daughters, Louis was a surrogate son. Gelber had been one of the men who had influenced Louis most intensely and had joined Grierson, Guthrie, and Southam as men who had shaped his career. In a letter to Mavor Moore he stated simply "We're all the poorer and weaker for not having Arthur fighting on our side."[34]

In 1999, Louis was working on *A School for Scandal* at Stratford. It was scheduled for a late-season opening, so the final rehearsals had to be held on the theatre stage in the middle of summer after the regular performance was over. Louis arrived back at his motel room early in the morning, totally exhausted. The next day he could not get up. Jan reserved the room for an extra two days, and kept him in bed. Finally, she drove him home to Toronto. It was still "I'll be all right," but Jan was worried as now he could not breathe easily. She found him, head down, barely able to speak. At this point she called an ambulance and, in late 1990s Ontario, the challenge became that of finding an emergency ward in the city that would accept a patient. Louis had been a patient at the Toronto General Hospital, so, after being turned away from three other hospitals, it was there that he was finally delivered. He remained there for 10 days of tests and medical attention.

It was clear that there was going to be no further remission. Constantly coughing blood, in a state of severe discomfort, Louis soldiered on. There was one bridge he wanted to cross; he was determined to complete the opera *Erehwon* with Mavor Moore. When, in February 2000, the opera was launched in Victoria, Louis decided it was time to wrap up his affairs. A week later, he called this writer to tell him that he had resigned from every board and committee to which he belonged; that with his son David's help he had closed his studio on Don Mills Road; that he was sending his valuable electronic equipment to the Royal Conservatory; and that he had sent all his remaining files to the Archives at York University. He had called Stratford to inform Richard Monette that he could not complete the score for that summer's production, Oscar Wilde's *The Importance of Being Earnest*, but assured Monette that Glenn Morley would be prepared to write the score. A few weeks earlier, as this writer sat in Louis's office, the phone had rung. On the other end of the line was one of Louis's favourite musicians, harpist Erica Goodman. She wanted a new piece for harp and strings for the fall of 2001 and Louis wanted very much to oblige. The piece would never be completed — a rare occasion when Louis could not fulfil his obligation.

In his Don Mills condominium, Louis was visibly uncomfortable, hooked up to oxygen and able only to leave his bed for short periods. He needed 24-hour nursing and he resented this intrusion on his privacy and Jan's. David had come up from Georgia and was determined to stay as long as his father was alive, but Louis was anxious about this imposition as well. He wanted to go to Baycrest — an institution he knew well from his mother's days as a volunteer — and the palliative ward there had a magnificent reputation.

Soon he was ensconced in a room where he was much happier and he quickly became a popular patient with nurses and medical staff on the floor. As well, it was easier to welcome guests and they came in considerable numbers. Although he lived only 10 days at Baycrest, there was an aura of celebration in his room. On a Tuesday afternoon, Elizabeth Bihl, the newly appointed Director of the Canadian Music Centre, came to see him, along with John Weinzweig, his closest composer colleague. Bihl simply wanted to meet him and for two hours he regaled her with a fascinating account of his life in the world of music. It was a joyous occasion, filled with reminiscences and laughter. Finally, a nurse intervened and Weinzweig and Bihl were sent away, but not before Louis called out "You must come back! I'm only up to the sixties!"

That same evening, Jan was preparing to make her morning trek to Baycrest. The telephone rang and it was Louis asking her to bring all the bank records and any papers he needed to sign. As well, he wanted his score for *Erehwon* — there were a few corrections he wanted to make. She filled a travelling bag, one she could wheel easily from the parking lot, and, early on Wednesday morning, she arrived to find Louis unable to sit up, hold a pen, or even speak clearly. That morning, with Jan at his side and holding his hand, he quietly died. Even in his last moments his mind was on others. He wanted bequests from his modest estate to go to his OAC Composers' Fund, and a sizeable contribution to go to Baycrest in honour of his parents. This money Jan directed to the palliative ward for the provision of amenities that would bring greater comfort to patients and assist nurses and medical staff.

It was the week of Passover in the Jewish calendar. Louis's funeral had to be delayed until the Sunday afternoon. For Jan, it was the end of one painful period and the beginning of another. "I cried for a year," she explained. Her own health broke down and an attack of pleurisy made it impossible for her to attend the funeral. It was a simple service held at his synagogue, Temple Sinai. Rabbis Dolgin and Pearlson, both friends of the family, officiated with quiet grace. Louis had wanted no eulogies — in his mind, they had been made redundant by the magnificent 80th birthday party at the St. Lawrence Centre two years before, and Jan, planning the funeral, was determined to follow his wishes. His legacy was his music, and selections of his work had been beautifully performed on that occasion, along with words of appreciation for his contribution to the cultural life of Canada. At the funeral, Glenn Morley gave a very short commentary on the life of this great man and his words rang true, flowing, as they did, from the many hours the two had spent working together. The Temple was filled with Louis's friends and colleagues, all saddened by his loss, but conscious of a life lived to the full.

A great Canadian had passed away.

Preface

1. Jordan Applebaum, interview with author, December 16, 1999. Louis's grandson was astonished at the broad range of interest in societal affairs that Louis exhibited. "He seemed to know something about everything." Professor Albert Breton, a noted Canadian economist, was equally impressed by Louis's command of political events during their work together on the Federal Cultural Policy Review.

Chapter 1. The Crucial Years

1. Gerald Tulchinsky, *Taking Root: The Origins of the Canadian Jewish Community*, Lester Publishing Limited, Toronto, 1992. Of the 2 million Jews who left the Russian and Austro-Hungarian Empires between 1880 and 1914, 75% came from the Russian Empire. "Here, a combination of social, political and economic factors had made the lives of Jews difficult since the mid-80s, and the pogroms that broke out in May of 1881 violently underscored the precarious position of the Jewish community in Czarist lands." [p.96].
2. Louis Applebaum, interview with author, January 16, 1999.
3. Irving Abella, *Coat of Many Colours, Two Centuries of Jewish Life*, Lester and Orpen Dennys, Toronto, 1990. [p.103]
4. Abella, Irving. *Growing Up Jewish*, McClelland and Stewart, Toronto. 1997. [p.vii] "There were Zionists and anti-Zionists, socialists, anarchists, Yiddishists, secular and Orthodox, each with their own agenda, each with their own plan, for the survival of the Jewish people in Canada."
5. Gerald Tulchinsky, *Taking Root: The Origins of the Canadian Jewish Community*, Lester Publishing Limited, Toronto, 1992. [p.158]
6. Stuart E. Rosenberg, *The Jewish Community in Canada*, Vol. II, "In The Midst of Freedom." McClelland and Stewart, Toronto, 1971. "If tailoring and the needle-trades are 'the Jewish industry', then music must surely be 'the Jewish art'. Jews are represented in every major profession and have

practiced every major art. Nevertheless Jews have not merely participated but have excelled in the world of music as performers, composers, conductors and teachers." [p.129] Rosenberg then lists the Canadian Jews who have "excelled" and even in 1971 it was a prodigious gathering of names: Singers George London and Maureen Forrester; Cellists Lotte and Dennis Brott, Zara Nelsova; Conductors Percy Faith, Alexander and Boris Brott, Victor Feldbrill, Eugene Kash; Impresario Walter Homburger; Pianists Leo Barkin, Anton Kuerti, Ellen Ballon, Greta Kraus, Ida Krehm, John Newmark; Strings: Ida Haendal, Hyman Goodman, Erica Goodman (Harp), Albert Pratz, Maurice Solway, Eli Spivak; Composers Neil Chotem, Harry Freedman, Srul Irving Glick, Oskar Morawetz, Morris Surdin, John Weinzweig, the Adaskins, Alexander Brott, Walter and Otto Joachim.

7. Louis Applebaum, interview with author, January 16, 1999.

8. Ruth Nusyna, interview with author, May 25, 1999. Even when Fanny Applebaum was in her 90s she continued to do volunteer work at the Baycrest Centre for Geriatric Care. Ironically, it was in the palliative ward at Baycrest that Louis was to die in April 2000.

9. Ibid.

10. David Applebaum, interview with author, January 12, 2000. It is David's analysis that Louis was a terrible businessman. He had no interest in money, and the goals of private enterprise invariably became undermined by non-profit goals.

11. Louis Applebaum, interview with author, January 16, 1999.

12. Gerald Tulchinsky, *Taking Root: The Origins of the Canadian Jewish Community*, Lester Publishing Limited, Toronto, 1992.[p.172]

13. Until 1952, Earl Haig Collegiate had served this entire jurisdiction. Even though the student body was 70% Jewish, Bathurst Heights held daily Bible readings, mostly and quite inappropriately from the New Testament, and designed somehow to reach the crucifixion by Easter.

14. Louis Applebaum, interview with author, January 16, 1999. If Louis had become a comic, Harbord would have had a much greater role in his career preparation. He remembers quite clearly a history teacher, Charles Girdler who organized the "oola-boola" club that operated as an extra-curricular activity at Harbord and played a vital role in the careers of Johnny Wayne and Frank Shuster. Shuster, whose roots included a grandfather who owned a theatre, the ASTA, in Rotterdam, recalls being told to read Perlman, Leacock and excerpts from "Punch" and then preparing skits which brought the house down at school assemblies.

15. *The Harbordite*, No. 40. Spring, 1997. The years at Harbord had an enormous effect on John Weinzweig's life. Even after graduation, Brian McCool played a role in his future. *The Harbordite*, No.33, Fall, 1993 reports Weinzweig's comment that "it was with his [McCool's] cooperation that on April 17, 1941, I presented an all-Canadian music program at Harbord Collegiate, the first of its kind in a public school. It was presented by the Ontario Department of Education under McCool's personal direction."

Harbord Collegiate has been more conscious of its past than perhaps any other Toronto secondary school. It has established its own archives and continues to publish a semi-annual periodical, *The Harbordite*, providing a rich source of information about its alumnae. In areas other than fine arts, the names include Eddie Goodman, a respected and politically active Toronto lawyer; Leonard Braithwaite, who after an active career in the Ontario Legislature became Ontario's Lieutenant Governor; Alan Collier, a major visual artist and social activist; Alan Borovoy, "Mr. Civil Liberties" in Canada; Stephen Lewis, former Leader of the Ontario New Democratic Party; Garfield Weston, a leading figure both as businessman and philanthropist; Louis Rasminsky, a Governor of the Bank of Canada; Kathleen Coburn, a world-renowned Coleridge scholar; Robert McClure, an outstanding medical missionary and Moderator of the United Church of Canada; Philip Givens, Mayor of Toronto; Alex Levinsky, outstanding Maple Leaf hockey player; and Harry Sonshine, a football star with the Toronto Argonauts. In the Rae Government of Ontario in the early 1990s there were two Harbord graduates who were members of the cabinet, Rosario Marchese, Minister of Culture and Communications, and Zanana Akande, Minister of Consumer and Social Services. They represent but a few of an alumnae that has made a unique contribution to this nation's political, intellectual, sporting, religious, and business life. It undoubtedly influenced Louis's broad interest in contemporary affairs and the varied ways he came to know about the world and to express that world in his music.

16. Louis Applebaum, interview with author, June 10, 1999. Applebaum's introduction to Gilbert and Sullivan at Harbord had important consequences. One of the first summer jobs he took was at a Jewish summer camp as music instructor and he, along with Johnny Wayne, found that the "Pirates of Penzance" was a splendid vehicle for involving campers in two months of rehearsal for a production on stage before parents when they came to collect their children at the end of the season.

17. Robert Stall, *Weekend* Magazine, June 14, 1975. [p. 10]. York University Archives, Louis Applebaum fonds, 1979-022/028[19]

18. Ruth Nusyna, interview with author, May 25, 1999. His sister confided that Louis was always receiving high marks at school, but much to her amazement, he "never studied."

19. Ibid.

20. *The Harbordite*, No. 27, Spring, 1991. [p.1]

21. Frank Shuster, interview with author, July 13, 1999. Frank Shuster remembers the card games, bridge and poker being the favourites, but Harry Sheffer remembers the poppy-seed cookies.

22. Ruth Nusyna, interview with author, May 25, 1999. These were the people who filled the Jane Mallet Theatre on the occasion of Louis Applebaum's 80th birthday, in some cases crossing the continent to be there.

23. Louis Applebaum, interview with author, January 16, 1999. Although Louis Applebaum did not experience overt, physically violent anti-semitism, other students at Harbord were most certainly aware of it. In *The Harbordite*, No.

42, Spring, 1998, Alvin Rakoff, who had lived on Baldwin Street, was interviewed. "But I remember, I was very young at the time, we were descended on by gangs on bicycles shouting 'Heil Hitler,' and trying to throw bricks and stones to try to break the windows. But they were soon seen off. A rather violent fight, I remember. A gang of about seven to ten of these hooligans were met by the old men with crowbars and soon dispatched. It wasn't a pleasant sight for a child."

24. Dr. Harry Sheffer, interview with author, April 10, 2000. While selling magazine subscriptions in the city of Peterborough, Louis was able to keep down the travel costs by sleeping at Harry Cherney's cottage on Chemong Lake. Even Harry's generosity couldn't rescue the enterprise, but Louis came to know Brian Cherney, who was to be a fellow composer, as well as a much younger offspring, Lawrence, one of Canada's finest oboists and an arts entrepreneur who worked with Louis in both roles.

25. George A. Proctor, *Canadian Music of the Twentieth Century*, University of Toronto Press, Toronto, Buffalo, London, 1980. [p.34].

Chapter 2. Moulding A Musician

1. Louis Applebaum, interview with author, January 16, 1999.
2. Ibid.
3. Irving Abella, *Coat of Many Colours*, Lester and Orpen Dennys, Toronto, 1990. "Ironically, while Max Lesses, a young Jew, was graduating with the gold medal from Queen's University, the university was lobbying for legislation that would make it totally 'Christian in character' and allow it to bar Jews." [p.130]
4. Clifford Ford, *Canada's Music: An Historical Survey*, GLC Publishers Limited, Agincourt, Ontario, 1982. [p12]
5. Louis Applebaum, interview with author, January 16, 1999.
6. Boris Berlin, interview with author, February 11, 1999. As the century ended, Berlin was 95 years old and very much a part of the musical life of Toronto, still teaching at the Royal Conservatory of Music. At the time of writing, one could enjoy his memories by climbing (as he did) to the third floor of the old McMaster Hall, the home of the Conservatory. He could be found amidst a room full of pianos on which he still inspired yet another generation of young people. (Boris Berlin died suddenly in the spring of 2001.)
7. Louis Applebaum, interview with author, January 16, 1999.
8. Boris Berlin, interview with author, February 11, 1999.
9. Ibid. The neighbour's daughter with whom Louis played duets was Laura Markovitz, and according to Louis's memory she was the girl that both sets of parents rather assumed might develop into a romantic interest. It would have been a perfect arrangement: the couple could have taken over the Applebaum-Markovitz partnership in the clothing company. Neither the relationship nor their performing interests bore out the parents' expectations.
10. Louis Applebaum, interview with author, January 16, 1999. There might be some dispute on the latter point. Ruth remembers that her career as a

potential piano virtuoso was aborted as she could never access the family piano for enough time to practice because Louis was there "making music" if not formally rehearsing.

11. Boris Berlin, interview with author, February 11, 1999.

12. Ibid.

13. Ruth Nusyna, interview with author, May 25, 1999.

14. *Canadian Jewish News*, Friday, July 26, 1974. York University Archives. Louis Applebaum fonds,1979-002/028[19]

15. Louis Applebaum, Speech to the Graduating Class of the Royal Conservatory of Music, November 22, 1971. Executive Director's Speeches, Ontario Arts Council files, RG 47-14-1. Archives of Ontario.

16. Clifford Ford, *Canada's Music: An Historical Survey*, G. L. C. Publishers Limited, Agincourt, Ontario, 1982. [p.176]

17. John Beckwith, "Music at Toronto, A Personal View", two lectures delivered in the fall of 1994 as part of the Thursday noon series of the Faculty of Music, University of Toronto, [pp.9–10]. Printed by the University of Toronto Press.

18. Ezra Schabas, *Sir Ernest MacMillan*, University of Toronto Press, Toronto, Buffalo, London, 1994. [p.127]

19. "Varsity Symphony Orchestra Premieres Work By Student" *The Varsity*, January 12, 1939. University of Toronto Archives, Fisher Library, Robarts Library. University of Toronto.

20. John Beckwith, "Music at Toronto, A Personal View," [p.18]. John Beckwith clearly explains the informal, indeed, quite unhelpful state of teaching and evaluation at the Faculty. The failure rate was quite incredible, but in the context of a music education, it didn't seem to matter. Composers are not commissioned on the basis of their academic qualifications.

21. Frank Shuster, interview with author, July 13, 1999. There are no records of the scores of the fraternity reviews to be found. However, the social commentary can be deduced from the snippet of a song Frank Shuster remembers, "We only breathe air from north of St. Clair." Shuster recalls a continuing professional contact with Louis over many years and even some 60 years after their Varsity campus days "felt very close to him." It is his analysis that, just as Wayne and Shuster were prepared for their career as entertainers and their success both in Canada and the U.S., so for Louis Applebaum these excursions into the genre of musical comedy were essential to the self-confidence he developed in moving into so many areas — film, radio, television, staged musicals — as well as the formal settings of churches, synagogues, concert halls, and ultimately the opera stage. In Shuster's view, it was this wide variety that was possible in Canada that could not be matched in the U.S. that led Applebaum to spend his life in this country.

22. *The Harbordite*, No. 25, Spring 1990.

23. Srul Irving Glick, interview with author, December 14, 1999. Glick is quite open about the fact that Louis Applebaum made possible his career. He was studying in Paris when Louis convinced him that he should return to Canada. When Glick did come back, he found that he could find no appro-

priate job and called Louis, who put him in contact with Geoffrey Waddington, the head of music at the CBC. Louis told Glick that he could join the CBC and used his own career as an example in convincing him that one could compose while working for an institution, indeed, could find inspiration in the work of music broadcasting. Glick went on to become a producer for some 23 years before taking on the role of composer on a full-time basis in 1985. After Louis's death, Glick wrote a choral work for the Elmer Iseler Singers "The Song of Eternal Light" for Peter Sigmundi and Valerie Kent and in memory of Louis Applebaum. It was given its world premiere on Friday, July 20, 2001 at the Festival of the Sound in Parry Sound. R. Murray Schafer tells a similar story. He was in London at the same time as Louis working on a project. Louis took the time to take him to the BBC and introduce him to all the producers and directors who would be able to help. [Interview: R. Murray Schafer with author July 31, 2001.] The reputation as "the wonderful guy" comes from countless such stories.

24. Jordan Applebaum, interview with author, December 16, 1999.
25. Ruth Nusyna, interview with author. May 5, 2000.
26. Louis Applebaum, interview with author, January 16, 1999. Many years later, Louis discovered that John Weinzweig and his wife, Helen, had been married on the same day by the same rabbi.
27. Frank Shuster, interview with author, July 13, 1999.

Chapter 3. The Seductive Screen
1. Louis Applebaum, interview with author, January 16, 1999.
2. Ibid.
3. Ibid.
4. Ibid. Jan's paintings testify to an enormous commitment to a highly exotic genre and technique that has drawn the interest of those who are connoisseurs of oriental art forms. Her visual arts library is extensive and her knowledge profound and far-reaching. She placed her career "on hold" for a lifetime in order to support Louis's work. She is a scholar in a field that has few practising "outsiders."
5. Eric Barnouw. *Documentary: A History of the Non-Fiction Film,* Oxford University Press, Oxford – New York – Toronto – Melbourne, 1983. [pp.35-45].
6. Ibid. [pp.65-66]
7. Ibid. [pp.72-73]
8. Louis Applebaum, Article, "Film Music," in Sir Ernest MacMillan, ed., *Music in Canada,* University of Toronto Press, Toronto, 1955. [p.1678]
9. Boris Berlin, interview with author, February 11, 1999.
10. James Beveridge, *John Grierson, Film Master,* Macmillan Publishing Company, Inc., New York, 1978. [p.33]
11. Eric Barnouw. *Documentary: A History of the Non-Fiction Film,* Oxford University Press. Oxford – New York – Toronto – Melbourne, 1983. [p.90]
12. Mackenzie King, in his youth, shared the social reform tendencies that

Grierson exhibited. Both experienced the generosity of the Rockefeller Foundation at an important point in their respective careers.

13. Louis Applebaum, "The NFB in the 1940s," in "John Grierson and the NFB," Papers presented at a conference held at McGill University, Montreal, Quebec, Oct. 29-31, 1981. [p.9].

14. Eric Barnouw. *Documentary: A History of the Non-Fiction Film.* Oxford University Press, Oxford – New York – Toronto – Melbourne, 1983. [p.89].

15. Louis Applebaum, interview with author, February 1, 1999. It was this style of working in film that was a major reason for his return to Canada after his success in Hollywood. Being responsible for music there meant that you had no role beyond and thus had little impact on the total production. Louis could not accept these kinds of limitations and he decided that making film in Canada was infinitely more satisfying.

16. Ibid. The core of this orchestra became, many years after Louis had left, the nucleus of the Ottawa Symphony Orchestra, which was, until the 1960s and the formation of the National Arts Centre Orchestra, the only source of symphonic music in the nation's capital except for the annual visits of the Montreal and Toronto Symphony Orchestras. This relationship was remembered and appreciated when Louis Applebaum returned some 20 years later to provide advice on the formation of the NAC Orchestra and to provide advice on the state of music education in Ottawa. Ironically, he found the Ottawa Symphony silent, as it was involved in a labour-management dispute.

17. Louis Applebaum, interview with author, September 7, 1999. A library of recorded music that was available to him was administered by an individual who had no commitment to the Canadian war effort and who expected "kick-backs" for every piece of music exhumed from the collection. Applebaum refused, outraged by this behaviour in the middle of a war, and he became known as "the guy who refused to give 'kick-backs.'"

18. Ibid. Applebaum became known, through dozens of stories, as the composer who never missed a deadline. That capacity to work to deadlines was very much the style that ruled his working life and, as Louis would concede, came from his days at the NFB. Ron Evans, a close colleague at the OAC, relates the story of a frantic producer coming to Louis on a Monday morning with a story of woe — he had to finish the film by the weekend, his music director had let him down, and could Louis do a rush job on the score? Louis asked him when it had to be completed. The director ruefully replied, "On Friday." The only further question from Applebaum: "Morning or afternoon?"

19. James Parr, interview with author, October 18, 1999. At the same time, Louis was candid in a conversation with Parr, an old friend and colleague. To Parr's question, "What do you like about conducting?" Louis smiled knowingly and replied with one word: "Power."

20. Ruth Budd, interview with author, March 31, 2000. Ruth Budd worked in Stratford for a full decade in the 1950s and 1960s. She took her young son at the age of 2, and when she stopped playing there, he was 12 years old and

felt quite badly used, as he thought that every kid went to a place like Stratford every summer.

21. Ezra Schabas, interview with author, April 7, 2000. Ezra Schabas became a close friend and associate of Applebaum, working with him at Stratford, at the CBC, at the Ontario Arts Council, and with the Canada Council. Eventually, he became the Principal of the Royal Conservatory of Music as well as a distinguished member of the Faculty of Music at the University of Toronto.

22. Charles Clay, Article on National Film Board, Montreal *Standard*, December 11, 1943. [p. 9]

23. Canadian author and CBC administrator Harry Boyle brought the membership of the OAC Board to tears with a heart-wrenching account of the longing of rural communities for the visual reality that only the NFB could give with its "travelling shows" in local schoolhouses during the Second World War. People drove for miles, bringing their children and staying all night.

24. Louis Applebaum, interview with author, February 1, 1999.

25. Kendall, who joined the National Research Council to work in the area of anti-submarine acoustics, eventually sold his laboratories in British Columbia in order to stay at the National Film Board, heading up the motion picture sound recording department and remained as a technical consultant to the NFB from 1948 to 1955.

26. Louis Applebaum, letter to Arthur Irwin, Commissioner, NFB, December 6, 1950. York University Archives, Louis Applebaum fonds, 1979-002/022 [431]. This must have been one of the first letters Irwin received in this position, as he took over the NFB as Commissioner in December of 1950. However, he had many other problems on his plate at that moment and could take no action.

27. Ibid.

28. *Dollar Days* was a 1943 NFB animated film about the evils of inflation and the importance of price controls. As an element of the soundtrack there was a catchy tune for the lines, "I'm your money, I'm your friend, yours to save, yours to spend." The incredible manipulation of the dollar sign through four minutes of film time drew considerable comment and contributed to McLaren's career as Canada's foremost film animator over the next decade.

29. Louis Applebaum to Ross McLean, July 15, 1946, Letter of resignation as Director of Music for the NFB, as of July 29, 1946. York University Archives, Louis Applebaum fonds, 1979 - 002/122 [438].

30. Alan Phillips, "Osmond Kendall's Marvellous Music Machine," *Maclean's* Magazine, June 11, 1955. [p.54]. York University Archives, Louis Applebaum fonds 1979 -002/030, [583a].

31. Pierre Berton, "He Sets Shakespeare To Music," *Mayfair* Magazine, May, 1954. [p.54]. York University Archives, Louis Applebaum fonds , 1979 - 002/030. [583b].

32. Ibid. [p.54]

33. Louis Applebaum, interview with author, February 1, 1999.

Chapter 4. An American Interlude.

1. Even after half a century, *Action Stations* is an impressive film. The visuals are striking — rough, unforgiving seas, violent naval action involving many victims contrasted with scenes of life at sea that included daily grog, singing, and dancing. The tension is riveting. Glorious, celebratory themes emerge as the seamen succeed in finding and sinking an enemy submarine. The feature concludes with a rousing rendition of the navy's unofficial theme song, "Roll Along, Wavy Navy, Roll Along."

   Some 22 years later, Louis Applebaum created an orchestral suite based on the music from *Action Stations*. This was unusual for Louis. He felt that the integrity of each film score was best maintained by its connection to the visual medium for which it had been written. However, he felt that the music for *Action Stations* was able to stand alone as a concert offering.

2. Louis Applebaum, interview with author, September 7, 1999.

3. Brochure: Hollywood Writers Mobilization First Writers Award Premiere, 1945. [Village Theatre, Los Angeles] York University Archives, Louis Applebaum fonds, 1979 - 002/030 [581]. The Awards Committee was made up of an array of actors who were to dominate the screen for the next five decades and included John Houseman, Walter Huston, Lena Horne, Alexander Knox, Edward G. Robinson, Orson Welles, Anne Baxter, Bette Davis, Greer Garson, and Katharine Hepburn.

4. Gerald Hawkins, "Liberty Profile: Louis Applebaum," *Liberty* Magazine, June 8, 1946. [p.19]

5. Louis Applebaum. NFB Newsletter, October, 1944, issued by the National Film Board, Ottawa, Canada. York University Archives, Louis Applebaum fonds, 1979 – 002/032 [604]. After Louis's first experience, he could never seriously consider Hollywood as a permanent venue for his work. "The invitation to Elysium came suddenly, so that I had little more than 16 hours en route in which to work up a case of nervous anticipation, but that was plenty. The nervousness left abruptly, however, when, on riding into town with the studio ambassador who had come to meet me, I was asked, 'So you're from Canada, eh: — a big town, ain't it?' After that I didn't feel such a hick."

   The visit to Hollywood also outraged his Canadian nationalism. "It really hurt that I should have been a foreigner, that so many people I subsequently met knew little more about Canada than that the Canadian Rockies are beautiful and that Quebec must be a charmingly quaint place where the streets are narrow and where French is spoken and that we have a small, brave army helping the Americans win the war. And that it is cold up there. They knew a bit about the unfortified boundary line, too. Haven't we an information service in the U.S.? I must ask Grierson."

6. Ibid.

7. A comparison of the lives of Bernstein and Applebaum reveals similarities. Both were born in 1918, to Jewish parents. The fathers of both were businessmen with no musical background who attempted to discourage their sons from pursuing a career in music though both displayed and early interest and talent.

413

Though both thought of themselves as essentially composers, they conducted a broad range of music. Both wrote for the ballet stage, the concert hall and works for chamber groups. Both remained in the traditional tonal patterns of the past, though both experimented with the twelve-tone system. Both were comfortable with the jazz idiom in their musical expression. Both looked to Roy Harris for instruction and to Aaron Copland for inspiration. Both were attracted to film and television early in their careers, Bernstein as a narrator and a conductor ("Omnibus," "Young People's Concerts"), Applebaum to radio and television theatre productions and to CBC's "Junior Magazine," as a producer, narrator, and conductor of youth programming. Both made great contributions to the wider cultural life of their respective nations; Bernstein was a conductor-ambassador to the Soviet Union, South America, Israel, and virtually every country in Western Europe and Asia; Applebaum made his contribution as an arts administrator giving advice to arts councils and arts organizations at every level and writing policy reports that changed his nation. Both were tied to a single city throughout most of their peripatetic lives, Bernstein to New York and Applebaum to Toronto. Both received honorary degrees from prestigious universities in their respective countries. Both were to receive the highest honours their country can give: Bernstein the Career Achievement Citation, Kennedy Center, and the Gold Medal, American Academy of Arts and Letters; and Applebaum, the Companion of the Order of Canada and the Canadian Council of the Arts Diplome d'honneur.

8. John Grierson, Message to staff of the NFB, NFB Newsletter, November 1945. York University Archives, Louis Applebaum fonds, 1979-002/032.[604].

9. Ibid. The Cold War soon overtook the peace, and John Grierson was never able to fulfil the destiny he had set out for himself. In September 1947, Igor Gouzenko fled the Soviet Embassy in Ottawa and revealed that there was a Soviet spy ring operating there. This revelation began a hunt for spies that entrapped Grierson himself. His secretary, Freda Linton, was a close friend of Fred Rose, the Communist Member of Parliament who became implicated in the Soviet plot. Though Linton successfully defended herself and was exonerated from any wrongdoing, Grierson's name appeared in documents she used in her defence. That was enough to implicate Grierson, if not in Canadian eyes, most certainly before American tribunals. John Weinzweig also found himself on RCMP lists, having written a ballet called *Red Ear of Corn* at a time when the colour "red" had ideological implications.

10. Louis Applebaum, interview with author, September 7, 1999.

11. John McLean, "'No Thanks' to Hollywood Offers," Ottawa *Evening Standard,* March 23, 1946. York University Archives, Louis Applebaum fonds, 1979-002/028 [02].

12. Ibid.

13. Gerald Hawkins, "Liberty Profile: Louis Applebaum," *Liberty* Magazine, June 8,1946.[p.118].

14. *Maclean's* Magazine, May 1, 1946. [p.22].

15. Ibid. [p.44].
16. Louis Applebaum, interview with author, September 6, 1999.
17. Script: *Lost Boundaries*, 1949. York University Archives, Louis Applebaum fonds 1979-002/003,[29].
18. *Time* Magazine, July 4, 1949.
19. *Canadian Film Weekly*, April 4, 1951.
20. *Toronto Daily Star*, September 13, 1949.
21. *Film Music Notes*, September-October, 1949. Vol. ix, Number 1. [p.7] York University Archives, Louis Applebaum fonds, 1979-002/028 [26]
22. Ibid, [p.7]
23. *Canadian Film Weekly*, April 4, 1951,Toronto. York University Archives, Louis Applebaum fonds 1979 -002/003 [463].
24. Fred Zinnemann, letter to Louis Applebaum, November 11, 1950. York University Archives, Louis Applebaum fonds 1979 - 002/024 [486].
25. Louis Applebaum, interview with author, September 7, 1999.
26. Mavor Moore, letter to Louis Applebaum, June 27, 1950, York University Archives, Louis Applebaum fonds. 1979 - 002/022[438].
27. Program of Works by Young Canadians, January 11, 1942, York University Archives, Louis Applebaum fonds. 1979 - 002/032. [602]. While Louis was off in Hollywood on the *G. I. Joe* assignment, the NFB called on John Weinzweig, who was in the RCAF and stationed at Rockcliffe, to compose a couple of film scores. The extra income allowed John to bring his wife, Helen, to Ottawa for six months at the end of the war. (John and Helen Weinzweig, interview with author, September 12, 2000.)
28. NFB Notes on *Canada Carries On* Series, 1945. York University Archives, Louis Applebaum fonds, 1979 -002/030[582].
29. In the early 1990s, the author chaired a meeting organized by SOCAN, by then the sole performing rights society for Canadian composers. It was attended by SOCAN "serious music" composers along with conductors and managers of symphony orchestras in Canada. R. Murray Schafer gave an impassioned speech, indicating that he had earned more money from royalties for "serious music" than any of his colleagues. The amount came to $7000. His question was, "If this is the highest, how are the rest of you surviving?" He wanted to see some strategy that would enhance the remuneration of "serious" composers. As early as 1970 and as late as 1998, Louis would report that there were probably only two composers living off their writing of "serious" music — the two Harrys (Somers and Freedman.)
30. Sir Ernest MacMillan, Ed., "Film Music," *Music in Canada*, University of Toronto Press, Toronto. 1955.[p.167]
31. Louis Applebaum, "Analysis of the *Best Years of Our Lives*," *Film Music Notes*, Volume XXXI, No.4, 1947. Quoted in Roger Manvell and John Huntley, *The Technique of Film Music*, Communication Arts Books, Hastings House, Publishers, New York, 1957. [p.150]
32. Charles Clay, "Louis Applebaum." Montreal *Standard*, December 11, 1943, [p.9]

33. John Kraglund, *The Globe and Mail,* June 14, 1962. [p.50] The problem of "being in a hurry" certainly resonated with Louis, with his years of break-neck activity at the NFB. He was quite aware that even in the context of John Grierson's team approach, the composer of the film music comes in after all else has been completed and when the scheduled time for production has ended. The deadline at the best of times was only days away. In an interview years later, Louis outlined the problems of being a film composer and these issues were undoubtedly in his mind as he faced the next phase of his career.

Question: Working under time pressure like this, has there ever been a time when you simply dried up?

Answer: No, because you can't. It just can't happen.

Question: Have you ever looked at your work afterwards and felt, "My God. If I hadn't had to rush that thing through it could have been so much better"?

Answer: Absolutely. I don't know what you do about it. I happen to have a pattern of living that's different from most other composers. I have no time in which to fulfill other musical drives. I may want to sit down and write a string quartet but I just don't have the time. ("Interview: Louis Applebaum," *Canadian Composer,* January 1974. [p.14])

34. Ibid. All these illustrious composers were conscious of the degree to which their film work might trivialize their reputation. The career of Erich Wolfgang Korngold has been a constant reminder of how the film world could deflect one from more serious purposes. Korngold had been considered a major force in music composition in Europe, but when he was driven from Austria by Hitler's annexation, he settled in Hollywood, where he wrote film scores for 15 Warner Brothers productions. Although two of his scores won Academy Awards and he had what was obviously a highly successful career, there has always been the sense that he was diverted by his Hollywood experience from becoming a truly great 20th-century composer.

35. Bob Blackburn, "Conducts Music from the Red Pony," Toronto *Telegram,* June 15, 1962. York University Archives, Louis Applebaum fonds, 1979 - 002/028. [16]

Chapter 5. Returning Home

1. Peter Goddard, "How a Dual Career Got Rolling in a Traffic Jam." The *Toronto Star,* Monday, April 6, 1998. [Section C, p.10]

2. NFB Promotional Document, *The People Between,* issued from 620 Fifth Avenue, New York. York University Archives, Louis Applebaum fonds, 1979-002/004[39].

3. Pierre Berton, *My Times, Living With History,* Doubleday Canada Limited, Toronto, 1995. [pp.29-30]

4. Agnes Fischer, letter to Louis Applebaum, July 10,1947. York University Archives, Louis Applebaum fonds, 1979/002/004[39].

5. NFB Film Commentary on *The People Between.* York University Archives, Louis Applebaum fonds, 1979/002/004.[39] The film was described in a

press release as a description of China after the war between Chiang Kai-Shek and Mao Tse-Tung (*sic*; later conventionally transliterated as Mao Zedong), emphasizing life in rural communities where 98% of the people had no schooling. However, even in these circumstances, people were voting in local elections. Louis's comment to the author emphasized that the film was so politically volatile that it "was not shown for years."

6. Examples of Louis's negotiations with government department and agencies abound. In 1943, Louis had written the score for *Platoon*, made for the Canadian Army, with the officers and men of the Canadian Army as the main figures in the production. Another 1943 film, *Handle with Care*, made for the Department of Munitions and Supply, concerned the dangerous materials that men and women were working with in the wartime production of shells and other explosives. It was a dull subject, so marches and lively tunes were essential. Even the general public found the film informative, and its production demanded active support of the Department as well as those running the munitions factories.

7. Peggy Rooke, "Film Music," *Canadian Review of Music and Art*, 1947, Volume 6, No's 1 & 2, [p.25] York University Archives. Louis Applebaum fonds, 1979 – 002/028 [02].

8. Gerald Hawkins, "Liberty Profile: Louis Applebaum," *Liberty* Magazine, June 8, 1946. [p.19]

9. David Mackenzie, *Arthur Irwin, A Biography*. University of Toronto Press, Toronto Buffalo London, 1953. [p.231]

10. *Canadian Film Weekly*, Volume 15, No.49, December 20, 1950. York University Archives. Louis Applebaum fonds, 1979 - 002/028[03]

11. Lotta Dempsey, "No Place Like Home Toronto Composer Finds" *The Globe and Mail*, Thursday, October 27, 1949.

12. Pierre Berton, "He Sets Shakespeare to Music," *Mayfair* Magazine, May 1954, [p.30], York University Archives, Louis Applebaum fonds. 1979 - 002/030[583b]. In the same year, Louis worked with Norman McLaren on a film that was simply an explanation of how he made synthetic sound on film. *Pen Point Percussion* showed exactly how sound "looks" when drawn directly on film. It was an appropriate effort to capture how McLaren, certainly a genius of international stature, had produced such incredible films, and Louis had, by this time, become his right-hand man in this work, having not only the capacity to compose in the traditional fashion but a nurtured interest in synthetic sound production as a result of his own Composer-tron experiments.

13. Ibid.

14. David Mackenzie, *Arthur Irwin, A Biography*. University of Toronto Press, Toronto Buffalo London, 1953. [p.256].

15. Script: *Adult Education*. U.S. Army. 1950.[p20] York University Archives, Louis Applebaum fonds. 1979 – 002/001[01]. Ironically, it was a Canadian and a friend of Louis, Roby Kidd, who became the world's most respected exponent of the concept of life-long learning. The reason that the International Council on Adult Education has its office, not in New York or

Geneva, but in Toronto, is that this was the city in which Roby Kidd worked and wrote until his death in 1981.

16. George Stoney, Potomac Film Producers Incorporated, letter to Louis Applebaum, October 24, 1957. York University Archives, Louis Applebaum fonds, 1979 – 002/003[24].

17. George Stoney, letter to Louis Applebaum, February 6, 1954. York University Archives, Louis Applebaum fonds, 1979 –002/001[03]. Louis's name was the only one to appear twice on the program of the Flaherty Awards, as he had written music for another award winner, *And Now, Miguel,* about a Mexican boy who wants to be a sheep-herder. This film had been completed, not without rancour as Joseph Krumgold, the producer, had to prod Louis with notes expressing his frustration, "What's the matter with the script? If you think it stinks why don't you tell a guy?" (Letter: Krumgold to Louis Applebaum, September 27, 1951. York University Archives, Louis Applebaum fonds, 1979-002/001[04].)

18. Letter, Nicholas Read to Louis Applebaum, February 7, 1957. York University Archives, Louis Applebaum fonds, 1979-002/002[22]. Read had been the producer of the film *Hard Brought Up* and in negotiating with Louis about a second feature, *None Goes His Way Alone,* stated, "I am not going to ask you again, as I did for Hard Brought Up, to do a charity job."

19. Ibid. George Stoney, letter to Louis Applebaum, October 15, 1954. *Hard Brought Up* was a complete success. "You deserve great credit for helping Nick [Nicholas Read] make a creditable film out of one of the most difficult script assignments one could imagine."

20. Script: *None Goes His Way Alone,* Television, Radio and Film Commission, The Methodist Church, Nashville, Tennessee, 1957. York University Archives, Louis Applebaum fonds, 1979-002/004 [34].

21. Script: *Varley,* National Film Board, 1952. York University Archives, Louis Applebaum fonds, 1979 – 002/006 [58].

22. "CBC Wednesday Night," 1948. Production Files, CBC Reference Library, Toronto. "CBC Wednesday Night" included a major drama presentation, whose quality can be gauged by reference to the *CBC Times,* a periodical which provided information to CBC listeners. For example, the second program on December 10 featured T. S. Eliot's *Murder in the Cathedral,* followed on December 17 by *Peer Gynt,* adapted by Lister Sinclair. But as well, there was music, often Canadian, performed by such ensembles as the CBC Vancouver Orchestra. Political and social comment was also included. In short, "CBC Wednesday Night" became a weekly intellectual journey that has no parallel in modern radio broadcasting, although the CBC Radio "Ideas" programs do continue that tradition in their examination of the intellectual underpinnings of the modern age.

23. Script: Hazel Robinson, "The Perilous Dream," "CBC Wednesday Night" 1949. York University Archives, Louis Applebaum fonds, 1979 – 002/013 [241]. In 1949, Louis wrote the music for two other productions that shared the "CBC Wednesday Night" series with "The Perilous Dream." "The Seven

Who Were Hanged" was a play that examined the manner in which each condemned man faced death and thereby exposed the meaning of his own life. As well, Britten's opera *Peter Grimes* was being prepared for offering to a "CBC Wednesday Night" audience and Louis took over its musical supervision and had to produce new scoring for this dramatic interpretation. This intervention had interesting implications. Within a few years Louis would be adding Britten's opera repertoire to his presentations at Stratford as part of his Stratford Music Festival. York University Archives, Louis Applebaum fonds, 1979 – 002/015[261].

24. Hazel Robinson, letter to Louis Applebaum, November 13, 1949. York University Archives, Louis Applebaum fonds.1979 - 002/013. [241] Today such a program would have a very limited audience, but in these years radio had extraordinary listeners with a degree of loyalty that became legendary. People tuned every Sunday to "Jake and the Kid" and every week to "CBC Wednesday Night." But the present obsession simply with the size of the listening audience has put the Corporation at constant risk and any whiff of "elitism" is used as an argument for cutting its government support.

25. CBC Manitoba Flood Relief Radio Program, 1950. York University Archives, Louis Applebaum fonds, 1979 – 002/016[268].

26. Radio Script: "The Year of Decision," United Nations, 1950. York University Archives, Louis Applebaum fonds. 1979 – 002/014[251] Louis was a perfect choice; he had already addressed the subject of atomic weapons in his film music in 1946 when Ragan Productions had employed him to write the score for *One World or None*. The film asked the basic question, How, then, shall we use this energy? It sought to shock by positing the image of what the Hiroshima bomb would have destroyed if it had been dropped on New York City, not an impossible situation if the development of this weapon were connected to the improvements in rocketry that the Nazis had achieved in World War II. The idea that the U.S. could be the battleground of any future war was put forward seriously and graphically. Atomic power meant the end of civilization or "a cohesive force that makes one world possible," the script proclaims. Script Outline: *One World or None*, Ragan Productions, New York. York University Archives, Louis Applebaum fonds, 1979 -002/004[35].

In 1952, Louis was commissioned to write the score for an RKO film, *Operation A-Bomb*. It seems inconceivable now that this film could have been made, documenting as it did the development of the atomic bomb from the Yucca Flats in Nevada to its use at Hiroshima. The film crew followed men of the U.S. Marine Corps who were being used as guinea pigs to determine the impact of the bomb in battle conditions, and concluded with the hope "that this awesome force may serve only peace – in a world without war." Louis did his best to make his music as pregnant with doom as possible. York University Archives, Louis Applebaum fonds 1979 – 002/004[36].

Another UN radio script soon followed. "Tomorrow for Two" depicted the despair faced by displaced persons from the camps of Europe through the lives of two who were confronted by advice such as, "there is so much misery … are you going to carry it all in your heart? Be hard." Radio Script. "Tomorrow for Two," United Nations, [p.8]. York University Archives, Louis Applebaum fonds 1979 – 022/016[250]. In 1956, Louis was approached once again by the UN to do the music for a radio play, "The Diplomat." It was a satire on the career of a diplomat moving all the way from Neanderthal man to Dag Hammarskjold, then Secretary-General of the United Nations. The voices of Michael Redgrave, Basil Rathbone, Orson Welles, and John Drainie were heard, but *Variety* Magazine, October 31, 1956, commented, "No less excellent was the music and sound effects. Louis Applebaum did special composition and scoring as telling as Redgrave's delivery." *Variety* concluded that for this program "not to reach a national television audience would be unpardonable."

27. Script: *Hamlet,* "CBC Wednesday Night" Production, 1951. This was Louis's first score for *Hamlet.* He was to do several more for television and the Stratford stage. This one, however, was an unusual commission as it was to be for two audiences: the regular "CBC Wednesday Night" listeners would hear it first, and then it was to be adapted for a series of six half-hour school broadcasts at 10:15 in the morning. Of all his *Hamlet* scores, this one proved the most difficult as both audiences had to be kept in mind and the revisions for morning productions were substantial. He received $100 for each educational segment and $300 for the "CBC Wednesday Night" version. York University Archives, Louis Applebaum fonds 1979 – 002/015[257].

28. Script: Jean Anouilh's adaptation of *Antigone.* "CBC Wednesday Night", February 11, 1953.[p.1] York University Archives, Louis Applebaum fonds, 1979 – 002/115 [252].

29. Ibid. [p.54]

30. Script: Harry Boyle, "Friends for Christmas," CBC Production, 1950. York University Archives, Louis Applebaum fonds. 1979 – 002/008[87].

31. Nathan Cohen, "After 25 Years CBC Stage Is All We Have," *Toronto Daily Star,* January 11, 1969. [p.33]

32. Script: "Coloured Buttons," "CBC Stage '52," 1952. York University Archives, Louis Applebaum fonds, 1979 – 002/013[223].

33. Script: "The Paper Railroad," "CBC Summer Stage" 1951. York University Archives, Louis Applebaum fonds, 1979 – 002/012[224]. This play was repeated on CBC in 1955 as part of the "Stage" series.

34. Script: Harry Boyle, "Strike," "CBC Summer Stage," 1954. York University Archives, Louis Applebaum fonds, 1979 – 002/013 [237].

35. Script: Charles Israel, "Prophecy at Dawn," "CBC Summer Stage," 1954. York University Archives, Louis Applebaum fonds, 1979 – 002/013 [236].

36. Script: Stanley Mann, "Bartholomew Webster, Age 83," "CBC Summer Stage," 1954. York University Archives, Louis Applebaum fonds, 1979 – 002/013[228].

37. Script, "Madwoman of Chaillot," "CBC Wednesday Night," June 15, 1955. York University Archives, Louis Applbaum fonds, 1979-002/015[259]. The program's cast was filled with names that appeared week after week on "CBC Wednesday Night" and other drama series, including Ruth Springford, John

Drainie, Bud Knapp, Paul Kligman, Kate Reid, Frank Perry, Ed McNamara, and Tommy Tweed.

38. Script, Harry Boyle, "The Thawing Wind," "CBC Wednesday Night," April 18, 1956, York Univeersity Archive, Louis Applebaum fonds, 1979 – 002/016 [266].

39. Brochure, *Dreams That Money Can Buy*, [p.1], York University Archives, Louis Applebaum fonds, 1979 - 002/028. [020].

40. Louis Applebaum's Lecture Notes for *Dreams That Money Can Buy*. York University Archives, Louis Applebaum fonds, 1979 - 002/028[15].

41. Bosley Crowther, "Calder Constructions," *New York Times*, April 24, 1948, York University Archives, Louis Applebaum fonds 1979 - 002/028. [020].

42. *Saturday Night* Magazine, November 15, 1949. [p.21] It was reported in the same issue [p.31] that "Anticipating trouble with Marcel Duchamp's famous painting 'Nude Descending a Staircase,' he [Richter] had superimposed a picture of anthracite coal going down a chute, but for the censors there was, apparently, too much coal and the sequence was cut from a minute and a half to a minute." The road for art films was not easy even in post-war North America. There was strong antipathy toward the exposure of the intimate parts of the human body on film.

43. Louis Applebaum's Lecture Notes for *Dreams That Money Can Buy*. York University Archives, Louis Applebaum fonds 1979 - 002/027[547].

44. Lotta Dempsey, "No Place Like Home Toronto Composer Finds," *The Globe and Mail*, Thursday, October 27, 1949. York University Archives, Louis Applebaum fonds, 1979 - 002/027[547].

45. Gerald Pratley, *Saturday Night* Magazine, August 9, 1952. [p.21], York University Archives, Louis Applebaum fonds 1979 - 002/028[02]. Pratley also wrote a most succinct comment that Louis treasured: "I look forward to the day when the standard applied by critics in responsible journals may have the effect of influencing a producer to choose a master rather than a hack to score his next picture and when those artists who are composing for films today will be encouraged in the knowledge that their work will receive in these journals the attention it deserves." Gerald Pratley, in Roger Manuel and John Huntley, *The Technique of Film Music*, for the British Film Academy, Communication Arts Books, Hastings House, Publishers, New York, 1957. [p. 282]

Chapter 6. The Stratford Miracle

1. Tom Patterson, interview with author, March 15, 2000. Tom Patterson was "stunned" by Applebaum's positive response. Patterson had given his "spiel" while being driven through central Toronto. Louis, "in his inevitable low key way just announced that, 'anything you want me to do… I'll do it.'" When Patterson sought advice from someone beyond Canada's shores, it was to Boyd Neel that he turned. "He was here under the auspices of Columbia Artists Management that ran Community Concerts of Canada, an organization that set up community groups to sponsor Columbia's artists. That year my mother was president of the Stratford branch. She

made an appointment for me to see Neel at the Queen's Hotel in Stratford where he was staying. I went with some trepidation … . We sat in the lobby of the hotel and I outlined the whole idea with great enthusiasm, throwing in the idea that we could also present music during the Festival. To my delight, he was even more interested in my idea than several of the Canadians I had talked to had been. Our conversation gave me a great boost. Now I could say that an international star from England agreed with the idea." Tom Patterson and Allan Gould, *First Stage*, McClelland and Stewart, Toronto, 1987. [p.38]

2. Louis Applebaum, interview with author, February 1, 1999.

3. Laura Pogson, interview with author, September 2, 2000. Pogson is a lifetime Stratford citizen with an intense devotion to the Festival. Her description of Stratford in 1953 through the eyes of a child is fascinating. It was a baseball and hockey town and the strength of that sports commitment along with other community interests, has, in her view, saved Stratford from becoming a Disneyland-like theme park.

4. Louis Applebaum, interview with author, February 1, 1999. The scoring for "Richard III, 2 percussion and 6 brass," for "All's Well … 1 percussion 2 trumpets, 5 strings and a harp." Louis's confidence in Guthrie was increased when, approaching his house one day, he heard a Bach fugue being played on the piano. It was Guthrie, who Louis claims was "a musical guy" and gave support to Louis's expansion of his role from "mere composer and conductor" to Music Director.

5. Louis's experience in sound production was an unexpected asset. The orchestra pit being on the side and not, as with the proscenium stage, directly in front of the footlights, presented a challenge. Thus even from the floor of the tent structure there was a sound delay problem unless the conductor slightly anticipated the cue. When the permanent structure was built, the orchestra "pit" was placed over the stage. Musical sound in the Festival Theatre became even more complicated when the conductor was no longer visible to those on stage. Closed-circuit television later provided the needed link. However, in the more complex scores, either for drama or music theatre, the problems were enormous.

6. Louis Applebaum, interview with Pat Quigley, January 1992. VHS Tape, Butch Blake Archival Program, Stratford Festival Archives, Stratford, Ontario.

7. Norman Campbell once commented that the royalties from these fanfares must be making Louis rich. Actually, even though he kept artistic control of these works, Louis donated these fanfares to the Stratford Festival in perpetuity, and received not a penny for their performance. At the beginning of the 1990s, it was estimated that the three fanfares had been played 18,000 times since 1953. Certainly, with the exception of the National Anthem, they are the most-played Canadian works ever written. Louis refused one request to make use of these works on the basis that the fanfare was quite exclusive to the Stratford, Ontario, context. However, he did allow an Australian theatre company to use a fanfare for one of its productions.

8. Elliot Hayes, Notes for liner notes, "Forty Seasons of Music from the Stratford Festival," CD ATTIC ACD 1378. It is suggested that during Jean Gascon's tenure as Artistic Director there was an effort to save money and provide a change by ceasing to play the fanfares before and during intermissions of plays at the Festival Theatre. There was a terrible uproar that ended any chance of this happening.

9. Tyrone Guthrie, *Mayfair* Magazine, October, 1953, p.27. York University Archives, Louis Applebaum fonds, 1979 –002/122 [430].

10. Louis Applebaum, interview with author, February 1,1999.

11. Louis Applebaum, first draft of an article for Clarke Irwin, "The Stratford Story" Toronto, 1968, [p.1] York University Archives, Louis Applebaum fonds, 1979 – 022/025[499].

12. Louis Applebaum, Script, CBC "This Week," 1954. York University Archives, Louis Applebaum fonds, 1979 – 002/022 [423].

13. Louis Applebaum, interview with author, June 10, 1999. The NFB was a unique enterprise that stressed collegial activity. In the early 1940s at the NFB, a handful of talented composers, including Louis, were used to working together, had witnessed the effect of music within the field of documentary film production, and were confident that music could communicate just as dramatically in other contexts, whether live or through the broadcast media.

14. John Weinzweig, "Recollection," The Program of the New Music Concerts 20th Anniversary Season, February 24, 1991 (40th Anniversary of the Founding of the Canadian League of Composers.) Weinzweig recounts how he, Harry Somers, and Sam Dolin were at Weinzweig's house. Helen, John's wife, offered to make supper. "Soon after we were talking about the problems of composing in Canada. They, too, were experiencing the sense of isolation in a career that held out little hope of publication and recording, the high cost of reproducing extended works, and the unlikely prospect of their performance."

   They were evidently prodded by Helen "to make up their minds" and at that moment decided to organize the Canadian League of Composers. Very quickly the group was enlarged to some 20 members and several meetings took place in a few months. As well as Louis, Harry Freedman, Andy Twa, Phil Nimmons, John Beckwith, and Barbara Pentland became early members.

15. Louis Applebaum, Script, "This Week," CBC, 1954. York University Archives, Louis Applebaum fonds, 1979 – 002/022[423]. Within months Louis, along with Nimmons, Dolin, Freedman, and Twa, became members of a committee to secure a charter from the Federal Government. They were successful. The League was launched. John Weinzweig remembers that at this time it took him three years to complete a violin concerto, as he had to spend his time organizing the League and selling tickets to its concerts. (John Weinzweig, interview with author, August 29, 2000.)

16. Louis Applebaum, interview with author, February 1, 1999. Though both Weinzweig and Louis had great respect for MacMillan, they had little confidence in his commitment to Canadian music even though he himself was a composer of some stature. Thus, they hired as conductor, Louis's old friend from

NFB days, Geoffrey Waddington. Sir Ernest was somewhat "put off" but came to be a supporter of his composer colleagues. There was something of a trend at work in North America, as in the same year Philadelphia's Leopold Stokowski, a supporter of American composers, along with Koussevitsky in Boston, had presented two concerts of American music at the New York Museum of Art that included the works of Elliot Carter, Alan Hovhaness, Henry Cowell, and Ulysses Kay, as well as the concert of Canadian compositions.

17. Louis Applebaum, First Draft of an article for Clarke Irwin, "The Stratford Story," Toronto, 1968. [p.2] York University Archives, Louis Applebaum fonds, 1979-022/025[499]

18. Mary Jolliffe, interview with author, August 29, 2000. Even her worthy efforts turned out badly. In a hastily created program, she referred to Louis as "Louse Applebaum" and was embarrassed when Tyrone Guthrie, who referred to her as "darling-girl," pointed it out.

19. Louis Applebaum, first draft of an article for Clarke Irwin, "The Stratford Story," Toronto, 1968. [p.2] York University Archives, Louis Applebaum fonds, 1979-022/025[499]

20. Ibid.

21. There were moments of bliss to be found in this season. Robertson Davies, previously a Shakespearean actor, the publisher of the Peterborough *Examiner* in the 1950s, but more importantly an enthusiastic supporter of the Festival, wrote: "The performance of *Oedipus Rex* is a triumph for all concerned with it …. A. E. Houseman said that he knew true poetry when he heard it by the prickling of the hair on his scalp. I, too, know this feeling and time and time again during Stratford's *Oedipus Rex* I felt this sensation of mingled terror and delight. Can there be higher praise?" Robertson Davies, *Saturday Night* Magazine, July 31, 1954.[pp.9-10].

22. Louis Applebaum, interview with author, February 19, 1999.

23. Louis Applebaum, interview with author, February 15, 1999. There was, however, one problem that could not be solved with the provision of a new structure: the weather. The summer of 1955 brought another heat wave and the "Casino" (later to become the Third Stage and now appropriately called the Tom Patterson Theatre) held the heat magnificently. Isaac Stern played a recital in the hall, and at his feet, at the conclusion of the event, Louis observed, "there was a pool of sweat large enough to sail a boat."

24. Louis Applebaum, interview with author, February 15, 1999.

25. Ibid.

26. Letter, Tyrone Guthrie to Louis Applebaum, February 5, 1955. York University Archives, Louis Applebaum fonds, 1979 – 002/023[458].

27. Ezra Schabas, interview with author, July 7, 1999. This ensemble, known as the Festival Singers, became Canada's primary professional choir. The singers were prompted to organize themselves as a professional choir by Louis's and Ezra Schabas's proposal that the ensemble participate in several concerts during the Festival weeks of the summer.

28. Ibid. Schabas's analysis of Neel's capacity was that "he was an amiable man with a clear beat, good at baroque, but otherwise an amateur." Neel was most appreciative of Louis's role. "The ultimate success of the venture was due almost entirely to his [Applebaum's] work and enthusiasm .... When we realize that Lou Applebaum, practically single-handedly, dealt with the arranging of the entire Festival in a most efficient way, we marvel at the achievement." Boyd Neel, "Music at the Festival," in Robertson Davies, Tyrone Guthrie, Boyd Neel, Tanya Moiseiwitsch, *Thrice the Brinded Cat Hath Mew'd, A Record of the Stratford Shakespearean Festival,* Clarke, Irwin and Company Limited, 1955. Toronto. [p.102] One finds considerable dichotomy in any objective analysis of the Boyd Neel intervention. Ross Parmenter's description was "as good an orchestra as any on this continent." John Pettigrew, Jamie Portman, *Stratford: The First Thirty Years,* Macmillan of Canada, Toronto, 1985 [p.11].

29. Dr. Leslie Bell, "The Man Behind the Music Festival," *The Star Weekly,* May 25, 1955. [p.12] York University Archives, Louis Applebaum fonds, 1979-002/027[535]. Louis had approached Franchot Tone, a very elegant and articulate artist, and one, he believed, who would bring flair and excitement to the text. Tone wanted a four-figure fee. Louis responded, "I'm afraid that is out of our class," to which Tone replied, "I never lower my price, so I'll tell you what I'll do — I'll come for nothing." The Applebaum strategy had triumphed. (It was a short-lived "triumph." In the end, Tone was unable to fulfil his commitment but the production was nevertheless a highlight of the Stratford Music season.)

30. Ibid. Louis established the concept of partnerships long before the term became so popular in the 1990s. He was able to share the costs of Schwarzkopf's participation with the Conservatory and reduce his own financial commitment. That season, Stratford Music presented Sunday afternoon concerts of sacred music in cooperation with the Canadian Council of Christians and Jews, which covered not only the direct costs of the concerts but also enabled Stratford Music audiences to hear Healey Willan's choir from St Mary Magdalene Church (Toronto), John Cozens's St. John's Evangelical Lutheran choir (Toronto) as well as the choirs from Beth Tzedec Synagogue and St. James' Cathedral, both from Toronto, and the St. George's Cathedral choir from Kingston and the Columbian choir from Windsor.

31. Louis Applebaum, interview with author, February 1, 1999.

32. At the first concert, the Iseler Singers sang a *Song of Welcome* by Healey Willan and the Hart House Orchestra played Honegger's *Symphony #3.* and although subsequent concerts in July had Glenn Gould playing Mozart, Beethoven, and Schubert, and Isaac Stern and Alexander Schneider tackling the Bach and Mozart concertos for two violins, the first orchestral offering by Boyd Neel was a study in musical obscurity for that time: Dittersdorf's *Symphony in C,* Hamerik's *Symphony Spirituelle,* a concerto by Holst, and a great but largely unknown work, *Verklarte Nacht* by Schoenberg. Such a repertoire would have been considered a courageous presentation in Toronto

or even in New York, but in Stratford it approached box-office insanity. Though subsequent Hart House Orchestra concerts featured Bach, Haydn, Elgar, and Vivaldi, there were also generous offerings of Britten, Bartok, Richard Strauss, and Françaix. Even Stravinsky's "A Soldier's Tale" was on the edge of tolerance for most concert-goers of this decade.

33. John Kraglund, "Music in Stratford," *The Globe and Mail*, June 14, 1955. [p.12]

34. Dr. Leslie Bell, "The Man Behind the Music Festival, *The Star Weekly*, May 28, 1955,[p.12].

35. The *Varsity*, September 21, 1955, [p.8]. York University Archives, Louis Applebaum fonds, 1979-025/022[494].

36. Louis Applebaum, "Report on the Inaugural Stratford Music Festival," August 8, 1955 [p.1]. York University Archives, Louis Applebaum fonds, 1979 – 002/025[497].

37. Ibid. [p.5]

38. Ibid. [p.5]

39. Stratford Festival News Release #2. February 29, 1956. York University Archives, Louis Applebaum fonds, 1979 – 002/033[622]. Louis made the point that "This is the first time that good jazz had been thoroughly integrated into a serious music festival."

40. John Kraglund, "Stratford Opera is a Triumph," *The Globe and Mail*, July 29, 1956. York University Archives, Louis Applebaum fonds, 1979 – 002/029 [06]. A day later Kraglund, not noted for effusive appreciation in his reviews, was also moved by another offering, an all-Beethoven concert by the Festival Orchestra conducted by Heinz Unger, with Claudio Arrau at the piano: "Music, soloist, conductor, and orchestra were superbly matched. It was one of those musical experiences which, despite the law of gravity, almost lifted the listener out of his seat." John Kraglund, *The Globe and Mail*, July 30, 1956. York University Archives, Louis Applebaum fonds. 1979 – 002/029[06].

41. George Kidd, Toronto *Telegram*, July 9, 1956. York University Archives, Louis Applebaum fonds 1979 – 002/029[06].

42. Louis's confidence in Canadian artists and music was paying off. A fine concert in which Reginald Stewart conducted the Festival Orchestra with Maureen Forrester singing another commissioned composition, Harry Somers's *Five Songs for Dark Voice* (a piece she was to sing many times in many recitals in Canada and abroad) was one of the highlights of the season. Glenn Gould not only performed but presented his own composition, String Quartet, Op. 1.

43. John Kraglund, *The Globe and Mail*, January 3, 1957. York University Archives, Louis Applebaum fonds, 1979 – 022/029[06] John Cook, Organist at St. Paul's Cathedral, London, and the man who was to give Louis some relief in both composing for Stratford productions and conducting, wrote to Louis: "Some of the highbrows are raising their eyebrows at the Ellington-and-Co. side of things, which amused Audrey and me. We think it's a terrific idea, and I can hardly wait. I'm particularly excited at the thought of hear-

ing Art Tatum whose recordings have always amazed me. I mean excited!!!"
John Cook, letter to Louis Applebaum, March 16, 1956. York University
Archives, Louis Applebaum fonds, 1979 – 002/017[283].

44. Jacqueline Rosenfeld. *Mayfair* Magazine, November, 1956. [pp. 36-7].

45. Gerald Pratley, interview with author, September 14, 2000. Canada's foremost film expert was to observe: "Stratford is the first place in North America
to stage a European-type international film festival where the emphasis was
not on stars and 'hype' but on the serious consideration of the art form." G.
Pratley, Stratford Festival Publication, 1957. York University Archives, Louis
Applebaum fonds, 1979 – 002/033[624].

46. Vic Polley, "Report of the Box Office Manager," Stratford Shakespearean
Festival, 1956. York University Archives, Louis Applebaum fonds, 1979 –
002/025[097]. Polley noted that "It should be borne in mind that any highly competitive music programme planned at the same time as Drama could
and does draw patrons from the plays." However, he displayed considerable
ambivalence, indicated by his concern that raising the ticket prices for concerts to $3.50 had meant "that some quite worthy and impecunious groups
have been deprived of the opportunity of sharing the marvelous talent that
more provident clients have chosen to ignore."

47. Robertson Davies, *Saturday Night* Magazine, [p.15] York University
Archives, Louis Applebaum fonds. 1979 – 002/029 [07].

48. Barry Ulanov, *Downbeat* Magazine, September 5, 1956. York University
Archives, Louis Applebaum fonds. 1979 – 002/025 [494]

49. Louis Applebaum, interview with author, February 1, 1999.

50. John Pettigrew, Jamie Portman, *Stratford: The First Thirty Years*, Macmillan of
Canada, Toronto. 1985. [pp.105 –6]

51. Lenore Crawford, *London Free Press*, August 11, 1956. York University
Archives, Louis Applebaum fonds. 1979 – 002/029 [07].

52. Script: Jesuit Marian Year pageant, CNE Coliseum, Toronto, October 8 – 16,
1954. York University Archives, Louis Applebaum fonds, 1979 –
002/017[285]. An indication of the minimal remuneration for such a project can be determined by the fee Louis received. He collected 4 cents a bar
per instrumental line with the choral arrangement segments returning 25
cents per line. Louis received $1,682.59 for the entire project.

Chapter 7. Return to Stratford.

1. Louis Applebaum, interview with author, March 30, 1999. It was a new
experience in another way. Instead of receiving a commission for composition and thereby an immediate guarantee of income, he would receive a percentage of the box office revenues. *The Centaur*, later changed to *Ride a Pink
Horse*, was, however, a financial disaster. It did not get "on the boards" until
late 1958 and was remounted in May, 1959 when it was expected to recoup
its original losses. By May 19, 1958, Louis received a letter from Jean
Roberts, Production Manager at the Crest: "I am sure Donald [Donald
Davis, Director of the Crest Theatre] has told you this, but to make doubly

sure, as audience sales for *Ride a Pink Horse* have been almost nil, we are closing this production on Saturday May 23rd. We are sorry it is not the Box Office success we had hoped it might be – but better luck next time." Jean Roberts to Louis Applebaum, May 19, 1959. York University Archives, Louis Applebaum fonds, 1979 – 001/018[297]

2. Harry Freedman, interview with author, September 11, 2000.
3. Mavor Moore, Toronto *Telegram*, May 8, 1959. [p. 34]
4. Mavor Moore, *Toronto Daily Star*, May 9, 1959. [p. 27]
5. Scott Young, *The Globe and Mail*, May 1, 1959. [p.18]
6. Ron Johnson, "Music Backed by Taxes," *Toronto Daily Star*, May 2, 1959.
7. Herbert Whittaker, *The Globe and Mail*, Toronto, May 8, 1959. [p. 23]
8. Louis Applebaum, interview with author, March 30, 1999.
9. "Applebaum Resigns," Stratford *Beacon Herald*, August 10, 1956. York University Archives, Louis Applebaum fonds 1979 – 002/029 [06].
10. Leslie Bell, *Toronto Daily Star*, July 5, 1957. York University Archives, Louis Applebaum fonds. 1979 – 002/029/ [09] Louis was to write the music for four productions of *Hamlet*, both at Stratford and on the CBC. The music for the 1957 production was described as "refreshingly dissonant and effectively dramatic." Peter Mellors, Toronto *Telegram*, July 7, 1957. [p. 3]
11. Robertson Davies, *Saturday Night* Magazine, July 20, 1957. York University Archives, Louis Applebaum fonds. 1979 – 002/027 [537]. This was indeed a magnificent *Hamlet*, with Christopher Plummer in the lead role, William Hutt as Polonius, Frances Hyland as Ophelia, Lloyd Bochner as Horatio, and Douglas Campbell as Claudius.
12. Louis Applebaum, "A Proposal for Music at Stratford," Stratford Shakespearean Festival, September 16, 1957. York University Archives, Louis Applebaum fonds. 1979 – 002/025 [498] [p.1]
13. Ibid. [pp.1-2]
14. Ibid. [p.2]
15. Ibid. [p.2]
16. Ibid. [p.3]
17. George Kidd, Toronto *Telegram*, Saturday, December 7, 1957, [p.36]. York University Archives, Louis Applebaum fonds, 1979 – 002/029[09].
18. *Detroit Jewish News*, January 17, 1958. [p.11] York University Archives, Louis Applebaum fonds.1979– 002/030[01].
19. Festival Brief to the Canada Council, 1958. [p.3] In this brief a mention is made of Louis's proposal to "establish a group of world-famous musicians" in the Festival's request for $75,000. York University Archives, Louis Applebaum fonds, 1979 – 002/025[498].
20. Lenore Crawford, *London Free Press*, July 23, 1958, [p.4] Crawford wrote: "The fourth annual season of the Stratford Shakespearean Festival of Music opened tonight in the Avon Theatre with a magnificent fanfare written especially for this gala opening by Music Festival Director, Louis Applebaum."
21. Helen McNamara, Toronto *Telegram*, July 23, 1958. [p.29] York University Archives, Louis Applebaum fonds. 1979 – 002/030 [566b].

22. Herbert Whittaker, *The Globe and Mail,* July 31, 1958. [p.27] Jacob Siskind, writing in the July 30 edition of the *Montreal Star,* was even more laudatory, referring to *The Beggar's Opera* as "one of the most enjoyable operatic productions I have ever witnessed and that it is the most satisfying event in the four seasons of musical festivities here. The lion's share [of credit] must go to Louis Applebaum who has conducted and rehearsed the work from the start … [and] has whipped these bits of musical froth about until the audience is left heady and giddy with sheer delight." On the other hand, Graham George was critical of Louis's efforts, complaining about the fact that this "piece de resistance" of the season had attracted able and experienced players in the orchestra and that "Mr Applebaum would do well to consider that these players are 'bridle-wise', he would get even better results with a shorter beat. Occasionally, his highly musical but too sumptuous conducting caused a sluggishness which his players did all they could to overcome." Graham George, "Music at Stratford: Tale of a Comet" *Canadian Music Journal,* 1958. York University Archives, Louis Applebaum fonds, 1979 – 002/029 [10].

23. Ken Johnson, "Stratford Enriched by Music Recital," *The Globe and Mail,* July 24, 1958 [p10] 1979 –002/030[566a].

24. Louis Applebaum, interview with author, February 1, 1999.

25. Jacob Siskind, "Stratford's Music in Decline," *Montreal Star,* August 2, 1950, [p21] 1979 – 002/029[14].

26. Score for *Much Ado About Nothing,* York University Archives, Louis Applebaum fonds 1979 – 002/029[14].

27. Letter, Glenn Gould to Louis Applebaum, November 2, 1958. York University Archives, Louis Applebaum fonds, 1979 – 002/025 [474]. A second handwritten and undated note from Gould proposes that he take on the suggested duties in 1960 though he doubted recording as a trio with the other artists Louis had suggested would be possible as they were under contract with different recording companies. Gould was a strange colleague, with most disconcerting habits. The Chief Archivist at York University, Kent Hayward, tells the story that Louis had told him of one trip to Stratford in the heat of the summer with all the windows up and with no air conditioning to relieve the discomfort. Gould insisted on driving, wearing an overcoat as always, and Louis was sweating profusely and succumbing to heat prostration when the car lurched. Obviously a tire had blown. Never was Louis so happy to change a tire on what was the most excruciating trip he ever took from Toronto to Stratford.

     Gould's preoccupation with his health is illustrated by a Jan Applebaum story. Gould arrived at her kitchen while she was peeling onions. Her eyes and nose were running and Gould immediately asked "Do you have a cold?" Before she could answer "no," without apology or explanation he was out of the door and down the street.

28. Louis Applebaum, interview with author, February 1, 1999. After renovating the "Casino" an even more appropriate venue was found — an abandoned theatre some blocks away but still close enough to be part of the Festival

complex. This theatre had been left to hundreds of rats as well as the disintegration of several decades and Louis found himself heavily involved once again in the process of renovation.

29. Eric McLean, *Montreal Star*, July 31, 1959. York University Archives, Louis Applebaum fonds, 1979-002/028 [10] Mollie Graham reported in the Stratford *Beacon Herald* of July 27, 1959 that *Orpheus* had "closed after 17 performances with the cast being given an ovation which surpassed even that of the opening night." It was her opinion that "under the baton of Louis Applebaum, the Festival's music director, the orchestra added a great deal to the performance where it might have detracted from it." Nevertheless, in spite of her conclusions that *Orpheus* "should be classified as an outstanding success for the Stratford Festival and had received excellent reviews in other newspapers and had been acclaimed by the public and had brought people to the Festival who have never been here before," it was not a financial success. There was only a 54% house on average and the production cost $25,000 more than it brought in. Louis Applebaum, Stratford Music Festival Report, 1959.

30. Eric McLean, *Montreal Star*, July 31, 1959. York University Archives, Louis Applebaum fonds 1979 – 002/028 [10].

31. Mollie Graham, Stratford *Beacon Herald*, August 6, 1959, [p.6] York University Archives, Louis Applebaum fonds, 1979-002/028[10]. Lenore Crawford, *London Free Press*, August 6, 1959, was equally moved. "Louis Applebaum, festival music director, scheduled an all-Bach program with some fear. He need not have worried; the performance was a unique experience in Ontario musical heritage and its popularity was evidenced by wild applause that greeted every number."

32. Mollie Graham, Stratford *Beacon Herald*, August 10, 1959, [p.6] York University Archives, Louis Applebaum fonds, 1979-002/028[11]. This was not the only triumph of the 1960 season. In a letter to William Judd, Columbia Artists, August 6, 1960, Louis was obviously ecstatic while writing "Tomorrow we are playing a chamber music program, all-Beethoven, and could easily have sold 8,000 tickets for this event. Whether it is Stratford, Sunday afternoon, the Festival Theatre, Glenn Gould or a combination of all these that attracts the hordes, I dare not say but the interest is certainly high." York University Archives, Louis Applebaum fonds, 1979 –025[505]

33. Oscar Shumsky, interview, Stratford *Beacon Herald*, August 7, 1959. [p. 6] York University Archives, Louis Applebaum fonds, 1979 – 002/028[10].

34. Ralph Thomas, *Toronto Daily Star*, 1964, York University Archives, Louis Applebaum fonds. 1979 – 002/028 [17]. Lynn Harrell, who joined as a young cellist and then went on to a stellar career as a soloist, was quoted as saying "This is one of the most exciting places I have ever seen" in the Thomas article.

35. Louis Applebaum, "Stratford Music Festival Report – 1959" York University Archives, Louis Applebaum fonds, 1979 – 002/025 [498]. In spite of Louis's role in developing the Film Festival, it was not a part of Stratford Music. Thus this contribution counted for little. This was unfortunate as, in 1959,

the Film Festival "took off" with an outstanding gathering of film art from the U.S., U.S.S.R., and the U.K., as expected, but also films from Hungary, Germany, China, India, Sweden, and Italy. The audience sky-rocketed to double that of the year before and the Film Festival ended with a surplus.

36. Louis Applebaum, interview with author, June 10, 1999.

37. Tyrone Guthrie, letter to Louis Applebaum, November 30, 1959, York University Archives, Louis Applebaum fonds, 1979-002/030 [564] Guthrie would come to Stratford and also direct Shakespeare's *King John*. However, he would give his main attention to Gilbert and Sullivan.

38. Morris Duff, "Shostakovich Ousts Jazz at Stratford," *Toronto Daily Star*, January 8, 1960. York University Archives, Louis Applebaum fonds, 1979 – 002/030[564]. Also noted in the article was the return of Glenn Gould. Louis commented "no one can play Bach like Gould" and both were delighted to be working together again. It was also noted that there would be an International String Congress sponsored by the American Federation of Music at which top students in Canada would be enrolled.

39. Louis Applebaum, "Notes for comments to Workshop participants," unpublished, August 6, 1960. Louis wanted the orchestra players to realize that the Workshop existed "because the Festival thinks the workshop is a valuable thing," and "it pours money into the workshop. It is here as a service to you. This is the Festival's contribution to the musical life of this country." He stressed the importance of this synergistic experience the musicians were engaged in as excellence in orchestral performance, as he believed great music emerges from "an ensemble of players who get along with each other."

40. Report of the Meeting of the National Youth Orchestra Advisory Committee, 1960. York University Archives, Louis Applebaum fonds, 1979 – 002/024 [484].

41. Letter, Walter Susskind to Louis Applebaum, April 5, 1960. York University Archives, Louis Applebaum fonds. 1979 – 002/024[484]. This collection of activities proved a cause of some confusion for Peter Dwyer, now responsible for the support of music at the recently created Canada Council. Having been asked for money from all these purveyors of training opportunities, Dwyer wanted to know what the relationship of the Civic Orchestral Workshop was to the National Youth Orchestra and what the relationship of both was to the Stratford Shakespearean Festival. Louis replied that after initiating a successful orchestral workshop for highly trained professionals, there was a need for supplementary programming for music teachers, students, choirs, opera groups, etc., and that Stratford Music had investigated the advantage of bringing these "amateur" players into contact with professional players already on site, hence the Civic Orchestral Workshop. The proposed NYO, Louis emphasized, was a completely separate operation.

42. Graham George, "Composers's Conference," *Saturday Night* Magazine, September 17, 1960. [p.17]. York University Archives, Louis Applebaum fonds, 1979 – 002/025 [506]. (The titles of the conference panels are revealing: "New Aspects of Tonality," "Performance Problems of Contemporary

Music," "The Training of a Composer Today," "Theatrical Music ... ballet, film, stage and television," "Music by Synthetic Means," and "The Public and the Composer." Louis's interests are revealed, particularly his enthusiasm for music written for film and television, as well as the training that could best produce a composer. The whole question of the contemporary composer and the relationship with audiences was also addressed. York University Archives, Louis Applebaum fonds, 1979 – 002/034[633].) In George's view "the chief cause of whatever failure there was, lay with the representatives of the more traditional modes of thought, who put up a much less vigorous case for their point of view than the serialists." As in Canada, the great battle at the Conference was between the young composers struggling to be heard against traditional composers who held the fort of public support. It was valuable for Canadian composers, who felt both isolated from the rest of the world and overwhelmed by the American music juggernaut, to understand this reality.

43. Louis Applebaum, interview with author and Ezra Schabas, retired Principal of the Royal Conservatory of Music. On Friday, April 15, 2000, the author arrived at the palliative ward of the Baycrest Hospital to find Louis and Schabas reminiscing about their Stratford days. Louis repeated his contention that the Composer's Conference had dramatically changed the self-perception of Canadian composers, a view with which Schabas wholeheartedly agreed. Five days later, Louis Applebaum died.

44. Alfred Frankenstein, "Canada Shows Rest of World She Belongs on Musical Map," *Toronto Daily Star*, August 20, 1960. York University Archives, Louis Applebaum fonds, 1979 – 002/030 [564].

45. Laura Pogson, interview with author, September 21, 2000.

46. Ezra Schabas, interview with author, January 25, 2000.

47. Udo Kasements, *Toronto Daily Star*, Saturday, August 18, 1962. [p.17] York University Archives, Louis Applebaum fonds, 1979 – 002/028[16].

48. For example, the 1962 season included concerts dedicated to the works of Schoenberg, Webern, Lucas Foss, and Hindemith. Certainly there was a 20th-century repertoire emphasis to be found, and the National Festival Orchestra, along with Gould and Marshall as soloists, concentrated on contemporary works. Even modern dance benefited that season, as the highly celebrated Grant Strate choreographed a work to the music of a contemporary composer.

49. Louis Applebaum, interview with author, March 17, 2000. Blaik Kirby saw the working of a "formula" that he believed "appeals not only to the masses and classes but even the musicians themselves." They played Gilbert and Sullivan and were rewarded with the Sunday concerts (now made possible by revisions to the *Lord's Day Act* of Ontario) as well as Saturday morning chamber music recitals. It also worked financially as G & S paid for the serious music. The system "devised by Louis Applebaum in 1959" continued to operate effectively. Blaik Kirby, *Toronto Daily Star*, June 23. 1962. [p.29] York University Archives, Louis Applebaum fonds, 1979 – 002/025[502]

50. Udo Kasements, *Toronto Daily Star*, Saturday, August 18, 1962. [p.17]

51. Lenore Crawford, *London Free Press*, August 15, 1970 [p.31]. York University Archives, Louis Applebaum fonds, 1979 – 002/028 [20].

52. Louis Applebaum, quoted by Lenore Crawford, *London Free Press*, August 15, 1970. York University Archives, Louis Applebaum fonds. 1979 – 002/028. [20] It could be argued that Berthold Carriere, the Music Director for many years, has fulfilled Louis's hope for a training program for potential music theatre performers, at least on a practical level. The Stratford musical productions do indeed emphasize the dramatic elements of these works as well as their compositional values. The participants must act and dance as well as sing. There is a commitment to the integration of music and theatre, and Louis's vision has been partially, though informally, achieved.

Chapter 8. On the Road with Gilbert and Sullivan

1. John F. Kennedy, October 26, 1963, quoted in William Manchester, *The Glory and the Dream*, Little, Brown and Company, Boston – Toronto, 1973, 1974. [p.1209]

2. Ibid, p.1386. The rising anger of American youth can be gauged by the extent of protestation at the height of the 1960s decade. "Between January 1 and June 15 of 1968 there were 221 major demonstrations, involving nearly 39,000 students on 101 American campuses."

3. J. L. Granatstein, *Canada 1957–1967: The Years of Uncertainty and Innovation*, McClelland and Stewart Limited, Toronto, 1986. [p.8]

4. Pierre Berton, *1967: The Last Good Year*, Doubleday Canada Limited, Toronto, 1997. [p.15]

5. Jan Applebaum, interview with author, October 11, 2000. Louis was anxious that Jan accompany him as often as she could. Jan modestly assumes that the main reason for this penchant for company on his many trips was in order that all his travel needs could be met — transportation plans, laundry, accommodation and dining arrangements, all fell to Jan's expert ministrations. Louis did not agree that it was simply a matter of personal convenience. He truly enjoyed Jan's company during the hours he could free himself from administrative and creative activity. Louis Applebaum, interview with author, March 30,1999.

6. Tyrone Guthrie, Article, "Pinafore Coupled With Shakespeare," New York *Herald Tribune*, June 19, 1960. York University Archives, Louis Applebaum fonds, 1979 – 002/026[505]

7. Louis Applebaum, letter to Tyrone Guthrie, February 25, 1959. York University Archives, Louis Applebaum fonds, 1979 – 022/025. [504] The *New York Times* special correspondent covering touring productions noted "Dr. Guthrie and Mr. Applebaum have successfully overcome that headache of all opera directors – finding singers who can act and actors who can sing." *The New York Times*, August 3, 1960. [p.5]

8. Orchestra Special Correspondent, *The New York Times*, August 3, 1960. [p. 5] The roster of the National Festival included musicians who were first-chair players with Canada's most prestigious orchestras, particularly the TSO.

Harry Freedman, a member of that orchestra, thinks there was an extraordinary collection of first-rate musicians at that point in the TSO's history from which Louis could draw, including violinists Hyman Goodman, Isidor Desser, Morry Kernerman, and Harold Sumberg; violist Stanley Solomon; bassoonist Nicholas Kilburn; clarinetist Stanley McCartney; French horn, Eugene Rittick, trumpeter, Joe Umbrico and oboeist, Stanley Wood. [Harry Freedman, interview with author, September 11, 2000.]

9. Tanya Moiseiwitsch , letter to Louis Applebaum, [handwritten, no date], York University Archives, Louis Applebaum fonds, 1979 – 002/025 [506].

10. Clifford Hulme, Review, *Brantford Expositor*, July 16, 1960, Clippings Files, Stratford Festival Archives, Stratford, Ontario.

11. Jacob Siskind, Review, *London Free Press*, July 16, 1960. Clippings Files, Stratford Festival Archives, Stratford, Ontario.

12. *The Globe and Mail*, September 10, 1960. York University Archives, Louis Applebaum fonds, 1979-002/025[506].

13. Howard Taubman, *The New York Times*, September 8, 1960. [p.41] York University Archives, Louis Applebaum fonds, 1979 – 002/025[506]

14. John Chapman, New York *Daily News*, September 8, 2960. [p.66] York University Archives, Louis Applebaum fonds, 1979 – 002/025 [506].

15. CBC Times, Volume 13, No. 14. October 8, 1960. This program was a popular international offering, as sales to networks in foreign countries exceeded all expectations. By 1963, *Pinafore* had been purchased by the New Zealand Broadcasting Corporation (the first such sale in the CBC Television's short history) as well as by the BBC, NBC, and the Australian Broadcasting Corporation. Thus, it became the first Stratford production to be seen by millions of people around the world. It is not unthinkable that in 1961, many Canadians, Americans, and citizens of Commonwealth countries would have connected the Stratford, Ontario, Shakespearean Festival with Gilbert and Sullivan rather than with the Bard of Stratford-on-Avon.

16. Alan Brien, "Voyage of Discovery," *Sunday Telegraph*, February 12, 1962. York University Archives, Louis Applebaum fonds, 1979 – 0023/025[514]

17. Andrew Porter, *Financial Times*, February 9, 1962. York University Archives, Louis Applebaum fonds, 1979- 002-025[514].

18. Noel Goodwin, *Daily Express*, February 9, 1962. York University Archives, Louis Applebaum fonds, 1979-002/025[514].

19. *Evening Standard*, February 9, 1962. York University Archives, Louis Applebaum fonds, 1979-002/025[514].

20. Stanley Eichebaum, "Guthrie's Bouncing, Jovial Pinafore," *San Francisco Examiner*, August 1, 1962. [p.2].

21. Theresa Loeb Cone, "Review" *Oakland Tribune*, July 31, 1962, Clippings Files, Stratford Festival Archives, Stratford, Ontario.

22. Stanley Bligh, Vancouver *Sun*, August 10, 1962. [p.23] There is little doubt that the Stratford experience with musical productions like *Orpheus* and the Gilbert and Sullivan operettas increased Louis's confidence in his conducting. Working in film and radio had provided little motivation to acquire a style that was not

only effective musically but also pleasing visually for an observant public. *Variety* Magazine, on July 18, 1963, described Louis Applebaum's conducting at the Greek Theatre in Los Angeles as "being first class." Reporting on the same performance, the Los Angeles *Herald-Examiner* of July 17, 1963, called attention to the fact that "Louis Applebaum conducts admirably." York University Archives, Louis Applebaum fonds, 1979 – 002/025[506].

23. T. Headley, RCA, letter to Louis Applebaum, June 7 1962. York University Archives, Louis Applebaum fonds, 1979 – 002/025[505]. RCA was quite blunt about the commercial prospects, concluding: "any decision by us to release the subject recordings would be premised on two considerations – as an aid in publicizing Canadian art and talent and the prestige value in so doing." The Stratford proposal apparently failed to meet the considerations outlined.

24. Jan Applebaum, interview with author, October 11, 2000.

25. Louis Applebaum, interview with author, February 1, 1999.

26. Michael Parver, letter to Louis Applebaum, August 21, 1964. York University Archives, Louis Applebaum fonds, 1979-002/025[511] He informed Louis of the problems to be faced. "Needless to say, money is at a premium and our current audit and examination of the situation shows that if we even come out without a loss on the tour we will be doing well. We are fighting for our very life every inch of the way. We need your help as far as understanding goes. The production must be good but we cannot squander on it."

27. Louis Applebaum, letter to Joseph Stopak, July 9, 1964. York University Archives, Louis Applebaum fonds, 1979 – 002/025[511]. Stopak was to take over conducting from Louis after the rehearsals and opening night in Los Angeles, and share conducting duties in other cities on the tour.

28. Alfred Frankenstein, *San Francisco Chronicle*, October 7, 1964. York University Archives, Louis Applebaum fonds, 1979 – 002/025[511].

29. After a seven-week run at the Phoenix in New York, the tour was to carry on to St. Petersburg, Atlanta, Tuscaloosa, Birmingham, Louisville, Columbus, Indianapolis, Cleveland, St. Louis, Kansas City, and Detroit.

30. Louis Applebaum, letter to Tyrone Guthrie, February 1, 1961. York University Archives, Louis Applebaum fonds, 1979 – 022/025[507].

31. Lenore Crawford, Review, *The Pirates of Penzance, London Free Press*, July 8,1961. York University Archives, Louis Applebaum fonds, 1979 –022-025[508].

32. Ron Evans, Review, *The Pirates of Penzance*, Toronto *Telegram*, July 8, 1961. York University Archives, Louis Applebaum fonds, 1979 – 002/025[508]. Evans, who viewed the opening in New York, headlined his review "Pirates Triumph in New York, Stratford Show Shines Like a Gem." He felt however that although it was Guthrie's show, "Mr. Campbell should be credited with the sharp edge on last night's presentation." Norman Campbell, who had triumphed with the television presentation of *Pinafore*, had taken over the direction of the *Penzance* tour.

33. Ron Evans, Review of *The Pirates of Penzance* at the Phoenix Theatre, New York, Toronto *Telegram*, September 7, 1961. York University Archives, Louis

Applebaum fonds, 1979 – 002/025[513] Louis also indicated in the article, "It's been quite a grind." Indeed, it had been. There were 11 new members to work into the cast and this had meant hard work for everybody. He told Evans, "We got down here on Wednesday, held the first rehearsal Thursday, a run-through Saturday, dress rehearsal on Sunday and here we are." Some of this pressure was picked up in a review by Blaik Kirby who observed the impact of a less-committed instrumental ensemble on the production, "The Company's New York orchestra, however, is nowhere up to Stratford standards." Obviously, the loss on tour of the National Festival Orchestra was a real blow.

34. Norman Campbell, interview with author, September 18, 2000.

35. *Variety* Magazine, July 18, 1962. York University Archives, Louis Applebaum fonds, 1979 – 002/025[507]. Leon Major was to give artistic leadership to a new acting company at the St. Lawrence Centre, a centennial project of the City of Toronto. After a number of other ventures, he taught in the Fine Arts Department at York University but was eventually enticed to the United States where he has pursued an outstanding career, particularly in the directing of opera productions in many different cities.

36. John Kraglund, Review, "The Gondoliers," *The Globe and Mail*, July 7, 1962. Clippings Files, Stratford Festival Archives Stratford, Ontario.

37. George Kidd, Review, *The Gondoliers*, Toronto *Telegram*, July 7, 1962, Clippings Files, Stratford Festival Archives. Stratford, Ontario.

38. Ed Hocura, Review, *The Gondoliers*, *Hamilton Spectator*, July 7, 1962. Clippings Files, Stratford Festival Archives, Stratford, Ontario.

39. Ted Miller, "Japanese Joy," Guelph *Guardian*, July 6, 1963. Clippings Files, Stratford Festival Archives, Stratford, Ontario.

40. W. J. Pitcher, Review, *The Mikado, Kitchener-Waterloo Record*, July 6, 1963. Clippings Files, Stratford Festival Archives, Stratford Ontario.

41. John Kraglund, Review, *The Mikado, The Globe and Mail*, July 7, 1963, Clippings Files, Stratford Festival Archives, Stratford, Ontario.

42. Louis Applebaum, letter to Charles P. Tuck, April 2, 1963. York University Archives, Louis Applebaum fonds. 1979 – 002/025[502]

Chapter 9. Television Beckons

1. "Takes CBC Post," *The Globe and Mail*, Toronto, September 14, 1960. [p.22] The emphasis given to "serious" music, particularly contemporary Canadian music, was extraordinary. Waddington had been Music Advisor to the CBC from 1947, and had formed the CBC Opera Company in 1948 at a time when there was not a single opera company in the country and only broadcasts of the Opera School at the Royal Conservatory had successfully filled this gap in CBC's programming. By 1952, as Director of Music, Waddington had established the CBC Symphony Orchestra, soon to be considered "one of the world's greatest." The author is indebted to John Peter Lee Roberts, Supervisor of Music, English Radio Network, CBC, whose account in an article, "Communications Media" in *Aspects of Music*, edited by Arnold Walter, has been

most helpful on the subject of the CBC's contribution to the performance of music in the 1950s and 1960s.

2. CBC Annual Report, quoted by J. P. L. Roberts, "Communications Media," in Arnold Walters, *Aspects of Music*, University of Toronto Press, Toronto, 1969. [p.183]

3. Frank Peers, *The Politics of Canadian Broadcasting*, University of Toronto Press, Toronto, 1969. [p.415]

4. Ibid. [p.416]

5. Ibid. [p.389]

6. Ibid. [p.444] A splendid account of the Diefenbaker Government's efforts to strengthen the private broadcasters and weaken the CBC can be found in Knowlton Nash, *Swashbucklers: The Story of Canada's Battling Broadcasters*, McClelland & Stewart Ltd., Toronto, 2001.

7. Louis Applebaum, interview with author, March 30, 1999.

8. Eric Nicol, script, "The Big Dig," CBC-TV Broadcast, January 1, 1955. York University Archives, Louis Applebaum fonds, 1979 – 002/013[221]

9. Norman Campbell and Elaine Campbell, interview with author, September 18, 2000. Louis was to work with producer and director Norman Campbell on a wide variety of programs. By the mid-1950s Campbell had achieved an unparalleled reputation with stellar productions at the newly established National Ballet, a 90-minute presentation of *Swan Lake* in 1956 and *Coppelia* the following season. He had even mounted a production of Gilbert and Sullivan's *Pirates of Penzance* with Godfrey Ridout conducting, a full four years before the series of G&S operettas which Louis and Guthrie initiated with CBC Television using the Stratford productions. Campbell tells of Applebaum's dexterity in conducting the studio orchestra in the basement of the CBC building on his knees behind piles of paint cans. He was not aware that Louis had acquired this physical flexibility from conducting in the pit at the Stratford Festival tent.

10. Shakespeare script, *Hamlet*, CBC-TV, April 24, 1955. York University Archives, Louis Applebaum fonds, 1979 – 002/013 [220]. The cast included Lloyd Bochner (Hamlet), Kate Reid (Ophelia), Esse W. Ljungh (Claudius), Douglas Rain (Laertes), Patrick McNee (Horatio), David Gardner (Rosencrantz), Tony Van Bridge (Marcello), William Hutt (Bernardo), Eric Christmas (Gravedigger), Earle Grey (First Player), Jack Creeley (Osric), and Frank Peddie (Ghost).

11. CBC Times, March 11-17, 1956. CBC Press and Information Service, Toronto

12. Alex Barris, Column on "Graphic," *The Globe and Mail*, May 12, 1956.

13. CBC "First Performance" Series, 1956. Production Files, CBC Reference Library and Archives, Toronto.

14. Joseph Schull, Script, "Black of the Moon," CBC "First Performance" Series, 1956. York University Library, Louis Applebaum fonds, 1979 – 002/007[81].

15. Arthur Hailey, Script, "Timelock," CBC "First Performance" Series, 1956. York University Archives, Louis Applebaum fonds, 1979 – 002/008 [84].

16. "Our Lady's Tumbler," adapted by Ronald Duncan, CBC Television, "On Camera" Series, December 1955, Production Files, CBC Reference Library, Toronto

17. Script: Len Peterson, "Party Line," CBC Christmas Feature, December 25, 1956. York University Archives, Louis Applebaum fonds, 1979 – 002/011[193]. A week later, on December 31, 1956, a program of some significance was aired. The Stratford Festival had been commissioned, with Michael Langham and Norman Campbell as co-directors and Brian Jackson as designer, to present Lister Sinclair's adaptation of *Peer Gynt*. The familiar story of the jokester/trickster whose greed and thoughtlessness had produced chaos for everyone around him had attracted other composers, notably Edvard Grieg. Louis eschewed the works of his predecessors and brought new lyrical quality to the music that enhanced the text read by a cast including Douglas Rain, Powys Thomas, Eric Christmas, Amelia Hall, Roberta Maxwell, and William Needles. It was an appropriate production to grace a special night.

18. CBC Times, February 2 – 8, 1958. CBC Reference Library and Archives, Toronto. It was a masterly piece of work involving 250 people from Halifax to Calgary. Louis had been given all the information he needed to compose the music; for example, there would have to be a Citadel March, misty Hebrides sounds as well as music for the high seas, Scottish dances accompanied by bagpipes in Cape Breton and a Canadian boating song. The history (including the expulsion of the Acadians) and the fishing economy would be carefully covered and even Yvon Durrell, a former boxing champion and by this point a working fisherman, would be interviewed. Louis had lots to work with. [Script, "Tower Trail to the Sea," CBC-TV, Opening of the Maritime Network, York University Archives, Louis Applebaum fonds, 1979 – 002/014[242].

19. Ron Poulton, review of "Memo To Champlain", CBC–TV, Toronto *Telegram*, July 27, 1958. It was clear that the CBC had not solved the bilingual problems posed by the script, but it was also apparent that the basic theme of constructing a message to French Canada's founder did not make sense in historical or geographical terms as the program proceeded. It was an important occasion. The CBC President, Davidson Dunton, could boast that in a mere 6 years, "CBC-TV was now providing instantaneous visual communication to 3 million Canadian homes with a potential audience of 12 to 14 million people through the presence of 8 key CBC stations and 40 privately-owned stations." Nevertheless people were looking not for statistics but for a moment of dramatic meaning. The program failed to provide this element. Script, "Memo to Champlain," CBC-TV, July 1, 1958. Opening of the Coast-to-Coast Network. York University Archives, Louis Applebaum fonds, 1979 – 002/009[103].

20. Sandra Lock, review of "Memo to Champlain," Toronto *Telegram*, July 12, 1958.

21. Review, "Junior Magazine," Toronto *Telegram*, Saturday, February 8, 1958, TV Section. [p.11]

22. Norman Campbell and Elaine Campbell, interview with author, September 18, 2000.

23. *CBC Times*, October 23, 1960 York University Archives, Louis Applebaum fonds, 1979 – 002/030[582].

24. *CBC Times*, April 15 – 21, 1961. CBC Reference Library and Archives, Toronto.

25. John Roberts, "Communications Media," in *Aspects of Music in Canada*, edited by Arnold Walter, University of Toronto Press, Toronto, 1969. [p.217]

26. Ibid. [p.190]

27. Louis Applebaum, interview with author, March 30, 1999.

28. William Shakespeare, script, *Two Gentlemen of Verona*, Stratford Tour, 1957. York University Archives, Louis Applebaum fonds, 1979 – 002/019[308]

29. Louis Applebaum, letter to George Anderson, Toronto, January 31, 1958. Casting was not without its difficulties as Louis had to inform George Anderson of "the difficulty of having an actor play guitar ['Who is Sylvia?'] on stage. Jeremy Wilkins can play guitar passably ... a member of Equity ... for first verse or 2, then pit orchestra can pick it up." It was worth the trouble. Louis's rendition of "Who Is Sylvia?" has become a classic and is included in the recording of his work for the CD *Fanfare: The Stratford Music of Louis Applebaum*, produced by Glenn Morley, August, 2000.

30. Louis Applebaum, letter to Michael Langham, December 6, 1960. York University Archives, Louis Applebaum fonds 1979 – 002/018[292]. The "few things in NY" were undoubtedly the major CBS "The Twentieth Century" series that this network regarded as a major contribution to America's understanding of the post-war age. Louis had been engaged to write three of these special programs. The first, "The Week That Shook the World," was not unlike the CBC program "7 Days to Victory" that he had scored in 1955, except CBS chose to focus on the week before Poland fell. However, that commission was followed by "Patton and the Third Army" and "Rommel," both the kind of film for which Louis was developing a distaste. He was able to make use of his NFB-developed skills but, although the series received considerable attention and accolade, it was not a series he found particularly to his liking. However, these CBS commissions (and a further special, "The Desperate Years," a dramatization of the American Civil War) paid well and came at the right time, in a year when Louis left one job, moved to a larger home, and took on CBC duties which did not provide full-time remuneration but took up time he might have spent composing.

Chapter 10. The Making of a Culture

1. Arnold Walter, *Aspects of Music in Canada*, University of Toronto Press, Toronto. 1969. [p.17]. It was a modest commitment. In its first nine years, the Canada Council gave out $11,350,000 to the performing and visual arts and $4.5 million of that sum had gone to music, by far the best organized of all the disciplines in effectively making its case.

2. A. W. Trueman, letter to Louis Applebaum, November 11, 1957, York University Archives, Louis Applebaum fonds, 1979 – 002/021[408].
3. Louis Applebaum, interview with author, March 30, 1999. There was some irony in the fact that Louis was wrestling with these arguments for public subsidy at the same time as he was engaged in his first foray into the administration of a private company, Group Four Productions.
4. W. B. Herbert, Director of the Canada Foundation, letter to Louis Applebaum, February 19, 1959. York University Archives, Louis Applebaum fonds, 1979 – 002/021[408]. Herbert's letter concludes with an accolade that Louis appreciated deeply. He had performed "a wonderful demonstration of good will and voluntary help."
5. Louis Applebaum, letter to Peter Dwyer, Canada Council, April 5, 1960. York University Archives, Louis Applebaum fonds, 1979 – 002/021[408].
6. Louis Applebaum, letter to Peter Dwyer, Canada Council, August 17, 1964. York University Archives, Louis Applebaum fonds, 1979 – 002/021[407].
7. Ibid.
8. Alan Neil, letter to Louis Applebaum, August 26, 1967. York University Archives, Louis Applebaum fonds, 1979-022/021[408].
9. David Silcox, interview with author, September 13, 2000.
10. Louis Applebaum, letter to D. Silcox, February 28, 1967, Canada Council. York University Archives, Louis Applebaum fonds, 1979 – 022/021[408].
11. Peter Dwyer, letter to Louis Applebaum, December 3, 1965, York University Archives, Louis Applebaum fonds, 1979 – 002/021[409]. The invitation had financial implications for Louis, adding modestly to his income when his company, Group Four Productions, was in decline financially and his regular income as a staff member at CBC had disappeared. Now, for his advice, he would receive $50 a day and his expenses in travelling from Toronto to Ottawa. After eight years of voluntary commitment to arts granting policy, Louis was now to receive remuneration.

    The Advisory Art Panel was a distinguished group of people. The Chairman was Vincent Tovell, of CBC and previously UN broadcasting renown, and members included writers Earle Birney and Kildare Dobbs; Artistic Directors Herman Geiger-Torel of the COC and John Hirsch of the Manitoba Theatre; actor and future Director of the National Theatre School Jean-Louis Roux, who would eventually chair the entire Canada Council; and finally Walter Herbert, Director of the Canada Foundation.
12. A. W. Trueman, letter to Louis Applebaum, April 14, 1961. York University Archives, Louis Applebaum fonds, 1979, 002/021 [417] Louis invited panelists Winters and Pentland but added as well composer John Beckwith, TSO conductor Walter Susskind, and composer Jean Papineau-Couture.
13. Peter Dwyer, letter to Louis Applebaum., April 23, 1963. York University Archives, Louis Applebaum fonds, 1979 – 002/022[413] Louis chose, as possible participants, composers Weinzweig, Somers, Joachim, Morel, Anhalt, Charpentier, and the Adaskins; conductors Feldbrill, Susskind, and Mehta; scholar Helmut Blume; administrator, the CBC's Geoffrey Waddington; arts

writers Geoffrey Payzant and Kenneth Winters; and from the U.S., composers Aaron Copland and Howard Hanson.

14. Louis Applebaum's Notes, Meeting at Stanley House, July, 1963. York University Archives, Louis Applebaum fonds, 1979 – 002/022[413]

15. Louis Applebaum, letter to Peter Dwyer, August 21, 1963. York University Archives, Louis Applebaum fonds, 1979 – 002/022[413]

16. Sir Ernest MacMillan, letter to Louis Applebaum, August 16, 1963. York University Archives, Louis Applebaum fonds, 1979 – 002/022[413]. The Canadian Music Council was something of an "ad hoc" organization, having been brought into existence by Sir Ernest at the time of the Massey Commission's desire to interview organizations that represented the various arts disciplines before producing its report. However, in the late 1950s and early 1960s it produced an excellent journal, edited by Geoffrey Payzant, who was to write the first, and many would say the most thoughtful, biography of Glenn Gould.

17. Report of the Canadian Conference for the Arts "Seminar '65." York University Archives, Louis Applebaum fonds, 1979 – 002/022[419]. At the helm of the CCA at this point was Arthur Gelber, a successful businessman whose interest in the arts and whose generosity, both of time and money, were to become legendary. His only experience as an artist had been on stage at Upper Canada College, one of the most prestigious independent schools in the country, but his whole life had been devoted to the arts. He played a major role in the development of the St. Lawrence Centre and the National Arts Centre, and was the most relentless champion of the Ontario Arts Council. His work on behalf of arts organizations like the National Ballet, as well as individual young artists such as Arthur Ozolins, was extraordinary. He had some success in encouraging his fellow businessmen to support the arts. A strong Liberal, his influence on Parliament Hill was considerable.

18. Louis Applebaum, "Seminar '65," Agenda and Notes, January 19 – 25, 1965. [p.1] York University Archives, Louis Applebaum fonds, 1979 – 002/022[419]

19. Ibid. [p.13]

20. Ibid. [p.15]

21. Ibid. [p.30]

22. Louis Applebaum, "Seminar '65," Agenda and Notes, York University Archives, Louis Applebaum fonds, 1979 – 002/022[419]. As a teacher in the City of Peterborough, the author remembers, with considerable warmth, the magnificent year of arts activities that took place in a city during the centennial year in a community that did not even have a performing arts venue. Month after month, the cultural feast went on with such groups as "Les Feux Follets" filling the city's major ice rink.

In fact, Louis's fears were not unfounded. The largesse of 1967 was followed by the restraint of 1968, and organizations had severe difficulties, as the Advisory Art Panel discovered to its regret when a Memorandum from Peter Dwyer spoke of real austerity after "magnificent increases."

In October 1968, the Canadian Conference of the Arts presented a brief that stated the case graphically. "A study of the arts in Canada carried out during the past two months shows clearly that there is an economic crisis of unprecedented severity ... the freeze on federal appropriations for the arts will, in the next budget year, create a regression, and if the austerity policies continue for three years, the nation's arts assets will deteriorate to the deplorable conditions of ten years ago." [Canadian Conference of the Arts, "A Crisis in the Arts, A Brief to the Federal Government," unpublished, October, 1968]

23. The Canadian Council for the Arts, "Building the Kind of World We Want to Live In," First Draft of a Report for "Seminar '66," York University Archives, Louis Applebaum fonds, 1979-002/021[409].

24. Peter Dwyer, letter to Louis Applebaum, November 9, 1965. York University Archives, Louis Applebaum fonds 1979 – 022/021[415].

25. Louis Applebaum, "Survey of the Position of the Professional Musician" York University Archives, Louis Applebaum fonds, 1979 – 002/022[415].

26. Louis Applebaum, letter to Peter Dwyer, October 7, 1966. Louis was determined that his report would not gather dust. This letter was written after many months of study and consideration, yet when Dwyer requested a billing for all this effort Louis responded with typical disregard for personal remuneration. "Finally, you ask that I propose a fee for effort. The answer is simple; the fee is nil. I couldn't dream of taking from the Canada Council for an undelivered job." This generosity came at a time of real financial difficulty for Louis. Because he was freelance composer, his income came from many sources and he kept a very detailed account of his receipts and expenditures. After leaving the CBC in 1962 his income was reduced to $7,482.25; in 1964, it was $8,562.18; in 1965 it was $11,240.87. (The reduction in his income in these years can be gauged by the fact that in 1951 he earned $16,276.50.) By 1966, it was just reaching rational levels as his commissions, CAPAC contracts, and Canada Council daily fees brought in $28,893.52. [Louis Applebaum Account books, York University Archives, 2000 –009/023[02]. Vincent Tovell, who hired him for many CBC programs, recounts that Louis never negotiated a fee, he just assumed that Tovell would "do the right thing" on the basis of his budget for the program.

27. Louis Applebaum, "Toronto's Orchestral Resources," A Study prepared for the Province of Ontario Council for the Arts and The Canada Council.[unpublished] Toronto, January 23, 1968. York University Archives, Louis Applebaum fonds, 1979 –002/022[416].

28. Ibid. [pp.3-4] Louis even thought that a third orchestra of about 20 would serve the not-yet-in-place St. Lawrence Centre, the Festival Singers, and any other choral or dramatic groups in Toronto who might require an orchestra of modest size. Louis had dismissed the idea of a "super-orchestra" of 150 members who could be grouped and regrouped for all occasions required by all four major arts institutions; there were a number of reasons for this, mostly centering around the diminution of the quality of sound and the loss of any "togetherness" that might produce great playing. His experience with the Stratford Festival Orchestral Workshop had led him to a belief (that he never lost) in the psychological elements of great orchestral performance.

29. Ibid. [p.16].
30. Ibid. [pp.18, 20]
31. Minutes of the Advisory Arts Panel of the Canada Council, June 2-3, 1967.[p.7] York University Archives, Louis Applebaum fonds, 1979 –002/021[410].
32. Ibid.
33. Ibid., [p.4]
34. Vincent Tovell, interview with author, April 1, 1999.
35. David Silcox, interview with author, September 13, 2000. In Silcox's opinion, Louis was exactly the person the Canada Council needed in its first decade, when virtually every decision established a benchmark and every determination initiated a tradition. The Council, after years of restraint that characterized the late 1980s and 1990s, has revived with expectations of much more generous treatment in the 2000s. Appropriate funding and a new Chair, Jean-Louis Roux, with a background of enormous achievement in the arts and their administration, have given its supporters new hope.
36. There were times in the 1980s when the arm's-length role of the Canada Council was threatened and political interference seemed imminent. It took a courageous and articulate Tim Porteous, the Council's Director in the 1980s, to put his job on the line in order to ward off the possibility of having a crippled and craven Council unable to arouse the respect of the artistic community.

Chapter 11. A Performing Arts Centre for a Nation

1. Hamilton Southam, interview with author, August 23, 2000.
2. G. H. Southam, Opening statement at a panel discussion before the Canadian Music Council Annual Conference, Ottawa. Saturday, April 2, 1966. York University Archives, Louis Applebaum fonds, 1979 – 002/024[476].
3. G. H. Southam, letter to Louis Applebaum, February 23, 1964. York University Archives, Louis Applebaum fonds, 1979 – 002/024[476]. Along with the invitation came all the documents that had been produced in the previous year, "A National Centre for the Performing Arts, A Study Prepared for the National Capital Arts Alliance, October, 1963" and "A National Centre for the Performing Arts, A Submission to the Government of Canada by the National Capital Arts Alliance, November 8, 1963" as well as laudatory press releases from the Prime Minister's Office, December 23, 1963, and February 17, 1964.

   The Advisory Committee Louis was to chair was a stellar gathering of major figures involved in each of music, opera, and dance from Ottawa and across the country. The membership included Herman Geiger-Torel, Director-General of the Canadian Opera Company; Mrs. Louis Rasminsky, Chair, Women's Committee of the Ottawa Symphony Orchestra; Arnold Walter, Director, Faculty of Music, and Principal of the Royal Conservatory, University of Toronto; Celia Franca, Artistic Director, National Ballet of Canada; Zubin Mehta, Conductor, Montreal Symphony Orchestra; Frederick Karam, Director, Ottawa Choral Society; Wallace Russell, a Theatre Advisor in

Toronto; and Mme Ludmilla Cheriaeff, Artistic Director, Les Grands Ballets Canadiens. Ex officio members were Hamilton Southam, Coordinator of the NAC project, and Nicholas Goldschmidt, representing the Centennial Committee that would be organizing performing arts events in 1967.

4. Minutes of the Performing Arts Steering Committee Meeting #3, July 29, 1964. York University Archives, Louis Applebaum fonds, 1979 – 002/024[473]. By this time, as well, the general outline of the building had been decided. There would be a large hall for opera and concerts seating 2100, a theatre accommodating 850 to 900, and a small studio space appropriate for a couple of hundred people.

5. Proposal for a Canadian Centre for Performing Arts, Memorandum for the Secretary of State. York University Archives, Louis Applebaum fonds, 1979 – 002/024[472]

6. Minutes of the Centre for the Performing Arts Steering Committee #4, August 24, 1964. York University Archives, Louis Applebaum fonds, 1979 – 002/024[473].

7. Ibid.

8. Hamilton Southam, Speech, *Entre Nous*, Special Edition, April 2000, "A Tribute to Hamilton Southam," National Arts Centre, Ottawa.

9. Louis Applebaum, Annex to the Minutes of the Meeting of the Canadian Centre for the Performing Arts Steering Committee, August 24, 1964. York University Archives, Louis Applebaum fonds, 1979 – 002/024[473]. This is not an understanding that governments at all levels have grasped. The City of North York, before it became a part of the new amalgamated City of Toronto, built a splendid performing arts centre with a recital hall that has the city's finest acoustics, then handed it over to an entrepreneur who ultimately came to grief and had to abandon his commitments to the facility. A fine building languished in a trough of minimal use and limited influence. Although effective leadership is now turning around this disaster, the lesson to all politicians caught up in the ideology of privatization is clear.

10. Louis Applebaum, letter to Humphrey Burton, Head, Music and Arts Programs, CBC Television, January 19, 1967. York University Archives, Louis Applebaum fonds, 1979 – 002/024[479]

11. E. Schabas, Associate Professor, Faculty of Music, University of Toronto, letter to Louis Applebaum, Chair of the Advisory Committee on Music, Opera and Dance, February 15, 1965. York University Archives, Louis Applebaum fonds, 1979 – 002/024[480]. In a recent conversation with the author, Schabas admitted that at the end of the controversy he had changed his mind and supported the full symphony orchestra as an appropriate ensemble for the NAC.

12. Louis Applebaum, interview with author, March 30, 1999. Louis was not only concerned about the lack of local support that might damage the future of the orchestra, but also disconcerted by the expectation that it would be a national institution. "Why would the people in Regina care about an orchestra playing in Ottawa?" was his question. His answer was that they would

care only through the creation of an orchestra that could spend a good part of its time on the road.

13. E. Schabas, letter to Louis Applebaum, February 15, 1965. York University Archives, Louis Applebaum fonds, 1979- 002/024[480].

14. Louis Applebaum, "A Proposal for the Musical Development of the Capital Region."[unpublished] National Arts Centre, May 20, 1965.

15. Ibid. [p.1].

16. Ibid. [p.2]

17. Ibid. [p.4]

18. Ibid. [p. 7]

19. Ezra Schabas, "Ontario Community Orchestras. A Report for The Province of Ontario Council for the Arts and the Ontario Federation of Symphony Orchestras," 1966, [unpublished] Toronto. His Report presented a rather sad picture of some 15 community ensembles, all amateur or at best pseudo-professional (that is, with a few professionals in first chairs of each instrumental section), trying to survive with little assistance from either the public or private sector. Schabas's solution to their rather pathetic quality of music was to create Regional Orchestras serving several communities, properly supported by the whole region. Thus it would be possible for each ensemble to reach professional status. Along with playing several series of concerts, the Regional Orchestral would be a valuable resource to each Board of Education in the region. Schabas too had realized that the future for audience and financial support lay in the involvement of the schooling system.

20. Louis Applebaum, "Memorandum to File, April 28, 1965." York University Archives, Louis Applebaum fonds, 1979 – 002/024[485] Father Guindon became one of the most loved figures in Ontario's university system. As the President of the University of Ottawa, his term far surpassed that of any of his presidential colleagues in length of tenure. Louis was much impressed by his openness and affability. The University of Ottawa had a strong commitment to teacher education and many graduates of the proposed music program would end up in the classroom.

21. Louis Applebaum, "Memorandum to H. Southam, May 7,1965." York University Archives, Louis Applebaum fonds, 1979 – 002/024[485]. The provision of instrumental teaching in strings, woodwind, and brass was essential in Louis's view, as this activity would provide jobs for the Centre's orchestral players and would also assure quality players from the Region who would be available to the Centre's orchestra in the future. At this point the establishment of a Conservatory was very high on Louis's list of priorities.

22. Louis Applebaum, "Memorandum for Mr. Southam," May 25, 1965. York University Archives, Louis Applebaum fonds, 1979-002/024[485]

23. Letter, W. W. Boss to Louis Applebaum, November 11, 1965. York University Archives, Louis Applebaum fonds, 1979 – 002/024[479]

24. Louis Applebaum, "A Plan for a School of Music at the University of Ottawa, September 27, 1965." (unpublished) [pp.4-5].

25. Robert Cram, interview with author, September 13, 2001.

26. Louis Applebaum, Notes for article on the NAC, February 19, 1966. York University Archives, Louis Applebaum fonds, 1979-002/024[476].

27. Barbara Clark, letter to author, October 29, 2001.

28. Ibid.

29. Article: "At the National Arts Centre, Queen Unveils Plaques 'Midst Poetry, Music.'" *Ottawa Journal,* Thursday, July 6, 1967. It was a song that had little resonance beyond this single occasion.

30. G. H. Southam, Opening Statement at a panel discussion before the Canadian Music Centre's Annual Conference, Chateau Laurier Hotel, Ottawa, Saturday, April 2, 1966. York University Archives, Louis Applebaum fonds, 1979 – 002/024[476]

31. Judy LaMarsh, Secretary of State, House of Commons Debates, Thursday, June 9, 1966. Vol. III, No. 94, 1st Session of the 27th Parliament of Canada. The bill as later amended occasioned an uproar in the House as it included a clause that John Diefenbaker, now in Opposition, regarded as an assault on his "One Canada" theme. The amendment had attempted to assure a broad representation, on the Board and in the administration, from those speaking each of Canada's official languages. Diefenbaker responded with a speech that achieved considerable fame: "I believe in one Canada. I believe there must not be in this nation first- and second-class citizens." The Bill and its Amendment passed, but not without considerable debate.

32. Hamilton Southam, "Feasibility Study Regarding the Creation of a Resident Orchestra Within the National Arts Centre," October 2, 1967. [unpublished] A Memorandum to the Board of Trustees, National Arts Centre. Ottawa. York University Archives, Louis Applebaum fonds, 1979 – 002/024[476].

33. Louis Applebaum, Memorandum to Hamilton Southam, February 22, 1967. Arguments re Size of National Arts Centre Orchestra. York University Archives, Louis Applebaum fonds, 1979 – 002/024[476].

34. Hamilton Southam set the record straight years later with a letter indicating that contrary to his article, the Board of the NAC had not been reluctant in its support of Louis's smaller orchestra because budget considerations had destroyed all options. Indeed, "once the facts had been assembled, the Board decided to accept the Applebaum recommendation. This was the Board's decision and not one forced upon it by the Government. The Board's decision, I should emphasize, was not taken reluctantly, but enthusiastically."

35. Joseph Siskind, Review of NAC Orchestra Inaugural Concert, Montreal Gazette, October 8, 1969. York University Archives, Louis Applebaum fonds, 1979 – 022/028[18]

36. Hamilton Southam, A Tribute to Hamilton Southam, A Special Edition of *Entre Nous*, April 2000. National Arts Centre, Ottawa.

Chapter 12. A Venture Into the Market

1. John Ralston Saul, *Reflections of a Siamese Twin, Canada at the End of the Twentieth Century*, Penguin Books, Toronto, 1997. [p.107].

2. Louis Applebaum, interview with author. March 31, 1999.

3. David Applebaum, interview with author, January 12, 2000. David believed that his father should have remained wedded to the public sector. As one who had engaged in business quite widely, he was convinced that Louis's lack of interest in money meant that he never looked for the "deal" that would really make him some money. Even in real estate, with any entrepreneurial spirit, the houses that Louis owned during all his years in Toronto could have made him a considerable profit if he had bought and sold strategically. He was simply not interested.

4. Jan Applebaum, interview with author, December 15, 2000.

5. Louis Applebaum, interview with author, March 31, 1999.

6. Louis Applebaum, "Perspective" Column, *Toronto Daily Star*, September 28, 1962. York University Archives, Louis Applebaum fonds, 1979 – 002/028[17]. Louis was obviously finding it hard to make things happen. In this same article there is rare evidence of discouragement in a man universally regarded as an irrepressible optimist. "The real trouble in Canada is that people get into jobs they aren't qualified for and you can't dislodge them. This is especially true of the film, television, and theatre business." The article concluded with a poignant commentary on his own frantic life. " ... days aren't long enough." He couldn't see enough of his own family, to say nothing of "conversing and playing bridge with friends."

7. "Domino" was really more than a mere game show. It was produced in five different Canadian cities, was an hour long, and ran five days a week. "It was designed to provide educational entertainment and included interviews, do-it-yourself projects, an almanac section, and a regular series of sketches on famous people and events." Louis Applebaum to Patricia Barber, May 15, 1964. York University Archives, Louis Applebaum fonds, 1979 – 002/023[449]. There were even plans to take the show, to be renamed "Ringo," to the United States ... "possibly Los Angeles and the east coast in January." These plans came to nothing.

8. Louis Applebaum, interview with author, March 31, 1999.

9. Statements of support for "En France." York University Archives, Louis Applebaum fonds, 1979 – 002/025[445].

10. Louis Applebaum, *Toronto Daily Star*, September 16, 1963. York University Archives, Louis Applebaum fonds, 1979 – 002/023[445].

11. Bruce Raymond, letter to Louis Applebaum, November 15, 1965. York University Archives, Louis Applebaum fonds, 1979 – 002/024[446].

12. Richard Rosenberg, letter to Mr. Pierre Tisseyre, Societé des Auteurs et Compositeurs Dramatiques, October 26, 1965. York University Archives, Louis Applebaum fonds, 1979 – 002/024[446].

13. Leo Clavier, letter to Louis Applebaum, September 10,1979. York University Archives, Louis Applebaum fonds, 1979 – 002/023[451] When the Ontario Department of Education was contacted about the program, Leo Clavier reported to Louis that Group Four's attention should be directed to Grade 12 and 13 as students at that level had more money for books. On the question of censorship, Group Four was advised that this was left up to the editor of

the materials, but that "particularly in Grade 9 to 11, anything which would prove embarrassing to a lady teacher is left out." Leo Clavier, Note to Louis Applebaum re conversation with J. R. McCarthy, Director of Curriculum, Department of Education. York University Archives, Louis Applebaum fonds, 1979 – 002/023[451]

14. Milan Herzog, Director of Production, Encyclopedia Films, letter to Louis Applebaum, President, Group Four Productions, May 15, 1962. York University Archives, Louis Applebaum fonds, 1979 – 002/021[408]

15. Louis Applebaum, letter to Milan Herzog, December 4, 1962. York University Archives, Louis Applebaum fonds, 1979-002/021[408].

16. Louis Applebaum, interview with author, November 17, 1999.

17. "Bridge of Love," prospectus, York University Archives, Louis Applebaum fonds, 1979 – 002/023[443]. Susan Rubes was to make a great contribution to the theatre life of Toronto when she and her friends established the Young People's Theatre (now the Lorraine Kimsa Theatre for Young People), an institution that has introduced thousands of children and youth to the excitement and relevance of fine drama.

18. Proposal, "A Canadian TV Times." York University Archives, Louis Applebaum fonds, 1979 – 002-023[457].

19. Louis Applebaum, letter to J. Hyman, American Corporation, New York, September 4, 1962. York University Archives, Louis Applebaum fonds, 1979 – 002-023 [443].

20. Louis Applebaum, interview with author, November 17, 1999.

21. David Bairstow, letter to Louis Applebaum, August 1, 1963. York University Archives, Louis Applebaum fonds, 1979 – 002/023[454].

22. Louis Applebaum, letter to Leo Clavier, September 6, 1963. York University Archives, Louis Applebaum fonds, 1979 – 002-023[454]. Bairstow was obviously a colourful character, one who saw infinite possibilities in this new mid-century interest in the Arctic. C. S. Robertson, who had commanded HMCS *Labrador* through the Northwest Passage in 1954 to great acclaim, had suggested that Canada and Russia should establish a treaty for Arctic cooperation, similar to the 12-nation Antarctic Treaty. Louis was attracted to the idea that film production might be a part of such cooperation. Needless to say, at a time when U.S.–U.S.S.R. relations were cool, this suggestion was not pursued by a Canadian Government anxious to keep Canada-U.S. relations as warm as possible. Bairstow was also a visionary who could arouse Louis's expectations. He saw that such a film could include " ... ancient Phoenicians ... . Vikings ... . Italian balloonists, madmen like Fridtjof Nansen, who learned to hibernate in winter like an animal, Dutchmen like Vitus Bering who served Russian emperors (Peter the Great) and not least people like Stefansson, who lived for two years at Bellevue Hospital in New York to prove that all-raw-meat was a perfectly balanced diet." David Bairstow, letter to Louis Applebaum, December 22, p3. York University Archives, Louis Applebaum fonds, 1979 – 002/023[457].

23. Proposal: Group Four and Seven Arts. York University Archives, Louis Applebaum fonds, 1979 – 002/023[450].

24. Proposal: Group Four and the Travel Show. York University Archives, Louis Applebaum fonds, 1979-002-023[455].

25. Proposal to the Centennial Commission. York University Archives, Louis Applebaum fonds, 1979 – 002/023[450].

26. Minutes of the Committee on the Canadian Universal and International Exhibition, Montreal, 1967. [p.9]. York University Archives, Louis Applebaum fonds, 1979 – 002/033[450]. On the Committee he was able to give valuable advice that "various forms of Canadian expression would have to be moulded together and should reach out to something new. The production should not be a restatement." No doubt this perception led Louis to try to put together an ice show that would exhibit Canadian familiarity with the sport of figure skating but would also have a musical score composed by Duke Ellington, his old friend from Stratford days. It did not "fly" either.

27. Jan Applebaum, interview with author, October 5, 2000.

28. In the late 1970s, when Louis and the author were both invited to be on the Planning Committee at TVOntario, I remember vividly an offhand comment during an informal conversation about royalty fees, which for him, that year, had been less than $100. Knowing little of the nature of his work and its focus on commissions, I was shocked that a man of his pre-eminence would be so lacking appropriate remuneration for his work.

29. David Applebaum, interview with author, January 12, 2000.

30. Ibid. As early as the 1970s David had realized there would be a market for "talking books" and could have made a fortune when the concept later became popular. He saw the way sound and images could be utilized in the tourist business and in real estate. David returned to the United States and eventually found his life's work in the university, working on communications and the marketing of Brenau University's technological capacity.

31. Jordan Applebaum, interview with author, December 16, 1999.

32. Ibid. After Louis's death, it was Jordan who, more than any other person, took care of Jan, ensuring, for example, that her finances were in order. Indeed, when Jan suffered a broken wrist a year later, it was Jordan who took her to the hospital and made sure she was cared for. Bob Sirman, who was an Assistant to Robert Welch, Ontario's cultural minister, while Louis was with the Ontario Arts Council, became quite close to Louis and remembers fondly Jan's Sunday luncheons he shared with Louis and Jordan. After lunch, Louis and Sirman would always go down to the park and to the swings and slides so that Jordan could have an outing. Robert Sirman, interview with author, August 3, 1999. The weekend with Jordan, often with Louis taking him to the Science Centre or a museum, was a commitment that went on for many years. Jordan became a second son for Jan and Louis.

Chapter 13. The Composer's Champion

1. Phil and Noreen Nimmons, interview with author, January 26, 2001.

2. CAPAC had been established in 1925 as the Canadian Performing Right Society, (CPRS) to administer the repertoire held by copyright by the Performing Right Society of Great Britain. Soon, the American Society of Composers, Authors, and Publishers (ASCAP) arranged with the PRS of Great Britain to jointly administer the performing rights of both organizations and thus became a joint owner of CPRS. Canadian composers were invited to join and thus have the same protection as their colleagues in the U.K. and the U.S. Between 1947 and 1962, as more Canadian composers became members, steps were taken to establish an organization owned and administered by Canadians (CAPAC- the Canadian Association of Publishers, Authors and Composers.) The 1940s spawned a second performing rights organization, BMI Canada Limited (Broadcast Music Incorporated Canada Limited.) As the broadcasting industry came to dominate music performance in the United States, this organization came to attract composers linked to radio and, subsequently, television production. With a different focus, BMI became "the most active publisher of serious music in Canada," attracting many Canadian composers to join the ranks of American creators. Both institutions had their own monthly publications and supported the Canadian Music Centre when it came into existence at the end of the 1960s. Louis had joined CAPAC before BMI had really begun its recruitment at the end of the 1940s, and remained as an active member from 1945 to 1990, when SOCAN (Society of Composers, Authors and Music Publishers of Canada) resulted from a merger of CAPAC and BMI. However, throughout that period the two societies carried on an active competition for members, a competition that drew the ire of the Canadian League of Composers on occasion.

3. Ontario Legislature, Estimates of the Department of Education, March 27, 1952. York University Archives, Louis Applebaum fonds, 1979 – 002/027[421].

4. CBC Programs, "Talks" Department, Program, "This Week," May 29, 1954. York University Archives, Louis Applebaum fonds, 1979 – 002/022[421] Louis's leadership was apparent from the outset. In balloting for the 1954-55 League Council, Louis received strong support, tied for most votes with John Weinzweig, John Beckwith, and Sam Dolin. Quite often in these years, meetings of the executive were held at Louis's home at 5 Wellwood Avenue in Toronto. By 1955 the League had even entered the field of music publication, producing "Fourteen Piano Pieces," all by Canadian composers.

5. Canadian League of Composers, Report to Members, June 1953. York University Archives, Louis Applebaum fonds, 002-022[423] Louis had arranged to have his own feature film *And Now, Miguel* shown at one of the Towne Cinema evenings. The following season Louis scheduled his NFB production *A Thousand Million Years* which featured an unusual orchestration of three bass and contra-bass, clarinets, flutes, English horn, celeste, viola, and harp. Also, he featured *The Stratford Adventure*, for which he had contributed the score, in a later film night. He was determined to see that the composing of music for film was given appropriate recognition. At the time, this was not a view that had wide

support from his colleagues, even those who had to indulge in such commissions on occasion in order to make ends meet financially.

6. Noreen Nimmons, interview with author, January 26, 2001. Composer Norma Beecroft was the first president of the "Associates," as they were to be known, with Ruth Somers as vice-president and Helen Weinzweig as corresponding secretary. The bond that the "Associates" shared was the knowledge that their husbands were obsessed beyond all hope with the making of music. Noreen Nimmons recounts a fundraising meeting at which Helen Weinzweig was driven to hysterical laughter when a recently married wife of a young composer suggested that funds might be raised by selling, at auction, items which had been produced through the hobbies their husbands pursued. Helen could not contain her mirth at the suggestion that composers might have hobbies – composing music was their vocation, their hobby, their religion ... their entire life.

7. Louis Applebaum, interview with author, November 17, 1999.

8. Brief to the Canada Council, Canadian Music Associates, 1957. York University Archives, Louis Applebaum fonds, 1979 – 002/022[423].

9. M. Hockley, Detroit, Michigan, letter to Louis Applebaum, October 18, 1955. York University Archives, Louis Applebaum fonds, 1979 – 002/022[423]. This letter was typical of the letters coming through Louis's hands in these years. Mr. Hockley wrote that he had heard there was "quite a renaissance up in Canada." He wanted a work that Louis had written ... preferably a violin sonata. Louis had to refer him to other Canadian composers who had recently produced such a work. In another instance, the League was asked to assist in providing a list of works by Jewish composers written from 1950 to 1955. The list included Louis's works "Cry of the Prophet" (1952) and his 1955 arrangements of "Oif'n Veg Shteht a Beim" and "Unsev Rebbenyu" as well as works by Weinzweig, Morawetz, Brott, and Freedman. The League, with no infrastructure, with no paid employees, had nevertheless become the repository of all there was to know about Canadian "serious" music composition.

10. Kenneth LeM. Carter, letter to Louis Applebaum, February 20, 1958. York University Archives, Louis Applebaum fonds, 1979 – 002/021[408].

11. Inside the front door of the St. Joseph Street Chalmers House where the CMC now has its headquarters there is a large brass plaque honouring those who generously gave support to this new home established in 1984 through the support of the Chalmers family. Jan and Louis Applebaum's names are to be found on the plaque.

12. Keith Macmillan, "National Organizations" in *Aspects of Music in Canada*, Arnold Walter, ed., University of Toronto Press, Toronto, 1969. [p.303]

13. Report to the Membership of the Canadian League of Composers, 1965. York University Archives, Louis Applebaum. 1979 – 002/022[425] Other members who were elected included Beckwith, Freedman, Kenins, Ridout, Somers, Twa, and Weinzweig.

14. Report to the Membership of the Canadian League of Composers of the Annual Meeting in Montreal, December 19, 1965. York University Archives, Louis Applebaum fonds, 1979 – 002/022[425].

15. Minutes of the Annual Meeting of the Canadian League of Composers, December 19, 1965, Montreal. York University Archives, Louis Applebaum fonds, 1979 – 002/022[425].

16. Report of the Annual Meeting of the Canadian League of Composers, 1966. York University Archives, Louis Applebaum fonds, 1979 – 002/022[425]. Louis's role in the League was much more modest in the years that followed. There was one last piece of business – the 20th anniversary celebration took place in 1971, appropriately, in terms of the League's perception of its national role, in Victoria, B. C. The theme was "20 Years and After" and Louis, now an elder statesman at age 53,was asked to chair a panel on "The First 20 Years." His panelists were not just among the mature founding members of the League (Weinzweig, Coulthard, and Beckwith along with Joachim), but were among the most distinguished as well. A second panel, "The Next 20 Years," was chaired by the League President, Sam Dolin, and included as panelists both "old" and "new" faces with Gabriel Charpentier, Robert Aitken, Murray Adaskin, Norma Beecroft, and John Hawkins taking part.

    Twenty pieces of Canadian music were performed, with the only sour note coming from a particularly nasty review by Bill Thomas in the Victoria *Daily Colonist*: "The really significant thing is that the music is dull beyond belief. It is totally devoid of excitement."

    It was at this conference that John Weinzweig uttered the much-quoted observation:

    > "When we are 25 we are young Canadian composers,
    > When we are 45 we are young Canadian composers,
    > When we are 55 we are young Canadian composers,
    > When we are dead, well, we are Canadian composers."

17. Report, "The Many Activities of the CAPAC-CAB Committee." *The Canadian Composer*, October 1966 [p.34]. The Committee made use of the Canadian Music Centre to supervise the recordings and to "assist in their promotion."

18. Ibid. Some outstanding recordings came out of the CAPAC-CAB project. A concerto album featured two concertos, the first by Oskar Morawetz, with Anton Kuerti at the piano, and the second a concerto for two pianos by Roger Matton, with the Canadian duo-pianists, Bouchard and Moriset. Another disc, *Scored for Ballet*, featured works by Louis as well as Robert Fleming, Pierre Mercure, John Weinzweig, and Morris Surdin. These were quality recordings in every way and received considerable praise. Louis was even successful in bringing Duke Ellington back to Canada to play the work of Canadian Norm Symonds. Ellington, Louis stated with great appreciation, "gets nothing" and simply "lent his name to the project" as a performer.

19. Article: "The Many Activities of the CAPAC-CAB Committee," *The Canadian Composer*, October 1966.

20. Clyde Gilmour, Toronto *Telegram*, August 24, 1967. York University Archives, Louis Applebaum fonds, 1979 –002/028[18].

21. Blaik Kirby, "Lou: Canada's No.1 Record Salesman," *The Globe and Mail*,

July 8, 1967. York University Archives, Louis Applebaum fonds, 1979 – 002/022[18].

22. Ibid.

23. Louis Applebaum, "An Audience for Canadian Recordings," Annual Meeting and Conference of the Canadian Music Council, April 6,7,8, 1967, at the University of Toronto and the Lord Simcoe Hotel.

24. Minutes of the Meeting of the Arts Advisory Committee of the Canada Council, September 21-22,1967. York University Archives, Louis Applebaum fonds, 1979 – 002/021[410].

25. William Littler, "Louis Applebaum, the music booster," *Toronto Daily Star*, July 19, 1969. [p.59] It was in this article that Littler coined the description of Louis that was to follow him throughout his life – Canada's "best known unknown composer."

26. Louis Applebaum, interview with author, November 17, 1999.

27. Louis Applebaum, letter to "Bill" [William St. Clair Low] February 8, 1971. York University Archives, Louis Applebaum fonds, 1979 – 002/022[430].

28. William St. Clair Low, letter to Louis Applebaum, March 1, 1971. York University Archives, Louis Applebaum fonds, 2000 –009/002[19].

29. Louis Applebaum, interview with author, November 17, 1999.

30. Ibid. Louis believed that Mills had actively engineered the pre-eminent role in place of any form of "equal" leadership structure that Louis had been led to expect. In retrospect, John Mills was most successful as CAPAC's CEO and can be credited with securing from the CRTC the "Canadian content" regulations that provided the base support for the amazing domination of Canadian performers in the North American market in the last years of the 20th century.

31. Jan V. Matejcek, interview with author, May 14, 2000. Jan Matejcek replaced Louis at CAPAC after a remarkable career as an arts manager in Europe, having come with the Czech delegation to the International Composer's Conference in Stratford, having been in charge of music for the Czech Pavilion at Expo 67 and then having fled Czechoslovakia in 1969 after the Soviet invasion of the country in 1968. He credits Louis as the Canadian who helped him secure a visa through his contacts in the Canadian government. After replacing Louis at CAPAC, Matejcek soon after left to join BMI. This "musical chairs" development was to be important many years later when the merging of the two organizations became a crucial issue.

32. Isaac Kleinerman, letter to Louis Applebaum, December 3, 1959. York University Archives, Louis Applebaum fonds, 1979 – 002-022[428].

33. Isaac Kleinerman, letter to Louis Applebaum, October 22, 1964. York University Archives, Louis Applebaum fonds, 1979 – 002/022[428].

34. Script: "Commonwealth of Sound," CBC Special, 1962. York University Archives, Louis Applebaum fonds, 1979 –002/007[76]. Canadian writer George Whalley was responsible for the script, and narrators were the familiar announcers Lamont Tilden and Bud Knapp. Louis had, once again, been brought in to do a special program of some lasting significance. It was a program of contrasts – the quiet description of a cricket match at Lord's and the

excited screams of Foster Hewitt as Bob Pulford scored a Leaf goal, the atmosphere of a Sotheby's auction and that of the Winnipeg cattle market. It was Louis's music that miraculously gave the program its continuity and order, with appropriate bridges, sometimes a minute or two, but more likely a few seconds in length. The appropriate musical expression might not inspire a lyrical line, but the opportunity to enhance the message was, as always, Louis's purpose.

35. Script: "It's All Yours" CBC Radio Special, 1963. York University Archives, Louis Applebaum fonds, 1979 – 002/009[99]. The program was produced and written by Keith MacMillan and had as hosts Tommy Tweed, Allan McFee, and John Rae along with Max Ferguson.

36. Article: "Affectionately Hockey," "Camera Canada" Series, *CBC Times*, April 7 –12, 1962. [p.4]. Modern technology allowed viewers to "experience the bumps and bruises through a short-wave radio strapped to Eddie Shack's shoulder."

37. Newspaper Clippings, "The Looking Glass People," CBC, 1963. Program Files, CBC Archives, Reference Library, Toronto.

38. Allan Wargon, letter to Louis Applebaum, March 14, March 24, and April 20, 1961. York University Archives, Louis Applebaum fonds, 1979 – 002/009[104,115]. By the time the program was aired, a fourth segment devoted to magic tricks had been added.

39. File, "And Then We Wrote" CBC Production, 1967. Program Files, CBC Reference Library and Archives, Toronto. Cast members included Veronica Tennant, Billy O'Connor, and Arlene Meadows. It was the CBC at its very best, celebrating the creative excellence that has been the proud product of Canadian artists and doing it in an entertaining manner. Once again, Norman Campbell was Louis's director on the project, a collaboration that invariably brought Louis great satisfaction.

40. Script: Bertold Brecht's *Mother Courage*, CBC Festival Production, 1964. York University Archives, Louis Applebaum fonds, 1979 –002/011[190] The play is filled with irony. "In a sense it's a war because there is fleecing, bribing, plundering, not to mention a little raping, but it's different from all other wars because it's a holy war."

41. Ibid.

42. Review of "The Mask," *Canadian Film Weekly*, November 15, 1961. [p.12]

43. Review of "The Mask," *Variety* Magazine, New York. October 27, 1961. York University Archives, Louis Applebaum fonds, 1979 – 002/004[30].

44. Clyde Gilmour, Review of "The Mask," Toronto *Telegram*, November 10, 1961. York University Archives, Louis Applebaum fonds, 1979 – 002/004[30].

45. Article, *The Canadian Composer*, November 18, 1968. [p18]

46. Bill Mason, letter to Louis Applebaum, September 1966. York University Archives, Louis Applebaum fonds, 1979 – 002/022[428].

47. Paul McIntyre, letter to Louis Applebaum, December 16, 1974. York University Archives, Louis Applebaun fonds, 1979 – 002/028[18].

48. Nathan Cohen, "Re God Save the Queen," *Toronto Daily Star*, June 14, 1963. [p.17] Cohen's initial outrage was matched by that of J. Burke Martin

in the *London Free Press.* "Louis Applebaum contributed some effective incidental music and I assume that he must also take responsibility for the scoring of the National Anthem which preceded the play. It sounded the way 'God Save the Queen' might be arranged by the Modern Jazz Quartet in one of their more dissonant moods. It deserved the snickers it got." J. Burke Martin, "First Night Play Seen Poor Choice" *London Free Press,* June 18, 1963. [p.16]. Louis did not believe that being a Canadian automatically made one a humourless monarchist.

49. Louis Applebaum, letter to David William, February 9,1966. There were other steps needed to support a beginning director at Stratford. Some scenes demanded the playing of ancient instruments [sackbut and early trumpets]. Louis assured him that the Stratford ensemble could play these instruments, but only after "diligence and effort they put into training themselves to play with skill and artistry" and warned William that there could be a disaster. "But I should shudder to think of the miserable sounds that twist the stomach when such instruments are played by Stratford-type musicians."

50. Heather Robertson, Review of "Nicholas Romanov," Winnipeg Tribune, March 10, 1966,[p.36]. Even the dialogue was fatally flawed. "Czar Nicholas and his wife sound like love spats between Dick Van Dyke and his wife or between Lucy and Desi."

51. Herbert Whittaker, Review of "The Last of the Czars," *The Globe and Mail,* July 13, 1966. York University Archives, Louis Applebaum fonds, 1979 –002/017[289]. The reviews could not have been more mixed. Nathan Cohen suggested that that the play had convinced him that a cause of the Russian Revolution had been sheer boredom and that "Michael Bawtree's play is bad theatrical hokum." (Review, Nathan Cohen, "The Last of the Czars," *Toronto Daily Star,* July 13, 1966.) Ron Evans, the Toronto *Telegram's* critic, was positively euphoric. "Today I exult. The Festival has found a brilliant new playwright ... the play is stunning ... It is exciting intelligent, witty, colourful, compassionate theatre ... . Bawtree ... [is] capable of making a contribution, not only to the Festival, to Canadian Theatre but to the English-speaking theatre at large." (Review, Toronto *Telegram,* July 13, 1966.) York University Archives, Louis Applebaum fonds, 1979 – 002/017[289].

52. Score and script: *Antony and Cleopatra,* Stratford Festival production, 1967. York University Archives, Louis Applebaum fonds, 1979 – 002/016 [272 and 273]. A hand written note from "Nora" to Louis Applebaum, dated March 30,1967, accompanied an item that must have been helpful to Louis as he composed the score. "Enclosed is a tape of Robin making noises and singing. The first part was actually done in rehearsals. The second part is Robin at home going through the first act of the play [scenes 1-17]."

53. Script, "Four Variations for Corno Di Bassetto," Shaw Festival, 1969. York University Archives, Louis Applebaum fonds, 1979 – 002/016 [277]. The production was essentially a collection of readings of Shaw's critiques and ruminations about music, interspersed with musical selections. There was lots of mate-

rial available as, on the whole, Shaw disliked composers and musicians and was quite blunt in his comments. "To me it seems obvious that Brahms is nothing more than a sentimental voluptuary with a wonderful ear" and went on to dismiss his "execrable requiem." [p.18] "It should be made a felony to play a musical instrument or sing anywhere but in a soundproof room" [p.19] Of Schubert symphonies, "they are charming but brainless." [p.20]

54. William Littler, Review, "Back to Methusalah is a Total Disaster," *Toronto Star*, York University Archives, Louis Applebaum fonds, 1979 – 002/016[277].

Chapter 14. A Troubled Arts Council

1. Thomas S. Axworthy, Pierre Trudeau, *Towards a Just Society: the Trudeau Years*, Viking Press, Markham, 1990. [p.23] He was setting his course in the wake of the most dramatic moment of Canada's centennial year, the intervention of Charles de Gaulle, a guest who took the opportunity of arousing those French-speaking citizens for whom separation was a cause, with his declaration, "Vive le Québec libre."

2. Louis Applebaum, interview with author, April 1, 1999. Jan Applebaum, whom Louis regarded as his most accurate advisor in matters of character assessment, found Trudeau a fascinating dinner partner. "He always recognized me and remembered who I was. He looked you straight in the eye when conversing, not allowing his gaze to stray over the crowd in search of some distinguished and influential guest whose attention he needed to attract. And he listened."

3. Walter Pitman, "Pierre Elliott Trudeau – Tribute to an Artist" *Artspaper*, Autumn 2000, Arts Education Council of Ontario, Toronto. Volume 11, Issue 1. [p.14]. Professor Albert Breton, Trudeau's Special Advisor, 1970-1979, was astonished to find that this prime minister spent his time reading poetry. "The tables in his office were piled high." Albert Breton, interview with author, May 25, 2001.

4. D. Paul Schafer, Andre Fortier, "Review of Federal Policies for the Arts in Canada: 1944-1988," prepared for the Department of Communications, Canadian Conference of the Arts, 1989.

5. Thomas S. Axworthy, Pierre Trudeau, *Towards a Just Society: the Trudeau Years*, Viking Press, Markham, 1990. [p.33] The government's efforts to limit U.S. influence were limited in their impact as trade diversification was impossible. But at the end of the Trudeau era, "Canadians owned more of their own economy" than in the 1960s and indeed "owned more of the American economy" than ever before.

6. Ibid. [p.37] The advice was taken as the CRTC, the broadcasting regulatory agency, was given power to prohibit foreign ownership of broadcast outlets and increase Canadian content regulation for both radio and television and, finally, the Canadian publishing industry was given support. The exemption on *Time* magazine from Canadian tax laws affecting advertisers in foreign publication disappeared, along with the right of Canadian advertisers to make use of commercial messages on American border television stations without tax penal-

ty. All these steps strengthened the role of broadcasting and publishing as the chains that now linked the people of Canada as tracks of steel had once done.

7. Roy MacSkimming, *For Art's Sake, A History of the Ontario Arts Council, 1963–1983*. OAC, Toronto, 1983.[p17-18]

8. Louis Applebaum, "The Professional Musician," included in the Proceedings of the Ontario Music Conference, Material for Small Group Discussion, Conference Aims and Structure, Programs Division, Government of Ontario, 1966.[unpublished] The other four workshops: Music Education in Elementary Schools, Music Education in Secondary Schools, The Role of the University in Music Education, and, Music in the Community. The participants, over 100 in number, included virtually the full roster of leaders in the music performance and music education fields across the province: Boris Berlin, Hyman Goodman, Walter Homburger, Herman Geiger-Torel, Carl Morey, Charles Peaker, Sir Ernest MacMillan, Hamilton Southam, Alexander Brott, John Weinzweig, Ezra Schabas, Peter Dwyer, John Sidgewick, and Leila Rasminsky, as well as general educators Lloyd Dennis, Zack Phimister and Kenneth Preuter. Many of the ideas in Louis's paper on "The Professional Musician" were to be included in another document that he prepared soon after on a commission from both the Canada Council and the POCA. This task arose out of a conflict between the CBC and the TSO that had to be resolved, but came to be a matter of how to utilize the orchestral resources of Toronto in a way that would benefit the musicians as well as the CBC, the TSO, the National Ballet, and the COC, all of whom were competing for a small number of excellent instrumentalists.

9. Ibid. The recommendations stressed the importance of a continuous curriculum for every student that would include music appreciation, choral work, and sight-reading programs for every student to Grade 6, with music theory and history, violin, chamber groups, orchestral, and wind instruments from Grade 4 to 13.

Although these recommendations were never legislated into effect, they did inspire music teachers in classrooms in schools across the province. POCA even set up CARE, the Centre for Arts Research, under Paul Schafer with an initial $50,000 budget, but it soon became apparent that even with its links with the Ontario Institute for Studies in Education, this was stretching the mandate beyond the tolerance of the Government.

10. Minutes of the Music Committee, Province of Ontario Council for the Arts, Thursday, October 13, 1966. [unpublished]. [p.3]. "Through a planned and experimental program of integration and correlation of English, History, Languages, Mathematics etc. with music and other arts devise and assess a model integrated curriculum feasible for implementation throughout the entire school system." Document, Recommendations of the Ontario Music Conference to the Department of Education, Province of Ontario Council for the Arts. (unpublished) The Committee had a membership that now included, Ezra Schabas, Elmer Iseler, Keith Bissell, Arnold Walter, Arthur Gelber, Walter Ball (just appointed as music officer at POCA) and Paul Schafer of the POCA staff.

11. Roy MacSkimming, *For Art's Sake, A History of the Ontario Arts Council, 1963–1983.* OAC, 1983, [p.21] The OAC as well as the Government might have been warned by his statement that the "arts are just as necessary for the spiritual welfare of man as hospitals are for his physical well-being." The state of the future could be glimpsed in Milton Carman's first Executive Director's Report at the end of the 1963-64 Annual Report where he identified a "section devoted to dreams and high hopes." Carman went on to talk about a "Peace Corps for the Arts," a scheme in which professional artists would be sent into the four corners of the province "to train and inspire amateurs." Carman was a man with a cause, and his isolation from some Council members and staff came from such single-mindedness.

12. Ron Evans, interview with author, July 18, 1999. By 1968, POCA had already strained its relations with the Robarts government beyond redemption with a document it referred to as "the Keiller MacKay Five-Year Plan," cleverly giving weight to its demands for the next half-decade by invoking the name of the highly respected Chairman of the Council. Certainly the Five-Year Plan had all the trappings of a normal budget document and was entirely within the POCA's mandate; however, the program directions and increased allocations which it proposed were such as to frighten any politician or change-resistant civil servant. Louis arrived precisely in the middle of the time span this plan purported to cover.

13. Charlotte Holmes and James Norcop, interview with author, March 30, 1999. Charlotte had been the second person to join the staff of POCA (only Naomi Lightbourn had preceded her). Her expertise was in theatre and ballet and was essential to the early years of the Council's success. In the next phase of the Council's development when discipline officers were required Holmes took both of these, along with film. James Norcop, a singer and music administrator, made his greatest contribution to the OAC by developing support for touring and finding markets for Canadian artists. A yearly extravaganza called the OAC "Contact" that brought concert presenters and artists and arts organizations together became an event that received both national and international attention.

14. Naomi Lightbourn, interview with author, March 5, 1999. Naomi Lightbourn had been the first person hired by the new Council. Her experience as an arts administrator and journalist was greatly prized. She remained with the Arts Council for the rest of her career, and her contribution as a Community Arts Officer was incomparable. Her analysis of Carman's role as he took his leave was that he had been "out of it" for some months before he resigned in the fall of 1970. By that point the Council was "rudderless."

In an article written shortly after Louis's succession to the directorship, Betty Lee, introducing the incumbent to *The Globe and Mail* readers, mentioned in passing Carman's self-description as "one of the beautiful freaks." "There was Milton the Great, suppressing his celebrated ego to 'fly as high as I can as a human being,' to spurn the System, study Zen, and wear love beads." She contrasted Louis's lifestyle as "No lovebeads for Applebaum. No engrossing love affair with group therapy … No pot or hash." Betty Lee, "Applebaum a man with $2.5 million for art" *The Globe and Mail,* May 15, 1971.

15. Minutes of the Meeting of the Province of Ontario Council for the Arts, October 4, 1970. Ontario Arts Council Archives, OAC Offices, Toronto. It was fair treatment. Carman had infuriated and exasperated the Council, but he had moved it many miles along the path toward being an effective agency. James Norcop believed that Carman's first years at the POCA were "truly brilliant." Whether his subsequent behaviour was due to the stress of conflicting perceptions of the OAC's proper role or a bizarre lifestyle choice, he had deserved generous treatment. Louis himself could state in a speech at the CNE Music and Flower Day Director's Dinner that "thanks to the vision and to the enterprise of Milton Carman, I have been able to move into a vital and productive organization."

16. Naomi Lightbourn, interview with author, March 5, 1999.

17. Louis Applebaum, interview with author, March 30, 1999. He had known Naomi Lightbourn both from Stratford days and when she had been an assistant to Walter Homburger at International Artists. Charlotte Holmes had been with the National Ballet, for which he had composed music and had been part of the team that produced a film on the Company some years before. Ron Evans had been the arts critic for the Toronto *Telegram* and had followed Louis's work at Stratford and, when on tour, to far-flung venues across the continent.

18. Minutes of the Province of Ontario Council for the Arts, September 22-23,1971. Minute Books, Ontario Arts Council, OAC Offices, Toronto.

19. Louis Applebaum, Speech to the Annual Meeting of the St. Lawrence Centre, June 2, 1971. Ontario Arts Council Files, RG47:14-1, TB101, Archives of Ontario.

20. In 1971, the OAC needed $30,000 to cover its expenditure deficit and wanted to request a supplementary grant. Robert Welch, by then the Council's Minister, refused to approach the Provincial Treasurer as he believed it would hurt the OAC's chance for an increase in the following budget year. However, at the year's end, he found money in his budget so the Council could conclude its year in the black. In 1972, the Government was anxious to assist the major performing arts organizations, and gave more than the promised allocation to the OAC on the basis that promises had been made and must be kept for a higher allocation to those institutions. In 1973, when the Royal Commission on Book Publishing reported, a substantial increase came to the Council in order that the recommendations of the Commission could be accommodated. The OAC grant was increased on the basis that the extraordinary increase would go the literary program and thereby assist the publishing industry. In each case, the financial base of the OAC was increased. Through a strong restraint against raising administrative costs, more and more resources were dispensed to more clients each year of Louis's tenure. This meant that whenever the Council came under some criticism, one charge that could not be laid against it was that its administrative costs were excessive.

21. John White, speaking at a University Affairs Conference, quoted in the Minutes of the Meeting of the Province of Ontario Council for the Arts, September 22-23, 1971. Minute Books, OAC Archives, OAC Offices, Toronto. White, a highly intelligent MPP from western Ontario, argued that Ontario had reached a plateau of economic prosperity at which cultural expansion was appropriate. White was, in later years, to make a significant contribution to the work of the Province in the field of protecting its heritage.
22. Louis Applebaum, Minutes of the Select Committee on Economic and Cultural Nationalism, Ontario Archives, Ontario Arts Council Files, RG 47 –14 – 1. Archives of Ontario.
23. Nathan Cohen, Column, *Toronto Daily Star,* March 11, 1971. [p.26]
24. Janice Dineen, "How the Arts Council Brings Culture to the Ontario Hinterland," *Toronto Daily Star* [no date], York University Archives, Louis Applebaum fonds, 1979 – 022-028[10].
25. Article, "Volpone Score Is Applebaum's Swan Song," *London Free Press,* Monday, July 26, 1971. [p.19] The director, David William, had very specific ideas about the kind of music he wanted. "Volpone strikes me as one of the most sadistic works in English literature." He wanted to "preserve the quality of fable" ... and yet achieve "some kind of cultural contact with the people" and depict "a society that has overdrawn its spiritual reserves and is dancing and debauching on the edge of its own grave." David William to Louis Applebaum, April 3, 1971. York University Archives, Louis Applebaum fonds, 1979 –002 – 019[309].

    The critics were divided on the success of the music in achieving what they thought should be an attack on avarice and duplicity. Herbert Whittaker, in his *The Globe and Mail* review, July 28, 1971, thought William had been "assisted nimbly by that talented composer Louis Applebaum, to make sure that every scene is presented with the utmost flourish and dispatch," but Urjo Kareda, complaining of the length of the play, commented in the *Toronto Daily Star,* July 28, 1971, that "the designer, Annina Stubbs, and composer, Louis Applebaum, make a busy contribution, and though they work their way through various styles with colourful gusto, their assistance proves clever rather than useful."

    When he was asked how he could have produced this score in the midst of the first frantic weeks of a new job filled with dramatic conflicts, he answered his questioner with no hesitation. "I compartmentalize – when I sit down to write music, I put everything else out of my mind. When I'm figuring out a budget for POCA, I put all my mind on that. Always I've had deadlines – I grew up with them and so far I've never missed one."[Ibid]

26. David William, letter to Louis Applebaum, November 3, 1971. Government of Ontario Archives, OAC Files. RG 17 –15, TR 123.
27 Lenore Crawford, Article, *London Free Press,* August 25, 1972. York University Archives, Louis Applebaum fonds, 1979–022/028[19]
28. Review, "Stratford Festival's *Othello,*" *The Globe and Mail,* June 7, 1973.
29. David William, letter to Louis Applebaum, March 10, 1973. York University Archives, Louis Applebaum fonds, 1979-002/018[295]. Though the letter

includes some gratuitous advice on musical accompaniment, it reveals as well the clarity of William's understanding of the play. He wanted Louis's music to support "the psychological factor – principally expressed in the conflict within Othello himself. Beginning in a state of high and noble security, proudly conscious of his exotic lineage and culture, yet firmly committed to the service of Venice and Christianity — and a great warrior, in an age when military life was still a source of romance, heroism and beauty. As the play progresses, this moral sovereignty disintegrates, the leader becomes the led, the lover becomes the hater, the representative of the highest authority known in the civilized world descends to a hellish chaos … ."

30. McKenzie Porter, Toronto *Sun*, June 13, 1977, [p29]

31. McKenzie Porter, "Winter's Tale a Smash Hit," Toronto *Sun*, June 11, 1978. [p.65]

32. Robin Phillips, quoted in article, "Interview with Robin Phillips," Stratford *Beacon Herald*, 1975 Special Festival Edition, York University Archives, Louis Applebaum fonds, 1979 – 002/030[577] Robin Phillips did wish to see music revived at the Festival, and the brilliant young conductor Robert Cooper, who was at that time conducting the Ontario Youth Choir, was brought in to play a role in 1978 that would move Phillips's commitment along. The choir was involved in the Festival's opening reception in 1979, but in 1980 Phillips wanted a young but professional choir to be involved in *The Beggar's Opera* and in four mainstage concerts to be hosted by Stratford stars such as Hume Cronyn and Jessica Tandy, Peter Ustinov, William Hutt, and Phillips himself. The experiment was pronounced a success. However, 1980 was the year that Phillips was standing down as artistic director. The Board first selected a British director to replace him and then, when that did not work out, a triumvirate of Canadian actors. In the chaos, the revival of music faltered. (Robert Cooper, interview with author, January 13, 2000.)

33. Article "Louis Applebaum: The Festival's first music man," Stratford *Beacon Herald* Special Festival Edition, Section F [p.6]. York University Archives, Louis Applebaum fonds, 1979 – 002/030[579]. Once again in this interview, Louis acknowledged the reduced role of music at the Festival, but took some responsibility for the earlier success in the face of the reality that "he did his own secretarial work" as there was no money for administration, and remembering that though "we had a lot of exciting activities in the 1950s and 1960s … unfortunately, they never really focussed into a stable pattern." "The Festival's first music man says he is disappointed the music program here isn't bigger that it was 10 years ago. 'That's someone else's worry though. I've done my job at Stratford', says Louis Applebaum. 'It's up to others to take the music to new plateaus.'" Both Robin Phillips and Louis were aware that there was a movement in opera toward greater dramatic realism, and both saw Stratford as the place where singers could gain the acting skills to address this new world, but neither could make it happen.

34. Jan Applebaum, interview with author, May 18, 2001.

35. Letter. Vincent Tovell to Louis Applebaum. October 7, 1971. York University Archives, Louis Applebaum fonds, 1979-002-008[96]. In another letter dated September 19, 1972, Tovell further indicated his interest in the music of the series: "My first impulse then is to use music suggestively and in a fashion which is exceedingly vivid." (Letter, Vincent Tovell to Louis Applebaum, September 19, 1972, Ibid.[97])

36. Knowlton Nash, *The National Dream*, CBC Publications, Toronto, 1972. Program Files, CBC Archives, Toronto. In the previous few years, the Corporation had produced "The Tenth Decade," an account of the political struggles of John Diefenbaker and Lester Pearson; "The Days Before Yesterday" a review of Canada's politics from Laurier to St. Laurent; and "First Person Singular," an account of the legacy of Lester Pearson.

37. "The National Dream," CBC–TV Network Promotion, July 5, 1973. Program Files, CBC Archives, Toronto. As his work for "The National Dream" was coming to an end, Louis was engaged by the CTV Network to write two of the segments for a series, "Five Self-Portraits," a series of five hour-long documentaries on the people of Canada and the influence of geography on their character and lifestyle. His work on the "The National Dream" had directed his attention to the areas he chose as his contribution to the series, "The Prairies" and "The Mountains." In the former there was reference to a theme that influenced his work on hearings associated with the Federal Cultural Policy Review in the 1980s. "But remarkable people and even more remarkable politics have come out of places like this. Many of the new political ideas of this century have struggled into being here … with tipped-back chairs and thumbs hooked on overall straps … . CCF, Social Credit, Progressives, Reconstructionists …." [York University Archives, Louis Applebaum fonds, 1979-002/007, [73] and [74].

38. Tony Thomas, Article on Louis Applebaum, *Stereo Guide*, Spring Issue, Toronto, 1974. Although Louis's music was widely applauded, there were discordant notes. A letter to the editor published in *The Globe and Mail,* May 6, 1974 from R. A. Young in Sudbury provided unsought advice. "Concerning the music, it is dreadful at times but why not Gordon Lightfoot's classic Canadian Railroad Trilogy?" "The National Dream" was sold to networks around the world including the BBC and TV-Ireland and has been repeated on the CBC and other networks several times since its original broadcast.

39. CBC Network Promotion Release, February 16, 1973, "Hiss the Villain, Cheer the Hero," "The Purple Playhouse," Program Files, CBC Archives, Toronto. The CBC had a strong position on the decision to provide this series. "Evil – whether it be demon, drink, lust or avarice – was always cast down by Good, usually in the form of a handsome young Hero who saved the proud beauty from A Fate Worse than Death in the nick of time. Black and white conflicts couched in purple prose." In his introduction, Robertson Davies put it a little more elegantly: "The theatre of Queen Victoria's reign was dominated by a particular kind of drama. Just as the

Elizabethans liked blood and plenty of it, the Victorians wanted moral contests – vice pitted against virtue, with Virtue Triumphant ... Black and White contests couched in purple prose."

40. Script. Harry Rasky, "The Wit and Wisdom of GBS," CBC Television Production, 1972. York University Archives, Louis Applebaum fonds, 1979 – 002/016[269].

41. "Next Year in Jerusalem," CBC Television Network Promotion Release, March 18, 1974. Program Files, CBC Archives, Toronto.

42. "Travels Through Life with Leacock," CBC Network Production Release, February 2, 1975. Program Files, CBC Archives, Toronto.

43. "Homage to Chagall, The Colours of Love," CBC Network Promotion release, March 17, 1978. Program Files, CBC Archives, Toronto. The film was invited to the Moscow International Film Festival in the year after it was completed. "The film is the only entry and the only documentary at this year's festival. It is also the only CBC show ever shown there. It was nominated for an Oscar and an International Emmy, and later received a National Documentary Award in the U.S." In 1989, "Homage to Chagall" was invited to the Leningrad Film Festival. The CBC Department of Communications reported that "It has become one of the most-seen art films," and Rasky, finding himself in the midst of the Gorbachev reforms, observed "I am honoured to help share in the new spirit of openness. Since the film is also a great spiritual document in which Chagall declares 'God is Love', I think it should be shared by many people in Russia, the birthplace of Chagall." (CBC Department of Communication release, December 21,1988. Program Files, CBC Archives, Toronto.) When Louis was asked to speak on musical composition to the National Ballet School students in 1978, he used this film as an illustration of his work.

44. "Arthur Miller on Home Ground," CBC "Spectrum Series", CBC Network Promotion Release, September 28, 1979. Program Files, CBC Archives, Toronto.

45. "Journey Without Arrival," CBC-TV, "Images of Canada Series," CBC Network Promotion Release, No. 79, March 15, 1976. CBC Library and Archives, Toronto.

46. Al Johnson, letter to Louis Applebaum, June 28, 1977. York University Archives, Louis Applebaum fonds, 1979 – 002/022[406].

47. "Nellie McClung," CBC "First Performance," CBC Network Promotion, February 7, 1978. Program Files, CBC Archives, Toronto. The program was repeated two years later after its initial airing in 1976.

48. "Sarah," CBC Network Production, CBC News Release, October 21, 1977. Program Files, CBC Archives, Toronto.

49. "Stacey," CBC Network Promotion release, November 16, 1978. Program Files, CBC Archives, Toronto.

50. "The Masseys," CBC Television, 1978-1979, "The One to Watch," September 14, 1978. Program Files, CBC Archives, Toronto. Glenn Morley, his collaborator, was the single speaker at Louis Applebaum's funeral, completed Louis's final commitment to a Stratford production in 2000, and pro-

duced and conducted the posthumous CD, *Fanfare, The Stratford Music of Louis Applebaum.*

51. "The Making of the President," Network Promotion release, September 6, 1978. Program Files, CBC Achives, Toronto.

52. Ray Conologue, "The Peking Man Mystery," *The Globe and Mail,* October 7, 1978.

Chapter 15. Cultural Czar

1. D. Paul Schafer, *Culture: Beacon of the Future,* Adamantine Press Limited. United Kingdom, 1998. [pp. 5-11] Paul Schafer was hired by Milton Carman as an economic adviser because of his particular interest in arts funding issues. Though he originally had a two-month contract, Schafer became involved in several projects at the Council, especially the Ontario Theatre Study. This project produced a significant report, "The Awkward Stage," certainly the most extensive look at the province's theatre community ever attempted, even though it had been initiated simply to examine the collapse of both the Crest Theatre and the Canadian Players Foundation. Schafer left the OAC in the early 1970s to give leadership to a Council-influenced arts administration program at York University and later at Scarborough College, University of Toronto.

2. "The Keiller MacKay Five Year Plan," Province of Ontario Council for the Arts, November 1968, Ontario Arts Council Files, 47 –15, TB 121. Archives of Ontario. This plan represents the triumph of the systemic approach to arts funding as opposed to the piecemeal support of particular arts organizations. It included a comprehensive program of Coordinated Arts Services (CAS), which was to assist the promotion of all major art organizations and the Centre for Arts Research in Education (CARE.)

3. Minutes of the Ontario Arts Council Meeting, September 12,13, and 14, 1972. [p.5] Minute Books, Ontario Arts Council Files, OAC Offices,Toronto. Louis had already connected his enthusiasm for the wider cultural interest of Council with the role of arts education. At the Annual Meeting of the St. Lawrence Centre in the spring of 1971, he stated, "When we separate the artistic elements from other aspects of our lives we are denying ourselves, as teachers, our most valuable and influential tool," and pointed out how "foolish it was to divorce art from history or mathematics or sociology or science." Speech to the Annual Meeting of the St. Lawrence Centre, Executive Director's Speeches, Ontario Arts Council Files, R647:14 –1 TB101, Archives of Ontario.

4. Louis Applebaum, letter to Richard Doyle, Editor, *The Globe and Mail,* December 8, 1971. Ontario Arts Council Files, RG 47-14-1, TB101, Archives of Ontario. The idea behind the "Music Box" was that of expanding the perception of children about learning on different levels, encouraging the use of all the senses as well as experiential ways of understanding. To some extent, the OAC found itself sharing the unpopularity of Ontario's new institution devoted to graduate studies in education but also to somewhat more questionable research into new ways of teaching and learning. Because of the

emphasis on graduate programs, academically respectable faculty with advanced degrees had to be found outside of Canada. As a result, a disproportionately large number of professors from the U.K., the U.S., and even Australia had to be recruited, most of whom knew little of the Ontario educational system. This, along with the Music Box and other "way-out" experiments, aroused opposition on all sides. The reaction to these learning "boxes" was thus simply the mountaintop of conservative reaction to experimental efforts on the part of both OAC and OISE.

5.   Ontario Arts Council Policy Meeting, November 23 –34, 1972, Ontario Arts Council Files, 24 –15 T121, Archives of Ontario. This meeting put into focus a number of Louis's other priorities. In literature, it was "emerging authors" who would be given special assistance. In visual arts, it was not galleries that would be emphasized, but the "economic support" of artists; and in music, funds which would allow schools to commission works would receive highest priority. Indeed, "composers would work with professional groups in preparing the compositions for them and would work directly with school choirs and orchestras in composing pieces." In drama, a program of funding was proposed that would assist "potential playwrights to learn their craft."

6.   Minutes of the Ontario Arts Council Policy Meeting, November 23 –24, 1972.[p3] Ontario Arts Council Files, 47 –15 T121, Archives of Ontario. A part of that accessibility had to be in the area of arts education. By this time, though, the wider role for the OAC recommended by the Music Conference as well as the MacKay Report had been rejected as unfeasible by the Minister of Education. There was one role that the OAC was able to salvage. This involved supporting schools who invited artists to spend time in classrooms with both students and their teachers, together with support for music, dance, and theatre performances in schools, and Linda Zwicker became an important part of that initiative. "Artists in the Schools" programs became a very high priority. Louis never stopped advocating on behalf of these programs. "Is there any reason why we can't organize a process that would give every child in every school an opportunity to participate, say even twice a year, in high-class music-making and a couple of times a year in a theatre piece and another in, say, dance movement?" Louis Applebaum, Speech to the Art Liaison Committee of the Toronto Metro School Board, "Showcase 72," February 28, 1972, Executive Director's Speeches, Ontario Arts Council Files, R647 – 14 – 18 TB101, Archives of Ontario

7.   Louis Applebaum, Speech, Arts Liaison Committee, Metro Toronto School Board, "Showcase 72," February 28,1972. Executive Director's Speeches, Ontario Arts Council Files, RG - 47 – 14 – 18 TB101, Archives of Ontario.

8.   Louis Applebaum, quoted in David Billington, article in *The Citizen*, Ottawa, September 15, 1974, [p.77]. York University Archives, Louis Applebaum fonds, 1979 – 022/028[19].

9.   Ron Evans, interview with author, July 8, 1999.

10.   Naomi Lightbourn, interview with author, March 5, 1999. By the late 1960s, this "democratic" involvement of all officers in every decision had become an

aspect of the battle between Council and staff. Carman had seen the "dry-run" as a way of manipulating the decision-making to advance his own agenda of support for the small and the experimental in place of the commitment to the large and established (the "dinosaurs," as the major art organizations were coming to be called.) Actually, by 1969 and 1970, the staff used the collegial system to block his more bizarre proposals for funding inappropriate causes.

11. James Norcop, interview with author, March 30, 1999. James Norcop had arrived in the late 1960s and had endured the leaderless months before Milton Carman's departure. Although first involved with the Coordinated Arts Services project, his report on touring and its acceptance expanded the market for hundreds of individual performers and gave Ontario audiences, particularly those in smaller communities, a choice of Canadian artists never before available.

12. Naomi Lightbourn, interview with author, March 5, 1999. All the officers at the OAC were constantly made aware of the problems of regional disparity. Although Louis's work on orchestras had concentrated on the Toronto scene, his friend Ezra Schabas's Report on Ontario Community Orchestras in 1966 had examined the state of some 15 orchestras outside the province's capital. Rarely had a report stated the point so starkly. "The orchestral situation in the northern part of the province is frightening. It is a vast musical slum ... How poverty-stricken must communities be?"[p. 51]

13. Janice Dineen, article, "How the Arts Council Brings Culture to the Ontario Hinterland," York University Archives, Louis Applebaum fonds, 1979 – 022/028[19].

14. Louis Applebaum, handwritten note for a speech in Oshawa, June 5, 1971, Ontario Arts Council files, RG 47-14 -1, Box 101, Archives of Ontario. It is not clear whether this entire segment was an original expression or whether Louis copied the thoughts of some other person in his description. In any case, it reveals very clearly what he had come to believe about arts education and its significance in the lives of children.

15. Frank McEachren, Minutes of the Ontario Arts Council Policy Meeting, November 23 –24, 1972, [p.10] Ontario Arts Council Files, RG – 47 –15 –1 T121, Archives of Ontario.

16. Elizabeth Murray, Minutes of the Ontario Arts Council Policy Meeting, November 23-24, 1972, [p.9], Ontario Arts Council Files, RG –47 –15 –1 T121, Archives of Ontario.

17. Louis Applebaum, Minutes of the Ontario Arts Council Meeting, September 25 –26, 1972.[p.3], Ontario Arts Council files, RG47 – 15 –1, T121, Archives of Ontario. Louis had also reported to Council that a management consultant firm had been retained by the Ministry of Colleges and Universities (the Ministry to which the OAC and other cultural agencies now reported, having been transferred from the Ministry of Education.) Louis was unperturbed by this development.

18. Ibid. [p.5]

19. Louis Applebaum, interview with author, June 10, 1999.

20. Minutes of the Ontario Arts Council Meeting, February 13 -14, 1975. [pp.2-4] OAC Minute Books, OAC Offices, Toronto.

21. Ibid.

22. Roy MacSkimming, *For Art's Sake, A History of the OAC from 1963–1983,* OAC, Toronto, 1983. [p.40]

23. Louis Applebaum, interview with author, June 10, 1999. There were civil servants who had little patience with all this "precious concern" for artistic independence and the time-consuming consultative process that it demanded. There were others who very much supported Louis and his staff in their effort to protect the integrity of the Council and its work, including Douglas McCullough, Andrew Lipchak, Norman Best, and Linda Loving. In the background, close to Minister Robert Welch and close to Louis as a personal friend, was the figure of Robert Sirman, who later came to work at the OAC.

    In spite of his disappointment, Louis remained the consummate gentleman in his relations with civil servants, and with Robert Welch and his successors as minister. He never allowed his personal frustration to affect his decisions or behaviour in such a way that his Council could be disadvantaged.

24. Report on the Special Program Review, November 21, 1975. Ontario Arts Council Files, RG47-14-1, Archives of Ontario. There were always minor blazes to be extinguished. Exactly three years later, the Standing Procedural Affairs Committee of the Ontario Legislature brought forth a report that stated, "The Arts Council should discontinue the practice of granting money to individuals and groups outside Ontario," and "The Arts Council should discontinue the practice of granting money on a continuing basis to schools and school boards." Louis was able to respond that, because the National Ballet School was in Ontario, there was more money coming to Ontario from other provinces than was going out as a result of this practice of supporting national training institutions. Also, he made the point that at this time in Canada's history "closing provincial borders" would be a foolish step to take. As well, he was able to make the point that there was no continuing funding to schools and school boards as had been assumed in the second resolution. (Minutes of the Ontario Arts Council Meeting, November 1978, OAC Minute Books, OAC offices, Toronto.)

25. Louis Applebaum, Speech, Dunning Trust Lectures, Executive Director's Speeches, 1976, Ontario Arts Council Files, RG 647 – 14 –1,TB 134, Archives of Ontario.

26. Louis Applebaum, *Mermaid Inn* column, *The Globe and Mail,* October 27, 1977. [p.5]

27. Minutes of the Executive Committee of the Ontario Arts Council, December 13, 1978. Ontario Arts Council Minute Books, OAC Offices, Toronto.

28. Louis Applebaum, letter to Lan Adomian, August 8, 1972. Executive Director's CAPAC and Personal Correspondence, Ontario Arts Council Files, RG 47 – 15 TRI 23, Archives of Ontario.

29. Louis Applebaum, letter to Reuven Frank, June 25, 1977. York University Archives, Louis Applebaum fonds, 1979 – 002/021[406].

30. Ibid.

31. Louis Applebaum, draft of *The C-Channel Story*, unpublished, York University Archives, Louis Applebaum fonds, 2000 – 009/005. [20]

32. Ibid. Eventually, other Canadian theatres and musical organizations could be brought on "generating a major production/distribution/ promotion venture in Canada to operate world-wide in its sales/promotion activities."

33. Robert Anderson, "New Audiences, New Dollars," June, 1978.   York University Archives, Louis Applebaum fonds, 2000 – 009/005[03] Louis proposal in response was that a three-member co-op be set up for one year, to include Stratford and the National Arts Centre, that a Stratford theatre production and a Glenn Gould recital be produced as an experiment. But if after one year there were no positive results, the idea should be abandoned.

34. Louis Applebaum, *The C-Channel Story*, (unpublished), York University Archives, Louis Applebaum fonds, 2000-009/005. [20]

35. Robert Anderson, letter to Louis Applebaum, handwritten note, February 8, 1979. York University Archives, Louis Applebaum fonds, 2000 – 009/005[03]. Anderson made it plain to Louis that it would be "difficult if not impossible to find someone other than you with the experience and stature to bring this off."

36. Louis Applebaum, letter to Robin Phillips, July 1, 1978. York University Archives, Louis Applebaum fonds, 2000 – 009/005[03] This letter was written on Canada Day, exactly five years before the demise of LAMB and C-Channel.

37. Louis Applebaum, memorandum to LAMB Board of Directors, January 17, 1980. Even though he was only an advisor, Louis sought, as well, to secure the goodwill of the new Minister of Culture and Recreation, indicating that LAMB's C-Channel would extend audiences for Ontario's performing arts. Louis's attitude to C-Channel was so focussed on benefiting the arts that it would never have occurred to him that there was a hint of conflict of interest with his role as Executive Director of the OAC.

38. LAMB: Intervention re CBC–2, December 23, 1980, for hearing before the CRTC, January 14, 1981. The CBC was also prevented from moving ahead on a joint proposal with CTV for a pay-TV service.

39. Hamilton Southam, letter to Douglas Fullerton, April 12, 1980. York University Archives, Louis Applebaum fonds, 2000 – 009/005[05]

40. Ed Cowan, memorandum to LAMB Board, March 26, 1982. York University Archives, Louis Applebaum fonds, 2000 – 009/005[13] After CBC's anger over LAMB's opposition to the CBC-2 application had blown over, Hamilton Southam had a private conversation with Al Johnson, the CBC's President. Johnson's advice: "Were he in our shoes, he said he would argue strongly for the licensing of one channel only, presenting C-Channel by itself or C-Channel packaged with another application. The licensing of both would guarantee the failure of both or all of them." Johnson understood the frailty of the pay-television world and was absolutely right in his analysis. (Confidential Memorandum: Southam to LAMB Board, September 1981. York University Archives, 2000-009/005[13])

41. Minutes of the LAMB Board Meeting #13, March 1,1981. York University Archives, Louis Applebaum fonds, 2000 – 009/005[11]. A letter was sent to Louis indicating that his position had been put in trust until such time as his current commitments left him free to join LAMB.

42. Ed Cowan, memorandum to LAMB Directors, June 18, 1981. York University Archives, Louis Applebaum fonds, 2000 – 009/005[12]

43. C-Channel February 1983 Programme Guide. York University Achives, Louis Applebaum fonds, 2000-009/006[14] A production of *Swan Lake* by the Royal Ballet, Covent Garden, graced the first evening's programming, but on the following night, the Montreal Jazz Festival was emphasized along with Tony Van Bridge's one-man portrayal of G. K. Chesterton in "Somewhere the Trumpets are Blowing," and within a few days the National Ballet's specially commissioned ballet *Newcomers* filled the screen. Sondheim's musical *Sweeney Todd* was the featured presentation but there were outstanding films, *The French Lieutenant's Woman* being only one of several.

44. Memorandum of Agreement, Louis Applebaum and LAMB, January 4, 1983. York University Archives, Louis Applebaum fonds, 2000-009/005[16].

45. Ed Cowan, memorandum to LAMB Board, May 1983. York University Archives, Louis Applebaum fonds, 2000 – 009/006[05] Jamie Portman, Southam News wrote "C-Channel – the only pay-TV service with credibility in its overall programme philosophy." *The Globe and Mail* reported that "C-Channel takes the approach that quality is better than quantity," and Michelle Landsberg, writing in the *Toronto Star*, said, "I applaud all this juicy programming ... a two hour block of superior children's programming – fresh, sumptuous, exciting and appealing." Perhaps the most thoughtful response came from Helmut Bierman, in the St. John's *Times Record*: "For those with more discriminating taste and those who appreciate the finer things in life, a blend of classic movies, recent quality movies and the arts, it seems that the best, and perhaps the only choice is C-Channel."

46. Jan Applebaum, interview with author, May 18, 2001.

47. Ed Cowan, interview with author, September 5, 2001.

48. Louis Applebaum, letter to M. Michel Dupuy, Minister, Canadian Heritage, December 20, 1993. York University Archives, Louis Applebaum fonds, 2000 – 009/006[02].

49. A short item appeared in the Executive Committee Minutes of the OAC, October 13, 1978. "Representatives of the P. C. Party led by David MacDonald have met with several OAC representatives, Thursday, October 13 to discuss arts policy," Minute Books, OAC Archives, Toronto. When the Conservative Government was elected a few months later, David MacDonald, now Secretary of State, found that he had as his under-secretary Pierre Juneau, from whom the proposal for a cultural review actually came.

50. Louis Applebaum, letter to Arthur Gelber, November 6, 1979. Minutes of the Meeting of the Ontario Arts Council, January 1980, Addendum, OAC Minute Books, OAC Offices, Toronto. No doubt the "other ventures" were associated with LAMB.

51. Minutes of the Meeting of the Ontario Arts Council, January 1980, OAC Minute Books, OAC Offices, Toronto.

52. Ezra Schabas, interview with author, July 7, 1999.

53. Louis Applebaum, Speech. "Some Thoughts About Graduate Programs," University of Calgary Symposium, March 1980. York University Archives, Louis Applebaum fonds, 2000 – 009/009[20]

54. T. H. B. Symons, interview with author, July 4, 2001.

55. Paul Schafer, interview with author. July 26, 1999.

56. James Norcop, interview with author, March 30, 1999.

57. Ron Evans, interview with author, July 28, 1999.

58. Charlotte Holmes, interview with author, March 30, 1999.

59. Naomi Lightbourn, interview with author, May 5, 1999.

60. Ibid.

61. Louis Applebaum, interview with author, February 1, 1999. Louis was even more enthusiastic about the support for the arts by the Russian people, and simultaneously more concerned about the dangers of outside influence on the creative artist. In a speech to the Temple Sinai congregation shortly after he had returned from Moscow, he said: "artistic participation is common to the whole population. Everyone goes to plays and opera ... to concerts and ballet. You have 40 or 50 magnificent repertory companies functioning, each equipped and housed superbly. You get an abundance ... a richness ... that is hard for us to appreciate. For, you see ... the artist ... the composer ... the actor ... the writer .... They make up the aristocracy .... They are respected and honored .... Demigods." However, Louis saw there was "a price to pay." The "contemporary public is the final arbiter and controller of creative effort." This, he believed, "can only lead to creative stagnation and self-destruction. The artist is also the servant and must serve immediate practical ends ... must be immediately understood." Speech to Mount Sinai Temple, November 21, 1958. York University Archives, Louis Applebaum fonds, 2000 – 009/009 [20].

Chapter 16. A Cultural Policy for a Nation

1. Arnold Edinborough, "Now Time for a Royal Commission on the Arts," *Financial Post*, September 18, 1976. [p. 42]

2. Pierre Elliott Trudeau, Juno Awards Celebrations, March 31, 1979. Quoted in the Introduction to Part I, "Canadian Cultural Development" in "A Strategy for Culture," Canadian Conference of the Arts, Ottawa, December, 1980.

3. Gina Mallet, "Will MacDonald do it all for our arts?" *Toronto Star*, June 30, 1979. York University Archives, Louis Applebaum fonds, 2000 – 009/006[08].

4. Hon. David MacDonald, interview with author, May 25, 2001. MacDonald had surprised his senior officials by having the results of his pre-election findings and observations printed and bound, so that at the first meeting with his prospective ministerial colleagues, when normally the new Minister is presented with briefing books expressing the collective wisdom of the departmental heads, he could make the occasion instead an exchange of documents.

This was something that had never happened before and likely has never happened since.

5. Louis Applebaum, interview with author, July 6, 1999.

6. Terms of Reference, Chairman of the Advisory Committee on Cultural Policy, October 23, 1979. York University Archives, Louis Applebaum fonds, 1989 – 018/024 [134]. The extent of the "internalization" of the review process can be assessed not only from list of first appointees, but also from Louis's responsibilities as set out in his job description as Chairman. He was to "participate in meetings of the Executive Committee chaired by the Under-Secretary of State." At these meetings it was expected that "the need for on-going policy development will be identified" and "proceedings of the Parliamentary Inquiry [will be] discussed and followed up where appropriate." Also, the Ministry Executive Committee would be the place where "the planning for the implementation of the recommendations of the Parliamentary Inquiry would be reviewed prior to discussion within the Advisory Committee and submission of implementation options to the Minister" would take place.

7. Jan Applebaum, interview with author, May 18, 2001. Louis had not known Breton, and both he and Jan visited him in order to make an initial contact. Louis was not taken with Breton, finding him rather cool and reserved, and was sure that his economics background would bring him to unhelpful conclusions about the arts and a lot of "bottom-line" reaction that was inappropriate. Also he was a close friend of both Trudeau and Pierre Juneau. Louis had failed to catch the full measure of the man, but Jan had no reservations and assured Louis that by the end of the process, he would have had no more valuable colleague. This turned out to be an accurate observation.

8. News Release Communique, Advisory Committee, Advisory Committee on Cultural Policy, November 7, 1979. York University Archives, Louis Applebaum fonds, 1989 – 018/024[134] There were other significant Canadians who ultimately came to serve on this Committee and its successor, the Federal Cultural Policy Review Committee: Ted Chapman, who became a Vice-Chairman; Jean-Louis Roux; Sam Sniderman; Robert Landry; Alain Stanke; Hilda Lavooie-Franchon; Mary Pratt; Max Tapper; and Rudy Wiebe.

9. Notice: "The Astounding Electrifying Mystifying Joint Parliamentary Committee Game." York University Archives, Louis Applebaum fonds, 1989 – 018/024[132]. Staff at the Secretariat of State were sending around a notice of a pool that had been organized. It informed potential participants that they would be asked to guess who the Chair would be and to select the names of five MPs and five Senators most likely to take their places on the Joint Committee. All entrants in the game were asked to place a list of their selections and $1.25 in an envelope. The winner would get all proceeds. "LOTO CANADA offers nothing like this." Contestants were advised that in their selection of Chair, a Conservative would be a more likely choice, "if they are in power, of course." Little did the organizers of the game realize how prescient the comment was.

10. Albert Breton, Economic Rationale for Cultural Policy, Report to the Advisory Committee on Cultural Policy, December 1979. York University Archives, Louis Applebaum fonds, 1983 – 003/001[01].

11. Albert Breton, interview with author, May 25, 2001. Apparently, the Prime Minister, Joe Clark, had decided that he would re-create the 1957–1958 scenario when John Diefenbaker, confronted by the Liberals, had leaped from a minority government to the largest majority in House of Commons history.

12. Agenda, Second Meeting of the Advisory Committee on Cultural Policy, December 12,13,14, 1979 York University Archives, Louis Applebaum fonds, 1983 – 003/001[1].

13. Louis Applebaum, Memorandum to Louis Toussignant, December 21, 1979. York University Archives, Louis Applebaum fonds, 1979 – 2000 – 009/003[16].

14. Sol Littman, "Politicians are Wooing the Arts," *Toronto Star*, February 17, 1980. [p.B2] York University Archives, Louis Applebaum fonds, 2000 – 009/003[16].

15. Ibid.

16. Louis Applebaum, Aide-Mémoire, Luncheon Meeting, February 29, 1980. York University Archives, Louis Applebaum fonds, 2000 – 009/003[20].

17. Ibid.

18. Ibid.

19. Louis Applebaum, Aide-Mémoire, Meeting, Chairman's Committee, March 3, 1980. York University Archives, Louis Applebaum fonds, 2000 – 009/003[20].

20. Ibid.

21. Memorandum: To the Hon. Francis Fox from the Advisory Committee on Cultural Policy, 1980. York University Archives, Louis Applebaum fonds, 1983 – 003/002[11a]. Many questions followed in this memorandum, but the answers were not entirely satisfactory. To the question "Would the Minister set up a Canadian Cultural Industries Council?" the reply came back that it "was not ruled out as a possibility." When the Committee asked, "Would the Federal Government set up a Cultural Industries Division?" the answer came back that it "was under comprehensive study." To the inquiry "What was the Minister's position on the Capital Cost Allowance for the Recording Industry?" the Committee was informed that "it was under study." An even more important question, "What was the position of the Minister in regard to the Canadian Association of Broadcasters' wish to diminish the Canadian content regulations of the CRTC?" provoked only the observation that "there was no plan for change."

22. Sam Sniderman, interview with author, October 1, 2001.

23. Advisory Committee on Cultural Policy, Memorandum to the Hon. Francis Fox, Secretary of State. York University Archives, Louis Applebaum fonds, 1983 – 003/002[11a]. The fact that Francis Fox promised a long-awaited revision of the copyright legislation gave Louis some hope that the Review could make a difference.

24. Louis Applebaum, interview with author, July 6, 1999. Louis's hope for a restraint on the size of the Committee was also irretrievably destroyed as Francis Fox continued to appoint more members. By the time the FCPRC's "Summary of Briefs and Hearings" was published in January 1982 there were 20 members. However, the later appointees were, in nearly every case, outstanding additions, including Jean Louis Roux, a close colleague of Louis from NFB days; Max Tapper, an arts entrepreneur; the already mentioned Sam Sniderman; and author Rudy Wiebe. Mary Pratt, an artist from the East Coast, replaced Alex Colville, who had resigned to take a role on a selection committee for a Director of the National Gallery. As a result of this expansion, two vice-chairs were needed, and Albert Breton and Ted Chapman took on these roles. Most important of all, the members of the Advisory Committee, without exception, were asked to join the FCPRC, and all agreed, except Alex Colville and Shirley Gibson. It was a generous political action on the part of Fox to accept all the appointees of his predecessor and political opponent, David MacDonald, and one much appreciated by Louis and his Advisory Committee colleagues.

25. Louis Applebaum: Notes on the Fourth Meeting of the Advisory Committee on Cultural Policy, March 13/14, 1980. York University Archives, Louis Applebaum fonds, 2000 – 003/001[02].

26. Draft Summary – Broadcasting Review, Document introduced at Fifth Meeting of the Advisory Committee on Cultural Policy, April 10–11, 1980. York University Archives, Louis Applebaum fonds, 1983 – 003-001[02].

27. Louis Applebaum, Memorandum to Pierre Juneau, May 2, 1980. York University Archives, Louis Applebaum fonds, 1989 – 018/024[134].

28. Hansard, May 6, 1980. Commons Debates. York University Archives, Louis Applebaum fonds, 1983 – 003/001[03].

29. Hansard, May 14, 1980, Commons Debates. York University Archives, Louis Applebaum fonds, 1983 –003/001 [03].

30. Louis Applebaum, Aide-Mémoire, Chairman's Committee, March 3, 1980. York University Archives, Louis Applebaum fonds, 2000 – 009/003[20].

31. Federal Cultural Policy Review Committee, "Speaking of Our Culture: Discussion Guide." Ottawa, January 1981. Briefs were invited with a submission deadline of February 9, 1981. Although there was the suggestion that the brief should be no longer than 25 pages, it was clear that longer documents would be accepted. As well, the sponsors of the brief were to indicate whether they wished to appear before the FCPRC at one of the 18 hearings. Though not designed to limit or restrain debate, "Speaking of Our Culture" did set out the principles and objectives of the Committee quite specifically. In particular, it made it clear that "formal education" (as well as science and scientific research, sports and recreation) would not be addressed by the Committee, since except as "it relates to specialized professional training of teachers, [it] would not be within the scope of the Review."

32. T. H. B. Symons, interview with author, July 4, 2001.

33. Louis Applebaum, interview with author, March 30, 1999.

34. Ibid.
35. Federal Cultural Policy Review Committee, "Summary of brief and hearings" Information Services, Department of Communications, January, 1982. [p.ii]. By the time the initial lists of intervenors had to be established there were over 1100 documents ranging in size from a page or two to well over a 100 or more pages. Even after the hearings, briefs continued to come in and by September, 1981, the Committee had received over 1,300 documents.
36. David Ellis, interview with author, September 7, 2001.
37. Albert Breton, interview with author, May 25, 2001.
38. Tom Symons, interview with author, July 4, 2001.
39. Sam Sniderman, interview with author, October 1,2001.
40. Joy Cohnstaedt, interview with author, October 23, 2001.
41. Mary Pratt, interview with author, July 14, 2001.
42. Jean-Louis Roux, interview with author, September 28, 2001. The experience was invaluable for a man who was to become the Chairman of the Canada Council some two decades later.
43. Ibid.
44. FCPRC Hearings: Saskatoon, May 25, 1981. York University Archives, Louis Applebaum fonds, 1983 – 003/003[36].
45. FCPRC Hearings, Saskatoon, May 25, 1981. York University Archives, Louis Applebaum fonds, 1983 – 003-003[36]. At that same hearing it was stated that multicultural arts "must not only be recognized but seen as an incredible opportunity." The multicultural issue came up again and again and was never resolved to the satisfaction of many groups whose cultural expression reflected other lands.
46. FCPRC Hearings, Ottawa, April 13 –16, 1981. York University Archives, Louis Applebaum fonds, 1983 – 003/003[34b].
47. Ibid.
48. FCPRC Hearings, Quebec City, May 15, 1981. York University Archives, Louis Applebaum fonds, 1983 – 003/003[36]. In 2001 the U.K. decided to give free admissions to all public art galleries.
49. Albert Breton, interview with author, May 25, 2001. This matter was an ongoing frustration for Louis, whose objective in life was to see every person in Canada enjoy the artistic experiences that would enrich his or her life. Louis had seen that the under-funding of the arts was creating an elitism that would ultimately damage every arts institution. By the 1990s, Louis was on the Board of the Stratford Festival and confessed to Breton that he was terribly upset about the cost of attending performances at Stratford. This was one of the reasons that, knowing of Breton's close friendship with Trudeau, Louis never stopped asking his colleague why this Prime Minister, who was such a cultured individual, could not have done more to support the arts.
50. Vincent Tovell, interview with author, April 1, 1999. The same treatment was meted out to Father Levesque who appeared on another occasion in the Province of Quebec.
51. Mary Pratt, interview with author, July 14, 2001.

52. Louis Applebaum, Journal, York University Archives, Louis Applebaum fonds, 2000 – 009/023[03].

53. Louis Applebaum, letter to Ian Morrison, December 7, 1981. York University Archives, Louis Applebaum fonds, 1983 – 003/002[12].

54. Ian Morrison, quoting Louis Applebaum, e-mail message to author, June 30, 2001.

Chapter 17. The Report: Achievement and Disappointment

1. Federal Cultural Review Committee, "Summary of Briefs and Hearings, Discussion Guide," January 1982, Ottawa. In some ways this 237-page volume was as effective as the final Report, which, though slightly longer, could not express the anger and frustration of the artistic community with the same passion.

2. Ibid. [p.132] Despairing thoughts came upon Louis on occasion in his last years. Alexina Louie, a most successful Canadian composer, worked with Louis on numerous committees in the 1980s and 1990s and at one point, after a most discouraging revelation of the hardships suffered by artists and composers, he asked her poignantly, "Where did we go wrong?" (Alexina Louie, interview with author, September 28, 2001.)

3. Ibid. [p.134].

4. Ibid. [p.134].

5. Ibid. [p.136].

6. Ibid. [p.123].

7. Ibid. [p.174].

8. Sam Sniderman, interview with author, October 1, 2001. Sniderman had lost touch with Louis after school days until, in the 1960s, Louis became involved with CAPAC and the Canadian Association of Broadcasters' crusade to put Canadian music on record. Louis had "used" Sniderman to entice RCA to do a series of recordings. During those years Sniderman tried to mediate the relationship between CAPAC and BMI Canada, the two Canadian performing rights organization, as he felt the war between them was helping neither. He was unsuccessful. Sniderman disagreed with Louis's obsession with classical music composers as he felt that many popular composers faced similar disadvantages.

9. Canadian Conference of the Arts, "A Strategy for Culture," Ottawa, 1980. [p.xi] Also caught in all the confusion of a change of government, the CCA was not sure whether the Advisory Committee would continue its work or some new mechanism might be established.

10. Jean-Louis Roux, interview with author, September 28, 2001.

11. Louis Applebaum, "Aide-Mémoire: Re Meeting with Pierre Juneau" October 21, 1981. York University Archives, Louis Applebaum fonds, 1983 – 003/002[20].

12. Minutes of the Planning Committee, October 29, 1981. York University Archives, Louis Applebaum fonds, 1983 – 003/002[20].

13. Louis Applebaum, Handwritten note accompanying Agenda, Meeting of the Federal Cultural Policy Review Committee, November 12 – 13, 1981. York University Archives, Louis Applebaum fonds, 1983 – 003/002[20].

14. The Canadian Conference of the Arts, "More Strategy for Culture," Ottawa, 1981. [p.iv] The Conference recommended that a special joint committee of the Senate and House of Commons be set up to make specific recommendations within eight months, thereby taking the issue out of the hands of the FCPRC entirely. Once Juneau and Dorais departed, though, there was a significant escalation of confidence in the FCPRC.

15. David Ellis, interview with author, September 7, 2001.

16. Jean-Louis Roux, interview with author, September 28, 2001

17. Joy Cohnstaedt, interview with author, October 23, 2001.

18. Albert Breton, interview with author, May 25, 2001. Breton had engaged Louis in countless conversations on the subject of creativity, and both men agreed that the same creative process was involved in composing a musical piece and writing a book on economics.

19. Sam Sniderman, interview with author, October 1, 2001.

20. Report of the Federal Cultural Policy Review Committee, November 1982, Information Services, Department of Communications, Government of Canada. [p.350]. This support was not enthusiastically received on all sides. There were artists who questioned the process of adjudicating grants for every discipline, and felt it was too easy for an "inside" group to gain control of the process. Even Mary Pratt, who fully recognized the importance of the Canada Council, felt that the FCPRC was too much influenced by both members and staff who had participated in the work of the Council, and who found it hard to engage in the critical appraisal of its functions that might have led to a more efficient and effective granting body. In 1980, Louis's commitment to a strong funding body led him to write to Margaret Thatcher, the British Prime Minister, complaining that "your efforts to overcome your severe economic problems have led to dramatic cuts in the budgets of the British Council" and the Arts Council of Great Britain. "The damage that could result to the goodwill and to the good name of England are, in my view, very real."

21. Report of the Cultural Policy Review Committee, Information Services, Department of Communications, Government of Canada, November, 1982. [p.354]

22. Louis Applebaum, "Notes on a TV Broadcasting Policy," August 28, 1981. York University Archives, Louis Applebaum fonds, 1983 – 003/003[19b] [pp.1-3] Louis had no reservations about the value of the CBC but was constantly disappointed by irrational bureauratic positions. One example suffices. Louis was asked by a distinguished film composer, David Raksin, to secure a CBC film for teaching purposes. Louis's reply on February 23, 1963, outlines his frustration. "This incredible bureaucracy is now devoid of logic and reason and has tied itself into inextricable knots. It seems the CBC cannot make a print available to an educational institution like the University of Southern California under any conditions." Louis's advice was to write to the CBC's Director of Network Programming. Raksin would then "get back a formal refusal with the 800 excuses he chooses to select" which then could be used to create a "stink" that could

be used in an appeal to the Prime Minister. (Louis Applebaum, letter to David Raksin, February 26, 1963. York University Archives, Louis Applebaum fonds, 1979 – 002/022[438].)

23. Louis Applebaum, "Aide-Mémoire – Some views expressed by Al Johnson at a lunch," (unpublished) February 19, 1982 York University Archives, Louis Applebaum fonds, 1983 – 003-002[25b].

24. Louis Applebaum, Journal, April 14, 1982. [no page number]. York University Archives, Luis Applebaum fonds, 2000 – 009/ 028[03].

25. David Ellis, interview with author, September 7, 2001.

26. Jacques Hébert, "Notes on the CBC," April, 1982, unpublished, York University Archives, Louis Applebaum fonds, 1983 – 003/002[25b] [pp.1-3].

27. Ibid. [p.4]

28. Report of the Federal Cultural Policy Review Committee, Information Services, Department of Communications, Government of Canada, Ottawa, November, 1982. [p. 354]

29. Louis Applebaum, "Aide-Mémoire – Meeting with Pierre Juneau" August 11, 1982. York University Archives, Louis Applebaum fonds, 2000 –009/002[20].

30. Sam Sniderman, interview with author, October 1,2001.

31. Joy Cohnstaedt, interview with author, October 23, 2001.

32. Louis Applebaum, interview with author, July 6, 1999.

33. Louis Applebaum, "Notes on Copyright." A paper included in the Minutes of the meeting of the FCPRC, September 1-2, 1982. York University Archives, Louis Applebaum fonds, 1983 – 003/003[29a]. Jean-Louis Roux believed that the FCPRC had played a major role in moving this policy along. (Interview, Jean-Louis Roux with author, September 28, 2001.)

34. Report of the Federal Cultural Policy Review Committee, November, 1982. Information Services, Department of Communications, Government of Canada. Ottawa. [p.350].

35. Ibid. [p. 351] The orchestra has continued to be, never as much as in the new century, the jewel of the capital city's cultural scene. With the present leadership, the orchestra is reaching the heights it scaled under Mario Bernardi's baton in its earliest days. On September 11, 2001, NAC Director-General Peter Herrndorf released a new five-year plan that would see the orchestra tour more vigorously and even provide "master class" leadership in training future string players. Unfortunately, other events on that day meant that this exciting plan received little attention.

36. Mary Pratt, interview with author, July 14, 2001.

37. Sam Sniderman, interview with author, October 1, 2001. Even this most out-going member of the Committee had come to the conclusion that "I did not like the people I was working with." By this point, the broad interest and understanding that Sniderman had achieved during the hearings had eroded and "I was not interested in other sectors. I was here to represent the recording industry."

38. Minutes of the Meeting of the FCPRC, August 16-17, 1982. York University Archives, Louis Applebaum fonds, 1983 – 003 /003[28a].

39. T. H. B. Symons, interview with author, July 4, 2001.

40. Louis Applebaum, "Aide-Mémoire re distribution of the Report," October 14, 1982. York University Archives, Louis Applebaum fonds, 2000 – 009/003[20] Even the distribution of the Report had its political ramifications. It had been decided that November 16 should be the date of the release of the Report. In mid-October, a conversation with Leo Dorais revealed that before the release, the Minister wanted to write to all his cabinet colleagues whose ministries had been mentioned and to all CEOs of cultural agencies, enclosing a copy of the Report in order that they could, in turn, advise the Minister of what their own reactions would be by the date of the Press Conference. A day later, Louis heard that the Minister had 50 copies of the Report and was about to distribute them. The Reports would thus be going out to interested parties a full month before the official release to the Press. Louis returned the call to Leo Dorais informing him that "It would be disastrous, unreasonable, and unacceptable for the Minister to distribute the Report as proposed," that "such a distribution would in fact take the Report out of our hands," and that "immediate press leaks would be inevitable."

41. News Release: Report of the Federal Cultural Policy Review Committee, November 16, 1982. York University Archives, Louis Applebaum fonds, 2000-009/003[25].

42. Ibid.

43. FCPRC Press Conference, November 16, 1982. "Draft Statement for Mssrs. Applebaum and Hébert." York University Archives, Louis Applebaum fonds, 2000 – 009/003[25].

44. Adele Freedman, William Johnson, "Applebert report called 'laudable but impractical'," *The Globe and Mail,* November 17, 1982. [p15]

45. Judy Steed, "Juneau says the report goes too far," *The Globe and Mail,* November 17, 1982.

46. Mary Pratt, interview with author, July 14, 2001. She made the point that in rural Newfoundland, the CBC was crucial to her intellectual wellbeing. "I painted with Allan McFee as a kind of leprechaun on my palette," she recounts.

47. Harry Rasky, Letter to the Editor, *The Globe and Mail,* November 19, 1982. Rasky was equally upset about the FCPRC treatment of the NFB, as his mention of John Grierson indicates. Although it did not receive the same attention, the Committee's recommendation that the NFB "should be transformed into a centre for advanced research and training in the art and science of film and video production" was considered equally ridiculous (in some cases by citizens who had never knowingly seen an NFB production.) It was difficult for Louis to be a part of any process that seemed to end the filmmaking role for the very operation that had launched his career as a composer. However, where the CBC was still a dominant player in broadcasting, the NFB's role had decreased as a presence in the filmmaking world, with dozens of private companies making films and receiving awards. Louis was aware of the extent to which the NFB had moulded his talent as well as those of many

others who were now developing the art in Canada, and was anxious that this function should not be lost. Yet even his close friend of some 40 years, George Stoney, reading a story of the Report in *Variety*, was driven to write, "For years I've known serious and profound changes were needed at the Board. But to cut it off from production is to kill what it does best. It's about like saying 'end Israel' because one (very rightly) disagrees with current government policy toward Palestinians." (George Stoney, letter to Louis Applebaum, December 6, 1982. York University Archives, Louis Applebaum fonds, 2000 –009/003[19].)

48. Michael Valpy, "Give up?" *The Globe and Mail*, November 18, 1982.

49. Louis Applebaum, rough outline, "*Mermaid Inn* Column #1," for *The Globe and Mail*, [no date] York University Archives, Louis Applebaum fonds, 2000 –009/003[19].

50. Albert Breton, Letter to the Editor, *The Globe and Mail*, November 30, 1982. In the same issue of the *The Globe and Mail*, a Letter to the Editor from Peter Herrndorf reacted strongly to the line in the Report that the CBC "has been suffering from a hardening of the creative arteries." Herrndorf was adamant that "Nothing could be further from the truth. It is the creative home for hundreds of the country's most gifted and innovative producers, directors, writers, performers, journalists, and craft people … they produce the kinds of programs that have made it possible for the CBC to win five international Emmies in the past six years – more than any other competing network."

51. Christopher Mark's "Arts Reporting Service," Washington, D. C., January 17, 1983. No. 308, [pp.1-2]

52. Jean-Louis Roux, interview with author, September 28, 2001. Roux played a unique role as a French-speaking member of the Committee, contributing to Louis's efforts to keep his Committee united and focussed. An example of his sensitivity came in the context of Louis decision to personally host a dinner for the members of the Committee when they were in Toronto. Jan Applebaum was made aware of the divisions within the Committee, in this case, the gulf between French and English-speaking members, that even the warmth of the Chinese restaurant could not overcome. As hostess, Jan felt quite uncomfortable. The event was putting a dent in the family finances but, even more, the lack of conviviality in the room was not serving the Committee's interests well and certainly not lessening Louis's frustrations. However, the next morning there came a simple gesture that indicated that one Committee member had noticed Jan's discomfort: Jean-Louis Roux sent her a bouquet of flowers. Louis's appreciation was manifested in a telephone call to Roux that went well beyond the simple "thank you" such a gesture would have normally elicited.

53. Louis Applebaum, interview with author, June 10, 1999. Vincent Tovell, one of Louis closest associates at the CBC and earlier, still expresses sorrow for saying, at a forum discussing the Report at the St. Lawrence Centre in Toronto, that the "Report had done more damage to the CBC than any document ever written." He knew he had hurt Louis and was shocked by his

own fury. He felt that Louis, with his commitment to the individual artist, could not concede that institutions like the CBC do support individual artists, in spite of being weighted down with bureaucracy. (Vincent Tovell, interview with author, September 5, 2001.)

54. T. H. B. Symons, letter to the Honourable Francis Fox, Secretary of State, March 7, 1983. York University Archives, Louis Applebaum fonds, 2000 – 009/003[19].

55. Joy Cohnstaedt, interview with author, October 23, 2001.

56. Albert Breton, interview with author, May 25, 2001.

Chapter 18. Aftermath and Renewal

1. Louis Applebaum, letter to Mary Pratt, undated, but in reply to her letter of May 3, 1983. York University Archives, Louis Applebaum fonds, 2000 – 009/003[19].

2. Robert Gourd, letter to all FCPRC presenters from the Chair, Standing Committee on Communications and Culture, December 1982, York University Archives, Louis Applebaum fonds, 2000 – 009/003 [19].

3. Mary Pratt, letter to Louis Applebaum, January 18, 1983. York University Archives, Louis Applebaum fonds, 2000 – 009/003[19].

4. Louis Applebaum, Letter to Mr. W. T. Herbert, MP (Vaudreuil) House of Commons, Ottawa, York University Archives, Louis Applebaum fonds, 2000 – 009/003[19].

5. Forrest Nickerson, Canadian Cultural Society of the Deaf, letter to Louis Applebaum, December 16, 1982. York University Archives, Louis Applebaum fonds, 2000 –009/003[19]. As a copy of the letter was forwarded to the Governor-General, Louis was asked to assist in composing the reply, but while agreeing "the cause is valid" he had to admit "the Committee has no life" and could therefore not redress the omission. To Mr. Nickerson he could only reply, "the Committee had decided to deal with a number of particular social groups in rather general terms" and that "the general tone of the Report supports you."

6. Guy Sylvestre, National Librarian, letter to Louis Applebaum, November 30, 1982. York University Archives, Louis Applebaum fonds, 2000 – 009/003 [19]. This letter was misdirected and Louis could only apologize that his reply came so much later than it should have. Sylvestre's letter included an observation that Louis could appreciate. " … but I must say that I was not surprised to find that broadcasters found that the only thing that really mattered was broadcasting."

7. Press Release: Social Science Federation. York University Archives, Louis Applebaum fonds, 2000 – 009/003[23].

8. Jane Martin, letter to Robert Fulford, Editor, *Saturday Night* Magazine, January 25, 1983, [copy to Louis Applebaum].

9. Joy Cohnstaedt, handwritten note to Louis Applebaum, December, 1982. York University Archives, Louis Applebaum fonds, 2000 – 009/025[11]. The note included a much-appreciated comment: "just a short note to say it was

a pleasure to work with you on the FCPRC, a challenge and an unforgettable experience. Throughout your presence and leadership made the difference to me and my admiration for your role grows."

10. Mary Pratt, letter to Louis Applebaum, May 3, 1983. York University Archives, Louis Applebaum fonds, 2000 – 009/003[19].

11. Louis Applebaum, letter [handwritten copy] to Mary Pratt, May 18, 1983. York University Archives, Louis Applebaum fonds, 2000 -009/003[19].

12. John D. Elvidge: "A Study of the Influence of Advice on Cultural Policy Making," undergraduate thesis, York University [not published, no date] York University Archives, Louis Applebaum fonds, 2000 – 009 061 [no file]. It is clear that Louis gave interviews to the author that proved invaluable in assessing the impact of the Report.

13. Ibid. [p.20] Elvidge does concede that in spite of the problems faced by the FCPRC, and the political morass into which it was dropped and finally submerged, "the document has not been without impact."

14. Howard Knopf, interview with author, December 14, 2001. Howard Knopf had played clarinet in Louis's orchestras in the 1960s and 1970s, regarding him as "a fine conductor, firm and demanding, who got the job done." Knopf went into law, concentrating on copyright legislation, and spent much time with Louis in his CAPAC roles.

15. Jan Matejcek, letter to Louis Applebaum, October 28, 1981. SOCAN Files, SOCAN Head Office, Toronto.

16. John Mills, letter to Louis Applebaum, November 18, 1981. York University Archives, Louis Applebaum fonds, 2000 – 009/002 [18].

17. John Mills, letter to Freeman M. Tovell, Cultural Affairs Division, Department of External Affairs, May 26, 1972. SOCAN Files, SOCAN Head Office, Toronto.

18 John Mills, letter to Louis Applebaum, January 19, 1982. SOCAN Files, SOCAN Head Office, Toronto.

19. Paul Hoffert, interview with author, December 8, 2001. Along with Jan Matejcek, Paul Hoffert was a key figure. Louis had met Hoffert many years before when a percussionist was needed during a recording session with the TSO; Hoffert's talents were evident and Louis had hired him. The relationship was picked up again when Hoffert became the Principal of the Blue Mountain School of Music, established close to Collingwood, Ontario, and Louis's OAC was a source of support for such enterprises. Finally, Louis had encouraged Hoffert to apply for OAC commissioning money at a time when he was engaged in the important enterprise of writing extended "serious" pieces for outstanding popular instrumentalists. Hoffert paid back his "debt" to the OAC with interest by becoming its able Chair from 1994 to 1997.

Hoffert was also alert to the fact that much of the problem of merging revolved around who would hold the major positions in the administration of the new society after the smoke had cleared. Gordon Henderson was also an essential ally and when he was convinced of the need for a merger had much to do with securing the government's approval of the move.

Unfortunately, only one of either Louis or Henderson could be the President of the new performing rights society, SOCAN. It was left to Paul Hoffert to carry on the informal negotiations that would make it possible for Louis to become the first SOCAN President.

20. Minutes of the Meeting of the Board of CAPAC, June 2, 1986. SOCAN Files, SOCAN Head Office, Toronto.
21. Louis Applebaum, interview with author, January 6, 2000.
22. Paul Hoffert, interview with author, December 8, 2001.
23. John Mills, Stephane Vane, "Political Climate," Memorandum to all CAPAC members, 1977. York University Archives, Louis Applebaum fonds, 2000 – 009/002[17] The document comments on the "marked change in the attitude of Quebec board members ... reflecting the new political climate of Quebec... the directors vote as a bloc on all issues .... 'Pop' composers in Quebec want to organize their own performing rights society .... They may attempt to move the head office to Montreal... There was even the threat of a demand for 'a preferential formula for Quebec writers' ...."
24. Louis Applebaum, letter to Richard Flohil, April 9, 1979. York University Archives, Louis Applebaum fonds, 2000 – 009/002[18].
25. Howard Knopf, interview with author, December 14, 2001.
26. Minutes of the CAPAC/PROCAN Merger Negotiating Committee, March 30, 1989, SOCAN Files, SOCAN Head Office, Toronto.
27. Minutes of the SOCAN Communication Committee, July 24, 1990. SOCAN Files, SOCAN Head Office, Toronto.
28. Minutes of the SOCAN Communications Committee Meeting, September 24, 1990. SOCAN Files, Head Office, Toronto.
29. Howard Knopf, interview with author, September 14, 2001.
30. Akides Lanza, letter to Louis Applebaum, March 17, 1989. York University Archives, Louis Applebaum fonds, 2000 – 009/002[17].
31. Amendment to the Minutes of the CAPAC Board of Directors, December 11, 1989, Board of Directors Meeting, January 11, 1990. York University Archives, Louis Applebaum fonds, 2000 – 009/002[18].
32. Louis Applebaum, letter to Murray Adaskin, November 29,1989. York University Archives, Louis Applebaum fonds. 2000 – 009/025[17].
33. Minutes of the Meeting of the SOCAN Communications Committee, June 18, 1991. SOCAN Files, Head Office, Toronto.
34. Michael S. Horwood, letter to Louis Applebaum, February 15, 1992. SOCAN files, Head Office, Toronto.
35. Bill Houghton, letter to Louis Applebaum, October 2, 1991. York University Archives, Louis Applebaum fonds, 2000 – 009/009 [07].
36. Louis Applebaum, letter to Bill Houghton, October 25, 1991. Ibid.
37. In 1991, the author was involved in organizing an International Conference on Arts Education at OISE and Louis Applebaum joined the Steering Committee. From this Conference came an Arts Education Council of Ontario which involved arts consultants and teachers and, some years later, professional artists who were teaching in the classroom. When this body created an Arts Education

Institute to provide courses for teachers, particularly those who were not spe-
cialists and taught at the elementary level, Louis, through the SOCAN
Foundation, provided the funds to have a composer on the teaching staff of the
Institute during its summer program, a contribution that had a profound effect
on the quality of the program. It focussed attention on creativity, as teachers
learned to make music and teach their students to do so.

38. Kate Taylor, *The Globe and Mail,* January 10, 1992, York University
Archives, Louis Applebaum fonds, 2000 –009/006[08].

39. Minutes of the Meeting of the SOCAN Distribution and Tariff Committee,
March 22, 1992. SOCAN files, Head Office, Toronto.

40. Louis Applebaum, interview with author, January 6, 2000.

41. Alexina Louie, interview with author, September 28, 2001.

42. Gary Kulesha, "SOCAN," *Bulletin of the Canadian League of Composers,*
March 1993. York University Archives, Louis Applebaum fonds, 2000 –
009/010[26].

43. Glenn Morley, interview with author, January 5, 2002.

44. Alexina Louie, interview with author, September 28, 2001.

45. Terry Crowley, "Louis Applebaum: An Appreciation," [unpublished] a presentation to the author, November 21, 2001.

46. Edward Johnson Music Foundation, "Notes from the Special Meeting of the
Board of Directors," Saturday, October 18, 1986, at the Millcroft Inn, [p.1].
Files of the Edward Johnson Music Foundation, Guelph, Ontario.

47. Ibid. [p.5]

48. Gloria Dent, Leonard Conolly, editors, *Guelph and its Spring Festival,*
Edward Johnson Music Foundation, Guelph, Ontario, 1992. [pp.133-134]

49. Nancy Coates, interview with author, November 21, 2001.

50. Edwina Carson, interview with author, November 21, 2001.

51. Gloria Dent, Leonard Conolly, editors, *Guelph and its Spring Festival,*
Edward Johnson Music Foundation, Guelph, Ontario, 1992. [p 137]

52. Kathryn Elton, letter to Louis Applebaum, June 27, 1989. York University
Archives, Louis Applebaum fonds, 2000 – 009/004 [17]. It was Louis's view
that "I was called upon to provide a band-aid for one year," but a note [no
date] from one of Marcia Shortreed (Administrator), Kathryn Elton
(Director of Marketing and Publicity), and Carol Ann Douglas,
(Coordinator, Fund-raising), and signed by all three of them, put their admiration quite frankly: "It looks as though we will have a Festival. I [we] can
hardly thank you enough for pulling us through this year." Louis had realized that the health of such an enterprise depends on the morale of the small
staff and that the events of the previous year had left it devastated. He set
about restoring that sense of confidence and, in a few months, succeeded.

53. Eleanor Ewing, "Louis Applebaum, O.C., LL.D. (1918-2000)," an insert to
the Guelph Spring Festival Program, Saturday, June 3, 1989, Guelph, Ontario.

54. Eleanor Ewing, interview with author, November 21, 2001. Louis was not
above giving very practical advice. Eugene Benson remembers quite vividly
Louis's advice that the Festival would have to raise its Artistic Director's salary

to attract a candidate of sufficient quality. As a one-year advisor Louis had no hesitation in offering such totally objective observations. (Eugene Benson, interview with author, November 21, 2001.) Louis's Guelph Spring Festival year unfortunately took place at a time when Jan was not well, suffering from an ailment that not even doctors could diagnose or give any relief for, other than advice that she would have to work her way through it. In a letter explaining her absence from Louis's tribute, she thanked Murdo and Elizabeth MacKinnon for " all the happy times that I had in Guelph whenever I had the good luck to participate in all the wonderful parties and music and conversation and kindness we were a part of." (Jan Applebaum, letter to Murdo and Elizabeth MacKinnon and Friends of the Guelph Spring Festival, May 10, 2000. Guelph Festival Archives, Guelph, Ontario.)

Chapter 19. "I want to be remembered as a composer."

1. On Saturday, August 30, 1997, the *The Globe and Mail* devoted an entire page [C12] to the subject of recorded music from old films, first in an article headlined "Focussing on Hollywood's classic film scores." Remarking on the degree to which Max Steiner and Erich Korngold had been "discovered" during the 1970s, thanks to the dazzling series of RCA recordings produced by George Korngold, Erich's son, the article goes on to observe that "Today, once again the record industry is leading the way to a new appreciation of Hollywood movie music and the most neglected composers who created it." A second article on the same page, headlined "A Prodigy in the recording studio," describes the work of Robert Townsend, who was born in Whitby, Ontario, and "is already Hollywood's premier producer of movie soundtrack recordings." Making use of all the new technology that allows the most attractive sound to be extracted from aging film, this young man, only 31 at the time the article was written, already had 400 recordings to his credit.

2. Max Wyman, a west coast music critic, wrote after a 1970 Vancouver Chamber Orchestra concert which featured the "Concertante" that it "is a work of depth and interest and by my reckoning, is among the better works by modern composers. The first movement has some moments of extreme beauty and an aura of happy childhood ease, and this was performed with style and elegance." (Max Wyman, Music Commentary, York University Archives, Louis Applebaum fonds, 1979 – 022/028 [18].) Marguerite Buck wrote of the Regina Symphony Orchestra's playing of the "Three Greek Dances," drawn from two NFB film soundtracks: "This was a short colourful performance introducing intriguing rhythms, tambourine and other percussive effects and some oriental melodic effects." (Marguerite Buck, Regina *Leader-Post,* March 14, 1960.)

3. "Five Snapshots" was commissioned by the Toronto Senior Strings and received its premiere in the last year of Louis's life. However, it is to be programmed by the Toronto Symphony Orchestra in the 2002-2003 Concert Series in a performance under the baton of Victor Feldbrill, the conductor of

its first performance. The work is one of compelling lyrical passages for the English horn and splendid string accompaniment filled with pleasing harmonic content. It is an example of the work of a dying composer wishing to record the sounds of what he believed to be his major composition, the opera *Erehwon*. (This composition was also played in Victoria by that city's symphony orchestra almost as an introduction to the launching of the opera.)

4. "A Song for the National Arts Centre" featured choir and orchestra and demanded forces that would be assembled very rarely by any ensemble wishing to repeat the work. As well, the lyrics were so specific to that one event that the piece, through praised at its first performance, never became part of the Canadian choral repertoire.

5. Having one's music be "remembered" was a challenge to every person making music in the 20th century. Technological development in that century meant that the sounds of compositions written in the 17th, 18th, and 19th centuries dominated the electronically recorded and transmitted music routinely heard by the general public, and thereby influenced the selection of "live" music in the symphony hall or recital venue. As a result, "classical" or "serious" music came to mean the compositions of Bach, Beethoven, and Brahms, with some attention to Berlioz, and Bruckner on the programs of the more distinguished orchestras. Yet, Louis often commented on the fact that the great commanding presences of this world of classical music represented only a fraction of the music composed in all these centuries. Music, unlike literature, is dependent on the interest of its performer, who is, in turn, dependent for an income on the popularity of his or her repertoire. Yet Louis's colleague Harry Freedman laments the plight of the music creator who finds himself not just in daily competition with his contemporaries, but, through the magic of recording, with every other composer down through the ages. But in spite of all this technological sophistication, we still tend to hear only the works of a few popular composers. Forgotten entirely are those who have composed countless works for salon and chancel, for classroom and town hall. Their compositions have been lost, or ignored, and thereby forgotten except by the odd antiquarian musician or musicologist who may dig up a manuscript either to round out a recital program or provide a footnote in a scholarly article. When such an item is found we are left wondering how many other compositions have been forgotten and how much delight and inspiration we have been deprived of as a result.

6. Louis Applebaum, Score, "Graydon Overture," 1956. York University Archives, Louis Applebaum fonds, 1979 – 022/023. [466] It is recorded that Louis was paid $50 for this commission.

7. Louis Applebaum, Carl Sandburg, Score and libretto, "Counting," 1999. York University Archives, Louis Applebaum fonds, 2000 – 009/032[13].

8. "Action Stations," a suite taken from his early NFB film, was an exception to this rule, and, in spite of its energizing effect on his career, he was unwilling to create other exceptions. His "Suite of Miniature Dances" from a Stratford production of *All's Well That Ends Well* was also a rare exception that Louis

could explain as a segment of music uncharacteristically isolated from the action of the play. Some years ago, after viewing Harry Rasky's film *The Mystery of Henry Moore* (1986), and discovering that Moore was by then quite ill and unlikely to live much longer, the author suggested to Louis that a suite drawn from that film would have enormous emotional appeal. Louis rejected the suggestion on the spot. (In this case, the soundtrack was drawn from the work of other composers as well as music specially composed for the film, but that was not the problem. Louis felt the music was inextricably woven into the visuals and words of Rasky and could not be extricated.)

9. Lazare Saminsky, " Canadian Youth" in *Living Music of the Americas*, 1951. [p.22] A copy of this publication can be found in the library of John Weinzweig, who was kind enough to share the volume with the author.

10. James Neufeld, *Power to Rise, The Story of the National Ballet of Canada*, University of Toronto Press, Toronto, Buffalo, London, 1996. [p.68]

11. S. Roy Malley, "Ballet Delights Sparse Audience," Winnipeg *Tribune*, April 6, 1954 [p.3] York University Archives, Louis Applebaum fonds, 2000 – 009/026 [11].

12. Russell McNaughton, "Folk Drama Into Dance – Dark of the Moon Done as ballet by Canadians" *Detroit News*, February 15, 1954. York University Archives, Louis Applebaum fonds, 2000 – 009/26 [11]. The National Ballet of Canada at that time in its development could afford neither a travelling nor a pick-up orchestra.

13. John Gardner, "The Theatre and Its People," Windsor *Daily Star*, February 18, 1954, [p.25].

14. John Kraglund, "Music of Toronto – Louis Applebaum's Score Blends Well with Dance in Dark of the Moon," *The Globe and Mail*, January 29, 1954. York University Archives, Louis Applebaum fonds, 2000 – 009/026 [12].

15. Ibid.

16. Nathen Cohen, "Ballet Comments," *Toronto Daily Star*, February 9, 1961. [p.34]

17. Ibid.

18. Herbert Whittaker, "Showbusiness – Poor Barbara Allen Seeks Place in Moon," *The Globe and Mail*, February 9, 1961. York University Archives, Louis Applebaum fonds, 2000 – 009/026 [11]. Three years later Louis took two segments of the Barbara Allen score, "Revival Meeting" and "Finale," creating an orchestral setting which has received many performances. York University Archives, Louis Applebaum fonds, 2000-009/059[03].

19. Louis didn't forsake the dance stage entirely. As early as 1957 he had provided choreographer Janet Baldwin with a score for piano and percussion which was called "Legend of the North" and in 1967 he had composed a short dance piece, "Homage," which was danced by the National Ballet at the opening of the National Arts Centre a couple of years later. The work was choreographed by Grant Strate, one Canada's most famous dance creators. Twenty years later Louis wrote "Balletic Overture" choreographed by Robert Desrosiers, this time for the National Ballet's 35th Anniversary Gala, and in the 1990s "The Legend

of Sleepy Hollow" for the Danny Grossman dance troupe. (This was a production for one of Lawrence Cherney's "Musical Monday" series programs at the Young People's Theatre.) Finally, in 1996, "Buffalo Jump," a piece choreographed by Michael Greyeys, was provided with an Applebaum score, and for the last eight years of his life he worked with Danny Grossman to create another version of "The Nutcracker." Together, they wanted to present a dance based on the original story that would have a very different message than the production that has become such a favourite Christmas offering. After much work, some initial funding from David Mirvish and continual revision of the concept and the score, it became obvious that Danny Grossman could not find the necessary resources to mount such a production. All of Louis's work over the all these years remains intact, but unheard. It was a major disappointment for Louis who wanted to test himself in the creation of another extended work. However, after such an auspicious beginning, Louis's repertoire devoted to dance is not as large as one might have expected.

20. Louis Applebaum, interview with author, June 10. 1999. It is somewhat ironic that Louis had such esteem for Stravinsky, a composer who had no admiration for colleagues who wrote for film and television. In an uncharacteristically pungent aside, Louis once suggested that "Stravinsky had little respect for anyone but Stravinsky."

21. Ibid.

22. Ibid.

23. Mary Willan Mason, comment to author. On February 18, 1968, CBC Radio presented a Tribute to Healey Willan who had died two days earlier, on the 16th. It was a program in which Willan's colleagues and students were asked to comment on his work. Louis was one of several chosen, along with Godfrey Ridout, Elmer Iseler, Horace Lapp, and others. Louis was asked to evaluate Willan's music place in the composition of church music, a bizarre topic for a Jewish colleague. However, Giles Bryant, who was to succeed Willan as organist and choirmaster at St. Mary Magdalene Church in Toronto and who was to become the expert on Willan's music, heard the program and pronounced to the author that "he [Louis] got it exactly right. He may have been Jewish but he understood exactly what Willan was about." (Giles Bryant, comment to author, May 15, 2001.)

24. Score: "Passaglia and Toccata," York University Archives, Louis Applebaum fonds, 2000-009/051[13]. This composition is an obvious example of Louis's use of traditional forms. In 1986, he was commissioned to write a selection for a wind ensemble at Wilfred Laurier University. Impressed by the University's prowess on the football field, Louis wrote a Passacaglia "introduced by a sort of cheerleader call which returns to a different guise later in the movement." The Toccata "recalls a sports stadium image with a straight forward sports march." In a typical Applebaum aside on the score, the composer assures the young musicians that "the contrasting dynamics, colours, and rhythms that surround the march should encourage the players to enjoy the performances."

25. Score: "Dialogue with Footnotes for Symphony Orchestra and Jazz Band" was commissioned by a Toronto radio station, CJRT, in celebration of the Toronto Sesquicentennial and Ontario's Centennial, and was first performed by the CJRT Orchestra, conducted by Paul Robinson, and the Boss Brass in Massey Hall, Toronto, December, 1988.

26. Score: "The Polanyi Fanfare," York University Archives, Louis Applebaum fonds, 2000 – 009/026[01]. A particular joy was the fanfare he wrote for a University of Toronto's celebration of Professor John Polanyi's Nobel Prize. In a typical gesture of generosity he returned his fee as a donation to the Department of Chemistry.

27. William Littler, "Symphony Previewed in Opening of 66th Season of the TSO," *Toronto Daily Star.* York University Archives, Louis Applebaum fonds, 2000 – 009/032[07]. There was some irony in this collaboration of the deceased Godfrey Ridout and Louis Applebaum. Ridout was considered the ultimate ultraconservative contemporary composer, who once declared himself an embarrassment to his colleagues who were more comfortable with the results of modern compositional techniques. "A listener to these phrases might almost have been forgiven for suspecting Ridout of a deathbed conversion to modernity but no, the music quickly reverted to Olde English type with sweeping tune in the strings before heading down the Appian Way as if accompanying a victory procession in Hollywood." Few composers would have been able to bring off such a re-scoring with integrity and with such respect to the composer of the original version.

28. A very poignant story reveals the private behaviour of Louis Applebaum in the setting of these RCM celebrations. The person given responsibility as Artistic Director for the success of the occasion was Edwina Carson. She had enlisted a willing Louis Applebaum to assist her in the organizing of the concert, and the event with all its trappings had given an enormous boost to the reputation of the institution in its efforts to secure its future. Carson had worked many months to make a success of this venture. Early on the morning after, Carson, in the midst of the inevitable exhaustion, faced the task of paying all the bills, handling all the complaints, and generally concluding the affair. She was startled to see the door open and her mentor and assistant Louis Applebaum turn up. He said nothing. Realizing her vulnerability in the wake of such an event, he just sat down, not even removing his heavy overcoat, silent for some moments. Then he uttered just one word that convinced Carson that it had gone well. "Wow." That Louis could have realized the terrible loneliness of the "morning after," and have taken the trouble to appear and utter an appropriate congratulatory expression, became her overarching memory of the RCM celebration. A few more moments of silence and he proceeded out of the office and down the hall.

29. Score: "Ode to a Birthday City." York University Archives, Louis Applebaum fonds, 2000-009/059 [01].

30. Louis Applebaum, "Shakespeare on Stage," President's Lecture, Convocation Hall, University of Toronto, July 24, 1963. [p.2] York University Archives, Louis Applebaum fonds, 2000 – 009/009 [02].

31. Ibid.

32. Ibid.

33. Ibid. An example of the Notes he received from Michael Langham for the 1960 production of *Romeo and Juliet* indicates why Louis could not allow his music to be sent off to theatre groups simply wishing to enhance their own productions with bridges from act to act and scene to scene. In Act I, Scene 5, starting at line 94, "a gentle, romantic mood...20 seconds... With no dialogue. Then, in a dreamlike manner, music needs to cease – leaving us suspended in mid-air. The dancers likewise become frozen – the lovers are now in their own world – nothing exists for them except each other. Reality needs to come crashing back with a big, final swirl to dance, loud, shattering and conclusive." For opening of Act 3, Langham wanted "hot, nervous, tense, irritable accompaniment" and for the entry of the household, "ritualistic, slow, but lyrical then after, say 15 seconds, chorus speaks over music. At conclusion of chorus, change mood suddenly for tableaux to break up ...." Michael Langham, Notes for Stratford Festival's *Romeo and Juliet*, 1960. York University Archives, Louis Applebaum fonds, 1979 – 007/019 [301 & 302].

34. Sydney Johnson, Review, Stratford Festival 1966 Production of *Twelfth Night*, Montreal *Star*, June 9,1966. York University Archives, Louis Applebaum fonds, 1979 – 002/028[18].

35. Nathan Cohen, Review, Stratford Festival 1967 Production of *The Merry Wives of Windsor, Toronto Daily Star*, July 25, 1967. York University Archives, Louis Applebaum fonds, 1979 –002/030[574].

36. Pat Sykes, "Lou Applebaum: Instant Composer," Stratford *Beacon Herald* Special Festival Edition, 1968. [p. F24] York University Archives, Louis Applebaum fonds, 1979 – 002/030[575].

37. Review, Stratford *Beacon Herald*, June 20, 1961. York University Archives, Louis Applebaum fonds, 1979 – 002/030 [568].

38. J. Corigliano, letter to Louis Applebaum, August 25, 1987. York University Archives, Louis Applebaum fonds, 1979 – 002/024[487].

39. Louis Applebaum, letter to J. Corigliano, September 20, 1987. Ibid.

40. Robertson Davies, Louis Applebaum, Sketches, script: "The Harper of the Stones," York University Archives, Lous Applebaum fonds, 2000 – 009/028 [24 –26].

41. Ron Hambleton, *Toronto Star*. May 6, 1991. York University Archives, Louis Applebaum fonds, 2000 – 009/032[12].

42. Paul Quarrington, Louis Applebaum, Libretto and Score, "So You Think You Are Mozart," York University Archives, Louis Applebaum fonds, 2000 – 009/032[12].

43. Robertson Davies, Louis Applebaum, "A Holly Wreath," score and libretto commissioned in December 1980, and revised 1995. York University Archives, Louis Applebaum fonds, 2000 – 009 028 [28]. The libretto, characteristically written with the audience in mind, begins:

    "Noel, Noel, No, No, Noel.

    From Massey College we wish you well … "

and ends,

> "All Massey Fellows that do here make merry,
> Spend the life everlasting in Heaven's library,
> And may all their enemies go to hell, Noel, Noel...."

Louis notes on the revised score explained "At the first performance, the conductor, in frustration and exasperation at the extended coda, threw the unbound pages into the air before the last bars could be completed."

44. Louis Applebaum, "Concerning Some Links Between New Creation and the Public," an unpublished paper for the Federal Cultural Policy Review Committee, January 18, 1982. York University Archives, Louis Applebaum fonds, 1983 – 003/002[22]. As the new century opens, the symphony concert is in question, and many symphony orchestras across the continent find themselves in deep trouble financially. As early as 1962, Louis foresaw the impact of the visual technology of television on the entertainment expectations of audiences. "There is not enough show business in our concerts. They should be presented in an exciting way for those who derive part of their musical pleasure from what they see." (quoted in the *Toronto Daily Star*, April 14, 1962. York University Archives, Louis Applebaum fonds, 1979 – 008/002[16].)

45. Mike Boone, "Massey documentary superb tribute to a great actor," *Ottawa Citizen*, Entertainment Section, D2, January 20, 1984.

46. Ibid.

47. Michael Bawden, "Canadian drama makes history live," *Toronto Star*, October 15, 1988.

48. Ray Conlogue, "Much Ado takes a sober tack," *The Globe and Mail*, August 16, 1987.

49. Robert Crew, "Stratford's Shrew shines on CBC-TV," Toronto Star, April 1, 1989.

50. Press Release, "Karsh: The Searching Eye," CBC Department of Communications, No. 159, July 24, 1990. CBC Archives, Toronto.

51. Louis Applebaum, interview with author, January 6, 2000. Jan Applebaum does not entirely agree with this perception, as she constantly chided him "you're going to kill yourself" with all the angst and frustration of seeking to have the opera produced.

52. Mavor Moore, "Remembrance" [unpublished], at the Tribute to Louis Applebaum, "A Fanfare Farewell," Festival Theatre Auditorium, Monday, August 21, 2000.

53. Mavor Moore, email to Louis Applebaum, August 3, 1995. York University Archives, Louis Applebaum fonds, 2000 – 009/020[12].

54. Mavor Moore, interview with author, November 28, 2001. Tyrone Guthrie, who had been the director of the Bernstein-Hellman production, had advised him that it was a lose-lose situation. If *Candide* was successful, Moore's version would be seen as repetitive and derivative; if *Candide* flopped, no producer would touch another version.

55. Ibid.

56. Louis Applebaum, email to Mavor Moore, July 16, 1997. York University Archives, Louis Applebaum fonds, 2000 – 009/020 [12].

57. Louis Applebaum, email to Mavor Moore, July 31, 1997. York University Archives, Louis Applebaum fonds, 2000 – 009/020 [12].

58. Louis Applebaum, email to Mavor Moore, August 14, 1997. York University Archives, Louis Applebaum fonds, 2000 – 009/020. [05].

59. Louis Applebaum to Niki Goldschmidt , by Fax, May 1, 1997.

60. Louis Applebaum, email to Mavor Moore, January 21, 1998. York University Archives, Louis Applebaum fonds, 2000 – 009/020 [12].

61. Mavor Moore, email to Louis Applebaum, December 30, 1988. York University Archives, Louis Applebaum fonds, 2000 – 009/020 [12].

62. Mavor Moore, email to Louis Applebaum, November 20, 1999. York University Archives, Louis Applebaum fonds, 2000 – 009/021[12]. By this time Louis's health was failing fast and Moore was anxious to keep him informed, but took on the role of the aggressive author himself rather than involve Louis in the unpleasant negotiations..

63. Mavor Moore, interview with author, November 28, 2001.

64. Mavor Moore, email to Louis Applebaum, November 25, 1999. York University Archives, Louis Applebaum fonds, 2000 – 009/021[12].

65. Louis Applebaum, Draft Program Notes for *Erehwon*, Pacitic Opera Victoria, February 2, 2000, York University Archives, Louis Applebaum fonds, 2000 – 009/020 [20].

66. Allan Boss, "Erehwon: A world within an opera," *The Globe and Mail*, February 19, 2000.

67. Brian Cherney, interview with author, December 1, 2001.

68. Fine's poem, printed in the program, reminded people in the hall that the object of their collective adulation was in fact, ending that journey. The last lines read,

> Birth is a beginning
> And death a destination;
> But life is a journey,
> A sacred pilgrimage
> To life everlasting.

69. Larry House, letter to Louis Applebaum, May 25, 1998. York University Archives, 2000 – 009/020[04].

Chapter 20. The Sage

1. Article, New York Tribune, October 7, 1947, York University Archives, Louis Applebaum fonds, 1979 – 002/028[02]

2. Stefanos Karabekas, interview with author, October 6, 2000. Karabekas had been Louis's student in the mid-1970s. Although he had graduated in industrial administration in his native land, Greece, he had come to Canada in the early 1970s, enrolled in political economy at York University, and signed up for Louis's course. It was, Karabekas states, Louis's influence that led him to pur-

sue music studies. "I had never met such a wonderful man – he was father, friend, mentor, and teacher." Though he had taken only some courses at the Conservatory in theory and harmony, he began composing and presented Louis with his compositions. Louis encouraged him as he did other aspirants. He always had time to meet with his students no matter how busy he was. After reading a score that Karabekas had written, he declared his music "very Greek … Mediterranean … like Jewish music." Karabekas saw Louis as "really a musicologist … he always saw the cultural component." The budding composer was advised that he should apply for an OAC grant in order to buy time to compose and was consoled when he failed to secure one. Louis convinced him that he should join the Canadian League of Composers and the Canadian Music Centre, where he met other composers, notably John Weinzweig. Karabekas advanced his career by gathering and conducting his own orchestra that performed across southern Ontario. He included his own music in the repertoire, but also the work of Louis Applebaum, specifically the "Finale" from the ballet *Barbara Allen.* On seeing the program, Louis's response was, "What about other Canadian composers?"

3.   Glenn Morley, interview with author, October 6, 2000.

4.   Louis Applebaum, quotation from Michael Schulman, *Sound Advice – Words and Music,* published by SOCAN, February 1994, Vol. 1, Number 2. [p. 11]

5.   Paul Hoffert, interview with author, December 8, 2001.

6.   Louis Applebaum, letter to David Raksin, February 5, 1995. York University Archives, Louis Applebaum fonds, 2000 – 009/026 [01]. Louis was only a part-time academic appointment, and, as such, was vulnerable to the ebb and flow of university financing. His minimal salary is also explained by the nature of his appointment. For the last three decades, universities have survived by exploiting part-time instructors and graduate students whose workload may be half that of a full professor but whose annual stipend might be only a twentieth as much.

7.   Louis Applebaum, "Some Thoughts About Graduate Programs in Music," University of Calgary Symposium, March, 1980. York University Archives, Louis Applebaum fonds, 2000 – 009/009 [20] At this lecture Louis illustrated the personal cost of working in the arts. Using his own experience, he described the interchange with a class of law students on the subject of remuneration for creative work. He had asked them what they thought his royalty income per year might be for public performance of his work. Though conceding that most of his music was written on commission and much was for specific occasions, nonetheless his Stratford fanfares, his Christmas choral offerings, and his pieces for piano were quite popular. The prospective lawyers responded with guesses of his annual income from such sources that ranged from $5,000 to $48,000. Louis revealed to a shocked class that three years before it had been $27 but in the big year that followed it had reached $72.

8.   Louis Applebaum, "Some Notes Regarding the School of Music," University of Windsor, [unpublished] July 28, 1985.[p.6] York University Archives, Louis Applebaum fonds, 2000 – 009/010[23].

9. Louis Applebaum, LL.D., O.C., O.Ont., David Elliott, Ph.D., "External Evaluation of the Department of Music, University of Saskatchewan," [unpublished] 1980. York University Archives, Louis Applebaum fonds, 2000 – 009/010[20 -21] It was the judgment of the authors that "Few post-secondary music departments in the world are as poorly designed as this one."

10. Ibid. [p.6] Although most of the criticisms of the evaluation were directed at the University, Louis and David Elliott found it necessary to accord the criticisms of students some validity. There were a small number of professors who were not pulling their weight. "Many students feel cheated by superficial, irrelevant and/or repetitive course content and the high rates of teacher absences in specific cases." The evaluators were amazed that the majority of faculty did not even attend student concerts or recitals. This was obviously an educational community in deep trouble.

11. David Elliott, interview with author, December 14, 2001.

12. Ibid. Louis and David Elliott found that the University of Saskatchewan had some good people on its music faculty who needed support, and both evaluators were determined to supply it. The process was eased by the fact that Louis was completely trusted by the dedicated faculty members. Fortunately, they found one vice-president whose children were engaged in music studies, and who, with a strong report in hand, could take action. They were right. New appointments and a renewed commitment from the University reversed the slippage into academic oblivion.

13. Catherine Smalley, "An Evaluation of the Performing Arts Programme of the Laidlaw Foundation," [unpublished] June, 2000. [p. 3]

14. Ibid. [p.13] Nathan Gilbert, the Foundation's Director, was determined to broaden the reach of the Foundation's impacton the performing arts, to encourage smaller and lesser-known arts organizations to apply. In Louis Applebaum, Wallace, Himes, and Zemans, he saw members who would champion the more fringe-like innovators.

15. Ibid. [p. 13] 16.

17. Donald Himes, interview with author, January 14, 2002. Himes, as a musician, found himself in the shadow of this living legend, yet he discovered that although Louis might come to a swifter decision in the area of a music discipline application, he did so by accepting other members' views when they might not be necessarily his own.

18. Robert Wallace, interview with author, January 11, 2002. Wallace openly credits Louis with the development of his own style as Chair. "Lou had the capacity to listen carefully and incorporate all the ideas tumbling out around the table before bringing the Committee to a decision." He guided rather than controlled. It was not just the decision, but also the process that brought about the decision, that was important. At the same time, he was not willing to allow the discussion to go on indefinitely; he "did not mince his words." He left Wallace and all his colleagues on the Committee with a realization that the giving out other people's money was a heavy responsibility.

19. Ibid.

20. Nathan Gilbert, interview with author, December 5, 2000.

21. Ibid.

22. Louis Applebaum, quote in article, *Toronto Daily Star*, April 14, 1962.

23. Suzanne Bradshaw, interview with author, November 30, 2001.

24. Richard Monette, interview with author, November 30, 2001. Monette has many stories to tell. Referring to himself as "musically unsophisticated," he speaks of occasions when he asked Louis for music for a scene and then had to ask whether there was a tune to be found in Louis's composition. This often occasioned a session with Louis at the piano playing and singing "in that awful voice" the phrases of lyrical content he had composed.

   On one occasion, Monette received more than he bargained for. In Shakespeare's *Antony and Cleopatra*, as the heroine expired there was a blast of trumpets that nearly shook Monette from his chair, at which Monette cried out "Lou, it's only Cleopatra dying! It's not the end of the world!" Always flexible, Louis suitably reduced the accompaniment in volume and intensity.

25. Linda Intaschi, interview with author, December 14, 2001. Intaschi served on the Board of the Stratford Festival with Louis for several years and commented that Louis "constantly reminded the Festival Board that Stratford had moved away from its commitment to music."

26. Richard Monette, interview with author, November 30, 2001. Monette states without hesitation that Louis was loved "by everyone at Stratford," but particularly by Bert Carriere, who literally broke into tears on hearing of Louis's final illness. Monette had never seen Carriere so visibly shaken by any event in all their long Stratford history together. Monette's description of Louis was that "he had all the inspiration of an artist with none of the temperament."

27. Bert Carriere, interview with author, December 11, 2001. Carriere very candidly states that Louis was "the greatest person I have ever known. He taught me not only the tricks of musical composition, but how to approach the Festival administration. Louis knew how to achieve effects with the least amount of trouble. At a point in a play where there was a need for a loud dissonance, Louis would tell the orchestra – 'pick a note and play it loud' and to the technicians – 'tape it.' At another point, he called out in the midst of rehearsal, 'whoever is closest to the bass drum, hit it!'" Carriere comments on Louis's capacity to see his musical contribution revised in the best interests of the total production. He had a pride in his workmanship, but the play as a whole was his first concern. When a lyrical line of music for a cue was reduced by two bars, Louis's only comment was, 'It was a beautiful cue; now it's shorter.'"

   In the late 1990s, Carriere realized when Louis was composing the score for *She Stoops to Conquer* that his health was failing. Carriere went to Louis's studio and asked, "Would you like me to conduct this?" This offer to replace him on the podium of the recording session brought tears of appreciation to Louis's eyes.

28. James Parr to Louis Applebaum, April 29, 1997, York University Archives, Louis Applebaum fonds, 2000 – 009/020[04]. Two years before his untimely death in 1999, Parr produced a CD, *When Music Sounds*, consisting solely of his own songs, sung by James Leatch accompanied by Dona Jean Clary.

29. Erica Goodman, letter to Louis Applebaum, October 9, 1997. York University Archives, Louis Applebaum fonds, 2000 – 009/020[04].

30. Michael Wood, letter to Louis Applebaum, August 27, 1995. York University Archives, Louis Applebaum fonds, 2000-009/026 [02].

31. Louis Applebaum, letter to "The Adaskins," December 28, 1994. York University Archives, Louis Applebaum fonds, 2000 – 009/026[04].

32. Louis Applebaum, letter to Susan Habkirk, February 4, 1994. Susan Habkirk had been a colleague at the Ontario Arts Council and had left to provide leadership to the "Prologue" operation.

33. Morris Wolfe, "Martin's room," *Toronto Life*, October 2000. The description of this tradition was included in a biographical piece on Martin Cohnstaedt, Joy Cohnstaedt's husband, a man of courage and humanity.

34. Louis Applebaum, e-mail to Mavor Moore, January 6, 1998. York University Archives, Louis Applebaum fonds. 2000 – 009/021[12]. Mavor Moore wrote a "Lives Lived" column for *The Globe and Mail* on Arthur Gelber's contribution to the arts and occasioned a reaction from Louis. "Your 'Lives Lived' piece brought tears to Jan's eyes and left me numb. We have lost a unique and irreplaceable shaper of our society, leaving us poorer by far." (Louis Applebaum to Mavor Moore, e-mail message, January 15, 1998. Ibid.)

Acknowledgements

T here are so many people to thank. The first person is obviously Louis Applebaum. Over a lifetime he collected an enormous mountain of papers that fortunately was placed in the York University Archives. I cannot adequately express my appreciation to the staff of that institution, particularly the Chief Archivist, Kent Howarth, his assistant, Suzanne Dubeau, and an especially helpful member of the archive staff, Sean Smith. Their continuing efforts to see that every document came to my attention, to gather together the last files that were placed in their care after Louis's death, made the biography's completion possible. The York Film Archives, and Kathy Elder's willingness to find examples of Louis's work in this collection, was most important.

As well I want to thank Leone Earl, the manager, and her staff at the CBC Reference and Design Library, as well as Gail Donald, co-ordinator of the CBC Radio Archives, for their assistance in "mining" the enormous record of Louis's work in the records of the CBC.

Jane Edmonds and her staff at the Stratford Festival were endlessly helpful, as was the staff of the Ontario Archives, particularly Senior Archivist Wayne Crockett. Loryl MacDonald of the University of Toronto Archives was most accommodating, and Stephen Campbell provided invaluable guidance in accessing the files of the Ontario Art Council.

There were a number of persons who read all or part of the typescript and their advice and assistance was crucial. Ezra Schabas, Paul Schafer, Robert Sirman, Ruth Nusyna, James and Charlotte Norcop, Michael Rock, Paul Spurgeon, Jan Applebaum, and my wife, Ida, all made an enormous contribution, though, I am sure, even their combined efforts could not save the author from errors and misinterpretations.

There was a host of people who knew Louis well and to whom the author turned for information and opinion. I have listed them below but

I cannot adequately express my appreciation for the many hours they spent speaking of their knowledge of Louis's contribution to the cultural life of their country. I was particularly fortunate to be able to spend many hours with Louis before his death in April 2000. There were countless moments after that date when I would have benefitted from his presence but having his initial involvement was a major advantage.

Another phalanx of associates put me in touch with persons and sources of documents, and their involvement was an advantage indeed. Francoise Dutan helped me find the NFB products of Louis's skill, but others, particularly Pat Quigley at the Stratford Festival, paved the way to that institution's involvement. Cynthia Floyd provided valuable materials from the files of the Music School at the University of Ottawa and Rick Macmillan gave me significant assistance in finding documents and pictures in the SOCAN files. David Parsons forged the first links with the Canadian Music Centre and Elizabeth Bihl has assiduously maintained that connection throughout the writing of the volume.

I must concede my ignorance of the universe of technological communication and only my sons, Mark and Wade, kept the typescript in existence through the years, and without the help of Brian Stewart of IBM the typescript might have disintegrated in the latter stages. In such a project there are always an army of people at one's side who find a person or suggest a source — Peter Fisher, Jo-Anne Bentley, Sonia Koerner, Andrea Vagianos, Janet Stubbs, Ian Morrison, Kimberley Briggs, Giles Bryant, Murdo and Elizabeth MacKinnon, Gloria Dent, Eugene Benson, Eleanor and Don Ewing, Neil and Edwina Carson, Nancy Coates, Srul Irving Glick, David Gardner, Arthur Bielfeld, and John Lawson were all conscripts in this formidable force, many of them friends of Louis's anxious to be helpful. Alan Thompson was thankfully available to provide copying of text when necessary.

I came to write this biography for one reason — to enhance the understanding of Canada's cultural life through the examination of a great life. I had met Louis Applebaum in the '70's when both of us occupied seats around the Board Table at TV Ontario as members of the Long Term Planning Committee during the tenures of Ran Ide and Jim Parr. I was much impressed by both the quiet humility and the evident intelligence of this prolific composer — at that time, Executive Director of the Ontario Arts Council. I knew little of his work even though he occupied a distinguished position in Canada's artistic community. I soon realized that my ignorance was widely shared.

As the '80's arrived I was called by Louis's friend and mentor, Arthur Gelber, to consider succeeding Louis Applebaum as the Director of the

OAC, as Louis had accepted the Chair of what was to become the Federal Cultural Policy Review Committee. Louis could not have been a more generous mentor. We soon developed a close friendship that was characterized by frequent meetings in his studio where soup and sandwiches were prepared by the host. It was a short leap to the decision that here was a man whose experiences would reveal much of the nature of Canadian cultural development in the 20th century.

Without the generous financial assistance of the SOCAN Foundation, the Arthur Gelber Foundation, and the Laidlaw Foundation and the involvement of the Canadian Music Centre in administering the project, *Louis Applebaum: A Passion for Culture* would never have been contemplated. Rick MacMillan, Nancy Gelber, and Nathan Gilbert collectively responded to the financial needs of the project and deserve my appreciation

Finally, the staff of the Dundurn Group — Kirk Howard and his colleagues, Beth Bruder, Barry Jowett, Tony Hawke, Jennifer Scott, and Kerry Breeze — has made the process of publishing this volume a truly pleasurable experience. I could not be more appreciative of their efforts.

Arden, Ontario
October 2002

Interviews

Applebaum, David	January 12, 2000
Applebaum, Jan	October 5, 2000
	October 12, 2000
	December 15, 2000
	May 18, 2000
Applebaum, Jordan	December 16, 1999
Applebaum, Louis	January 16, 1999
	February 1, 1999
	March 30, 1999
	June 10, 1999
	July 6, 1999
	November 17, 1999
	January 6, 2000
	January 27, 2000
	March 17, 2000
Beckwith, John	April 25, 2000
	April 4, 2001

Berlin, Boris   February 11, 1999
Bradshaw, Suzanne   November 29, 2001
Breton, Albert   May 25, 2001
Campbell, Norman and Elaine   September 18, 2000
Carriere, Bert   December 11, 2001
Carson, Edwina   June 5, 2002
Cherney, Brian   December 11, 2001
Cherney, Lawrence   January 17, 2001
Clarke, Barbara   September 24, 2001
Cohnsteadt, Joy   October 23, 2001
Cooper, Robert   January 13, 2000
Cowan, Ed   September 5, 2001
Cram, Robert   September 12, 2001
Elliott, David   December 14, 2001
Ellis, David   September 7, 2001
Evans, Ron   July 28, 1999
Freedman, Harry   September 11, 2000
Gilbert, Nathan   December 5, 1999
Goldschmidt, Nicholas   January 15, 2001
Hoffert, Paul   December 8, 2001
Himes, Donald   January 14, 2002
Intosci, Linda   December 4, 2001
Joliffe, Mary   August 29, 2000
Karabekas, Stefanos   October 6, 2000
Knopf, Howard   December 14, 2000
Lightbourne, Naomi   May 5, 1999
Louie, Alexina   September 28, 2001
MacDonald, Hon. David   June 21, 2001
Matejcek, Jan   May 14, 2000
Monette, Richard   November 30, 2001
Moore, Mavor   November 28, 2001
Morrison, Ian   June 30, 2001
Morley, Glenn   June 1, 2000
                                       June 14, 2000
                                       January 5, 2002

Nimmons, Phil and Noreen   January 26, 2001
Norcop, James and Charlotte   March 30, 1999
Nusayn, Ruth   May 1, 2000
                                       May 25, 2000
Parr, Jim   December 14, 1999

Patterson, Tom	March 15, 2000
Pogson, Laura	September 21, 2000
Pratley, Gerald	October 5, 2000
Pratt, Mary	July 14, 2001
Rock, Michael	January 15, 2001
Roux, Jean-Louis	September 28, 2001
Schabas, Ezra	July 7, 1999
	January 25, 2000
	August 30, 2000
Schafer, Paul	July 26, 1999
Sheffer, Harry	January 4, 2000
Shuster, Frank	July 13, 1999
Silcox, David	September 13, 2000
Sirman, Robert	August 3, 1999
Sniderman, Sam	October 1, 2001
Southam, Hamilton	August 23, 2000
Symons, Thomas H.B	July 4, 2001
Tovell, Vincent	April 1, 1999
	September 8, 2000
Traugott, Eric	February 5, 2001
Wallace, Robert	January 11, 2002
Weinzweig, John and Helen,	September 12, 2000